HUTTON'S GUIDE
TO MARTIN GUITARS
1833- 1969
BY GREIG HUTTON

ABOUT THE COVER

"Young Woman Playing a Guitar" was painted by G. P. A. Healy. The painting is dated "1834" and, since it is known that Healy left for Europe by 1835, the date can be confirmed. It is generally thought that Martin did not have regular guitar styles until the 1850's but in 1834 Martin did record the sale of a number of style 10, 18, 36, 40 and 45 guitars. At this early date the style number was the retail price of the guitar while from the 1840's the style number reflected the wholesale price. The guitar in the painting is one of the style 45 guitars and fits the description in the text on page 77 (also see Figure 59). Martin sold at least three style 45 guitars in 1834. One was sold to a Mrs. W. M. Robinson, another was sold to a Mrs. Dupre and the last was sold wholesale to Mr. Atwill, who operated Atwill's Music Saloon at 201 Broadway and was one of Martin's earliest customers. It is intriguing to think that the young lady in the painting might be either Mrs. Robinson or Mrs. Dupre."

Greig

ISBN 978-1-57424-411-3
SAN 683-8022

Cover Design by James Creative Group

Copyright © 2022 CENTERSTREAM Publishing
P.O. Box 17878 - Anaheim Hills, CA 92817

www.centerstream-usa.com | centerstrm@aol.com | 714-779-9390

Foreword

Chapter 1 - A Short History of the Martin Guitar Co.

Chapter 2 – Shop and Factory Locations

Chapter 3 – Important Business Relationships

Chapter 4 – Development of Martin Guitars (Designs, Shapes and Sizes)

Chapter 5 – Development of Martin Guitar Styles

Chapter 6 – Dating Early Martin Guitars 1833 to 1867

Chapter 13 – Martin Instrument Development in the Late 19th and 20th Century

Chapter 14 – Technical Information

Chapter 14 – Technical Information (cont.)

Chapter 15 – Some Musicians and Their Martin Guitars

Chapter 16 – Martin Employees

FOREWORD
by Dick Boak
Sifting History

Many companies have shallow history, or a story that is not particularly interesting. That is not the case with C. F. Martin & Co. The company has tremendous historical depth – the extended story really starts in the late 1700s, well before C. F. Martin's famed emigration to America in 1833. In addition to the transitions between and biographies of more than six generations of the Martin family, there is also the gradual growth of the company itself and the employees, the dealers and end users that sought the company's unparalleled product, and the indelible mark that Martin made on a nearly two centuries of American musical culture.

Over the years, many individuals have taken an interest in Martin's fascinating history. The members of the Martin family thought that the story of C. F. Martin's dispute with the Violin Maker's Guild was interesting enough to capture and pass on to future generations. The reputation that C. F. Martin established was certainly a great source of pride for the extended tentacles of the family, but when Mike Longworth authored "Martin Guitars A History" in 1975, he established a framework upon which future authors could investigate specific aspects and eras of the Martin legacy.

When Mike retired in the mid-1990s, there was of course a gaping hole to be filled and I was the de facto person to fill it. Mike had prepped me somewhat by giving me a small notebook that detailed the many locations of important documents and artifacts.

In 1995, I was contacted by Richard Johnston and Jim Washburn who expressed their desire to visit Nazareth and pull historic files that might be relevant for the book "Martin Guitars: An Illustrated Celebration of America's Premier Guitar Maker" that they were writing. I knew there were several dozen boxes of historic documents and letters in the North Street attic, and I offered to let them search those files during their subsequent visit. Inside the boxes we excitedly uncovered bundles of letters wrapped with twine and covered with a thin layer of Brazilian rosewood sawdust. Though missing several key years, this correspondence covered nearly seven decades from the 1880s through the 1940s, providing a perfect snapshot of how and with whom Martin's business was conducted. Washburn and Johnson returned the relatively small percentage of borrowed files after their research concluded and their groundbreaking book was published in 1997.

When the Visitor Center expansion of the Sycamore Street factory was initiated by Chris Martin in 1998, I participated in meetings about the design of the new Martin Museum, but I also requested and was given space for the consolidation of the company archives. As construction concluded, the new Archive room was fitted with a sliding rack system with plenty of shelving, and the North Street files were brought to Sycamore Street where I gradually I gradually tried to assimilate everything. There were also pockets of other valuable materials scattered throughout various Martin locations: Artist relations files, photographs, and advertising materials from my office area; Board of Directors minutes, Martin family files, photographs, and PR files from various cabinets; antique tools and bracing patterns no longer needed in production – these all came together in one central and secure spot. Perhaps the most interesting and valuable archives were the antique sales journals that dated back to the C. F. Martin Sr.'s first shop on Hudson Street in New York City. Philip Gura, a professor from the University of North Carolina, had published his research on the origins of the banjo, and learning about the Martin archives, he visited the factory to see the files firsthand. He was certainly enthralled, and in a great leap of faith, I entrusted him with the loan of the precious early journals. The wonderful result was the publication of his 2003 book "C. F. Martin & His Guitars, 1796-1873."

Later in 2003, my first book "Martin Guitar Masterpieces: A Showcase of Artist's Editions Limited Editions and Custom Guitars" was published. This, too, was a positive experience for me, and in 2008, after a long research collaboration with co-author Richard Johnston, our two-volume set "Martin Guitars–A History (Book One)" and "Martin Guitars–A Technical Reference (Book Two)" provided a needed update to Mike Longworth's original text.

As early as 2010, co-editors Robert Shaw and Peter Szego solicited topical essays from musicologists David Gansz, Richard Johnston, David LaPlante, Arian Sheets, and James Westbrook for their 2013 book "Inventing the American Guitar: The Pre-Civil War Innovations of C.F. Martin and His Contemporaries." This academic effort had brought several dozen early Martin instruments together for close inspection and chronological dating. The book and the associated instruments would eventually provide the basis for the unprecedented exhibition of Early Martin Guitars at the Metropolitan Museum of Art in New York City. This exhibit was an incredible honor for Martin – a fact that cannot be over-stated.

Concurrently with the essays, Peter Szego enlisted the expertise of Greig Hutton, who was already a fervent Martin guitar enthusiast, to expand upon Philip Gura's initial research into the guitars made by C. F. Martin. Hutton had done extensive research on the Canadian postal system and the historic equipment utilized to process Canadian mail, so he was well-versed and extremely thorough in his approach to research in general.

Accordingly, I received Greig into the Archives for his initial visit. Equipped with a laptop, an external hard drive, and a digital camera mounted on a vertical frame with photographic copy stand, he proceeded to capture several thousand selected images from the pages of the 1830s sales journals and related correspondences of C. F. Martin Sr.

My plan for the archives had always been to first consolidate everything into one location, then to gradually organize the files by date and/or topic into archival acid-free folders and boxes. With these organizational steps complete, the mind-boggling next steps were to somehow digitize the vast number of archive documents that I had estimated to be more than 100,000 in number. Given the demands of my job, I envisioned that this would take many years to accomplish, but here I was, watching Greig Hutton dive eagerly into this part of the job. Of course, he had agreed to share his image captures with me, but beyond the mere images, were the organization of the files, the keywording, the cross-referencing, and the actual assimilation and comprehension of the content of the documents. This was just what the archives needed!

When Greig completed his work on the pre-Civil War era of C. F. Martin Sr.'s lifetime, he requested permission to "keep going" into the later 1800s, and then further yet into the World War I and World War II time periods that would establish Martin's "Golden Era." Of course, I saw this as extremely useful and extended Greig's access to encompass the entire scope of the Martin Archives. Over the course of several years, Greig visited Nazareth several dozen times and spent countless hours capturing images that eventually totaled more than 200,000 photographs. Back in London, Ontario during the periods of time between visits, Greig would organize and assimilate these vast amounts of information, entering everything into his personal searchable database.

In the meantime, I participated in several other books projects that emerged from the Archives. In 2014, I gathered historic photographs for Arcadia Publishing's Images of America Series – "C. F. Martin & Co." In 2018, historian Larry Bartram detailed the fascinating story of the Martin ukulele that went to the North Pole with Admiral Byrd in: "A Stowaway Ukulele Revealed: Richard Konter & the Byrd Polar Expeditions." And lastly, in 2016, Jim Washburn and I assembled "The Martin Archives: A Scrapbook of Treasures from the World's Foremost Acoustic Guitar Maker."

It was perfectly clear to me that each of these book projects was adding tremendous depth and scope to the archives and making valuable information accessible to the greater community of Martin enthusiasts.

While I was busy with these projects, I was intensely aware that Greig was hard at work up in Canada on this very book, and now, after more than a decade, Greig Hutton adds his work to the long legacy of Martin. He has established himself, more or less (I'd say more!) as the Mike Longworth of our time. There is certainly no one else on the planet that knows as much about the history of Martin guitars as Greig does, and I personally thank him for sharing his knowledge with those of us who are anxiously waiting to receive it!

Dick Boak
Nazareth, PA

———————

Dick Boak is an illustrator, musician, luthier, woodworker, and author who had the distinct honor of working for the Martin Guitar Company from 1976-2018. During his 41+ years with the company he managed the Martin Museum and archives, founded the in-house advertising department, and initiated the Limited Edition guitar program that produced signature models for more than one hundred legendary artists including Steve Miller, John Mayer, Eric Clapton, Paul Simon, Mark Knopfler, Tom Petty, Joan Baez, Johnny Cash, Rosanne Cash, Marty Stuart, Willie Nelson, Sting, Laurence Juber, and Crosby, Stills & Nash. Now retired, he continues to pursue his illustrative art, music, writing, and love of guitars in Nazareth, PA
www.dickboak.com

FOREWORD
by George Gruhn and Joe Spann

At the time of this writing, C.F. Martin & Company has been in business without a break for 189 years, longer than any other presently existing or defunct guitar company on the planet. Their company records are unmatched for comprehensive scope and depth of detail. No other fretted instrument company has an archive to compare. Many researchers would be daunted simply by the sheer size of the raw data, to say nothing of the tasks of organization, reduction and synthesis required. However, in this book, author Greig Hutton has managed to combine the historical archive, along with a lifetime of first-hand observations and produced the definitive reference work, surpassing everything written previously about C.F. Martin & Company, or any other American guitar manufacturer. It provides researchers, dealers and collectors of today with new insights and a greater depth of knowledge than we have ever had available to us.

The work of an archivist is quite different from the work of an essayist. There are plenty of guitar company reference works in which an author talks about his personal experiences. This book has some elements of that, but there is no substitute for the kind of archival work that was done. Looking at instruments, repairing instruments, or even making instruments gives us some great insights, but there are other insights that this book provides that cannot be obtained in this way. Even a lifetime of in-hand examination cannot approximate the historical accuracy of a work like this one that is compiled from the original company records. This is work that often requires meticulous, detailed examination and interpretation of handwritten documents. Assembling this information was a monumental task.

This book is a very welcome addition to our library and would be to anyone else who is interested in the history of Martin guitars. No other book that we have encountered in the marketplace covers Martin's archives as deeply, from the very earliest records of the 1830's, and on to the present day. No one else we know has taken as much time and effort to go through tens of thousands of pages in the Martin archives, a task that required years of work, and produced a cross-referenced and accessible book covering the topic in this depth. Even so, it should be noted that this book does not cover the entirety of information available, and additional facts and photos may be found on the author's website (www.theguitarphile.com)

In the history of guitar company reference works, this book simply has no peer, no equal, no better.

George Gruhn and Joe Spann
Nashville, Tennessee
May 12th 2022

Chapter 1
A Short History of the Martin Guitar Co.

The history of C. F. Martin & Co. can be divided into five easily distinguishable periods:

1) C. F. Martin in Europe (1794-1833)

2) C. F. Martin in New York (1833 to 1839)

3) C. F. Martin Nazareth PA (1839 to 1867)

4) C. F. Martin & Co., Nazareth PA (1867 to 1898)

5) C. F. Martin & Co., Nazareth PA (1898 to 1969)

Between 1833 and 1867 guitars received a "C. F. Martin/New York" name stamp. The guitars made between 1833 and 1839 usually have the Stauffer body shape. From 1867 to 1898, the stamp was altered to "C. F. Martin & Co./New York". From 1898 to 1969 the name stamp became " C. F. Martin & Co./Nazareth PA".

1) C. F. Martin in Europe 1794 to 1833

Christian Frederick Martin was born on January 31, 1796 in Neukirchen, Saxony[1]. His father, Johann Georg Martin (1765-1832), was a member of the Cabinetmakers' Guild and was credited by one source with "perfecting" the guitar in Neukirchen[2].

Some of the labels in early Martin guitars proclaim Martin as a "**pupil of the celebrated Stauffer**". This would be Johann Georg Stauffer (1778-1853), the famous Viennese violin and guitar maker. Evidence of Martin's employment by Stauffer is indirect but there is no reason to doubt C. F. Martin worked for Stauffer in Vienna and even rose to the level of foreman in Stauffer's shop[2] as will be demonstrated.

Martin, having been born in 1796, would probably have started an apprenticeship with Stauffer when he was 14 or 15 (i.e. in 1810-1811). Recent research has uncovered a notice in the January 2, 1811 edition[3] of the Weiner Zeitung newspaper containing some information on Stauffer's apprentices at the time:

"**The local civil violin and lute maker Georg Stauffer has submitted a document to His Majesty in which he offered – in addition to his taxes – to voluntarily give ten percent of his total business revenue in 1811, without deduction of prior expenses to the I&R Bancozettel redemption fund. Spurred by this example his five apprentices:**

Johann Götz, Johann Buckschek, Franz Fink, Bernhard Enzensberger and Mathias Hametter also obliged themselves to give one gulden per week from their income in the same purpose."

Because C. F. Martin is not included in this list, it has been suggested that he may not have worked for Stauffer at all. However, he could have started his apprenticeship later that year. An interesting note appears in a scrapbook for the Martin and Ruetenik families: "**Cosacks (sic) plundered & burned 5 villages visible from Dresden in the year 1812 & 1813 when grandfather was 16 & 17 years old.**"[4] It is not clear if this means C. F. Martin was present in Saxony in 1812 and 1813 but he may have had to delay taking up his apprenticeship with Stauffer due to the Napoleonic wars.

Because of a lack of documentary evidence, there has always been a question as to whether C. F. Martin actually worked for Stauffer, even though C. F. Martin had clearly mastered the Stauffer-style guitars that he made in his store in New York during the 1830's.

The following is an excerpt from page 44 of the "**Historical Review for the Joint Celebration of the Musical Instrument Makers' Guild (formerly Violin Makers' Guild) and the String Makers' Guild, of Mark Neukirchen, commemorating the years of their foundation, 1677 and 1777**", published in German by the Guilds in 1927. The excerpt provides contemporary documentary evidence that C. F. Martin did indeed work for Stauffer and became a foreman in his shop:

"**The cabinet makers said in reply (to a complaint from the Violin Makers' Guild) that the violin makers has no vested right in the making of guitars and that the 'discovery of the guitar' had been brought about by travelers some 30 to 35 years before and had been perfected by the cabinet maker George Martin, and submitted a testimonial from the wholesaler Christian Wilhelm Schuster that *Christian Frederich Martin who 'for a number of years has been foreman in the factory of the noted violin and guitar maker, Johann Georg Stauffer of Vienna'*, had produced guitars, 'which in point of quality and appearance left nothing to be desired** and which marked him as a distinguished crafts-man.' Under date of July 9th, 1832 the authorities again permitted the cabinet makers to continue making guitars because these instruments were not mentioned in the Articles of the Violin Makers' Guild. In a revision on August 31st, 1837 the Guild named the guitar in Article 2 as one of the instruments included in its rights and in Article 5 allowed the presentation of a guitar as a Masterpiece. In spite of this the strife was not ended. Against the violent protests the cabinet makers were allowed, on the 19th of November 1853, to form their own Guild with a guitar as a Masterpiece. Not until the reorganization of the whole Guild System did the guitar makers, who had previously belonged to the cabinet makers' trade, join the Musical Instrument Makers' Guild." (the complete excerpt from pages 41 to 44 can be seen in note 2 for Chapter 1).

The testimonial provided by Schuster was made prior to Martin's departure for the United States and indicates Schuster was familiar with both C. F. Martin and his work.

By early 1825 C. F. Martin was employed by Karl Kühle[5], a pedal harp maker in Vienna, although it is not recorded what type of work Martin performed. Karl Kühle was the father of Ottilia Kühle, who became C. F. Martin's wife on April 25, 1825. The records for the marriage indicate that from February 1825 C. F. Martin had been living at Spittelberg No. 95, while the Kühle family was nearby at Spittelberg No. 98.[3]

Further confirmation of C. F. Martin's relationship

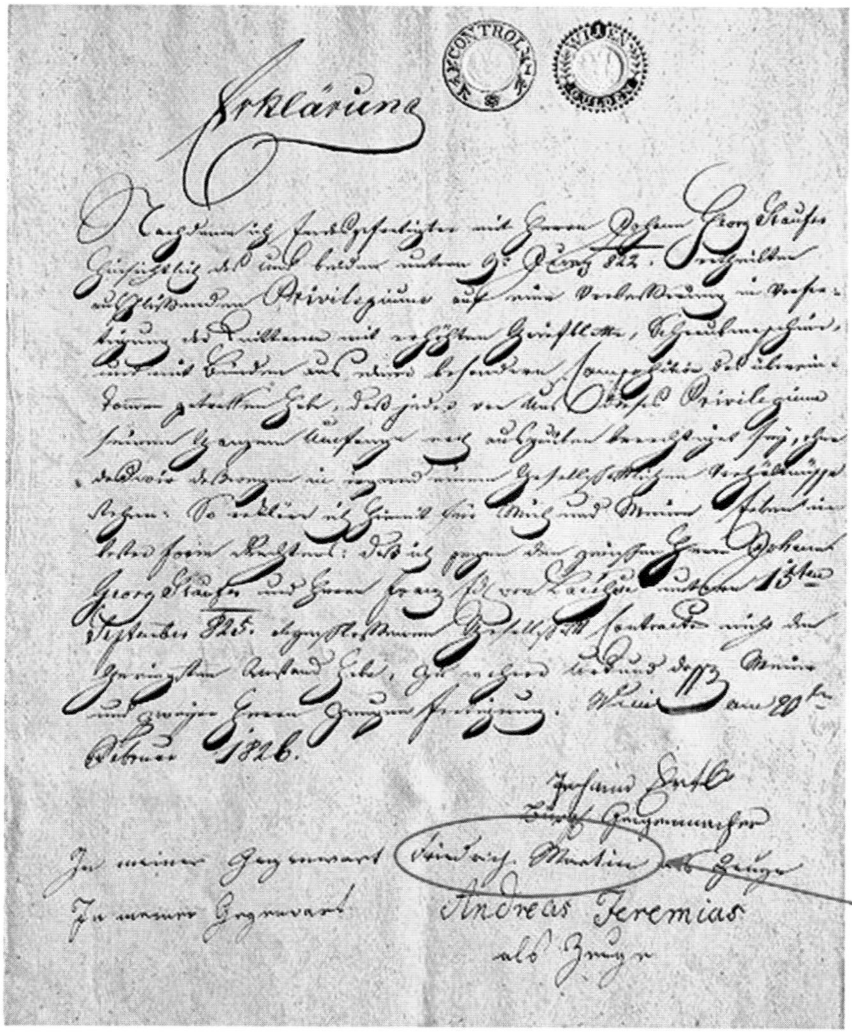

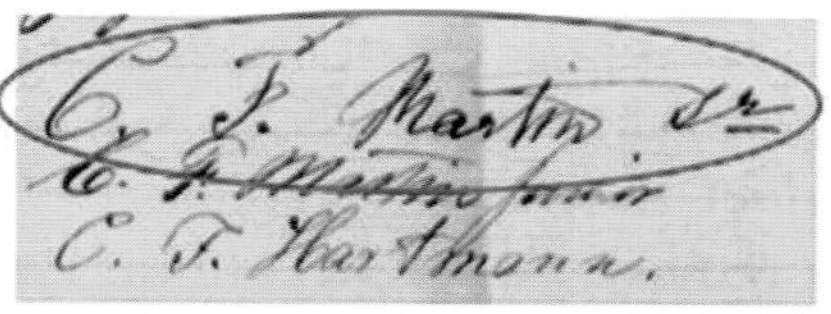

Figure 1
1826 Declaration Signed by C. F. Martin Sr.

Declaration

Because I, the undersigned, have reached an agreement with Mr. Johann Georg Stauffer that the excluding patent which was granted to both of us on 9 June 1822 concerning the improvement of guitars with elevated fingerboards, screw machines and metal frets made of a special alloy can be used by both of us to its full extent without entertaining any business relationship because of this. Therefore for me and my heirs I declare it formally legal: that I bear no the slightest objection against the business contract which on 15 September 1825 was concluded between Mr. Johann Georg Stauffer and Mr. Franz von Lacasse. In witness whereof my and the two witnesses' signatures. Vienna 20 February 1826.
Johann Ertl
Civil luthier
In my presence **Fredrich Martin** witness
In my presence **Andreas Jeremias** witness

with Stauffer comes from a legal document dated in Vienna on February 20, 1826[3] that was witnessed and signed by C. F. Martin (Figure 1). The document itself is of more than passing interest since it records the transfer of a patent jointly owned by Johann Ertl and Johann Georg Stauffer to the sole ownership of Stauffer. The patent covers the invention of the elevated fingerboard, screw machines and frets of a special alloy. This document proves that C. F. Martin must have been held in high esteem by Stauffer since he was asked to act as a witness, even though he was no longer employed by Stauffer. It implies Martin had, at some point, worked for Stauffer and also proves that C. F. Martin was familiar with the elevated fingerboard and other features that appeared on many of the guitars he made in New York. The second witness, Andreas Jeremias (1797-1838), was a contemporary of Martin's and another well known Viennese guitar maker (Hofmann et al 2011).

In case there is any doubt on the identity of "Frederich Martin" in the declaration, the signature on this document closely matches the signatures of C. F. Martin Sr. found in the Martin Guitar Co. archive.

Martin's first child, C. F. Martin Jr., was born in Vienna on October 2, 1825 and was baptized on October 22. Emilie Martin, C. F. Martin's second child followed on April 27, 1827 and was baptized on May 2. Heinrich (Henry) Schatz signed the baptismal certificate (Figure 2) as Emilie's godfather, thus proving his close relationship with the Martin family and the fact that both he and C. F. Martin were still living in Vienna[3] at that time.

C. F. Martin returned to Neukirchen in Saxony in 1828[6] where he probably took up working along side his father.

No instruments made in Neukirchen by either Christian Frederick Martin or his father have been found to date, nor is it likely one will ever to be discovered. The wholesale instrument trade in Neukirchen was controlled by a few prominent families. They actively discouraged artisans from identifying their work, to prevent them attempting to establish a market for their own instruments.

The continuing dispute with the Violin Makers' Guild and the death of his father on May 6, 1832[7] were probably the main reasons for C. F. Martin's decision to immigrate to the United States. C. F. Martin under-

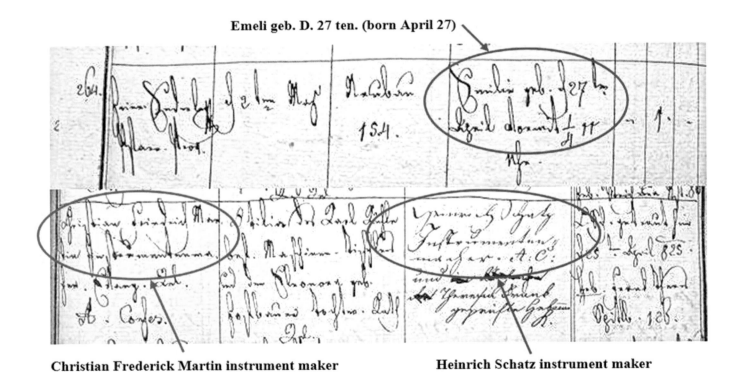

Emeli geb. D. 27 ten. (born April 27)

Christian Frederick Martin instrument maker   Heinrich Schatz instrument maker

Figure 2
1827 Baptism Record for Emelie Martin

stood the merit of his musical instruments and could see no way to move forward in the confining guild system of his native land. He had doubtless also heard glowing reports of the opportunities in America from his friend, Henry Schatz, who had immigrated to the United States around 1830, and he could expect help settling in New York from Schatz and the large German community already in the city.

2) The New York Period 1833 to 1839

C. F. Martin and family sailed from Bremen on September 8, 1833[8] aboard the ship "Columbus" and arrived in New York on November 6[9]. Louis Schmidt, 18 years old at the time, arrived on the same ship. Schmidt was almost certainly Martin's apprentice from Neukirchen.

"Francis Kuhle, age 31, merchant" also appeared on the manifest, possibly a brother of Martin's wife, Ottilia.

Martin took up residence in New York and immediately began the establishment of his business. Until now it had not been known where Martin lived between his arrival and the opening of his store at 196 Hudson St. in May 1834. However, the earliest ledger does provide one clue. On August 1, 1834 there is an entry for "the Rent to Mr. West & Cholay" for $47.50. In this period rent was generally paid at the end of each quarter[10], so this rent payment covered the period from May to July 1834. The rent seems too low for 196 Hudson Street, as we know the rent during the 1836 and 1837 period was $100 per quarter, and was always paid to a Mr. McVickar.

There is no West & Cholay in the 1834 edition of Longworth's American Almanac. However, there is a **West & Scholey** listed as "silkhatters" at 157-158 Broadway. This may be where the Martin family was living prior to the move to 196 Hudson Street. The building at 157-158 Broadway must have been quite large as Longworth's American Almanac lists 9 other businesses at this address. A certain F. Delhoyo is recorded as operating a boarding house at 158 Broadway in 1834, so Martin may have been subletting rooms above the hat shop of West & Scholey.

The first expense in the 1834 ledger is for a "**trip to Philadelphia**" dated April 29, 1834[11]. Of the total

expense of $9.25, "carriers" received $0.25, probably for the transport of a crate to 196 Hudson Street. The first musical instrument shipment recorded in the ***Rechnungsbuch Merz*** was made to Henry Schatz in Philadelphia[12] (T. F. Merz in Neukirchen supplied musical merchandise to Schatz and later C. F. Martin). It seems likely that Martin took passage to Philadelphia to pick up a portion of one of these shipments.

To be completely accurate, the first shipment to Schatz recorded in the ***Rechnungsbuch Merz*** was made in July 1834. However, the shipment was marked as "Box 3" so it is reasonable to assume Boxes 1 and 2 were shipped to Schatz at an earlier date and the "trip" mentioned above was to pick up a portion of one of these earlier shipments.

Some notes written by C. F. Martin in the 1834 Martin ledger concerning Louis Schmidt and Jacob Hartman have only recently been translated and reveal several interesting and important new facts. Louis Schmidt, as mentioned above, was C. F. Martin's apprentice and as noted by Martin in a June 4, 1834 entry: **"from this date I am giving him weekly $4 and board and lodging"**.[13,14]

Jacob Hartman was another early employee of Martin's although it is not known what relationship he may have had to Martin or whether he might have been related to August Hartman, one of Martin's suppliers in Germany. In a June 1, 1834 entry Martin noted for Hartman: **"to this date all has been reckoned up, I pay the remainder $15.00, I give from today room and board and $1 per week, for this he manages for me all my business proceeds in the city"**.

In effect, both Schmidt and Hartman were members of the Martin family.

Since Hartman's duties involved "handling all (Martin's) business proceeds in the city", this would seem to indicate that Martin, from the very beginning, intended to concentrate on building guitars. This is certainly borne out by the guitar sales for 1834. Martin carefully separated "instruments which I made myself" from the other store sales. The first ledger book covers sales and expenses from late May to early November 1834 and in that period of 5 months C. F. Martin and Louis Schmidt, possibly with some help from Schatz and Hartman, made 29 guitars, an average of 5 guitars per month.

The first recorded sale at 196 Hudson Street was for some strings on May 26, 1834[15], but there are also a few entries indicating Martin collected monies for at least two guitars that were sold prior to the store opening.[16]

Considering that Schmidt and Hartman were boarding with him, Martin would have started his business immediately upon arriving in New York, making guitars and taking in repair work. Martin would have sold his guitars directly to teachers and music stores, so was developing a market for his instruments even before his store at 196 Hudson St. opened in May 1834.

The ledger book for 1835 is missing but Jacob Hartman must have stopped working for Martin prior to the end of 1835 since Charles Bruno was keeping Martin's books by January 1, 1836. Like Hartman, Bruno would have managed the shop and otherwise looked after Martin's business affairs. Jacob Hartman continued to appear regularly in the Martin ledgers from 1836 to 1838 for the payments made to him for repairing brass instruments. Hartman does not appear in the city directory so was probably one of the many craftsmen who occupied small shops at the rear of other businesses. He may even have worked independently out of 196 Hudson St.

Henry Schatz only rarely appears in the 1834 ledger. From June to August 1834, Schatz was paid a total of only $11.50[17]. He may have been helping Martin and Schmidt from time to time but he had his own musical instrument business to operate in Philadelphia, although confirming documentation has yet to be found.

Martin & Schatz formed some form of business relationship about January 1835. Several guitars were shipped to J. G. Miller of Philadelphia on March 3, 1835 and Miller was offering "Martin & Schatz" guitars for sale in a newspaper advertisement[18] on March 18 (Figure 3). The ledger entry recording the shipment to J. G. Miller appears to be in Schatz's hand writing.

Further confirmation of the business relationship is a notice in the April 13, 1835 edition of The Evening Post (New York) advertising undelivered letters at the

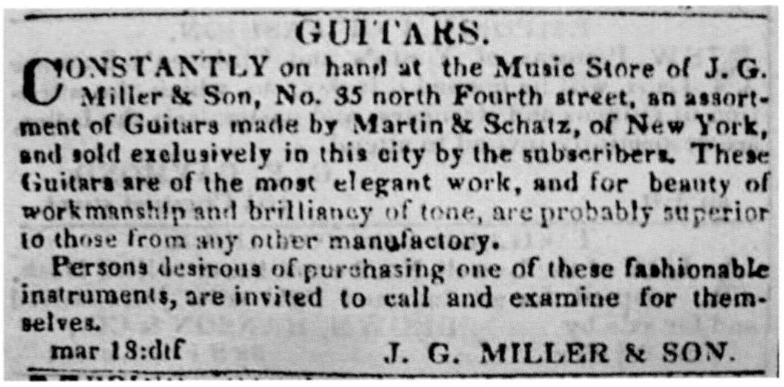
GUITARS.

CONSTANTLY on hand at the Music Store of J. G. Miller & Son, No. 35 north Fourth street, an assortment of Guitars made by Martin & Schatz, of New York, and sold exclusively in this city by the subscribers. These Guitars are of the most elegant work, and for beauty of workmanship and brilliancy of tone, are probably superior to those from any other manufactory.

Persons desirous of purchasing one of these fashionable instruments, are invited to call and examine for themselves.

mar 18:dtf J. G. MILLER & SON.

Figure 3
March 18, 1835 Advertisement for Martin & Schatz Guitars Published in the Philadelphia National Gazette

post office, including a letter for "Martin & Schatz".

T. F. Merz made several shipments to "Martin & Schatz" commencing in April 1835[19] and we know that Merz was informed Martin & Schatz partnership by late January 1835. The T. F. Merz correspondence demonstrates that Merz originally exported musical instruments and supplies to Schatz. Schatz had accumulated a debt of about 2,000 rixdollars ($1,600 in US currency) by the end of 1834 and had not notified Merz about the Martin & Schatz partnership until after it happened. However, Merz knew C. F. Martin personally so was not too upset with the new arrangement, even though he had every right to expect more consideration, as he was, in effect, financing Schatz and, later, Martin & Schatz.

Shipments of musical merchandise continued to be sent to "Martin & Schatz" until September 1836[20]. Schatz purchased land at Millgrove PA in December 1835[21] and had moved there by April 1836 or earlier as Martin paid the postage for a letter from Schatz in Millgrove on April 28[22]. (Author's note: At the time, letters were usually sent unpaid, the receiver being required to pay the postage). It appears the Martin & Schatz partnership may have continued as late as August or September1836 as the next C. F. Martin label (type 4) came into use about October 1836. Untangling the partnership and obtaining permission from Merz to transfer the trade debt from Martin & Schatz to C. F. Martin may have accounted for the delay.

At this point Merz was not happy. Schatz had built up a considerable debt, formed a partnership with Martin and then abandoned that partnership, leaving C. F. Martin to carry on the business with the accumulated debt. Whatever Merz' misgivings, he continued to export goods to Martin at an increasing rate and the debt continued to increase.

Throughout 1835 and 1836 Martin steadily increased musical imports from Germany as his business grew. By late 1836 or early 1837 business had increased to the point where another location became necessary. Martin started paying rent on 212 Fulton Street from February 1, 1837[23] although the first sale at that location wasn't recorded until April 1[24]. Starting in late March, the ledger for 196 Hudson Street shows moneys being received from C. F. Martin, sometimes twice a day. From this it would appear that C. F. Martin was running the 212 Fulton Street location himself and that it was his policy to keep as little cash as possible in the new store. The style of writing in the ledger makes a subtle change about March 21, 1837 and it appears that another employee began keeping the books at 196 Hudson Street, just as the 212 Fulton Street opened.

Unfortunately, the opening of 212 Fulton Street coincided with the Panic of 1837[25]. The Panic had an immediate and very negative effect on Martin's sales. After May 10, the ledgers often record only one or two sales entries per day whereas previously there had often been four or more.

The sudden change in business climate caused C. F. Martin to quickly close the 196 Hudson Street shop. The last sale at 196 Hudson Street was recorded on June 9, 1837, although rent was paid to the end of July.

Interestingly, the ledger contains several clues that C. F. Martin continued to live and work out of 196 Hudson Street after the store closed, giving up the storefront but working and living on a floor above. On May 4, 1838 Bruno "Paid ($45) to Professor McVickar the balance of the last quarter's rent for the house No. 196 Hudson St."[26] and charged the $45 to Martin's account. A number of guitars from the 1837 to 1838 period have labels with an additional hand written endorsement "& 196 Hudson Str." An entry in the ledger dated August 17, 1838 notes a charge for carrying a piano from "Mr Opel's, 196 Hudson str to the store at 212 Fulton str"[27].

In the period following May 10, 1837 the ledger contains numerous small expenses for "bank note lists". The Panic of 1837 resulted in the disappearance of coinage from circulation. There was no Federal Reserve system so private banks issued their own bank notes, often issuing bank notes with a total value many times the value of specie actually on hand. The Panic resulted in a sudden demand by the public to convert bank notes to coinage. The banks had to refuse to exchange bank notes for coinage or go bankrupt. So it was prudent to have purchased "bank note lists" to see which banks had failed, thus rendering their issued bank notes worthless.

On May 1, 1838 Martin and Bruno entered into a co-partnership that was advertised in The Morning Courier & New York Enquirer[28]. The advertisement reads:

COPARTNERSHIP
C. F. MARTIN having taken C. BRUNO into copartnership, the business in future will be conducted under the firm of MARTIN & BRUNO at 212 Fulton street (late 196 Hudson st.) C. F. MARTIN Manufacturer and Importer of Musical Instruments New York, May 1, 1838

Longworth's American Almanac for 1837-1838 records Bruno as a "bookseller" at the 212 Fulton Street, while the directory for 1838-1839 also shows Bruno selling musical instruments. There are separate listings for C. F. Martin, Martin & Bruno and Charles Bruno. At the time, it was the normal practice of Longworth's directory to give individuals from partnerships their own listings.

By 1838 it appears Martin had made up his mind to make the move to the Nazareth area, as both he and his wife visited Nazareth during that summer. His other actions during 1838 also tend to support this assertion. Martin probably formed the partnership with Bruno in the hope that the business in New York would continue and he would maintain an outlet for his instruments. Martin also appears to have been helping Louis Schmidt, his apprentice and long-term employee, open his own business. Schmidt continued in Martin's employ until the middle of 1838 but was purchasing musical supplies from Martin throughout that year. A payment of $100 to Schmidt on August 23, 1838[29] may have been a loan of start-up capital. The city directory for 1838-1839 confirms Louis Schmidt had his own musical instrument business operating at 92 Chatham Street.

Bruno sent money to Mrs. Martin in Nazareth via "Mr. Clewel (sic)" in June 1838[30] and again in November[31], so it is entirely possible Mrs. Martin and the children were already in the Nazareth area. Many purchases for wine and bread were made by Bruno between June and October 1838 and charged to C. F. Martin's account. Only a few entries for wine were recorded in the ledger prior to June 1838.

When all these details are considered, it appears C. F. Martin had decided on the move by the beginning of 1838 and had moved his family to the Nazareth by the end of May that year. Martin stayed on by himself in New York to establish the Martin & Bruno partnership. At the same time, C. F. Martin was helping Louis Schmidt launch his own business.

Sales were slow through 1838 and this likely contributed to the breakup of the Martin & Bruno partnership. From the edger entries it appears the Martin & Bruno partnership only lasted until the end of September 1838. From the start of the partnership on May 1, Bruno had been very diligent in charging non-business expenses to C. F. Martin's account. This strict accounting ended at the end of September although Bruno continued to work for Martin until late November[32].

Having failed to find a partner to continue the business in New York, Martin sold his stock in trade to Ludecus & Wolter, another music store located in New York, on May 29, 1839[33].

Comparing the handwritten entries in the Martin ledgers after November 1838 and the inventory listing sold to Ludecus & Wolter on May 29 demonstrates that Edward Ludecus was working with C. F. Martin from at least January 1839. This would have been a very prudent arrangement for both parties. C. F. Martin received help with the bookkeeping and Ludecus & Wolter would have learned the business and been able to take a detailed inventory.

The sale to Ludecus & Wolter included not only Martin's stock in trade but also his relationship with T. F. Merz. From the Rechnungsbuch Merz ledger we know that T. F. Merz began shipping directly to Ludecus & Wolter on October 23, 1839 and even continued using the same sequence of box numbers previously used for shipments to C. F. Martin[34].

3) C. F. Martin Nazareth PA (1839 to 1867)

As his family was already in Nazareth there was nothing keeping Martin in New York and he probably made the move to Nazareth in June 1839.

Thus Martin's sojourn in New York had come to an end. The impression, gained from studying the archival material, is that Martin was not really interested in the retail music trade and was focused, from the beginning, on building guitars. His New York business was a means to an end. He had the contacts in Neukirchen for the importation of musical merchandise and the revenue from the retail store helped support his family as well as several employees.

A recently discovered document in the Martin Guitar Co. archive shows that C. F. Martin leased part of a farm house from William L. S. Gross in Bushkill Township from April 1, 1839 to April 1, 1840. For $30 per quarter the Martin family had use of the kitchen, two bed rooms, washroom, cellar, one-half of the garden, a share of the stable and, most importantly, "**all the old shop**". Although the exact location of this farm house has yet to be confirmed, it was in Schoeneck on the west side of North Broad Street. It is probably the house directly across from the Schoeneck church and is very close to Martin's modern factory. This was Martin's first guitar shop in the Nazareth area. It was about 1-1/4 miles south of the farm of Henry Schatz.

On December 21, 1839 Martin purchased 8 acres of land from Philip Deringer in Cherry Hill on the southern edge of Bushkill Township. The deed specified that the property included a "**messuage tenement**", an archaic legal term for a dwelling and associated outbuildings. The property was purchased for $1,250 and, because land was worth about $50 per acre at the time, the lot must already have had a house and other buildings. Although a family picture claims Martin "built this home" it is clear that the house, barn and the shop at the end of the house were already in existence when the Martin family moved in.

Once in the Nazareth area Martin went back into partnership with Henry Schatz. A few guitars are known with a new type of Martin & Schatz label (type 7) without a New York street address. Fortunately, the three known examples of the type 7 label have hand-written serial numbers that maintain continuity with the serial number sequence used by Martin guitars in New York.

Martin & Schatz, wanting to maintain an outlet for their products in New York, appointed Ludecus & Wolter as their agents in the city. For Ludecus & Wolter this was such an important business arrangement that it was noted in their entry in the 1839 edition of Longworth's American Almanac (Figure 4). C. F. Martin also used the Ludecus & Wolter address, at 320 Broadway, for the company's entry (Figure 5).

For a time Ludecus & Wolter even used sales receipt forms left over from the Martin & Bruno partnership, as evidenced by the receipt in Figure 6. Recently a Martin violin came to light, identified because it contained a Martin label (Figure 7). Ever thrifty, Martin had just clipped the title box out of one of his sales forms and used it as a label for the violin! This also nicely dates the violin to 1838 or 1839.

The evidence is thin but it appears the Ludecus & Wolter agency started in June 1839 and was possibly terminated as early as August 1839 due to a lack of sales activity. The Martin & Coupa agency replaced

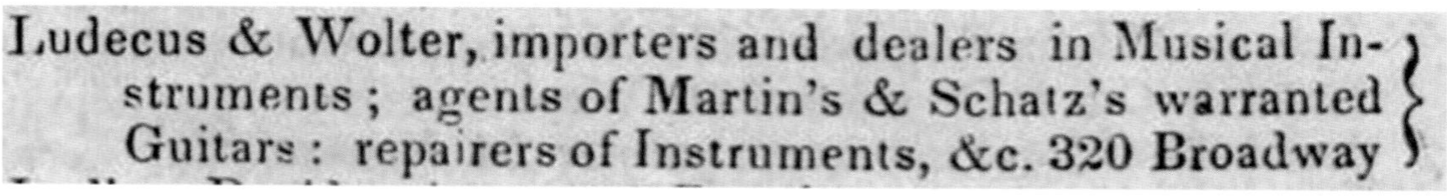

Ludecus & Wolter, importers and dealers in Musical Instruments; agents of Martin's & Schatz's warranted Guitars: repairers of Instruments, &c. 320 Broadway

Figure 4
Entry for Ludecus & Wolter in the 1839-1840 edition of Longworth's American Almanac

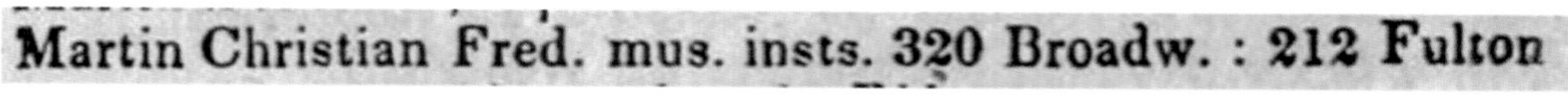

Martin Christian Fred. mus. insts. 320 Broadw. : 212 Fulton

Figure 5
Entry for C. F. Martin in the 1839-1840 edition of Longworth's American Almanac

Figure 6
Entry for Ludecus & Walter sales order dated August 13, 1839 using left-over Martin & Bruno forms (E-Bay photo)

Figure 7
Label Inside 1838 or 1839 Martin Violin

Ludecus & Wolter at the same time[35] or possibly the agency was split between Ludecus & Wolter and Coupa.

The renewal of the Martin & Schatz partnership may have only been intended as a temporary arrangement. Instrument production in the Nazareth area probably took place at Martin's first residence in Schoeneck from June 1839. As mentioned earlier, Martin rented part of a farm house in Schoeneck, including "all of the shop". This shop was an old blacksmith's forge and is still in existence. By the time Martin moved into his own house in Cherry Hill in late December 1839, or shortly thereafter, the partnership with Schatz seems to have come to an end. By that time Martin had a work force that included himself, C. F. Martin Jr. and C. F. Hartmann, his nephew, so he may not have needed Henry Schatz. There is also the possibility that Schatz continued to work for Martin as an employee but we will probably never know as the ledger books for the 1840's are missing.

Only three guitars from the 1839 to 1840 period are documented with type 7 labels. One has the Martin & Schatz label AND a Ludecus & Wolter label[36], the second has the Martin & Schatz label AND a Martin & Coupa label[37] and the last only has the type 7 label[38]. The archival records are very spotty for 1839 and 1840. Only a few guitars were recorded as being sold to Ludecus & Wolter, the latest one on March 8, 1840[39]. The last sales entries are from March 26, 1840 but these guitars were sold to John Coupa[40]. Records from May 1839 to February 1840 are completely missing. This period may define the second Martin & Schatz partnership since sales and expenses for this partnership would probably have been kept in a separate ledger.

From late August 1839 Martin set up an sales agency for New York with John. B. Coupa at 385 Broadway. The ware rooms were above the Samuel C. Jollie & Co. music store (Figure 8). The case labels of this period confirm the upstairs location of the shop (See Case Labels on pages 126 and 127).

No written agreement between Martin and Coupa has been found in the archive although one probably existed. Whether there was a formal agreement or not, this was a most successful business arrangement. Martin had an outlet for his guitars in the booming New York musical scene with a well known concert guitarist and teacher managing the guitar depot and looking after the company's business affairs in the city. Equally valuable, Coupa provided feedback to Martin and introduced him to many artists and different types of music. Coupa was in a unique position to influence the development of Martin guitars.

Guitars that were sold from 385 Broadway Street received a Martin & Coupa (Type 8) label. Martin also had a network of other dealers in the eastern US, the Southern states and even the West, which at that time meant Ohio. Guitars sold to other dealers did not receive the Martin & Coupa label unless they were wholesaled from 385 Broadway. The agency for Martin guitars in New York continued until John Coupa's death on May 18, 1850[41].

Most of the records covering 1840 to 1850 are missing but by 1850 Martin reported a workforce of 6, although the expense records do not seem to support this, and a capacity of 250 guitars per year. The expense ledgers are very sparse for the 1850's but it appears the core workforce consisted of C. F. Martin Sr., C. F. Martin Jr., C. F. Hartmann and Henry Goetz. Martin may have employed a few more workers for making cases but it doesn't appear this was full-time work. That same year he installed a steam engine to power a saw and a lathe[42]. A lathe may seem to be an odd piece of equipment for making guitars but its real purpose was probably for winding strings.

As a result of Coupa's death, C. F. Martin Jr. moved to New York at the beginning of June 1850 to handle the business at 385 Broadway Street. The sales' records he kept were spotty and only covered to October 1850[43]. Guitar shipments to New York and expenses were recorded separately and cover up to January 1851[44].

On January 1, 1851 Martin drew up a business agreement for the sales agency in New York City with guitarist Charles De Janon[45]. Martin paid for the ware rooms at 385 Broadway Street and De Janon was allowed to use the rooms for teaching free of charge. The agreement was valid until February 1, 1852. The correspondence with De Janon reveals he was not as astute a businessman as Coupa and the agreement was not renewed. In fact, De Janon continued to owe money to Martin for a number of years.

Figure 8
Advertisement for Samuel C. Jollie & Co.
store at 385 Broadway ca 1839-1840
The Martin & Coupa depot was located on the second floor.

It is not known how long Martin maintained the location at 385 Broadway but the last mention of rent appears in a letter dated 1853[46].

The Martin archive contains numerous letters from dealers complaining about slow deliveries of guitars during the period from 1851 to 1858. Production figures through this period are remarkably stable and Martin seems to have been content with selling 200 to 300 guitars per year even when a greater demand existed for his instruments.

Sales dropped to under 100 guitars per year in 1861 and 1862. This may be as a result of the beginning of the Civil War but it is known C. F. Martin Sr. suffered a stroke around this time period and the drop in

production may reflect his absence from the factory. The drop in sales was not related to workers enlisting in the army because the work force does not seem to have changed at all. Regardless, sales rebounded strongly in 1863 to 221 instruments and over 300 in 1864. Unfortunately, the sales records for June 28, 1864 to August 4, 1867 are missing.

On July 20, 1867 articles were drawn up between C. F. Martin Sr., C. F. Martin Jr. and C. F. Hartmann to form a new company, C. F. Martin & Co. The establishment of the C. F. Martin & Company ended the first chapter of the Martin story.

See Appendix G for an estimate of guitar production covering the years from 1833 to 1867.

What was C. F. Martin Sr. like?

It might be best to look at what his immediate family thought of him. The following excerpts, from a biography written in 1913 by C. F. Martin Sr.'s granddaughter, Clara Ruetenik-Whittaker, give some insight into his personality:

"...on all his pictures grandfather looks strictly honest, upright, firm, yet kind and pleasant.

... I can well imagine him among his guests, a genial, hospitable, modest personage, putting himself into the background, yet beloved and respected by all.

... he must have found a keen delight in his creative abilities. Nor was he satisfied with anything mediocre – he was anxious to produce the very best that can be produced."

These observations fit well with what can be gleaned from his correspondence. Close examination of Martin instruments of the 1830's and 1840's show that C. F. Martin Sr. was constantly experimenting, always seeking to improve the tone of his instruments. In fact, of the twenty or so pre-1840 Martin guitars examined, practically no two are exactly the same in terms of bracing.

C. F. Martin Sr. was never hidebound in his approach to the design and construction of his instruments and was open to the influences around him. John B. Coupa played a particularly important role in introducing Martin to Spanish guitar players and their instruments but it was his open attitude that allowed him to absorb this influence into his own instruments. Martin began experimenting with Spanish features on his guitars in 1837 and by 1840 had dropped the traditional Stauffer guitar shape for Spanish-shaped guitars. Nor was the shape of the guitar the only change Martin made. The 50 or so Martin & Coupa guitars from the 1840's examined for this book, especially those made before about 1842, show a wide variety of top bracing patterns and differences in construction details.

4) C. F. Martin & Co. (1867 to 1898)

The formation of C. F. Martin & Co. began a long period of relative stability, compared to the frenetic period of innovation that characterized Martin during the 1840's and 1850's.

C. F. Martin Sr. had been in declining health for some time before the formation of the company in 1867 and passed away in 1873, so the driving force for innovation waned. It is just as likely that Martin had perfected the guitar for the musical tastes of the period, so further changes to their product line were unnecessary. C. F. Martin Jr. also seemed content to leave marketing of Martin instruments to C. A. Zoebisch while he concentrated on manufacturing.

The product range and many construction features of Martin guitars had been perfected, although minor variations in purfling used for the top, sound hole, end block and back stripe are not uncommon. Sales records are complete from the formation of C. F. Martin & Co. in August 1867 until September 1884. The sales ledgers are missing from late 1884 until July 31, 1898 although partial sales records, for 1888 to 1890 and 1892 to 1893, have been reconstructed from the C. A. Zoebisch & Sons correspondence in the archive.

This period for Martin was dominated by two major financial upheavals, The Panic of 1873 and The Panic of 1893.

The Panic of 1873 was an event that had long-term consequences for Martin's business. The Panic was a financial crisis that triggered a severe international economic depression in both Europe and the United States that continued until 1879. This depression was known as the "Great Depression" until the Depression of the 1930's usurped that name and is now often called the "Long Depression" instead. The Panic was caused by a fall in the international demand for silver as a result of Germany's decision to abandon the silver standard after the Franco-Prussian war. Western U. S. mines provided much of the world's silver at the time and the reduction in demand led to a dramatic fall in silver prices. As a result, the U. S. government passed the Coinage Act of 1873 which essentially demonetized silver and put the United States on the gold standard.

The financial depression did not seem to affect Martin's sales until several years after the Panic began. From 1873 to 1875 Martin's guitar sales averaged about 225 per year. However, in 1876 Martin only sold 50 instruments and 1878 was another poor year with only 64 guitars being shipped. Sales of Martin guitars did not recover to pre-1873 levels until 1883. The sales records are missing from 1884 to 1898 but it appears the late 1880's was a period of strong sales growth and by 1893 Martin was manufacturing about 480 to 500 guitars per year.

C. A. Zoebisch & Sons acted as master distributor for Martin guitars in the United States from 1868, although Martin continued to sell directly to a few dealers until at least 1884. This sales policy may have continued until 1893 but the point is moot due to the lack of sales ledgers. The archival correspondence has been carefully reviewed for the 1868 to 1897 period and, for the most part, Martin guitars were handled by C. A. Zoebisch & Sons. As might be expected Zoebisch was extremely jealous of its business relationship with C. F. Martin & Co. Throughout this period there is a steady stream of correspondence extolling the benefits of dealing solely through Zoebisch and complaints about music dealers attempting to get local agencies so they can deal directly with Martin. C. A. Zoebisch was also a firm believer that his policy of supporting dealers was the correct approach and he was constantly arguing with Martin about the discount that should be offered to teachers. Martin did occasionally appoint local agents. For example, W. H. Keller (a relative of F. H. Martin's wife) received the agency for Easton PA in 1887 and became one of Martin's more active dealers until well into the 20th century.

The original 1867 C. F. Martin & Co. partnership included C. F. Martin Sr., C. F. Martin Jr. and C. F. Hartmann. The partnership was revised on January 1, 1880 by the surviving partners, C. F. Martin Jr. and C. F. Hartmann. Although C. F. Martin Sr. had died in 1873, it had taken time to wind up his estate, thus explaining the delay in the new agreement. The two partners were co-owners of the business although C. F. Martin Jr. retained ownership of the factory and rented it to the company for $75 per year.

Based on clues in the ledger books, it appears the partnership was dissolved around April 1885 and C. F. Martin Jr. became the sole proprietor. It has been suggested that C. F. Hartmann was ousted from the partnership but as co-owner it is difficult to see how this could have happened. It should be remembered that Hartman would have been about 65 years old in 1885 and had been working for the company for more than 45 years. Since Hartmann's son did not seem interested in the guitar business, Hartmann may have decided to sell his shares in the company while continuing to work at the factory as an employee, which he did until retiring in 1892.

C. F. Martin Jr.'s health began to fail during the late 1880's and at the beginning of July 1888 Frank Henry Martin, C. F. Martin Jr.'s only son, began to keep the ledger books. C. F. Martin Jr. died in Nazareth on November 15, 1888 and the ownership of the firm passed to F. H. Martin, only 22 years old at the time. The responsibility of managing the business and supporting his mother and several unmarried sisters must have been considerable burden, but in this he would have been aided by his very experienced factory workers (C. F. Hartman, 49 years with the company, Henry Goetz, 38 years with the company, and Reinhold Schuster, more than 20 years with the company). Frank Henry also inherited the long-standing business relationship with C. A. Zoebisch & Sons which would allow him the time to gain experience before forging his own path.

Although only a few years of sales can be pieced together from 1888 to 1893, Zoebisch was clearly dictating the size, style and quantities of guitars being produced by the Martin factory. Zoebisch would order guitars on monthly or semi-monthly "lists" that averaged between 25 guitars per month in 1888 but which increased to 30 guitars per month by 1893. Production was about 280 guitars in 1888 but gradually increased

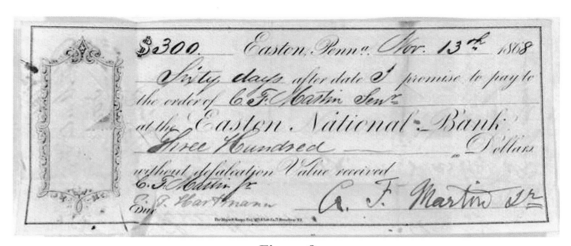

Figure 9
Check with Signatures of C. F. Martin Sr., C. F. Martin Jr. and C. F. Hartmann

to about 480 to 500 guitars in 1893.

The Panic of 1893 was another serious economic depression in the United States and triggered a series of events that changed Martin forever and eventually cost C. A. Zoebisch & Sons its master distributorship.

The Panic of '93 was caused by the collapse of a railroad building bubble, resulting in a series of bank failures. Compounding the railroad bubble was a run on the gold supply as huge quantities of silver were being produced by new Western U. S. mines, thus depressing silver prices. The Panic of '93 was the worst economic depression the United States had experienced to that time and the U. S. economy did not begin to recover until 1897.

Although the first sign of trouble was the bankruptcy of the Philadelphia & Reading Railroad on February 23,1893, it was not until July 19 that the Zoebisch correspondence noted bank failures and financial troubles. From this point until the end of 1893 Zoebisch correspondence include numerous statements about the slowness of business, shortage of money, continued bank failures and inability to collect debts.

Zoebisch, to emphasize the poor business environment, started to report the number of guitars in stock. At one point, on October 16, 1893, Zoebisch reported 168 on hand, equal to about 4 months' production. However, by November 28 the guitars on hand had fallen to a more manageable figure of 84 instruments.

Near the end of the year, on December 21, Zoebisch wrote Martin to tell him 81 guitars were in stock and

that Martin should consider shutting down for a time due to lack of business. With the sharp drop in business Martin entered into discussions with Zoebisch about building mahogany guitars to be priced below style 17. Martin does not appear to have added mahogany guitars to the product line at this time but one prototype was shipped on May 4, 1894, two more in June 1894 and one in August 1894.

Although the correspondence after 1893 is somewhat fragmentary, it appears Zoebisch never again controlled the output of Martin factory. Zoebisch continued to play a role in selling Martin guitars as he had 65 guitars in stock on March 9, 1894 and 106 guitars on hand on November 8, 1895. As with most changes made by Frank Henry Martin, the termination of the Zoebisch master distributorship was implemented over a period of time, especially considering their long and cordial business and personal relationships.

Zoebisch continued to be the largest distributor of Martin guitars but by 1894 Frank Henry Martin must have realized that it was becoming more and more risky to rely on only one agent. Martin as a company needed to broaden its base of dealers. Martin was also well aware of the many complaints from dealers who had to deal through Zoebisch.

Martin began collecting intelligence on musical instrument dealers in a number of markets. For instance, J. M. Holland, son of the guitar teacher Justin Holland, provided some very interesting insights into dealers known to him in New Orleans and Chicago when he wrote to Martin on May 17, 1895.

Martin began making prototype mandolins in 1895, against the Zoebisch's advice, and began to explore how to market them. F. H. Martin continued to move cautiously as illustrated by a letter written to him by Joseph Flanner, a music dealer in Milwaukee, on June 12, 1895. Flanner accepted the Martin agency for mandolins in Milwaukee but expressed disappointment that the agency did not include guitars. This policy did not last long, though, as Flanner noted in a November 19, 1895 letter that he had just learned he could now buy guitars directly from Martin.

At the same time The Chicago Music Co. in a letter dated November 8, 1895 complained about the way Zoebisch did business in Chicago and commented that Zoebisch was "poor".

C. F. Albert of Philadelphia was also an early dealer of Martin mandolins and by December 1895 must have also received the agency for guitars because an order for guitars was placed by him on December 11.

The Martin archive contains a large number of letters from Zoebisch in 1892 and 1893 but no correspondence for the years 1895 and 1896, although the archive does contain a number of invoices from C. A. Zoebisch & Son for guitar machines, shellac and other musical supplies. The correspondence for these years may have gone missing but it is clear Zoebisch's reign as sole agent of Martin instruments had ended by 1895. C. A. Zoebisch Jr. was 71 years old in 1895 and just did not have had the drive or energy to adapt to the changes in the music business environment.

Martin named Chicago Music Co. as an agent for Martin mandolins at some point in 1895 or 1896. Chicago Music Co. must have been tardy in paying its bills because F. H. Martin wrote them a letter on September 2, 1896 laying out terms of business and, having received no reply, removed their agency for Martin mandolins. That cancellation of their agency got Chicago Music's attention because, in a letter dated October 3, they apologized for the late response and delays in payment and stated they wanted to take advantage of the discount for cash payment in the future.

That didn't end the problems with Chicago Music Co., however, because they were put into receiver-ship in 1897 by one of their creditors. Chicago Music Co. complained to Martin that the receivership didn't need to happen but that did not stop them from making low offers to creditors for monies owed.

By 1897 Zoebisch's relationship with Martin had been seriously eroded. Just the same, he continued to advise Martin to stick to the old business model of selling through dealers and limiting the discount offered to teachers. Zoebisch commented on the Chicago Music receivership in several letters and must have felt vindicated in his negative opinion of a company that had been trying to undermine his relationship with Martin for some time.

Nevertheless, Martin's business with Zoebisch continued to fade. On December 15, 1898 Martin made a final sale to C. A. Zoebisch & Sons, a 00-28 (serial number 8255).

In the April 13, 1901 edition of the Music Trade Review, there is an interesting report on page 20:

"Zoebisch Sells to Pollman

C. A. Zoebisch & Son, the old-time musical merchandise house of this city, have sold out their entire stock to August Pollman, including the agency for a number of lines which they represented. For some time past the Zoebisch concern has been cutting down their advertising and, as a consequence, their business suffered in the competition now so keen. This illustrates the fact that it is impossible for a concern to progress or hold its own to-day without being believers in the value of trade papers and printers' ink properly utilized."

Although this article is more than a little self serving, as Zoebisch had regularly advertised in the Music Trade Review for many years, it does indicate that Zoebisch had entered a period of decline beginning with the Panic of 1893, eventually leading to the company being sold in 1901.

Confidence in the economy was restored after 1898 with increasing gold supply coming from the Klondike and the economy began 10 years of steady growth.

See Appendix G for an estimate of guitar production for 1867 to 1898.

5) C. F. Martin & Co., Nazareth PA (1898 to 1969)

1898 to 1915

The years from 1898 to 1915 cover the period from the introduction of serial numbers for guitars to the beginning of ukulele production. Also in 1898, Martin changed the stamp applied to their instruments to read "C. F. Martin & Co./Nazareth PA" instead of "C. F. Martin & Co./New York".

Although ledgers and other records are quite complete from August 1898, practically no correspondence exists in the Martin archive for the years 1898 to 1922. This is unfortunate, because this period covers the introduction of 000 size guitars, the development of style 45 instruments and the appearance of the first ukuleles.

Sales varied considerably from 1898 to 1905. In 1904 and 1905 sales were down significantly and more mandolins were sold than guitars. Frank Henry Martin' foresight in adding mandolins to the product line in 1895 now bore fruit. Otherwise, Martin, as a company, may not have survived the early 1900's.

Sales almost doubled between 1905 and 1906 and F. H. Martin must have felt he needed to concentrate on manufacturing while leaving wholesale marketing to others because on September 1, 1906 Buegeleisen & Jacobson of New York City was named the sole agent for Martin guitars in the U. S. as recorded in the sale ledger:

"Buegeleisen & Jacobson appointed sole agents for United States (to the trade) excepting old customers. Discount uniform 50% net 30 d(ay)s less 2% 10 d(ay)s except on Pacific Coast"

Martin already had Southern California Music Co. and Sherman, Clay & Co. handling the wholesale business on the West Coast, which account for the proviso "except on the Pacific Coast".

The 50% discount seems incorrect, though, as Buegeleisen & Jacobson actually received a 64% discount. From January 1907 Buegeleisen & Jacobson seem to have had their own special price list amounting to a 64% discount whereas Martin ledgers usually recorded the retail prices of instruments and then applied an appropriate discount depending on whether the customer was a dealer, teacher or professional musician.

In the period just before September 1906 the total number of employees at Martin, including Frank Henry Martin, amounted to only 7 people. F. H. Martin clearly expected the increase in sales to continue because he added 4 workers in September to keep up with demand.

By April 1907 the discount offered to Buegeleisen & Jacobson had been reduced to 60% and was continued until February 1911 even though their purchases had been falling for some time.

As the company had in 1837, 1873 and 1893, C. F. Martin & Co. had to weather another economic upheaval in 1907. The Panic of 1907, also known as the 1907 Bankers' Panic, was a financial crisis beginning in October of that year. The 1907 panic eventually spread throughout the U. S., with many state and local banks and businesses being forced into bankruptcy. The panic might have deepened even further if financier J. P. Morgan and other New York bankers had not intervened to shore up the banking system with their own money, as the United States did not then have a central bank to inject liquidity into the market. One of the long-term results of the Panic 1907 was the establishment of the Federal Reserve System in 1913. Panic of 1907 Martin caused a dramatic drop off in business in 1908, although business bounced back nicely in 1909 and remained fairly steady through 1915.

The popularity of bowl-back mandolins had been waning for some time when Martin added flat back mandolins to the product line in 1914. This helped to fill the gap in the loss of sales for bowl-back mandolins but the less expensive bowl backs continued to be offered into the early 1920s.

In 1915 Frank Henry Martin decided to take advantage of the Hawaiian craze and began to manufacture ukuleles. The next chapter in the Martin story was at hand.

1916 to 1928

This period was extremely important to the long-term future of C. F. Martin Guitar Co. and for the development of the product line that was to echo for the following 50 years. The tremendous increase in sales as a result of the addition of ukuleles to the product line allowed Frank Henry Martin to expand the factory in 1917 and again in 1927, with a resulting large increase in the work force.

This was also the period where gut strings began to give way to steel strings.

The year 1917 was a very important one for the Martin Guitar Co. Since the 1830's Martin had been a small family-owned factory with an equally small work force that never exceeded 18, during the sales boom of the 1890's, and was only 7 workers as late as

not particularly successful, but where would C. F. Martin Guitar & Co. be without Dreadnought guitars?

As recorded in the sales ledger, the company was incorporated as C. F. Martin & Co. Inc. on January 1, 1921. On that date Frank Henry Martin sold the property and good will of C. F. Martin & Co. to the new corporation. The actual corporation was organized on February 12, 1921 with F. H. Martin as president, C. F. Martin III as vice president and H. K. Martin as secretary.

Although Martin no longer had a sole sale agent, the factory did set up a number of master distributors or "jobbers" to cater to specific regions of the country.

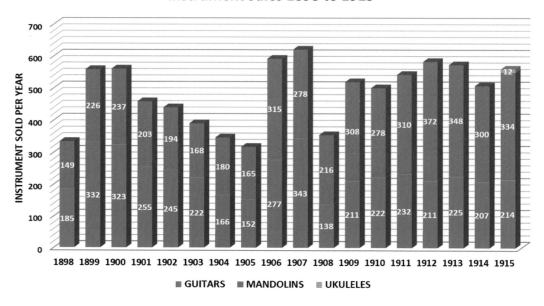

Instrument Sales 1898 to 1915

Figure 10
Instrument Sales 1898 to 1915

the beginning of 1916. In 1917 Frank Henry Martin expanded the factory to the east with the addition of a one floor brick building. Following the family tradition, F. H. Martin paid for the building himself and rented the factory to the business. The detailed employee records in the Martin archive end in December 1922 but at that time 37 employees worked for Martin, including 28 factory workers, 3 foremen, 3 office workers, a salesman, a packer and a janitor.

In 1916 another seminal moment was reached with the production of the first Dreadnought guitars for Charles H. Ditson & Co. of New York. This addition to the product line was unappreciated at the time and

A few customers, Rudolph Wurlitzer Co. being the prime example, had so many branches that they became, in effect, master distributors to themselves.

From 1922 to 1924 Martin offered a "Customer's Line", or "C Line", to those jobbers who wanted to offer Martin-made instruments under their own brand names. These guitars had slightly simpler design features, often the sound hole decoration had a single ring instead of 3 rings, but were priced the same as regular Martin instruments. By the end of 1924 having a separate line of instruments made less sense when ukulele sales were booming and the "Customer's Line" was dropped.

Instrument demand continued to grow into the early 1920's, so Frank Henry Martin, at his own expense, erected a new building in 1924. It was available for occupation in the fourth quarter of that year.

Martin flirted with tenor banjos between 1922 and 1925 but dropped them due to the surge in demand for ukuleles. The Martin tenor banjos were well received by dealers and players but were relatively plain and never developed the necessary traction for continued inclusion in the product line.

With the huge increase in the demand for ukuleles in 1925, Frank Henry Martin decided to expand the new building, only erected in 1924, by adding an floor and

more fully in a separate section (see page 206).

The period from 1916 to 1928 also marked the transition from gut strings to steel strings. F. H. Martin resisted this change as best he could but by 1927 he admitted in a letter that 9 out of 10 guitar players were currently using steel strings. The subject will be covered more fully in the section on "The Transition to Steel Strings" (page 313).

It has often been suggested that the 1920's saw an increase in top bracing in order to handle the increased tension of steel strings. This theory is not supported by the company correspondence, at least for the early to middle 1920's. On May 16, 1922 Martin replied to

Instrument Sales 1916 to 1927

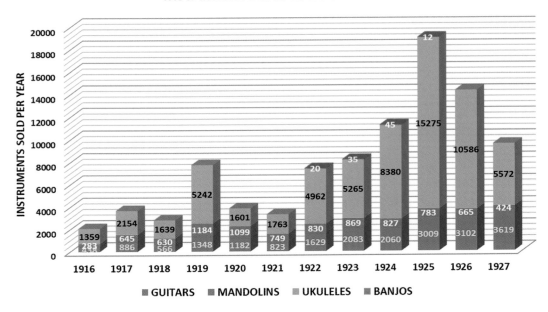

Figure 11
Instrument Sales 1916-1927

attic. The decision to expand the factory was made by mid-1925 and the new floor was finished and occupied by September 1925 so Martin may have already laid the groundwork for the expansion earlier in the year.

Ukulele sales peaked in 1925 and began to taper off in 1926 and 1927. The Hawaiian craze was on the wane. Musical tastes had begun to change, resulting in an increasing demand for tenor banjos and guitars, so Martin was prompted to add tenor guitars to the line in early 1927. The development of Martin tenor guitars is a very interesting story and will be covered

an inquiry from W. J. Dyer :

"We have your letter of the 9th and note that you wish to have the sample Guitars which we are making with your trade name "Stetson" constructed so that they can be strung with steel string. This is largely a matter of regulation because all Martin Guitars are fully guaranteed when strung with Steel as well as strung with Gut and Silk Strings, although we regularly use the latter.

If you find that almost all of the Guitars sold are used with Steel Strings we would suggest that you

instruct us to regulate and string them that way here. Even if they are specially constructed for Steel Strings the regulation would be too high for that purpose if we make it for Gut Strings. This, you will of course readily understand".

Conventional wisdom holds that the 2-17 guitar was the first Martin guitar constructed for steel strings. This is a misinterpretation of the 1922 advertising card that Martin printed which stated the 2-17 guitars were offered with "**steel strings only**". Up to this time Martin offered their guitars with either gut, steel or Hawaiian strings, at the buyer's option. As the 2-17 guitar was the least expensive member of the line, Martin decided to offer the 2-17s with steel strings only in order to reduce costs, and also as a reflection that steel strung guitars were becoming more popular. Only a year later, in 1923, Martin changed 0-18 guitars to steel strings only, although more expensive guitars were still available with gut or Hawaiian strings. You could still get a 2-17 or 0-18 with gut or Hawaiian strings but with an extra charge for the change in regulation

1928 to 1944 - "The Golden Era"

"The Golden Era" is defined as the period between development of Martin guitars fully capable of handling the tension of steel strings and December 1944 when Martin stopped scalloping the top braces of their guitars.

By the late 1920s', with 90% of their guitars being sold with steel strings, Martin became aware that some strengthening of their guitars was needed. There is little documentary information describing what changes were made and when. However, a letter dated March 6, 1929 provides some idea of Martin's thinking:

"It is quite true that the early Martin Guitars were hardly strong enough for steel strings. In recent years, however, Guitars have been used almost entirely with steel strings so we have found it necessary to make our Guitars stronger. They are now built in such a way that we guarantee for use with steel strings, either in the Spanish or the Hawaiian style. In fact, all our Guitars are strung at the factory with steel strings unless they are ordered otherwise."

The only documented change occurred in March 1928 when Martin increased top thickness of their guitars. The increase was small, only an additional 1/64", but the increase in stiffness was significant. Top bracing was also strengthened. The actual changes were not recorded although, at some time later, the brace width was increased from 1/4" to 5/16".

By 1927, Martin's sales of flat-back mandolins, and the industry-wide demand for mandolins in general, had been sliding for several years. Even at this late stage in the mandolin market, Frank Henry Martin, with the encouragement of a few dealers, began to explore the possibility of adding carved-top mandolins to the line. Martin was well aware of the carved-top mandolins offered by Gibson and Lyon & Healy and, in fact, Martin contacted Guy Hart at Gibson to find out the kind of spindle machine they used for carving Gibson mandolin tops. No competitive animus existed between the management of Martin and Gibson so Guy Hart was happy to share this information. In the end Martin bought the same brand of spindle machine used by Gibson. The carved-top mandolins entered production in 1929 and although they did not increase mandolin sales, they at least helped to stabilize sales through the first few years of the Great Depression. Mandolin sales were slow through the remainder of the 1930's and manufacturing was terminated on all types of mandolins in 1942, mostly as a result of wartime labor shortages.

It is well documented that Martin began to manufacture the 14-fret Orchestra Model guitars in late 1929. The development of this new type of guitar was strongly influenced by Perry Bechtel who, with the waning in popularity of plectrum banjo music, was looking to transition to a plectrum style guitar for band work. The result was the extraordinary OM-18 and OM-28 guitars which were very popular for several years and helped boost Martin's sales results through 1930 and 1931.

By mid-1931 it was becoming clear that sales of Martin's 12-fret guitar line was on the wane. This was partially due to the Depression but also due to changing musical tastes, especially with the increasing popularity of radio music and live performances. The OM guitars were a godsend at the beginning of the Depression but Martin continued to adapt to the new realities by adding more products to their line.

Charles Ditson died in New York on May 14, 1929. The parent company, Oliver Ditson Co., took over the New York branch but sold out to The Theodore Presser Co. in 1931. This allowed Martin to begin making Dreadnought guitars for their own account.

Incidentally, the first Martin Dreadnought was not a D-1 or a D-2 but actually a special order D-21 that was stamped in April 1931. The initial Dreadnought models offered were the D-1 and D-2 but the designation was changed to D-18 and D-28 respectively by late 1932. All the D-1 and D-2 guitars were made for the Chicago Musical Instrument Co. It wasn't until the introduction of the D-18 and D-28 guitars that other dealers were allowed to purchase Dreadnought

was not really specific to a particular size but was an indication that the guitar had a 14-fret neck. With the success of the OM-18 and OM-28, Martin decided to offer a number of their smaller body guitars as Orchestra Models. The 0-18 guitar was the first to be made with the 14-fret neck when a few 0-18S guitars were made as "Model 32" prototypes in January and early February 1932. Martin could immediately see they had a winner on their hands and put the "Model 32" 0-18 in full production by late February 1932. The first "Model 32" 0-17s appeared in March 1932, followed by the first 14-fret 00-17 guitars in January 1933 and the first 14-fret 00-18's in June 1933. It was Martin's intention that all Model 32 guitars would have a "dark top" finish but a few of the first 0-18 gui-

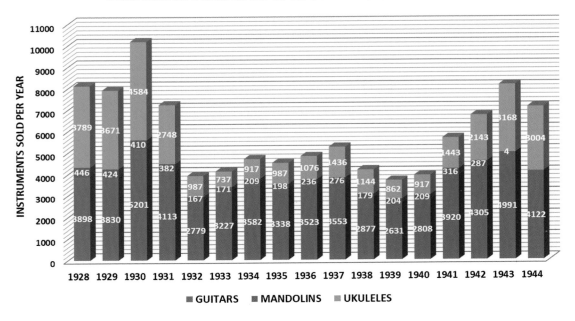

Figure 12
Instrument Sales 1928 to 1944

guitars. The 12-fret Dreadnought guitars were always special order items only, they were never made for inventory.

Since Martin already had the machinery for making carved-top mandolins it was natural for them to look at using the same equipment for making carved-top guitars. The C-1, C-2 and C-3 guitars all entered production by the third quarter of 1931. A budget model R-18 was added in early 1933 with a formed instead of a carved top.

The Orchestra Model terminology used by Martin

tars may have natural tops. Interestingly, the budget members of the Model 32 line, the 0-17 and 00-17 guitars, had the sunburst finish applied to their sides and back, not just the top. For some reason, with the exception of a few custom orders, the 00-21, 00-28 and 00-42 guitars kept their original 12-fret necks. In 1934 the 14-fret 000-18 and 000-28 models replaced the OM-18 and OM-28. The 000-21 and 000-42 14-fret guitars were added to the product line in June 1938, although one special order 14-fret 000-42 guitar was made in each of the years 1932 and 1934.

Sales still lagged in 1933, even with the addition

of the Orchestra Model 14-fret and the carved-top guitars. The company, on its own initiative, made a monumental decision that would affect Martin for decades to come; they made a prototype 14-fret D-28 in January 1934. Like the small body 0-17 and 0-18 14-fret guitars of 1932, the 14-fret D-28 was an immediate success. The dealer feedback was very positive and Martin made the first production batch of D-28 guitars in March 1934, followed by the D-18's in April of the same year. Sales of the new 14-fret guitars were strong and helped lift Martin's sales out of the doldrums of 1932 and 1933. More trouble was still on the horizon, though, as the years 1938, 1939 and 1940 saw a further drop in sales compared with the sales levels of 1934 to 1936.

Martin continued to add more designs to the line when they launched the deluxe large bodied F-7 and F-9 guitars in 1935. Sales were good for the first year but had tapered off sharply by 1938. In order to try to revive the line Martin brought out the more budget oriented F-1 and F-2 models in 1940. Sales were small but adequate through 1942 but war-time labor shortages forced Martin to terminate F model production in 1943.

Frank Henry Martin had always been a promoter of gut string guitars for classical music. In 1930 he corresponded with George Krick, a guitar teacher and Martin dealer in Philadelphia, who was in touch with Andres Segovia. F. H. Martin was interested to know what brand of guitar Segovia played and the strings he used. The increased interest in classical guitar music due to Andres Segovia and the encouragement of Krick appears to be among the reasons that Martin decided to launch the "G" model classical guitars beginning in 1936 (although one 00-21G was made in 1934). The initial "G" models (00-18G, 00-28G and 00-42G) were based on the regular 12-fret Martin body with a 24.9" scale. However, starting in 1938 Martin switched to what they referred to as an "OM" body with a 25.4" scale length, although the necks still joined the body at the 12th fret. The reason for the switch in body style is related to the increase in scale length to 25.4" (645 mm) which was closer to the then popular 650 mm classical guitar scale length. The body of the OM-shaped G model guitars is 3/4" shorter than the 12-fret 00 size guitar and the total length of the G model is 1/8" less. This allowed a 12-fret neck with a 25.4" scale to be fitted to the G model guitar body without a significant shift in the location of the bridge.

As can be surmised, the years from 1928 to 1944 were challenging years for Martin and profitability was often difficult to maintain. Below are a few comments for each year concerning profitability and the factory work force. The workforce only includes actual shop workers, not foremen or management.

1928 Small loss, 37 workmen

1929 Small loss, 36 workers

1930 Business better than 1930 (possibly due to Orchestra Model guitars), small profit, 38 men

1931 A 20% drop in sales but still a small profit, 34 men, 4 day work week

1932 Small loss, 34 workmen, reduction in hourly pay and institution of a three day work week

1933 Small loss, 34 men, slight increase in pay, 32 hrs per week increasing to 40 hrs towards the end of the year

1934 Small profit, under the NRA (National Recovery Administration), 40 men employed at 40 hours per week

1935 Small profit, the NRA was terminated in May 1935 after the Supreme Court declared it unconstitutional but Martin still honored the spirit of the NRA and employed 41 men at 40 hrs per week, new lacquer spraying equipment installed resulting in faster and better work

1936 Small profit, 33 men at 40 hours per week

1937 Small profit, 36 men by the end of the year, wages increased slightly

1938 Small profit, 27 men employed at 28 to 32 hours per week

1939 Small loss, 26 men employed at an average of 34 hours per week

1940 Small profit, 26 men at 40 hrs per week

1941 Small profit, 26? men at 40-50 hrs per week, demand exceeded production so overtime was paid, shortage of metal parts but plenty of wood available, may need to turn over part of facility to war work

1942 Martin was not able to secure any war work contracts, large demand for guitars, it is not recorded how many workmen were employed (it could have been as few as 17) but the work week was 50 hours. Some comments by C. F. Martin III in the corporate meeting minutes contain some very interesting information:

"Beginning March 1 Limitations Orders L-37 and L-37A of the War Production Board limited the use of critical materials in musical instruments to 75% of the quantity, by weight, used in 1940 and to 10% of the total weight of each instrument. To meet these limitations we made these changes:

a) Ebony bars were substituted for steel to reinforce guitar necks
b) Fewer guitar and more ukuleles were made
c) All mandolins and tiples were discontinued.

2) There was difficulty getting practically all materials, including wood. On some cases it was necessary to use substitutes at higher prices which could not be offset because our selling prices were frozen at the level of the October 1941 list, including the 10% Federal Excise Tax.

3) The demand for guitars rose sharply, largely because music dealers could not get other types of instruments, the manufacture of which was stopped entirely. This demand, with the decrease in our production, made our deliveries several months slow. Beginning about September 1 available goods was allotted to customers in proportion to their 1941 purchases and no new customers were accepted.

4) Uncertain as to the steadiness of employment here nine men left in Spring, mostly to work in munitions plants. One was drafted for military service and one was hired, making a net reduction of nine workers. Except during June and

July a 50 hour week was in effect all year with no change in the wages rate."

1943 Labor and material restriction kept production well under demand, small profit, orders now booked out 8 months with many orders turned down, 2 women were on the workforce but it is not clear how many men were employed

1944 C. F. Martin III became General Manager on November 1, 1944, materials not available, 29 men and women on workforce at 50 hrs per week, salesman John Shea dismissed November 1, 1944 (had been on part time and half pay since March 1, 1943).

It can be seen that the workforce through the 1930's averaged 34 to 37 men although this figure dropped to 26 or 27 for the last few years of the decade. Considering the economic conditions, when Martin was forced to reduce their workforce, they kept the most experienced and capable workers and as noted by C. F. Martin III in early 1931: **"(At the end of 1930) there were thirty-eight men on the payroll, all trained and capable of the high quality work."** It is little wonder that 1930's Martin guitar are considered some of the finest ever produced by Martin.

Although 1940 had been a bit of a struggle for Martin, by 1941 demand for guitars exceeded production and this continued throughout the rest of the war years, even though prices were fixed and not allowed to increase.

The year 1944 was one of change for Martin Guitar; C. F. Martin III took over the reigns of the company and some of the design features of Martin guitars were altered (including the dropping of scalloped bracing and simplification of fingerboard inlays). These events may be related. C. F. Martin III was conservative by nature and, faced with fixed selling prices and the high demand for his products, may have sought ways to reduce costs and increase production. Eliminating scalloped braces would have saved a little time and simple dot inlays, instead of slotted diamond and square inlays, would have been a slightly less expensive alternative.

Another possible reason that Martin ceased using scalloped braces was that some players began using extra heavy strings on their guitars. Although there is nothing in the Martin archival material to corroborate this, George Gruhn, the well-known musical instrument expert, had the opportunity, early in his career, to talk to musicians active in the 1950's and 1960's who indicated they did use extra heavy strings on their instruments. It is also possible that extra heavy strings were used on 1930's and 1940's Martin guitars. Individual musicians may have overloaded their guitars with extra heavy strings but whether this became such a problem that Martin was forced to make heavier top braces is a topic for further discussion and research.

Through the 1930's and 1940's Martin mostly bought strings in bulk from the Mapes Piano String Co. and packaged them to sell under their own brand. The author has undertaken a small, and in no way complete, study of Martin and other brands of strings from period by purchasing old strings on E-Bay and examining strings from old guitar cases. These were measured to ascertain their gauges. For those strings marketed for guitar use, the author has not found any strings that would be considered heavier than currently available medium strings (although Martin did offer heavy strings in the 1950's).

1945 to 1969

The elimination of scalloped bracing in late 1944 marked a clean break with the past. Only the herringbone purfling used on the tops of style 28 guitars remained as a tie to the past, but even this feature was gone by early 1947.

The hectic pace of innovation initiated by the Great Depression and the material and labor difficulties of the war years were over. The period through 1961 was one of steady and conservative growth, with the exception of one off-year in 1947. From 1962 the phenomenal growth of folk music, with its emphasis on acoustic instruments, lead to large increases in guitar sales.

However, it is only by looking at the monthly sales that one gains a feel for the frenetic nature of business experienced by Martin during this period.

From 1944, and for each year thereafter until 1969, there were one, or occasionally two, months that accounted for a very high percentage of the yearly sales. We know that, during this period, Martin often had more demand for instruments than the factory could fill. A case in point is the situation in October 1957 (see Figure 14) when D-28 guitars were back ordered for 12 months and D-18 guitars for 10 months. It is not known why such a large proportion of sales occurred in only one month each year. It might be related to sales taken at trade shows or Martin may have simply held orders until the factory had a chance to catch up on backlogs.

It would seem that with the steady sales growth and increasing quantity of backlogged orders during the 1950's caused Martin to consider the idea of increasing the factory capacity to meet demand. One intermediary step taken to address the capacity problem during 1960 and 1961 was to drop less popular lines of products and free up production for models with larger demand. As a result, 00-17 guitars were discontinued on February 10, 1960, 0-17T guitars on March 15, 1960 and 0-15 guitars on March 27, 1961. Somewhat later, T-15 tiples, uke 1, uke 2 and concert ukes were discontinued on August 22, 1966.

The gigantic increase in sales in 1962 and 1963 finally forced Martin's hand, the requirement for more factory space became an imperative. The following is an excerpt from the February 1, 1964 of The (Easton) Express-Times:

"Ground was broken this morning for the $500,000 plant of the C. F. Martin Co. of Nazareth on Beil Avenue in Upper Nazareth Township. The 131-year-old firm specializes in making guitars and ukuleles. The eight-acre property was purchased from Schoeneck Farms. The building will be constructed of pre-cast concrete panels. The present location of C. F. Martin is 10 W. North St., Nazareth. The new structure, expected to be completed in July, will provide about 36,000 square feet, or about twice that of the present building. C. F. Martin, the president of the company, said that within three years the number of workers employed by the firm is expected to double. The company presently employs 75 people."

The move to the new factory on Sycamore St. in Nazareth took place between June 26 and July 7, 1964, during the normal factory vacation period. In 1964 it was decided to drop hot hide glue in favor of "cold" glue. The change occurred on a batch of 0-16NY guitars stamped on September 2, 1964. The first serial number was 197207.

Several changes occurred in 1967 that are of interest to collectors. Martin began using black acetate pick guards with a batch of 00-21 guitars stamped on June 14, 1967, the first serial number being 222313. Around November 1967, the steel T-bar neck reinforcement was replaced by steel square

plates returned to regular production in 1988 with serial number 478093, a prototype Guitar of the Month HD-28PSE.

From the perspective of collectors, and as a convenient place to end the time frame covered by this book, a major change occurred in 1969 when Martin replaced Brazilian rosewood with East Indian rosewood for the bodies of their guitars. There is no explanation to be found in the archival material but the subject is well covered on page 54 of C. F. Martin & Co.: A History by Mike Longworth (3rd edition, 1988, paperback version):

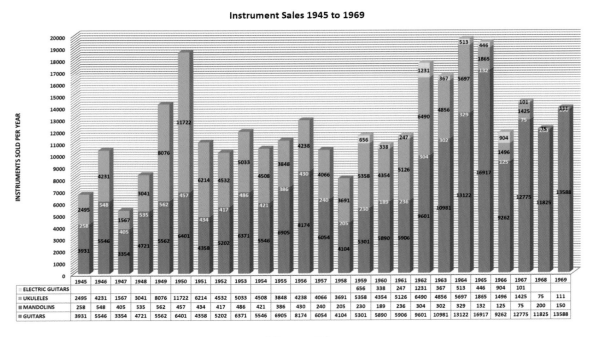

Instrument Sales 1945 to 1969

	1945	1946	1947	1948	1949	1950	1951	1952	1953	1954	1955	1956	1957	1958	1959	1960	1961	1962	1963	1964	1965	1966	1967	1968	1969
ELECTRIC GUITARS															656	338	247	1231	367	513	446	904	101		
UKULELES	2495	4231	1567	3041	8076	11722	6214	4532	5033	4508	3848	4238	4066	3691	5358	4354	5126	6490	4856	5697	1865	1496	1425	75	111
MANDOLINS	258	548	405	535	562	457	434	417	486	421	386	430	240	205	230	189	236	304	302	329	132	125	75	200	150
GUITARS	3931	5546	3354	4721	5562	6401	4358	5202	6371	5546	6905	8174	6054	4104	5301	5890	5906	9601	10981	13122	16917	9262	12775	11825	13588

Figure 13
Instrument Sales 1945 to 1965

tubing. As with other changes in Martin's long history these change may not have occurred abruptly so tortoiseshell pick guards and the steel T-bar may appear after the dates mentioned above.

Another change happened in 1968 when Martin substituted Brazilian rosewood for the maple that had used for bridge plates to that point. Mike Longworth recorded that the change occurred with serial number 235586, a batch of 0-18 guitars stamped on May 6, 1968. Initially, the change seems to have occurred on smaller-bodied guitars only and the first Dreadnought to have a Brazilian rosewood bridge plate was serial number 242454, a D-18 stamped on January 8, 1969. Maple bridge

"In the 1960's Brazil placed an embargo on Brazilian rosewood logs which Martin required. Their purpose was to attract industry to Brazil by demanding that the logs be sawn in Brazilian mills. This was unsatisfactory, and Martin changed to a similar product, East Indian rosewood from India.

To the experienced eye, the difference in appearance between Brazilian and Indian rosewood is discernible, but in tone and quality Martin has found them to be equal. In addition to the embargo, there is another problem with Brazilian rosewood. The available supply of rosewood trees, large enough that the

processed wood is wide enough for two-piece **Dreadnought backs, was depleted. The shortage of wide pieces led to the introduction of the D-35 with a 3-piece back, in 1965**."

On November 10, 1969, Martin introduced East Indian rosewood on shop orders 105 (D-21), 106 (D-28), 107 (D-35), 108 (D-35), 109 (D12-35), 110 (D12-35), 116 (D-28) and 117 (D-28). Interestingly, shop order 115, another batch of D-28 guitars, seems to have been made from Brazilian rosewood. The change to East Indian rosewood for Dreadnought guitars occurred at serial num-

ber 254498. However, two batches of Brazilian rosewood D-41 guitars were made after this serial number and a least one batch of 000-28 guitars were made in early 1970 with Brazilian rosewood (shop order 208 stamped on January 16, 1970). This would suggest Martin continued to discover small quantities of Brazilian rosewood for a while, so other examples may come to light. Martin also used up smaller Brazilian rosewood back and sides, not just on D-35 guitars, but on some smaller model guitars, since a N-20, from a batch stamped on May 4, 1970, has been reported with a Brazilian rosewood body.

DELIVERY TIME in MONTHS after RECEIPT of ORDER
* Prompt shipment from stock   Oct.25,1957

Spanish Guitars

ORCHESTRA MODEL

(Flat top, 14-fret neck)

12	0-15	Concert Size	$ 87
12	00-17	Grand Concert	100
8	0-18	Concert	115
8	00-18	Grand Concert	125
6	000-18	Auditorium	145
10	D-18	Dreadnaught	170
8	000-21	Auditorium	195
6	D-21	Dreadnaught	220
*	000-28	Auditorium	235
12	D-28	Dreadnaught	270

STANDARD MODEL

(Flat top, 12-fret neck)

3	5-18	Junior (¾)	$ 95
4	00-21	Grand Concert	175

CLASSIC MODEL

(Flat top, Nylon strings)

4	00-18G	Grand Concert	$ 140
4	00-28G	Grand Concert	230

Tenor Guitars

5	5-15T	Junior (¾)	$ 70
4	0-17T	Concert	85
3	0-18T	Concert	110

Tiples

1	T-15	Mahogany	$ 68
5	T-18	Mahogany	87
*	T-28	Rosewood	120

Ukuleles

2	0	Standard	$ 27
*	1	Standard	37
*	2	Standard	43
*	3	Standard	65
*	1-C	Concert	45
2	1-T	Tenor	55

Mandolins

*	A	Flat Model	$ 68
*	2-15	Carved Model	150

Warranty

All Martin instruments are warranted without time limit against defective material or imperfect workmanship.

Figure 14
1957 Martin Price List Showing Delivery Times

Notes for Chapter 1

1) Baptismal certificate for C. F. Martin in the Martin Guitar Co. archive.

2) Excerpt from pages 41 to 44 of the "Historical Review for the Joint Celebration of the Musical Instrument Makers' Guild (formerly Violin Makers' Guild) and the String Makers' Guild, of Mark Neukirchen, commemorating the years of their foundation, 1677 and 1777", published in German by the guilds in 1927 (see pages 23 and 24 in Martin Guitar: A History by Richard Johnston & Dick Boak):

"Out of the stipulation in the Guild Articles that only Masters of the Guild might produce violins and 'similar wares' there arose a long drawn-out dispute between the Violin Makers' Guild and the cabinet makers' trade. Beginning about the year 1800 certain cabinet makers were building guitars, in particular Johann Georg Martin, Christian Frederich Martin, Carl Gottlieb Wild and Carl Frederich Jakob, later on August Paulus, Johann Frederich Düurrschmidt, Heinrich Schatz, Christian Gottlieb Seifert, and Christian Frederich August Meinel, nicknamed 'on the hill.' In memoranda of May 25th and July 9th, 1826 the violin makers, who had already complained of the state of affairs in 1807, demanded an injunction against the 'bunglers' and asserted that they themselves belonged to the 'class of musical instrument makers and therefore to the class of artists', 'whose work not only showed finish but gave evidence of a certain understanding, a cultured taste', while the cabinet makers by contrast were 'nothing more than mechanics' and 'their product consisted of all kinds of articles known as furniture'. With asperity the violin makers asked: 'Who is so stupid that he can not see at a glance that a grand-father's armchair or a stool is no guitar, and such an article appearing among our instruments must look like Saul among the Prophets. And just as little would a violin or guitar finished by a master hand, when it had become old, figure in a lot of new carpenter style goods but it would, like a nightingale gaming gaily colored parrots, remain unnoticed'. Besides that, the violin makers pointed out, among the 120 Masters of the Guild 'about 40 members made guitars exclusively'. Finally they warned that the cabinet makers employed outside help, that a certain Dressel in St. Petersburg and a certain Bormann in Langenheim, in the Duchy of Nassau, had already established themselves, and that there was a great danger that the guitar making industry would be dragged into foreign lands. Although this application was rejected September 26th 1826, five years later the violin makers again asked that the cabinet makers be enjoined from making guitars, saying: 'Our Guild of the Violin Makers that has existed in this manufacturing center for 150 years is entitled to the exclusive right of making everything under the category of violins and related instruments, being all such as have a soundboard and strings in the manner of a violin and by a combination of the two produce tone, which includes Basses, Cellos, Zithers, Lutes, Mandolins, Guitars and Harps. The cabinet makers, they charged, has stolen the patterns from models which were furnished them by the violin makers for the purpose of fitting cases and packing boxes, and had then presumed to guitars on their own account. The violin makers felt all the more dissatisfied because in Klingenthal, which was 'only a village' the cabinet makers were forbidden to make guitars. Moreover, they said, the cabinet makers already had an 'extra and very profitable support' from the violin makers since they 'build the many cases and packing boxes needed for the transportation of instruments'. Also, that the Guild Articles of the violin makers made severe requirements for a Masterpiece; the cabinet makers on the contrary did not have to undergo this test and in consequence their work would injure the standing of local products in the foreign market.

The cabinet makers said in reply that the violin makers has no vested right in the making of guitars and that the 'discovery of the guitar' had been brought about by travelers some 30 to 35 years before and had been perfected by the cabinet maker George Martin, and submitted a testimonial from the wholesaler Christian Wilhelm Schuster that Christian Frederich Martin who 'for a number of years has been foreman in the factory of the noted violin and guitar maker, Johann Georg Stauffer of Vienna', had produced guitars, 'which in point of quality and appearance left nothing to be desired and which marked him as a distinguished craftsman.' Under date of July 9th, 1832 the authorities again permitted the cabinet makers to continue making guitars because these instruments were not mentioned in the Articles of the Violin Makers' Guild. In a revision on August 31st, 1837 the Guild named the guitar in Article 2 as one of the instruments included in its rights and in Article 5 allowed the presentation of a guitar as a Masterpiece. In spite of this the strife was not ended. Against the violent protests the cabinet makers were allowed, on the 19th of November 1853, to form their own Guild with a guitar as a Masterpiece. Not until the reorganization of the whole Guild System did the guitar makers, who had previously belonged to the cabinet makers' trade, join the Musical Instrument Makers' Guild."

3) From research by Michael Lorenz in the Vienna city records, http://michaelorenz.blogspot.co.at/2014/03/stauffer-miscellanea.html

4) There is an interesting note in a scrapbook of the Martin and Ruetenik families in the Martin Guitar Co. archive that states: "Cosacks (sic) plundered & burned 5 villages visible from Dresden in the year 1812 & 1813 when grandfather was 16 & 17 years old."

5) Certificate in the Martin Guitar Co. archive from Karl Kühle, dated March 3, 1825, stating that C. F. Martin was being employed at a weekly salary of 18 guilders Vienna currency (equal to 9 thalers or, roughly, US $9.00). This certificate was probably needed by C. F. Martin to prove he had the means to marry Ottilia Kühle. This document proves C. F. Martin was working for Kühle by 1825 and may have been working for him even earlier.

6) Eulogy notes in Martin Guitar Co. archive for C. F. Martin Jr.'s 1888 funeral.

7) Funerary memorial card for Johann George Martin in the Martin Guitar Co. archive.

8) From C. F. Martin's 1833 Saxony passport, in the Martin Guitar Co. archive.

9) Passenger manifest for the ship "Columbus", New York, November 6, 1833

10) 01-STORE LEDGER 1834-1837, page 186, translation from original German

11) 01-STORE LEDGER 1834-1837, page 6, translation from original German

12) 21-RECHNUNGSBUCH MERZ, page 1, entry dated July 16, 1834

13) 01-STORE LEDGER 1834-1837, page 196, translation from original German, entry dated June 2, 1834

14) 01-STORE LEDGER 1834-1837, page 199, translation from original German, entry dated June 1, 1834

15) 01-STORE LEDGER 1834-1837, page 161

16) 01-STORE LEDGER 1834-1837, pages 160 and 183

17) 01-STORE LEDGER 1834-1837, pages 185 and 186

18) Advertisement in The National Gazette, Philadelphia, PA, March 18, 1835

19) 21-RECHNUNGSBUCH MERZ, page 7, entry for box 9 dated April 25, 1835

20) 21-RECHNUNGSBUCH MERZ, page 24, entry for boxes 20 and 21, dated Sept. 3, 1836

21) Henry Schatz bought 55 acres, including a house and other out-buildings, from Samuel Siegfried on November 4, 1835

22) 02-JOURNAL 1836-1839, page 36, entry dated April 28, 1836

23) 04-JOURNAL 04-1837 TO 11-1838 BRUNO, page 4, entry dated May 1, 1837. It was customary at this time to pay rent at the end of each quarter.

24) 04-JOURNAL 04-1837 TO 11-1838 BRUNO, page 1, entry dated April 1, 1837.

25) The Panic of 1837 was a financial crisis in the United States caused primarily by credit speculation. Some banks had issued paper money to as much as five times the value of real money (coinage) they had on deposit. The bubble burst on May 10, 1837 in New York City, when every bank stopped payments in gold and silver coinage. The Panic resulted in a five-year depression with many bank failures and record-high unemployment.

26) 04-JOURNAL 04-1837 TO 11-1838 BRUNO, page 42

27) 04-JOURNAL 04-1837 TO 11-1838 BRUNO, page 65

28) The notice appeared in The Morning Courier & New York Enquirer from May 5 to May 8, 1838.

29) 04-JOURNAL 04-1837 TO 11-1838 BRUNO, page 66

30) 04-JOURNAL 04-1837 TO 11-1838 BRUNO, page 51, June 7, 1838

31) 04-JOURNAL 04-1837 TO 11-1838 BRUNO, page 94, November 16, 1838

32) As one of his last acts as an employee of C. F. Martin, Bruno purchased a $35 guitar for himself on November 20, 1838. 03-ACCT 1837-39 NEW YORK, page 1-1

33) 06-LUDECUS & WOLTER INVENTORY LISTING, page 18

34) 21-RECHNUNGSBUCH MERZ, page 58, entry dated October 23, 1839, shipment of boxes 33 and 34 to Ludecus & Wolter in New York

35) The Longworth American Almanac for 1840-41 lists Martin selling musical instruments at 385 Broadway. As was common with Longworth, Coupa was also listed at the same address in a separate entry.

36) Martin & Schatz guitar, serial number 1296.

37) Martin & Schatz guitar, serial number 1304.

38) Martin & Schatz guitar, serial number 1341

39) 03-ACCT 1837-1839 NEW YORK, page 45-1

40) 03-ACCT 1837-1839 NEW YORK, page 30-1

41) The Martin Guitar Co. archive contains a number of letters written by John Coupa to C. F. Martin during 1849 and early 1850, the last dated February 7, 1850. Coupa died on May 18, 1850, The New York Genealogical and Biographical Record

42) Letter from Philip Deringer, September 22, 1850

43) There are 8 pages of expenses in the archive recorded by C. F. Martin Jr. between May 27 and October 1850.

44) 07-DAYBOOK 1850-51, records guitars received by C. F. Martin Jr. at 385 Broadway from June 2, 1850 to January 23, 1851.

45) The business agreement between C. F. Martin Jr. and Charles De Janon dated January 1, 1851 is in the Martin Guitar Co. archive.

46) In a letter dated May 4, 1853 the landlord, a certain J. Grosvenor, requested payment for the last quarter's rent.

47) Cleave's Biographical Cyclopaedia Homeopathic Physicians and Surgeons, Galaxy Publishing Company, Philadelphia PA

1873.

The following is a portion of a short biography of William Frederick Schatz, the son of Henry Schatz that contains some interesting information (highlighted by author):

"William Frederick Schatz MD, of Columbus, Ohio, was born in Millgrove, Northampton county, PA on January 23, 1839. **His father, Henry August Schatz, manufacturer in Europe and America of the celebrated Schatz guitars, was born in Saxony in 1808, and emigrated to the United States in 1830.** His mother, Caroline Wigand, was a sister of the late Dr. Henry Wigand, of Dayton O., one of the oldest homeopathic physicians in the West. **The elder Schatz, in 1849 (error, should be 1850), took his family to Germany that his children might have facilities for a more thorough education than he deemed obtainable in the United States.** After passing through the common schools of Saxony, the subject of this sketch graduated in the Gewerken School at Marknewkirchen (sic), Saxony with the highest honors. In order to avoid conscription he left Germany in 1858, and on his arrival in America was engaged as teacher in the Moravian Boarding School for boys at Nazareth, Pa. In 1862, he enlisted a company of 100 days' men for the 38th Regiment Pennsylvania Volunteer Militia, and was elected captain. On the abandonment of military life he determined to resume his medical education, previously begun, and for that purpose joined his uncle, Dr. Henry Wigand, at Springfield, O. Notwithstanding his determination to practice homoeopathy, having been literally born and bred a homoeopathist, he devoted the winters of 1862 and 1863 to study in the Ohio Medical College of Cincinnati. The two following winters he attended the Hahnemann Medical College at Chicago, where he graduated with distinction in 1864. Soon after graduation he began to practice as a partner Dr. J. H. Coulter, in association of whom he remained until the summer of 1866, when he again went to Europe to attend the University at Leipzig. **His father died during his absence, and on his return, after a period of two years, he located in Columbus.**"

48) Henry Schatz's passport May 30, 1850 application gives his age as 44 years

48A) Vogtlandischer Geigenbau, Bernhard Zoebisch, page 266

49) Schatz appeared in the Boston Almanacs from 1845 to 1850 but was not listed in the 1842 edition. See Appendix F.

50) From Charles Bruno's passport application dated December 22, 1870.

Chapter 2
Shop and Factory Locations

Shop Locations in New York 1833 to 1939

C. F. Martin opened his first shop at 196 Hudson Street at the beginning of May 1834. This location probably had two or three floors. Since there are no records documenting separate housing for his family, the 196 Hudson Street location served as both store and living space. The retail store would have occupied the front and the shop the back part of the first floor with the living quarters being located above on the second floor. The building at 196 Hudson, according to the 1834 edition of Longworth's American Almanac, was the on the right hand side of the street, the second house south of Broome Street. There is currently a small park, numbered 222 Hudson, at this location.

By 1837 business was good enough for C. F. Martin to open another location at 212 Fulton Street. The ledger records quarterly rent being paid to Mrs. Morris for 212 Fulton Street on May 1, 1837. As the rent was paid at the end of each quarter the new location must have been rented by February 1. The shop at 212 Fulton was located on the south side of the street, probably the third house above Church Street on the left hand side of the street. At the time Church Street ended at Fulton. This location is now under the World Trade Center.

The need for a new location was probably a result of increased instrument and general musical merchandise sales. Martin had begun to import guitars from Germany by early 1836 and was also buying some guitars from Henry Schatz. Large purchases from T. F. Merz for all sorts of musical products meant more space was needed.

As a result of the Panic of 1837, Martin had moved out of 196 Hudson Street by August 1, 1837. The ledger records $21.69 in taxes being paid on August 2 and a

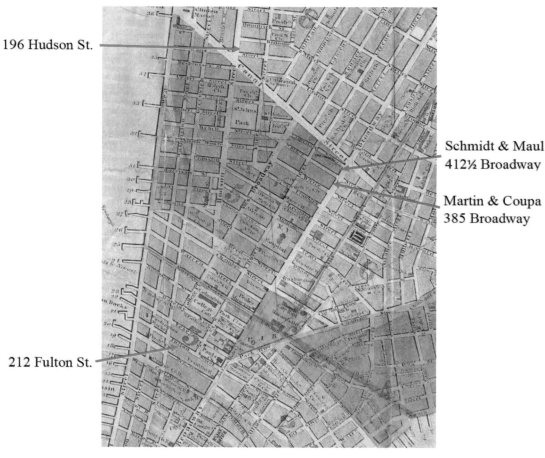

Figure 15
Martin's Shop Locations in New York 1834 to 1839

final rent payment on August 26 for $110, covering May, June and July. These are the last expenses recorded for 196 Hudson Street. However, Martin may have continued to live at 196 Hudson Street and use it as a work shop for a short time after June 1837. For the remainder of his time in New York C. F. Martin carried on business at 212 Fulton Street only.

Curiously, the New York City Directory for 1837-38 shows both C. F. Martin and Charles Bruno located at 212 Fulton. The Martin & Bruno partnership did not start until May 1, 1838 so it is possible that Bruno was already operating another business out of 212 Fulton, although the ledger does not indicate whether Bruno contributed to the rent.

The map in Figure 15 is a detail of a 1835 map of Manhattan, showing the shop of C. F. Martin, Schmidt & Maul and Martin & Coupa. The locations are from city directories of the 1830's and are slightly different from modern maps, as street numbering has changed over time.

Properties in Schoeneck, Cherry Hill and Nazareth

From clues in the ledger books it appears that C. F. Martin moved his family to the Nazareth area in the summer of 1838 while he remained in New York to wind up his business. It is unknown where the Martin family may have stayed but it may have been with one of the Clewell families in the area since Charles Bruno forwarded money to Ottilia Martin via "Mr. Clewel (sic)" in June 1838 and again in November.

Martin did rent part of a farm house from William L. S. Gross of Bushkill Township (in Schoeneck just north of Nazareth) in the spring of 1839. A copy of a lease agreement is in the Martin archive and details that Martin's share of the house included the kitchen, two bedrooms, washroom, right in the cellar, half the garden, a share of the stable and "all the old shop". The lease ran from April 1, 1839 until April 1, 1840 with rent set at $30 per quarter. The "old shop" was probably where C. F. Martin first produced guitars in the Nazareth area. Interestingly, the lease agreement

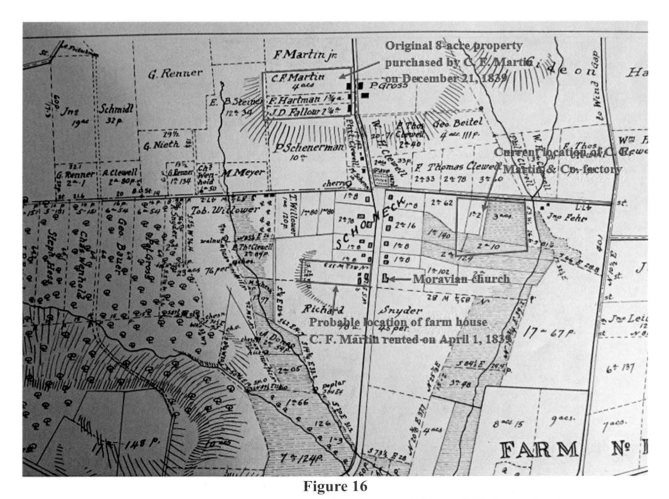

Figure 16
Location of C. F. Martin's Properties in Schoeneck and Cherry Hill, Pennsylvania

states that C. F. Martin was already a resident of Bushkill Township.

On December 21, 1839 Martin purchased 8 acres of land from Philip Deringer in Cherry Hill on the southern edge of Bushkill township. The deed specified that the property included a "**Messuage tenement**" which is an archaic legal term for a dwelling and associated outbuildings. Although a family picture indicates Martin "built this home" it is more likely that the house, barn and, possibly, the shop at the end of the house were already in existence when the Martin family moved in.

On April 30, 1844 Martin sold two acres of his Cherry Hill property to C. A. Zoebisch and another 2 acres of the remaining property to C. A. Zoebisch on July 25, 1845.

Zoebisch must not have had these two properties for very long as later maps of Cherry Hill show that one 2 acre lot was owned by C. F. Hartmann and the furthest south lot was owned by either J. D. Fallow or F. Clearland. In the mean time, C. F. Martin Jr had purchased the property to the north of the original homestead.

On October 2, 1857 C. F. Martin Jr. bought a block of land from the Congregation of the United Brethren for $699.98. The purchase included lots 29, 31, 33 and 35 of the Nazareth town plan. These lots fronted along North Main Street for 285 feet, with lot 29 bordering North St. on the south. All lots were 250 feet deep.

Lot 29, presently 201 North Main St., was where C. F. Martin Sr. lived, with the factory being built on the east side of the house. C. F. Martin Jr. built a house on lot 33 and, on September 27, 1860, sold lot 31 for $2,050 to C. F. Hartmann. Lot 31 included a house.

C. F. Martin Sr. bought lots 33 and 35 from C. F. Martin Sr. on April 9, 1866 for $2,000. It appears this purchase was to create an asset for the eventual beneficiaries of C. F. Martin Sr.'s estate.

C. F. Martin Sr. died on February 16, 1873 and on May 1, 1873 the heirs of C. F. Martin Sr. (C. F. Martin Jr., H. H. Martin, Emelia C. Martin, wife of W. J. Ruetenik and Ottilia R. Martin, wife Henry A. Troeger) sold lots 33 and 35 for $2,400 to Reinhold Schuster, who had been employed at the factory since 1867. Lot 33 included the house occupied by C. F. Martin Jr. up to that point. So now lot 29 became the home of C. F. Martin Jr. and contained the factory, lot 31 was the home of C. F. Hartmann and lot 33 was the home of Reinhold Schuster.

The 1917, 1924, 1925 ad 1927 factory expansions all took place on the original lot 29. This continued to be the Martin Guitar Co. location until 1964 when a new factory was built at 510 Sycamore St.

Figure 17
Recent Photograph of C. F. Martin Sr.'s House in Cherry Hill

Chapter 3
Important Business Relationships

1833 to 1898

HEINRICH (HENRY) A. SCHATZ (1806-1867)

Heinrich Anton Schatz was born in Neukirchen, Saxony on January 23, 1806[1].

An addendum to the document used by the Markneukirchen violinmakers' guild in their action against the cabinetmakers' guild indicates that Schatz spent two years and 5 months learning guitar making in Vienna, almost certainly at the shop of Stauffer. Schatz made a request to be allowed to join the violinmakers' guild but never received a reply.

Frustrated by the intransigence of the violinmakers' guild Schatz immigrated to the US some time after 1827. The Rechnungsbuch Merz records that Schatz was importing musical instruments to Philadelphia by 1833 as indicated by accounting for a bill of exchange dated August 6, 1833.

From June to August 1834, C. F. Martin paid Schatz a total of only $11.50. Schatz may have been helping Martin and Schmidt in the shop at 196 Hudson Street but he doesn't appear to have been working there on a full-time basis.

A recently discovered letter from T. F. Merz dated November 1834 clearly indicates Schatz was operating his own musical instrument business in Philadelphia. Schatz even asked Merz about sourcing "a piano-forte, jacconet (light weight cotton fabric), lace, Swiss clocks and music boxes" from Neukirchen.

Martin & Schatz formed some sort of business partnership by about January 1835. The Rechnungsbuch Merz records that shipments continued to be made to "Martin & Schatz" until September 1836, although it would appear that Schatz had moved to Millgrove, Pennsylvania by April 1836.

On November 4, 1835 Schatz purchased 55.79 acres of land at Millgrove from Samuel Siegfried for the sum of $1,400. The property included a house, which is still in existence.

When C. F. Martin moved to Nazareth in mid-1839 the Martin & Schatz association was resurrected, although it only lasted until early 1840.

On April 8, 1844 Schatz sold 29.75 acres, including the house, to Daniel Schlabach for the sum of $1,163.28 and the remainder of the property to Paul Siegfried for $736.72.

Schatz subsequently moved to Boston where he made guitars from 1844 to 1850[2]. Most Schatz guitars made in Boston contain a label. Schatz used several addresses in Boston and the labels are a very useful tool for dating Schatz guitars made in Boston (see Appendix F).

Schatz moved his family back to Germany in 1850. Prior to his departure Schatz wrote a letter from Boston to Martin on April 29, 1850 offering him some purfling. Schatz's application for a passport was dated May 30, 1850 and from the passport application we get a physical description of Henry Schatz. He was 5'-7" tall, had hazel eyes, a low forehead, a Grecian nose, a small mouth, round chin, black hair, sallow complexion and a spare face.

In a letter addressed to the Martin family dated June 4, 1850, Mrs. Schatz stated the family was hoping to leave for Bremen June 20 aboard the steamer "Hermann".

His son, William Schatz, returned to the US in 1858 to avoid conscription for military service[3] in Germany. Henry Schatz, however, remained in Germany and died in Neukirchen on December 28, 1867.

CHARLES BRUNO (1806-1884)

Charles Bruno was born in Hanover, Germany on May 6, 1806[4].

Bruno emigrated from Germany to Macon, Georgia in 1832[5]. He founded a musical import business and store in Macon by 1834 but in the same year moved to New York.

Charles Bruno appears to have become an employee

of C. F. Martin in late 1835 because from January 1, 1836 the Martin sale books and ledgers are in his handwriting. Bruno ran the store at 196 Hudson Street and otherwise looked after C. F. Martin's business affairs, just as Jacob Hartman had done before him. With Bruno looking after the day-to-day business activity C. F. Martin was free to concentrate on guitar building and repair work. If this was the reason for hiring Bruno, it was clearly the correct one as guitar production increased from an estimated 60 instruments in 1835 to 98 in 1836. Production in 1837 fell to 68 guitars as a result of the Panic that year.

Charles Bruno was listed as a book seller at 212 Fulton Street in Longworth's New York City Directory for 1837-1838. The same edition shows C. F. Martin selling musical instruments at both 196 Hudson Street and 212 Fulton Street. From this it would appear that Bruno was employed by Martin at the 212 Fulton Street location and was allowed some space to sell books on his own account. Martin continued to run a retail store at 196 Hudson Street until June 9, 1837, and, afterwards, at 212 Fulton Street alone. However, it does appear Martin continued to live and work out of the 196 Hudson address.

On May 1, 1838 Martin and Bruno entered into a co-partnership[6].

Sales in 1838 remained slow due to the lingering effects of the Panic of 1837 and the ledger seems to indicate the partnership ended around the end of September 1838.

From the beginning of May until the end of September 1838 Bruno had kept very detailed records. Martin continued to operate the separate manufacturing location at 196 Hudson Street and Bruno was very careful to charge any expenses not directly related to the Martin & Bruno partnership to C. F. Martin's account. This detailed accounting ended around September 21, 1838 indicating some change in the business relationship. However, Bruno continued to keep the books for Martin until the end of November[7].

The main reason C. F. Martin entered into the partnership with Bruno was that he had already decided to move to the Nazareth and wanted a partner to whom he could sell the business in New York, along with its considerable debt, while maintaining an outlet

for his instruments. T. F. Merz corresponded directly with Bruno during this period and there can be no doubt Bruno was well aware of the actual state of the business, especially with respect to its debt to Merz. Having failed to find the suitable partner in Bruno, C. F. Martin sold his stock in trade to Ludecus & Wolter at the end of May 1839.

Until now, the whereabouts of Bruno from the end of 1838 until his reappearance in New York in 1849 was a mystery. Fortunately, the Rechnungsbuch Merz records that Bruno began importing musical instruments to his store in Macon, Georgia in June 1839[8].

As mentioned previously, Bruno had founded a music store in Macon, Georgia in 1834. It is known Bruno was keeping the books for Martin by early 1836 and returned to Macon in late 1838 or early 1839, where he owned Bruno's Music Store. It is not known if Bruno's music store in Macon continued to operate from 1836 to 1838 while he was in New York.

In October 1840 Bruno formed a partnership with Samuel Stanley Virgins and the store became Bruno & Virgins. A second branch of Bruno & Virgins was opened in Columbus, Georgia about 1846[9].

Bruno moved back to New York by 1849 where he formed a number of partnerships in the music business; Bruno & Cargill (1851-1853), Bruno, Wiessenborn & Co. (1854-1857) and Bruno & Morris (1860-1863)[10].

Martin sold Charles Bruno (and later Bruno & Morris) 286 guitars between May 1858 and May 1864 and another 40 guitars between September and December 1867, making him the largest Martin dealer after C. A. Zoebisch & Sons. It appears that C. A. Zoebisch became Martin's master distributor in 1868 because no direct sales to Bruno are recorded in the ledger books after 1867. This change prompted Bruno to have copies of Martin guitar made in Neukirchen as reported by C. A. Zoebisch in several letters dated 1869. In the 1870's Bruno advertised their own line of guitars and was also selling Tilton Impovement guitars. Bruno could still buy Martin guitars from C. A. Zoebisch, as detailed in a letter dated 1870, but chose not to deal with his long-time rival. Several years later the company of C. Bruno and Son was formed.

Martin did not start selling direct to C. Bruno & Son again until early 1902, when C. Bruno & Son was a thriving wholesale music business in New York. C. Bruno & Son was a very successful music and musical instruments business and lasted well into the 20th century, eventually being acquired in August 1971 by Kaman Corp., maker of Ovation guitars.

JOHN B. COUPA (1808-1850)

John B. Coupa, full name Jean Baptiste Coupa, was a concert guitarist, teacher and businessman. He originally settled in Boston[11] but later moved to New York. Coupa was well known in concert circles during the 1840's and played with a variety of other musicians including Benedid and Madame De Goni[12].

of the Martin & Coupa agency in New York. It is also possible Coupa applied these labels to used guitars that had originally been shipped to other dealers, in which case these guitars could be from the period after 1840.

De Ferranti, the famous Belgian guitarist, visited the US in 1846 and 1847. Coupa and C. F. Martin were undoubtedly familiar with him and developed a "Ferranti" model that was discussed in their correspondence, although it is not clear what features this model had.

The archive contains a number of letters from Coupa to Martin during 1849 and early 1850. The letters cover a wide variety of business subjects but also contain personal information. Some of the letters

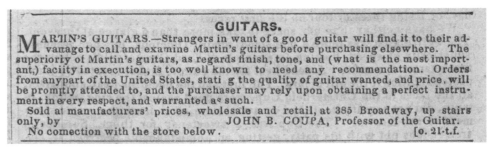

Figure 18
1849 Advertisement for Martin Guitars[19]

The first mention of John Coupa in the Martin records is dated March 9, 1837: "**Repaired a Guitar for Mr. Coupa, 198 Broadway**"[13]. Coupa also bought a guitar with a polished sound board on May 11, 1837[14] and another on August 17 with "**Spanish neck and bridge**"[15]. In an entry dated September 25, 1837[16], Coupa had a "**new Spanish bridge**" put on a guitar that was in for repairs.

It appears Coupa's original studio was located at 198 Broadway. However, the city directory for 1838-1839 shows Coupa at 385 Broadway[17], so he couldn't have been at the 198 Broadway address very long. An entry in a Martin ledger shows Coupa had moved to 385 Broadway by at least July 1838[18].

Several guitars have recently come to light containing a John B. Coupa label (type 9). The original "198" of the street address has been inked out and replaced with a hand written "385". That would seem to date those guitars with a type 9 label to the period between the middle of 1838 and early 1840, at the beginning

mention that Coupa's daughter, Susan Angelica Coupa (referred to in the correspondence by her pet name "Petite"), was severely ill. Unfortunately, the little girl did not recover and died on July 5, 1849[20].

Coupa was only 42 years old when he died on May 17, 1850[21,22] after a short illness.

As a result of John Coupa's demise C. F. Martin Jr. moved to New York by early June 1850[23] to run the business at 385 Broadway.

In the sales notes kept by C. F. Martin Jr. is a record, dated October 16, 1850, for "Commision on Mrs. Coupas piano $5.00". Clearly, Mrs. Coupa was settling her affairs prior to her eventual return to England. Susan Frances Coupa died in 1898 in Chelsea, UK at age 80[23].

CHARLES DE JANON (1834-1911)

The Martin ledger on November 25, 1836 records that

"Mr. De Jannon (sic) has paid for repairing a guitar and some strings"[25]. This probably refers to Leopold De Janon, a well know guitarist.

Charles De Janon was born in Cartagena, Columbia in 1834 and emigrated with his family, including 9 older siblings, to New York in 1840. He displayed extraordinary musical ability from an early age and learned to play the piano and violin. By 1843, however, he

Figure 19
Photograph of Charles De Janon

had taken up the guitar and stayed with that instrument for the rest of his life[26].

After John Coupa died C. F. Martin Jr. ran the ware-room at 385 Broadway from June 1850 until January 1851. C. F. Martin Jr.'s stay in New York had always been intended to be a temporary arrangement, until a new agent could be found. An agreement was drawn up by Martin on January 1, 1851[27] giving De Janon the sole agency for New York. Martin was to provide and insure the sale room and De Janon was to operate

the depot but was allowed to carry on teaching at 385 Broadway at no charge. De Janon was allowed a 33% discount on his retail sales, any commissions offered by him were to come from his percentage. Wholesale orders from Martin customers were to be directed to Martin with no compensation although De Janon was entitled to a 5% commission on the first sale of a new wholesale account. The agreement was in effect until February 1, 1852. De Janon carried on regular correspondence with Martin during 1851 but the arrangement must have been unsatisfactory as the agreement was not renewed.

At only 17 years of age in 1851, De Janon was probably too young and inexperienced to run the business at 385 Broadway. As reflected in his letters, he was soon behind in his payments to C. F. Martin and remained indebted to him for a number of years. However, this did not effect Martin's long term relationship with De Janon as he bought a number of Martin guitars between 1869 and 1889.

De Janon died in New York on February 10, 1911.

C. A. ZOEBISCH & SONS

Carl A. Zoebisch Jr. (1824-1911) arrived in New York on January 21, 1842[28]. On the passenger list he is identified as an instrument maker. Zoebisch purchased land from Martin in Cherry Hill and one source suggests he may actually have worked for Martin[29], although this is doubtful.

Carl A. Zoebisch Sr. (1801-?) and his family arrived in New York aboard the bark "Sir Isaac Newton" on September 20, 1845[30]. His occupation was recorded as "mechanic", a term meaning a craftsman or artisan.

Gura (2003) reports that the family settled in the Lancaster, Pennsylvania area and established themselves as musical instrument dealers[75]. The family imported musical instruments but also manufactured their own brass instruments.

By 1847 C. A. Zoebisch Sr. and his sons (Carl Jr., Hermann Ernst and Bernhard) moved to New York and established C. A. Zoebisch & Sons at 411½ Broadway, directly across the street from Schmidt and Maul at 412½ Broadway. In the 1848 edition of Doggett's Directory, Charles A. Zoebisch was listed at

189 Mott St. as an instrument maker and C. A. Zoebisch & Sons was located at 171 Mott St.

C. A. Zoebisch Sr. and his son Bernhard returned to Neukirchen in 1869 to organize the export of parts to New York for reassembly.

The first sale of Martin guitars to Zoebisch occurred on June 7, 1855[32]. Although they may have been family friends, they did not enjoy the extra 5% discount off the wholesale price, usually offered to Martin dealers, until their third order on September 29, 1855. By October 16 of the same year they were receiving the extra 10% discount afforded to larger dealers.

From June 1855 to May 1864 C. A. Zoebisch & Sons bought 702 guitars, making them the largest Martin dealer at the time.

It appears C. A. Zoebisch & Sons became Martin's master distributor and sole agent in 1868. They were operating from their location at 46 Maiden Lane in New York at the time. This arrangement was not without its critics as many customers corresponded with Martin to complain about having to deal with Zoebisch. Complaints usually revolved around the rigid pricing structure and Zoebisch's supposedly poor service. However, the arrangement worked well for Martin as C. F. Martin Jr., with only a small work force at the factory, could concentrate on manufacturing guitars rather than having to spend a large portion of his time on correspondence and marketing. When guitar sales greatly rapidly between 1888 and 1893, Zoebisch began sending monthly lists of guitars to be manufactured. Zoebisch did indeed control the output of the factory through this period.

The deterioration of Zoebisch's relationship with Martin began with the Panic of 1893. It became clear to Frank Henry Martin that Zoebisch's sole agency no longer served the interests of the Martin factory. Frank Henry Martin moved cautiously but by 1895 Martin began to set up new wholesale accounts, Zoebisch's sole agency was at an end. Zoebisch's sales gradually decreased until 1898, when they made their last guitar purchase. Several years later, in April 1901, C. A. Zoebisch & Sons sold out their stock and remaining sales agencies to August Pollman.

TRAUGOFF F. MERZ

T. F. Merz was a Neukirchen musical instrument wholesaler who supplied C. F. Martin with much of the musical merchandise for his New York stores. The Musical Instrument Museum in Markneukirchen, Germany has in its collection the T. F. Merz ledger book covering the years 1828 to 1840, which provides a detailed inventory of most of the shipments made to C. F. Martin. The Merz ledger book is divided into three sections: sales within Europe, sales to the U. S. and duplicate letters. Duplicate letters were necessary because the only way to retain a copy of an important letter was to write it out a second time. The letters are not only interesting in themselves but are historically important. Due to the importance of the information contained, some of the Merz letters have been translated and are quoted in their entirety.

The earliest relevant document in the records is a bill of exchange for 200 Thalers (a thaler being roughly equal to one dollar in US currency) received from Heinrich Schatz on August 6, 1833.

The following letter was sent by T. F. Merz to Heinrich Schatz in Philadelphia on November 24, 1834:

"After the departure of my most recent letter on October 4, in which we sent you the bill for 3 crates of instruments, I received your letter dated Oct. 12; I was glad to see in the post script of this that the crate of accordions, No. 3 (Author's note: shipped July 16), **arrived in safety in your harbour. I hope the quality of the instruments will meet your expectations. On the 21st of this month we sent another box of instruments, No. 7, to Bremen for you. You will find the invoice for this enclosed; please send us its total amount of (Rixdollars) 222/22/10…"**

A Rixdollar was a money of account (i.e. there was no Rixdollar currency) valued at 80 cents in US currency. A Rixdollar was divided into 72 Grotes and 1 Grote was divided into 5 Schwaren. Therefore, 222/22/10 stood for 222 Rixdollars, 22 Grotes and 10 Schwaren.

From the letter of exchange and the letter above we learn a number of interesting facts:

1) The original business relationship that T. F. Merz developed in the United States was with Henry Schatz in Philadelphia, not C. F. Martin in New York, and that Schatz had been importing from Merz from at least 1833.

2) From the Merz ledger we know that box 3 mentioned in the letter was shipped from Neukirchen on July 16, 1834, boxes 4, 5, and 6 were shipped on September 29 and Box 7 was shipped November 21 the same year. It follows that Box 1 and Box 2 must have been shipped prior to July 1834.

3) We know that C. F. Martin journeyed to Philadelphia in late April 1834 and paid for something to be carted from the ship to his shop. It seems quite probable that Martin went to Philadelphia to meet with Schatz and select musical instruments and supplies from boxes 1 and 2 for his new store at 196 Hudson Street in New York.

Merz recorded receipt of a letter from Schatz in New York on February 27, 1835. Box 9 in the sequence was shipped to Martin & Schatz on April 25, 1835, so it is clear this February 27 letter announced to Merz the formation of the Martin & Schatz partnership and also ordered more musical instruments and supplies. We also learn that Schatz had now moved to New York. This is confirmed as Merz replied to the February 27 letter on March 3 (although, unfortunately, this letter was not duplicated). By chance Merz got the address for the store on Hudson Street wrong and the "Evening Post" edition of April 13, 1835 contains an advertisement for an undeliverable letter sent to "Martin & Schatz" (undeliverable letters were sent to the "dead letter office" and then advertised in local newspapers). When an invoice for box 8 was sent on April 28 it, too, was sent to the wrong address: 119 Hudson Street.

Since the letter received by T. F. Merz on February 27 was probably in transit for a month or more, the Martin & Schatz relationship must have been formed sometime during January 1835. The Martin & Schatz partnership could not have begun much earlier because the large debt Schatz owed to Merz would have required him to inform Merz about the change in security on his property. Unfortunately, there are no Martin ledgers covering the period from December 1834 to January 1836 so details of the partnership and

Schatz's actual role in the business will likely never be known.

Schatz had accumulated a debt of about 2,000 rixdollars ($1,600 in US currency) by the end of 1834 and had not notified Merz about the Martin & Schatz partnership until after it happened. Merz, however, knew C. F. Martin personally (see letter to Charles Bruno dated April 19, 1838) so was not too upset with the new arrangement even though he had every right to expect more consideration as he was, in effect, financing Schatz and, later, Martin & Schatz.

Shipments of musical merchandise continued to be sent to "Martin & Schatz" until September 1836. Schatz purchased land at Millgrove PA in December 1835 and had moved there by April 1836 at the latest since Martin paid the postage for a letter from Schatz in Millgrove on April 28. (Author's note: At the time, letters were usually sent unpaid, the receiver being required to pay the postage). It appears the Martin & Schatz partnership may have continued as late as August 1836. A new C. F. Martin label (type 4) probably came into use during September 1836.

The Merz ledger book only records notes on shipments, invoices and payments received (in the form of letters of exchange) between 1835 and 1838 so details on the demise of the Martin & Schatz partnership are absent. At this point Merz was not happy. Schatz had built up a considerable debt, formed a partnership with Martin and then abandoned the partnership, leaving C. F. Martin to carry on the business with the accumulated debt. Whatever Merz' misgivings, he continued to export goods to Martin at an increasing rate and the debt continued to rise.

Merz sent a letter to C. F. Martin on March 27, 1838:

**"Neukirch(en) March 27, 1838
To C. F. Martin in New York**

I am now in possession of your 3 letters dated September 30 of last year and January 23 and February15 of this year, and my purpose in writing this letter is to answer them. First I want to acknowledge receiving the 400 (Rixdollars in louis d'ors) (author's note: a louis-d'or was another money of account) sent to me, 60 days after (sight) to Bremen which I gratefully credit to you with

reservation of the correct receipt of the 113 1/3 Louis D'or with pr ct 453 (Rixdollars) 8 (schwaren). I ask you to credit this against the enclosed Porto of 1 (Rixdollars) 19 (schwaren) to Bohemia for your letter of Sept 30 of last year, with the enclosure. I do not think it is necessary for me to describe to you what a troublesome year the past one has been for me; you can imagine for yourself the extent of my troubles if you consider the relationship I now have with you and the horrible times we have just endured. May we never experience another year like this one.

You asked me if I want to continue carrying out your business, and I am very willing to do so, but take as much care to pay me promptly as I always take to provide you with the best and least expensive wares; you should take this into consideration in the orders mentioned if I should carry them out, because my financial circumstances absolutely do not require a further extension of credit, that you would not demand or need either. I cannot continue the way things have gone before; just be sure that I always get my money back after 1 year. I could rightfully demand several hundred (Rixdollars) in interest for waiting that long, but I do not want to do this; surely this proves how committed I am to your interests. I leave it up to your propriety to determine how this is managed. I will take care of the items ordered as well as I can. From the 400 (Rixdollars) enclosed I have designated 200 (Rixdollars) for guitar machines, 150 (Rixdollars) for recorders (in German: B Flöte) and the rest for a spinning wheel and other articles. I have spoken with our music teacher Pezolt regarding the music supplies you requested from me on February 31, 1837 (sic). He tells me it would indeed be possible to procure the music suppliers, but they could not be found anywhere for recorders and (CSE) clarinets, but only S(oprano) recorders and B(ass) and A(lto) clar(inets). We could actually get them for the first instruments, but they would have to be thoroughly reworked and it would take a full ¼ year to do this, and he also couldn't obligate himself to delivering such work for 50 (Rixdollars) when they would only cost half this much for the S(oprano) recorders. Now I want to get your response to this before I get the music supplies, as well as the 3 clarinets and 2 recorders from Vienna. I will try to get the rest of the items ordered by

Mr. Bruno in your last letter, the wares mentioned above soon and send them. One can count on quicker service from the workers than in 1836. Everything is also less expensive but most of it is just ordinary work. The better (items) have maintained their prices, particularly (ordinary) violins are inexpensive now."

This letter is particularly interesting because the it explains the frustrations of Merz but also indicates C. F. Martin Sr. had his own share of frustration and even broached the subject of discontinuing the business arrangement. This must has alarmed Merz, with such a large amount of property in far-away America, and he attempted to sooth Martin's bruised feelings.

In April 1838 Merz wrote to Charles Bruno:

"April 19, 1838

To Mr. Bruno in New York

Your last letter of March 5 reached me today and I will not neglect to send you the requested answer right away and in this to be just as upstanding toward you as you seem to be towards me. My thanks for what you told me about Mr. M(artin) and his situation. Since you are intending to make your relationship to him even closer than it has been previously, I can tell you that your description does not make me especially happy; nor does it particularly surprise me. Although Mr. M(artin) did not so openly tell me about his situation, I could still imagine what it was. I have endured many worries on his account and especially in the past year. May God grant that everything turns out all right. I did not miss the shadows you cast over me about him. I always found cause to complain about his ignorance in commerce and especially about the little respect for order this subject requires. At the top of this order, however, stands the timely completion of what a person has promised, and it is precisely here that Mr. M(artin) has unfortunately revealed the greatest lack of order. Therefore, I desire nothing more sincerely than that he would find a man who could compensate for this deficit, and if you were to be this man I would be particularly happy about this since, at least in the thoughts you revealed in your letter, you are very much in agreement with me. You expressed the desire to learn about my relationship to Mr. M(artin) is, and I will fulfill this desire.

A you know, M(artin) was previously with S(chatz). The latter was actually the reason that I decided on shipments to America. This had barely left when I received the notification that Schatz had entangled himself with M(artin) in this confusion. I did not see anything disadvantageous for me; I knew both men to be upstanding. However, this tie did not last long. S(chatz) separated himself and bought his own way without worrying about me. When he left the transaction, I was owed more than 2,000 (Rixdollars) and it was his responsibility to ask first if I were satisfied; however, he did not seem to feel this way or did not want to and believed he was doing enough if he informed me with a few words that he had withdrawn and I needed to transfer my ownership to Mr. M(artin) as well. I did not answer S(chatz) but I continued my association with M(artin) through which my ownership grew to 3,040 (Rixdollars) 23 (schwaren) 77 (groten). Without the considerable interest which I could take because my ownership stretched back to 1835. Of the preceding sum, however, the current year's remittance of 400 (Rixdollars) in gold or 453 (Rixdollars) 8 (groten) must be subtracted. This is how things stand with Mr. M(artin). My request is not insignificant and if I assure you that I am not especially happy but am the father of a family I'm sure you will believe me that I often look westwards full of worry. At the same time I am not opposed to continuing my association with Mr. M(artin). I will manage to sell the 400 Rixdollars because things cannot continue as they were previously when I always sent 5 to 600 (Rixdollars) of wares for 200. My property can no longer grow but will more likely dwindle and when his business takes a favorable turn it is quite possible I have entrusted Mr. M(artin) with my property with the stipulation that he return it to me within a year. That is precisely what is not being done and about which I have the most complaints. I requested my entire property but I only received 400 (Rixdollars) despite an order with the transmittal of the second (bill of exchange) of 7 to 800. Things cannot continue in this way with transactions like this; I will be ruined. You are reasonable man so I know you will understand this and find it appropriate that, if Mr.

M(artin) requests his order to be carried out in a prompt and proper manner, which I have always done, then I must insist on equally punctual payment on my side. Only in this way can our association continue and be mutually beneficial."

This long letter is full of previously unknown information and fills in many details of C. F. Martin's business in New York:

1) It confirms that Charles Bruno had been working for Martin for some time.

2) Merz complained about Martin's lack of business acumen to a party who might be able to ameliorate the situation. This is more than a little ironic since Bruno had been running the retail store and keeping Martin's books since 1836. It is not hard to imagine Bruno must have had some input into what stock, and how much, was carried by the store. Rather than an indication of Martin's lack of business sense, this would seem to confirm the assertion, mentioned elsewhere in this book, that C. F. Martin had no real interest in retail business, as he had always hired others to look after the store. Martin knew he made a superior product and chose to concentrate his efforts on making guitars.

3) It implies that the Martin & Bruno partnership was already under discussion and Charles Bruno took the sensible, if slightly underhanded and self-serving, opportunity to sound out Martin's largest single supplier who was owed a large amount of money. This debt would become a payable for any new partnership.

Merz wrote a letter to Martin & Bruno on June 8, 1838:

"New York Martin & Bruno June 8, 1838

I refer to my most recent letter to Mr. Martin dated March 27, and since then I have received 2 letters from Mr. Martin dated February 18 and March 31 and one from Mr. Bruno dated April 23. In the latter, you informed me of your association through the firm of Martin & Bruno; I have taken note of your reciprocal signatures and send you my sincere congratulations for your association. Mr. Martin informed me on March 31 that he is taking over sole ownership of my goods that have accrued by May 1 and that he alone would satisfy me; however, I am not in agreement with this. I much prefer that until May 1 Mr. Martin, as well as Mr. Bruno, remains responsible for all my property. In any case when Mr. Bruno began, he found a good portion of the wares I had sent before May 1, and in addition, I used all the payment for my goods to continue carrying out their orders; therefore, these payments became part of their mutual property. Honorable Mr. Bruno, you will not find improper my request that you share responsibility for my property with Mr. Martin until May 1. Negotiate with the latter about any differences in the above matters. Therefore, I have repeated your part of the account of the interest already charged to the new firm, to the repeated request of Mr. Martin. If you look through this and find it correct, then send the balance in my favor for 2,744 (Rixdollars) 2 (schwaren) 11 (groten) by May 1 and inform me of what has happened. The Brazil wood sent to me is already floating on the Elbe. I hope to be able to share with you an agreement about this. Invoice for Box 29 has been sent."

In this letter Merz, who was already aware of the possibilities, agrees to the transfer of his security to the Martin & Bruno partnership.

Merz sent a long letter to Martin & Bruno on October 16, 1838:

"New York, Martin & Bruno, 16 October 1838

I still find myself waiting for your reply to my letter of June 9 with the invoice for box number 29. Hopefully it will arrive and bring me the information I requested about my assets and also the report of wares sent. I did, however, receive two of your letters, dated May 24 and June 12, and I will reply to these in more detail below. I want to inform you first of the receipt of the Fernambuco. I cannot express my amazement at Mr. Martin and how he could send me such goods. The veneer is especially an object of my annoyance. Many guitar makers have looked at it; they all shake their heads and shake my hand again to leave without buying anything, and they think Mr. Martin sent me something that he himself couldn't use. The carpenters and Pianoforte builders have taken

away any of my hopes of earning my money back. Concerning the whole pieces, a lot of them simply cannot be shown. Mr. Martin must surely know that bows are supposed to be made from wood of a particular length and also be free of knots. What has been sent is mostly of this very blemished nature, and I only hope of gradually selling a small portion of it. For these reasons I regret I am not able to share any sales reports today. If Mr. M(artin) had sent me anything salable, I would have been put in a position of being able to make an appropriate shipment of instruments. I have just had to spend about 50 Rixdollars for out of pocket expenses/transaction fees that I will not see again for a long time. And as badly as things are going with this wood, it looks like equally sad and unfavorable circumstances might spread all over all the circumstances of my business dealings with you. Now I would like to answer your letters of May 24 and July 12. In the spring I had much hope of a rapid improvement in circumstances through the news of Mr. Bruno's entry into your business; now this hope has also disappeared and when you ask me to help you I am left standing here again as clueless as I was before, since you do not consider how I might be helped first, so that I would be in a position to offer you help again. The boundless trust I had for Mr. Martin and Schatz moved me to give everything that I had to gradually to put them in a position of founding a respectable business; this would not only help them make a profit, but also ensure that I made a respectable gain. However, now instead of reaping the blessing of my efforts and my trusting devotion, I must unfortunately concede that my plan has completely failed. Therefore, Mr. Martin I give my serious and urgent admonition to you especially to return my assets to me. Not just to take it away from you, but rather so that I will be able to use it again for new shipments (still hoping in a successful outcome). However, I can no longer make shipments without receiving money first, because I have nothing more. I have become a poor man through my devotion. My wife's property, which consists of a house and some land, is property that belongs to her and is not to be sold; it cannot and may not be touched, without committing the most atrocious sin against her and her children, especially for an undertaking which has such little guarantee as that with you. Therefore I ask you once again to do everything in your power to enable me to send you goods once again, because trade, when it is carried out thoroughly and properly, is usually the best means of making a profit. And if you can't send me thousands at once, just send me hundreds. Something can be purchased for that, especially in earthenware goods which are still extremely inexpensive. In return you can count on my honesty, of which I have always given proof, that I will purchase goods for you of the highest quality for the least expensive price. If the trade improves, I will naturally require my investment back, and you can continue to work with your own money. This would also be he case, however, if you neglect your association with me or enter into agreements with other people to provide for your needs.

I must also tell you that I was extremely surprised - indeed I can hardly deny that I was outraged – to read in your letter of July 12 that you could have afforded to make some payments to me at that time if you had not first had to satisfy L. Schmidt and that the reason you had to satisfy him first was so that he would not be able to embarrass you in Neukirchen. Now I ask you how you could be embarrassed in N(eukirchen)? Is he buying wares here for your account? Should it not be completely meaningless to you what he writes here about you if you know how you stand with me now, and if you fulfill your obligations to me? Just let Schmidt and others wait on you for once as well; won't I be able to offer you more advantage than they can?"

Obviously, the payment situation had not improved with the formation of Martin & Bruno and Merz was so desperate as to request the return of his goods if large payments were not quickly forthcoming.

At the same time Merz sent a second letter directly to Charles Bruno:

"New York C. Bruno 16 October 1838

I have received your recent letter of June 9. I did not answer it promptly since I had already informed you of the most important matters relevant to this in my letter to your firm of that same date. Some time ago Hartmann here brought me a private letter from you to him dated August 15. Since you ask for various news from me in this letter, I asked him to leave it with me so I could answer these things since I do not have a close confidential relationship with him, and I am in a better position to give you information about these things than is he. In this letter you wanted to know my general thoughts about your business with Martin. You will find enough about this in my letter of today to Mr. M(artin) and I should add that I fear Martin behaved quite negligently with my small amount of money. Although you assured me in your letter of June 9 that his wealth was still considerably higher than his debts, I still cannot keep from having justified doubts about this assurance until you inform me what assets he actually has. He does not have a house; he does not have property; there are shortages in his supply of goods, and he does not have cash because he has not sent me any. So where is his wealth? Further, you ask Hartman what my circumstances are like. Today I described these to your firm most faithfully; I personally have nothing more!! Finally, you want to know if you can rely on me in every respect, specifically when you also carry out your obligations to me? If by this you mean to ask whether I will carry out your assignments in the best possible manner and use the money to be sent for that purpose, then I give you my most sacred assurance that I will always do this. However, if you mean that you will not carry out your obligations towards me until I made new shipments to you from my own pocket, then I must refuse this for the simple reason that my account is empty. So much for Hartman's letter. Now I turn to you, honorable Mr. Bruno, with the most urgent request that you use your powers and unite them with those of Martin and to try everything to continue the work you began. Indeed, although you say you have no assets, in your letter to me there is proof that you could help if you just wanted to. Because you say you enjoy the favor of a wealthy girl, but you do not want to marry until you are independent. You are indeed independent, since you are the companion of M(artin) and no longer his servant. So why then do you not want to marry? As a spouse you will have the right, indeed even the duty, to protect the wealth of your wife, even to invest it productively. Could you then use it in a better manner than if you use it, or at least part of it, in trade? It cannot be lost, since there is insurance against shipwrecks, and when the goods are sold you will not let the profits disappear. You also say you have investments in real estate that you would suffer damage through sale and if that were true, it would not help. But it is better to suffer some harm in a side business if the primary business is helped through this. And – couldn't you take out a capital loan on these investments? You would not need to sell them all. Truly, you could help if you just wanted to!"

Clearly, Charles Bruno had opened a back channel to T. F. Merz in the letters of June 9 and August 15 quoted above. Bruno may have begun to have second thoughts about the Martin & Bruno partnership and even seems to have been trying to cut a side deal for his own account. Indeed, Bruno may not have waited for the reply to his two letters and made the move to end the Martin & Bruno partnership in September 1838. Bruno may have decided that the large debt that would payable to Merz was not to his liking and had hopes of buying musical goods from Merz for his own store.

The following letter was sent by Merz to Edward Baack:

"New York, E Baack August 27, 1839

At the suggestion of Mr. G. D. Meyer in Hamburg I allow myself to ask for your assistance in the following matter. Mr. C. F Martin, brother-in-law of David Hartmann with whom you are well acquainted, has previously engaged in trading instruments there and since 1834 has gradually accumulated a debt in the amount of 3,240 (Rixdollars) 4 (schwaren), owed to me. Recently this man, tired of trade, sold part of his stock of wares to a certain E. Ludecus for 2,576 (Rixdollars) 9 (schwaren) and sent me the enclosed note as security for this amount. Since this Ludecus is completely unknown to me and the note was issued in the most frivolous, non-binding manner, I wrote to Martin on August 12 that I could not acknowledge Ludecus as the debtor of the said amount nor the note as security. On the contrary he would remain the individual obligated to me.

Now, however, I no longer want to bear the sole responsibility for managing this matter which I so important to me, and I ask you to assist me out of kindness and humanity. Mr. Meyer will make this request his own.

Martin is an upstanding man and certainly does not intend to deceive me, but he has allowed himself to be deceived by the silver-tongued Ludecus and has thus taken away the worldly possessions of a business in the lightest manner. In the enclosed letter to Martin, which you should read through and have sent to him properly sealed, I address this account until October 1 of this year. Then follows Martin's last letter to me, in which he acknowledges his significant debt to me, although not with payment. You are also receiving a letter from Ludecus in which he treats the matter in a much more binding manner than in his note and together these things give me hope that my property might be restored to me. The most important thing is to join with Martin in taking steps against Ludecus to get the 2,576 (Rixdollars) 9 (schwaren), if not in cash at least as well guaranteed as possible, along with the promise that I will receive payment soon. Martin will not fail to provide his support in this matter, and I would prefer for the matter to be resolved amicably, but in a manner that increases my security.

How that will be managed, however, I must leave entirely up to your wise judgment. Only in the most extreme case should you begin a legal case if you discover warrant, and you would have to have this carried out according to your legal counsel in the manner of the nation there. If my own interests do not forbid it, I do not want to be an obstacle to his leaving there either. I should soon receive 500 (Rixdollars?) from Braunschweig for him and for this I will send him goods. Only his father does not seem to want to do anything for him, because he also wrote that his son should not expect any financial support from him. Martin must have some wealth, as can be seen from the letters he has already written. He is also supposed to own a small property, probably where he currently resides in Nazareth."

Obviously, Merz was not pleased to hear that Martin had sold his property to Ludecus & Wolter without his permission. It was such a concern that Merz took steps to hire an agent to look after his interests in New York. However, Merz was incorrect on one thing.

Martin did not own his own property in the Nazareth area until December 1839, although Merz may have been referring to the farmhouse Martin rented in Schoeneck in April 1839.

The letter sent by Merz to C. F. Martin, as mentioned in the letter above, is as follows :

"Nazareth, C. F. Martin, August 27, 1839

I refer to my letter of the 12th of this month in which I told you that I absolutely could not acknowledge Ludecus as my debtor for the amount of the goods turned over to him of 2,576 (Rixdollars) 9 (schwaren), but rather I will rely on you for this; I also asked you immediately to find means to get better security for me for the sum mentioned than the note that was sent provides. According to your request, I am enclosing a summary in which the interest up to October 1, in accordance with your wishes, is only calculated at 4%. As you see, all my assets up to that point add up to 3240 (Rixdollars) 4 (groten) which you will find correct. The sales invoice for the Pernambuco sold thus far also follows. Now, dear Mr. Martin, I need to inform you that Mr. E. Baack in New York will assist me with the goods you sold Ludecus for the amount of 2,576 (Rixdollars) 9 (schwaren). This gentleman will deliver this letter to you and request that you immediately discuss with him the means and ways necessary to get the said amount, or at least to guarantee it. Exert all means to meet my demands and do not forget how cordially and well advised I have always treated you, and that therefore my desire to regain my property once and for all is justified. If your views do not agree with those of Mr. Baack, but you obviously are trying to achieve what is best for me, then I will try to meet you in a cordial manner so that we can part ways in friendship and Mr. Baack will not be forced to suggest means that would only be unpleasant for you and for me. Besides the 2,576 (Rixdollars) 9 (schwaren) I should also receive 663 (Rixdollars) 19 (schwaren) which you should give Mr. Baack, as I sincerely desire, as soon as possible; hopefully you will be satisfied if I set the date this is due at one year from today."

A letter was also sent to Edward Ludecus on the same date as the two letters above:

"New York. E. Ludecus August 27, 1839

I have received your letter dated June 15. Since you and Mr. Martin mention that your father would pay the 2,576 (Rixdollars) 9 (schwaren), the amount for which you took over Martin's stock, so I asked him what I should hope for in this regard. Unfortunately, however, I received unsatisfactory news and since I do not know the older gentleman at all, you will not think badly that I cannot assign the amount above to you and must hold Mr. Martin alone responsible for this. I have already informed Mr. Martin of this and agreed to consult with you about this. Otherwise I remain constantly at your service. I also need to tell you that Mr. [Keith/with] Geller in Braunschweig writes on the 9th of this month that he will soon send me 500 (Rixdollars?) for your account and when I receive this I will send you goods; I am waiting for a more detailed description of these from you."

A letter was also sent to G. D. Meyer in Hamburg:

"Hamburg G.D. Meyer August 27, 1839

In return for my recently sent letter of the 22nd of this month, the contents of which I confirm, I have received your honorable letter of the 20th of this month. I am happy to see, my friend, that you are willing to help me with my demands to Martin, which is why I am turning over to you the enclosed letters that are relevant to this. Please read through them and send them on to Mr. E. Baack with the necessary comments.

Concerning your comments about my delivery to you, I assure you that I would be very embarrassed to get the amount due only through Baack. Let me to get interest from 2 months from the date the invoice was issued. I will begin this with the next delivery and with that I will be able to make it. Is that alright with you? I would also like to add that I counted the 4 J. Violins from M in crate No 46 at 13 (Rixdollars) 2 (schwaren), but since they cost only 2 (Rixdollars) 16 (groten) per piece, so I credit you with 1 (schwaren) 16 (groten) and ask you to forgive my mistake."

This flurry of activity must have finally been settled to Merz's satisfaction as Merz made several shipments to Charles Bruno in Macon, Georgia during 1839 and continued to supply musical goods to Ludecus & Wolter in 1839 and 1840.

However, it does appear Martin still owed Merz some money as late as November 1843 as Merz noted such in an entry in his ledger.

1898 to 1969

BUEGELEISEN & JACOBSON

Although the sole sales agency with C. A. Zoebisch & Son had ended in the 1890's, C. F. Martin & Co. came to an agency agreement with Buegeleisen & Jacobson, a major musical wholesale business in New York. On September 1, 1906 the following details were recorded in the sales ledger:

"Buegeleisen & Jacobson appointed sole agents for United States (to the trade) excepting old customers. Discount uniform 50% net 30 d(ay)s less 2% 10 d(ay)s except on Pacific Coast"

Martin already had Southern California Music Company and Sherman, Clay & Co. handling the West Coast.

The 50% discount seems incorrect, though, as Buegeleisen & Jacobson actually received a 64% discount. From January 1907 Buegeleisen & Jacobson seem to have had their own special price list that still amounted to a 64% discount. Usually Martin ledgers recorded the retail prices of instruments and then applied the appropriate discount depending on whether the customer was a trade, teacher or professional account.

In the period just before September 1906 the total personnel of Martin, including Frank Henry Martin, amounted to only 7 people. F. H. Martin must have been extremely busy handling the normal business affairs of his company. He must have been planning on appointing a sole agent for some time and, expecting a surge in orders, he added 4 workers in September to boost production.

By April 1907 the discount had been reduced to 60%. Buegeleisen & Jacobson continued to receive the 60% discount until February 1911 even though purchases had been falling for some time.

The sole agency probably have come to an end around 1911 but B & J continued to buy Martin guitars. B & J even participated in the "Customer's Line" between 1923 and 1926 when they ordered Martin 2-17 guitars and style 0 ukuleles that were stamped "S. S. Stewart".

Buegeleisen & Jacobson continued to purchase Martin guitars until 1954 and the company survived into the early 1970's.

SOUTHERN CALIFORNIA MUSIC CO.

Southern California Music Company was founded in Los Angeles in 1880. By 1916 Southern California Music Co. had become a large retail and wholesale music chain with branches in Los Angeles, Pasadena, Riverside and San Diego. At this time the company's main branch was located at 332-334 South Broadway in Los Angeles.

Southern California Music began selling Martin guitars in 1902 although sales did not really take off until 1913. Until mid-June 1913 Martin's largest dealer in Southern California had been Lindsey Music Co. of

Figure 20
Southern California Music Co. (ca. 1924)

Los Angeles. Southern California Music Co. began buying larger quantities of Martin instruments in November 1913 so there is a possibility SoCal purchased Lindsey Music Co.

Southern California Music Co. and Sherman, Clay Co. were Martin's two largest dealers on the West Coast. In 1915, Southern California corresponded with Martin and was granted a territory stretching southward from Bakersfield to San Diego.

In mid-1916 Southern California Music ordered some sample guitars from Martin with spruce tops and koa wood back and sides. Six guitars of each of three different styles were order, these being similar to 0-18, 0-21 and 00-28 guitars. Martin shipped the first eighteen guitars on July 10, 1916. One of the prototype 0-18 koa guitars is in existence and differs from a normal 0-18 in having a single sound hole ring and no serial number.

The company sent a very interesting letter to Martin, dated August 11, 1916, requesting that the tops be changed to koa and the asking that the guitar decoration also be changed. The company supplied three sample Nunes ukuleles to illustrate the decoration desired for future guitars. The Model 1350 (0-18K) was to be similar to the prototype in decoration with a single sound hole ring and black binding, the Model 1400 (0-21K) was to have a three-ring sound hole decoration with "rope" purfling for the inner ring plus black binding and the Model 1500 (00-28K) was to be similar in decoration to Model 1400 but with the "rope" purfling added around the top of the guitar and with body and neck to be bound with white celluloid. The sample Nunes model 53 ($5.00), model 52 ($6.25) and model 51 ($8.00) ukuleles were returned by Martin on November 24, 1916. The guitar decoration for the Model 1350, 1400 and 1500 guitars changed over time and became more like regular Martin guitars. The fan bracing of the original models was eventually changed to X-bracing. By October 1919, the special SoCal serial number range had been dropped in favor of Martin's regular serial numbers.

Southern California Music supplied koa logs to Martin for their early koa guitars. At least two shipments of koa logs were made by Southern California Music Co, the second being on November 15, 1917. This was more than sufficient koa wood to cover production of all koa guitars until April 1921, at which point Martin began buying their own supply of koa.

Martin applied a special series of serial numbers for the koa guitars made for Southern California Music Co. The first 18 guitars were not serialized although they were accounted in the serial number sequence since the first serialized guitar was assigned serial number 19. Serial numbers 19 to 262 are recorded in the sales ledger (with the exception of serial numbers 124, 137, 141 and 142. These are probably all model 1350 guitars, similar to Martin 0-18K guitars).

Southern California Music Co. opened a new store in 1923 at 806-808 South Broadway in Los Angeles but had moved before the end of the 1930's.

The last Martin guitar purchase was made by the company on April 1, 1939. Between 1902 and 1939 the Southern California Music Co. bought about 2,100 Martin instruments.

The history of the Southern California Music Co. after 1939 is not known but the company, mostly involved in selling pianos, was in existence until just a few years ago.

SHERMAN, CLAY & CO.

Sherman, Clay & Co. was a San Francisco-based retailer of musical instruments and publisher of sheet music.

The company began as a music store founded in 1853 by A. A. Rosenberg with a location at the corner of Kearny and Sutter streets. Leander Schutzenbach Sherman (1847-1926), who had been employed as a clerk by Rosenberg, bought out his employer in 1870. Sherman took on a Major Clement C. Clay (1836-1905) as a partner in 1879. Sherman, Clay & Co. was incorporated in 1892. During the 1890's, the company sold imported music, pianos and musical instruments and also had a factory for the manufacture of pianos and church organs.

By 1894, the company had four store locations: San Francisco, Oakland, Seattle and Portland, Oregon.

The 1906 San Francisco earthquake destroyed the San Francisco location, and forced the company to operate out of the Oakland location. The headquarters returned to San Francisco in 1907 when a new building was constructed.

A new store was constructed in San Francisco in 1909 on the southwest corner of 14th and Clay, with Sherman, Clay & Co. as the tenant.

Based on the letters in the Martin archives, Sherman, Clay & Co. relocated several times in the 1920's and 1930's. In 1922 the company was located at 741 Mission Street but by 1924 had moved to 536 Mission Street and by 1932 had returned to a location at Kearney and Sutter streets.

The company was sold to Bernard Schwartz, of San Francisco, in 1957. The company had 21 location in the 1950's and had expanded to 28 stores by 1965, all located California, Oregon or Washington, although its headquarters remained in San Francisco. The next stage in the company's history was to expand beyond the West Coast. By the mid-1970's it had established a national presence, including stores in Manhattan, Kansas City, Seattle and Los Angeles. In the 1980's, the company had grown to 60 stores. From that point the company began a long period of downsizing and all its retail stores were closed by 2013.

Sherman, Clay & Co. sold about 4,350 Martin instruments between and July 1918 and November 1967. Between 1918 and 1932 the company bought sixty-four style 42 and 45 guitars including five OM-45 Deluxe guitars, one being the prototype OM-45 Deluxe (serial number 42125) made famous by Roy Rogers.

RUDOLPH WURLITZER CO.

Although chiefly known for its pianos, organs and juke boxes, Rudolph Wurlitzer & Co. played a very important role in helping the Martin Guitar Co. survive the early years of the Great Depression.

The Wurlitzer family had been involved in the musical instrument trade in Saxony as far back as 1659. Franz Rudolph Wurlitzer (1831–1914) was born in Schoeneck, Saxony, located less than 10 km from the instrument-making center of Markneukirchen. After emigrating to the United States he founded the Wurlitzer Company in Cincinnati in 1853. The company

originally imported stringed, woodwind and brass instruments from the Wurlitzer family in Germany. Wurlitzer enjoyed great success providing musical instruments to the U.S. military during the American Civil War and Spanish–American War.

Wurlitzer began manufacturing its own pianos in 1880, adding coin-operated pianos in 1896. Wurlitzer further increased manufacturing when World War I interrupted imports from Europe. After Franz Wurlitzer's death in 1914 the company was successively directed by his sons Howard, Rudolph and Farny.

As well as having a number of manufacturing subsidiaries, Wurlitzer also operated a chain of retail stores for selling the company's products. From the Martin correspondence it is clear that Wurlitzer had built up a chain of at least 40 stores during the 1920's and

RUDOLPH WURLITZER CO.				
CITY	STATE	START	END	QUAN
East St. Louis	IL	1925	1926	2
Greensburg	PA	1927	1927	1
Atlanta	GA	1931	1931	1
Oakland	CA	1930	1931	28
Memphis	TN	1931	1932	2
Huntington	WV	1932	1932	2
Blythwood	SC	1934	1934	1
San Francisco	CA	1923	1934	481
Pontiac	IL	1934	1934	1
Kansas City	MO	1930	1935	134
Niagara Falls	NY	1926	1935	55
Akron	OH	1933	1936	15
Pittsburgh	PA	1924	1936	386
Syracuse	NY	1926	1937	91
Youngstown	OH	1930	1937	111
Brooklyn	NY	1937	1938	10
Dayton	OH	1925	1938	344
Louisville	KY	1924	1938	342
Middletown	OH	1932	1938	39
Piqua	OH	1928	1938	18
Springfield	OH	1927	1938	101
St. Louis	MO	1925	1938	297
Ashland	KY	1930	1939	82
Hamilton	OH	1929	1939	70
Milwaukee	WI	1925	1939	193
Rochester	NY	1927	1938	217
Columbus	OH	1924	1942	238
Flint	MI	1942	1942	1 (a D-45)
Cleveland	OH	1924	1946	1,014
Chicago	IL	1923	1954	1,434
Wyandotte	MI	1959	1959	1
New York	NY	1922	1961	5,533
Philadelphia	PA	1924	1963	571
Buffalo	NY	1925	1967	682
Chicago	IL	1967	1967	21
Cincinnati	OH	1921	1967	3,522
De Kalb	IL	1959	1967	6
Detroit	MI	1925	1967	1,985
New York	NY	1967	1967	11
Philadelphia	PA	1967	1967	9
Valley Stream	NY	1967	1967	6

Figure 21
Total Instrument Sales by Rudolph Wurlitzer Co. Branch

1930's, some in quite small cities. As to be expected, the Depression had a negative effect on the company's business and Wurlitzer began closing stores by the mid-1930's, including shutting down their two California locations, Los Angeles and Oakland, in 1934. Between 1935 and 1939 another seventeen stores were closed and by the 1960's only a few larger stores, Cincinnati, Cleveland, Detroit, Buffalo, New York and Philadelphia, were still selling Martin instruments.

Wurlitzer started buying Martin instruments in 1921 and participated in Martin's "Customer's Line" or "C Line" in 1922, these guitars having a slightly different design and no serial numbers. However, by the end of 1922 Wurlitzer began buying regular Martin instrument with serial numbers, even though they continued to use their own model numbers when ordering and the instruments continued to receive the Wurlitzer stamp.

Wurlitzer seems entered a period of decline from the early 1960's, as evidenced by a number of questionable transactions. In 1964, Wurlitzer bought out the Henry C. Martin Band Instrument Company of Elkhart, Indiana, a manufacturer of brass wind instruments. In 1967, Wurlitzer became the sole distributor of Holman-Woodell guitars, sold under the Wurlitzer brand. Wurlitzer then switched buying to Welson, an Italian guitar maker, but had abandoned the guitar market entirely by 1969.

In 1973, Wurlitzer sold its jukebox brand to a German company. The Baldwin Piano Company purchased Wurlitzer's U. S. factory and piano and organ brands in 1988 and moved production overseas. In 1996, the Gibson Guitar Corporation acquired The Baldwin Co., including its Wurlitzer assets. Gibson acquired Deutche Wurlitzer Jukebox and Electronics Vending brand in 2006 thus reuniting the Wurlitzer product lines under one banner. Baldwin ceased using the Wurlitzer name on pianos by 2009 and Gibson now uses the Wurlitzer brand name exclusively for jukeboxes and vending machines. Gibson continues to manufacture Wurlitzer jukeboxes and vending machines at a factory in Hullhorst, Germany.

Between 1921 and the end of December 1967 Wurlitzer sold 21,444 Martin instruments. Since the Martin archival material covered by this book ends in 1967, it is not known when Rudolph Wurlitzer Co.

ceased buying Martin instruments.

COAST WHOLESALE MUSIC CO.

Coast Wholesale Music Co. was a wholesale musical instrument sales company founded in San Francisco on August 1, 1928. A connection must have already existed between the owners of Coast Wholesale and Martin since purchases of Martin instruments had begun by the middle of September 1928. Coast Wholesale Music Co., with branches in San Francisco and Los Angeles, distributed Martin instruments to many music stores on the West Coast that were too small to order Martin product directly.

In late 1967 Kaman purchased Coast Wholesale Music Company and added the music distribution business to the company's Ovation Guitar manufacturing operations.

During its years in operation Coast Wholesale Music Co. was Martin's single largest customer. In the period between September 12, 1928 and November 3, 1967 Coast Wholesale purchased over 61,000 Martin instruments, accounting for about 26.8% of Martin's total production.

Notes for Chapter 3

1) Vogtlandischer Geigenbau, Bernhard Zoebisch, page 266

2) Schatz appeared in the Boston Almanacs from 1845 to 1850 but was not listed in the 1842 edition (see Appendix F)

3) See note 47 in Chapter 1

4) From Charles Bruno's passport application dated December 22, 1870.

5) The Musical Instrument Makers of New York: A Directory of the 18th and 19th Centuries, Nancy Groce, page 23

6) The notice appeared in The Morning Courier & New York Enquirer from May 5 to May 8, 1838.

7)) 04-JOURNAL 04-1837 TO 11-1838 BRUNO, page 94, last entry dated November 29, 1838

8) 39-RECHNUNGSBUCH MERZ, pages 48 to 50, entry dated June 4, 1839, shipment of boxes 1, 2 and 3 to C. Bruno in Macon

9) History of Columbus Georgia, page 98, published by Thomas Gilbert, Columbus Ga. 1874

10) The Musical Instrument Makers of New York: A Directory of the 18th and 19th Centuries, Nancy Groce, page 23

11) Coupa boarded at 6, Sewall Place, Boston, Massachusetts, and was an instructor of French, The Boston Directory, 1830, Charles Stimpson, Jr. Boston. The 1832 edition of The Boston Directory shows Coupa at the same address as a professor of music. Coupa in not listed in Stimpson's Boston Directory for 1834, 1835 or 1836.

12) Strong on Music, 1836-1850, Vera Brodsky Lawrence, pages 142 and 223

13) 02-JOURNAL 1836-39, page 116

14) 02-JOURNAL 1836-39, page 134

15) 05-INVENTORY PURCHASES 1837-38, folio 16

16) 04-JOURNAL 04-1837 TO 11-1838 BRUNO, page 17

17) The store at 385 Broadway was located on the west side of the street just north of White Street.

18) 04-JOURNAL 04-1837 TO 11-1838 BRUNO, page 58, entry dated July 12, 1838

19) Spirit of the Times, September 1, 1849. Volume 19, No. 28

20) Death record states: "Canterbury NY July 5, Susan Angelica dau John and Susan Coupa 8y 1m"

21) Coupa died on May 18, 1850, The New York Genealogical and Biographical Record

22) Coupa's death notice in the Evening Post on Saturday, May 18, 1850

23) 07-DAYBOOK 1850-51, records guitars received by C. F. Martin Jr. at 385 Broadway from June 2, 1850 to January 23, 1851.

24) (United Kingdom) Deaths registered in October, November and December 1898, page 70

25) 02-JOURNAL 1836-39, page 90

26) The Guitar & Mandolin, Philip J. Bone, page 162

27) Articles of Agreement between C. F. Martin and Charles De Janon, January 1, 1851, in Martin Guitar Co. archive

28) Passenger manifest, New York, January 21, 1842

29) "Brass scholarship in review: proceedings of the Historic Brass Society ...", Stewart Carter, Historic Brass Society, pg 90 and 91

30) Passenger manifest for bark "Sir Isaac Newton", New York, September 20, 1845

31) C. F. Martin and His Guitars 1796-1873, University of North Carolina Press, Philip F. Gura, 2003, page 136

32) 08-SALE 1852-59 ledger

Chapter 4
DEVELOPMENT OF MARTIN GUITARS (DESIGNS, SHAPES AND SIZES)

EARLY MARTIN GUITARS (1834 to 1839)

BODY SHAPES

Of the twenty-seven pre-1840 Martin guitars studied for this book, all those made before the third quarter of 1838 have the rounded body shape associated with Stauffer guitars; that is, the upper bout is nearly as wide as the lower bout.

The Martin ledgers record the first "Spanish" guitar was sold in late 1837[1] but the first guitar examined with the Spanish shape, the upper bout noticeably narrower than the lower bout, dates to late 1838. Either an early Martin Spanish-shaped guitar is still to be discovered or Martin was referring to features such as fan bracing, a tie bridge or a cedar neck when noting "Spanish". Serial number 1275, made about February 1839 is the earliest Martin guitar examined with a more Spanish shape. The new shape retains the relatively rounded bottom of the Stauffer shape but differs from Martin's later Spanish guitars which had a flatter bottom. As the new shape is a transitional stage between the Stauffer shape and the fully Spanish shape used after 1840 it will be referred to as the "transitional Spanish shape" in subsequent discussions. The center points for the bottom radii of the lower bout of the transitional Spanish shape are further from the bottom of the guitar than Martin's regular Spanish guitars. This gives the lower bout of the transitional Spanish shape a more rounded appearance when compared to the flatter appearance of the later Spanish guitars. By early 1840 Martin had perfected the shape of his Spanish guitars, a shape that survived for the rest of the 19th century and is still used for small body 12-fret guitars to this day. Martin experimented with the body dimensions and thickness of his instruments for several years after 1840 but never again returned to the Stauffer shape.

MATERIALS

Martin used a variety of types of wood for the back and sides of his early guitars. The most commonly encountered are bird's-eye maple, Brazilian rosewood, brazilwood (pernambuco) and zebrawood (gonçalo alves). The 1839 ledger records several guitars were made of "valnut", probably Spanish walnut, and one of these is extant (serial number 1293, made about June 1839). Guitars made in this period have either one-piece or two-piece backs.

The backs are commonly veneered with another wood: either spruce, mahogany or rosewood. It is not known if the veneering was intentional or a convenient way to utilize veneers too thin for use on their own. However, purchases of "furniers" (German for veneers) of zebrawood, bird's-eye maple and mahogany appear in a 1836 ledger entry so veneering may have been normal practice on Martin's early guitars. Around the same time Martin also bought 2-1/2 tons of "brazil-wood" and would, presumably, have cut this wood thick enough to make veneering with other woods unnecessary.

All early Martin guitars made between 1834 and very

Figure 22
1838 Martin & Bruno Guitar (missing serial number) and
1839 Martin & Schatz Guitar (serial number 1296)

early 1840 have very fine-grained spruce tops, very different from the typically available America spruce. Dendrochronology studies have convincingly proven that this top wood is European spruce, some of it more than 50 years old in1834. C. F. Martin clearly bought a good supply of European spruce with him from Saxony as it lasted him six year, during which time he made about 400 guitars. Martin did buy some spruce in 1834 but this was probably used for veneering with more expensive woods for guitar backs or for braces or lining.

The Martin ledger in 1834 mentions a purchase for "whitewood", which could be any wood with a light color, but probably means either poplar, tulipwood, basswood or cottonwood. The "white wood" was used for constructing the necks, headstocks and "ice cream cone" heels of Martin's guitars. This type of neck was generally finished black although higher grade guitars had necks veneered with ebony and a few had necks inlaid with alternating strips of ebony and ivory. Many of the surviving pre-1840 Martin guitars have a clock key mechanism that allows adjustment of the necks angle, these guitars always have an elevated fingerboard.

Ebony was used for the bridges and fingerboards.

Ivory was used for binding, bridges, saddles and nuts.

Mahogany was used for veneering with more expensive woods for the backs of guitars and also for bridge plates.

TOP BRACING

When discussing top bracing, only the bracing below the sound hole is considered. The earliest Martin guitars have simple ladder bracing with one straight ladder brace and a second ladder brace at a more oblique angle. This did not remain the norm for long, though, for almost no two Martin guitars between 1834 and mid-1838 have exactly the same bracing pattern. It is hard to describe the variety of bracing patterns encountered because they vary from almost no bracing at all (but with a long and wide bridge plate), to a number of different one-brace and two-brace patterns. See page 88 for a few representative sketches. The earliest three-strut fan braced guitar seen is serial number 1160, made about June 1837. This guitar retains the Stauffer body shape but is fitted with the new bracing pattern and an early version of a pyramid bridge. From about August 1838 to the end of 1839, the three-strut fan brace became the normal bracing pattern, so Martin had probably determined this type of brace gave the best combination of strength and tone. Clearly, Martin was open to experimenting with bracing to improve the tone of his guitars and tried many different bracing patterns during this period.

BRIDGES

The earliest Martin guitars have ebony moustache bridges. Martin referred to these as **"steg mit herzchen"** ("bridge with little hearts"), which nicely describes the abalone hearts inlaid into the down-turned corners of the bridge. The down-turned corners are also a distinctive feature of Martin guitars as most Stauffer guitars, as well as many Stauffer copies, have up-turned corners. The moustache bridge was used until about September 1837 and was replaced by the "shield" type bridge. A few pyramid bridges are encountered in the period, with the earliest dating, as mentioned previously, to around June 1837. Whereas the moustache and shield bridges were made for guitar pins, the early pyramid bridges were always made as tie bridges.

BRIDGE PLATES

The earliest Martin guitars do not have bridge plates but bridge plates, usually made of mahogany, do appear by 1835. These bridge plates take a variety of forms; some are rectangular while others have pointed ends and a few have long thin "wings" that tie into the linings on either side of the lower bout, almost like a top brace.

DECORATION

For the most part, Martin guitars from the 1834 -1839 period have understated and elegant decoration. Very few of the less expensive Martin guitars have survived from the period so it is not known the level of decoration but it may be assumed that the purfling and sound hole decoration were plain lines. The higher priced instruments generally had fancier purfling, abalone inlays around the sound hole and, sometimes, ivory bridges and ivory binding, as well as adjustable necks and Vienna one-side screws. Martin made a small number of very fancy guitars; these had "thumbnail" abalone inlays around the top edge of the guitar, ivory binding on the body, neck and the head stock, and fancier inlays around the sound hole. One fancy early guitar recorded has an ivory fingerboard, an ivory veneered neck and an ivory bridge.

EARLY MARTIN GUITARS (1839 to 1852)

BODY SHAPE

Around February 1839, probably under the influence of John B. Coupa, Martin altered the shape of his guitars from the Stauffer shape to the transitional Spanish shape. This new shape was only used until early 1840, when the shape was changed again to the more recognizable Spanish shape. The Spanish shape established in 1840 was used for the remainder of the 19th century, although Martin tinkered with the size and depth of his guitars throughout the 1840's.

Correspondence from 1849 indicates John Coupa ordered "Paez" and "Ferranti" models from C. F. Martin. It is not known what is meant by "Paez" unless it is a misspelling of "Pagez", indicating Martin was making guitars based on instruments by that Spanish luthier.

A clue to what is meant by the "Ferranti model" may be provided by the following entry on page 22 of "A History of the Guitar" by James Ballard:

"In 1846, M. Ferranti, guitarist to the king of Belgium, brought with him a guitar of large circular form, something like the Legnani pattern. It had an extra sounding-board, of the kind mentioned in Experiment No. 6. The instruments made from this model have almost exclusively been made by Schmidt & Maul."

The Ferranti family still has two Lacote guitars once owned by Marco de Ferranti[2] and have kindly supplied photographs of these two instruments.

It is not known what Coupa meant when he ordered the "Ferranti" model but no Martin guitars after the late 1830's have been seen with this shape. Possibly Coupa was referring to a guitar with an extra sound board, as one early Martin guitar with an extra sound board has been reported.

Figure 23
1839 Martin & Bruno guitar (SN 1296) and ca. 1840-1842 Martin & Coupa guitar (right)

Figure 24
Lacote guitars once owned by Marco Aurelio Zani De Ferranti

RENAISSANCE BODY SHAPE

The last style of body encountered has become known as the "renaissance" shape. The "renaissance"-shaped guitars, although only making up a minority of early Martin guitars, came in four distinct varieties. These were made over a larger range of dates than covered by this section but are all included here for reference.

On type 1 guitars the sides meet the body tangentially but are twisted (or warped) to blend gracefully into the shape of the heel. On type 2, the most commonly encountered variety, the guitar has small shoulders that meet the neck at a 90 degree angle. On type 3 the

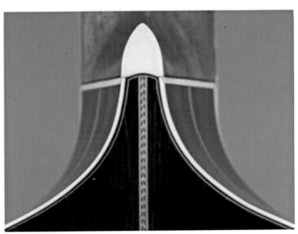

Figure 25
Type 1 Renaissance Body
Circa 1842-1843

Figure 26
Type 2 Renaissance Body
Circa 1840's to 1850's

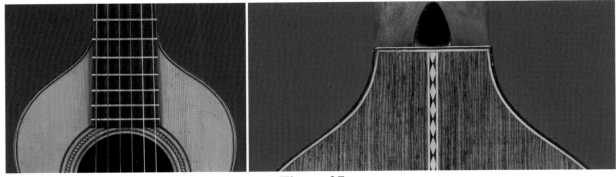

Figure 27
Type 3 Renaissance Body
Circa 1850

Figure 28
Type 4 Renaissance Body
1859-1860

sides meet the neck tangentially but the sides do not blend into the heel. The type 1 body shape appears to come from the 1842 to 1843 period . The type 2 body shape was used from the 1840's to the 1850's. The type 3 body shape dates to around 1850.

The type 4 shape is the body style associated with the five 10-string guitars made by Martin in 1859 and 1860. Martin made four 10-string harp guitars for Olaf Erickson of Richmond, Virginia in 1859 and 1860 plus one more for Bruno & Morris of New York, also in 1860.

Martin did not have a terminology for the "renaissance" shape. In a letter dated October 30, 1853, a music teacher in Alabama ordered a "renaissance" guitar but had to include a little sketch of the shape he wanted. Martin didn't have a clear way for identifying this shape.

MATERIALS

In the 1839 to 1852 period Martin used mostly Brazilian rosewood for guitars bodies although guitars made of bird's-eye maple, pernambuco and mahogany exist. As a carry over from the previous section, it is possible a few guitars were made of "valnut" (probably Spanish walnut). Guitars from the period always have two-piece backs.

The backs of guitars are still commonly veneered with another wood; either spruce, mahogany or rosewood, but this practice decreased as time went on.

A very few early 1840 guitars appear to have been made with the last of the very fine-grained European tops Martin brought with him from Saxony in 1833. After the European spruce was exhausted Martin began using locally grown red spruce.

Martin continued to use "whitewood" (poplar, tulip-wood, basswood or cottonwood) for the ebonized necks with an "ice cream cone" heel but also used Spanish cedar for the Spanish necks on some of his guitars. Some of the Spanish necks have a one piece heel, contiguous with the rest of the neck, but heels are known constructed of two or even three pieces.

Ebony was used for the bridges, fingerboards and occasionally as a veneer between the head stock and neck on Spanish guitars. Spanish necks in this period were always constructed of two pieces, the head stock and the neck being separate.

Ivory was used for binding, bridges, saddles and nuts. A few guitars have been seen which have veneers of ivory and ebony separating the head stock and neck.

Mahogany was used for veneering with more expensive woods for the backs of guitars and also for bridge plates. Mahogany guitars may also be encountered as it is known Martin used mahogany for guitar bodies between 1852 and 1856.

TOP BRACING

Although a few unusual bracing patterns have been

observed, in general top bracing can be broken into several distinct periods. From circa 1840 to 1841 Martin was using three-strut fan bracing and from 1842 to early 1843 switched to a five-strut fan. All the guitars from this time frame had a tie bridge. Beginning in 1843 Martin began using an early form of X-bracing. You can visualize this bracing pattern by putting your hand flat on a table to represent a five-strut fan brace. Now, imagine you remove the middle finger and extend the first and third fingers upwards until they cross. You will note the thumb and small finger are still splayed like in the fan brace and are not parallel to the first and third fingers. The driving rationale for the invention X-bracing was probably that Martin wanted to use pin, not tie, bridges. A three or five-strut fan brace made it difficult to drill holes in the top for the pin bridge without damaging the braces themselves. An X-brace freed up space below the X so a pin bridge could be easily installed. The crossing of the main braces to form an X greatly increased the strength of the bracing and, at the same time, opened up the lower bout area for producing a better tone.

Martin did continue to use the three-strut fan bracing pattern on his size 3 and 2½ "student model" guitars until the end of the 19th century but almost all other guitars were given X-bracing. The early X-bracing is somewhat variable as some guitar have the outrigger braces (thumb and small finger) that are still not parallel but slant in the opposite direction. The early form of X-bracing survived to about 1848 but by 1850 Martin was experimenting with plain X-bracing without a tone bar or finger braces. By about 1852 one tone bar and one finger brace were added to the plain X-bracing pattern to create a pattern similar to, if not exactly the same as, modern bracing.

Other bracing patterns are encountered and probably indicate Martin's willingness to try new ideas, always seeking to improve the tone of his guitars.

BRIDGES

A few 1840 guitars have a shield bridge but, with this exception, Martin changed over to pyramid bridges. These bridges were the norm until 1930. The early pyramid bridges, circa 1840 to 1842, were tie bridges with a large L-shaped ivory saddle. From circa 1843 Martin used pin bridges almost exclusively.

BRIDGE PLATES

Bridge plates from the period are made of a thin veneer of mahogany, generally with pointed ends, that extend under and past the fan or X-braces.

DECORATION

Martin continued to make his instruments with understated decoration. As to be expected, more expensive guitars styles received finer purfling for the top, back stripe and end decoration, ivory binding and/or an ivory bridge and abalone purfling and inlay around the sound hole.

Although it is generally believed Martin didn't establish a specific product line until the late 1850's, the little correspondence that exists from the 1840's proves that Martin did produce guitars with at least some standardized forms of decoration as will be examined later. Some models that would be recognizable with guitars produced later in the 1850's include 3-17, 2½-26, 2-27 and 1-26, even if some variation in purfling is encountered.

MARTIN GUITARS (1852 to 1867)

DESIGN

The basic design remained the Spanish-shaped guitar with a 12-fret neck but Martin began to increase the size of the bodies. The 0 size body was added in 1852 and became quite popular for concert use, guitars with this size are relatively common. The 00 size body was added in 1858 but remained relatively rare with only ten guitars being made between 1858 and 1884. The 00 size became more common in the 1890's but production never exceeded much more than about a dozen guitars per year in the late 19th century.

MATERIALS

The records are quite complete from 1852 to 1864, although there is a gap in the records from 1864 to 1867. The vast majority of guitars made in this time frame have Brazilian rosewood bodies although some mahogany guitars were made between 1852 and 1856. The records also indicate three maple guitars were made in 1853 and 1854. Guitars from this period always have two-piece backs.

Some guitars from the period are still seen with backs veneered with spruce although this practice decreased as time went on.

Locally grown red spruce was used for guitar tops during these years.

Martin used "whitewood" (poplar, tulipwood, basswood or cottonwood) for ebonized necks. Generally, the ebonized neck with the "ice cream cone" heel was used for less expensive models (styles 17, 18, 20 and 21) and for parlor guitars in style 34. Spanish cedar was used for the necks in styles 22, 23, 24, 26, 27 and 28 guitars. Style 30 guitars received a mixture of ebonized and Spanish cedar necks.

Ebony was used for the bridges and fingerboards.

Ivory was used for binding, bridges, saddles and nuts.

TOP BRACING

The three-strut fan bracing pattern was used for size 3 and 2½ "student model" (style 17) guitars. All other guitars were made with X-bracing, a single tone bar and finger braces. Exceptionally, a few guitars up to style 24 have been encountered with fan bracing.

BRIDGES

Only pyramid bridges, in either ebony or ivory, were in use during the period.

BRIDGE PLATE

Bridge plates from the period are made of a thin veneer of mahogany, generally with pointed ends, that extend under and past the fan or X-braces.

DECORATION

By 1852 Martin's product line was well established and had become formalized by 1858 with the introduction of the size and style code. The purfling used on specific models, such as "herringbone" on style 28 guitars, became normalized although some variation in the top purfling, back stripe and end decoration is encountered.

MARTIN GUITARS (1867 to 1898)

MATERIALS

This period starts with the formation of C. F. Martin & Co. on July 20, 1867. The sales records are complete, if not very detailed, from 1867 to 1884 but almost completely missing from 1884 to 1898.

All guitars made in this time frame have Brazilian rosewood bodies although Martin may have experimented with mahogany guitars in the aftermath of the Panic of 1893. Guitars always have two-piece backs.

During these years Martin used solid veneers for the backs of guitars thus ending the previous practice of sometimes veneering backs of guitars with spruce, or some other type of wood.

Locally grown red spruce was used for guitar tops at the beginning of this period. At least as late as 1888 Martin still buying from a local supplier in Effort PA, just north of Nazareth. By 1890 Martin was buying Adirondack spruce from several suppliers. In 1894 Martin began purchasing White Mountain spruce from New Hampshire and continued with this source through to the end of this period.

Martin continued to buy poplar for making ebonized necks. Generally, the ebonized neck with the "ice cream cone" heel was used on the style 17 guitars. All other styles of guitars had Spanish cedar necks.

Ebony was used for the bridges and fingerboards.

Ivory was used for binding, bridges, saddles and nuts.

TOP BRACING

The three-strut fan bracing pattern was used for size 3 and 2 ½ "student model" (style 17) guitars. All other guitars were made with X-bracing, a single tone bar and finger braces.

BRIDGES

Only pyramid bridges, in either ebony or ivory, were in use during the period.

DECORATION

By 1867 Martin's product line was well established and decoration was quite predictable. However, by about the mid-1870's the wide strips of purfling Martin had used for the end decoration of some models was giving way to plainer rectangular or trapezoidal ebony and ivory end decorations. Beginning in 1896, Martin, at the request of customers, began to add fingerboard inlays to some guitars. This usually took the form of three pearl dots but a few guitars received fancier snowflake inlays (a 1897 0-42 is known with snowflake inlays at the 5th, 7th and 9th frets). A curious thing about the dot inlays is that they were not centered between the frets but were offset to be nearer to the lower fret.

MARTIN GUITARS (1898 to 1969)

DESIGN

This final period covered by this book is one of frenetic innovation as Martin reacted to changes in musical taste and the increasing affluence of the American population.

This period begins in early 1898, when Martin began adding serial numbers to guitars (mandolins had been made with serial numbers since 1895 so it is a mystery why Martin waited so long to serialize guitars) and ends with the switch from Brazilian rosewood to Indian rosewood at the end of 1969.

A large number of new products were developed between 1898 to 1969. As to be expected, not all of the additions to the product line were successful but more than a few can only be considered as prescient from today's point of view. The list below documents some of the more important changes:

1) Bowl-back mandolins (1895 to 1925)

2) First 000 size guitar (1901)

3) Fancy 00-42S guitars (1901-1903)

4) Style 45 guitars developed (1904)

5) Style 17 mahogany-bodied guitars (1907)

6) Flat-back mandolins (1914 to 1969)

7) Ukuleles added to product line (1915-1916)

8) Development of the Dreadnought guitar (1915-1916)

9) Bodies of style 18 guitars changed from Brazilian rosewood to mahogany (1917)

10) Use of ivory eliminated (1917)

11) Mahogany topped 2-17 guitars, offered in steel string only (1922)

12) "Customer's Line" or "C Line" guitars (1922 to 1924)

13) Style 18 guitars offered in steel string only (1923)

14) Tenor guitars (1927 to 1969)

15) Carved-top mandolins (1929 to 1964)

16) Orchestra Model (OM) guitars with 14-fret long scale necks (1929 to 1933)

17) Pyramid bridges replaced by belly bridges in April 1930

18) Carved-top model C guitars (1931 to 1943)

19) D-45 guitars (1933 to 1942, 1968 to 1969)

20) OM guitar designation changed to 14-fret 000 guitars with short scale (1934)

21) Bar frets replaced with T-frets (1934)

22) Ebony neck reinforcement changed to steel T-bar (1934)

23) Carved top F model guitars (1935 to 1943)

24) G series classical guitars (1936 to 1962)

25) Style 45 guitars dropped (1943)

26) Scalloping of top braces eliminated (1944)

27) Use of herringbone purfling on top of style 28

guitars dropped (1946)

28) C series classical guitars (1961 to 1969)

29) N series classical guitars (1968 to 1969)

MATERIALS

Martin guitars made between 1898 and 1907 all have Brazilian rosewood bodies. In 1907 Martin, in order to have a competitively priced entry-level guitar, began to offer style 17 guitars with mahogany bodies. Around April 1917 Martin dropped style 17 guitars and changed style 18 guitars to mahogany bodies. Style 21 to 45 guitars retained Brazilian rosewood bodies through the rest of the period covered by this book. In 1922 Martin revived style 17 as an all ma-hogany guitar and added the even plainer style 15 in 1940.

Guitars always have two-piece backs of solid wood.

From 1898 to 1913 Martin used White Mountain spruce from New Hampshire for the tops of their instruments. From 1913 Martin changed to a compa-ny in Cincinnati who supplied West Virginian spruce. Beginning in 1919 Martin started to buy Adirondack spruce from a supplier located in Dolgeville, New York but continued to buy supplies of spruce from the Cincinnati firm from time to time until the supply of red spruce, from both sources, dried up towards the end of 1941. Martin was able to buy small supplies of Vermont spruce from 1949 to 1952 and again in 1955.

Martin began buying Sitka spruce from Posey Manu-facturing Co. in Hoquiam WA in 1918 and this com-pany was Martin's sole supplier for Sitka spruce, with the exception of a few trial orders from other com-panies. Martin used the Sitka spruce on some guitar and mandolin tops around 1919 but found the natural dark-colored streaks in the Sitka unsuitable for the tops of instruments, as long as red spruce was avail-able. Thereafter, Martin continued to buy Sitka spruce for making braces, where the darker color issue was not an issue. However, Martin also used Sitka spruce for the tops of carved-top instruments because the Sitka had fewer imperfections than red spruce. With the disappearance of red spruce in 1941, Martin was forced to use Sitka spruce for the tops of their instru-ments and, with the exception of the Vermont spruce

mentioned above, continued to use Sitka spruce for the rest of the period.

Martin bought pre-seasoned German spruce for guitar tops from 1957 until at least 1963. Martin almost certainly continued buying German spruce tops after-wards but the detail purchasing records end in 1963.

From 1898 to about 1920 ebony was used for all bridges and fingerboards. The records are a little unclear but it appears Martin had always used rose-wood for the fingerboards and bridges of ukuleles in style 2 or lower. Martin inventoried rosewood guitar fingerboards and bridges from 1920. Initially, these may have been leftover material when style 17 was dropped in 1917. Rosewood fingerboards and bridges were again in use when the 2-17 guitars were launched in 1922, although the catalogs did not des-ignate rosewood fingerboards until 1925. Rosewood was also used on some mandolins around 1919 to 1920, as well as tiple fingerboards and bridges from at least 1925. Rosewood was used for the bridges of C-1 guitars from 1931. Rosewood fingerboards and bridges appeared on style 18 guitars by 1941. Style 21 guitars had rosewood fingerboards from around 1956.

Rosewood was also used for bridge plates on all gui-tars from serial number 235586 (1968).

Ivory was used for binding, bridges, saddles and nuts until April 1917. Thereafter ivory was replaced by white celluloid (ivoroid) for binding although ivory continued to be used for nuts and saddles into the 1960's. Ivory pyramid bridges continued to be used until 1920 on style 45 guitars.

TOP BRACING

All guitars were made with X-bracing although the number of tone bars and finger braces varied over time. Carved-top guitars had two longitudinal braces.

BRIDGES

Pyramid bridges were the norm for most guitars from 1898 to April 1930 when the belly bridge was intro-duced. Pyramid bridges were made of ebony and, later, Brazilian rosewood although ivory was used on style 34, 40, 42 and 45 guitars until April 1917. Straight bridge (rectangular bridge without the pyramid ends) first appeared on koa guitars in the 1926 catalogue.

Belly bridges were made of both ebony or rosewood depending on the grade of guitar and the time frame.

DECORATION

Decoration for most of the period relates to purfling and fingerboard inlays. Guitars up to grade 18 had plain white and black lines for purfling and the sound hole decoration plus graduated pearl dots for the fingerboard inlays. Style 21 retained the black and white lines but had herringbone for the sound hole decoration and pearl slotted square inlays on the fingerboard. Style 28 guitars had herringbone purfling with an ivory or, later, ivoroid inlaid sound hole decoration and slotted diamond and square fingerboard inlays. Style 30 and 34 used fancier purfling but were dropped from production relatively early in the 20th century, style 34 in 1907 and style 30 in 1917. Style 40, 42 and 45 had pearl purfling and sound hole decoration although the pearl purfling on style 45 was also applied to the sides and back. Styles 30, 34, 40, 42 and 45 had elegant pearl "snowflake" fingerboard inlays with the inlays beginning on the first fret for style 45 and on the third fret for style 42. On D-45 guitars the "snowflakes" were replaced by hexagonal abalone inlays in late 1938 although smaller body style 42 and 45 guitars retained the "snowflake" inlays until 1943, when production stopped for styles 42 and 45 (the last style 40 guitar being made in 1939).

Style 45 also received a very distinctive "flowerpot" or "torch" inlay in the head stock veneer from 1904 until 1931. When the C-2 and C-3 carved top guitars were introduced in 1931 they received a vertical "Martin" head stock inlay and this was also applied to style 45 guitars from that point. In 1932 the "Martin" headstock veneer was modified to "C. F. Martin" and remained in use until 1943.

PICK GUARDS

Martin began buying celluloid for mandolin pick guards by 1895. Martin usually bought celluloid for pick guards but, if the color of a particular delivery of celluloid was unsuitable, Martin would buy real tortoiseshell. Celluloid pick guards were special order features on Martin guitars until 1931 but from 1932 most steel string guitars were supplied with a pick guard. Tortoiseshell celluloid was replaced by black acetate for use on pick guards in early 1967.

NECK REINFORCEMENT

Initially the necks of Martin guitars had no reinforcement at all but at some point a rectangular bar of ebony was added to increase the stiffness of the neck. Due to the increased tension of steel strings Martin replaced the ebony neck reinforcement with a steel T-bar at the end of 1934. The steel T-bar was replaced with square steel tubing beginning with serial number 228246 in 1967.

THE FIRST SIZE "0" GUITAR (1854)

The first size 0 guitar was shipped to W. C. Peters & Son on April 25, 1854 and the second example on May 11, 1854 to G. P. Reed & Co. The first two guitars in this size appear to be either style 22 or style 23 based on the descriptions recorded in the 1852-1859 sales ledger, and both had peg heads for friction pegs. The first guitar sold for $24 and the second for $26. Martin may have charged a little extra for the new larger size guitars by adding a dollar or two to the normal wholesale price. The second guitar was supplied with a very fine case thus explaining another difference in price.

From 1854 to mid-1864 Martin made a total of seventy size 0 guitars, accounting for roughly 3% of production during that period. Of these seventy guitars only four or five were style 22, 23 or 24 guitars with ivory pegs.

The 1852-1859 sales ledger entries for both these guitars are illustrated in Figure 29. The description code Martin used for recording the features of the first 0 size guitar is as follows: 0 (size 0), one (quantity), Rose (rosewood body), Cedar (neck), Lines (purfling), plain (sound hole decoration. Author's note: this is the most problematic element of Martin's description as different types of purfling were used interchangeably), Black (edge, i.e., rosewood binding), Ivory (pegs), none (meaning no extra decoration), f (fine case), $24 wholesale price. The description of the second example is identical except that it received a ff (very fine) case and had a wholesale price of $26.

(Author's note: until about 1858 style 24 guitars had "lines" for purfling and a fancier grade of purfling, named "Ottilia" by Martin, for the sound hole decoration. Later style 24 guitars used the "Ottilia" pattern for purfling.)

figure 31 illustrates a normal sound hole decoration for the period, with black and white lines making up the inner and outer rings and an attractive "saw tooth" purfling pattern for the main sound hole ring. On the other hand, Figure 36 shows a very unusual sound

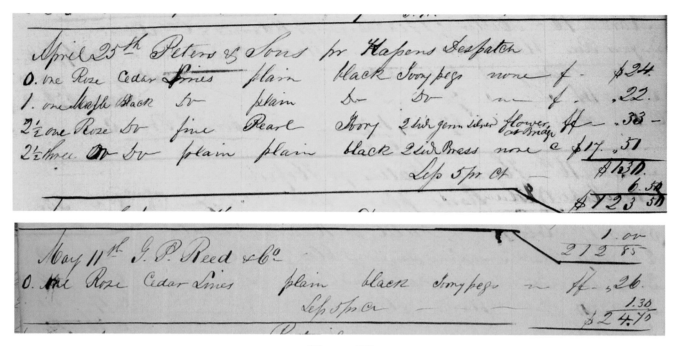

Figure 29
1854 Sales Ledger Entries for the First Two 0 Size Guitars

Remarkably, it seems that both of these earliest 0-size guitars still exist (Figures 30 and 33).

The guitar in Figure 30 is likely the first 0 size guitar because of its very unusual bracing pattern. The top bracing pattern is in the form of "nested diamonds" or "double diamonds" (Figure 32), totally unlike any other Martin bracing pattern. Martin appears to have experimented with bracing patterns when he increased the size of his guitars, just as he had when X-bracing was applied to the "De Goni" size 1 guitar in 1843. The 0-22 guitar otherwise fits well with the sales ledger description.

The guitar in Figure 33 is most likely the second 0 size guitar because it has X-bracing. Possibly, the "double diamond" bracing of the first 0 size guitar didn't yield the results Martin was seeking, so he returned to the tried and tested X-bracing. Just the same, some of the second 0-size guitar's other features are a little unusual, and are somewhat different from the first 0 guitar.

Comparing Figures 31 and 36 it will be noted that

hole decoration of only two rings; an outer ring of a single black line and an inner ring of "herringbone" purfling.

The end decoration of the first 0-size guitar is a plain trapezoid of inlaid ebony while the second guitar (Figure 34) utilizes a fancy piece of wide purfling. It can also be seen that on the side of the guitar in Figure 35 that there is an additional white line of purfling under the binding, usually only seen on style 23 or 24 guitars from the period.

Based on the above discussion, the first "0" size guitar is probably a 0-22 while the second example, even allowing for the unusual sound hole decoration, is likely a 0-23. Martin's usual practice at the time was to use the style number to indicate the wholesale price. For both guitars under Martin charged more than the style number. It is not known why this was the case unless Martin was attempting to charge a little more for larger guitars. Until the mid-1880's, however, guitars of a particular style were always priced the same, regardless of size.

Figure 30
1854 Martin 0-22 Guitar

Figure 31
Purfling and Sound Hole of 1854 Martin 0-22

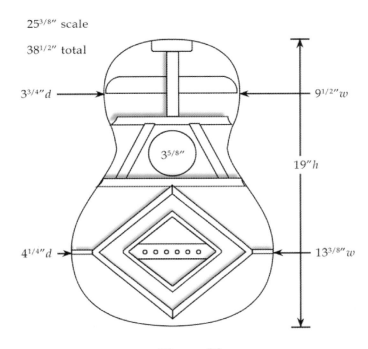

25³/₈″ scale

38¹/₂″ total

3³/₄″d

9¹/₂″w

3⁵/₈″

19″h

4¹/₄″d

13³/₈″w

Figure 32
Sketch of Bracing Pattern in 1854 Martin 0-22

Figure 33
Second 0-Size Guitar, a 0-23 from 1854

Figure 34
Detail of End Decoration on 1854 Martin 0-23 Guitar

Figure 35
Back of 1854 Martin 0-23 Guitar

Figure 36
Detail of Sound Hole of 1854 Martin 0-23 Guitar

THE FIRST SIZE "00" GUITAR (1858)

The first guitar of this size was custom ordered by W. C. Peters & Son of Cincinnati OH in a letter dated February 5, 1858 (see figure 37).

The guitar was shipped only three weeks later on February 26, 1858, a remarkably short amount of time for Martin at the time (see Figure 38).

Interestingly, the 0-27 and the 00-34 guitars bought at the same time were ordered with ivory pegs but were delivered with 2-side machines. Also, a 2½-34 was shipped instead of the 2-34 ordered and three 2½-17 guitars were shipped instead of the two ordered. It thus appears that Martin sometimes shipped what he had on hand and changed details to suit the styles ordered. (The vast majority of style 27, 30 and 34 guitars from this period were made with 2-side screws.) Although the 00 size guitar sold for $36 the description fits a style 34 guitar. Possibly, Martin decided to charge $2 extra for the larger body.

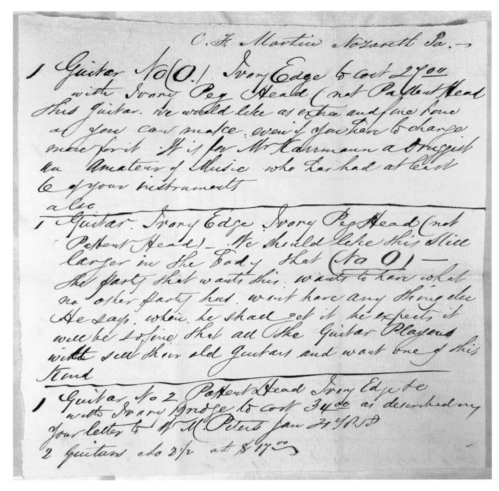

"1 Guitar No. (0) Ivory Edge to cost $27 with Ivory Peg Head (not Patent Head) this guitar. We would like a extra and fine one as you can make even if you have to charge more for it. It is for Mr. Karrmann a druggist an amateur of music who has had at least 6 of your instruments also

1 Guitar Ivory Edge Ivory Peg Head (not Patent Head). We should like this larger in the body that (sic) (No. 0) - the party that wants this wants to have what no other party has, won't have any thing else He says. When he shall get it he expects it will be so fine that all the Guitar Players will sell their guitars and want one of this kind.

1 Guitar No. 2 Patent Head Ivory Edge & with Ivory Bridge to cost $34.00 as described in your letter to W. M. Peters Jan. 21, 1858, 2 Guitars No. 2-1/2 at $17.00"

Figure 37
February 5, 1858 Letter Ordering First 00 Size Guitar

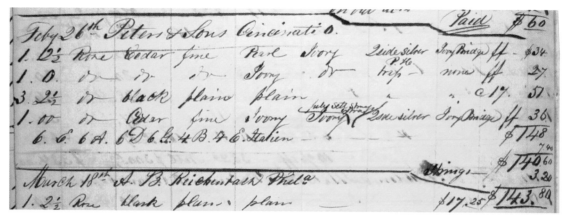

Figure 38
Sales Ledger Entry for February 26, 1858 Showing First "00" Size Guitar

SUTTER'S FORT MUSEUM
MARTIN 00-28 GUITAR ca. 1864-1867

Although only two pre-1867 size 00 guitars were recorded in the ledgers, a third pre-1867 00-size instrument exists in the collection of the Sutter's Fort Museum in California. The guitar has a "C. F. Martin/New York" stamp on the back strip, so there is no doubt it was made prior to August 1867.

All the style 28 guitars made before 1858, only a total of 7 in all sizes between 1854 and 1858, are described as having a pearl sound hole decoration.

This guitar has the ivory sound hole decoration and "zig-zag" back stripe that one would expect to see on a style 28 guitar from the later 1800's. This seems to point to the guitar being made in the period between July 1864 and August 1867, where there is a gap in the Martin records.

Confusingly, the guitar also has a German silver nut and a tie bridge, which are usually only seen on Martin guitars from the 1840's. There are no holes in the top that would indicate the original bridge was a pin bridge. The bridge is also unusual as it is slightly shorter than a contemporary pyramid bridge but also a little wider. It might be more accurate to describe the bridge as a "stop" bridge (the strings being knotted before being strung through the holes in the bridge and then over the saddle before attachment to the friction pegs).

This guitar contains a "Salvator Rosa/San Francisco/Montgomery St" label. According to the San Francisco city directories Rosa was located at several addresses on Montgomery Street between 1858 and 1867[3].

The top bracing is in the form of a "double X" although it might be better to call it "lattice" bracing as each of the four intersections of the double X-bracing are interlocked. This different form of bracing seems to follow Martin's predisposition to experiment with bracing patterns when increasing the size of his guitars (see the section on the first 0 size guitar above).

Figure 39
Sutter's Fort Museum Martin 00-28 Guitar
ca. 1864-1867

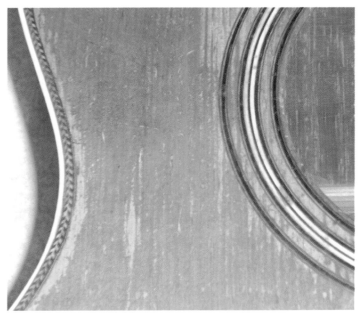
Figure 40
Detail of Purfling and Sound Hole Decoration

Figure 41
Tie Bridge on Sutter's Fort Museum 00-28 Guitar

Figure 42
Double-X Bracing Pattern in Martin 00-28 Guitar

THE FIRST SIZE "000" GUITAR (1901)

The demand for guitars for larger size appeared periodically in the Martin records during the 19th century. As detailed in the previous section, the first 00 size guitar resulted from a customer request in 1858. By the 1890's there was a growing demand for larger instruments.

On January 7, 1892 E. S. Sanford made an inquiry to Martin:

"**Can you make a bass guitar with finger board not much longer than the regulation size that can be tuned down to G. Of course, you would have to use large strings. Could any effect be produced on my 00 with large strings. If so, will you wire me a set of silver strings and send them to me for trial.**"

Sanford received a reply from Martin because he sent another letter on January 11:

"**Thank you for your prompt reply to mine.**

I note your remarks about the suggested bass guitar.

The "large ones" are as much superior to 0-28 as this size is to the 1-21 in quality.

I have two 00's the trebles of both are excellent and that being the only weak point. I consider these guns(?) as does Romero. I find they are most satisfactory tuned ½ tone or full tone below French A. They are richer and respond quicker. Of course, when you want brilliancy put 'em up to French A."

It is not known if Martin proceeded with this "bass" guitar but other manufacturers were quick to fill the demand for larger sized instruments. In a letter from C. A. Zoebisch & Son dated December 2, 1893 reported:

"**A customer has a party who wants a larger gtr than the 00 – and gives the size of what the(y) call (Lyon & H.) a Washburn Contra Bass style of the following dimensions:**

Across body back of Bridge 15 inches

Across body above sound hole 10 ½ inches

Length of scale 27 ½ inches

If this is not explicit enough, it is to be made exactly like the Washburn as above. We want a handsome Instrument. I would ask you to write us immediately the probable cost and length of time to make such a Guitar. They don`t give the narrow size of the body and we would have to find out at Pond or write them to send us a drawing of the body. Let us know at once what you think about it & prices if you wish to wish to change style like 00-28 & finer, also like 00-21 finish."

A postcard from Zoebisch continued the correspondence on December 19, 1893:

"We sent you yesterday drawings of that guitar wanted, now let us know at once whether you have wood large enough, as we can report(?) & when you could have one ready."

Unfortunately, there is nothing more in the Martin correspondence to say whether this special guitar was made or not. At 15" wide it would have been similar in size to the later 000 guitars. However, a letter from

Figure 43
Front and Back of the First 000-21 Guitar

Joseph Flanner, a Martin dealer in Milwaukee, in February 1896 infers that 00 size guitars were still the largest regularly made instruments.

The first documented 000 size guitar was a 000-21 (serial number 9156) shipped to Henry Spahr on November 7, 1901 (see Figure 43).

This guitar was discovered more than 30 years ago in New Jersey but the top was in poor condition. Dana Bourgeois attempted to save the severely thinned top but it was eventually replaced by T J Thompson to return it in playable condition. The original top, fortunately, was kept with the guitar and was used as the pattern for the replacement top. The top is dated "Jan. 28, 1901" in pencil. The letters "H.L.K." are also rubber stamped under the top indicating Martin employee Harry L. Keller, who worked for Martin from 1888 to 1901, was responsible for building this custom instrument.

Although the top is dated January 28, 1901 the guitar was not delivered, or in this case, was not picked up at the factory, until November 7. This is a surprisingly long amount of time as Martin was usually able produce a guitar in as little as 3 or 4 weeks in this period. Maybe Martin used the extra time to manufacture forms and otherwise work out the details of the new design. If forms were being produced it would seem to indicate Martin was intending to add the larger 000 size to the line.

Befitting its status as the 000 prototype, this guitar displays a number of unusual features. The scale length 24¾" is slightly shorter than the 25.4" scale found on most 000's. The lower bout measures very close to 15", the normal specification for 000 size Martins, but the upper bout measures almost 11" or close to ¼" wider than normal. The body is also 1/8" deeper and the body shape is slightly different than later 12 fret 000-size instruments.

DATE	SERIAL NO.	MODEL	COMMENTS	DEALER	SHIPPING DATE
1901	9156	000-21	EXTRA LARGE 000 BUT DEEP, OR. LEATHER CASE ($3.75)	H. SPAHR	07/11/1901
1901	9374	000-28	DUPLICATED SERIAL NUMBER, 10 STRINGS		24/12/1901
1902	9392	000-21	10 STRINGS, FRICTION PEGS		10/05/1902
1902	9393	000-21	10 STRINGS		18/04/1902
1902	9429	000-21	2 NECKS, 12 EXTRA STRINGS		03/02/1905
1902	9437	000-21	2 NECKS, 12 STRINGS		04/09/1902
1903	9660	000-21	FRICTION PEGS		13/08/1903
1904	9934	000-21		H. SPAHR	27/10/1904
1904	9935	000-28		H. SPAHR	27/10/1904
1904	9965	000-28		H. SPAHR	30/12/1904
1905	10009	000-21	IMPORTED MACHINES ($2 UPGRADE TO GERMAN SILVER MACHINES)	H. SPAHR	28/03/1905
1905	10010	000-28/30	EXTRA FOR STYLE 30 FINGERBOARD, $3.00, Imported Machine, $2.00	H. SPAHR	10/03/1905
1905	10054	000-21	12-STRING HARP GUITAR		20/06/1905
1906	10163	000-28	2 NECK 12-STRING HARP GUITAR, VIENNESE (STAUFFER) HEAD ON SECOND NECK		28/04/1906
1906	10176	000-21		H. SPAHR	11/05/1906
1906	10201	000-45(S)	SPECIAL TO ORDER	H. SPAHR	01/10/1906
1906	10329	000-18	MADE TO ORDER IN CURLY MAPLE, EXTRA FOR INLAYING & BRIDGE ($1.50)	H. SPAHR	16/01/1907
1907	10576	000-21	SPECIAL BORDER EXTRA $0.75, IMPORTED GERMAN SILVER MACHINES, $1.25	H. SPAHR	14/06/1907
1907	10706	000-45	HARP GUITAR, DUPLICATE SERIAL NUMBER, TAN LEATHER CASE TO ORDER, $7.20		31/12/1907
1909	10916	000-21			12/12/1910
1909	10921	000-40	EBONY BRIDGE, STEEL STRING, MACHINE SUPPLIED (FOR DISCOUNT)	H. SPAHR	30/07/1909
1910	11063	000-28	FRICTION PEGS		18/04/1910
1910	11131	000-28	FRICTION PEGS		04/10/1910
1911	11230	000-45	BLACK LEATHER CASE ($8.50)		28/01/1911
1911	11234	000-18			13/09/1911
1911	11241	000-45	FRICTION PEGS, RUSSET LEATHER CASE EXTRA PADDED ($5.90)		20/05/1911
1911	11248	000-45	MADE TO SPECIFICATIONS WITH SEVEN STRINGS		19/07/1911
1911	11275	000-45			30/08/1911
1911	11276	000-28			31/07/1911
1911	11280	000-28	FRICTION PEGS, BLACK LEATHER CASE ($5.60)		21/11/1913
1911	11281	000-17	HARP GUITAR, 12 STRINGS, BINDING ON BACK EXTRA $1.00	H. SPAHR	05/09/1911
1911	11332	000-28			12/02/1912
1911	11333	000-28	BLACK LEATHER CASE ($5.20)		31/10/1911
1911	11334	000-18			12/04/1912
1911	11335	000-18			07/12/1912
1911	11353	000-45	FRICTION PEGS, IN MARTIN MUSEUM (CFM III PERSONAL GUITAR)		
1911	11354	000-45			31/01/1913
1911	11365	000-21	12-STRING HARP GUITAR	H. SPAHR	24/11/1911

Table 1
List of 000 Size Guitars Made Between 1901 and 1911

The surviving original top demonstrates how Martin modified their normal X-bracing to fit the larger size body. The prototype bracing pattern didn't satisfy Martin, however, as the pattern was changed for later 000 size guitars. When this transition occurred is unknown.

The guitar was ordered by teacher and dealer Henry Spahr of Jersey City, New Jersey. Spahr had organized a guitar and mandolin club so he may have been looking for a guitar with a larger volume, although we will never know how he convinced Martin to actually produce the larger bodied guitar.

The guitar has 20 frets instead of the more usual 19 frets seen on other early 000 size guitars. Around 1900 William Foden, the well known professional guitarist, began specifying 20 frets on the Martin

guitars he purchased. Spahr may have been aware of this development and requested the same feature for this guitar. However, judging by the other early 000's examined, Spahr reverted to 19-fret guitars for subsequent orders.

It is quite clear that Spahr was a driving force in the development of the 000 size Martins as illustrated in Table 1. Spahr purchased thirteen early Martin 000 guitars between 1901 and 1911, almost certainly for his students and music club. It can also be seen that the new larger body size was quite popular for harp guitars.

A remarkable photograph of the "Spahr Mandolin and Guitar Club", circa 1910, was discovered several years ago (Figure 44). The distinguished gentleman in the middle of the photo with the baton is Henry Spahr.

Figure 44
Spahr Mandolin and Guitar Club, Circa 1910

The photograph is of good enough quality to be able to distinguish that at least 3 mandolins and 5 guitars are Martin instruments. And all the Martin guitars appear to be early 000 guitars! Based on special features, some of these guitars can even be identified in the table.

Although not all the guitar fingerboards can be seen only one guitar has 20 frets (back row, third from the right, see Figure 45). It clearly has the slotted square inlays associated with style 21 guitars and is probably the first 000-21.

Figure 45
Detail of First 000 Guitar, Note the 20-Fret Neck

As is sometimes encountered in Martin guitars of this vintage, the serial number is stamped in the end of the head stock (see Figure 46). Interestingly a "H. SPAHR/J. C." stamp appears above the serial number (the "J. C." stands for Jersey City, the location of Henry Spahr's business).

A 1903 00-42 (serial number 9665) has come to light with a similar "H. SPAHR" stamp. Another early 000-21 (serial number 10009) appeared on the vintage guitar market in early 2013. This guitar also has the

"H. SPAHR/J. C." stamp although it was now located under the C. F. Martin stamp on the back of the head stock.

The only significant difference between serial number 9156 and 10009 is that the first 000-21 had 20 frets whereas serial number 10009 has 19 frets.

The Martin archive does not contain any correspondence from this period so only the discovery of other early 000's ordered by Spahr will be able to determine when Spahr changed from 20 to 19-fret necks.

Figure 46
Serial Number Stamped on End of Head Stock

THE "KEALAKAI" GUITAR (1916)

The Martin Dreadnought guitar is the world's most widely recognized and copied guitar. Today, the Martin Dreadnought guitar has established a dominant position in the acoustic guitar market. Interestingly, the first Dreadnought guitars were meant be played as Hawaiian guitars and were far from a commercial successful

It is well known that the first Dreadnought guitars were made for Charles H. Ditson & Co. What is less well known is that an earlier "extra large guitar" was made and was the basis of the Ditson Dreadnought. The "extra large guitar" had the same shape as a contemporary 12-fret 000 size guitar but the body was ½" longer and ½" wider.

Martin shipped an "**extra large**" style 17 guitar (serial number 12210) to Major Kealakai in Chicago on March 25, 1916. Mekia (Major) Kealakai was a famous Hawaiian musician and band leader who had been playing on the mainland since the turn of the century and was working the Vaudeville and Chautauqua circuits out of Chicago when the guitar was ordered in late 1915.

NEW USE FOR STEEL GUITAR

Instrument Found to be Excellent for Making of Talking Machine Records—Another Hawaiian Instrument Soon to be on Market

A new steel guitar called the "Dreadnought," and said to produce the biggest tone of any instrument of its kind, is now being used in the making of phonograph records. It is also said to be an excellent instrument for use in auditoriums and large halls. Chas. H. Ditson & Co. will soon have the above instrument ready for delivery and at the same time will introduce to the American public another Hawaiian instrument never before used to any extent in this country, called the Terapatch, a Hawaiian "fiddle." H. L. Hunt, manager of the musical merchandise department of the Ditson store, left Thursday for Boston and after several days' stay will make a tour of the larger cities of the West. His trip will include a visit to the new Lyon & Healy store in Chicago. The tour is Mr. Hunt's annual pilgrimage in the quest of new ideas and includes both business and pleasure.

Figure 47
1916 Announcement for "Dreadnought" Guitar

Martin shipped another "extra large guitar" to David Manaku on June 29, 1917. The ledger records the following details:

"1 Gtr Style 17, Extra large, Made with special bridge & nut adjuster for Hawaiian playing, Duplicate of one sold Major Kealakai 3/25/16"

It is not known definitively if David Manaku was a member of Major Kealakai's Royal Hawaiian Band. However, the guitar was shipped to The Garrick Theater in Chicago and, since it is known Major Kealakai was touring out of Chicago, it is reasonable to assume that David Manaku would have known Kealakai and may even have been a member of his troupe.

The August 19, 1916 edition of Music Trade Review contains an article on page 47 concerning the naming of a new Ditson Dreadnought guitar (Figure 47).

In the article above, Henry Hunt, who worked for Charles H. Ditson & Co. in New York, made the earliest known comment on the "Dreadnought" guitar and its intended use. This article came out immediately after the prototype Ditson model 222 (Ditson serial number 172), was received by Ditson on August 9, 1916, so Hunt must have been talking about this particular guitar. Another interesting part of the article is the comment that Hunt made an annual trip "in quest of new ideas". It seems quite apparent that Hunt saw the Kealakai guitar in the Martin factory in late 1915 or early 1916 (or was already acquainted with Major Kealakai as a result of his travels) and realized the larger size guitar would make a fine addition to the line of Ditson Hawaiian guitars already being manufactured by Martin. All that had to be done to make it distinctively "Ditson" was to widen the waist to make it similar in appearance to the other Ditson guitars.

The "Dreadnought" name was devised by Henry Hunt and was an allusion to the British all-big-gun battleship of the same name. The original Dreadnoughts had 12-fret necks that subsequently morphed into the iconic 14-fret Martin Dreadnought guitars.

A demand for large Hawaiian guitars did not materialize and the Ditson Dreadnoughts were, from a purely commercial viewpoint, spectacularly unsuccessful! There were, however, a harbinger of successes to come.

Seven Ditson Dreadnoughts were shipped in 1916 (four 222 and three 111 guitars), two model 111's in 1917 (serial numbers 214 and 215) and another two 111 guitars in 1921, with the very last Ditson serial numbers (570 and 571). Twenty-one more Ditson 111 guitars, with regular Martin serial numbers, were shipped between 1923 and 1930 for a grand total of twenty-eight 111 and four 222 guitars.

Therefore, only 32 Ditson Dreadnoughts were made between 1916 and the introduction of the first Martin D-1's and D-2's in 1931.

The Martin archives contains a considerable amount of evidence showing the Kealakai guitar was the original template for the Ditson Dreadnought guitar.

The original wooden pattern for the Kealakai guitar is still in the Martin archive. Pencil notes on the

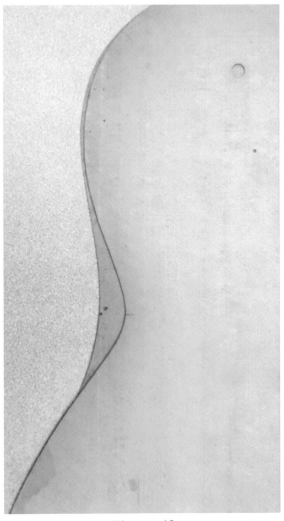

Figure 48
Kealakai Pattern over Ditson Pattern
Showing its Narrower Waist

pattern state "**1/2" longer than 000 both length and breadth**" and, more importantly, "**Braces, scale & sound hole used for Ditson Dreadnought without change**". The reverse of the pattern details that the sound hole was 4" in diameter and the guitar had 20 frets with a "**00 scale**" length (i. e. 25.4").

The wood pattern for the original Ditson Dreadnought is also in the archive. The notes on this pattern include "**Deichman pattern**" and "**Ditson Dreadnought, 7/19/16, 00 scale, sound hole by Kealakai pattern**". The date mentioned is stamped into the pattern.

When the two patterns are laid one upon the other (Figure 48), it is immediately clear that the length of the body and the width of the upper and lower bouts are practically identical. The only significant difference between the two is the increased width and larger radius of the waist of the Ditson guitar.

A paper pattern for the Kealakai guitar in the archive confirms that Martin simply took a regular 000 guitar and added ¼" to all edges, thus increasing the lower bout to 15½", the upper bout to 11-1/4" and the body length to 21". The paper pattern also illustrates the 5-strut fan bracing dates used on the Kealakai guitar and dates it to February 2, 1916. An additional note, "**Used for Ditson Dreadnought-7/24/16**", provides further evidence that the Ditson Dreadnought was indeed based on the Kealakai guitar (Figure 49).

Figure 49
Note Confirming the Bracing Pattern of the Kealakai Guitar was Used for the Ditson Dreadnought

The archive also contains a paper sketch for an unusual shaped bridge with the note: "**Kealakai Extra large guitar 1916**" (Figure 50). This is the same bridge design Deichman used for the Dreadnought guitar he made in February 1917.

Although unusual, similar bridge designs had been in the market for some time. The February 12, 1898 edition of Music Trade Review has an article promoting a Grunewald harp guitar with a bridge very much

Figure 50
Paper Pattern for the Unusual Bridge Used on the Kealakai Guitar

like the Kealakai guitar (figure 51). Other Hawaiian instruments from the early part of the 20th century had similar unusual shaped bridges (Figure 52).

Figure 51
1898 Grunewald Harp Guitar

Figure 53 shows a photo of Kealakai's Hawaiians from The Lyceum Magazine[4]. The guitar being played just behind Major Kealakai is one of the two Kealakai guitars made, the unusually shaped bridge can be seen just below the right hand of the guitarist.

The photograph shown in figure 54 is in the Martin archive but is not accompanied by any documentation. It clearly shows a Martin guitar with the extra large Kealakai bridge. At first glance it may be mistaken for the Kealakai guitar but closer examination reveals that it is actually a Martin 0-30 guitar. Research indicates this guitar was also owned by Major Kealakai but that he sold it to a student when Kealakai was on tour in England in 1919 or 1920. This narrative is further supported by Figure 55 which is a photo of said student with the 0-30 guitar.

Major Kealakai also owned a 1910 Martin 00-21 (serial number 11157) that was returned to Martin for a new top in 1917. The guitar in Figure 56 appears to be that 00-21 guitar. The guitar does not appear to have ivory binding on the body or the neck so it can't be the 0-30 in figures 54 and 55. The 00-21 also has a Kealakai bridge that may have been added when the guitar was re-topped by Martin in August 1917.

The second Kealakai guitar was ordered by David Manaku in June 1917 and can be seen in Figure 57.

Figure 52
Hawaiian Musical Group from the Early 20th Century

Kealakai's Hawaiians

is one of the original Hawaiian companies, and they have a long record of success.

Major Kealakai and his wife, Princess Ulnwehi, are of royal blood and are well known for their Victrola records. Major Kealakai is a composer as well as an interpreter.

This company scored a great triumph on the Midland Chautauqua this season.

Address

Lora Gooch
Manager

Auditorium Bldg.
Chicago

Figure 53
1917 Photograph of Major Kealakai and the "Kealakai" Guitar

Figure 54
Martin 0-30 with Extra Large Kealakai Bridge

Figure 55
Albert Cramer, Student of Major Kealakai,
with Martin 0-30

Major Kealaka of Royal Hawaiians at Star Theater "First Half."

Figure 56
Major Playing Martin 00-21 Guitar with
Extra Large Kealakai Bridge

Figure 57
David Manaku with the Second Kealakai Model Dreadnought Guitar

DATE	COMMENTS
(February) 1916	Kealakai top pattern with notes: 1) **1/2" longer than 000 both length and breadth** 2) **Braces, scale & sound hole used for Ditson Dreadnaught without change**
(February) 1916	Bridge pattern for **"Kealakai Extra large guitar 1916"**
February 2, 1916	Bracing pattern for Kealakai guitar and note **"Used for Ditson Dreadnaught-7/24/16"**
March 26, 1916	Extra large style 17 shipped to Major Kealakai
July 19, 1916	"Deichman" top pattern with note **"Ditson Dreadnaught, 00 scale, sound hole by Kealakai pattern"**. The date **"7-19-16"** is stamped into the pattern.
August 9, 1916	Ditson 222 shipped to Charles H. Ditson & Co.
December 30, 1916	Three D-111 and three D-222 guitars shipped to Charles H. Ditson & Co.
June 16, 1917	Two D-111 guitars shipped to Charles H. Ditson & Co.
June 29, 1917	Second extra large Kealakai guitar shipped, probably serial number 12734 or 12688

Table 2
Kealakai Guitar and Dreadnought Guitar Time-Line

12-FRET DREADNOUGHT GUITARS

All the original Ditson Dreadnoughts and a number of early Martin Dreadnought guitars had 12-fret necks. Tables 3 and 4 document all known 12-fret Dreadnought guitars made to the end of 1933. After the beginning of 1934 Dreadnought guitars were made with 14-frets, with the exception of a few special order 12-fret instruments.

The switch to the 14-fret neck also coincided with Martin's decision to start making the Dreadnoughts in quantity. Until the end of 1933, Dreadnought guitars had always been viewed as "build-to-order" specials only.

As can be seen in the tables a number of the early

MODEL	SHOP ORDER	DATE SHIPPED	QUAN	SERIAL NUMBER	COMMENTS
EXTRA LARGE STYLE 17		MAR. 25, 1916	1	12210	MAJOR KEALAKAI PRE-DREADNAUGHT GUITAR
DITSON 222		AUG. 9, 1916	1	71	
DITSON 222		DEC. 30, 1916	1	172	
DITSON 111		DEC. 30, 1916	3	173-175	
DITSON 222		DEC. 30, 1916	2	176-177	
DITSON 111		JUNE 6, 1917	2	214-215	
EXTRA LARGE STYLE 17		JUNE 29, 1917	1	UNKNOWN	DUPLICATE OF KEALAKAI PRE-DREADNAUGHT GUITAR
DITSON 111		JAN. 5, 1921	2	570-571	
DITSON 111		DEC. 22, 1923	1	19734	ORDERED FOR ROY SMECK, DARK FINISH

Table 3

MODEL	SHOP ORDER	DATE STAMPED	QUAN	SERIAL NUMBER	COMMENTS
DITSON 111	19	MAR. 25, 1924	1	20306	DARK WOOD, STAINED TOP
DITSON 111	134	OCT. 20, 1924	1	21539	DARK FINISH, INLAID PICK GUARD-MANDOLIN STYLE
DITSON 111	193	FEB. 23, 1925	1	22276	
DITSON 111	7	APR. 21, 1925	1	22528	DARK FINISH
DITSON 111	42	MAY 13, 1926	1	25054	CALLED "DREADNAUGHT 18" ON INVOICE
DITSON 111		NOV. 26, 1926	4	27961-27964	DARK FINISH
DITSON 111	161	NOV. 23, 1927	2	33983-33984	DARK FINISH INCLUDING TOP
DITSON 111	270	MAY 29, 1928	2	35957-35958	DARK FINISH INCLUDING TOP
DITSON 111	273	JUNE 28, 1928	2	36213-36214	
DITSON 111	378	FEB. 5, 1929	2	37857-37858	DARK FINISH
DITSON 111	613	FEB. 3, 1930	1	41215	8 STRINGS, WIDTH AT NUT 2 1/8", WIDTH AT 12TH FRET 2 9/16"
DITSON 111	859	NOV. 26, 1930	2	44997-44998	DARK FINISH INCLUDING TOP
D-21	985	APR. 14, 1931	1	46590	DITSON DREADNAUGHT #21 SPEC.
D-1	1013	MAY 22, 1931	1	47052	19 FRETS, BLACK BINDINGS, B & W BORDER
D-1	1013	MAY 22, 1931	1	47053	20 FRETS, CELLULOID BINDINGS, B/W/B BORDER
D-2	1014	MAY 22, 1931	1	47054	19 FRETS, STYLE 28 DESIGN
D-2	1014	MAY 22, 1931	1	47055	20 FRETS, STYLE 28 DESIGN
D-2	1082	AUG. 18, 1931	1	47996	
D-2	1096	SEPT. 9, 1931	1	48238	
D-18	1100	SEPT. 17, 1931	1	48324	19 FRETS (ORDERED AS D-1)
D-28	1100	SEPT. 17, 1931	1	48325	19 FRETS
D-2	225	MAR. 23, 1932	1	50562	"ARKIE" INLAID IN FINGERBOARD, 19 FRETS, GROVER HORIZ. MACHINES
D-2	229	APR. 4, 1932	1	50642	STYLE 28 DESIGN
D-28	282	JULY 21, 1932	1	51516	
D-18	313	OCT. 11, 1932	1	51978	
D-28	313	OCT. 11, 1932	1	51979	
D-28	321	OCT. 17, 1932	2	52036-52037	
D-18	358	DEC. 20, 1932	2	52507-52508	DARK FINISH
D-18	372	FEB. 1, 1933	1	52804	DARK FINISH
D-18	376	FEB. 9, 1933	2	52915-52916	DARK FINISH
D-45	396	MAR. 27, 1833	1	53177	"GENE AUTRY" INLAID IN FINGERBOARD
D-18	407	APR. 25, 1933	2	53341-53342	DARK FINISH
D-28	408	APR. 25, 1933	2	53343-53344	NATURAL FINISH
D-18	416	MAY 16, 1933	2	53424-53425	DARK FINISH
D-28	421	MAY 23, 1933	2	53504-53505	NECK WIDTH LIKE OM, PEG HEAD, #98 MACHINES
D-28	459	SEPT. 1, 1933	1	54218	
D-18	466	SEPT. 11, 1933	1	54250	
D-18	479	OCT. 3, 1933	1	54445	
D-28	480	OCT. 12, 1933	1	54546	LIGHT TOP
D-28	486	OCT. 19, 1933	2	54572-54573	LIGHT TOP
D-28	506	DEC. 15, 1933	1	54590	STAINED TOP
D-28	512	DEC. 28, 1933	3	55082-55084	LIGHT TOP

The Ditson Dreadnaught model designation has been simplified for this table. A number of model designations were used in the records for the earliest Dreadnaughts.

Table 4

12-fret guitars had dark finishes, similar to the finish originally specified for Ditson Dreadnoughts. More of these early Dreadnought guitars may have dark tops as Martin did not always record this feature in the sales or shipping records.

From table 5 it can be seen that the total production of 12-fret body Dreadnoughts made prior to 1934 was only 72.

MODEL	QUAN
DITSON 111	28
DITSON 222	4
D-21	1
D-1	2
D-2	7*
D-18	13
D-28	17
D-45	1

*One D-2 was a D-2S with a carved top

Table 5

Table 4 also illustrates how the sales of Dreadnought guitars were particularly weak between 1921 and 1924, which lead to some interesting correspondence between Martin and Ditson.

On January 23, 1924 Charles H. Ditson & Co. sought to order another "**D. M. 111**" like the one made for Roy Smeck. Martin made a response on January 25 with some interesting comments on Dreadnought guitars:

"**Thank you for your order of January 23rd; how-**

ever, before booking we wish to call this matter to your attention, that on the last order of this kind, that is the instrument made up for Mr. Smeck in December we found no profit for ourselves. Would you consider it advisable to order at least half a dozen at one time? If not, we will have to quote a somewhat higher price on this single order."

On January 29 Ditson made a more than interesting response:

"**Replying to your letter of the 25th inst., in reference to the guitar made up for Mr. Smeck, beg to say that we would like to order these in half-dozen lots if we had sale for them.**

We need one more for a special order. Unless there is a demand for these instruments, we will retire them, therefore, would kindly ask you to make the instrument and charge us the price that you think will cover your trouble and show profit for yourself.

There are one or two vaudeville players who insist on this sort of an instrument and if we find that there is enough of them we do not mind ordering them in half-dozen lots but, at present, we are undecided."

How ironic that the sales of the Dreadnought guitars in 1924 were so poor that Ditson contemplated retiring the model!

THE FIRST 14-FRET DREADNOUGHT GUITAR

The 14-fret Orchestra Model (OM) guitars appeared in late 1929 and 14-fret guitars in styles 0-17, 00-17, 0-18 guitars and 00-18 were added to the line in 1932.

However, Martin continued to make Dreadnought guitars as 12-fret instruments only until the end of 1933. Maybe this was because the early Dreadnoughts were made-to-order only and Martin did not considered them as inventory items.

On March 1, 1934 Martin sent the following letter to Chicago Musical Instrument Co.:

"**We are wondering what you think of the new**

Model D-28 Guitar we sent you last week with the fourteen-fret neck. Have you had it tried by anyone also familiar with the twelve-fret model, and what did they think of the tone?

We would like to go further along this line so we can hope you can let us have a report within a few days."

The letter clearly shows Martin had shipped a 14-fret D-28 guitar to CMI during February 1934. A check of the bookings ledger shows that this guitar was not ordered by any customer. Martin made the first 14-fret D-28 as a prototype, something Martin rarely did. The first 14-fret Dreadnought guitar was a D-28 with serial number 55260. It was stamped on January 22, 1934 and was shipped to Chicago Musical Instruments Co. on approval on February 12, 1934. The "first of many" was made and shipped in only 20 days! As can be seen from the shop order slip in Figure 58, "J. H. D." (John Deichman) was involved in making the prototype D-28 guitar.

The Martin archive does not contain a response to the March 1 letter. However, the feedback must have been very positive as the first production batch, for three 14-fret D-28 guitars, was stamped only a week later on March 8, 1934.

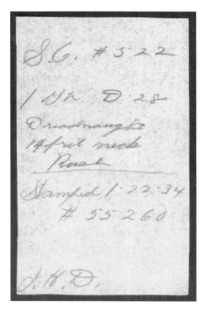
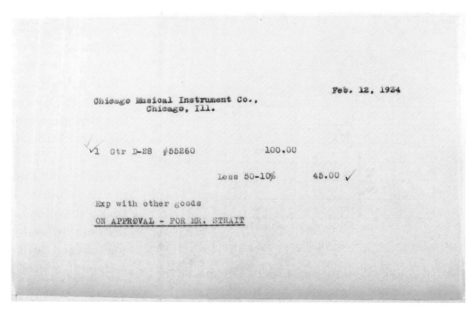

Figure 58
Shop Order Slip and Invoice for the First 14-Fret D-28 Guitar

Notes for Chapter 4

1) 04-JOURNAL 04-1837 TO 11-1838 BRUNO, page 26, December 30, 1837

2) Marco Aurelio Zani de Ferranti: Guitarist, Simon Wynberg, page 77, there is a description of the two guitars used by Ferranti and still held by the Ferranti family. One is quite large, about the same size as a "0" Martin.

3) The San Francisco city directories show Rosa located at 180 Clay St. from 1852 to 1854 and at 193 Clay St. in 1856. Rosa moved to 157 Montgomery in 1858, then to 618 Montgomery by 1863 and was located at 615 Montgomery between 1864 and 1867. By 1868 Rosa had moved to 624 Sac(ramento) Street.

4) The Lyceum Magazine, Vol 27, October 1917, pg 82

Chapter 5
DEVELOPMENT OF MARTIN GUITARS STYLES

Standardization of Styles (1833 to 1852)

It is a common misconception that Martin did not standardize his guitar models until 1858. The first use of the size and style designation (e. g., 0-28) occurred in a letter from Zoebisch dated August 25, 1856 but it did not come into general use with Martin until 1858. However, it is still possible to assign a model and size designation to pre-1856 guitars based on the size and price as recorded in the sales ledgers. Pre-1856 guitars will be shown in bold italicized font to indicate the size and style designations are an interpretation of the written descriptions in the ledgers.

In fact, Martin made a few standard models from the opening of his business in May 1834. The very first guitar sale, on May 9, 1834, was recorded as a "**very**

The early styles were identified by their retail price while guitars from the 1840's and later were identified by their wholesale price. Only a few of the early guitars were recorded with a style number but the design features recorded are consistent with the price.

Figure 59 illustrates an 1834 entry for a No. 45 guitar. C. F. Martin Sr.'s handwriting was more than scratchy so an attempt to clean up the description is shown in red. A loose translation would be "Mrs. W. M. Robinson, 1 very fine guitar, small Vienna machines, herringbone purfling, No.45 with box, incidentally sent with stained mahogany (case?), normal abalone (sound hole decoration?)". Some native German speakers might argue with the translation of "zarg" but the little sketch says it all.

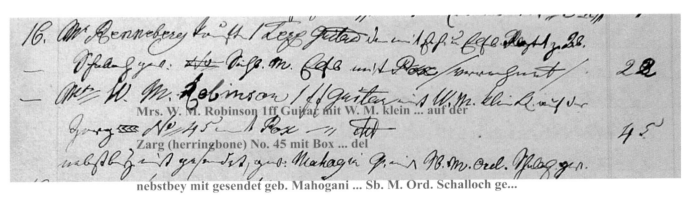

Figure 59
Entry Dated June 16, 1834 for a "No. 45" Guitar

fine guitar No. 40 with box" given to Joseph Atwill on commission. The retail price for this guitar was $40. Mr. Atwill was allowed a 33-1/3% commission so a wholesale price of $27 was entered into the ledger.

The 1834-35 ledger lists several other guitars with numbered styles: No. 10 (1 sold), No. 18 (1 sold), No. 36 (1 sold), No. 40 (2 sold) and No. 45 (2 sold). One No. 45 was sold at a retail price of $45 and the other was wholesaled for $32. The No. 40 guitars, as mentioned above, wholesaled for $27. The No. 36 was wholesaled for $27 so, presumably, only a 25% discount was allowed on this instrument.

No. 45 guitars were the most expensive Martin made at the time. The early 1834 guitar in the Martin Guitar Co. Museum is probably one of the No. 45 guitars.

There is practically no documentation in the Martin archives from the 1840's but one of these rare items is a June 30, 1848 letter from J. H. Mellor, Martin's dealer in Pittsburgh (see Figure 60):

"**Please send me via Philadelphia.....**

1 Mahogany Guitar with double side screw & case $15.00

3 Rosewood Guitar with double side screw & case $17.00

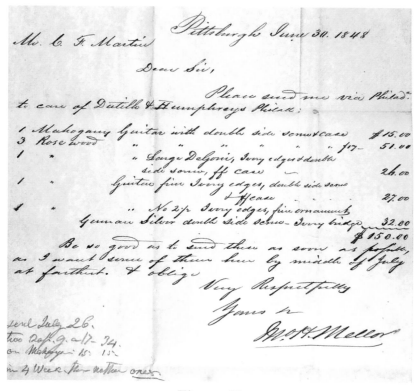

Figure 60
Letter from J. H. Mellor Dated June 30, 1848

1 Rosewood Guitar Large De Goni, ivory edges, double side screw, ff case $26.00

1 Rosewood Guitar fine, ivory edges, double side screw & ff case $27.00

1 Rosewood Guitar No. 2 ½, ivory edges, fine ornament, German silver double side screw, ivory bridge $32.00"

The three most expensive guitars are clearly a *1-26*, a *2-27* and a *2½-34*. Some of the details, such as purfling or sound hole decoration, may not be exactly the same as the models from the 1850's but it is a clear indication that Martin had begun standardizing his models by the late 1840's, at the latest, since the letter specifically mentions a "Large De Goni" or 1-26 model. The $15 and $17 guitars were probably size 3 "student" models.

The original "De Goni" guitar was built in mid-1843. Martin must have made this a standard model soon afterwards and communicated this to his dealers, as this 1848 letter illustrates.

Coupa also used a kind of code in ordering guitars from Martin but only by price, so styles must have been well understood between him and C. F. Martin.

Guitar Styles 1852 to 1867

In the 1840's and 1850's Martin had a more developed range of styles than previously thought. The list below is based on the wholesale price Martin charged dealers as well as design features documented in the 1852-59 sales ledger, the 1859-1864 day book and information gleaned from archival letters. Many styles became obsolete by the end of the 1850's as Martin reduced the number of the models on offer. The prices Martin charged for guitars in this period generally included a case.

Following is a list of styles and features associated with them:

Style 14
Size 3 and 2½, mahogany body, black neck, plain purfling and sound hole, rosewood binding, ebony pegs or two side brass tuners, common case (6 made from 1852 to 1853)

Style 15
Size 3 and 2½, mahogany (very occasionally rosewood) body, black neck, plain purfling and sound hole, rosewood binding, ebony pegs or two side brass tuners, common case (32 made from 1852 to 1855)

Style 16
Size 3 and 2½, mahogany or rosewood body, black neck, plain purfling and sound hole, ebony pegs or two side brass tuners, rosewood binding, ebony pegs or two side brass tuners, common case (89 made from 1852 to 1856)

Note: It is not possible to differentiate between styles 14, 15 and 16 based on the descriptions from the ledger. Style 14 may have had no binding and style 15 may have had only top binding. On the other hand, the pricing difference may have just reflected variation in wholesale pricing offered to dealers.

Style 17
Size 3 and 2½, rosewood body, black neck, plain purfling and sound hole, rosewood binding, two-side brass screws, common case. Style 17 is much more common than style 18. (1,041 made 1852 to 1864)

In the early 1850's about 30% of Martin's production was in the inexpensive models (i.e. styles 17 or lower).

Style 18
Size 3, 2½ and 2, rosewood body, black neck, single line purfling, plain sound hole, rosewood binding, usually two side brass tuners but sometimes ebony friction pegs, common case. (201 made 1852 to 1864)

Style 20
Size 2½ and 2, rosewood body, black (occasionally cedar) neck, single line purfling, plain sound hole, rosewood binding, two side brass tuners, common case. Style 20 is much more common than style 21. (351 made in all sizes)

Style 21
Size 1, rosewood body, black or cedar neck, single line purfling, plain sound hole, rosewood binding, two side brass tuners, common or fine case (120 made)

Style 22
Mostly size 2 (a few size 1 and 0), rosewood body, cedar neck, purfling variable (usually double lines but "De Goni" and "Spanish" also mentioned), usually plain sound hole (but "De Goni", "Small De Goni" and "Spanish" also mentioned), rosewood binding, usually two side brass screws (a few with ebony friction pegs), fine case. (154 made in all sizes)

Style 23
Mostly size 2 (a few size 1 and 0), rosewood body, cedar neck, purfling variable (usually double lines but "De Goni", "Small De Goni" and "Otilia" also mentioned), usually plain sound hole (but "De Goni", "Small De Goni" and "Squares" also mentioned), rosewood binding, usually two side brass screws (a few with ebony friction pegs), fine case. (70 made in all sizes)

Style 24
Mostly size 2½ (but also size 2, 1 and one recorded size 0), rosewood body, cedar neck, purfling usually double lines (but "Otilia" and "Spanish" mentioned), sound hole usually "Otilia"(but "Spanish" also mentioned), rosewood binding, two side brass screws, fine case. (150 made in all sizes)

Style 25
Scarce model seen 1852-57, mostly size 1 (but one recorded each in size 2½, 2 and 0), rosewood body, variable but usually "Spanish" purfling, "Ivory" or "Spanish" sound hole, white holly binding, ivory friction pegs or two side brass tuners, fine or very fine case. The main difference between style 25 and 26 is that the binding on style 25 is white holly rather than ivory. (13 made in all sizes)

Style 26
Mostly size 1 (but size 2½, 2 and 0 also recorded), rosewood body, cedar (occasionally black) neck, usually De Goni purfling ("Fine" and "De Goni Chain" also mentioned, usually pearl sound hole to 1858, usually ivory binding but sometimes with bound fingerboard, usually two side brass tuners but also ivory friction pegs, very fine case. (270 made in all sizes)

Style 27
Usually size 2½ and 2 (but also a few size 1 and 0), rosewood body, cedar (a few black) neck, "Fine" or "De Goni" purfling, pearl sound hole, ivory binding but most to mid-1854 also with bound fingerboard, usually two side brass tuners (but a few with German silver tuners), very fine case. (194 made in all sizes)

Style 28
Scarce model before 1858, size 2½ and 2, rosewood body, cedar neck, "Fine" purfling, pearl sound hole, ivory binding (one with bound fingerboard), two side German silver tuners, very fine case. Later models

were usually size 0 with ivory sound hole, ivory binding and bound fingerboard. (19 made in all sizes)

Style 30
Size 2½ and 2, rosewood body, usually cedar neck (a few black), "Fine" purfling, pearl sound hole, ivory binding but most before 1854 also have bound fingerboards, usually two side German silver tuners, very fine case. Later models have bound fingerboards. (65 made from 1852 to 1863)

Style 32
Size 2½, 2, 1 and 0, rosewood body, cedar or black neck, "Fine" purfling, pearl sound hole, ivory binding but a few with bound fingerboards, two side German silver tuners, some have a an extra ornament (usually called "flower" by Martin) below the bridge, very fine case. (19 made from 1852 to 1862)

Style 33
Size 2½ and 2, rosewood body, usually black neck, "fine" or "extra fine" purfling, pearl sound hole, ivory binding but most also have bound fingerboards, two side German silver tuners, "flower" ornament below the bridge, very fine case. (16 made from 1852 to 1863)

Style 34
Size 2½ and 2 (sizes 1 and 00 also mentioned), rosewood body, usually black neck, "fine" or "extra fine" purfling, pearl sound hole, ivory binding (before 1854 also specified with bound fingerboard), two side German silver tuners, ivory bridge, very fine case. Later models always have bound fingerboards. (102 made from 1852 to 1864)

Style 35
Size 2½ and 1, similar to style 34 but with one side Viennese machines (7 made from 1853 to 1860)

Style 40
Sizes 2½, 2 and 0, rosewood body, cedar neck, pearl purfling, pearl sound hole, two side German silver tuners, ivory bridge, very fine case. (6 made from 1854 to 1864)

Style 42
Rare model before 1859, size 2½ and 2, rosewood body, cedar neck, pearl purfling (including around fingerboard extension), pearl sound hole, two side

German silver tuners, ivory bridge, very fine case. (4 made from 1853 to 1858)

There are also a few more expensive guitars sold by Martin but extra cost seems to be associated with better quality cases or may indicate retail sales.

Guitar Styles 1867 to 1898

The sales ledgers are complete from 1867 to 1884 but are mostly missing from 1885 to 1898 except for some information from 1892 and 1893. The guitar styles had become fairly fixed by 1867 although Martin continued to allow some variation in the pattern of purfling used for the top edge of guitars. There is also an interesting variation in the back stripe purfling and the end decoration that deserves further study.

Style 17
Sizes 3 and 2½ "student" models, fan braced

Style 18
Almost always size 2

Style 20
Almost always size 2

Style 21
Usually size 1 to at least until 1884, some size 0 by 1892

Style 22
Only one 2-22 made after the formation of C. F. Martin & Co. in 1867

Style 24
Usually size 2 but a few size 2½ and 0 until at least 1884, usually only 2-24 in the 1890's

Style 26
Usually size 1 but other sizes made until at least 1884, usually only 1-26 in the 1890's

Style 27
Usually size 2 until at least 1884, a few 1-27 in the 1890's

Style 28
Size 0 and more rarely size 00

Style 30
Sizes 5, 2, 1, 0 until at least 1884, usually size 2 and 0 in the 1890's

Style 32
One 0-32 guitar made in 1877

Style 33
Two 00-33 guitars made in 1877

Style 34
Sizes 2, 1, 0 until at least 1884, usually size 2 and 0 in 1890's

Style 40
Size 2, 1, 0 until at least 1884, usually 2 and 0 in 1890's

Style 42
Sizes 2, 0, usually with neck screws, until at least 1883, size 2, 1, 0 and 00 in 1890's

It will be seen in the above lists that styles weren't offered in all sizes. For example, style 21 guitars were almost always size 1 while the less expensive style 17 guitars were only ever offered in sizes 2½ and 3.

Chapter 6
DATING EARLY MARTIN GUITARS 1833 to 1867

One of the goals of this book is to provide clues for dating Martin guitars made prior to 1867. The information in this chapter is not meant to be the final word on the subject but as a basis for further study and discussion. Also, the dating of early guitars is a theory based on currently available information. This theory will need to be tested, and adjusted accordingly, as more instruments come to light.

The first step in the process was to study the labels found in old Martin guitars and compare them to the information from the ledgers. The labels provide the best clues for dating guitars in the period from 1833 to 1840, although design features are also important to consider, and will be examined individually.

There are practically no records in the Martin archive from 1840 to 1850. This covers virtually the whole period of John B. Coupa's sole agency for New York City. About half of the guitars examined from this period have Martin & Coupa labels while the other half do not. Guitars sold by the factory to dealers outside of New York did not receive the label. The fact that half of Martin's sales came from the New York market emphasizes the importance of New York to Martin at the time.

Guitar Labels 1834 to 1840

All Martin guitars from 1834 to 1839, and many from 1840 to 1850, have a label affixed to the inside of the guitar and visible through the sound hole.

Martin had two store locations and a number of different business relationships in the period from 1834 to 1850. This information appeared on the labels and provides a very useful tool for dating instruments. The Martin records are somewhat spotty with regard to the purchasing of labels but it is possible to estimate the period of use of many of the labels, based on store location recorded on the label and design features of the guitars themselves. The first store was located at 196 Hudson St. and Martin conducted business there until June 9, 1837. A second location was in operation at 212 Fulton St. by April 1, 1837 so Martin had the two different retail locations operating for about 9 weeks.

The known types of labels are discussed below.

Type 1 and 2 labels are identical except that an extra note "**from Vienna, Pupil of the celebrated STAUFFER**" was added on the type 2 label. The "C. Frederick Martin" title blocks are also slightly different. These labels were made using the lithographic printing process. One of the advantages of lithography is the relative ease in making changes to the design. Type 1 is assumed to be the first label used because of the lack of the mention of Stauffer. The Type 2 label and Type 3 Martin and Schatz labels both mention Stauffer so are presumed to be consecutive. Why the Type 1 label does not mention Stauffer is unknown, possibly an oversight by Martin or the lithographer.

It is possible that the sequence of Type 1 and Type 2 labels is incorrect but this can only be determined as more instruments are discovered. However, at present, only one guitar with a type 1 label is recorded (on display in the Martin Guitar Co. Museum), whereas three guitars are known with the type 2 label. This would tend to support the idea that the proposed sequence of labels is correct.

From the Rechnungsbuch Merz we know that Martin & Schatz had a business relationship by at least March 1835 and this continued until March-April 1836, when it appears Schatz had already moved to Millgrove, Pennsylvania. The Type 3 labels were used during this period. However, T. F. Merz continued to make shipments to "Martin & Schatz" as late as September 1836. T. F. Merz may have forced the continuation of the Martin & Schatz partnership as security for the large amount of money owed to him, or until he was satisfied Martin could handle the debt alone.

Four guitars with the type 3 Martin & Schatz label were examined for this book. The cittern-shaped guitar in the collection of the Experience Music Project in Seattle displays a type 3 label which is slightly different from other type 3 labels encountered and suggests it was made in late 1836. The label in this guitar has a thin strip of paper glued over the text "**from VIENNA, Pupils of the celebrated STAUFFER**". It would appear Martin was signaling the end of the Martin & Schatz partnership while economizing by using the old label until a new one could be printed.

Most type 4 and all type 5, 6 and 7 labels have hand-written serial numbers. By carefully examining the monthly sales figures from the ledgers it appears that the type 4 label came into use around September 1836 (see Appendix H). The ledgers for this period are very detailed but no expense is recorded for the printing of the type 4 labels in this period, although the serial numbers do fit this theory. The type 4 label continued in use until late March 1837.

The type 5 labels, showing the new 212 Fulton Street address, were in use by early April 1837.

The Martin ledger records two payments for labels: one of March 21, 1837 (in the 196 Hudson Street ledger) and one on April 1, 1837 (in the new ledger started for the 212 Fulton location). These two separate entries are for the same expenses related to the printing of the type 5 label.

Logically, the type 4 labels must have been used before the type 5 labels because they have earlier serial numbers. There is no overlapping in the serial number sequence, so the labels do not appear to have been used concurrently.

Both the type 4 and 5 labels were printed without mention of Stauffer. Martin was well enough established by this point to make it unnecessary to refer

to his previous employer. Martin paid rent on 196 Hudson St. until July 31, 1837, although sales ended on June 9, 1837. Martin was only operating one retail business, at 212 Fulton, after June 1837 but he may have continued to live and have his work shop at 196 Hudson. This premise is based on the fact that a number of the type 5 labels (with serial numbers 1160, 1168, 1173, 1176 and 1188) have an additional hand-written endorsement "& No.196 Hudson str".

The type 5 label is of particular interest as it had two distinct periods of use. The first period of use lasted from April 1, 1837 until late April or early May 1838. After the end of the Martin & Bruno partnership, that lasted from May to September 1838, the type 5 label again was put into use. The second period of use covered October 1838 until May 1839, when Martin sold his business to Ludecus & Wolter. The type 5 labels from the second period of use do not have the "& No.196 Hudson str" endorsement because Martin was only operating from the 212 Fulton Street location during this time.

The Type 6 label was employed during the Martin & Bruno partnership that lasted from May to September 1838. To date only three guitars with the Martin & Bruno label have been examined.

Only three guitars have been seen with the type 7 label. The first example (serial number 1296) also has a "Ludecus & Wolter" label. The second example

MARTIN GUITAR LABELS 1834 TO 1850			
LABEL TYPE	PERIOD OF USE	SERIAL NUMBERS	COMMENTS
1	Early 1834	N/A	
2	Mid 1834 to late 1834	N/A	"from Vienna, Pupil of the celebrated STAUFFER"
3	Jan. 1835 to Sept. 1836	N/A	First "Martin & Schatz" label
4	Sept. 1836 to Mar. 1837	1114, 1130	One example known without serial number
5 (1st PERIOD OF USE)	Apr. 1837 to Apr. 1838	1160, 1168, 1173, 1176, 1188	"& 196 Hudson Str" written on label
6	May to Sept. 1838	1231, 1235	Martin & Bruno
5 (2nd PERIOD OF USE)	Oct. 1838 to May 1839	1275, 1293	
7	July 1839 to Mar. 1840	1296, 1304, 1341	Second "Martin & Schatz" label
8	Mar. 1840 to May 1850	N/A	Martin & Coupa label

Table 6
Guitar Labels - 1834 to 1850

(serial number 1304) has a type 7 label and a type 8 Martin & Coupa label. The third example (serial number 1341) only has the Martin & Schatz label. Research now suggests C. F. Martin resumed his business relationship with Schatz from mid-1839 until early 1840. Ludecus & Wolter had the Martin agency in New York for only a few months, from June to August 1839, and serial number 1296 is from this period. Coupa took over the agency in August 1839 thus explaining why the second example, serial number 1308, has both the Martin & Schatz and the Martin & Coupa label. It is estimated that serial number 1341 was made about the end of January 1840. The design features of these three guitars fit the 1839-1840 time frame and all have the transitional Spanish body shape. In these three cases the Martin & Schatz is the label of the "factory" and the second label indicates the holder of the "agency" for New York. See Table 6 for a listing of all known pre-1840 serial numbers.

The fourth example recorded with the type 7 label is in the "De Goni" guitar. This instrument can be dated to July 1843 and it is unknown why this label would have been used so late. It is possible Schatz aided in the construction of the "De Goni" guitar or it may have been the only label Martin had on hand. It wouldn't have received the Martin & Coupa label because it wasn't sold out of the depot at 385 Broadway. This guitar was hand delivered to Madame De Goni by C. F. Martin Sr. himself.

The Type 8 Martin & Coupa label is the commonest label encountered in early Martin guitars and was in use from August 1839 until the death of John Coupa in May 1850. Coupa operated the depot for Martin guitars in New York City and the instruments sold at the 385 Broadway depot received the Martin & Coupa label. Although there is little documentation, Martin had other wholesale accounts in the eastern United States and these would not have received the Type 8 label as the instruments were shipped direct from the factory. A number of guitars that are clearly from the 1840-1850 period have been seen without the Martin & Coupa label (e.g. the Colonel Wilkins guitar). In the population of guitars examined for this book, the split is exactly 50-50 between those guitars with the Martin & Coupa label and those without.

Recently two guitars have been discovered with Type 9 labels. These labels are not really associated directly

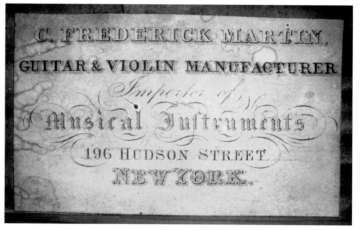

Figure 61
Type 1 Label
Early to mid-1834

Figure 62
Type 2 Label
Mid to late1834

Figure 63
Type 3 Label
January 1835 to September 1836

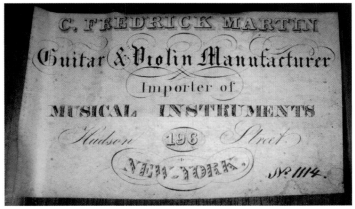

Figure 64
Type 4 Label (Serial Number 1114)
October 1836 to March 1837

Figure 65
Type 5 Label (Serial number 1173)
1st Period of Use: with "& No. 196 Hudson str" endorsement
April 1837 to April 1838
2nd Period of Use: without endorsement
October 1838 to May 1839

Figure 66
Type 6 Label (Serial Number 1231)
May to September 1838

Figure 67
Type 7 Label
1st Period of Use: June 1839 to March 1840
2nd Period of Use: July 1843

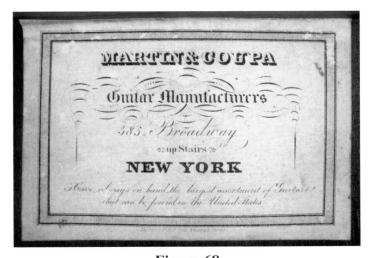

Figure 68
Type 8 Label
August 1839 to May 1850

Figure 69
Type 9 Label
1838 and later

with Martin but are included here for completeness. Both labels have "385" inked over the original address of 198 Broadway, where John Coupa had his first teaching studio. Coupa had been selling Martin guitars to his pupils since mid-1837 from the 198 Broadway location. A New York directory shows John Coupa at 385 Broadway from 1838 so it is reasonable to assume that Coupa applied these labels to guitars he sold in the period from 1838 until the he took over the Martin agency in August 1839.Coupa may also have applied these labels to used guitars he sold, in which case the type 9 label may have been used for a longer time frame.

Martin and Martin & Schatz always advertised themselves as manufacturer of violins as well as guitars. The sale ledgers contain sales for about a dozen violins that, based on their price, could have been made by C. F. Martin. A Martin violin exists that contains a C. F. Martin label (see Figure 7). As can be seen from Figure 6, the violin label is actually a cut-out portion of the sale receipt that was used by Martin during 1838 and 1839.

Top Bracing Patterns

Once the labels were put in sequence, the top bracing patterns were examined and put in order. The bracing sketches (Figures 71 to 84) are representations of some of the types of bracing patterns seen. The shaded areas on the sketches indicate the size and location of the bridge plate. The sketches are not to scale.

Ladder bracing (circa 1834-1838)

-seen in guitars with type 1, 2, 3, 4, and 5 label (Figures 71, 72 and 73. There are also transitional types of bracing in between ladder and fan bracing (Figure 75).

3-strut fan brace (circa 1837-1841)

-seen in guitars with type 5, 6, 7, and 8 labels, with the earliest being from 1837 (serial number 1160)
-from 1838 to 1842 most guitars have some form of fan-bracing (Figures 74, 76, 77 and 78)
-guitars from the 1840's with 3-strut brace fans have lower bouts measuring from 11.22" to 11.61" (i.e. size 3 and 2½), although some guitars in these sizes are encountered with 5-strut fan bracing

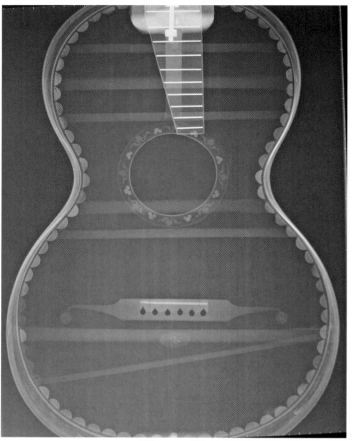

Figure 70
X-Ray of 1834 Martin Guitar

-a size 3 guitar with the 3-strut fan brace dated October 1844 has been reported
-after 1852 all size 3 and many of the size 2½ guitars are seen with 3-strut fan braces
-none of the 3-strut fan braced guitars have been encountered with purfling around the sides of the guitar which would point to the period before 1845

5-strut fan brace (circa 1842-1843)

-seen in guitars with and without the type 8 label and with the type 9 label (Figures 79 and 81)

Transitional bracing (circa 1842-43)

-seen in guitars with and without the type 8 label (Figure 80)

Early X-bracing (1843-1850)

-seen in guitars with the type 7 label and with and without the type 8 label (Figure 82)

Plain X-bracing (circa 1850)

-for a short period Martin used plain X-bracing without a tone bar but sometimes with a finger brace (Figure 83)

Normal X-bracing (1852-1867)

-this is the type of X-bracing that is immediately recognizable as the style Martin used for the remainder of the 19th century (Figure 84)
-bracing pattern includes a tone bar and one or two finger braces, later guitars may have two tone bars

It is possible that both the 3-strut fan and 5-strut fan patterns were used concurrently during the early 1840's for the size 3 and 2½ guitars. The 3-strut fan bracing is most commonly encountered but a number of guitars in these sizes have been examined with the 5-strut fan bracing pattern and even a few with the early type of X-bracing.

However, certain features, particularly the shape of the Spanish foot and the type of lining, appear to indicate the 3-strut fan bracing was used earlier than the 5-strut pattern. The guitars with the 3-strut fan brace always have the rectangular shaped neck block with the crescent shaped support beneath and solid lining whereas the 5-strut fan braced guitars always have a Spanish foot (either rectangular or pointed in shape) and kerfing blocks for the lining.

No guitars from the 1840's larger than size 2½ have as yet been encountered with the 3-strut fan top bracing.

Throughout the 1850's and 1860's, all size 3 guitars and many size 2½ guitars had 3-strut fan bracing patterns. At least one size 2 guitar has also been encountered with the 3-strut fan bracing.

For size 3 and 2½ guitars only, it appears Martin used the 3-strut fan bracing first (circa 1840-1845), switched to the 5-strut fan (circa 1845-1848), made a few X-braced guitars (circa 1848-1850) and finally returned to a 3-strut fan for the period following 1850. By 1852, size 3 guitars were almost exclusively plain "student" models in either mahogany or rosewood. The use of the 3-fan strut was likely related to their lower price.

For two short periods of time Martin experimented with transitional forms of bracing. The first period occurred between 1836 and 1837, as Martin moved towards fan bracing, and the second circa 1840 to 1843, when Martin experimented with variations of fan bracing that eventually led to X-bracing.

For the larger sized guitars, Martin used 3-strut fan bracing first (circa 1840-1842), switched to 5-strut fan bracing (circa 1842-1843) and began using the early form of X-bracing around the middle of 1843. By circa 1850, plain X-bracing was being used and by about 1852 X-bracing with a tone bar and finger braces became the norm.

It should also be mentioned that the 3-strut and 5-strut fan-braced guitars from the 1840's almost always have a tie bridge, only one or two exceptions being known. On a 5-strut fan braced guitar it would have been difficult to use a pin bridge as drilling holes in the top might damage a brace beneath. It appears one of the reasons Martin developed X-bracing was to free up an un-braced area under the bridge so that drilling holes for a pin bridge wouldn't hit a top brace.

By about 1850, a plain X-bracing came into use. Shortly thereafter the tone bars and finger braces were added to become the recognizable pattern still in use.

After putting the guitars in sequence, it is clear that C. F. Martin was experimenting with bracing in order to improve the tone of his guitars, eventually resulting in the perfection of X-bracing, . As he absorbed influences from a variety of sources, he experimented with different patterns of top bracing. Ladder bracing gave way to fan bracing and finally to X-bracing. Between these divisions guitars with atypical or anomalous bracing patterns are occasionally encountered.

It also appears Martin was never content to merely rest on his laurels as the size of his guitars increased. The first size 1 guitar (the De Goni guitar) may have been the final impetus for the development of X-bracing. The first size 0 guitar has a very radical "double diamond" bracing pattern. Although not a successful design it demonstrates that Martin, even into the 1850's, was not afraid to try something new. Although the first 00 size guitar has not yet come to light the bracing may be similar to the Sutter's Fort Museum 00-28, which has a double-X pattern top bracing.

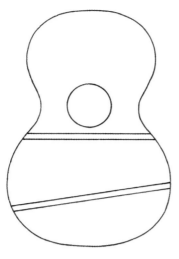

Figure 71
1834 Martin Guitar

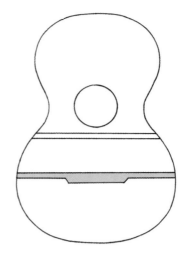

Figure 72
1835 Martin & Schatz Guitar

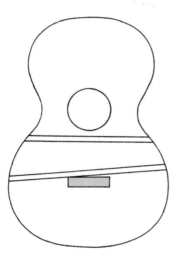

Figure 73
1836 Martin Guitar (Serial Number 1114)

Figure 74
1837 Martin Guitar (Serial Number 1160)

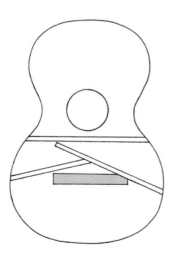

Figure 75
1837 Martin Guitar (Serial Number 1173)

Figure 76
1838 Martin & Bruno Guitar (SN Missing)

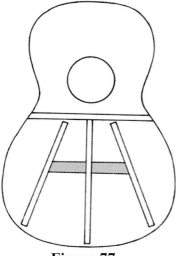

Figure 77
1840 Martin & Coupa Period Guitar

Figure 78
1840-1841 Martin & Coupa Period Guitar

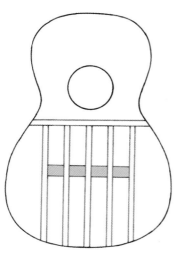

Figure 79
1842-1843 Martin & Coupa Period Guitar

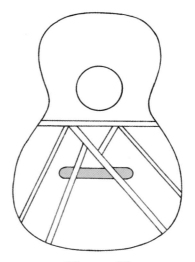

Figure 80
1842-1843 Martin & Coupa Period Guitar

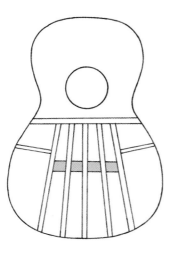

Figure 81
1842-1843 Martin & Coupa Period Guitar

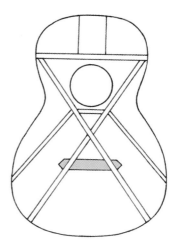

Figure 82
1843 Martin & Schatz "De Goni" Guitar

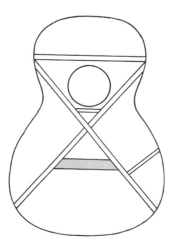

Figure 83
Ca. 1850 Martin Guitar

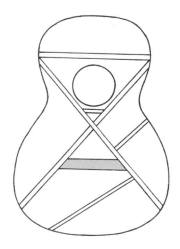

Figure 84
Ca. 1850-1852 Martin Guitar

Over 60 old Martins guitars were documented for this book. C. F. Martin started his career in the United States by duplicating the ladder braced guitars he had made in Europe. He then began a process of experimentation that, over a period of several years, resulted in the early form of X-bracing. C. F. Martin continued to try out different ideas over the next decade or so and it was not until the early 1850's that Martin finally perfected the now familiar form of X-bracing (although size 3 and some size 2½ guitars continued to have fan bracing).

In summary, Martin generally used ladder bracing from 1834 to 1838 and then changed to 3-strut fan bracing from circa 1837-41 and 5-strut fan braces circa 1842-1843. In the 1842 to 1843 period Martin experimented with several different types of bracing that resulted in the X-braced instrument made for Madam De Goni in mid-1843. The De Goni guitar may not have been the first guitar made with X-bracing but it is certainly the earliest dateable X-braced guitar.

Neck Blocks

Neck blocks, containing the dove-tail joint, can be useful for dating early Martin guitars. The following types of neck blocks have been encountered, although others may exist.

1) **Rounded neck block (circa 1834 to 1840)**

This type is found on most pre-1840 Martin guitars and are sometimes roughly shaped (Figure 85). Usu-

ally there is no C. F. Martin stamp on the neck block, although a few early Martin & Coupa guitars with this type of neck block can be found with a name stamp.

Figure 85
Type 1 Neck Block

2) **Rounded neck block with a crescent-shaped wood support beneath (circa mid-1839 to 1841)**

Not all of this type have a C. F. Martin stamp on neck block. It appears the earliest guitars from this period are missing the name stamp (Figure 86).

This type of neck block is encountered in the earliest part of the Martin & Coupa period. The thickness of semi-circular support varies considerably. Generally, the thicker supports appear to be on earlier guitars.

Figure 86
Type 2 Neck Block

3) Rectangular neck block (with chamfered corners) and rectangular or rounded "real" Spanish foot (circa 1841 to 1842) - Figure 87

Guitars with the rectangular or rounded Spanish foot appear to be from period immediately following the type 2 neck blocks. In this case the Spanish foot continues under the neck block to close off the dove-tail

A C. F. Martin name stamp does not appear on the neck block or the Spanish foot

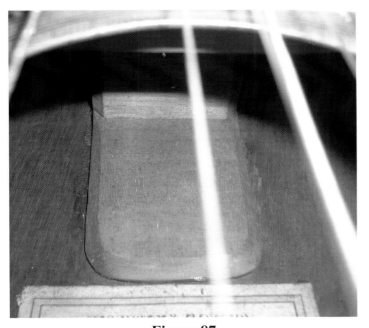

Figure 87
Type 3 Neck Block

4) Rectangular neck block (with chamfered corners) and shield-shaped "decorative" Spanish foot (circa 1843 to 1850) - see Figure 88

The Spanish foot in this type of neck block does not close off the dove-tail as in type 3. In effect, the Spanish foot has been reduced to a "decorative" feature.

The type 4 neck block was used for a relatively long period of time and there is considerable variation in the shape of this Spanish foot. A few guitars from this period are known without a Spanish foot.

Figure 88
Type 4 Neck Block

5) Rectangular neck block (with chamfered corners) but without a Spanish foot - Figure 89

This type of neck block became the norm about 1850 and is still the type used on Martin guitars with a dove-tail neck joint.

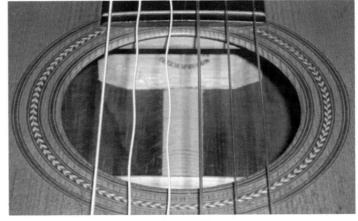

Figure 89
Type 5 Neck Block

Bridges

Bridges evolved over time as Martin changed from the early Stauffer-influenced guitars to Spanish-style instruments.

The first guitar made by Martin with a "Spanish bridge" was sold on August 4, 1837 (from Inventory Purchases 1837-38, see also figure 110). Martin sold his first "Spanish" guitar on December 30, 1837 to a "Mr. Bayard" for $31.25 and paid a commission of $7.00 to Mr. Schnepf. It is not known if this guitar had a Spanish-shaped body or just some special features (e. g., Spanish type bridge, Spanish neck or fan bracing).

Moustache bridges

Martin called these "**steg mit Herzchen**" or, literally, "**bridge with little hearts**". On Martin guitars the ends of the moustache bridges always turn down. This style of bridge is a hallmark of early Martin guitars.

These bridges are fragile and most of these bridges now show signs of being repaired or modified. The bridge illustrated is the only completely original example examined for this book.

The original moustache bridges have a fret wire saddle. Some also have five "trefoil" abalone inlays and a "box" made of thin German silver wire surrounding the inlays and bridge pins.

Moustache bridges are only seen on guitars with type 1, 2 or 3 labels (i. e., the 1834 to 1837 period).

Figure 90
Moustache Bridge on 1834 Martin Guitar

"Shield" bridges

Shield bridges are encountered on guitars with type 4, 5, 6, 7 and 8 labels (circa 1837 to 1840). The shape of the shield bridges evolved over time and their usage overlaps with the early "Spanish" style pyramid bridges.

The earliest shield bridges have a fret wire saddle but later examples have a drop-in ivory saddle.

Many shield bridges have an additional decoration below the bridge. Martin referred to the fancy decorations, of abalone and ivory, as "**flowers**" or "**ornaments**".

One curious feature of this type of bridge is the stag-

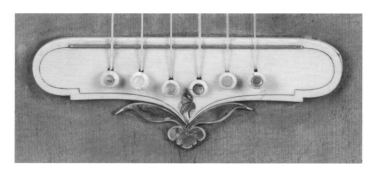

Figure 91
Shield Bridge on November 1836 Martin Guitar (Serial Number 1114) - Note the fret wire saddle

Figure 92
Shield Bridge on June 1837 Martin Guitar (Serial Number 1168) - Note fret wire saddle

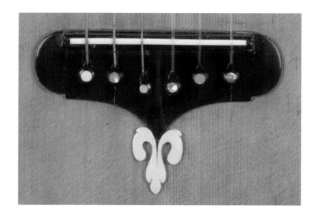

Figure 93
Shield Bridge on 1838 Martin & Bruno Guitar
Note the drop-in ivory saddle

gered positioning of the 3rd and 4th pins. Only one shield shaped bridge, in ivory, has been seen with the bridge pins arranged in a straight line.

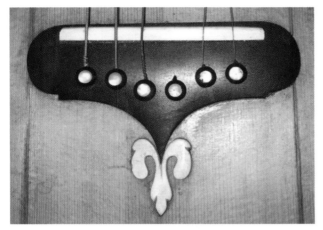

Figure 94
Shield Bridge on August 1838 Martin & Bruno Guitar (Serial Number 1231)

Figure 95
Shield Bridge on ca. 1840 Martin & Coupa Guitar

Figure 96
Shield Bridge on ca. 1840 Martin & Coupa Guitar

Pyramid Bridges

a) Prototype Pyramid Bridge (1837)

The bridge in Figure 97 may be an early version of a bridge that subsequently developed into the classic Martin pyramid bridge. This bridge appears on a 1837 Martin guitar (serial number 1160).

b) Pyramid tie bridges (1839 to 1843)

A more developed pyramid bridge appeared around mid-1839 (Figure 98). This particular bridge is interesting because it has a large ebony L-shaped drop-in saddle, whereas most L-shaped saddles were ivory (Figure 100).

This type of bridge has a raised center section and the rear edge of the bridge is flat or "scooped-out".

Figure 97
Very Early Tie Bridge on 1837 Martin Guitar
Serial Number 1160
This may be a prototypical pyramid bridge

Figure 98
Pyramid Tie Bridge on June 1839 Martin Guitar
Serial Number 1293
This bridges illustrates that shield and pyramid bridges were used concurrently for a time.

Generally, the ebony tie bridges have a flat or slightly concave back edge while the scooped-out edge of ivory tie bridges are more pronounced (Figures 99 and 101 to 104).

Tie bridges appeared during 1837 but were dropped about 1842 or 1843 when Martin switched from tie to pin bridges. However, at least one guitar with a tie bridge is known after this period, the 1864 to 1867 Sutter's Fort Museum 00-28 - see Figure 41.

c) Pyramid pin bridges (1843 to 1857)

These pin bridges retained the raised center section but the back edges are flat or very slightly scooped. It appears this style of pin bridge was in use from 1843 to 1857 (see Figures 105 to 108).

d) Pyramid pin bridges with rounded rear edge

This style of bridge came into general use about 1857 although a few have been encountered prior to that date (see Figure 109). This style of bridge was standard on Martin guitars for the remainder of the 19th and well into the 20th century.

Figure 101
Pyramid Tie Bridge on ca. 1841-1842 Martin & Coupa Guitar - See figure 102 for reverse side

Figure 102
Pyramid Tie Bridge on ca. 1841-1842 Martin & Coupa Guitar

Figure 99
1839 Martin & Schatz Guitar (SN 1304)
This bridge proves that shield and pyramid bridges were used concurrently.

Figure 100
Detail of Ivory Drop-In Saddle for Tie Bridge

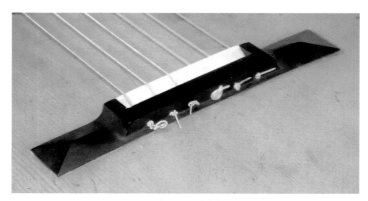

Figure 103
Pyramid Tie Bridge on ca. 1841-1842 Martin & Coupa Guitar

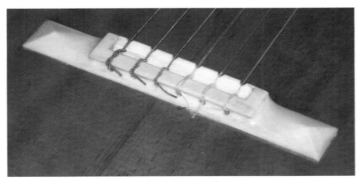

Figure 104
Pyramid Tie Bridge on ca. 1842-1843
Martin & Coupa Guitar

Figure 105
Pyramid Pin Bridge on ca. 1843-1846
Martin & Coupa Guitar

Figure 106
Pyramid Pin Bridge on the
Colonel Wilkins Guitar (1846)

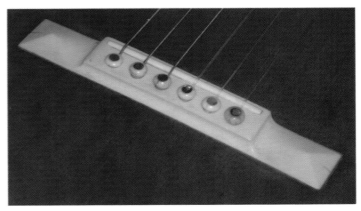

Figure 107
Pyramid Pin Bridge on ca. 1850 Martin Guitar

Figure 108
Pyramid Pin Bridge on 1857 Martin 5-21 Guitar

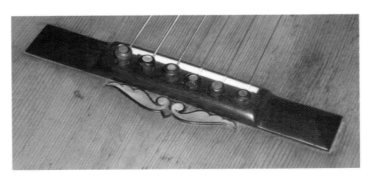

Figure 109
Pyramid Pin Bridge on ca. 1856
Martin 2½-32 Guitar

Head Stocks

Martin guitar offered three options with regard to the type of head stock used on his guitars. The three options, using Martin terminology, were: 1) Vienna machines or one-side screw, 2) two-side screws, also known as patent machines and 3) peg heads with friction pegs.

The Vienna screws are usually seen on the fancier grade of guitar. Customers could choose either a peg head or two side machines on the regular grade of instruments but a peg head was almost always used for the least expensive Martin models.

The earliest ledgers do not always record which type of head stock was used on each guitar although all three types were offered from the beginning. The ledger of **"INVENTORY PURCHASES 1837-38"** records a partial list of guitars brought into stock in 1837. Of the 27 guitars that can be identified as being built by Martin, 13 had peg heads, 7 had two-side machines and 7 had one-side machines.

If this list is representative, then about 50% of Martin guitars of the period should have peg heads and two-side screws and one-side screw head stocks would make up about 25% each. These figures are somewhat surprising since the large majority of pre-1840 Martin guitars examined for this book have Vienna machines. Only two guitars pre-1840 Martin guitars have been with two-side machines and, so far, only two more have been seen with peg heads. This statistical anomaly must reflect the higher survival rate of fancier grade guitars.

All three types of head stock are encountered in more equal numbers during the Martin & Coupa period (circa 1840-1850). However, the one side screw head stocks went out of use by the mid-1850's.

1) Vienna Machines or One-Side Screws

These tuners were made of either brass or nickel silver and were imported from Austria. As these machines were expensive, they are usually only seen on higher grade instruments.

The one-side machines are commonly encountered on guitars made prior to 1850. After 1850 only 7 guitars with the Vienna screws are recorded in the Martin ledgers, the last one being shipped in early 1855. However, the Martin records for 1850 to 1852 are spotty, so a few more may be discovered.

Of the 22 guitars with Vienna screws examined at least two styles are identifiable.

Only one Type A one-side screw has been seen and, interestingly, it is mounted on the earliest Martin guitar known (in the Martin Museum).

The remainder are all style B. The designs on the back of the type B machines are all unique except for the one illustrated in Figure 111, which has been seen twice. It is not known how many different designs exist because of the small population of these early guitars.

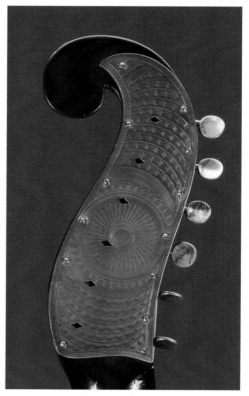

Figure 110
Type A One-Side Screw
Early 1834 Martin Guitar

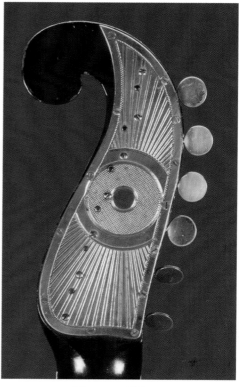

Figure 111
Type B One-Side Screw
Ca. 1835-1836 Martin & Schatz Guitar

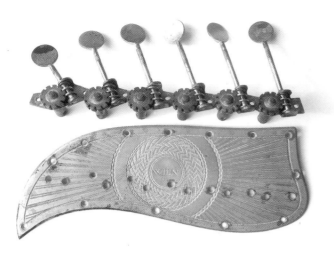

Figure 112
Internal Construction of One-Side Screw
1834 Martin Guitar

Martin sent a letter to "**C. Dumert at Vienna**" in June 1838[1] and there is a remarkable, although undated, letter in the Martin archive written by Charles Dumert to C. F. Martin discussing improvements in his machines and asking for another order. Based on the date, the letter was probably referring to the early one-side screws.

2) Two-Side Screws, also known as Patent Heads

Martin offered two-side screws as an option for head stocks from the beginning. The original machines were imported from Neukirchen and were mounted on head stocks with a rounded top and wide slots. The original machines are made of brass and have a somewhat crude appearance (Figure 113).

To date, only three early Martins guitars have been recorded with a rounded head stock but on one of these the original German machines were replaced with Ashborn tuners.

The next type of two-side machines encountered are on guitars from the early Martin & Coupa period (circa 1840-1842). The earliest type seen were manufactured in France and are stamped "Jerome".

The "Jerome" tuners come in a variety of grades but, generally, came in brass, plain or decorated, or in German silver with a decorated mounting plate. The decorated plates are sometimes referred to as "engraved" but the designs are stamped, not engraved.

Figure 113
Two-Side Screws on 1834 Martin Guitar

The stamped designs were made up of a number of small bits arranged in a circular pattern. These designs appear remarkably similar over a period of time, extending from the early 1840's to the late 1850's.

The different types of gears can be useful dating tools. The earliest Jerome tuners have gears that were manufactured with a smooth outside surface, looking almost like a washer. The tuners shown in Figure 114 have an 11 to 1 ratio while the ratio for Figure 116 is 10 to 1. The former has a gear of slightly larger diameter with a few more teeth.

The later Jerome tuners use a normal spur gear. The tuners illustrated in Figure 117 have a gear ratio of 12 to 1.

The machines used on the De Goni guitar (Figure 122) are the only known example of "Demet" machines seen on a Martin guitar and can be dated to 1843.

Figure 114
Ca. 1842-1843 Jerome Tuners

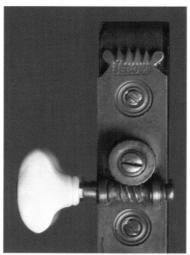

Figure 115
Ca. 1843-1850 Jerome Tuners

Figure 116
Ca. 1843-1850 Jerome Tunes

Figure 117
Ca. 1850-1852 Jerome Tuners

Figure 118
Ca. 1852-1857 Jerome Tuners

Figure 119
1853 Schmidt & Maul Guitar

Figure 120
Ca. 1855-1860 Jerome Tuners

Figure 121
Ca. 1850-1855 Unknown Tuners

Figure 122
1843 Demet Tuners

Demet machines were manufactured in France by Victor Auguste Demet who was born on December 15, 1804 in Beaucourt and died in Mirecourt on November 10, 1884. Demet is mentioned in the Mirecourt records as a watchmaker and a luthier.

A new style of stamped decoration was being used on Jerome tuners by the 1850's (Figure 119). These particular machines are mounted on a Schmidt & Maul guitar that is dated 1853 under the top.

The machines shown in Figure 120 are another style of Jerome tuner that appeared in the late 1850's. The stamped decorations are the same as the earlier versions but the backing plate has been shortened, so there is no longer enough room for the name stamp. This type of tuners are seen on guitars until well into the 19th century.

By the early 1850's Martin was using tuners by other manufacturers but, since we know that Martin was buying machines from a number of sources, a variety of different machines may be encountered. The tuners in Figure 121 may be early Seidel machines. It appears Martin ceased using "Jerome" machines and switched to Seidel tuners about 1857.

As with the machine gear ratio, the tuning buttons can also provide a clue to dating. The earliest Jerome machines have distinctive ivory buttons (Figures 115 to 117, 199 and 120) and the fancier grade of Jerome machines have attractive floral-pattern pearl buttons (Figures 114 and 118). By the early 1850's the buttons had been changed to an oblong shape (Figure 121) in either bone, ivory or pearl. The Demet tuner buttons (Figure 122) on the 1843 De Goni guitar are similar to those on the Jerome tuners from the same period.

The Martin archive contains a number of invoices from the 1850 to 1867 period that show Martin was purchasing guitar machines, sometimes called patent machines, from local sources including Rohé & Leavitt, C. A. Zoebisch & Sons, and Charles Bruno. Several letters in the archive specifically mention machines being sourced from "Paris". The suppliers mentioned above imported a wide variety of musical supplies from Europe so it probably didn't make sense for Martin to directly import tuning machines from Europe when he could just as easily buy them locally.

From the early 1850's Martin was generally procuring a number of different grades of machines:

a) Brass with bone or ivory buttons

b) German silver with ivory buttons

c) German silver with pearl buttons

The decoration and some other features must have varied somewhat as some invoices show pricing for as many as six different grades of machines. The brass two-side machines were usually used on style 24 guitars and below while the German silver machines were used on style 26 guitars and higher, with the exception of style 27 which had two-side brass screws. The German silver machines with pearl button were generally, but not always, used on style 34, 40 and 42 instruments.

3) Peg heads

Peg heads were used on roughly 50% of Martin guitars before 1840 but only two were examined for this book. The example illustrated in Figure 123 is on a 1838 Martin & Bruno terz guitar while the head stock shown in Figure 124 belongs to a Martin & Coupa terz guitar from circa 1840.

The second type of peg head (Figure 125) appeared about 1840 and was basically the same type used until well into the 20th century, excepting that the earlier examples are slightly more flared in shape. Peg head guitars were very common throughout the rest of the 19th century. This type of peg head is one of the features that differentiate Martin's "Spanish" guitars from his earlier instruments.

The radii in the upper corners of the peg head on higher grade instruments are slightly larger to allow for bending of the ivory binding (Figure 126).

In the early Martin guitars two small holes sometimes appear near the top of the peg head. These were used for attaching a "ribbon" or strap. Later, these holes were replaced by an ivory or ebony button attached to the back of the peg head. The two small holes appear intermittently from about 1840 to 1850.

Friction pegs were made of ebony or ivory. The ebony

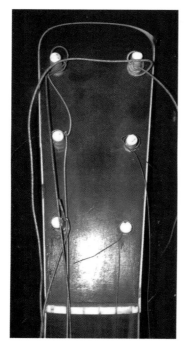

Figure 123
1838 Martin & Bruno (Serial Number 1231)

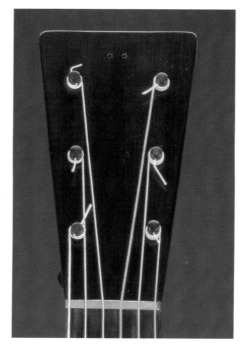

Figure 125
Ca. 1840-1841 Martin & Coupa

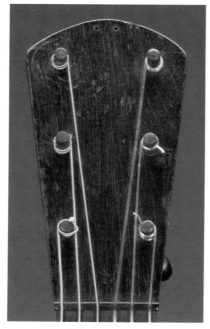

Figure 124
Ca. 1840 Martin & Coupa

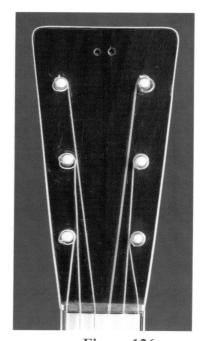

Figure 126
Ca. 1843-1850 Martin & Coupa

pegs were used on style 24 and lower and the ivory pegs on style 26 and above, although customers occasionally specified ivory pegs on lower grade instruments.

Martin purchased some pegs from Neukirchen before 1840 but, subsequently, friction pegs were sourced from U. S. suppliers.

Martin Stamp on Back of Guitar

A number of early instruments have a **"C. F. Martin/New York"** stamp impressed in the back of the guitar near the heel of the neck. This stamp was sometimes applied lightly and can be hard to see, especially on darker wood.

Many of the Martin guitars with either ladder bracing or 3-strut fan bracing (i. e., to about 1841) have this stamp. For some reason none of the guitars examined with 5-strut fan bracing or early type of X-bracing bear the Martin stamp in this position. So, most of the guitars between 1842 to 1850 do not have the Martin stamp on the back.

The Martin stamp resurfaced about 1850 but mostly disappeared by the end of the decade, excepting on guitars with black necks. For the most part, the Martin stamp appeared only on the lower priced 3-17 and 2½-17 guitars. This practice continued until the 1890's.

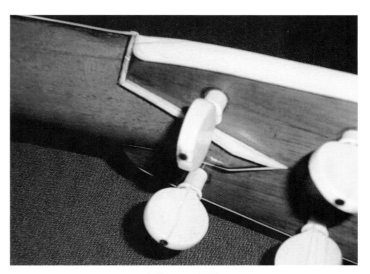
Figure 128
Ca. 1843-1846 Martin & Coupa Guitar

Figure 127
Back Stamp on 1834 Martin Guitar

Ebony and Ivory Veneered Joints

One of the more interesting features seen on some early Martin guitars are the thin ebony veneers applied between the head stock and neck volute and at the joint between the neck and the body of the guitar. In one case an ivory veneer was added to the ebony veneer at the joints to create a striking effect.

The ebony veneered joints are always seen on higher grade guitars. All examples seen have ivory binding, with either peg heads or two-side machines.

From the population of guitars studied, the ebony veneered joints are only seen with the 5-strut fan or early X-bracing. If previous assumptions on dating are accurate, guitars with this feature can be dated to the 1840 to 1848 period.

Figure 129
Ca. 1843-1846 Martin & Coupa Guitar

Laminated Backs

The backs of many early Martin guitars are laminated, or veneered, with a different type of wood. The guitars made of birds-eye maple are usually laminated with plain maple veneers. Rosewood guitars are laminated with veneers of spruce, mahogany or rosewood.

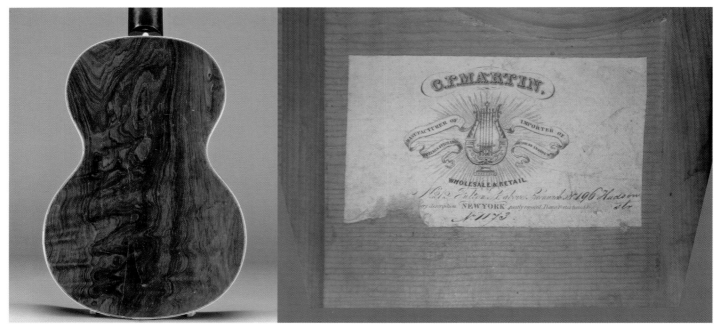

Figure 130
1837 Martin Guitar (Serial Number 1173) with Rosewood Back and Spruce Lining

It appears laminated backs were a standard feature on Martin guitars until 1841 or 1842.

Laminated backs continued to be used intermittently until at least 1854. One Martin customer, in a letter dated July 25, 1854, inquired why some Martin guitars were supplied with laminated backs and asked whether C. F. Martin counted them superior to guitars with solid backs.

It is not known whether a laminated back was an intended design feature or as an economy for using veneers that would not be thick enough for use on their own.

Nickel Silver Nuts

A number of old Martin guitars have been seen with German silver (nickel silver) nuts. In the population of guitars examined, nickel silver nuts are commonly seen on guitars with 5-strut fan or early X-bracing. The latest appears to be on a "renaissance" shaped Martin from 1853. From these observations it appears that the nickel silver nuts were in regular use from about 1841 to about 1853. However, the Sutter's Fort Museum 00-28, made between 1864 and 1867, also has a German silver nut.

Not all the guitars from this period have nickel sil-

ver nuts, although it is possible the original German silver nuts may have been replaced at some point. The only actual mention of a "**metal nut**" in the Martin archival material occurs in a letter from Peters & Son dated June 15, 1853.

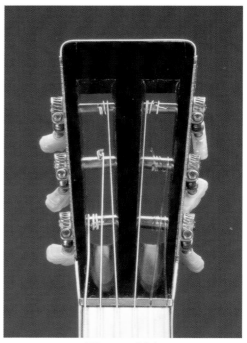

Figure 131
German Silver Nut on Ca. 1842-1843
Martin & Coupa Guitar

One-Piece and Two-Piece Backs

All Martin guitars examined with type 1 to 5 labels, from 1834 to early 1838, have one-piece backs.

The first two-piece back appears on a 1838 Martin & Bruno guitar (type 6 label, serial number 1231). The last one-piece back noted is on a 1839 Martin & Schatz guitar (type 7 label, serial number 1296).

Subsequently, all Martin guitars have two-piece backs, although the possibility of encountering a later one-piece back can't be discounted.

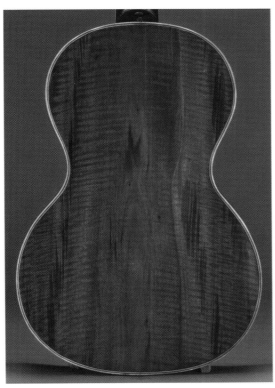

Figure 132
Typical One-Piece Back on Ca. 1835-1836
Martin & Schatz Guitar

Necks

The Martin ledgers record that three types of necks were employed in the 19th century:

1) **Black or "ice cream cone" heel**

2) **Cedar or Spanish heel**

3) **Neck screw** -similar to 1) but with a clock key mechanism for adjusting the neck angle

No pre-1840 guitar has yet been encountered with a cedar neck, the necks are always black regardless of the type of head stock used.

The **"ice cream cone"** heels on black necks were assembled from several pieces of wood and the head stock was glued to the neck with a simple V-notch joint. Figure 133 illustrates how the "ice cream cone" heel was attached to the neck with a wood key.

Figure 133
"Ice Cream Cone" Heel Construction
from a 1850's Martin Guitar

The Spanish necks of early Martin guitars were made of Cuban cedar (cedrela odorata). The earliest guitar encountered so far with a cedar neck is a ca. 1841-1842 Martin & Coupa guitar in the collection of The Farmers Museum in Cooperstown NY.

The head stock, regardless of tuners installed, was attached to the cedar neck with a complicated scarf joint and was further supported by a "volute", an extension of the neck. The length of the volute varies a good deal, especially in the 1840's, but does not appear to be a reliable tool for dating guitars.

It is generally assumed that the "ice cream cone" heels are encountered only on Martin's less expensive style 17 guitars. However, quite a large number of **'ladies' guitars'** (i.e. size 2 or 2 ½) in styles 27, 30, 32, 34 and 42 were made with a black neck and **"ice cream cone"** heel.

The black necks are made of painted "whitewood" (probably poplar) although the more expensive models occasionally had necks veneered with ebony. The black paint was a mixture of shellac and lamp black.

Cedar necks, with a Spanish heel, were commonest on mid-range Martin guitars (styles 20, 21, 22, 23, 24, 26, 27, 28). The neck was often made of two or even three pieces of wood, these joints being clearly visible on the heel of the neck (Figure 134). Whether this was simply a desire on Martin's part to economize or whether only small size lumber was available is unknown.

Figure 134
Two Piece Heel on ca. 1841-1842 Martin & Coupa

In the 1830's, Martin's more expensive guitars usually had a screw neck. However, to date, only one guitar from the 1840's has been seen with a neck screw. Only twelve more guitars were recorded with neck screws between 1850 and 1862.

Additionally, four style 42 guitars were made between 1853 and 1858. It is not known if these had a neck screws as this detail wasn't recorded. However, if not, why would pearl purfling around the fingerboard be necessary?

Eight more style 42 guitars were produced with a neck screw between 1871 and 1883. It appears this feature was dropped by 1892, at the latest, since no neck screw guitars have surfaced from the period and the price lists no longer indicated a neck screw as a feature of style 42 guitars.

Two different types of neck screws are encountered. The early guitars with a neck screw have a fingerboard elevated above the top of the guitar. The elevated fingerboard allows a clearance for pivoting of the neck when the neck angle is adjusted.

The second type, encountered from the 1850's to the 1880's, has the bottom of the fingerboard extension almost flush with the top of the guitar. The guitar top is cut out under the fingerboard extension so that the fingerboard can rotate into the recess provided.

Figure 135
Neck Screw on ca. 1871 Martin 2-42 Guitar

Lining and Kerfing

Two types of kerfing are encountered on early Martins guitars:

a) Solid lining

In a general sense continuous lining, similar to the lining used in violins, is encountered on all pre-1840 Martin guitars and continued to be used in small sized guitars until at least the 1850's. More study is needed here to define how far into the 19th century solid lining was used.

b) Individual kerfing blocks

Martin began to use individual kerfing blocks, a feature commonly seen on Spanish guitars, by the early 1840's. The size and spacing of the individual kerfing blocks vary widely at the beginning but gradually become more regular in size and more closely spaced as time went on. Individual kerfing blocks, closely spaced and regular in size and shape, continued to be used into the 20th century.

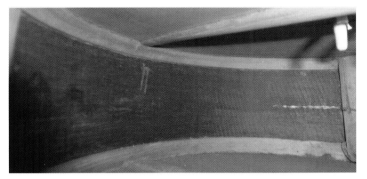

Figure 136
Solid Lining in ca. 1836 Martin Guitar
(Serial Number 1114)

Figure 137
Individual Kerfing Blocks in ca. 1841-1842
Martin & Coupa Guitar

Number of Frets

Martin rarely recorded the number of frets on guitars, so this section is based on observation of existing guitars. The sample of guitars, especially for the pre-1840 instruments, is small so exceptions are bound to be encountered. This information should be considered a basis for further study and discussion.

On the early Stauffer-shaped guitars the number of frets on the fingerboard depended on the period and whether the neck was adjustable or not:

LABEL TYPE	DATE	NUMBER OF FRETS	SCALE (NOMINAL)
1 to 3	1834-1836	22	24"
4 or 5 (FIRST PERIOD)	1837	21	24"
6	May-Sept. 1838	20	24"-25.59"
5 (SECOND PERIOD)	Sept. 1838-May 1839	18	24"-24.69"
7	June 1839-Mar. 1840	18	24"-24.5"
8	Mar. 1840-May 1850	18 or 19	24"-25"

Table 7
Number of Frets

The cittern-shaped Amadill sold on August 8, 1836 guitar has a type 3 Martin & Schatz label but only 18 frets.

During the Martin & Coupa period (i. e. 1840-1850) guitars had either 18 or 19 frets, although 18 fret guitars are seen more often. The "Renaissance" shaped guitars were made with 20 frets, although the "Elegant" guitar from 1854 has 19 frets.

From 1851 until around the middle 1880, all guitars featured 18 frets. By at least 1886 the 0-28 guitars gained an extra fret while the rest of the sizes and style remained at 18 frets until at least 1898.

By 1900 all sizes and styles had 19 frets, although William Foden in that year was presented a 0-42 guitar with 20 frets. For the remainder of the 20th century Martin six-string guitars had either 19 or 20 frets, depending on the model and period.

Strap Button on Back of the Guitar

A strap button, on the back of the guitar near the end block, is occasionally seen on early Martin guitars. The pin is usually a bridge pin that is mounted by drilling a hole into the end block, but larger pins are known. All the guitars examined to date with this feature have 3-strut fan bracing (also associated with the semi-circular support under the neck block). It appears this feature was only current for a short time in 1840 and 1841. However, a few later guitars can be found with a strap button to ca. 1844 and style 17 guitars continued to have strap buttons until at least the late 1850's.

The strap button in Figure 138 is unusually large and is possibly a replacement for the original bridge pin, but adequately shows the location of the strap pin.

Figure 138
Strap Button on Back of ca. 1840-1841
Martin & Coupa Guitar

Strap Button on Back of the Head Stock

A few pre-1840 Martin guitars have been seen with a large ebony strap button on the back of the head stock. These invariably have two-side screws or a peg head, there being no room for such a feature on guitars with a one-side screw.

The head stock strap buttons reappeared in the mid-1870's and are seen on some Martin guitars into the early 20th century. They are usually made of ebony but the more expensive models featured ivory strap buttons.

Guitar Decoration

C. A. Zoebisch & Son began using the size and style code (e. g., 0-28) in 1856 and by the end of 1858 Martin had brought it into general use.

Prior to 1856 Martin recorded the size, type of neck, wood used for the body and decoration of his guitars in the ledger book. This methodology gives a very clear idea of the features of any particular guitar and, combined with the price, allows a size and style code to be inferred. For example, the four guitars shown in Figure 139 are clearly a *2½-33*, two *2-22* and one *2½-20*.

C. F. Martin recorded the decoration of his guitars as: "**ornament**" (purfling), "**sound hole**", "**edge**" (type of binding), "**head**" (type of tuners), "**extra ornament**" (special features such as neck screw or ivory fingerboard) and "**case**" (c=common, f=fine, ff=very fine).

It was one of the intentions of this book to use the type of decoration employed by Martin as a tool in dating guitars. However, Martin tended to generalize the type of decoration used on particular grades of guitars. Certain types of purfling and sound hole decoration can be assigned to particular periods but the sample of guitars examined for this book is small compared to the types of marquetry encountered so

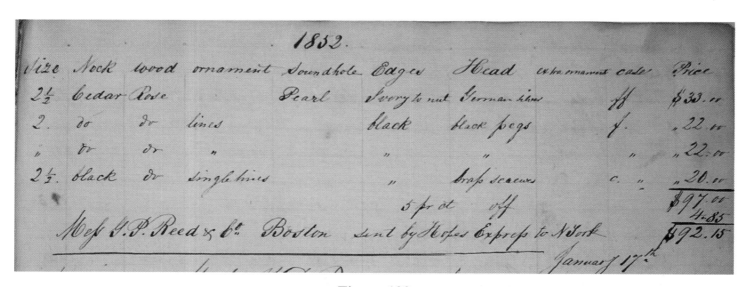

Figure 139
January 21, 1852 Entry from 1852-1858 Sales Ledger
Illustrating How Martin Recorded Design Features

conclusions on dating will have to wait the examination of a far larger group of instruments.

As an example, style 26 guitars prior to 1858 are described as having "**De Goni**", "**Spanish**" or "**fine**" purfling. From the many different types of purfling seen on style 26 guitars, Martin did not always use the same type of purfling but would sometimes substitute another type of purfling of equivalent value.

Martin appears to have sourced most of his marquetry from C. H. Burdorf in Hamburg, Germany. Heinrich Goetz purchased purfling on Martin's behalf when he was in Germany in 1854. Figures 140 and 141 are photographs of the Burdorf marquetry sample boards in the Martin Guitar Museum.

Associated Design Features

Considerable space above has been dedicated to examining in detail the design features of about seventy pre-1867 guitars. Particular focus has been placed on guitars from the 1830's and 1840's, since, until now, so little information has been available on guitars from this period.

This section provides a table of associated design features for attempting to date early Martins guitars. When considered altogether, the design features of early Martin guitars fall into identifiable groupings. Labels are the most useful clue since Martin used seven type of labels between 1834 and 1839 and an eighth type from 1839 to 1850, the whole of the Martin & Coupa period. As well, certain types of top bracing patterns tend to be associated with particular types of neck blocks and bridges.

It should be mentioned that the information displayed in Table 8 is based on assumptions as to when certain features were current. As more guitars come to light it may well be necessary to revisit these assumptions. However, so far these assumptions seem to fit fairly well with observed guitars.

LABEL TYPE	DATES	SERIAL NUMBER	NO. OF FRETS	BRIDGE	STRING ATTACHMENT	BRACING PATTERN	NECK BLOCK
1	Early 1834		22	Moustache	Pin	Ladder	Rounded
2	Mid to late 1834		22	Moustache	Pin	Ladder	Rounded
3	Jan. 1835 to Mar. 1837		22	Moustache or Shield	Pin	Ladder	Rounded
4	Apr. to June 1837	1114 to 1130	21	Shield	Pin	Ladder	Rounded
5	Apr. 1837 to Apr. 1838	1160 to 1188	21	Shield or Pyramid	Pin or Tie	Atypical Ladder or Translational Bracing	Rounded
6	May-Sept. 1838	1231 to 1235	20	Shield	Pin	Ladder or 3-Strut Fan	Rounded
5	Sept. 1838 to May 1839	1275 to 1293	18	Shield or Pyramid	Pin or Tie	3-Strut Fan	Rectangular
7	June 1839 to Mar. 1840	1296 to 1341	18	Shield or Pyramid	Pin or Tie	3-Strut Fan	Rectangular with Crescent-Shaped Support
8[1]	Aug. 1839-1841		18	Shield or Pyramid	Pin or Tie	2 or 3-Strut Fan	Rounded or Rectangular with Crescent-Shaped Support
8[1]	1841-1842		18	Pyramid	Pin or Tie	5-Strut Fan	Rectangular with Rectangular Spanish Foot
8[1]	1842-1843		18	Pyramid	Pin or Tie	5-Strut Fan	Rectangular with Pointed Spanish Foot
7, 8[1]	1843-1850		18 or 19	Pyramid	Pin or Tie	Early X-Brace	Rectangular with Pointed Spanish Foot
8[1]	1850		18 to 20	Pyramid	Pin	Plain X-Brace (No Tone Bar)	Rectangular with Pointed Spanish Foot or Renaissance Body
None	1852-1867		18 or 19	Pyramid	Pin	X-Brace with 1 Tone Bar	Rectangular or Renaissance Body

1) Not all Martin & Coupa period guitars have the Martin & Coupa label
2) Size 2½ and 3 "students' model" guitars retained 3-strut fan bracing

Table 8
Table of Associated Design Features for Dating 1834 to 1867 Guitars

Notes for Chapter 6

1) 04 - JOURNAL 04-1837 TO 11-1838 BRUNO, page 50, June 5, 1838

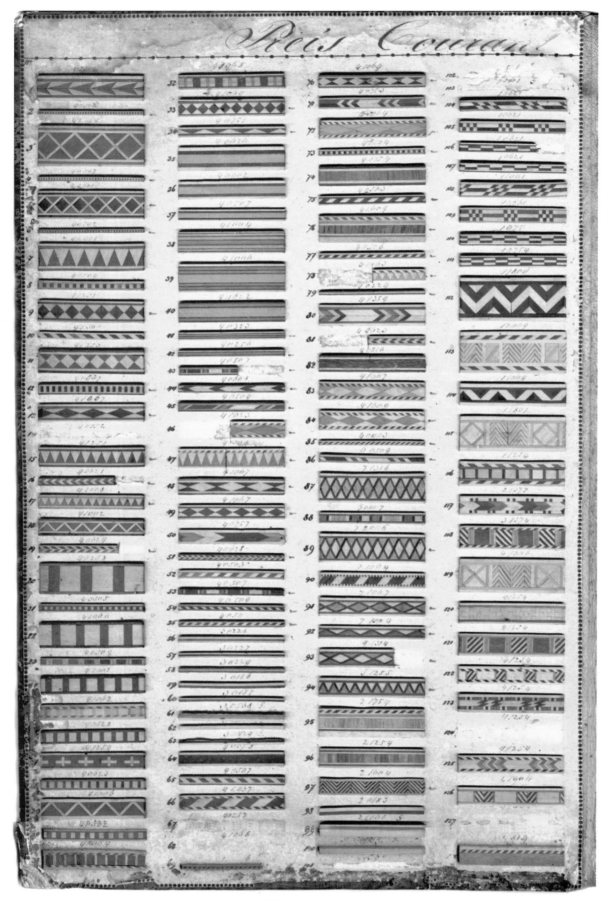

Figure 140
Burdorf Marquetry Sample Board-Part 1

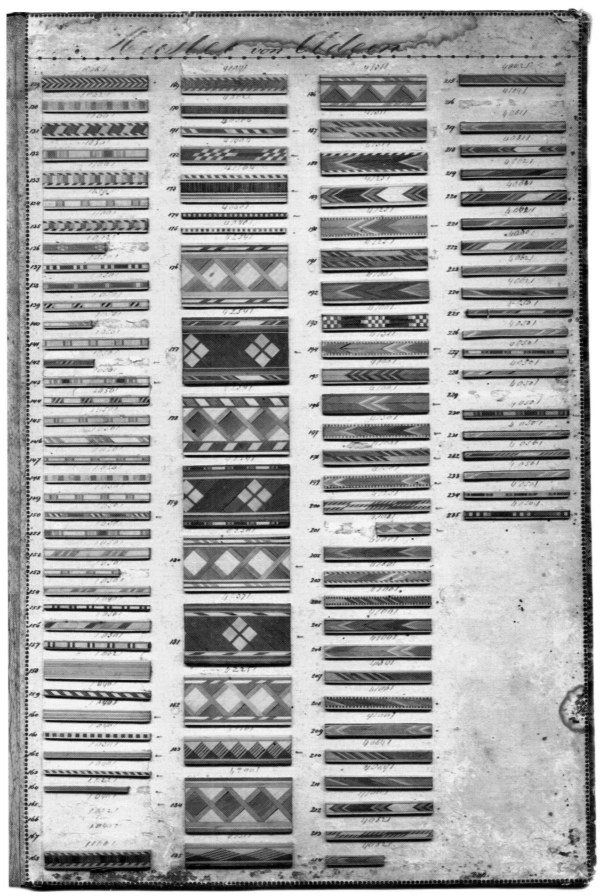

Figure 141
Burdorf Marquetry Sample Board-Part 2

Chapter 7
EARLY HIGH-GRADE AND PRESENTATION-GRADE GUITARS (1836 TO 1862)

C. F. Martin made high-grade guitars from his earliest period in New York. These expensive instruments were sometimes decorated with ivory fingerboards and beautiful "**thumbnail**" abalone inlays around the top. Many of the early Martin guitars that have survived are the high-grade instruments, probably because they were easily recognized as quality instruments and were preserved as treasured heirlooms.

By the early 1840's, probably under the influence of John Coupa, C. F. Martin had settled on a range of models with fairly conservative appointments. Although records from 1840 to 1850 are largely missing, a small number of fancy grade guitars have been seen with special features, including ivory fingerboards.

By the 1852 the highest grade Martin guitar normally available was style 34, although about two dozen extra fancy guitars were made up to 1864. Of these, only five guitars can be considered presentation-grade

DATE	QUAN	SIZE & STYLE	NECK	ORNAMENT	SOUNDHOLE	EDGE	HEAD	EXTRA	CASE
1853-02-01	1	1-38	CEDAR	FINE	PEARL	IVORY TO THE NUT	TWO SIDE GERMAN SILVER SCREW	NECK SCREW	VERY FINE
1853-02-15	1	2 1/2-35	BLACK	FINE	PEARL	IVORY TO THE NUT	ONE SIDE SCREW	IVORY BRIDGE	VERY FINE
1853-04-18	1	2 1/2-38	BLACK	FINE	PEARL	IVORY & BRIDGE	TWO SIDE GERMAN SILVER SCREW	NONE	CEDAR
1853-05-23	1	1-35	CEDAR	DE GONI	PEARL	IVORY	IVORY PEGS	NECK SCREW	VERY FINE
1853-12-13	1	2-70	BLACK	PEARL	PEARL	IVORY TO THE NUT	ONE SIDE SILVER	NECK SCREW, ?	CEDAR
1853-12-13	1	2 1/2-42	BLACK	PEARL	PEARL	IVORY & FINGERBOARD	TWO SIDE GERMAN SILVER SCREW	IVORY BRIDGE	VERY FINE
1853-12-26	1	2 1/2-35	BLACK	FINE	PEARL	IVORY TO THE NUT	ONE SIDE SILVER	IVORY BRIDGE	VERY FINE
1854-04-05	1	2 1/2-40	CEDAR	FINE	PEARL	IVORY TO THE NUT	TWO SIDE GERMAN SILVER SCREW, IVORY HANDLES	IVORY BRIDGE	VERY FINE
1854-05-04	1	2-160		CRYSTAL PALACE				CRYSTAL PALACE	POLISHED
1855-02-24	1	2 1/2-35	BLACK	FINE	PEARL	IVORY TO THE NUT	ONE SIDE SILVER	IVORY BRIDGE	VERY FINE
1855-04-06	1	2 1/2-48	BLACK	FINE	PEARL	IVORY & PEARL	TWO SIDE SILVER	IVORY BRIDGE	CEDAR
1856-12-28	1	2-160		CRYSTAL PALACE				CRYSTAL PALACE	ROSEWOOD
1857-07-13	1	0-50	CEDAR	FINE	IVORY ROUND HOOP DOUBLE	IVORY	IVORY PEGS	IVORY BRIDGE	VERY FINE
1858-11-02	1	2-42							
1858-12-21	1	2-42	CEDAR	PEARL AROUND THE HOOP	FINE	IVORY	2 SIDE SILVER	IVORY BRIDGE	FINE CEDAR
1858-12-21	1	2 1/2-42	CEDAR	PEARL AROUND THE HOOP	FINE	IVORY	2 SIDE SILVER	IVORY BRIDGE	BLACK
1859-08-29	1	1-35					GERMAN SILVER SCREW FINE	IVORY BRIDGE	
1859-11-15	1	2 1/2-160					CRYSTAL PALACE		
1860-03-19	2	1-35					DOUBLE LINES	NECK SCREW	
1861-02-19	1	2 1/2-40							
1862-02-23	1	2-65					FINE GUITAR	NECK SCREW	
1862-12-25	1	2 1/2-40							
1863-12-31	1	2-40							
1864-05-27	1	2 1/2-40							
1864-05-28	1	0-40							

Table 9
High-Grade and Presentation-Grade Guitars 1852-1864

110   Hutton's Guide to Martin Guitars (1833-1969)

instruments. Each of these five will further be examined in detail below. A few additional high-grade guitars may also have been made between mid-1864 and August 1867 where there is a gap in the records.

In Table 9, the size and style designations for guitars made prior to 1856 are shown in italics and are inferred from the sizes, decoration and prices recorded in the sales ledger. The size and style shorthand (e.g. 0-28) that Martin began to use in October 1856 are shown in normal font. The size and style short hand was originally only used on orders for C. A. Zoebisch & Sons and did not come into general use until the end of 1858.

Almost all of the fancier grade instruments are either size 2 or size 2½. Highly decorated instruments were mostly sold to "**ladies**" for parlor use.

The style 35 guitars in table 9 has the same features as a style 34 but had one-side screws. The last two guitars from 1860, that had a wholesale price of $35, were probably similar to style 24 guitars but these had neck screws, thus explaining the higher price.

The first style 38 appears to be a style 34 with a neck screw. The second style 38 guitar is probably a style 34 supplied with a cedar case, the reason for the additional cost.

The first style 40 guitar appeared in 1854 but only 6 were made in the 10 years to mid-1864.

The first style 42 guitar was made in 1853 and had pearl purfling and sound hole decoration as well as an ivory fingerboard (see further comments under the Martin 2-70 guitar below). Only four style 42 guitars were made between 1853 and 1858. The last two had abalone purfling (or "pearl around the hoop" as Martin quaintly put it) but did not have pearl sound hole rings. The 2-42 shipped December 21, 1858 was wholesaled at the higher cost of $47 as it was supplied with a fine cedar case.

Although not specified in the descriptions in the ledger, the style 42 guitars mentioned above may have had neck screws. In the period between 1870 and the 1880's, the style 42 guitars were always advertised with neck screws. The neck screw was also the reason that the abalone purfling was extended around the fingerboard extension. With a neck screw, the fingerboard extension could be lowered into an opening cut in the top of the guitar. The appearance of the guitar would thus be compromised without the abalone purfling surrounding the opening. This fingerboard extension purfling continued to be a characteristic of style 42 guitars even after the neck screw feature was dropped before the turn of the 20th century.

The only style 48 guitar had, what was described as, "ivory & pearl" binding and was supplied with a cedar case.

The "Crystal Palace" guitar appears several times in the ledgers as Martin sent the guitar to several dealers for display purposes. It was finally sold to C. A. Zoebisch & Sons in November 1859.

1857 Martin 0-50 Guitar

This guitar may not be fancy enough to be considered a presentation grade instrument but it was made with one person in mind, although as the result of an error! Martin made it as a personal guitar for Ossian E. Dodge (1820-1876), the well known musician, publisher and, by 1857, owner of a music shop in Cleveland.

In a letter dated June 1, 1857 Dodge had been asking to become a dealer for Martin guitars and then added:

"**Please state also if you can make me a plain guitar for $50.00 cash-which shall equal the one I have now that I got from you.**"

It is easy to see how Martin could have misunderstood this request. Dodge was a relentless self-promoter and $50 was considerably more than the normal wholesale price of Martin guitars so C. F. Martin probably assumed Dodge was looking for a high grade guitar for personal use.

In a letter dated July 30, 1857 Dodge had two things to gripe about (all emphasis per Dodge):

"**You will see by my first letter that I did not <u>order</u> a guitar but merely asked the <u>price of one</u>.**

The guitar has arrived and as it would not be delivered until the charges, $53.75, were <u>paid</u>, and I

did not want <u>you</u> to suffer from sending the instrument, <u>I paid the bill</u> and <u>now have the guitar</u>; but <u>it</u> <u>is</u> <u>not</u> <u>equal</u> <u>to</u> <u>my</u> <u>own</u>."

Dodge then went on to complain:

"I am told you would not sell your guitars to any man in this city at <u>wholesale prices</u> but Brainard! Is this so?

If so, you did wrong not to let me know it, as I am an <u>old</u> <u>customer</u>, an <u>editor</u> of the <u>only Musical Paper in the State</u> and have the <u>largest</u> <u>music</u> <u>store</u> <u>in Ohio</u>!!

...The guitar I now hold I cannot sell for more than $50 and the matter is placed therefore exclusively upon your honor."

Figure 142
Engraving of Ossian E. Dodge
from a 1854 Concert Pamphlet

If this guitar still exists, it should be easy to identify as it has a double purfling of ivory as well as ivory binding. It is the fanciest 0-size guitar made by Martin before 1867.

In the last letter from Dodge in the archive, dated November 9, 1857, it appears that Martin reached an accommodation with Dodge by allowing him a $15 credit on the guitar above. Dodge also ordered a size 1 guitar for $35 and reiterated his earlier request for a Martin dealership. This guitar was shipped on November 25, 1857. The written description for this guitar is close to a style 34 guitar in description but the guitar has an ivory instead of a pearl sound hole.

At this point C. F. Martin must have considered his business dealings with Dodge to be at an end ,and Dodge never did get the Martin dealership he wanted so badly.

Additionally, Dodge bought a 1-30 guitar with ivory friction pegs from Martin in December 1853. The engraving in Figure 142 appears to show that guitar.

1862 Martin 2-65 Guitar

A Martin 2-65 guitar was shipped to C. Reichenbach on February 23, 1862. The day book records this was a "f. g." (fine guitar) and had a neck screw. As Reichenbach received the usual dealer discount, this was not a retail sale, so the guitar must have had a high degree of ornamentation.

1853 Martin 2-70 Guitar

Colburn & Field in Cincinnati in a letter dated October 15, 1853 asked that Martin to:

"Please add to order, two of your finest finished guitars, one of them with ivory fingerboard & one of some other style."

The two guitars were shipped on December 13, 1853. One was a size 2 with a wholesale cost of $70, before an extra 5% discount. In the later Martin terminology this would have been a 2-70. It had a black neck, pearl sound hole, pearl purfling, ivory binding to the nut, one side screw, neck screw and came with a cedar case. There is also an indecipherable note possibly related to the type of bridge. The case was probably part of the reason for the high cost.

The other guitar was a size 2½ with a wholesale cost of $42. Like the guitar above it had a black neck, pearl sound hole and pearl purfling and ivory binding but differed in having an ivory fingerboard, two side German silver screws and an ivory bridge. It was supplied with a very fine black case. Except for the ivory fingerboard, this might be the prototype style 42.

Style 42 guitars were the only model regularly shown on later price lists with the screw neck.

The 1852 "Elegant" or "Lula" Guitar

There are three remarkable letters in the Martin archive related to this instrument. The following are excerpts from the three letters.

The first letter, from Peters & Sons, Cincinnati, Ohio, is dated October 12, 1852:

"N. B. Please write us at Cin(cinnati) the cost, or supposed cost, of a Guitar of the following description:

A Guitar of the very finest make (same shape as the fine one we have on con(signment)) with rosewood inside case. The Patent Head to be of Plated Gold and end of screws etc to be pearl tiped (sic). Frets to be Gold (18 carat) and the fingerboard to be covered with pearl, instead of ebony. The man is not particular about the price but wants the best in the country."

The second letter, dated November 8, 1852, continues:

"The gentleman who wants the elegant guitar is at our elbow. He wants as good a guitar as you can make for $100 wholesale. The head to be patent head – the metal part of the head to be galvanized with gold. The frets to be 14 carat gold – worth 50 cts per pennyweight. The spaces between the frets to be made of pearl.

There must be an extra case, of rosewood, such as the one we have of yours. Also, the shape of the instrument to be the same as the one we have. Above all, the gentleman wants to know soon he can have

the instrument, as it is for a lady who is about to be married."

The third and final letter, dated November 24, 1852, further defined the specifications:

"Make the fine Guitar, with a black neck veneered with ebony. Make the sounding board or top – pale yellow.

Make the Guitar, same size as the one we have on con(signment)

Make the neck a little narrower.

It must not cost us more than $110 dollars, but the frets must be gold as we last wrote you.

You must cheapen it a little on the Rosewood case and above all, don't forget to send it away within

Figure 143
Front View of 1852 "Elegant" Guitar

Figure 144
Detail View of 1852 "Elegant" Guitar

Figure 145
Detail of "Elegant" Guitar Tuning Machines

three weeks from the receipt of our letter."

In the August 1986 issue of Guitar Player magazine is an article by George Gruhn and Suzy Newton concerning this guitar. The article identifies an interesting feature not mentioned in the letters in the Martin archive. On top of the rosewood case the name "Lula" is inlaid in script letters, probably the name of the lady who received the guitar as a wedding gift. The article suggests the material for the inlay used was brass but it is more likely that left-over gold fret wire was used for the inlaid letters. The pictures in the article were later reproduced in "Acoustic Guitars and Other Fretted Instruments" by George Gruhn and Walter Carter, pages 20 and 21.

The pictures reveal a most unusual head stock, one not seen on any other Martin guitar of the period. Using this type of machine resulted in very narrow peg head slots. Martin selected these peculiar tuning machines because the dealer specified "**the Patent head to be of plated gold**". The external mounting plates of these unusual machines would have been much easier to plate than the machines Martin normally used.

This guitar has what is commonly known as the "renaissance" shape. Until the connection could be made between this guitar and the archival material, it was a matter of conjecture as to when these guitars were made. C. F. Martin did not record this different shape in the day book but we do know from correspondence that W. C. Peters & Sons had at least one more in stock with the same "renaissance" shape. This guitar is one of the few "milepost" instruments from the period because it can be accurately dated. We now know that the "renaissance" shaped guitars were made in the period from about 1843 to 1860. (See page 52, "10-string harp guitars").

The Ledger 1852-57 records this guitar as being shipped on December 27, 1852. For some reason this guitar was not recorded in the day book, so we do have the detailed description Martin usually made in this period. Since Martin couldn't have received the last letter (dated November 24, 1852) before November 25 or 26 at the earliest, it is incredible that he was able to make such a stunning instrument in the period of only one month! The final wholesale cost of the guitar was $110.

1853 "Crystal Palace" Guitar

The most expensive presentation guitar ever made by Martin was one of the two instruments sent to the Exhibition of the Industry of All Nations, which opened in New York in July 1853.[1] This trade fair was commonly known as the "Crystal Palace" exhibition after the building constructed to house the show. The fancy guitar Martin made for the exhibition is mentioned in Martin records and correspondence as the "Crystal Palace" guitar.[2]

Martin competed in Class 30, Musical Instruments, in the exhibition and displayed two guitars. Other competitors included William Baucher (sic, should be Boucher) who displayed a banjo and a guitar and C. A. Zoebisch & Sons and Bruno & Cargill who showed guitars, as well as other types of musical instruments, in their exhibits. Napoleon W. Gould displayed an improved transposing guitar and an improved banjo. Musical instruments were displayed in Division A, Courts 7, 8 and 9 of the exhibit hall.

(Martin also exhibited guitars at the 1876 Philadelphia Exhibition. See page 332 of official catalogue. Martin competed with Charles F. Albert, Moritz Gläsel of Neukirchen, Joaquim G. Araujo of Portugal, Lemenha Lims, Vicente Arias of Spain.)

Unfortunately, Martin did not record a detailed description of this instrument, as normally done during this period, possibly because it wasn't made as part of a dealer order and was meant for exhibition purposes only. The only detail Martin recorded in the sales ledger was that it was a size 2 guitar and was supplied with a polished rosewood case.

We are able to get a little more information on the appearance of this instrument because in 1922 a customer wrote to Martin and claimed to have purchased **"the guitar that won the prize at the Crystal Palace Exposition"**. In a letter dated March 30, 1922, F. H. Martin offered the following comments:

"It is true that my grandfather, C. F. Martin Senior, made a Guitar for exhibit at the Crystal Palace Exposition. I used to hear my father (C. F. Martin Jr.) and his partner (i.e., C. F. Hartmann) tell about it and later on it came here for repairs so I remember it very well. I understand it drew first prize, but that is really immaterial because all of the old gentleman's work was so fine that there was seldom anything to compare with it. This guitar was of rosewood, small size, with a black neck, rich and fine with pearl, and if I remember right, had solid ivory veneer on the fingerboard. The tone was agreeable, but small."

This was a very fancy guitar for the period and generated considerable interest for Martin. Ossian E. Dodge, the musician and song writer, tried for several years to convince C. F. Martin to sell to him the "Crystal Palace" guitar.

Martin kept the "Crystal Palace" guitar for several years and circulated it to a number of his dealers to be displayed at local exhibitions.

C. F. Martin valued this guitar at $160 wholesale, as recorded on May 4, 1854 when it was sold to Hilbus & Hitz. From the advertisement below it can be seen that the Crystal Palace guitar was put on display at Hilbus & Hitz "for a short time" at a retail price of $250. It clearly didn't sell at that time because the "Crystal Palace" guitar was finally shipped to C. A. Zoebisch & Sons on November 15, 1859 at a wholesale price of $125.

CRYSTAL PALACE GUITAR.—We have been favored by the receipt of C. F. Martin's fine Crystal Palace GUITAR, which will be on exhibition for a short time at the Music Depot of HILBUS & HITZ. Persons wishing to inspect a very superior and masterly piece of American workmanship, will do well to call early, as the time is limited for which it will be exhibited. Price of the Guitar $250. may 8—3t

Figure 146
Hilbus & Hitz Advertisement[3] for the "Crystal Palace" Guitar

It might be suggested that the "Elegant" guitar and the "Crystal Palace" guitar are actually one in the same instrument. Fortunately, Ossian Dodge made a comment in a letter to C. F. Martin, dated September 21, 1853, that clears this up:

"I saw a beautiful guitar of your make last winter in Springfield Ohio for which the lady said she paid $150 – you probably recollect it."

Peters & Sons paid a wholesale price of $110 for the "Elegant" guitar so a retail price of $150 seems reasonable.

Since no other Martin guitar in this period would have retailed for this price, the guitar Dodge saw was undoubtedly the "Elegant" guitar discussed above. Especially since we also know the "Elegant" guitar was meant for a woman and was delivered in January 1853 to an address in Ohio. As Dodge, in this same letter, was also encouraging Martin to sell him the "Crystal Palace" guitar, the "Elegant" guitar must be a different instrument.

Notes for Chapter 7

1) See page 96 of the official catalogue of the 1853 Crystal Palace Exposition which mentions that Martin exhibited two guitars

2) See letters from Ossian Dodge dated September 21, 1853 and November 5, 1853, Colburn & Field letter dated November 28, 1853, De La Cova letter dated December 1, 1853 and Hilbus & Hitz letters dated November 15, 1854 and November 20, 1854 for comments on the "Crystal Palace" guitar.

3) Evening Star, Washington DC, May 10, 1854

Chapter 8
DATEABLE GUITARS (1834 to 1857)

Unlike Schmidt & Maul, C. F. Martin did not date his guitars. Dating of early Martin guitars is only possible using the labels in the guitars as a starting point and an understanding of the evolution of design features. However, it is possible to date a few guitars by identifying unique features recorded in the ledgers or, in a few cases, in the archival correspondence.

This list of dateable Martin guitars below is based on the latest research into Martin's early guitars. For the guitars made prior to November 1836 the sale date is based on the type of label and certain design features, although at least one guitar can be accurately dated because it can be identified in the ledger. From November 1836 Martin began to write an serial number on the label and, based on close examination of the sales records, a fairly accurate sales date can be extrapolated (with an accuracy of no more than plus or minus two weeks. See Appendix H). However, it should be noted the dating of early Martin guitars is a theory based on fairly thin evidence and may need to be altered in the light of other guitars being discovered. (Author's note: this has already happened several times since research for this book began.)

1) Guitar with type 1 label (Martin Guitar Museum collection)

Made in the first half of 1834 (Figure 147)

2) Terz guitar with type 2 label (private collection)

Made from mid-to-late 1834 (Figure 148)

Figure 147   **Figure 148**

3) Guitar with type 2 label (The Guitar Museum collection)

Made from mid-to-late 1834 (Figure 149)

4) Guitar with type 3 label (private collection) (Several other guitars are known with this label and are from the same period, Figure 150)

Made between January 1835 and September 1836.

The Martin & Schatz partnership seems to have ended by September 1836 or even a little earlier.

Figure 149   **Figure 150**

5) The cittern-shaped "Amadill" guitar with a type 3 label (Museum of Pop Culture collection)

Sold on August 8, 1836 (Figure 151)

This cittern-shaped guitar has a very unusual label. A very thin strip of paper has been pasted over the part of the label stating "pupils of the celebrated STAUFFER". This would infer that the Martin & Schatz partnership had ended when this guitar was made. The term "Amadill" is not well understood but this cittern-shaped guitar must be the Amadill guitar as no other unusual guitars were noted in the Martin ledger book during this period.

6) Guitar with a type 4 label (Museum of Pop Culture collection)

Completed in September or October 1836 (Figure 152)

This is the only type 4 label seen without a serial number. Based on the sales records, Martin probably began the serial sequence around 1100. Clearly, this guitar was made before serialization of the labels began.

Figure 151   **Figure 152**

7) Guitar with type 4 label (serial number 1114)

Completed in late November 1836. It is likely the $63 "fine" guitar sold to John F. Nunns of Philadelphia on November 24, 1836 (Figure 153)

Type 4 labels were used from some time in September 1836 until March 1837. Only one other type 4 label, serial number 1130, is known and is dateable to January 1837.

8) Guitar with type 5 label (serial number 1160)

Finished in late May or early June 1837 (Figure 154)

This guitar may be the one sold to John B. Coupa on June 28, 1837. Although it still has the Stauffer-shaped body, this guitar has the earliest known Spanish feature, in this case a 3-strut fan bracing pattern.

This guitar is from the first period of use of the type 5 label, identifiable by the endorsement "& 196 Hudson Str" that appears on the label. Serial numbers 1168, 1173, 1176 and 1188 are also known from this period (dateable to June 1837, July 1837, July 1837 and November 1837 respectively.)

| **Figure 153** | **Figure 154** | **Figure 155** | **Figure 156** |

9) Guitar with type 6 label (in private collection)

11) Guitar with type 7 label (serial number 1296)

A terz guitar of unusual shape (serial number 1231)

Finished in August 1838 (Figure 155)

A second type 6 label (serial number 1235) is known, also dateable to August 1838. A third type 6 label exists but is missing the serial number (Figure 155).

10) Guitar with type 5 label (in the Martin Guitar Museum)

Serial number 1275. Transitional Spanish-shaped guitar. Finished late February or early March 1839

This guitar was made during the second period of use when the type 5 labels no longer had the "& 196 Hudson Str" endorsement, since Martin no longer had a store at that location (Figure 156)

Another guitar is known with a type 5 label AND a Ludecus & Wolter label. It has serial number 1293 and is dateable to May 1839. At the end of May 1839 Ludecus & Wolter bought out Martin's store stock and was awarded the sales agency for New York. This must be one of the last guitars Martin made in New York.

This guitar has a Martin & Schatz AND a Ludecus & Wolter label. This nicely proves Martin & Schatz was the "manufactory" and the agency of Ludecus and Wolter in New York was for selling guitars only.

This guitar was made during the period that Ludecus & Wolter had the agency for New York (June 1839-August 1839) and, assuming Martin was able to get production going very soon after arriving in Schoeneck, it was made in late June or early July 1839. It has the transitional Spanish-shape (Figure 157).

12) Guitar with type 7 and type 8 label (serial number 1304)

This transitional Spanish-shaped instrument contains both a Martin & Schatz AND a Martin & Coupa label. This guitar provides proof that Martin & Schatz were the manufacturers and Martin & Coupa was the sales agency for Martin & Schatz guitars in New York (i.e. Coupa was not a partner in Martin's factory in Schoeneck). As the serial number is very close to the previous guitar it was likely finished in September 1839, immediately after Coupa took over the sales agency for New York (Figure 158).

| **Figure 157** | **Figure 158** | **Figure 159** | **Figure 160** |

13) Guitar with type 7 label (serial number 1341)

Finished in February 1840 (Figure 159)

It will be noted that this guitar does not have a Martin & Coupa label like serial number 1304. It was shipped from the factory to one of Martin's regular clients and was not sold out of the "depot" in New York (see appendix H).

This is the last Martin & Schatz label known. Serial number 1341 on a type 7 label suggests the second Martin & Schatz partnership only lasted from June 1839 to around February or March 1840.

14) July 1843 - Martin & Schatz "De Goni" guitar

This guitar (see Figure 160) has a type 7 Martin & Schatz label with a remarkable handwritten endorsement "**Made for Madam De Gone** (sic)".

The late usage of the Martin & Schatz label is a bit of a mystery. Possibly Coupa needed a label for making the endorsement mentioned above and it was the only type available (also suggesting Martin & Coupa labels were applied in New York). Based on comparison with the writing in letters in the Martin archive, the endorsement on the label was penned by John Coupa

himself. The fact that Coupa signed the label should not be a surprise because of his close association with both De Goñi and C. F. Martin. Madam De Goñi used several spellings of her name and "de Gone" appeared in newspaper advertisements during 1842 and 1843.

The "De Goni" Martin guitar has a number of very interesting and early features.

a) It has the early type of X-bracing.

b) The kerfing blocks are glued in individually and are particularly crude looking, being quite variable in size and widely spaced.

c) The sound hole is quite small and the sound hole design is unusual for a Martin guitar. The sound hole decoration is so understated that it is almost invisible from just a few feet away. The purfling around the top is also unusual as the black lines are more prominent than the white lines.

d) The head stock slots are quite "open". The machine tuners are stamped "Demet" not "Jerome", as often seen on early Martins. In fact, it is the only recorded example of these machines on a Martin guitar. The barrels are tapered and are made of bone. One of the tuners has been removed and it appears the machine tuners are original to the guitar. One other set of these tuners is known but are not mounted on a guitar.

e) The nut, like many early Martins, is made of nickel silver.

The Martin archive has a letter from John Coupa, dated November 29, 1849, containing the following commentary:

"I have a guitar to be repaired, it is broke in the back, can you tell me how I can send it, or if you can do it when you come in the city. It is a fine guitar, one you made for Mrs. Degoni. I had it here more than one month."

This description fits well with the current condition of the De Goni guitar which has two repaired cracks on the back. The back was removed at some point although the repair appears to be very old. The back purfling and binding match that of the top and appear to be of the same age. This would appear to be a very rare example of a repair that can be attributed to C. F. Martin Sr. himself.

The Martin & Schatz "De Goni" guitar is a remarkable historic instrument. It firmly establishes that C. F. Martin had developed an early form of X-bracing by July 1843 by following their own development path.

15) 1846 Colonel John Darragh Wilkins Guitar

One well known Martin guitar was once a possession of Colonel John Darragh Wilkins and remained in the family until quite recently. The family maintains that Colonel Wilkins received this Martin guitar upon his graduation from West Point (Figure 161).

John Wilkins was born in Pittsburgh, Pennsylvania in 1822, the son of Captain John Holmes Wilkins, U.S. Army and Mary Darragh, daughter of John Darragh, first mayor of Pittsburgh. He received his early education in Lawrenceville and was appointed to West Point in 1842.

This guitar clearly comes from the Martin & Coupa period but is lacking a label. At the time, Martin had dealers in both Pittsburgh and West Point so the guitar likely came from one of those sources. Because it was not sold out of the 385 Broadway depot it would have

received a Martin & Coupa label.

John Wilkins graduated from West Point, 46th of 59, in the storied class of 1846. Also in this class were George B. McClellan (commander-in-chief of the Union armies in 1862), Thomas J. "Stonewall" Jackson, George E. Pickett (of Pickett's Charge fame) and 17 other future generals in the Unites States and Confederate States armies.

In July 1846, John D. Wilkins joined the U.S. Army as a 2nd Lieutenant under the command of General Taylor, and was ordered to join the 4th Infantry at Matamoros, Mexico in October of the same year.

Yale University has in its possession Wilkins' "Army Chronicle". Wilkins kept this journal from 1846 to 1848 and it records some of his adventures in the Mexican War.

In 1848, during the US army withdrawal from Mexico City, Wilkins' trunk was misplaced. Another officer promised to track down the wayward trunk but Wilkins' journal is full of concern for his missing possessions. On June 9, 1848 Wilkins noted in his journal that he was hoping to **"(increase) my wardrobe which consisted of the clothes I had on and a guitar..."**. His trunk eventually caught up with him but there is, unfortunately, no more commentary on his guitar.

Wilkins included a number of small ink and wash drawings in his chronicle. One of these shows two officers playing music in a room, one on a flute and the other on a guitar.

Wilkins later fought in a number of Civil War battles, first as a Captain in the 3rd US Infantry and, after 1864, as a Major in the 15th US Infantry. The 3rd US Infantry participated in the battles of Bull Run, the Peninsula Campaign, Manassas, Antietam, Fredericksburg, Chancellorsville and Gettysburg. The 15th US Infantry, in 1864, took part in the Georgia Campaign.

The guitar case, painted in a faux rosewood finish, still bears a number of old shipping labels. One identifies Wilkins as a Lieutenant Colonel, the rank he attained in 1873 with the 8th Infantry. The other states "Colonel Wilkins" which must be from the period after 1882 when he became Colonel of the 5th Infantry, the rank he held until his retirement in 1886.

Colonel Wilkins died on February 14, 1900 in Washington DC. He and his wife, Caroline, are both buried at Arlington National Cemetery, site 794[1].

Figure 161
Colonel Wilkins (ca. 1846)
Martin & Coupa Period Guitar

16) 1852-12-27 The "Elegant" or "Lula" guitar (see pages 113 and 114)

17) 1853-07 The "Crystal Palace" guitar (see pages 115 and 116)

18) 1856-08-08 Martin 0-26 presented to Henry Worrall

On July 12, 1856, David A. Truax, a Martin dealer in Cincinnati wrote to Martin to introduce Henry Worrall:

"I take pleasure in introducing to your acquaintance my old & much esteemed friend Mr. Henry Worrall who has been long & favorably known to the music public of our city as an excellent teacher of the Guitar.

He will make known to you his business with you. Any favors shown him will be thankfully received by

Your obedient servant, David A. Truax

P. S. If you have a price list now printed of your instruments, please send it to me as I wish to make order a large supply immediately."

On August 21, 1856 Martin received a very interesting letter from Henry Worrall:

"I did not get an opportunity to see Mr. Schubert in Philadelphia though I walked all about Franklin Square hunting for him. I shall hope to meet him some other time.

From making a longer stay in Philadelphia and New York than I at first anticipated I had not time left to make a stop in Boston and therefore did not get to see Mr. Hartman. I remained near two days in Montreal and from what I could see and hear I judge the guitar is very little played there.

I arrived here last Saturday, being the finish of my summer rambles, and have commenced preparing for the writers work – on Friday last, from a previous arrangement, I stopped at Glendale and played at a concert given to a Mr. Bickerdyke, at which Mr. Jos. Posso played, also Mad. Keve and Miss Staub. Mr. Posso claims an acquaintance with you. I did not have the new guitar but borrowed Mad. Keve's which is one of your make.

The guitar arrived today by Adams & Co. express, they were leaning against the door of my room when I went there in the morning. I shall not endeavor to tell you how proud I am of that guitar or how much I thank you for it, knowing I have not words to do so. It seems the whole town knew that I was about to receive an extra instrument and from noon to 7 o'clock there must have been twenty persons who called to see it, having heard of its arrival and I have played so much that all my fingers are sore and my thumb is blistered – I am delighted.

I have not taken Miss Babbs instrument to her yet but shall do so this evening, when she will be delighted too.

Everything looks promising as regards Guitars this winter, there will be an abundance of teaching to do and I hope the guitar will "look up". Both Mr. Peters and Truax & Baldwin have succeeded in getting a better quality of strings and express a desire to keep no more bad ones, that alone will do much good.

I shall hope to see you here soon, and nothing will prevent my being entirely at your service while you remain with us.

Please present my respects to your family with the assurances that I remember my pleasant little visit to Cherry Hill."

Worrall wrote again on December 1, 1856:

"My friend Mr. Schuyler who is teaching here has requested me to write to you to make him a guitar the same as the large one you made for me, and one quite as good if possible. He would like to have it by the 1st of January if you can make it by that time. He will dispense with the screw neck as he fears the expense. I having told him that I thought it would make a difference of $10.00 in the price.

Immediately on your answer in this and stating the price for the instrument, the money will be forwarded to you in advance. Please tell me how to forward it, if by letter or otherwise. Mr. Schuyler is a young and very promising player, and wishes to "come out" in January with one of your very best instruments.

I have had several enquiries as to the price (retail) of guitars the same as mine, and have said $75.00, I guessed at it. If I am not right please correct me as I expect you will have some orders for them soon. Also please state the difference in the cost without the 'screw neck'.

I have looked anxiously for you through September and October as many others have here, I had hoped Mr. Schuyler would see you here as he wished, and have deferred writing thinking you would yet visit our city.

P. S. Mr. Schuyler being a teacher expects to get the guitar at wholesale price."

From Worrall's first letter we learn, that during the summer of 1856, he had stayed with the Martin family in Cherry Hill and that Martin had made him a special guitar. The sales ledger shows that Martin made two guitars for Worrall and one was a PRESENT! The date of this letter is only four days after Martin shipped the guitars so there is no doubt it is the same guitar, and clearly illustrates the efficiency of the U. S. rail system in the 1850's. The special guitar would be very easy to identify, if it still exists, because it is a 0-26 guitar with a neck screw. Martin presented guitars to Madam De Goni in 1843 and Henry Worrall in 1856, the only such occurrences recorded in the 19th century. Later, in 1900, William Foden was gifted a 0-42 for "professional influence".

In the second letter Worrall talks about ordering another large guitar for a musician named Mr. Schuyler. Schuyler didn't order a guitar at this time but bought two 1-26 guitars in 1860 when he was living in Buffalo. It also appears Martin was planning a trip to Cincinnati to visit Worrall.

Although little known today, Henry Worrall (1825-1902) was a gifted musician and artist. The Worrall family generously donated his photographs, music and artwork to The Kansas Historical Society but without the interest of Michael Church at the KHS and the efforts of Brian Baggett to revive the music of Worrall, Henry Worrall may have continued to languish in obscurity. This would have been a shame indeed, because of Worrall's interesting association with the Martin Guitar Co.

Worrall was born in Liverpool and later emigrated to the United States. By the 1850's Worrall was living in Cincinnati and was teaching guitar at the Ohio Female College. He also co-founded the Cincinnati Sketch Club. He published his guitar instruction book "Worrall's Guitar School" in 1856 with W. C. Peters & Sons of Cincinnati, Ohio. Worrall also published music in the 1860's with A. C. & J. L. Peters in Cincinnati and with J. L. Peters & Brother in St. Louis, Missouri. W. C. Peters was an important dealer for Martin guitars in the 1850's and 1860's. Worrall's music was still being published in the 1890's by Oliver Ditson Co. in Boston. His most famous composition,

"Sebastopol", was one of the earliest guitar pieces written for open tuning.

Worrall moved to Topeka, Kansas in 1868 where he established another career as an artist, illustrator and decorator. Among other things, Worrall designed the Kansas pavilion for both the 1876 Philadelphia Exposition and the 1893 Columbian Exposition.

Worrall died in Topeka, Kansas in 1902.

In the early twentieth century, Worrall's popular guitar instrumentals in open tunings played a key role in the development of the guitar styles of southern rural folk musicians and country and blues musical idioms.

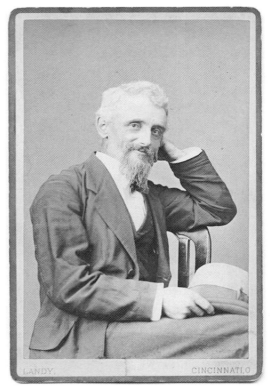

Figure 163
1870's Photograph of Henry Worrall

Figure 162
Engraving of Henry Worrall and His Guitar

Figure 164
Henry Worrall and His Wife
Playing Martin Guitars

Notes for Chapter 8

1) Obituary for Colonel John Darragh Wilkins, The Dispatch, Pittsburgh, Pa., February 20, 1900

Chapter 9
INSTRUMENT CASES AND CASE LABELS

Coffin Cases

Martin used wooden cases for their guitars during the 19th and very early 20th centuries. Until the 1887 Martin had a full-time work force of only four men. Martin made their own coffin cases when they had time but when guitar sales were brisk the making of cases was sub-contracted to farmers in the Nazareth area, who had time on their hands between the harvesting and planting seasons.

Cases were constructed of "whitewood" (poplar) and were finished with "canton" flannel lining and brass hardware. During the 1850's Martin sometimes purchased flannel material with attractive designs. Cases were painted black with a mixture of shellac and lamp black.

Martin records identify three grades of wooden (coffin) cases: COMMON, FINE and VERY FINE. A few expensive custom cases, in polished mahogany, rosewood or cedar, were also made.

Style 20 guitars and lower were supplied with common cases, style 21 could receive either a common or a fine case, styles 22 to 24 came in fine cases and styles 25 and above were sold with very fine cases.

The common cases were simple in construction and the hardware was very plain, with the hardware at the neck end of the case often only being a simple hook. Fine cases had a bolsters on the inside of the case to support the waist of the guitar and very fine cases were similar to fine cases but had better hardware.

The last year Martin regularly used coffin cases was 1898. Some wood cases appeared in inventories for a few years but each year the number decreased, and the value was progressively written down, until they disappeared around 1909.

Leather Cases

It appears that Martin bought some sample leather cases from Maulbetsch & Whittemore in 1895 but probably didn't use leather cases regularly until somewhat later.

Leather cases first appeared in the inventory of January 1, 1899, so must have been purchased at some point during 1898. Leather cases were purchased from Maulbetsch & Whittemore. Leather cases became the norm for Martin instruments through 1917. They appeared in the 1918 inventory but had virtually disappeared by 1920 (the inventory records for 1919 are incomplete). Leather cases were replaced by keratol covered hard shell cases from 1918 although leather cases still appeared on Martin's price lists until 1922 and were still special ordered, at the request of customers, until at least 1927.

Economy Cases

At different times Martin offered three different types of economy cases for their instruments.

Canvas Cases

Canvas cases first appeared in 1899 and continued in use until they were replaced by duck cases in 1904. Some canvas cases appeared in the 1905 inventory but were gone by 1906. Canvas cases reappeared from 1928 to 1930 when they replaced duck cases. The reason for the change being that canvas cases were 25-30% less expensive than duck cases.

Duck Cases

It is not known what differentiates canvas from duck cases but Martin was careful to separate them in the inventories. In 1905 duck cases were about 30% more expensive than canvas cases. Duck cases were Martin's main economy case offering from 1905 to 1928 when, as mentioned above, they were replaced again by canvas cases.

It is likely that both the canvas and duck cases were supplied by Maulbetsch and Whittemore.

Felt Bags

The least expensive case option were simple felt bags closed with a zipper. Felt bags were about 40-50% less than a comparable duck case. Martin sold felt bags from around 1920 to 1928. It is not known what manufacturer supplied the felt bags as the Martin correspondence is mostly missing in this period.

Hard Shell Cases

Keratol Cases

Martin's first hard shell guitar cases had a keratol (imitation leather) covering over a plywood body. The first keratol mandolin case was bought in 1917 but the first keratol guitar cases weren't purchased until mid-1918. The keratol cases replaced leather cases from 1918 and was Martin's main high-quality case from 1918 to 1930. There were two different grades of cases. Regular cases were lined with flannel material while the more expensive cases were lined with "plush". All instrument cases received a " Bull's Head" brand stamp which included the initials "M" and "W".

Maulbetsch & Whittemore was acquired by A. L. Felsberg & Co. in 1920 and continued to use the

Bull's Head brand but with the initials "F" and "F", even after the company name changed to The Felsberg Co. in 1922. Harptone Manufacturing Co. bought The Felsberg Co. in 1929 and also continued to use the brand but with the initials now being "B" and "C".

Most keratol cases were supplied by Maulbetsch & Whittemore (and later Felsberg and Harptone) from 1918 to 1929 although Geib & Schaefer received some orders in 1921 and 1922 and intermittently thereafter until 1930.

Style A, B, C and D Cases

In 1928 the line of instrument cases was changed to in include four different grades, from least to most expensive: A, B, C, and D.

Canvas cases became style A in 1928 but continued to be inventoried as "canvas" through 1930. Style B cases were originally referred to as "utility" cases in

DATE	STYLE	BODY	COVERING	LINING	HARDWARE	COMMENTS
1928-1930	A	STRAWBOARD	CANVAS	FLANNEL		END-OPENING
	B	CHIPBOARD	BLACK KERATOL	FLANNEL	NICKEL	UTILITY, SIDE-OPENING
	C	THREE-PLY WOOD	BLACK KERATOL	FLANNEL	NICKELED BRASS	SIDE-OPENING
	D	THREE-PLY WOOD	BLACK KERATOL	SILK PLUSH	NICKELED BRASS	SIDE-OPENING
JULY 1931	A	STRAWBOARD	CANVAS	FLANNEL		END-OPENING
	B	CHIPBOARD	BROWN ALLIGATOR GRAIN KERATOL	FLANNEL	NICKEL	SIDE-OPENING
	C	THREE-PLY WOOD	BLACK SEAL GRAIN KERATOL	PADDED DUVETYN	NICKELED BRASS	SIDE-OPENING
	D	THREE-PLY WOOD	BLACK SEAL GRAIN KERATOL	SILK PLUSH	NICKELED BRASS	SIDE-OPENING
MAR. 1935	B	CHIPBOARD	BLACK OSTRICH GRAIN KERATOL	FLANNEL		CHAIN STITCHED EDGES, KERATOL BOUND, STRING POCKET
	C	THREE-PLY WOOD	BLACK SEAL GRAIN KERATOL	DUVETYN FELT	NICKELED BRASS	SIDE-OPENING
	D	THREE-PLY WOOD	BLACK SEAL GRAIN KERATOL	SILK PLUSH	NICKELED BRASS	SIDE-OPENING
JULY 1937	B	CHIPBOARD	BLACK OSTRICH GRAIN KERATOL	FLANNEL		CHAIN STITCHED EDGES, KERATOL BOUND, STRING POCKET
	C	THREE-PLY WOOD	BLACK SEAL GRAIN KERATOL	DUVETYN FELT	NICKELED BRASS	SIDE-OPENING
	D	THREE-PLY WOOD	BLACK SEAL GRAIN KERATOL	PADDED RAYON SILK PLUSH	NICKELED BRASS	SIDE-OPENING
AUG. 1938	B	CHIPBOARD	BLACK OSTRICH GRAIN KERATOL	FLANNEL		CHAIN STITCHED EDGES, KERATOL BOUND, STRING POCKET
	C	THREE-PLY WOOD	BLACK SEAL GRAIN KERATOL	DUVETYN FELT	NICKELED BRASS	SIDE-OPENING
	D	THREE-PLY WOOD	BLACK SEAL GRAIN KERATOL	PADDED RAYON SILK PLUSH	CHROME PLATED	SIDE-OPENING
JULY 1940	A	FIBERBOARD	BROWN SHARK GRAIN KERATOL	FLEECE		SIDE-OPENING
	B	PROTEX FIBERBOARD	BLACK OSTRICH GRAIN KERATOL	PURPLE FLANNEL	NICKEL PLATED	SIDE-OPENING
	C	PLYWOOD	BLACK KERATOL	PADDED PURPLE FLANNEL	CHROME PLATED	SIDE-OPENING
	D	HEAVY PLYWOOD	FINE BLACK KERATOL	PADDED GREEN PLUSH	CHROME PLATED	SIDE-OPENING
MAY 1948	B	LAMINATED CHIPBOARD	BLACK GRAINED KERATOL	DUVETYN	NICKEL-PLATED	SIDE-OPENING
	C	HEAVY PLYWOOD	BROWN OR BLACK KERATOL	PADDED DUVETYN	NICKEL- PLATED	SIDE-OPENING
	D	HEAVY PLYWOOD	BROWN OR BLACK KERATOL	PADDED PLUSH	POLISHED NICKEL-PLATED	SIDE-OPENING
JULY 1949	B	LAMINATED CHIPBOARD	BLACK GRAINED KERATOL	DUVETYN	NICKEL- PLATED	SIDE-OPENING
	C	HEAVY PLYWOOD	BLACK KERATOL	PADDED DUVETYN	NICKEL- PLATED	SIDE-OPENING
	D	HEAVY PLYWOOD	GRAINED BLACK KERATOL	PADDED PLUSH	POLISHED NICKEL-PLATED	SIDE-OPENING

Notes: 1) Dates and descriptions are from the Martin case price lists
2) Only dates when description changes occurred are shown
3) The descriptions from July 1949 lasted until at least May 1957

Table 10
Design Features of Style A, B, C and D Cases

the 1928 to 1930 inventories.

The flannel-lined keratol cases and the plush-lined keratol cases became Styles C and D respectively. Table 10 details the features of the various styles of cases over time as per period Martin price lists.

Harptone received almost all of Martin's cases orders from 1930 to 1946 with only a few orders going to Lifton Mfg. Co. or Geib & Schaefer (Geib Inc. after 1937) , probably at customer request. Harptone remained Martin's largest supplier of cases after 1946 although Geib Inc. began to get more orders. This situation lasted through 1958.

As can be seen from Table 10, Style A cases only appeared on the price lists from 1928 to 1931 and again in 1940. This is a little odd as Martin always had at least a small inventory of style A cases through to 1940. A remnant stock appeared in the inventories every year until 1946, although in decreasing quantities and with the cost being written down each year.

Series 200 and 400 Cases

The 200 and 400 series of cases were introduced in 1959 and were the standard to 1965, when the detailed records end. The differences between the two grades of cases is not documented but Series 400 cases were about 3 times the cost of Series 200 cases. Table 11 is included to show the numbering system for cases of various types of instruments.

SERIES 200 AND 400 CASES		
SIZE	CASE #	CASE #
5	205	405
TENOR	209	409
0	210	410
UKULELE	212	412
CONCERT UKULELE	213	413
TENOR UKE	214	414
TIPLE	215	415
BARITONE UKE	216	416
00	220	420
FLAT MANDOLIN	225	425
000	230	430
CARVED MANDOLIN	235	435
D	240	440
ELECTRIC	245	445

Table 11
Numbering System for Series 200 and
400 Instruments Cases

With the introduction of the series 200 and 400 cases in 1959, Martin increased the number of suppliers. Prior to 1959 Harptone received the lion's share of the orders and Geib Inc. the remainder. From 1959 the orders were about evenly split between Harptone, Geib and a new supplier, I. Silber & Son. Harptone supplied mostly series 400 guitar cases, Geib a mixture of series 200 and 400 guitar cases while I. Silber & Son sold mostly series 200 guitar cases as well as ukulele, tiple and mandolin cases.

Much useful information on vintage guitar cases is available at: www.stevekirtley.org/vintagecases.htm

Case Labels

Early Case Labels - 1840 to 1850

A few Martin & Coupa guitars have been seen that have a label tacked to the inside of the case. There are three distinct types, all showing the depot location at 385 Broadway.

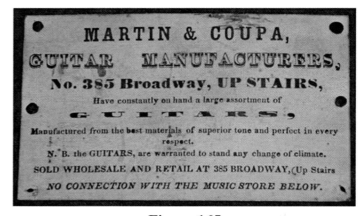

Figure 165
TYPE A Case Label

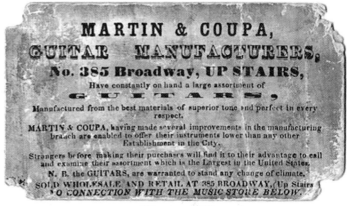

Figure 166
TYPE B Case Label

Figure 167
TYPE C Case Label

It appears the Type B and C labels were used after the Type A label because they both note "**improvements in the manufacturing branch**" in the body of the text. This closely matches an advertisement placed in the Baltimore Olio of February 1850 (see Figure 168) which describes Martin "enlarging his factory".

Since Martin purchased "cards" along with the Type 4 and Type 5 "papers" (i. e., labels), it is possible these cards could be found affixed to the inside pre-1840 guitar cases, although none have been seen to date.

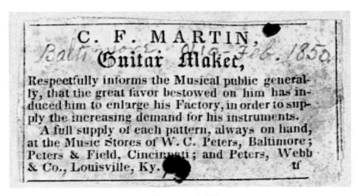

Figure 168
Advertisement for C. F. Martin Guitars in February 1850 Edition of "The Baltimore Olio"

No case labels have been seen in the period from 1850 to 1867, which is a little surprising since Martin carefully added labels to all guitars cases after 1867.

Later Case Labels - 1867 to 1898

Martin used at least five different types of cases labels in the period from 1867 to 1898.

Due to the scarcity of dated guitars from this period there are gaps in the periods of use for some of the case labels. It is also possible more types of labels may be discovered. The case labels and periods of use listed below are therefore offered as a starting point for further study. The periods of use shown below are from guitars that can dated with some accuracy or are dated underneath the top.

Martin used coffin cases until 1898, at which time they were replaced with leather cases.

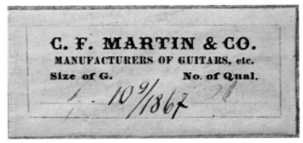

Figure 169
TYPE 1 Case Label
Period of Use: 1867-1873?

Most guitars from this period are not dated so it may be difficult to expand the range of use without finding guitars with unique features that are dateable. Fortunately, this particular label is dated.

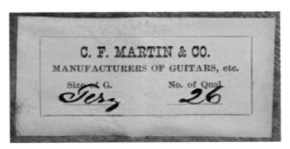

Figure 170
TYPE 2 Case Label
Period of Use: 1875? to 1886

Most guitars from this period are also undated. The early period of use can be estimated because the label above is associated with a 5-26 guitars. Only two were made, one in 1875 and one in 1877. By 1886, many most guitars were dated so the last years of use can be determined.

Figure 171
TYPE 3 Case Label
Period of Use: 1887 to 1888

Most guitars from this period are dated. So far, only guitars dated 1887 and 1888 have been seen with this label.

Figure 172
TYPE 4 Case Label
Period of Use: 1889 to 1893

All guitars from this period are dated. This type of label was used from 1889 to 1893.

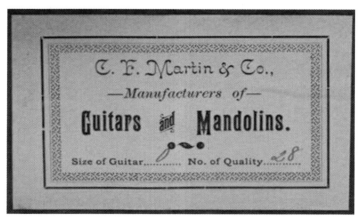

Figure 173
TYPE 5 Case Label
Period of Use: 1895-1898
Latest date seen: May 22, 1898

Chapter 10
SERIAL NUMBERS

Serial Numbers

In the period from late 1836 to early 1840 Martin wrote serial numbers on the various labels then being applied to guitars (see Chapter 6). Serial numbers between 1114 and 1341 have been encountered in existing instruments. It is estimated that this sequence of serial numbers started at around 1100 but the significance of this number is unknown. Between 1834 and late 1836 Martin made approximately 200 guitars and roughly another 240 guitars from later 1836 to early 1840.

A number of early Martin guitars are known with a serial number hand-written on the paper label glued inside the guitar. Two of these numbers has been seen on type 4 labels (No. 1114 and No. 1130), seven on type 5 labels (No. 1160, No. 1168, No. 1173, No. 1176, No. 1188, No. 1275 and No.1293), two on type 6 labels (No. 1231 and No. 1235) and three on type 7 labels (No. 1296, No. 1304 and No. 1341). Five of the type 5 labels, No. 1160, No. 1168, No. 1173, No. 1176 and No. 1188, have a hand written endorsement **"& No. 196 Hudson Str"** added to the bottom of type 5 labels and are from the first period of use of that label. Serial numbers 1275 and 1293 on type 5 labels are from the second period of use.

Inventory Numbers

Starting May 1, 1838 inventory numbers were also recorded in the ledger for a variety of musical instruments, although this system only seems to have been used for about 6 weeks. These inventory numbers may designate stock in which Bruno had no investment. Sales of this stock would accrue to C. F. Martin and not the Martin & Bruno partnership. This is confirmed by a number of entries for monies received for guitars sold before the partnership, monies in which Bruno had no share.

The problem with this theory is that the inventory numbering system was used for such a short period of time. C. F. Martin had a large inventory of musical instruments of various kinds at the beginning of the Martin & Bruno partnership and sales were not brisk enough in 1838 to significantly reduce the inventory

in only 6 weeks. On the other hand, we know that shipments from T. F. Merz to "Martin & Bruno" were made in June and August 1838. If Bruno paid for all or part of these shipments maybe his investment was considered equivalent to that of C. F. Martin. Or, possibly, sales were so poor the partnership was already failing and Bruno had just become an employee. Unfortunately, the answers to these questions will probably never be known.

On August 16, 1838 a "Spanish guitar Inv. No. 450, $35.00" was sold, the only guitar in the sales ledger recorded with an inventory number. The price suggests it was a Martin-made instrument.

Early Serial Numbers (1836 to 1840)

During the period from November 1836 to May 1839 production averaged a little less than 6 guitars per month. By comparing the range of known serial numbers with actual sale figures, it appears that serial number 1114 was made in November 1836. Since 11 guitars were sold in October 1836 it is likely that 1100 was the first serial number and, therefore, serialization began sometime in September 1836. It is not known why 1100 would have been chosen as the starting point for serialization. A total of forty-six guitars were sold between October 1836 and March 1837. Allowing for a few guitars made in September 1836, the full range of type 4 labels should probably be from 1100 to around 1149.

The ledger expenses show that type 5 labels were printed in early April 1837. Since the type 5 labels were likely put into service immediately, the first serial number for this type should be around 1150. Five of the type 5 labels (serial numbers 1160, 1168, 1173, 1176 and 1188) and all have **"& No. 196 Hudson str"** handwritten on the label to reference the two Martin locations at 212 Fulton Street and 196 Hudson Street. Based on the actual sales figures, serial number 1160 was made in May 1837, 1168 in June 1837 and serial numbers 1173 and 1176 were made in July 1837. Using the same logic serial number 1188 was made in November 1837. It is known that Martin stopped selling at the 196 Hudson Street story in early June 1837 but it is not clear why "**& No. 196 Hudson str**" continued to be written on the labels until well into 1838, unless the Martin family continued to live at 196 Hudson or C. F. Martin continued to use it as a work shop. Assuming the type 5 labels continued to be used until late April 1838, the full range of the first period of use for type 5 labels is probably from 1150 to about 1215.

Three guitars with type 6 labels are known although only serial numbers 1231 and 1235 are known. The third type 6 label is damaged and the serial number is unreadable. Continuing the logic described above, serial numbers 1231 and 1235 were both made in August 1838. Based on the ledger entries, it appears Martin & Bruno partnership may have ended in September 1838, even though Bruno continued to keep up the ledger until late in November 1838. Assuming the partnership ended in September 1838 the full range of serial numbers for the Martin & Bruno period should be from about 1216 to 1242. If, on the other hand, the partnership continued to November the range would be extended to serial number 1261, since 19 guitars were sold in October and November 1838. Only the appearance of guitars with serial numbers from this range will be able to test the theory above.

After the termination of the Martin & Bruno partnership C. F. Martin returned to using type 5 labels. The second period of use of the type 5 label covers the remaining period of time C. F. Martin spent in New York (i. e. September 1838 to May 1839). These labels do not display the "**& No. 196 Hudson str**" endorsement, as Martin's retail store had no further connection with the old location. The two guitars known from this second period of use have serial numbers 1275 and 1293. Serial number 1275 was made in March 1839 while serial number 1293 must come from the very end of Martin's tenure in New York in late May or early June 1839. It is estimated that 32 guitars were made between December 1838 and the end of May 1839 so the full range of serial numbers for the second period of use of the type 5 labels should be from about 1262 to 1293. This fits very well with the actual sale records and Martin's move to the Nazareth area because the next serial number (1296) is on a type 7 label and must have been made in Schoeneck!

See Appendix H for a graphic timeline of the serialized guitars made between 1836 and 1840.

Assuming serial number 1114 was made in November 1836 and serial number 1293 was made in May 1839, guitar production was about 179 instruments over 31 months or a little less than 6 guitars per month. This fits very well with the sales recorded in the ledgers. The sales for 1838 totaled only 52 guitars, although the records only cover as far as November that year. The records for 1839 are very spotty and incomplete so production may have been curtailed somewhat during C. F. Martin's move to Millgrove in June 1839, but only for the duration of the move. C. F. Martin and Henry Schatz re-established a business relationship at this time and Martin's nephew C. F. Hartman son arrived from Saxony in 1839. With some help from C. F. Martin Jr., who was 14 at the time, Martin would have re-established production immediately. Although Martin didn't buy his house in Cherry Hill until December 1839, it is now known he rented part of a farm house in Schoeneck in April 1839 with an "old shop". The "old shop" is still in existence and was once a blacksmith's forge. Therefore, in June 1839, Martin had a shop and a work force, and was in a position to begin make guitars immediately.

Whatever the reasons for the inventory numbering system mentioned above, none of the serial numbered labels were ever recorded in the Martin sales ledgers with the following exceptions.

At the back of the Ludecus & Wolter Inventory List from 1839 are entries for two guitars identified by serial number, although they do not appear to be part of the inventory sold by Martin. The two guitars are:

No. 1287 Rosewood guitar, Hamburg purfling & ivory binding, "oak leaves" and ivory in the sound hole, black neck with ivory binding, very fine Vienna machines with a black head, shield bridge with a "flower", valued at $40

No. 1288 Zebrawood guitar, Hamburg purfling & ivory binding, "oak leaves" and ivory in the sound hole, black neck with ivory binding, fine Vienna machines with a black head, shield bridge with a "flower", valued at $31

These two serial number fall between serial numbers 1275 and 1293 discussed above. If either of these two guitars is ever uncovered it will likely be found with a type 5 label from the second period of use (without the "& No. 196 Hudson str" endorsement).

The last three serial numbers, 1296, 1304 and 1341, are found on type 7 (Martin & Schatz) labels. The guitar with serial number 1296 contains a "Ludecus and Wolter" label and, being so close to serial number 1293, must come from June 1839. The guitar with serial number 1304 has both the type 7 **AND** a type 8 Martin & Coupa and, assuming Martin was able to re-establish guitar production in Schoeneck quickly, was made around September 1839. The last serial number known is 1341, and since the Martin & Schatz partnership ended in early 1840, must be one of the last guitars made during the partnership.

As only nine instruments separate serial numbers 1296 and 1304, the Ludecus & Wolter agency for New York was not a success and lasted only from May to August 1839. Clearly, Martin could make more guitars in his new shop than Ludecus & Wolter could sell and C. F. Martin decided to award the sales agency for New York to John B. Coupa, a move that was a great success during the decade of the 1840's.

However, to add further to the confusion, Martin kept another numbering system for guitars for a brief period of time. At the back of the inventory purchases ledger for 1837 and 1838 is a list of 48 guitars brought into stock in 1837, numbered consecutively from 1 to 48. Many of these numbers were recorded in the sale ledgers. Most were sold between April 1837 and January 1838.

Martin sold a total of 91 guitars in 1837 of which 27 were German-made. The inventory numbers were applied to the guitars as they entered stock and, therefore, cannot be strictly considered serial numbers.

1840 to 1898

From 1840 to 1898 Martin did not use serial numbers although, at times, dates were written under the top of guitars in pencil or blue crayon. The earliest guitar seen with a date is from 1874. It wasn't until the mid-1880s that most guitars were dated. Dates usually appear in the form "5/1888" (for May 1888) or "3/93" (for March 1893).

Many guitar, especially in the 1890's, were also initialed by Frank Henry Martin, although other initials

are known. The dating of tops continued up to 1916 or, possibly, early 1917 but the practice ceased during 1917 with the huge increase in production as a result of the ukulele craze. Frank Henry Martin simply didn't have the time to personally examine each instrument top.

SERIAL NUMBERS FOR MANDOLINS

Martin did not begin to regularly serialize guitars until 1898, although mandolins had received serial numbers from late 1895. It appears that the idea for serial numbers was a suggestion from a dealer. In a letter dated November 1, 1895 C. F. Albert of Philadelphia made a number of useful suggestions concerning construction details and decoration of Martin's new mandolins and added a reminder in a post script:

"Do not forget to number the mandolins."

The first 55 mandolins did not receive serial numbers but by late October 1895 Martin began serializing their mandolins. Why Martin did not apply serial numbers to guitars until January 1898 is a mystery.

SERIAL NUMBERS FOR GUITARS

The first guitar serial number recorded in the foreman's notebook was 8119 from January 19, 1898 although the style of guitar was not noted. The foreman always noted the serial number of the last instrument serialized on a specific date, so several other guitars from that date were also serialized. This is confirmed by the fact that the earliest serial number in the sales ledger is 8116, a style 1-21 guitar.

Even earlier serial numbers probably exist because the archive contains repair records for a 00-21 with serial number 8008.

The "**SALES 1898-1913**" ledger book begins in August 1898. Serial numbers were recorded for most guitars from that point. The first serial number recorded was 8086, a 0-28. The 1898 ledger contains records of a number of guitars sold without serial numbers that must have been in stock before serialization began.

It was suggested by Mike Longworth that the earliest serial number was Martin's estimate of the number of guitars they had made prior to 1898. However, close examination of the sales records shows that about 8,300 guitars were made between 1867 and mid-1898. To this figure must be added the estimated 440 guitars made in New York between 1834 and 1839 and the estimated 5,500 guitars made between 1840 and 1867 for a total of about 14,240 guitars. See Appendix G for the estimate of guitar production between 1834 and 1898.

Mike Longworth noted that the old "**C. F. Martin New York**" stamp continued to be used in guitars with serial numbers 8116 to at least 8129. Serial number 8129 was stamped on February 12, 1898 so the "**C. F. Martin Nazareth PA**" stamp was not put into use until at least a month after serial numbers were first used.

The introduction of serial numbers was not without its issues. Control of the allocation of serial numbers in the factory must have been an area of confusion, because a number of duplicate serial numbers exist, the most famous example being the two 1901 00-42S guitars known to exist with serial number 9372. About 280 duplicate serial numbers appear in the ledgers from 1898 to 1927. There is even one triplicate serial number! In 1922, serial number 17461 appears to have been used on one 2-17 and two 0-28 guitars (It may be suggested the two 0-28 guitars are the same guitar sold at two different times. However, in this case, the two guitars were sold to two different branches of Rudolph Wurlitzer Co. within 11 days of each other so are likely two separate guitars). Most duplicate serial numbers occurred between 1919 to 1923 when Martin was ramping up production to meet increased demand. It is easy to understand how simple it would be to duplicate some serial numbers in a busy factory environment.

A few gaps also exist in the records where serial numbers went unallocated or at least went unrecorded.

Martin had separate serial numbers sequences for early ukuleles and guitars made for the "C" line of customer branded instruments.

Martin had separate serial numbers for:

1) Mandolins from 1896

2) Ukuleles in 1916 (serial numbers 1-141)

3) Ditson guitars 1916-1921 (serial numbers 1-571)

4) Ditson mandolins in 1916 (serial numbers 1-44)

5) Ditson ukuleles in 1916 (serial numbers 1-167)

6) Southern California Music Co. guitars 1916-1918 (serial numbers 1-262)

A number of instruments made for other firms did not receive serial numbers at all:

1) Bacon Banjo

2) Beltone (Perlberg & Halpin)

3) Foden (later Foden Specials did have regular Martin serial numbers)

4) S. S. Stewart (Buegeleisen & Jacobson)

5) Stetson (Dyer Brothers)

Chapter 11
MANDOLINS

EARLY BOWL-BACK MANDOLINS 1895-1897

Little information has been previously published to explain why Martin entered the mandolin market in the 1890's. Longworth simply noted that Martin started producing mandolins in 1895 but, from the examination of correspondence, it is clear Martin had been aware of the mandolin craze for at least several years. A letter from Zoebisch dated October 6, 1892 lists prices of various types of mandolins, probably in response to a question from Martin on current market pricing of mandolins.

However, Martin had already been gaining experience with mandolins as they repaired one for Charles Loag in 1890 and on June 30, 1893 Zoebisch ordered 500 very fine mandolin tops from Martin, possibly for Fairbanks Banjo Co. who also produced mandolins.

In 1893 Martin started collecting information on mandolin designs and sought advice from mandolin dealers, players and teachers. This accelerated with the sharp drop off in guitar sales as a result of the Panic of 1893.

Zoebisch Advises– "Don't make mandolins"

I a letter dated September 16, 1893 Zoebisch promised to send a mandolin, "**one of an Italian maker**". Zoebisch followed up with another letter on September 21 with some intelligence on "**that Mandoline maker**" and mentioned the low price of his instruments and the large number of Italians already making mandolins.

In another letter on September 23, Zoebisch sought to discourage Martin from making mandolins by stating:

"**I wouldn't bother with Manolines, won't pay you, there are too many Italians & Swedes here who make them very cheap & good & the demand for them is falling off.**"

Zoebisch billed Martin for two sets of mandolin patent heads on December 27, 1893 so Frank Henry Martin was clearly not listening to Zoebisch's advice. In effect Frank Henry had no choice but to pursue

mandolin production. Guitars sales had collapsed due to the Panic but there was still strong demand in the market for mandolins.

INTERESTING CORRESPONDENCE

On January 11, 1894 George Flora, director of the Orpheus Concert Company in Philadelphia, sent a letter to Martin with some interesting information:

"**Your postal (i. e., post card) of the 10th at hand and in reply would recommend you to Mr. Henry M. Straton 141 N. 8th St. who I am satisfied will give you terms and prices that will be all right for guard plates & machine heads. He is the gentleman with whom I'm located and I know he will do the right thing by you for he wholesales quite extensively.**

How are the new mandolins coming on? Hope you will be successful. ..."

From this letter, and the fact that Zoebisch had supplied mandolin components as mentioned above, it can be assumed that Martin was making prototype mandolins by the beginning of 1894. Flora also appended a sketch of a mandolin top and some dimensions.

Flora followed up with another letter on May 9, 1894:

"**Mr. Morris W. Fenner, formerly of your place, informed me you have made some mandolins. I want to get a new instrument and if I can get you to make me one at a satisfactory figure and it will give as good satisfaction as your guitars I ask for no more. Can you refer me to anyone who has used one of your mandolins or have you any in stock? I expect to be in Nazareth before long, probably with Mr. Fenner, and will call and see you. Can you give me an idea for what you would make me up a good instrument? ...**"

Flora borrowed an early mandolin from Martin and offered some feedback in his letter of October 11:

"**How are you progressing with the new mandolin.**

I have been using the one you loaned me but the E and A strings don't seem to give perfect satisfaction, that is, they sound more or less harsh and woody beside the D & G. The 2 lower strings are all one could desire – but the upper one- instead of improving seem to get worse. I wish you could remedy the defect in some way. If you could - I could get the party I'm with (Mr. Straton) to take the exclusive in Phila. – and he's a hustler."

Apparently, Martin made a final decision to start manufacturing mandolins as Flora commented in his letter of October 13, 1894:

"Am pleased to learn of your determination re making the Mandolins. ..."

Flora acknowledged in a letter dated November 13:

"Your letter and Mandolin rec'd. I will give the mandolin a thorough test and report in the course of a few days. I have been making some observations on the Wyman (Keystone State) instrument and will write you full particulars in a few days."

The new Martin mandolin did not meet Flora's expectation as noted in his follow up letter of November 21:

"With further reference to yours of recent date re the mandolin will say – I have made a through test and am very sorry but it does not meet the requirements.

First – While the dimensions are all right – the shape is not at all desirable – being a little too clumsy. If you remember - the Washburn I showed you was a little deeper at the lower (string) end – and did not bulge so much at the sides. However, this is a very slight objection and can very easily be remedied.

Re the neck – while it is a little heavy – that is another difficulty easily overcome. I would prefer a thin neck. Now – re the next important - the tone - would say the D & G strings are very good – a singing sensation of the strings that you speak of is a good quality. The E & A strings are too harsh– having a woody tone. While the tone is very good it does not by any means compare favorably with a

Washburn or Keystone State. If you can make a mandolin in which the E & A are sweet – mellow- and at the same time penetrating and clean and devoid of that woody tone- your mandolin is a complete success. The D & G strings now are a vast improvement over some of the world or first class makes and as far as they go, are entirely satisfactory. Of course the model may have considerable to do with the tone. I note that all the good instruments come to more (or less) a tapering point where the neck joins the body (on the face) – and that they all seem to have that peculiar bulge or hump on the bottom opposite the sound hole about which you made the remark 'you thought that would not improve the tone'. Do you recollect that I refer to? If I could only see you - I could readily explain what I mean.

I enclose dimensions of a $60 Keystone State which I took. I notice in this they have a sort of dark brown shellac or something inside to bring it together and only have the face braced. It seems they are as yet experimenting as I have seen 2 or 3 different styles of making them. Then again – the size and shape of the sound hole may make a difference in the tone – producing that woody tone – as I have noticed all the instruments with a round sound hole are more or less harsh and are only made in cheap mandolins.

If you have occasion to come to (City) in the near future I'll be pleased to arrange to get and show you just exactly what I mean. It might possibly be an advantage to you. I would like your mandolin to be a complete success and can see no reason at why they can't be. The distance of the strings apart is all right. Just makes it nice to play. I will have the instrument boxed and returned to you in a day or 2 – or if you expected to some down soon – will keep it and we can then compare with other makes and notice the differences."

On October 8, 1894 W. B. Hornberger of Philadelphia sent some interesting intelligence on Griffith instruments and a connection with Beitel:

"Griffith & Co. are now located on 11th St. and are now pushing the sales of their own Mandolins and Guitars. The factory is located there. Mr. Beitel of Easton made them a sample Concert Guitar to sell at $38. I tried it, but could not say the tone was anywhere near as good as your make. The finish was very nice though. A little darker than yours and ornamented slightly different. The bridge was made of inferior wood too. Between you and I, I have heard that Griffith wanted to have him in their factory, or else take his whole output of Guitars and name them The Griffith. Haven't heard since what he intended to do."

Hornberger offered some more comments on in his letter of October 27:

"Am glad to hear you are going to make mandolins. See no reason why it should not be a success. There is a Mandolin by H. Zoerner sold here by Wanamaker and also Cutallis that for finish and tone beats the Washburn, Bruno and others all hollow. The prices seem reasonable too. I think you would like the model too. Don't know who supplies the trade. ... I have been writing for Catalogues of Mandolins & Guitars and have now a few. If you would care I could send them to you and when through you could return them again.

I think you would like this Zoerner Mandolin and am sorry I haven't one to show you. Of course, I am no judge, but my eye gets them occasionally. I know several players that speak well of it. One said 'It's the best mandolin on the market to-day'."

Note: Cutallis mentioned above is probably Prof. B. Cutillo who had a musical/photographic studio at 715 South 9th St. in Philadelphia

Hornberger continued to provide intelligence on the mandolin market in his letter of January 6, 1895:

"You are in all probability waiting for the retail price list of the Zoerner mandolins and I am very sorry I can not furnish you with the same. From what I can learn Geo. Bauer takes a great deal of the output of the factory and sells them as Bauer Mandolins. He buys them in a rough state and finishes them at his place on Chestnut St. They are very nice looking and he tells me he is doing very well, but of course he didn't say they were Zoerner mandolins. I have learned that elsewhere. He also handles a nice Guitar. I told you of them. His

mandolins run from $12 up and Guitars from $20 up. He told me he couldn't fill his orders for Guitars, had too many.

Stewart's last Journal devotes a lot of space to Bauer's instruments. Prof. Cutillo used to work for Zoerner and now handles his mandolins and teaches too. He buys them unfinished and puts the heads on and files the frets, etc. Prices run anywhere from $20 to $50. Prof. Fleishaner buys them finished and sells them as his only, great and wonderful mandolins. He has many pupils and I guess he does well. So you can see how the thing is worked. I saw some of the Griffith mandolins in the window several weeks and they were nicely inlaid and finished. I guess he does pretty well."

Hornberger followed up with another letter on March 26, 1895 listing music dealer and the instruments they handled:

"Yours to hand and will try and give you what information I can:

Ditson & Co. - Bay State Mandolins and Guitars

Griffith & Co. - Griffith Mandolins and I think also some of the Bruno make

Albert & Sons - Washburn Mandolins and Guitars. Carries nice lines too.

Weyman & Sons Manufactures the Keystone State Mandolins and Guitars and also retails them at three of their stores

Staton's Sell Keystone State as do quite a number of the smaller stores

The three first on the list are about the most prominent stores. Griffith is pushing his own mandolins very hard now. It's a nice one too.

When I see you again, I will try and tell you all I know in regard to the different dealers. The Mandolin & Guitar Clubs have been more prominent here this season than the Banjo. The mandolin is very much the "craze" now and I think you will get on the market at a favorable season. Of course the contest probably had something to do with it.

Stewart says 'create a demand for your (S. S. Stewart Banjos) goods by having contests' and I guess he's about right."

Throughout 1895 Martin continued to seek feedback on their mandolins as well as collect intelligence on dealers in particular markets (as mentioned elsewhere in this book Martin had to seek other outlets for their instruments as a result of the Panic of 1893). In particular, Martin corresponded with Charles F. Albert of Philadelphia, J. M. Holland (son of Justin Holland) in New Orleans, Joseph Flanner of Milwaukee, Chicago Music Co. and several smaller dealers.

In a letter dated May 13, 1895, Charles F. Albert offered the following comments on Martin mandolins:

"After thoroughly examining the mandolins you sent me, I find the workmanship very nice although there is not quite enough fancy work for the price. Now, in the first place, the necks are about ¼ of an inch too wide, and are filled (sic) the shape of a Guitar neck which is wrong. Also, the machine head is at least ½ or ¾ of an inch too wide, as you would find very few mandolin cases with which you could put your instrument as they now are. The tone is very good but I can get cheaper instruments fully as good. There is room for improvement, I think, and I do not wish to be understood as finding fault. ..."

J. M. Holland had some interesting comments on New Orleans instrument dealers in his letter of May 17.

"I just opened the box and was very pleased with the appearance of the instrument, for which I thank you very much. I had already spoken to Mr. Grunewald about the matter and in the morning shall send it to be displayed in his window, and will send my friends there to examine it. There are really only three stores here, The Grunewald Co. Ltd., Philip Werlein and Junius Hart. The Grunewalds are very well off, own their own and several other stores on the principal business street of the city, as well as a large hotel and considerable residence property. They have the agency for Steinway, Knabe, Sohmer, Fischer and other pianos, and do a very large business. Werlein has a store of finer appearance because of very recent

modern build, but he does not own it, and in addition to the current report that he is losing his mind, ill luck seems to pursue him for every once in a while he is burned out. He has a minister in charge of the store, and I do not like the way things are run. He does not own his business place, and the Lyon & Healy influence in the store has been strong on account of his having imported two men from the Chicago house that swear by it. Mrs. Junius Hart is attempting to run the business begun by her husband who died a year or so ago. She owns her place which, while on Canal Street, is about two squares from what is called the business center. The last two or three years of his life Mr. Hart was paralyzed, and could only in a small degree direct his business, but he had remarkable success, and from a small beginning was able in less than 20 years to leave his wife a full $100,000 dollars in property and stock. Time only can tell how she will succeed.

I think it advisable to place your mandolins for the present at least with the Grunewalds, as the best of the three stores, accepting Mr. Grunewald's assurance that your own instruments will not interfere with his as he is now making very few other than the cheap grade selling for $5 to $15. He agrees to advertise yours, and to display any placards or signs you may have as well as to distribute your price lists from his counters. He says also that he will keep a few of your wound strings in stock, and make a specialty of offering them to persons asking for good strings. He told me that he would also order one each of the other styles so as to be able to start with a line."

In early 1895, J. M. Holland informed his friend, Joseph Flanner, that Martin was undertaking the production of mandolins. Flanner was in touch with Martin because on May 15, 1895 he wrote:

"Received your favor of the 11th inst. Note prices quoted. I certainly will expect a very fine instrument for the prices. As you know both the Washburn & Bay State are instruments well known all over the country and those are the ones we must compete with. Can buy #1 Bay State for $7.00 and #3 Bay State for $12.00. They are guaranteed to be perfect and warranted; if anything happens to them they are replaced by new instruments.

You may send me three sample as you suggest, carefully boxed by freight. If they are perfectly satisfactory, I shall take hold of them properly and if anyone can do any business with your goods, I think I can."

The three samples mentioned in the letter above were received on June 12:

"The Mandolins have arrived. I like the E3 by far the best. The tone seems good but I think you might finish the cheaper styles a little more elaborate. Kindly let me know by return mail if the price quoted in the invoice is the very best you can do for me for spot cash upon receipt of goods. I am willing to accept the exclusive agency for Milwaukee for your Mandolins. I am sorry, however, that you cannot include your guitars. Fine goods should be handles by one firm only.

You must not look for much trade during our hot season. Most people leave for the country to remain away July, August and September. We are advertising your guitars and we have a great deal of competition to contend against. There is Bauman, Washburn and there is a young man here who imports Italian mandolins in large quantities of the finest quality. I am trying to induce him to give up that business and handle the Martin guitars."

By September 11, 1895 things had worked out well enough with Charles F. Albert that he was seeking a contract for the exclusive agency for Martin mandolins in Philadelphia:

"As soon as you sign the return Contract I will send you some suggestions I wish you to observe in making me the first sample lot of mandolins, and which I think will be of advantage and greatly improve your instruments. One of the mandolins you left with me, has the neck too thin and sharp at the edges, owing to the shape being too much like a Gibson neck which makes it unhandy to play on! I would not like to start out with an instrument in this shape. What would you propose for me to do?

In the meantime until I hear from you I will make preparations to get out circulars and advertising

matter for your mandolins. Send me Electrotypes of all your styles, not alone of mandolins but of Guitars also."

On October 17 Albert wrote again:

"I have been patiently waiting for a reply from you as I wrote to you some time ago in reference to the following. I repeat herewith that your suggestions in the contract are satisfactory & I agree to the same with one exception in reference to presenting instruments for advertising purposes wholly or in part as may be found fit for the benefit of introducing the mandolins as in such cases the instrument should be delivered through the agent in his territory, please be kind enough to attach this to the contract. I have been looking for the electros but not hearing from you I will say you might send me whatever cuts you have at present which will do until you make the different changes which you might mark in course of time as I want them for advertising purposes. I herewith order the following mandolins:

1 Mandolin Style A,
One Mandolin Style B
1 Mandolin Style S1
One Mandolin Style S2

and as per your promises you might make me a fine one so I can show it as a sample. I do not care to send a larger order as we have not decided to what shape neck yet. I would suggest that you send me an unfinished mandolin which has the neck nearly dressed down with the fingerboard on it, then I could dress it myself & which would show you a great deal more than I could write , this is especially for the upper part of the neck of which I have some important information."

None of these mandolin styles were listed in Martin's first mandolin catalogue of 1896. Martin was still experimenting with and developing the styles that would be offered to the market.

Albert continued his comments in his letter of November 1:

"I herewith send you the patterns for the rounding of the bridge & fingerboard, also patterns for the heads I would like to have on the mandolins, the one for the finer mandolins I think will look well if you put some mother of pearl or some other ornament of inlaying. I also send you a gauge for the strings from the 17th fret. My son thought also that the neck on the fine mandolin which I brought with me is too large. I think that the size of the neck which I made out with you will prove all OK. Another thing I have to mention to you is that we have overseen to fix a sce(d)ule of retail prices for the Mandolins which must be on the same idea as the list you fixed for your guitars leaving the teachers and dealers discount to the option of the agent of the mandolins I will send you my idea of prices in a day or two for your approval as such prices must be fixed for you catalogue. I also return you to the bridges & hope that you will find them OK.

P. S. ... do not forget to number the mandolins."

From this letter it appears it was the suggestion of Charles F. Albert that prompted Martin to start stamping serial number in their mandolins and, by 1898, guitars.

By November 30 Martin had made some changes to their mandolins that were well received by C. F. Albert:

"The mandolins have some to hand and I am so far, well pleased with them. You got the rounding of the top and sound holes pretty good and in time you will of course improve upon them. The 'crossbar' in front, near the sound hole is not yet quite the shape I like to have done. I will send you a pattern made up in the way I mean. I also find the strings at the upper end of the finger-board lie too close together and wish you in the next instruments to lay them further apart by bringing the 3 E and G strings closer to the edge of the finger-board.

The thickness of the neck is right. Also be very careful in making the cuts in the Bridge and little saddle where the strings are to rest – so that the strings rest firm to the extreme edge of same as will be seen in the diagrams I herewith enclose as otherwise the strings will jingle. ..."

Martin had also been in contact with Chicago Music Co. in early 1895 as evidenced by their letter of February 15, 1895:

"We are in receipt of your esteemed favor of the 13th inst. and feel that with your reputation as guitar makers, your mandolins can be nothing else than a success. We would like to buy these goods from you direct and represent the manufacture in the west. ... Would like to see line of samples as soon as they are out of you think favorably of what we propose."

Chicago Music Co. acknowledged receipt of sample mandolins on May 14:

"We are in receipt of yours of the 7th inst., also the three sample mandolins.

The workmanship on these instruments is of course the same as your work always is, perfection; but we believe if you made a different model neck, your instrument would meet with more hearty approval among the best mandolin players in this city. We think the fingerboard is too wide.

There is a mandolin made in this city by Sig. Tomaso that is very popular with every one who sees it, and we think it would be a pretty good plan if you would request us to ship you one of his instruments that you may see what they are. At the present time there is no business either in mandolins or anything else, and until there is demand, we can not say how your instruments will take; but we hope with you that they will meet with the same approval that your guitars always have.

If you would like to have us send you one of the Italian instruments for examination & measurement, we will do so cheerfully."

Apparently Martin was sent a Tomaso mandolin and used it as a model as reflected in the Chicago Music Co letter of June 15:

"We are very anxious to see your new production of mandolin made on the Tomaso model, and hope for great results. We think that your fine workmanship, and the old material which you have in the way of rosewood (having been in the manufacture of guitars so long) will be the prime factors in the production of tone.

One of the mandolins which you sent us, though they are all of the same model, is very good, but the others we are sorry to say, are not as well balanced as we hoped they would be. Of course, your name will always sell an instrument, and there are people who do not know whether they are getting a good toned instrument or not, and if we should sell these we should aim to place them in the hands of such people. ..."

On October 17, 1895 Chicago Music Co. ordered a number of mandolins (two Style A1 and one each in styles B, G1, G2 and G3). As in the order above by Charles F. Albert (on the same date) several styles were ordered that did not appear in Martin's first mandolin catalogue printed in 1896. It appears from the correspondence during 1895 that Martin had originally considered producing six different models although only four, G1, G2, G3 and G5, survived to make it into the 1896 mandolin catalogue. There are no records detailing the specifications for the style A1 or B mandolins though the dealers thought they were too plain for the price quoted by Martin. From the few clues available, it appears that style A was a plain mandolin with 9 rosewood and maple ribs.

Mandolin Production 1895 to 1897						
	A[1]	G1	G2	G3[2]	G5[3]	TOTAL
1895	1	?	?	?	?	78
1896	10	?	?	5	3	89
1897	?	1	?	1	1	42
						209

The archive contains only fragmentary information for 1895-1897 although the production totals for each year are accurate.

1) Style A mandolins were not included in the 1896 mandolin catalogue even though a number were made that year
2) Sometimes later misidentified as Style 4
3) Sometimes later misidentified as Style 6

Table 12
Mandolin Production from 1895 to 1897

There is a note in a foreman's notebook from the end of 1897 stating:

"Add 55 made before Oct. 1895, make total to Jan. 1st 1898, 210"

From this we learn that Martin had made 55 mandolins before serial numbers came into use in October 1895. Martin estimated that 210 mandolins had been made to the end of 1897. The last serial number in 1897 was number 155. In order to bring the serial numbers in line with the number of mandolins produced, Martin did not use serial numbers 156 to 209 and started 1898 with serial number 210.

Martin continued to collect information on competitive mandolins and Joseph Flanner, a dealer in Milwaukee, forwarded a Mauer mandolin to Martin for examination on December 8, 1896.

The first Martin instrument catalogue was for mandolins, indicative of the importance of mandolins to the company at that time, as the guitar market had not yet recovered. This catalogue was printed by Livermore & Knight with the first batch being shipped on April 18, 1896. Four mandolins were illustrated: Styles G1, G2, G3 and G5. Interestingly, three of the four mandolins illustrated have the mounting plate of the tuning machines on the front of the headstock. Later Martin mandolins always had the mounting plate on the back of the head stock.

STYLE G 1. Rosewood, 27 ribs with continuous binder, mahogany neck and head, ebony fingerboard with pearl position dots, orange colored face inlaid at sound hole and border with purfling, pearl inlaid guard plate, fine ebony bridge, engraved German silver machine head and tail piece.

Price $28.00

Figure 174
Style G1 Mandolin from 1896 Catalogue

STYLE G 2. Rosewood, ivory
bound, 27 ribs with continuous binder,
mahogany neck and head, ebony fingerboard with pearl position dots, white face
inlaid at sound hole and border with fine colored purfling,
pearl inlaid guard plate, fine ebony bridge, engraved German
silver machine head and tail piece.
Price $33.00

Figure 175
Style G2 Mandolin from 1896 Catalogue

STYLE G 3. Rosewood, ivory
bound, 27 ribs with continuous binder,
mahogany neck and head, both bound in
ivory, ebony fingerboard with finer position
dots, white face inlaid at sound hole and border with pearl,
finely inlaid guard plate, ivory bridge, finely engraved
machine head and tail piece.
Price $40.00

Figure 176
Style G3 Mandolin from 1896 Catalogue

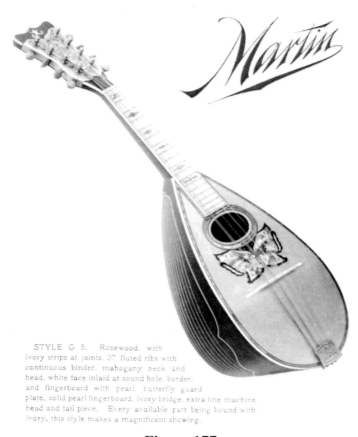

STYLE G 5. Rosewood, with
ivory strips at joints, 37 fluted ribs with
continuous binder, mahogany neck and
head, white face inlaid at sound hole, border,
and fingerboard with pearl, butterfly guard
plate, solid pearl fingerboard, ivory bridge, extra fine machine
head and tail piece. Every available part being bound with
ivory, this style makes a magnificent showing.

Figure 177
Style G5 Mandolin from 1896 Catalogue

BOWL-BACK MANDOLINS AFTER 1898

Around the middle 1898 Martin changed their line of
mandolins and increased the number of styles to 6.
The new styles appeared in Martin's 1898 catalogue.
The most obvious changes included the addition of
a decorative cut-out in the head stock and the use of
tuners that attached to the back of the head stock, with
the exception, for a time, of Style 1.

Figure 178
Mandolin Style 1 from the 1898 Catalogue

Figure 179
Mandolin Style 2 from the 1898 Catalogue

Figure 182
Mandolin Style 5 from the 1898 Catalogue

Figure 180
Mandolin Style 3 from the 1898 Catalogue

Figure 183
Mandolin Style 6 from the 1898 Catalogue

Figure 181
Mandolin Style 4 from the 1898 Catalogue

The style 1 illustration (Figure 178) shows the tuner mounting plate on the front of the head stock. A few style 1 mandolins dated from 1898 to 1900 are known with this type of machines. Style 1 was out of production during 1901 and 1902 and when the style re-appeared in the 1904 catalogue it had the same type of machines as other styles.

The following descriptions are from the 1898 catalogue plus some details provided through the examination of existing mandolins. All style 1 to 6 mandolins had rosewood bodies.

Style 1 - 18 ribs, 10 lines of black and white purfling (the middle black line and outer white line are noticeably thicker), rosewood binding, herringbone sound hole decoration, simple pick guard inlay smaller than in the illustration, pearl dot fingerboard inlays, ebony bridge, German Silver machines and tailpiece

Style 2 - 26 ribs, 10 lines of black and white purfling all the same thickness, rosewood bonding, fancy "rope" purfling for the sound hole decoration, inlaid pick guard similar to the illustration, fancy pearl inlays beginning at the 5th fret, ebony bridge, German Silver machines with pearl button, covered German Silver tail piece

Style 3 - 26 ribs, fine colored purfling (although the catalogue specifies this type of purfling, known examples have "line" purfling similar to Style 2), ivory binding, pearl sound hole decoration, inlaid pick guard similar to illustration, slotted diamond and square fingerboard inlays (5th to 15th frets), ebony bridge (although ivory bridges are known), machines and covered tailpiece like Style 2

Style 4 - 34 ribs, pearl purfling and sound hole decoration, ivory binding, fancier grade of inlaid pick guard, ebony bridge, snowflake fingerboard inlays beginning at the 5th fret, German Silver machines with pearl buttons and fine covered tailpiece

Style 5 - 34 ribs, pearl purfling, distinctive "corded" binding of pearl and tortoiseshell, pearl sound hole decoration, pick guard like Style 4, ebony bridge, fancy pearl inlay in fingerboard, machines and tailpiece like Style 4

Style 6 - 42 fluted ribs jointed by ivory, pearl purfling around top and around fingerboard extension, ivory bound body and fingerboard, pearl sound hole decoration, very fancy inlaid pick guard with pearl edge, ivory bridge, fingerboard with very fancy pearl inlay, extra fine German Silver machines and tailpiece.

Martin's fanciest mandolin, the Style 7, was introduced in 1900 but was not included in catalogues until 1904.

Style 7 - 42 fluted ribs jointed by ivory, pearl purfling around top, ivory bound body and fingerboard, ivory border around end of cap, pearl sound hole decoration, very fancy inlaid pick guard, ivory bridge, scroll design in pearl inlaid in the head and fingerboard, a narrow line of Japan pearl inlaid in cap on both sides, extra fine German Silver machines and tailpiece

At first glance a Style 7 mandolins looks much like a Style 6 model. The main difference between the two is that the Style 7 mandolin has extra wide abalone purfling around the edge and in the sound hole decoration into which is inlaid another fancy pattern in contrasting Japan pearl (Figure 184).

Figure 184
1904 Style 7 Mandolin

The level of decoration of the Style 7 mandolins, especially the head stock veneer and inlaid pick guard, evolved over time and became slightly plainer as time went on. A good example of this can be seen in the changes in Style 6 shown in Figure 185.

By 1910, the bowl-back mandolins were becoming obsolete as carved-top and flat-back mandolins began to dominate the market. Although Martin added flat-back mandolins to the line 1914, the company soldiered on with the bowl-back mandolins for quite some time. Slowly, the bowl-back models were dropped from production: Style 7 in 1917, Style 5 in 1920, Styles 4 and 6 in 1921, Style 3 in 1922 and Styles 1 and 2 in 1924. The less expensive Style 0, 00 and 000 mandolins lasted only a little longer.

Regardless of the eventual demise of the bowl-back mandolins, the sales chart for 1898 to 1915 (Figure 10) indicates how important these instruments were to Martin. For almost every year during this period mandolin production exceeded that of guitars. With sales of guitars from 1898 to 1915 being less than half of sales during 1888 to 1893, the bowl-back mandolins were just what Martin needed to keep the business afloat during some tough years. The bowl-back mandolins also provided a bridge to the next change in musical taste, when Martin added ukuleles to the product line in 1915.

Figure 185
1899 (left) and 1905 (right) Style 6 Mandolins

STYLE 6a MANDOLINS

On October 15, 1902 Martin shipped a Special Style 6 mandolin to Stratton & Handley of Lowell, MA. The specifications for this special mandolin were:

No. 6 shell and sound hole
Plain ivory border
No. 4 bridge & fingerboard
22 frets
Side guard not inlaid

The serial number for this instrument was not recorded in the ledger. However, it is likely either serial number 1067 or 1068 as these serial numbers are missing from the sales records.

This mandolin became the prototype for what became the Style 6a mandolin. A total of 41 Style 6a mandolins were made between 1902 and 1920. Almost all were sold to Stratton & Handley and, from 1910, J. A. Handley both located in Lowell MA.

As can be seen in Figure 186 the binding is like a Style 2 mandolin. The mandolin pictured is the 3rd Style 6a made and differs from the original specification in having an inlaid pick guard.

Stratton & Handley were, like Vahdah Olcott-Bickford with the Style 44 guitars, looking for an instru-

ment of the highest quality materials but with plainer decoration so the price could be kept lower. The retail price of the Style 6a mandolin in 1902 was $60 compared to $75 for a regular Style 6 mandolin and $100 for a Style 7.

Figure 186
1903 Martin 6a Mandolin (Serial Number 3127)

STYLES 0, 00 AND 000 MANDOLINS

In 1905 Martin added the plainer and less expensive model 0 mandolin. The Model 00 added in 1907 and Model 000 added in 1909 as an even less expensive option. The Style 0 and 00 mandolins had a rosewood body and Style 000 had a mahogany body. In the 1911 retail price list the price for a Style 0 mandolin was $20 while the Style 00 was priced at $15 and the Style 000 at $12.

Style 0 - rosewood body, 18 ribs, rosewood binding, ebony bridge and fingerboard, pearl position dots, plain tortoiseshell (celluloid) pick guard, nickel plated machines and tailpiece

Style 00 - rosewood body, 9 ribs, rosewood binding, ebony bridge and fingerboard, small position dots, celluloid pick guard, nickel plated machines and tailpiece

Style 000 - mahogany body, 9 ribs, rosewood binding, ebony bridge and fingerboard, celluloid pick guard, nickel plated machines and tailpiece

The last 000 mandolin was made in 1917 but styles 0 and 00 continued in production until 1925.

Bowl-Back Mandolas and Mando-Cellos

Martin made a small number of bowl-back mandolas and mando-cellos as detailed in Table 13:

	MANDOLA[1]	MANDOLA 1	MANDOLA 2	MANDOLA 4	MANDO-CELLO[1]
BOWL BACK MANDOLAS AND MANDO-CELLOS					
1900			1		
1902	1				
1907		3			
1908			1		
1909					4
1911		5			
1912		6		1	
1913		1			
1914		2			

1) Style not recorded

Table 13
Bowl-Back Mandolas and Mando-Cellos

FLAT-BACK MANDOLINS

Martin started making flat-back mandolins in August 1914 although they didn't appear in a catalogue until 1915.

The popularity of bowl-back mandolins had been in decline for some time by 1914 but, unfortunately, the correspondence in the Martin archive is missing for this period so the exact rationale for Martin's move into the flat mandolin market remains unknown. However, judging by which dealers bought the first flat-back mandolins, it would appear Martin was encouraged by Southern California Music Co., Charles H. Ditson & Co., Rose Music Co. of Seattle, Loomis Temple of Music of New Haven and Bergstrom Music Co. of Honolulu.

On May 7, 1915 a Style B was shipped to John E. Russell of New Bedford MA:

"Complimentary in acknowledgment of helpfulness in testing sample flat back in September 1914"

The flat-back mandolins appeared in 1915 with the introduction of five models: Styles A, B, C, D and E.

Style A - mahogany body, rosewood binding on front only, ebony bridge and fingerboard, small position dots, ebony nut, plain nickel plated machines and tailpiece, celluloid pick guard, square head stock

Style B - rosewood body, rosewood binding front and back, ebony bridge and fingerboard, pearl position dots, ivory nut, nickel plated machines and tailpiece nicely embossed, celluloid pick guard, shaped head stock with decorative cut-out

Style C - rosewood body, fancy colored purfling, pearl sound hole decoration, ivory binding, ebony bridge and fingerboard, "cat's-eye" and slotted square and diamond fingerboard inlays, engraved German silver tailpiece and tuners, celluloid pick guard, shaped head stock with decorative cut-out

Style D - rosewood body, pearl purfling and thinner pearl purfling on sides, pearl sound hole decoration, ivory binding, ebony bridge and fingerboard, snowflake fingerboard inlays, engraved German silver tailpiece and tuners, celluloid pick guard, shaped head stock with decorative cut-out

Style E - rosewood body, pearl purfling on front, sides and back, pearl sound hole decoration, ivory binding, ebony fingerboard, snowflake fingerboard inlays, engraved German silver tailpiece and tuners,

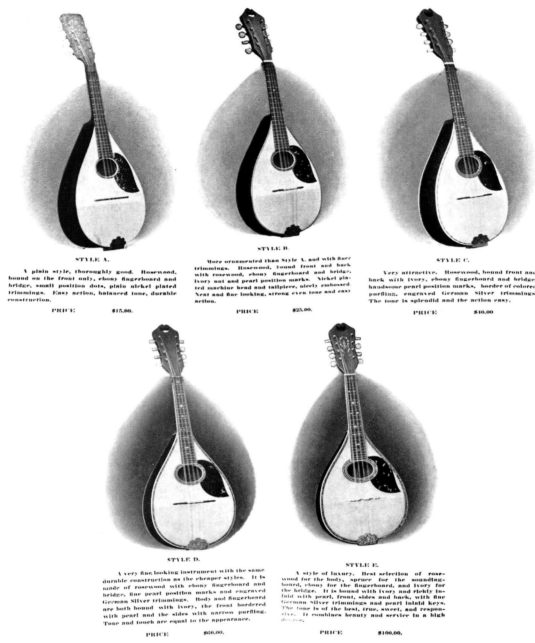

STYLE A.

A plain style, thoroughly good. Rosewood, bound on the front only, ebony fingerboard and bridge, small position dots, plain nickel plated trimmings. Easy action, balanced tone, durable construction.

PRICE $15.00.

STYLE B.

More ornamented than Style A, and with finer trimmings. Rosewood, bound front and back with rosewood, ebony fingerboard and bridge, ivory nut and pearl position marks. Nickel plated machine head and tailpiece, nicely embossed. Neat and fine looking, strong even tone and easy action.

PRICE $25.00.

STYLE C.

Very attractive. Rosewood, bound front and back with ivory, ebony fingerboard and bridge, handsome pearl position marks, border of colored purfling, engraved German Silver trimmings. The tone is splendid and the action easy.

PRICE $40.00

STYLE D.

A very fine looking instrument with the same durable construction as the cheaper styles. It is made of rosewood with ebony fingerboard and bridge, fine pearl position marks and engraved German Silver trimmings. Body and fingerboard are both bound with ivory, the front bordered with pearl and the sides with narrow purfling. Tone and touch are equal to the appearance.

PRICE $60.00.

STYLE E.

A style of luxury. Best selection of rosewood for the body, spruce for the soundingboard, ebony for the fingerboard, and ivory for the bridge. It is bound with ivory and richly inlaid with pearl, front, sides and back, with fine German Silver trimmings and pearl inlaid keys. The tone is of the best, true, sweet, and responsive. It combines beauty and service in a high degree.

PRICE $100.00.

Figure 187
Styles A, B, C, D and E from 1915 Mandolin Price List

celluloid pick guard, shaped head stock with decorative cut-out

Style AK - like style A but with koa body and top

Style BK - like style B but with koa body and top

In 1917 the Style D mandolin was dropped . At the same time Style C was upgraded, with its colored purfling being replaced by pearl purfling like the obsolete Style D.

It will be noted that mandolins from 1915 had "tear drop" celluloid pick guards. By 1917 the tear drop pick guards had been replaced by more rounded pick guards that became the norm subsequently.

The Style C mandolins only kept the pearl purfling from 1917 to 1920 and by around 1921 the colored purfling was resurrected and continued in use until the style was retired in 1934.

Koa wood Style AK and BK mandolins were added to the product line in 1921 although the Style BK only lasted until 1925.

The head stock of the Style A mandolin had always been squared off and the Style B may also have received this treatment with the introduction of decals in 1932 (although none was been recorded to date).

From 1914 to 1927 mandolin sales began to taper off and increasingly became less and less important to Martin's sales (see Figures 10 and 11).

As with the bowl-back mandolins, certain styles were dropped as time went on. Only 7 Style D mandolins were made; five in 1914 and two in 1917. The Style E mandolin ceased production in 1929, after a total of 62 had been made. Style C was dropped in 1934 and Style AK in 1937.

There was no mandolin production from 1943 to 1945. Production of Style A and B mandolin was relaunched in 1946 but that was the last year for Style B. The Style A was the last flat-back mandolin model made by Martin and continued in production until 1974.

Table 14 shows flat-back mandolin production from

YEAR	A	AK	B	BK	C	D	E
1914	44		35		13	5	3
1915	121		44		15		
1916	87		21		9		
1917	257		98		16	2	2
1918	282		77		8		1
1919	353		157		43		4
1920	710		394		82		4
1921	341	242	93	37	22		5
1922	372	69	49		12		
1923	451	172	97		22		2
1924	451	175	88		24		6
1925	410	100	150	6	12		12
1926	400	200	162		50		12
1927	300	100	50				
1928	200	100	25		12		
1929	250		50		19		5
1930	175				10		
1931	225	50	50		6		
1932	125	50			6		
1933	25						
1934	125	25			1		
1935	50	50	6				
1936	100	50	9				
1937	150	25	12				
1938	75		24				
1939	100						
1940	75		12				
1941	175		24				
1942	75		12				
1943							
1944							
1945							
1946	200		36				

FLAT-BACK MANDOLIN PRODUCTION 1914 TO 1946

Table 14
Flat-Back Mandolin Production 1915 to 1946

1914 until 1946.

FLAT-BACK MANDOLAS

Martin also made a number of flat-back mandolas between 1915 and 1941, plus one carved-top mandola in 1938, as documented in Table 15.

	MANDOLA A	MANDOLA B	TENOR MANDOLA A[3]	TENOR MANDOLA B[3]	TENOR MANDOLA B-CT[4]
1915	1				
1917		6[1]			
1919	4	3[1]	1[2,3]		
1920	18	12			
1921	11	7			
1922	12				
1923	6				
1926	1				
1927	13				
1929	10				
1931	12				
1932		3			
1934		2			
1935	6		6	4	
1936				3	
1937		3			
1938					1
1939				3	
1941		3			

FLAT MANDOLAS

1) SOMETIMES RECORDED AS MANDOLA BB
2) RECORDED AS TENOR MANDOLA AA
3) IT IS NOT CLEAR WHAT TDIFFERENCES EXIST BETWEEN THE MANDOLA AND TENOR MANDOLA MODELS
4) CARVED TOP, F-HOLES, DARK FINISH LIKE 2-15 MANDOLIN

Table 15
Flat-Back Mandola Production 1915 to 1941

CARVED-TOP MANDOLINS

During 1927 Martin began looking into the possibility of manufacturing carved-top mandolins. George Krick corresponded with Martin to encourage them to enter the carved top mandolin market as detailed in his letter of November 26, 1927:

"Perhaps you will recall the conversation we had on my last visit in Nazareth regarding your getting out a high grade flat model mandolin (carved back & top) similar to the ones made by the Gibson & Lyon & Healy companies. I brought this to the attention of several teachers here in Phila. (Mr. Tschkopp and Mr. Swiderski) and they are quite enthusiastic about the idea. I know there are many others that would welcome an instrument like that from your factory and hope you will go ahead with the plan in the near future. Would like Frederic to come & see me sometime & talk the matter over."

Frank Henry Martin was already well acquainted with the carved top mandolin market and the competitors in the field. Martin typed out two replies on November 28 but the first was crossed out and not sent. However, the first reply is included below as it provides some context as to Martin's awareness of the carved mandolin market:

"Your letter about carved mandolins is appropriate but I admit I have been delaying the work for a talk with Frederick and for that reason have done nothing about it. This morning we took up it up again and he will state (author's note: should be 'start') the foreman of our construction room, who is a violin maker, to carve one or two for a test. If there is a good future for this make mandolin we shall make what we can out of it. It does not seem possible that there will be a large market for it because there are already a large number of goods makes on the market. Perhaps you can explain this.

Frederick is not likely to visit you but will write you regarding the information as he gets along with the work."

The reply actually sent was slightly different and a little more positive:

"Your letter about carved mandolins is appropriate but I admit that I dread the work and for this reason have done nothing about it. This morning Frederick and I took it up again and he will start the foreman of our construction room, who is a violin maker, to carve one or two for a test. If there is a good future for this kind of mandolin we should learn all about it and get our share of the business.

Frederick is very busy and can hardly visit you but will write as he gets along with the work."

Although not definitively stated it seems likely that John Deichman, who was known as a violin maker, hand-carved the first carved top mandolin prototypes. Unfortunately, the correspondence for 1928 is missing so further details on the development of Martin carved top mandolins will have to remain a mystery.

Since making carved tops required the use of a multi-spindle carving machining, Martin contacted Guy Hart at Gibson Inc. in December 1927 to find out the types of machine used by Gibson. Hart answered that Gibson Inc. was using two different machines; one was a Curtis Carving Machine that was only rarely used for very large work and the other a carving machine supplied by The Tannewitz Works of Grand Rapids. Hart also kindly extended an invitation for Martin to see the machine in operation.

In early 1933 The Vega Co. send a letter to Martin asking what type of carving machine they are using for carved top instruments. From the reply we learn that Martin had purchased a Tannewitz Automatic Chair Seat Machine in December 1928.

The first carved top mandolins were style 20. The first batch was stamped February 6, 1929 so Martin did not wait long before putting their new carving machine into use.

In 1929 Martin produced mostly Style 20 carved-top mandolins. Although a few of the plainer Style 15 were made in 1929 this model did not really enter production until early 1930.

In 1936 Martin introduced f-hole mandolins and changed the style designations to 2-15 and 2-20 to reflect the design change. The first few Style 2-15 mandolins may only be stamped as Style 15 instruments. The Style 15 and Style 20 mandolins continued to be made concurrently with the Style 2-15 and 2-20 instruments until 1942.

A fancier Style 2-30 model was introduced in 1936 and continued in production until 1942. Only two oval sound hole versions of this style were ever made, a Style 30 in 1932 and a Style 30S in 1941.

Style 2-20 was dropped in 1941. One style 20 mandolin was made in 1942 and thirty Style 20S were made from 1949 to 1957. The last six Style 20S mandolins were made for Carlos De Filipis. The shop orders for 1949 to 1956 are missing but, since most of the Style 20S mandolins were shipped to the National Music Shop Inc., it is likely all were ordered by De Filipis.

Style 2-15 continued in production until 1964.

On December 13, 1927 Martin wrote to Julius Breckwoldt & Son about purchasing 5/8" thick dressed spruce for carved mandolin tops and purchased a small quantity a few days later for a trial. The type of spruce supplied was almost certainly the Adirondack variety.

In July 18, 1933 The Vega Co. asked Martin for their source of wood for carved top guitars. Martin replied on July 20:

"Spruce for Guitar tops that are to be carved must be absolutely clear and straight and we find it very difficult to get Eastern wood of the right quality so we find it best to use Sitka Spruce which we get from the Posey Manufacturing Company, Hoquiam, Washington. We order the Violin grade, quarter sawn, air dried, Spruce, four feet long, eight inches wide and two inches thick, resawing to one inch gives us a complete top with matched grain.

While we believe the Eastern Spruce to be superior in tone, it is not quite satisfactory for carving because it contains so many hidden defects. ..."

Charles H. Ditson & Co. must have queried Martin on the possible availability of carved top mandolas and mando-cellos because Martin wrote to Ditson on May 2, 1929:

"I reply to you letter of yesterday, it is a little too soon to say anything definitely about the Mandola and the Mando-Cello we are planning to make in our carved model line. We hope to work out these instruments during the summer so that they will be ready in Fall; but we cannot now give any idea as to the price."

Whatever the interest shown by Ditson, no carved top mandolas or mando-cellos were ever produced by Martin (not counting the single flat-back mandola A made with a carved top).

Chapter 12
MARTIN INSTRUMENTS MADE FOR OTHER FIRMS

CLAUDE GASKINS (1895-1899)

HARP MANDOLINS

Martin had only just begun to consider producing mandolins in 1894 when Frank Henry Martin decided to make a sample harp mandolin for a gentleman named Claude H. Gaskins of Shamokin PA, in the hopes of receiving a larger order. As explained in other parts of this book the years between 1894 and 1898 were very difficult ones for C. F. Martin & Co. and any sales were welcome.

In a letter dated January 21, 1895 Gaskins explained:

"I have invented a mandolin harp and have had it patented. I want to put it on the market and would like to have a sample lot made-about 12 or 15. It is something entirely new on the market, flat and is easy to make. Can you make up about 12 for me, that is to finish them complete. It will have the regulation fingerboard of a mandolin and the wood used is same as in guitars. If you thrust (sic, should be "trust") in favor of making them I will call on you with the model."

PATENTS ISSUED FEB. 8, 1896.

552,116. Stringed Musical Instrument. C. H. Gaskins, Shamokin, Pa. This invention combines the characteristics of a mandolin and harp, and is designed to increase the volume of sound and the tone of the instrument. A prolongation is provided on one side of the instrument, forming additional space for the sound to travel, in this space, and in the upper side thereof is provided a sound-opening. The finger board, frets, head and keys are arranged in

From Music Trade Review June 1896

Figure 188
Patent Announcement for Harp Mandolin

Martin replied on January 30 that he did not have sufficient seasoned rosewood large enough for the instrument but Gaskins pleaded in his February 1 response for at least one sample to show to prospective buyers.

Martin also offered some suggestions on construction and Gaskins agreed by leaving the details to Martin's judgment.

The next letter, from February 5, further discussed details of the instrument as it appears Martin offered to make it with a rounded back like an Italian style mandolin. Gaskins provided the following comment:

"Mr. Wagenseller (an associate, or possibly partner, of Gaskins) **and I have talked about the different styles of the mandolin and concluded you could make the first one flat on both sides and also make one with a convex back."**

He went on in the letter to specify the strings to be ½" longer than "regulation" and that the neck was to join the body at the 12th fret, while again leaving details to Martin's judgment.

On February 9, Martin sent a post card to Gaskins stating the first sample would soon be completed. In a letter from March 3 Gaskins expressed disappointment that he had not yet received the first sample as he had some sold and had already missed an opportunity for the instrument to be demonstrated to the State College Club in Williamsport. If the sample proved satisfactory Gaskins wanted to buy one or two dozen more and asked how long it would take to fill the order.

On March 8 Martin wrote Gaskins to let him know the sample would be finished by March 13 and Gaskins replied on March 10 that he would pick it up on that date.

In the next letter dated April 27 Gaskins acknowledged receiving a post card from Martin that **"the harps are finished"**. Although Gaskins had held out the possibility of an order for 12 harp mandolins, it appears only two more were made as Gaskins paid $30 for two harp mandolins on May 2, 1895 (plus an additional $6.50 for two cases). In a follow up letter dated May 16 Gaskins mentioned payment for the first batch was in the mail and that he wanted to visit Martin to **"write you up a contract for doz(en) or so."**

From a letter dated June 15, 1895 it is not clear whether a batch of 12 had been ordered. Since the letter goes on to state that Mr. Wagenseller had other priorities, the most likely scenario is that only the sample and the small batch of two instruments were made at the time. The accounts ledger records no sales to Gaskins between 1895 and 1899 so the promised order for 12 instruments did not happen.

Some time was to pass but in 1899 C. H. Gaskins & Co. ordered a number of harp mandolins in several different styles.

DATE SHIPPED	MODEL	QUAN	COMMENTS	PRICE (ea.)
March 13, 1895	Harp Mandolin	1	Sample	
April 27, 1895	Harp Mandolin	2	Probably style 21	$15.00
October 12, 1899	Harp Mandolin	1	Ivory bound, guard & machines like style 2 mandolin, herringbone purfling	$24.00
October 21, 1899	Harp Mandolin	5	Style 18, ebony guard	$13.50
October 28, 1899	Harp Mandolin	7	Style 18	$13.50
November 7, 1899	Harp Mandolin	6	Style 21	$15.00

Table 16
Harp Mandolins Made for Claude H. Gaskins

From Table 16 it can be seen that Martin made a total of 22 of these attractive and unusual instruments: 3 in 1895 and 19 more in 1899. None received serial numbers.

On March 1, 1901 Gaskins was shipped "1 piece of ivory 10-1/2" X 1-3/4" X 1/16" for "veneering". Possibly Gaskins was intending to veneer a fingerboard of one of his harp mandolins.

In *Martin Guitars: A Technical Reference (Johnston & Boak)* it is stated that the harp mandolin pictured on page 199 was made in 1901. However, there were no instrument sales to Gaskins in either 1900 or 1901. It was probably one of the style 21 harp mandolins shipped in 1899.

Figure 190
One of the Style 21 Harp Mandolins
Shipped on November 7, 1899

Figure 189
Back of Style 21 Harp Mandolin

HENRY SPAHR (1901)

As discussed in the section "First 000-Size Guitar" (pages 63 to 67), it would appear Henry Spahr was the driving force behind the introduction of the first 000-sized guitars in 1901. There is no correspondence to support this assertion but Spahr did purchase a majority of the early 000 guitars (see Table 1). As well, at least three examples are known with a special "**H. SPAHR/J.C.**" stamp, located on either the end of the head stock or on the back of the head stock. Martin may have initially considered the 000 guitar as the "Henry Spahr" model. It is not known if the "H. SPAHR" stamp was applied by Martin or Spahr himself.

However, by 1909 demand for 000-size guitars was beginning to increase and it became a regular part of the Martin line.

The larger body was also very convenient for the addition of another neck for making harp guitars, that were popular in the early 20th century. Five of the first six 000-size guitars were made as harp guitars during 1901 and 1902.

STRATTON & HANDLEY (1902-1909) and J. A. HANDLEY (1910-1920)

In the early 20th century a niche market developed for mandolins of the same quality as style 6 instruments but with somewhat less ornamentation. William Foden was shipped a style 6 mandolin with a plain side guard (serial number 1234) on June 9, 1903 and, likewise, Stratton & Handley of Lowell MA was shipped a special mandolin (style 6 shell with style 4 neck and binding, serial number 1276) on September 9, 1903.

The first mandolin designated as style 6a (serial number 1311, with side guard and 22 frets) was shipped to Stratton & Handley on November 27, 1903. The first 19 style 6a mandolins were sold to Stratton & Handley in the period 1902-1909. See Figure 186 in for photographs of a Style 6a mandolin.

The Stratton & Handley partnership must have ended by the end of 1909 because from 1910 to 1920 J. A. Handley purchased another 20 style 6a mandolins (another one was sold to a local Allentown customer).

DANIEL SCHUYLER'S MODEL "AMERICA" GUITAR (1907-1909)

Mike Longworth, in "C. F. Martin & Co.: A History", documented that two 0-28 "Model America" guitars were made in 1907 for Daniel Schuyler. These guitars are quite distinctive as they have a double body, a thin body being mounted beneath a regular size body but connected to the main body by an extended neck heel. A small notebook in the Martin archive contains the specifications for the Model "America" guitar.

Examination of the Martin Guitar archive correspondence, however, shows that Martin had been aware of this unusual guitar design for at least 15 years! In 1892 Martin received several letters from E. S. Sanford discussing a "Bini-Schuyler" guitar.

Sanford wrote to Martin on May 9, 1892:

"I have always said I would pay $100 for a guitar better than a Martin. I have heard an instrument this A. M. that is wonderful considering that it weighs at least twice as much as a 00. The singing power is there and were the tone equal it would be superior to yours.

The maker recognizes the fault and proposes to rectify it and if he does up goes my $100.

This is simply an attachment that can be placed on any guitar.

The owner is D. Schuyler. He has called upon Zoebisch and the old gentleman would not listen to him. From what I have seen of his invention take my word for it, it will pay for you to look into it. It will make another instrument of the Washburn and will make a Martin 00 sound like a harp."

More followed on May 16:

"I received your last note in reply to mine about Schuyler's attachment. There is certainly merit in it to some extent but tho (sic) old – has started out to make a guitar to put it on "as good as a Martin". He in ingenious but I have told him it is a ten year job he has undertaken and when he does make one he will think like all the rest of them, that it is better whether it is or not. My original

00 happened to be in Pond's at the time and with Romero present we tested them side by side. The 00 had the power but the Schuyler "out sang" it so that a sustained note on the b or g would sing through a bar andante 6/8 time. Had the E (treble) been any good it would have it would have done as well if not better. The attachment adds at least ½" to the depth of guitar which Romero said did not interfere with his execution altho (sic) at first awkward.

I have told the old fellow to buy the 00 and put it on and have himself money but he don't catch on. He will spend enough board(?) money to say nothing of cost of labor to pay for half dozen Martins before he learns that his invention is the attachment and not the guitar.

Here is a note of his to me and you will see what he is at. When I see it you shall hear all about it. Tear the letter up when you have read it."

Sanford followed up in a letter dated June 18:

"Last night I spent at Mr. Schuyler's residence in Brooklyn listening to Mr. Bini and his daughter which they played Schuyler's new guitar and I put up against theirs my 00. You can't make a "silk purse out of a sow's ear". The 00 was musical and the Bini-Schuyler combination was not but in everything else they handled you without gloves, particularly in the upper register. And had not Bini (he made the instrument) put the strings down so close he would have drowned you out completely.

I am so well satisfied that the improvement is responsible for this great improvement that I wish now to offer you my 00 to put it on and when Schuyler comes to Nazareth and you care to look into it I will send the instrument and pay you for your time etc as you think fit to charge. No one but your firm however can operate on the bowels of my darling. So if you won't that ends it.

I wish you would make a nut and bridge out of aluminum. You will get a tone from that that will surprise you. Schuyler has a bridge of his own that should make his fortune when it is perfected. It permits you to shorten or lengthen the strings at pleasures an inch thereby overcoming the great

difficulty of false strings. This is a neat and sightly affair and is the Eureka of the untrue strings business and I am sure when you see it you will say at once this is what we want. To return to has attachment I firmly believe it will increase the power of an 0-28 so that it will fill any hall that will hold 1,200 people and that is the only and great benefit to be had from it.

Your opinion is worth something in this matter because you are the practical man (mine is worth nothing). I shall always be ready to say that I was greatly deceived if you don't see the much in this man's invention at once.

You will hear from Schuyler before long."

Martin must have requested more information on aluminum because Sanford sent the following note followed on June 21, 1892:

"The peculiarity about aluminum that would seem to make it valuable is that when you hold it up and strike it sounds about the same as an old shoe would while if you lay it on wood and hit it will ring like silver. You can cut it like cheese into any shape you want and it is so soft a nut made from it would wear away under the bass strings.

Its quality of sounding on wood however seems to me valuable enough to monkey with on holidays. Mr. Zoebisch don't want to see Schuyler or to have anything to do with him. This is confidential."

Much later Martin made two "double-body" guitars for the same Daniel Schuyler, who referred to them as Model "America". The first Model America was shipped on January 28, 1907 and the second on June 21, 1909. These are the only examples ordered so the design can hardly be considered a success.

Interestingly, these guitars contain special labels, although neither guitar has a serial number. The 1907 example has a label dated "**1906**" as it was ordered in 1906 although not delivered until 1907. The 1909 guitar has a different type of label dated "**1909**".

As can be seen in Figures 193 and 194, this guitar is quite distinctive with its double body; a thin extra body being mounted beneath a regular size body but both being connected by an extended neck heel. Any attempt to reset such a long neck heel would be a tricky operation.

The guitar is based on the 0 body size and has typical style 28 appointments: herringbone purfling, ivory binding, zig-zag back stripe. The only thing that is unusual is the one piece neck. Style 28 guitars during this period generally had a two piece neck, with a head stock grafted to the main part of the neck by means of a scarf joint, and characterized by a volute glued to the back of the head stock for support.

Figure 191
Label in 1907 Model America Guitar

Figure 192
Label in 1909 Model America Guitar

Figure 194
Detail of Extended Neck Heel of
1907 Model America Guitar

Figure 193
1907 Model America Guitar

Figure 195
Head Stock on 1907 Model America Guitar

The bridge is very unusual ebony affair, probably designed by Schuyler himself (Figure 196).

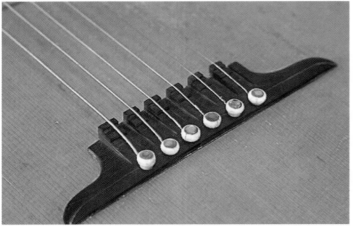

Figure 196
Detail of Bridge on 1907 Model America Guitar

The 1907 Model America has no serial or C. F. Martin stamp on the back of the head stock.

The 1909 Model America is a little different from the 1907 version. This guitar appears to have a replacement pyramid bridge but the footprint points to it having had a pyramid bridge from the beginning. The neck differs from the 1907 example in having a regular, for the time, neck with the neck glued to a separate head stock. This guitar also has no serial number but it does have a Martin stamp on the back of the head stock.

JOHN WANAMAKER (1909-1910)

John Wanamaker (July 11, 1838 – December 12, 1922) was a merchant whose business eventually developed into Wanamaker's Department Store.

Wanamaker's department store was the first department store in Philadelphia PA and one of the very first department stores in the United States. At its zenith in the early 20th century, there were two major Wanamaker department stores; one in Philadelphia and one in New York City (at Broadway and Tenth Street). By the end of the 20th century there were 16 Wanamaker's outlets. The chain was absorbed into Hecht's in 1995 and eventually became Macy's in 2006.

The Wanamaker's Grand Depot, as the first department store was called, opened in time to service the public visiting Philadelphia for the American Centen-

nial Exposition of 1876. In 1910, Wanamaker replaced his Grand Depot with a new store on the same site.

Figure 197
Wanamaker's in Philadelphia (ca. 1920)

The Wanamaker store in Philadelphia started buying instruments from Martin in 1904. From 1907 to 1910 some guitars were also purchased for the New York branch. Wanamaker continued to buy Martin guitars, mandolins and ukuleles until 1939, mostly for the Philadelphia store although a few were occasionally shipped to the New York store.

On December 18, 1909 ordered a number of special guitars and mandolins for both their Philadelphia and New York stores. Another smaller order was placed on May 20, 1910 for the New York store. Unfortunately, there is no correspondence to detail the variety of styles. The arrangement could not have been very successful as these were the only orders ever placed.

The "ladies" size guitar were probably size 2½ while "small" size were size 2. "Normal" referred to size 1 and "concert" was size 0.

JOHN WANAMAKER, NEW YORK					
DATE	STYLE	QUAN	STYLE	SIZE	BODY MAT'L
1909-12-18	GUITAR	2	D	SMALL	MAPLE
1909-12-18	GUITAR	2	E	STANDARD	MAPLE
1909-12-18	GUITAR	1	F	SMALL	MAHOGANY
1909-12-18	GUITAR	1	H	CONCERT	ROSEWOOD
1909-12-18	GUITAR	2	I	LADIES'	ROSEWOOD
1909-12-18	GUITAR	1	J	CONCERT	ROSEWOOD
1909-12-18	MANDOLIN	1	D	MAPLE	9 RIBS, NOT BOUND
1909-12-18	MANDOLIN	1	E	MAPLE	9 RIBS, BOUND
1909-12-18	MANDOLIN	1	F	ROSEWOOD	9 RIBS, BOUND
1909-12-18	MANDOLIN	1	H	ROSEWOOD	22 RIBS
1909-12-18	MANDOLIN	1	J	ROSEWOOD	26 RIBS
1910-05-20	GUITAR	3	D	SMALL	MAPLE
1910-05-20	GUITAR	3	E	STANDARD	MAPLE
1910-05-20	MANDOLIN	6	E	MAPLE	9 RIBS, BOUND

Table 17
Special Instruments Ordered by John Wanamaker in New York

JOHN WANAMAKER, PHILADELPHIA					
DATE	STYLE	QUAN	STYLE	SIZE	BODY MAT'L
1909-12-18	GUITAR	2	D	SMALL	MAPLE
1909-12-18	GUITAR	2	E	STANDARD	MAPLE
1909-12-18	GUITAR	1	F	SMALL	MAHOGANY
1909-12-18	GUITAR	1	H	CONCERT	ROSEWOOD
1909-12-18	GUITAR	1	J	CONCERT	ROSEWOOD
1909-12-18	MANDOLIN	1	D	MAPLE	9 RIBS, NOT BOUND
1909-12-18	MANDOLIN	1	E	MAPLE	9 RIBS, BOUND
1909-12-18	MANDOLIN	1	F	ROSEWOOD	9 RIBS, BOUND
1909-12-18	MANDOLIN	1	H	ROSEWOOD	22 RIBS
1909-12-18	MANDOLIN	1	J	ROSEWOOD	26 RIBS

Table 18
Special Instruments Ordered by
John Wanamaker in Philadelphia

The instruments had no Martin markings but received a Wanamaker stamp, of which two varieties are known. The TYPE 1 stamp was used at the Philadelphia store and the TYPE 2 stamp at the New York store. The guitars, and probably the mandolins, did not receive serial numbers.

| TYPE 1 | TYPE 2 |

Figure 198
Stamps Used in Wanamaker Guitars

To date, only two Wanamaker guitars have been reported, hopefully more will be found.

The first is a mahogany guitar that was probably meant to be size 2, although several dimensions are slightly less than expected. It will be noted it has a "Chicago" style pyramid bridge and a single ring rosette. Since it has the type 1 Wanamaker hand stamp on the neck block, it is the style F shipped to the Philadelphia store on December 18, 1909. The wholesale cost of this guitar was $7.50. The closest Martin equivalent was a style 1-17, which had a wholesale cost of $10.00. Martin didn't make a 2-17 at the time so made an adjustment in price to $7.50.

The second example is a concert size rosewood guitar with simple purfling and decoration, a single sound hole ring, a "Chicago" style pyramid bridge and a type 1 Wanamaker stamp. Wanamaker in Philadelphia was shipped two rosewood guitars on December 18, 1909, a style H and a style J. The wholesale price of the style H was $12.50 and the style J had a price of was $17.50. The prices are the same as Martin's regular 0-18 and 0-21 guitars respectively. Since this guitar is fairly plain it is almost certainly the style H.

Figure 199
Wanamaker Stamp on Neck
Block of Style F Guitar

Figure 200
Wanamaker Style F Guitar
(Shipped December 18, 1909)

Wanamaker also briefly participated in the "Customer Line" in 1922 when the New York branch ordered 50 style 0 ukuleles, while the Philadelphia branch only ordered one. These ukuleles probably received a Wanamaker stamp but none has yet been seen to confirm this.

WILLIAM FODEN AND
FODEN SPECIAL GUITARS (1912-1919)

William Foden (March 23, 1860-April 9, 1947) was a popular composer, arranger and teacher and was considered America's first native-born guitar virtuoso, being known especially for his mastery of tremolo. Foden was also a frequent contributor to music journals, writing regular columns for Cadenza, and later for its rival, Crescendo.

Foden was born in St. Louis MO where he learned to play guitar and mandolin. He began playing professionally in the 1880's and gained national attention from the early 1890's.

Figure 201
William Foden Playing a Washburn Guitar
Photograph by Fitz W. Guerin

Figure 202
Poster for Performance of "The Big Three"

In 1910 and 1911, Foden, along with Fred Bacon (1871-1948) on the banjo and Giuseppe Pettine (1874-1966) on the mandolin, undertook an eight-month long tour of the United States and British Columbia . The group was billed as "The Big Trio" and was described as **"banjo, mandolin and guitar royalty"**[1].

In 1911 Foden moved his family to Englewood, New Jersey. He would commute from Englewood to his studio on 42nd Street in New York City, where he taught guitar as well as other musical instruments. He published numerous work for mandolin, guitar, banjo, ukulele and Hawaiian guitar with William J. Smith & Co. and in 1920 and 1921 published his two volume "Grand Guitar Method".

Foden returned to St. Louis in 1939. Far from retiring, Foden continued to teach and arrange music for the guitar. He also conducted a brisk business selling sheet music until 1946,the year before he died.

Foden continued to corresponded with Martin until at least 1936 when he helped a certain Major Faulconer order a special 00-28G (serial number 65088). This guitar was made to shop order 357 which records the following details: "For gut strings only, Select material, 45 grade, no pick guard, loop bridge". From a 1936 letter Foden mentioned to Major Faulconer that he played a 0-42 (serial number 8721) in his early concerts and a 00-28 in his later career.

1900 Martin 0-42 Guitar Given to Foden "For Professional Influence"

Early in his career Foden promoted Washburn guitars but the made the switch to Martin guitars when Martin shipped him a 0-42 (serial number 8721) on March 10, 1900 **"for professional influence"**, documenting one of the few times Martin gave a guitar to an artist (the only other known cases being Madam De Goni in 1843 and Henry Worrall in 1856). The sales ledger contains the following notes on the guitar: **"Made to order, 20 frets, ebony bridge, thin round neck, strings close, regular width, position in binding of fingerboard 5, 7, 9, 15, 17"**. This is the earliest mention of a 20-fret neck on a Martin guitar.

On July 29, 1947 Arthur Hoskins wrote to Martin to inform them he had the guitar that the late Mr.

Figure 203
"The Big Three" Touring Car with Fred Bacon, Giuseppe Pettine and William Foden in the Back Seat

Foden had used when touring with Fred Bacon and was looking to have it repaired and refinished. Arthur Hoskins was a student and friend of William Foden and likely acquired the guitar from the estate for sentimental reasons. At a later date Hoskins donated Foden's papers, correspondence and extensive sheet music collection to the Missouri History Society, where it is now archived as the Foden-Hoskins Collection. Probably, these items were acquired at the same time as the guitar.

As further correspondence shows, this is the same 0-42 guitar (serial number 8721) mentioned above. Martin replied to Hoskins on July 31[2]:

"Your letter is of unusual interest because we remember clearly the guitar Mr. Foden used and we know it was a very fine instrument. Since we quite agree with you that few guitars have been used more worthily, we shall be happy to take special pains to recondition it for you."

Upon receipt of the guitar Martin reported on August 21, 1947[2]:

"**We received your Style 0-42 Guitar, No. 8721,** **formerly owned by Mr. Foden, and we find some** **work that should be done in addition to the refinishing. The Ivory bindings are broken and loose at several places and should be repaired; the neck is deeply worn under the first few frets and should be straightened there unless you wish to leave it that way for sentimental reasons. Straightening it would, of course, weaken it somewhat and it is already an unusually thin neck so it might be best to leave the hollows, if you don't mind the appearance. Before refinishing, we plan to glue all the cracks and replace worn frets, including some that are broken at the ends.**

Our records show that this guitar was made especially for Mr. Foden in 1900 and had some new features that he specified, including an Ebony bridge instead of the regular Ivory bridge, twenty frets instead of the regular nineteen in this model and a slightly thinner neck than usual. The top and back of the guitar show an usually high arch, probably due to swelling of the extra thin wood. This swelling may have been a factor in the fine tone of the guitar."

Foden bought 28 Martin guitars between 1900 and

1911, for sale to his students. Most of these were size 0 guitars. Although an important customer, Foden did not receive a full 50% dealer's discount but was given a 33-1/3% discount by Martin since he was considered a teacher rather than the owner of a retail store.

From another 1936 letter Foden mentioned to Major Faulconer that he played a 0-42 (serial number 8721) in his early concerts and a 00-28 later in his career.

Figure 204
William Foden and His 0-42 (Serial Number 8721)

FODEN SPECIAL GUITARS

The Foden Special guitars were built at the height of Foden's fame. After The Big Trio tour, Foden moved to New Jersey and opened a studio in New York. Foden was probably hoping to capitalize on his fame by selling special guitars to his students.

The Martin Guitar Co. archive still contains the cards made up to record the specifications for the Foden models. The cards are all dated March 6, 1917 and provide the following information.

STYLE A

Size 0 or 00, Corresponding to Style 18, 20 frets
Stained mahogany, front bound with rosewood and 2 pcs thin black and white
Back not bound
Rosette single ring black and white strips
Brace crossed pattern
Positions style 18, ebony nut
Brass machines, plain ebony pins
Celluloid side dots 5, 7, 9, 15 & 17

STYLE B

Size 0 or 00, Corresponding to style 21, 20 frets
Rosewood front edge similar to Style 21
Back edge and joint Style 21
Rosette single ring. Purfling in rosette Style 21, bordered on each side with veneer strips.
Brace crossed pattern
Positions 5, 7, 9 similar to Style
Celluloid side dots 5, 7, 9, 15, 17
Nickel & brass machine, inlaid pins

STYLE C

Size 0 or 00, Corresponding to style 28, 20 frets
Rosewood ivory bound. Front edge thin veneer style 5 black, 4 white
Back edge Style 28
Rosette single ring, 3 strips ivory bound with black & white veneer strips
Brace crossed pattern
Positions 5, 7, 9 special design. See card
Celluloid side dots 5, 7, 9, 15, 17
Nickel & brass machine, white pins
Fingerboard not bound

STYLE D

Size 0 or 00, Corresponding to style 30, 20 frets
Rosewood ivory bound. Front edge colored purfling.
Back style 30.
Rosette single ring. Like middle ring Style 30 with single black & white added against ivory.
Brace crossed pattern
Positions 5, 7, 9 special design. See card
Celluloid side dots 5, 7, 9, 15, 17
Fingerboard ivory bound.
German silver machine. White pins

STYLE E

Size 0 or 00, Between Style 40 and 45, 20 frets

Rosewood ivory bound. Front Style 40 (i. e. pearl edge like 42 but not around the fingerboard)

Back Style 45. Sides Style 45 except that pearl does not run around heel or end piece.

Rosette 3 rings Style 42. Brace crossed pattern
Fingerboard ivory bound. Head not inlaid.
Positions 3, 5, 7, 9, 12, 15 special design. See card.
Celluloid side dots 5, 7, 9, 15, 17.
German silver machine. White pins
Ebony bridge

Most Foden Special guitars were either size 0 or 00 although one each were made in sizes 2½ and 2.

No style A guitars were manufactured and this style was not included in Foden's price list (Figure 206). Probably, as explained in the his price list, Foden felt that rosewood was the best wood for creating good tone in a guitar.

There are two different Foden Special stamps in the Martin archive (Figure 205), although, so far, only the Type 2 stamp has been seen in existing Foden guitars. The Type 2 stamp was applied to the neck block and the back strip inside of the guitar.

A regular C. F. Martin & Co. stamp usually appeared on the back of the head stock but at least one Foden guitar is known with the Foden stamp in that position.

A capital letter, indicating the style of the guitar, was also applied to the neck block and sometimes to the back strip beside the Foden stamp.

TYPE 1   TYPE 2

Figure 205
William Foden and His 0-42 (Serial Number 8721)

Only the last five Foden Specials had Martin serial numbers. However, most, if not all, of the early Foden guitars were dated in pencil under the top and this is almost as good as a serial number! From this information any Foden guitar can easily be located in Table 19 (3 to 4 weeks was the average time between the date on the top and the shipping date).

Although Foden remained in New York until 1939, he didn't order any Martin instruments after 1919.

NO.	DATE SHIPPED	SIZE AND STYLE	SERIAL NUMBER	COMMENTS
1	1912-07-26	0 FODEN E	N/A	
2	1912-07-30	0 FODEN B	N/A	
3	1912-07-30	0 FODEN C	N/A	
4	1912-07-30	0 FODEN D	N/A	
5	1912-12-14	0 FODEN E	N/A	
6	1913-01-25	0 FODEN B	N/A	GUITAR REPORTED – TOP DATED "10/31/1912"
7	1913-04-22	0 FODEN E	N/A	GUITAR REPORTED – TOP DATED "3/14/1913"
8	1913-04-22	0 FODEN C	N/A	GUITAR REPORTED – TOP DATED "3/31/1913"
9	1913-06-18	0 FODEN D	N/A	
10	1913-06-18	0 FODEN E	N/A	
11	1913-06-18	0 FODEN D	N/A	7-STRING, GUITAR REPORTED
12	1913-10-28	0 FODEN B	N/A	
13	1913-12-08	00 FODEN D	N/A	GUITAR REPORTED -- TOP DATED "11/1/13"
14	1914-02-16	00 FODEN D	N/A	GUITAR REPORTED – TOP DATED "1/20/1914"
15	1914-02-26	00 FODEN B	N/A	
16	1914-02-26	00 FODEN B	N/A	
17	1914-06-22	00 FODEN D	N/A	DARK TOP
18	1914-06-27	00 FODEN D	N/A	IVORY BRIDGE, REPORTED ON UMGF (2016-07-05), ONE RING SOUNDHOLE DECORATION
19	1914-07-10	00 FODEN C	N/A	
20	1914-10-13	0 FODEN E	N/A	
21	1914-11-05	0 FODEN B	N/A	
22	1915-02-12	00 FODEN E	N/A	
23	1915-05-27	0 FODEN E	N/A	IVORY BRIDGE, IVORY PEGS, IVORY BINDING ON HEAD
24	1916-03-03	2 1/2 FODEN C	N/A	STAINED TOP
25	1916-03-21	2 FODEN B	N/A	SPECIAL CONCERT WIDTH NECK
26	1916-08-31	0 FODEN E	N/A	
27	1916-08-31	0 FODEN E	N/A	
28	1917-04-17	0 FODEN E	N/A	
29	1917-04-20	0 FODEN D	N/A	
30	1917-04-20	0 FODEN D	N/A	
31	1917-07-28	0 FODEN E	N/A	
32	1918-02-16	0 FODEN D	N/A	
33	1919-05-19	0 FODEN B	13538	
34	1919-05-19	00 FODEN B	13600	
35	1919-05-19	0 FODEN C	13595	
36	1919-05-19	00 FODEN C	13590	GUITAR REPORTED
37	1919-05-19	0 FODEN C	13598	HOLLY BINDING ON FINGERBOARD

Table 19
Foden Special Guitars

Notes for Chapter 12

1) The Guitar in America, Jeffrey Noonan, University Press of Mississippi

2) From correspondence in the Foden-Hoskins Archive, Missouri History Museum

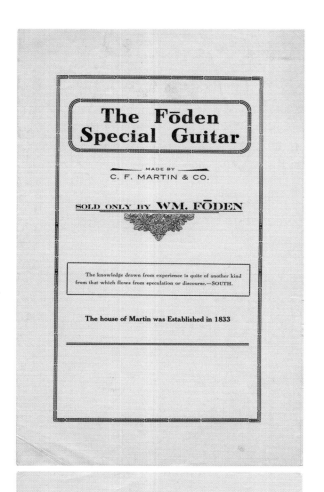

The Foden Special Guitar

MADE BY
C. F. MARTIN & CO.

SOLD ONLY BY WM. FODEN

The knowledge drawn from experience is quite of another kind from that which flows from speculation or discourse.—SOUTH.

The house of Martin was Established in 1833

---

nicely arched and finished, which becomes a part of the sound-board in its vibrations, and improves as the fibre of the wood settles in place. Our concert size is recommended for all-around use, the Bass and Treble being well balanced. The Grand Concert size has a very sonorous tone, and therefore excellent for club purposes. Their respective widths at the bridge are: Concert size, 13½ inches; Grand Concert size, 14½ inches.

Experience has proven that rosewood is the best material for the body, and spruce for the sounding board and braces; for the neck we use cedar and for fingerboards, ebony. The mode of finishing is hand polish, the same as is employed on pianos, a very clear varnish is made and the coating, by a special process is left thin; as this is rather an expensive method, it may be well to give the reasons for using it. They are: first, that a thin coating of varnish is less likely to hurt the tone; second, that it will not crack like a thick coat rubbed down; and third, being so thin and transparent it shows the beauty of the natural wood; in the selection of trimmings, wearing quality and appearance are both considered. All instruments are warranted free from defects of material or workmanship. If any prove otherwise they will be repaired or exchanged. Every guitar is examined by Mr. Foden before being shipped, and the purchaser can rest assured that it is in good condition when it starts on its journey. Correspondence invited.

The Foden Special Guitar

THE GUITAR, in one form or another, is very ancient, instruments of the lute family are found in many countries, differing in shape, but alike in so far, that they are of a convenient size to carry about. This seems to show, and the facts bear out the idea, that they are intended for use in a social manner particularly. The general use of the Guitar, Mandolin and Banjo, and the industry of making them, is an accepted fact, and in America it has developed remarkably of late years, so that now where once there were single players, there are scores and hundreds, organized into clubs and orchestras. Much pleasure has resulted from this turn of fashion, parents and friends enjoy many an evening's entertainment, and teachers find their work attractive and worthy of their best efforts. All these instruments, and in particular the guitar, are as well suited for solo playing, as for concerted performance, and in this respect there should be further development. Solo playing does not necessarily mean public performance: it may be only an hour's recreation by one's self, and in order that the greatest pleasure may be derived from such practice, it is absolutely necessary that the Guitar be properly balanced, and also have a sonority consistent with purity. The FODEN SPECIAL is designed with this object in view, and its powerful singing tone and easy action throughout its entire register makes it adequate for all purposes. To build a good guitar is not easy, nor can it be built for the price of a poor one, but *who*, that has a good one, regrets the extra cost? To build a guitar to give a singing quality of tone, requires care and patience; care in selecting the material, laying out the proper proportions, and attending to the many details which add to the player's comfort; patience, in giving the necessary time to finish every part. We gain delicacy of tone by having the wood of the proper thickness. The top, or sound-board, in particular, must be thin, gauged with care, and well smoothed on both the outside and the inside. The braces of the top must be properly made,

---

Description of the Different Styles

[handwritten: All dull finish. Celluloid binding instead of ivory]

Style B—Rosewood, with rosewood binding front and back, spruce top, rosette of black and white purfling, narrow black and white border, ebony fingerboard with pearl position dots on front and small dots on the side, ebony bridge, nickle plated machine head, 20 frets.

Concert Size	$50.00
Grand Concert Size	55.00

Style C—Rosewood, ivory binding front and back, spruce top with rosette of ivory and wood, black and white border, ebony fingerboard with pearl position dots on front and small dots on the side, ebony bridge, nickel plated machine head, 20 frets.

Concert Size	$65.00
Grand Concert Size	70.00

Style D—Rosewood, ivory binding front and back, spruce top, with rosette of pearl and ivory, border of fine black and white purfling, ebony fingerboard bound with ivory and inlaid with pearl position marks on front and pearl dots on the side, ebony bridge, German Silver machine head, 20 frets.

Concert Size	$80.00
Grand Concert Size	85.00

Style E—Rosewood, ivory bound sides and back, bordered with a narrow line of Japan pearl, spruce top bordered with pearl, rosette of pearl and ivory, ebony fingerboard bound with ivory and inlaid with pearl position marks on front and pearl dots on side, ebony bridge, German Silver machine head, 20 frets.

Concert Size	$125.00
Grand Concert Size	130.00

Smaller sizes than the above, can be made to order.

Net cash with order.

Transportation charges are to be paid by the purchaser.

Figure 206
Foden Special Guitar Price List

OLCOTT-BICKFORD
STYLE 44 GUITARS (1914-1938)

As detailed elsewhere in this book Vahdah Ol-cott-Bickford was a well-known classical guitar artist and teacher.

Early pictures show that she played Martin style 42 guitars. However, beginning in 1914, Vahdah Ol-cott-Bickford began to order special "Soloist" guitars from Martin. She desired to have a Style 45-quality guitar but with relatively plain decoration and no pearl inlaying. Later these guitars became known as Style 44. The style 44 instruments were always considered as special orders and never appeared in any Martin catalogue.

Figure 208
Purfling, Sound Hole Decoration and
Back Stripe of Style 44 Guitar

Figure 207
Olcott Quartette (ca. 1910)

The purfling was plain white and black lines, somewhat similar to Style 28 guitars after 1946. On the earliest guitars these white lines and binding may have been ivory but all later instruments had white celluloid lines. The sound hole decoration is unique to Martin with the white celluloid lines being more prominent than the black lines.

The back stripe is also unusual for such a high grade instrument, being only simple white and black lines instead of a strip of fancy marquetry.

A total of 37 Olcott-Bickford style 44 guitars were made. This figure differs from earlier publications which estimated the total was about 32 instruments. The difference exists because four guitars were recorded only as "Soloist" in the records and a fifth was

recorded only as a Style 44 guitar, without the body size being indicated. It is likely these five extra guitars will be either size 0 or 00 instruments. Refer to tables 20 and 21 for details on all the Style 44 guitars recorded in the Martin ledgers.

Even though Olcott-Bickford was the originator of the Style 44 guitars she could not order her special guitars directly from Martin, but had to place orders through an authorized Martin dealer. The normal dealer discount was 50% but the dealers probably only took a nominal mark-up because of Olcott-Bickford's special relationship with Martin and she probably bought the guitars for about 40% off list compared to the normal teacher discount of 20-25%.

Olcott-Bickford ordered most of her Style 44 guitars through Charles H. Ditson Co. in New York even after Olcott-Bickford returned to California in 1923. A few were ordered through other Martin dealers.

In 1918 Olcott-Bickford custom ordered two ¾-21 (i.e., 5-21) guitars with the Ditson body shape. These have Ditson serial numbers 315 and 316. Although the guitars have consecutive serial numbers they were made about 6 weeks apart. The first of these was for Olcott-Bickford's personal use and the second was made for one of her students. Olcott-Bickford probably received her guitar within a month of it being ordered. Clearly, one of her students liked the guitar so much he ordered one for himself, thus explaining the difference in order dates.

In 1922 Olcott-Bickford ordered four 0-44 and two 00-44 guitars in unfinished condition or "**in the white**". These guitars were French polished by a well-known violin maker in New York named Martin Lange, as indicated in the letter excerpts below.

On June 14, 1922 Ditson wrote to W. L. Currier of Boston concerning a Style 44 guitar:

"You will probably remember me as having met you at the Guild Convention. At that time, I had the pleasure of talking with you in reference to the Bickford-Olcott Artist Model Guitars. Mrs. Bickford was in our store to-day and found an exceptionally fine one and said that she liked it so much that she would be pleased to have you own this instrument as she was sure you would appreciate its quality.

His is the latest Model of the Artist Model Guitar, full concert size, peg head, in antique finish, at $130.

In the event that you should wish one of these instruments we shall be glad to pay the transportation charges to Boston and can send same to the Oliver Ditson Company, 179 Tremont Street, Boston, Mass., where you can call and examine same or, if you prefer, same can be sent to your residence."

Ditson wrote to H. F. Odell on June 22 concerning this guitar for Mr. Currier:

"We beg to advise that the guitar which has been shipped to you for Mr. Currier is the same guitar which was selected by Mrs. Bickford and upon which Mrs. Bickford played, pronouncing same to be one of the finest she ever played upon.

The guitar has also played upon by Mr. Johnstone Bane who was extremely enthusiastic in regard to its tone qualities and said that he considered the instrument one of the finest guitars he had ever played, having all the qualities of an old instrument.

We trust that Mr. Currier will find the instrument satisfactory in every way."

In a letter dated June 22, 1922 from H. F. Odell, publisher of "the Crescendo", it is learned that:

"We have today received the guitar from C. H. Ditson Company, New York. Please call in at your earliest convenience and see it.

Mr. Hunt writes us that the finish on these guitars is the highest grade violin varnish, done by Martin Lange, who is considered one of the greatest violin makers in the country. In a letter received this morning from Mr. Hunt, he said that Johnson C. Bane, noted guitarist, was in Ditsons and he played on this guitar. He pronounced it one of the finest guitars he had ever played upon and said it has all the quality of an old instrument."

A number of the Style 44 guitars have friction pegs as this was the choice of many classic guitar players in the American tradition. The four 2-44 guitars made in 1930 were all originally made with friction pegs. However, correspondence indicates some trouble was experienced with the ebony pegs and these were replaced with banjo-type tuners soon afterwards.

Table 21 shows the last three Style 44 guitars made had OM (Orchestra Model) bodies but, interestingly, two had 12-fret necks and only one had the 14-fret neck usually associated with the OM models.

NO.	MODEL	SERIAL NO.	COMMENTS	DEALER	SHIPPED DATE
1	SOLOIST (0-44?)	11675	"SOLOIST", IN EXCHANGE FOR #11691 WITH EBONY (STAMPED JUNE 6, 1913)	C. H. DITSON & CO.	05-03-1914
2	SOLOIST (0-44?)	11676	STYLE 44 "SOLOIST", SPECIAL WITH FLAT FINGERBOARD, HIGH NUT & PEARL FOR MARKS FOR USE OF MR. GEORGE B. ARLEINS IN HAWAIIAN STYLE PLAYING	SOUTHERN CALIFORNIA MUSIC CO.	15-04-1914
3	00-44	11682	"SOLOIST"	J. A. HANDLEY	15-11-1913
4	00-44	11683	"SOLOIST" FRICTION PEGS, ON APPROVAL TO GEORGE KENNEDY 1913-08-28	C. H. DITSON & CO.	25-05-1923
5	00-44	11690	"SOLOIST", 00 LEATHER CASE ($5.15)	J. A. HANDLEY	27-09-1913
6	SOLOIST (0-44?)	11691	SENT JULY 8, 1916, SPECIAL PRICE @ $45	C. H. DITSON & CO.	14-05-1917
7	00-44	11693	FRICTION PEGS, OLCOTT-BICKFORD, SERAIL NUMBER MAY BE 11673 OR 11613	SOUTHERN CALIFORNIA MUSIC CO.	29-05-1919
8	0-44?	11765	IVORY BRIDGE, SIZE NOT MENTIONED BUT PROBABLY SIZE 0	KOHLER & CHASE	10-04-1917
9	SOLOIST (0-44?)	11789	"SOLOIST"	WILLIAM J. SMITH & CO.	10-11-1917
10	SOLOIST (0-44?)	11790	SENT JULY 8, 1916, SPECIAL PRICE @ $45	C. H. DITSON & CO.	14-05-1917
11	000-44	12796	FOR MR. LOWE	KOHLER & CHASE	27-09-1917
12	000-44	13309		SHERMAN, CLAY & CO.	31-07-1918
13	000-44	13637	FOR W. R. KEARNS	C. H. DITSON & CO.	17-06-1919
14	00-44	13638	SPECIAL	SHERMAN, CLAY & CO.	17-06-1919
15	0-44	16727	"SOLOIST", IN THE WHITE, LESS $5.00 FOR NO FINISHING	C. H. DITSON & CO.	14-02-1922
16	0-44	16728	"SOLOIST", IN THE WHITE, LESS $5.00 FOR NO FINISHING	C. H. DITSON & CO.	14-02-1922
17	0-44	16984	"SOLOIST", IN THE WHITE, LESS $5.00 FOR NO FINISHING, EBONY PEGS	C. H. DITSON & CO.	14-04-1922
18	0-44	16985	"SOLOIST", IN THE WHITE, LESS $5.00 FOR NO FINISHING, EBONY PEGS	C. H. DITSON & CO.	14-04-1922
19	0-44	17126	"SOLOIST", KERATOL PLUSH CASE ($15.44)	E. H. ROYCE	20-07-1922
20	00-44	17638	"SOLOIST", IN THE WHITE	C. H. DITSON & CO.	04-12-1922
21	00-44	17639	"SOLOIST", IN THE WHITE	C. H. DITSON & CO.	04-12-1922
22	0-44	19009	STEEL STRINGS	SOUTHERN CALIFORNIA MUSIC CO.	28-09-1923
23	0-44	19010	STEEL STRINGS	SOUTHERN CALIFORNIA MUSIC CO.	28-09-1923

Table 20
Style 44 Guitars Made Between 1914 and 1923

NO.	MODEL	SERIAL NO.	SHOP ORDER	STAMPED DATE	COMMENTS	DEALER
24	0-44	29472	283	07-02-1927	EBONY PEGS, ORDERED BY MR. KITCHENER	C. H. DITSON & CO.
25	0-44	31212	SPECIAL	29-04-1927	"SOLOIST" DARK TOP, EBONY PEGS	C. H. DITSON & CO.
26	00-44	35099	208	24-02-1928	FOR SOPHOCLES T. PAPAS	CARL FISCHER INC.
27	0-44	35551	240	11-04-1928	SPECIAL LIGHT BRACES LIGHT, EBONY PEGS, TOP STAINED VERY LIGHT BROWN	C. H. DITSON & CO.
28	1-44	38721	450	29-05-1929	DITSON SPECIAL, OLCOTT-BICKFORD, ARTIST MODEL 450 (STAINED TOP), NO STYLE STAMP, SMALLEST DITSON-STYLE BODY	C. H. DITSON & CO.
29	1-44	39235	491	29-07-1929	DITSON OLCOTT-BICKFORD ARTIST MODEL	C. H. DITSON & CO.
30	2-44	42643	695	21-05-1930	OLCOTT-BICKFORD, 19 FRETS, SELECT DARK ROSEWOOD, LIGHT BRACES	OLIVER DITSON CO.
31	2-44	42644	695	21-05-1930	OLCOTT-BICKFORD, 19 FRETS, SELECT DARK ROSEWOOD, LIGHT BRACES	OLIVER DITSON CO.
32	2-44	43718	794	26-08-1930	GUT STRINGS, STAINED TOP, EBONY PEGS OLCOTT-BICKFORD MODEL	OLIVER DITSON CO.
33	2-44	43719	794	26-08-1930	GUT STRINGS, STAINED TOP, EBONY PEG), ONCE OWNED BY VAHDAH OLCOTT-BICKFORD	OLIVER DITSON CO.
34	0-44	46337	955	21-03-1931	MADE FOR W. J. KITCHENER, EBONY PEGS, GUT STRINGS	G. SCHIRMER INC
35	00-44G	70469	742	03-06-1938	FOR GUT STRINGS ONLY, OM BODY, REGULAT BRACING AS LIGHT AS POSSIBLE, SLOTTED HEAD, 12 FRET NECK OM WIDTH, 1/16" THINNER THAN USUAL, 19 FRETS, NECK & FINGERBOARD BOUND & INLAID LIKE STYLE 45, OLD STYLE HEAD VENEER, REGULAR PIN BRIDGE, STYLE 28 PINS, D & J MACHINE HEADS	G. SCHIRMER INC.
36	00-44S	70803	765	21-07-1938	ORCHESTRA MODEL BODY, FINGERBOARD BOUND WITH TOROISE SHELL FIBERLOID, PLAIN ROSEWOOD HEAD, 14 FRET FINGERBOARD 1 3/4" WIDE, 45 POSITION MARKS, #98G ENGRAVED MACHINES, BLACK BRIDGE PINS, STYLE 18, BODY BOUND AND INLAID LIKE STYLE 21	COAST WHOLESALE MUSIC CO.
37	00-44G	70854	776	28-07-1938	O. M. BODY, LIGHT BRACING FOR GUT STRINGS ONLY, 19 FRET, 0 SCALE, 12 FRET NECK WIDTH 1 3/4", THICKNESS 1/16" THINNER THAN USUAL, NECK & FINGERBOARD BOUND AND INLAID STYLE 45, STYLE 21 BACK CENTER STRIP, PLAIN ROSEWOOD HEAD VENEER, NAME TRANSFER BACK OF HEAD, STYLE 28 BRIDGE PINS, D & J #33 MACHINE HEADS, DECAL ON BACK OF HEADSTOCK	G. SCHIRMER INC.

Table 21
Style 44 Guitars Made Between 1927 and 1938

C. H. DITSON & CO. and OLIVER DITSON CO. (1915-1931)

It is worth briefly examining the history of the Oliver Ditson Co. due to the number of important names in the musical business that were associated, one way or another, with Ditson during the 19th and early 20th centuries.

Oliver Ditson was born in Boston on October 20, 1811. As a young man Ditson was first employed by the Parker Music Co. but became in 1834, when he was only 23, a partner in a new company named Parker & Ditson.

In 1845 Oliver Ditson hired fifteen-year-old John C. Hayne at $1.50 per week. Hayne must have been very successful in the business because on his twenty-first birthday, September 9, 1850, Hayne began to share in the profits of the store and on January 1, 1857, was made a business partner when the company name changed to Oliver Ditson & Co.

In 1864, P. J. Healy and George W. Lyon were established in Chicago with the capital of Oliver Ditson & Co., under the name of Lyon & Healy.

On March 4, 1867, Oliver Ditson & Co. purchased the music plant, stock and good will of Firth, Son & Co., of New York City. Oliver Ditson with this acquisition established a New York branch house under the name of Charles H. Ditson & Co., managed by his eldest son Charles.

In 1875, the purchase of the catalog of Lee & Waxx of Philadelphia, led to the opening of J. E. Ditson & Co. in Philadelphia, under the management of another son, James Edward Ditson. J. E. Ditson died in 1881 but the Philadelphia branch continued until 1910, when it was finally closed.

On December 21, 1888, Oliver Ditson, the pioneer of music publishing in America, died at the age of seventy-seven. The surviving partners, John C. Haynes, Charles H. Ditson and the executors of Oliver Ditson's estate, then organized a new corporation, Oliver Ditson Company, with Mr. Haynes as president.

With the death of John C. Haynes on May 3, 1907, Charles Healy Ditson became president of the corporation.

Ditson began to purchase Martin guitars and mandolins in 1902. The majority of the early purchases were shipped to Charles H. Ditson & Co. in New York, although a few were shipped to J. E. Ditson & Co., the Ditson branch in Philadelphia. Oliver Ditson Co. in Boston commenced buying Martin instruments in 1910, by which time J. E. Ditson & Co. had closed.

Charles H. Ditson died in New York on May 14, 1929 and Oliver Ditson Co. took over the operation of the New York branch. The latest letter in the Martin archive on Charles H. Ditson & Co. letter head is dated September 25, 1929 and by October 22 Oliver Ditson Co. was using their own letter head in New York. The Ditson companies were now clearly in decline. The last purchase from the New York branch was a D-111 ordered on November 11, 1930 and the last instrument ordered from the Boston branch was on January

6, 1931. Later in 1931 the Oliver Ditson Co. was bought out by the Theodore Presser Company.

Mandolins with a Ditson Stamp (1915 to 1926)

The wide-waisted Martin Ditson guitars are well known but mandolins were the first special instruments ordered by Charles H. Ditson & Co. The first special mandolins were ordered in 1915 by Charles H. Ditson & Co. and the first 45 mandolins received a special series of serial numbers. Initially, there was a little confusion with the Ditson designations but this was quickly straightened out. The specification cards in the Martin Guitar Archive lay out the details of the styles. The specification cards are all dated July 23, 1915.

Style 1517

- Bowl 14 ribs, plain cap, like 00
- Rosette same width as 00, white holly center
- Border like 00
- Side guard extending to edge at both ends
- Head & neck, fingerboard & bridge like 00
- Machines and tailpiece like 00
- Ditson stamp and serial number

Style 2250

- Bowl 18 ribs, exactly like Martin 0
- Rosette all of thin black & white
- Border like style 18 guitar, with maple strip under binding
- Celluloid side guard, same shape as 1517
- Head & neck, fingerboard & bridge like 0
- Machines and tailpiece like 0
- Ditson stamp and serial number

Style 2538

- 22 ribs, large cap like No 1, no small cap
- Rosette black & white purfling & blocks, blocks in center, veneers outside
- Border like rosette of style 18 guitar, using maple instead of holly
- Fingerboard not bound, card of positions in box
- Celluloid side guard, pearl inlaid
- Style A Handel machines, Plain nickel tailpiece
- Bridge like No. 1
- Ditson stamp and serial number

Style 3035

- 26 ribs, large cap like No. 2, no small cap
- Rosette colored purfling in center similar to No. 2
- Border like style 18 guitar, no strip under binding
- Celluloid side guard pearl inlaid like 2538
- Fingerboard celluloid bound, card of positions in box
- Machines, tailpiece & bridge like No. 2
- Ditson stamp and serial number

Style 3540

- 26 ribs, large cap like No. 3, no small cap
- Rosette pearl & wood without ivory
- Celluloid binding with very narrow light colored purfling
- Celluloid side guard pearl inlaid like 2538 and 3035
- Fingerboard celluloid bound, card of positions in box
- Machines, tailpiece & bridge like No. 3
- Ditson stamp and serial number

As can be seen from the specification above styles 1500 and 1517 were similar in design and price to regular style 00 mandolins. Mandolin styles 2000 and 2250 were similar to a regular style 0 mandolin but were priced at $9.50, slightly less than the $10.00 normal price. Mandolin styles 2500 and 2538 were equal in price to the regular style 1 mandolin. Style 3000 and 3035 mandolins were priced the same as regular style 2 mandolins while Styles 3500 and 3540 were equal in price to the regular style 3 mandolin.

The mandolins shown in Table 22 were purchased exclusively by Charles H. Ditson in New York and were delivered between July 1915 and June 1916.

From 1918 to 1926 Martin mandolins with a Ditson stamp were purchased almost exclusively by Oliver Ditson Co. in Boston. Some were shipped with both the Martin and Ditson stamps and some with the Ditson stamp only, but almost all had the regular Martin serial numbers. The only Ditson-stamped mandolins bought by Charles H. Ditson in this period were the twenty-five style AK mandolins shipped in late 1922. For some reason these twenty-five mandolins did not receive serial numbers.

DITSON MANDOLINS		
DITSON STYLE	**QUAN**	**SERIAL NUMBERS**
MAND 1500	1	1
MAND 1517	10	6, 7, 8, 9, 36, 37, 38, 39, 40, 41
MAND 2000	1	2
MAND 2250	10	10, 11, 12, 13, 30, 31, 32, 33, 34, 35
MAND 2500	1	3
MAND 2538	4	14, 15, 16, 17
MAND 3000	1	4
MAND 3035	4	18, 19, 20, 21
MAND 3500	1	5
MAND 3540	7	22, 23, 24, 25, 43, 44, 45
MAND A	4	26, 27, 28, 29

Table 22
Special Ditson Mandolins - 1915 to 1916

To add to the confusion both Oliver Ditson Co. and Charles H. Ditson & Co. made numerous purchases of regular Martin instrument throughout this period that were not ordered with a Ditson stamp. From early 1926 to the end of the company in early 1931 only regular Martin mandolins were bought.

Guitars with a Ditson Stamp
(1915 to 1926)

Design

The distinctive shape of the Martin Ditson guitars was determined by the type of music played on them. Since they were intended to be played on the lap as Hawaiian steel guitars, a narrow waist as found on normal guitar was not necessary. So Ditson decided on a design with a wider waist which also provided Ditson guitars with a very recognizable shape.

Sizes

The first Martin Ditson guitar was shipped to Charles H. Ditson & Co. on February 28, 1916 although the design had been in the works for several months. The Martin Guitar Archive contains a paper pattern with the following information:

Ditson Steel Gtr
Own Model 12/22/15
Length 17-3/4
Width above 8-7/16
(Width) bend 7-3/16
Width) below 11-1/8

Initially there were two different sizes; DS (Ditson

DITSON MANDOLINS					
DITSON STYLE	QUAN	DATE SHIPPED	COMMENTS	BRANCH	SERIAL NUMBERS
MAND 1500	1	1915-07-15	MAND 1500 ($7.50)	C. H. DITSON & CO.	1
MAND 2000	1	1915-07-15	MAND 2000 ($9.50)	C. H. DITSON & CO.	2
MAND 2500	1	1915-07-15	MAND 2500 ($12.50)	C. H. DITSON & CO.	3
MAND 3000	1	1915-07-15	MAND 3000 ($15.00)	C. H. DITSON & CO.	4
MAND 3500	1	1915-07-15	MAND 3500 ($17.50)	C. H. DITSON & CO.	5
MAND 2250	4	1915-08-24	MARTIN MAND 2250 ($9.50)	C. H. DITSON & CO.	10, 11, 12, 13
MAND A	2	1915-08-24	MARTIN MAND A ($7.50)	C. H. DITSON & CO.	26, 27
MAND 1517	4	1915-08-30	MAND 1517 ($7.50)	C. H. DITSON & CO.	6, 7, 8, 9
MAND 2538	4	1915-08-30	MAND 2538 ($12.50)	C. H. DITSON & CO.	14. 15. 16. 17
MAND 3035	4	1915-08-30	MAND 3035 ($15.00)	C. H. DITSON & CO.	18, 19, 20, 21
MAND 3540	4	1915-08-30	MAND 3540 ($17.50)	C. H. DITSON & CO.	22, 23, 24, 25
MAND A	2	1916-02-10	MAND A, DITSON STAMP? ($7.50)	C. H. DITSON & CO.	28, 29
MAND 2250	6	1916-03-28	DITSON MAND 2250 ($9.50)	C. H. DITSON & CO.	30-35
MAND 1517	6	1916-04-14	DITSON MAND 1517 ($7.50)	C. H. DITSON & CO.	36-41
MAND 3540	3	1916-06-27	DITSON MAND 3540 ($17.50)	C. H. DITSON & CO	43-45
MAND A	6	1918-07-30	DITSON STAMP	OLIVER DITSON CO.	6188, 6191, 6193, 6196, 6200, 6212
MAND B	5	1918-07-30	DITSON STAMP	OLIVER DITSON CO.	6249, 6251, 6255-6257
MAND B	1	1918-09-28	DITSON STAMP	OLIVER DITSON CO.	6282
MAND 00	6	1918-09-28	DITSON STAMP	OLIVER DITSON CO.	6302-6307
MAND 0	6	1918-09-28	DITSON STAMP	OLIVER DITSON CO.	6308-6313
MAND B	2	1918-12-20	DITSON STAMP	OLIVER DITSON CO	6354, 6355
MAND A	4	1918-12-28	S.D. (STAMPED DITSON)	OLIVER DITSON CO	6132, 6134, 6142, 6154
MAND A	11	1919-03-29	MAND A, OLIVER DITSON STAMP	OLIVER DITSON CO.	6517-6519, 6523-6525, 6527-6530, 6532
MAND A	6	1919-04-07	OLIVER DITSON STAMP	OLIVER DITSON CO.	6533-6537, 6539
MAND B	5	1919-04-07	OLIVER DITSON STAMP	OLIVER DITSON CO.	6505-6507, 6511, 6513
MAND A	1	1919-04-23	OLIVER DITSON STAMP	OLIVER DITSON CO.	6489
MAND B	1	1919-04-23	OLIVER DITSON STAMP	OLIVER DITSON CO.	6509
MAND B	6	1919-04-30	OLIVER DITSON STAMP	OLIVER DITSON CO.	6504, 6508, 6510, 6512, 6514, 6515
MAND A	1	1919-04-30	OLIVER DITSON STAMP	OLIVER DITSON CO.	NOT RECORDED
MAND B	4	1919-05-26	MAND B, DITSON STAMP	OLIVER DITSON CO.	6633-6636
MAND 0	6	1919-07-30	DITSON STAMP	OLIVER DITSON CO.	6758-6763
MAND B	6	1922-10-21	DITSON STAMP	OLIVER DITSON CO.	9219, 9221, 9228, 9229, 9592, 9602
MAND C	3	1922-10-21	DITSON STAMP	OLIVER DITSON CO.	9613, 9616, 9618
MANDOLA A	1	1922-11-23	DITSON STAMP	OLIVER DITSON CO.	9853
MAND AK	12	1922-12-12	DITSON STAMP	C. H. DITSON & CO	NO SERIAL NUMBERS
MAND B	6	1922-12-15	DITSON STAMP	OLIVER DITSON CO.	10010-10015
MAND AK	13	1922-12-16	DITSON STAMP	C. H. DITSON & CO	NO SERIAL NUMBERS
MAND A	12	1923-01-10	DITSON STAMP	OLIVER DITSON CO.	10085-10096
MAND A	12	1923-02-23	DITSON STAMP	OLIVER DITSON CO.	10234-10245
MAND A	4	1923-04-23	DITSON STAMP	OLIVER DITSON CO.	10308, 10320, 10328, 10340
MAND A	12	1923-05-03	DITSON STAMP ONLY	OLIVER DITSON CO.	10371-10382
MAND B	6	1923-08-31	DITSON STAMP ONLY	OLIVER DITSON CO.	10597-10602
MAND B	6	1923-11-05	DITSON STAMP	OLIVER DITSON CO	10702-10707
MAND A	4	1923-11-21	DITSON STAMP ONLY	OLIVER DITSON	10793, 10794, 10796, 10799
MAND A	8	1923-12-06	DITSON STAMP ONLY	OLIVER DITSON	10791, 10792, 10795, 10797, 10798, 10800-10802
MAND A	4	1924-02-26	DITSON STAMP	OLIVER DITSON	11022-11025
MAND A	8	1924-02-29	DITSON STAMP ONLY	OLIVER DITSON	11021, 11026--32
MAND A	12	1924-08-16	DITSON STAMP	OLIVER DITSON	FROM ORDER BOOK
MAND B	6	1924-08-16	DITSON STAMP	OLIVER DITSON	FROM ORDER BOOK
MAND A	12	1924-10-31	DITSON STAMP	OLIVER DITSON	FROM ORDER BOOK
MAND A	4	1926-03-09	DITSON STAMP	OLIVER DITSON	FROM ORDER BOOK

Table 23
Mandolins with Ditson Stamps

Standard) and DC (Ditson Concert).

The Ditson Standard dimensions are considerably smaller than a regular Martin size 1 guitar and are, in fact, somewhere between size 2½ and size 2.

The original dimensions for Ditson Concert guitars is not in the Martin archive and it is now evident these guitars were made in two different sizes. The original paper pattern in the Martin archive indicates the size was "enlarged from the old pattern" on May 22, 1917. The updated size had a lower bout dimension of 13-5/16" while the original pattern had a lower bout width of 12-3/4". Since a regular size 0 Martin guitar has a lower bout width of 13-1/2" and size 1 has a lower bout of 12.75", the original Ditson Concert size

was only slightly larger than a size 1 and even the updated Ditson Concert size was still smaller than a size 0. It appears that the waist and upper bout dimensions of the updated Ditson Concert size remained the same. No Ditson Concert guitars were shipped between April 21, 1917 (ending at serial number 189) and August 31, 1917 (beginning at serial number 269) so all Ditson Concert guitars made after August 1917 will have the wider lower bout.

The Ditson Dreadnought was based on the Kealakai guitar which itself was based on the shape of a 000 guitar, but increased by 1/2" in all dimensions. The obvious difference between the Kealakai guitar and the Ditson Dreadnought is the wider waist of the latter. Being based on the original 000 size guitar and the Kealakai, the original Ditson Dreadnoughts should have a lower bout of 15 ½", although actual guitars measure slightly less.

On July 6, 1917 Ditson added three new sizes: from smallest to largest; Child's Guitar, Ditson ¾ size and Ditson Terz. These designations were a little confusing and were renamed on March 11, 1918: Child's Guitar became Ditson ¼ size, Ditson ¾ size became Ditson size ½ and Ditson Terz became Ditson ¾ size. These are all rare guitars as only seven Ditson ¼ size, seven Ditson size ½ and eleven Ditson ¾ size guitars were made.

Figures 209 and 210 show the specification cards for the Ditson Small Guitars. They were designed on July 6, 1917 and went through two updates of specification, one on December 1, 1917 and the other on March 9, 1918. The Small Ditson Guitars were renamed on March 30, 1918 (see Figure 211).

There are a few changes noted on the specification cards for the Small Ditson Guitars. The sound hole diameters are slightly smaller on the card dated March 9, 1918. As well, the scale length of the Child's Guitar (later Ditson ¼ size) was changed from "0 scale with nut at 6th fret" to "Lima scale with nut at 4th fret". The length of the Lima scale is unknown but it can't be referring to a 17" tiple scale or the resulting scale, that would begin at the 4th fret, as the scale would be too short. The first order of Ditson Small Guitars was made on March 30, 1918 so it is unlikely any of these guitars from the December 1, 1917 specification card were ever made.

There was also a second designation for each Ditson guitar that combined the style of each guitars with its size. The standard sizes were designated 1, 2 or 3 while the concert sizes were 11, 22 and 33. The Ditson Dreadnoughts were made as models 111 or 222, none of the fancier 333 guitars being made.

Styles

Ditson guitars have three levels of decoration: Style 1, Style 2 and Style 3. Style 2 guitars had celluloid bindings "exactly" like a style 2 ukulele, a celluloid heel and inlaid ebony pins. Style 1 Ditson guitars were like style 2 except they had rosewood binding and plain ebony pins. Style 3 Ditson guitars were based on style

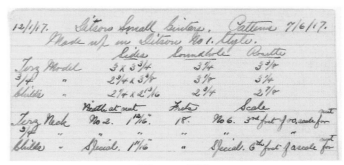

Figure 209
Specifications for Ditson Small Guitars, December 1, 1917

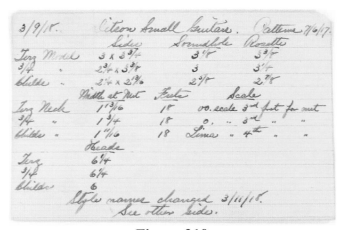

Figure 210
Specification for Ditson Small Guitars from March 9, 1918

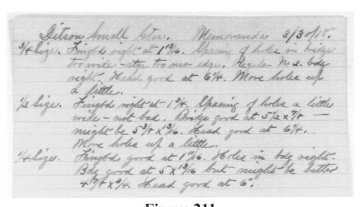

Figure 211
Ditson Small Guitars Renamed on March 30, 1918

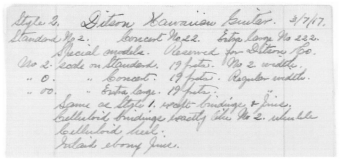

Figure 212
Specifications for Style 1 and Style 2 Ditson Guitars

3 ukuleles but had more elaborate fingerboard inlays and an inlay on each side of the bridge.

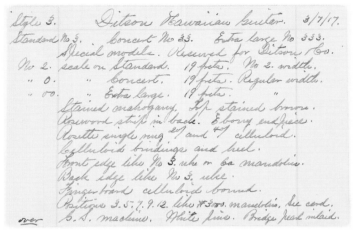

Figure 213
Specifications for Style 3 Ditson Guitar

In March 1919 another Ditson model, ODS or Oliver Ditson Special, was added to the line. These were ordered as 1-18 and 0-18 guitars, although they were based on the original Ditson styles 1 and 11. The ODS guitars were almost all shipped to Oliver Ditson Co. in Boston. These guitars were slightly different from a regular Ditson 1 or 11 guitars as they had a three ring sound hole rosette rather than a single ring (see Figure 214) and were ordered with no Martin stamp.

Figure 214
Oliver Ditson Special (ODS) 1-18 Guitar
(Serial Number 367)

Between June and August 1918 Charles H. Ditson & Co. were shipped a new series of guitars referred to as D. M. for Ditson Model. Up to this point Ditson guitars had always had mahogany bodies and although some 1-18 D. M. guitars were ordered the remainder of the guitars had rosewood bodies. The rosewood bodied D. M. guitars were offered with normal Martin style designations as 1-21, 1-28, 1-30, 1-42 and 1-45. There were no further orders for these guitars after August 1918.

In Mid-1918 Vahdah Olcott-Bickford special ordered two ¾-21 guitars. These were Ditson ¾ size (terz) guitars with rosewood bodies.

Decoration

The specification cards indicate the level of decoration but some variation has been encountered. The two earliest shipments of guitars of DS (Ditson 2) guitars (serial numbers 2 to 19) had three ring rosettes instead of the later single ring rosettes. The single ring rosettes matched the specification cards that called for decoration like Martin ukuleles.

Figure 215
Fingerboard of Ditson 33 Guitar
(Serial Number 20)

As well, the earliest Ditson 33 guitars had fancier inlays than later examples. Figure 215 shows an early Ditson 33 (serial number 20) with fancy banjo-style inlays beginning at the first fret of the fingerboard and Figure 216 illustrates the large "flower" inlays on the ends of the Chicago-style bridge. Later Ditson 33 guitars had "snowflake" inlays beginning at the third fret and simplified inlays on the wings of the pyramid bridge (see Figure 217).

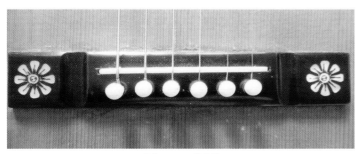

Figure 216
Chicago-style Pyramid Bridge on Ditson 33 Guitar
(Serial Number 20)

OLIVER DITSON COMPANY, BOSTON   7

THE DITSON "HAWAIIAN PROFESSIONAL" GUITARS
American Made

No. 3

Ditson Quality of the better kind, beautiful antique Spanish model, graceful simplicity, manufactured for us under our own special supervision, carefully constructed of the best material, responsive true scale. Every instrument thoroughly tested before shipment, used, recommended and sought by the most prominent professional players.

No.		Each
1	Standard size, old dark mahogany back and sides, spruce top, dark finish with rosewood bound edge, sound hole inlaid around edges with rings of ebony, dark smooth rubbed mahogany neck, ebony heel, rosewood veneered head piece, ebony fingerboard, German silver frets, pearl position dots, ebony bridge with white bone saddle, brass machine head, white buttons, polished body	$25.00
11	Concert size, same description as No. 1	30.00
111	Extra Grand, same description as No. 1	35.00
2	Standard size, old dark mahogany, back and sides, ebony stripe through center of back, spruce top, dark finish, sound hole inlaid around edges with purfling, top and back edges bound with white celluloid, dark, smooth rubbed mahogany neck, ebony heel, rosewood veneered head piece, ebony fingerboard, German silver frets, pearl position dots, ebony bridge with white bone saddle, brass machine head, white buttons, bright polished body	35.00
22	Concert size, same description as No. 2	40.00
222	Extra Grand, same description as No. 2	45.00
3	Standard size, selected, old dark mahogany, back and sides, ebony stripe through center of back, extra selected spruce top, dark finish, sound hole bound with white celluloid, and inlaid around edges with rings of white celluloid and ebony, top and back edges bound with white celluloid, dark smooth rubbed mahogany neck, celluloid heel, rosewood veneered head piece, ebony fingerboard bound with white celluloid, German silver frets, pearl position designs, pearl inlaid ebony bridge, with white bone saddle, nickel plated machine head, white buttons, French polished	50.00
33	Concert size, same description as No. 3	55.00
333	Extra Grand, same description as No. 3	60.00

Figure 217
From Oliver Ditson Co. and Charles H. Ditson & Co. catalogue circa 1918-1920

Construction Details

Ditson guitars varied from normal Martin practice in several areas.

The neck block of Martin guitars are made of two pieces of mahogany, the main body and a thinner piece that closes off the bottom of the dove tail. Ditson guitars are quite often seen with two pieces of mahogany making up the body of the neck block.

Martin used Chicago-style pyramid bridges on the Ditson guitars rather than Martin pyramid bridges. The Chicago-style bridges have a truncated pyramid at each end of the bridge, resulting in a flat surface that could be used for inlay work. The Martin purchasing records indicate that "special #34" bridges were purchased in 1916 and 1917. It is not known what "#34" meant nor is the name of the supplier.

The fingerboard inlays for the D. M. (for example, 1-28) guitars were simplified in some cases. The fingerboard inlays on one 1-28 has the usual style 28 diamond and square inlays, but the inlays were left unslotted. The inlay work for Ditson guitars does not appear in the Martin purchasing records so there is a possibility these inlays were supplied by Ditson and only applied by Martin.

Tables of Ditson Guitars

Tables 24 to 27 list all shipments of Ditson guitars and Martin guitars with Ditson stamps. This listing is not exhaustive. There are many orders, mostly placed by Oliver Ditson Co., where is not clear if the guitars ordered received a Ditson stamp or not. As more guitars are uncovered this listing may need to be expanded.

DITSON MARTIN GUITARS AND MARTIN GUITARS WITH DITSON STAMPS					
MODEL	QUAN	DATE SHIPPED	DESCRIPTION	BRANCH	SERIAL NUMBERS
DM SPECIAL	1	1916-02-18	DITSON SPECIAL, OWN MODEL	C. H. DITSON & CO.	1
DS 2	6	1916-03-28	STYLE LIKE NO. 2 UKULELE	C. H. DITSON & CO.	2-7
DS 2	12	1916-04-29	DITSON STANDARD 2	C. H. DITSON & CO.	8-19
DC 33	1	1916-05-12	DITSON CONCERT 33	C. H. DITSON & CO.	20
DS 3	1	1916-05-31	DITSON STANDARD 3	C. H. DITSON & CO.	26
DC 33	5	1916-05-31	DITSON CONCERT 33	C. H. DITSON & CO.	21-25
DS 3	5	1916-06-29	DITSON STANDARD 3	C. H. DITSON & CO.	27-31
DC 33	5	1916-06-29	DITSON CONCERT 33	C. H. DITSON & CO.	32-36
DS 3	5	1916-07-31	DITSON STANDARD 3	C. H. DITSON & CO.	49-53
DC 33	4	1916-07-31	DITSON CONCERT 33	C. H. DITSON & CO.	66-69
DS 1	6	1916-08-07	DITSON STANDARD 1	C. H. DITSON & CO.	37-42
DC 11	6	1916-08-07	DITSON CONCERT 11	C. H. DITSON & CO.	54-59
DS 2	4	1916-08-07	DITSON STANDARD 2	C. H. DITSON & CO.	43, 45-47
DS 2	2	1916-08-09	DITSON STANDARD 2	C. H. DITSON & CO.	44, 48
DC 22	6	1916-08-09	DITSON CONCERT 22	C. H. DITSON & CO.	60-65
DC 33	1	1916-08-09	DITSON CONCERT 33	C. H. DITSON & CO.	70
DD 222	1	1916-08-09	DITSON DREADNOUGHT 222	C. H. DITSON & CO.	71
DS 1	5	1916-10-24	DITSON STANDARD 1 (NEW STYLE)	C. H. DITSON & CO.	117-121
DC 11	5	1916-10-25	DITSON CONCERT 11	C. H. DITSON & CO.	78, 80-83
DC 11	6	1916-10-30	DITSON CONCERT 11	C. H. DITSON & CO.	73-77, 79
DS 1	2	1916-10-31	DITSON STANDARD 1	C. H. DITSON & CO.	110, 112
DS 1	6	1916-11-02	DITSON STANDARD 1	C. H. DITSON & CO.	107, 109, 111, 114-116
DC 11	6	1916-11-07	DITSON CONCERT 11	C. H. DITSON & CO.	85, 86, 89, 91, 93, 95
DS 1	7	1916-11-11	DITSON STANDARD 1	C. H. DITSON & CO.	98, 101, 103, 105, 106, 108, 113
DC 11	6	1916-11-11	DITSON CONCERT 11	C. H. DITSON & CO.	72, 84, 88, 94, 96
DS 1	5	1916-11-16	DITSON STANDARD 1	C. H. DITSON & CO.	97, 99, 100, 102, 104
DC 11	2	1916-11-16	DITSON CONCERT 11	C. H. DITSON & CO.	87, 92
DS 2	6	1916-11-29	DITSON STANDARD 2	C. H. DITSON & CO.	123, 125, 126, 129-131
DS 2	12	1916-12-05	DITSON STANDARD 2	C. H. DITSON & CO.	132, 134-138, 140-142, 144-146
DS 2	7	1916-12-15	DITSON STANDARD 2	C. H. DITSON & CO.	122, 124, 127, 128, 133, 139, 143
DC 22	7	1916-12-15	DITSON CONCERT 22	C. H. DITSON & CO.	148, 152, 153, 157, 159, 160, 162
DC 22	6	1916-12-28	DITSON CONCERT 22	C. H. DITSON & CO.	147, 149-151, 155, 164
DC 22	11	1916-12-30	DITSON CONCERT 22	C. H. DITSON & CO.	156, 158, 161, 163, 165-171
DD 111	3	1916-12-30	DITSON DREADNOUGHT 111	C. H. DITSON & CO.	173-175
DD 222	3	1916-12-30	DITSON DREADNOUGHT 222	C. H. DITSON & CO.	172, 176, 177
DC 22	1	1917-01-09	DITSON CONCERT 22	C. H. DITSON & CO.	154
DS 3	6	1917-04-21	DITSON STANDARD 3	C. H. DITSON & CO.	178-183
DC 33	6	1917-04-21	DITSON CONCERT 33	C. H. DITSON & CO.	184-189
DC 11	4	1917-05-31	DITSON CONCERT 11	C. H. DITSON & CO.	203, 211-213
DS 1	2	1917-06-04	DITSON STANDARD 1	C. H. DITSON & CO.	190, 197
DC 11	6	1917-06-04	DITSON CONCERT 11	C. H. DITSON & CO.	202, 204-206, 208, 209
DD 111	1	1917-06-04	DITSON DREADNOUGHT 111	C. H. DITSON & CO.	214
DS 1	3	1917-06-06	DITSON STANDARD 1	C. H. DITSON & CO.	193-195
DC 11	2	1917-06-06	DITSON CONCERT 11	C. H. DITSON & CO.	207, 210
DD 111	1	1917-06-06	DITSON DREADNOUGHT 111	C. H. DITSON & CO.	215
DS 1	4	1917-07-31	DITSON STANDARD 1	C. H. DITSON & CO.	228, 232, 236, 238
DS 1	6	1917-08-03	DITSON STANDARD 1	C. H. DITSON & CO.	222, 226, 235, 260, 262, 268
DS 1	6	1917-08-07	DITSON STANDARD 1	C. H. DITSON & CO.	227, 230, 233, 237, 240, 261

Table 24
Ditson Guitars Shipped February 18, 1916 to August 7, 1917

DITSON MARTIN GUITARS AND MARTIN GUITARS WITH DITSON STAMPS					
MODEL	QUAN	DATE SHIPPED	DESCRIPTION	BRANCH	SERIAL NUMBERS
DS 1	9	1917-08-09	DITSON STANDARD 1	C. H. DITSON & CO.	219. 223. 229, 239, 241, 247, 248, 251, 257
DS 1	10	1917-08-13	DITSON STANDARD 1	C. H. DITSON & CO.	220, 224, 225, 231, 242, 245, 246, 255, 258, 259
DC 11	1	1917-08-24	DITSON CONCERT 11	C. H. DITSON & CO.	274
DS 1	6	1917-08-24	DITSON STANDARD 1	C. H. DITSON & CO.	231, 234, 236, 243, 250, 254
DC 11	1	1917-08-27	DITSON CONCERT 11	C. H. DITSON & CO.	281
DC 11	4	1917-08-30	DITSON CONCERT 11	C. H. DITSON & CO.	273, 276, 286, 292
DC 11	18	1917-08-31	DITSON CONCERT 11	C. H. DITSON & CO.	269-272, 275, 277-280, 282-285, 287-289, 291, 293
DC 11	1	1917-09-05	DITSON CONCERT 11	C. H. DITSON & CO.	290
DS 1	9	1917-09-05	DITSON STANDARD 1	C. H. DITSON & CO.	244, 249, 252, 253, 263-267
¼	6	1918-03-30	DITSON ¼ GUITAR	C. H. DITSON & CO.	297-302
½	6	1918-03-30	DITSON ½ GUITAR	C. H. DITSON & CO.	303-308
¾	6	1918-03-30	DITSON ¾ GUITAR	C. H. DITSON & CO.	309-314
¼	1	1918-02-28	DITSON ¼ GUITAR	C. H. DITSON & CO.	296
½	1	1918-02-28	DITSON ½ GUITAR	C. H. DITSON & CO.	294
¾	1	1918-02-28	DITSON ¾ GUITAR	C. H. DITSON & CO.	295
¾-21	1	1918-07-16	FOR MRS. BICKFORD (ORDER ENTERED 1918-05-30, "1 GTR DITSON ¾, SOLO GUITAR FOR MRS. BICKFORD, ROSEWOOD, WHITE TOP, ROSETTE & BORDER LIKE DITSON 1, BACK LIKE MARTIN 21, FINEST POSSIBLE", ORANGE TOP	C. H. DITSON & CO.	315
DITSON TERZ ¾-21	1	1918-08-30	ROSEWOOD, DITSON GUITAR, TERZ MODEL, EXTRA SELECTED WOOD, FOR MRS. BICKFORD'S STUDENT	C. H. DITSON & CO.	316
DS 1	5	1918-11-30	DITSON STANDARD 1	C. H. DITSON & CO.	321, 324, 327, 330, 331
DS 2	3	1918-11-30	DITSON STANDARD 2	C. H. DITSON & CO.	319, 326, 333
DS 3	2	1918-11-30	DITSON STANDARD 3	C. H. DITSON & CO.	325, 328
DS 1	8	1918-12-21	DITSON STANDARD 1	C. H. DITSON & CO.	322, 323, 334-336, 341-343
DS 3	1	1918-12-30	DITSON STANDARD 3	C. H. DITSON & CO.	318
DS 2	5	1918-12-30	DITSON STANDARD 2	C. H. DITSON & CO.	337, 339, 346, 348, 358
DS 1	6	1918-12-30	DITSON STANDARD 1	C. H. DITSON & CO.	338, 340, 344, 345, 347, 349
DS 1	6	1918-12-31	DITSON STANDARD 1	C. H. DITSON & CO.	320, 350, 353-355
DS 2	2	1918-12-31	DITSON STANDARD 2	C. H. DITSON & CO.	351, 352
DS 3	3	1918-12-31	DITSON STANDARD 3	C. H. DITSON & CO.	317, 329, 332
1-18	3	1918-12-31		C. H. DITSON & CO.	13375-13377
0-18	6	1918-12-31		C. H. DITSON & CO.	13402-13409
1-18	3	1918-12-31		C. H. DITSON & CO.	13410-13412
DS 2	1	1919-01-18	DITSON STANDARD 2	C. H. DITSON & CO.	359
DS 2	1	1919-01-31	DITSON STANDARD 2	C. H. DITSON & CO.	357
DC 11	6	1919-01-31	DITSON CONCERT 11	C. H. DITSON & CO.	211, 271, 275, 277, 282, 289 (RETURNS)
DS 1	1	1919-01-31	DITSON STANDARD 1	C. H. DITSON & CO.	265 (RETURN)
DC 22	2	1919-01-31	DITSON CONCERT 22	C. H. DITSON & CO.	147, 159 (RETURNS)
DS 3	1	1919-01-31	DITSON STANDARD 3	C. H. DITSON & CO.	183 (RETURN)
DS 33	1	1919-01-31	DITSON CONCERT 33	C. H. DITSON & CO.	67 (RETURN)
DS SPECIAL	1	1919-02-13	DITSON STANDARD SPECIAL, SELECTED ROSEWOOD, IVORY PEGS	C. H. DITSON & CO.	360
DS 1	1	1919-02-13	DITSON STANDARD 1	C. H. DITSON & CO.	356

Table 25
Ditson Guitars Shipped August 9, 1917 to February 13, 1919

MODEL	QUAN	DATE SHIPPED	DESCRIPTION	BRANCH	SERIAL NUMBERS
			DITSON MARTIN GUITARS AND MARTIN GUITARS WITH DITSON STAMPS		
1-18 ODS	1	1919-03-25	OLIVER DITSON STAMP 1-18	C. H. DITSON & CO.	370
1-18 ODS	10	1919-03-25	1-18, OLIVER DITSON STAMP	OLIVER DITSON CO.	361, 363-365, 369, 371-375
¾-DM 1	1	1919-03-31	¾ SIZE DITSON MODEL 1	C. H. DITSON & CO.	13521
0-18 ODS	1	1919-03-31	0-18 OLIVER DITSON STAMP	C. H. DITSON & CO.	383
¾-DH	5	1919-04-02	¾ SIZE D. H.	C. H. DITSON & CO.	13519, 13520, 13522-13524
1-18 ODS	1	1919-04-07	OLIVER DITSON STAMP	OLIVER DITSON CO.	362
0-18 ODS	6	1919-04-07	OLIVER DITSON STAMP	OLIVER DITSON CO.	376, 380, 382, 384-386
0-18 ODS	4	1919-04-23	OLIVER DITSON STAMP	OLIVER DITSON CO.	377-379, 381
1-18 ODS	3	1919-04-23	OLIVER DITSON STAMP	OLIVER DITSON CO.	366-368
1-21 DM	5	1919-06-24	1-21 DITSON MODEL	C. H. DITSON & CO.	429, 435, 437, 448, 449
1-18 DM	9	1919-06-26	1-18 DITSON MODEL	C. H. DITSON & CO.	390, 393, 394, 398, 402, 407, 410, 411, 415
1-18 DM	11	1919-06-28	1-18 DITSON MODEL	C. H. DITSON & CO.	391, 392, 396, 397, 404, 408, 413, 417, 420, 453, 453
1-21 DM	1	1919-06-28	1-21 DITSON MODEL	C. H. DITSON & CO.	431
1-18 DM	12	1919-06-30	1-18 DITSON MODEL	C. H. DITSON & CO.	389, 395, 418, 419, 421, 425, 426, 456, 458-461
1-18 DM	12	1919-07-08	1-18 DITSON MODEL	C. H. DITSON & CO.	387, 388, 399, 401, 403, 405, 409, 412, 416, 424, 455, 462
1-18 DM	4	1919-07-11	1-18 DITSON MODEL	C. H. DITSON & CO.	400, 414, 423, 457
1-21 DM	8	1919-07-11	1-21 DITSON MODEL	C. H. DITSON & CO.	432, 434, 436, 438, 440, 444, 447, 450
1-21 DM	8	1919-07-18	1-21 DITSON MODEL	C. H. DITSON & CO.	427, 430, 439, 441, 443, 445, 446, 451
1-28 DM	3	1919-07-18	1-28 DITSON MODEL	C. H. DITSON & CO.	491, 494, 501
1-18 DM	1	1919-07-23	1-18 DITSON MODEL	C. H. DITSON & CO.	406
1-21 DM	2	1919-07-23	1-21 DITSON MODEL	C. H. DITSON & CO.	428, 433
1-18 DM	2	1919-07-26	1-18 DITSON MODEL	C. H. DITSON & CO.	422, 454
1-21 DM	1	1919-07-26	1-21 DITSON MODEL	C. H. DITSON & CO.	442
1-30 DM	4	1919-07-26	1-30 DITSON MODEL	C. H. DITSON & CO.	481, 486, 488, 489
1-42 DM	4	1919-07-26	1-42 DITSON MODEL	C. H. DITSON & CO.	468, 471, 473, 476
1-30 DM	1	1919-07-29	1-30 DITSON MODEL	C. H. DITSON & CO.	482
1-42 DM	7	1919-07-29	1-42 DITSON MODEL	C. H. DITSON & CO.	467, 469, 470, 472, 474, 475, 478
1-45 DM	4	1919-07-29	1-45 DITSON MODEL	C. H. DITSON & CO.	463-466
1-28 DM	6	1919-07-30	1-28 DITSON MODEL	C. H. DITSON & CO.	492, 493, 495, 497, 499, 500
1-30 DM	7	1919-07-30	1-30 DITSON MODEL	C. H. DITSON & CO.	479, 480, 483, 484, 485, 487, 490
1-42 DM	1	1919-07-30	1-42 DITSON MODEL	C. H. DITSON & CO.	477
1-28 DM	3	1919-08-09	1-28 DITSON MODEL	C. H. DITSON & CO.	496, 498, 501
DS 3	12	1920-04-21	DITSON STANDARD 3	C. H. DITSON & CO.	515-526
DS 2	12	1920-05-08	DITSON STANDARD 2	C. H. DITSON & CO.	503-514
DS 1	22	1920-06-08	DISTON STANDARD 1	C. H. DITSON & CO.	527, 528, 530-540, 542-546, 548-550
DS 1	3	1920-06-29	DITSON STANDARD 1	C. H. DITSON & CO.	529, 541, 547
DS 3	6	1920-07-17	DITSON STANDARD 3	C. H. DITSON & CO.	516-518, 520, 521, 523 (RETURNS)
DC 33	12	1920-07-31	DITSON CONCERT 33	C. H. DITSON & CO.	552-563
DC 11	6	1921-01-05	DITSON CONCERT 11	C. H. DITSON & CO.	564-569
DD 111	2	1921-01-05	DITSON DREADNOUGHT 111	C. H. DITSON & CO.	570, 571
TIPLE	6	1922-12-11	DITSON STAMP	OLIVER DITSON CO.	17684-17689
T-18	2	1923-01-23	DOTSON & MARTIN STAMP	C. H. DITSON & CO.	17737, 17740
TIPLE	6	1923-01-27	DITSON STAMP	OLIVER DITSON CO.	17750-17755
0-18	2	1923-02-01	DITSON STAMP	OLIVER DITSON CO.	17836, 17837
0-18	1	1923-02-23	DITSON STAMP	OLIVER DITSON CO.	17862
2-17	6	1923-04-23	DITSON STAMP	OLIVER DITSON CO.	18149-18154
2-17	12	1923-05-04	DITSON STAMP ONLY	OLIVER DITSON CO.	18233-18244
0-18	3	1923-05-24	OLIVER DITSON STAMP	OLIVER DITSON CO.	18341, 18342, 18344
00-18	3	1923-06-09	OLIVER DITSON STAMP	OLIVER DITSON CO.	18389-18391
0-18	1	1923-07-31	DITSON STAMP	OLIVER DITSON CO.	18741

Table 26
Ditson Guitars Shipped March 25, 1919 to July 31, 1923

MODEL	QUAN	DATE SHIPPED	DESCRIPTION	BRANCH	SERIAL NUMBERS
			DITSON MARTIN GUITARS AND MARTIN GUITARS WITH DITSON STAMPS		
T-18	6	1923-08-18	DITSON STAMP ONLY	OLIVER DITSON CO.	18940, 18943, 18944, 18949-18951
0-18	2	1923-08-18	DITSON STAMP ONLY	OLIVER DITSON CO.	18742, 18743
T-18	6	1923-08-18	DITSON STAMP ONLY	C. H. DITSON & CO.	18941, 18942, 18945-18948
T-18	4	1923-12-20	DITSON STAMP	OLIVER DITSON CO.	19616, 19622, 19624, 19627
DD 111	1	1923-12-22	DITSON DREADNOUGHT 111	C. H. DITSON & CO.	19734, FOR MR. SMECK
2-17	12	1924-02-01	DITSON STAMP ONLY	C. H. DITSON & CO.	19735, 19737-19746
0-18	3	1924-02-14	DITSON STAMP	OLIVER DITSON CO.	19906, 19908, 19915
DD 111	1	1924-04-22	DARK FINISH	C. H. DITSON & CO.	NO SERIAL NUMBER RECORDED
T-18	3	1924-03-04	DITSON STAMP	C. H. DITSON & CO.	FROM ORDER BOOK
TIPLE	12	1924-04-04	DITSON STAMP	OLIVER DITSON CO.	FROM ORDER BOOK
DD 111	1	1924-08-16	DITSON DREADNOUGHT 111	C. H. DITSON & CO.	FROM ORDER BOOK
T-18	12	1924-10-31	DITSON STAMP	OLIVER DITSON CO.	FROM ORDER BOOK
2-17	6	1924-10-31	DITSON STAMP	OLIVER DITSON CO.	FROM ORDER BOOK
0-18	3	1924-10-31	DITSON STAMP	OLIVER DITSON CO.	FROM ORDER BOOK
DD 111	1	1925-01-27	DARK FINISH	C. H. DITSON & CO.	FROM ORDER BOOK
2-17	12	1925-03-02	DITSON STAMP	OLIVER DITSON CO.	FROM ORDER BOOK
0-18	6	1925-03-02	DITSON STAMP	OLIVER DITSON CO.	FROM ORDER BOOK
00-18	3	1925-03-02	DITSON STAMP	OLIVER DITSON CO.	FROM ORDER BOOK
0-21	3	1925-03-02	DITSON STAMP	OLIVER DITSON CO.	FROM ORDER BOOK
DD 111	1	1926-01-26	DITSON DREADNOUGHT 111	C. H. DITSON & CO.	FROM ORDER BOOK
T-18	12	1926-03-09	DITSON STAMP	OLIVER DITSON CO.	FROM ORDER BOOK
2-17	12	1926-03-09	DITSON STAMP	OLIVER DITSON CO.	FROM ORDER BOOK
0-18	6	1926-03-09	DITSON STAMP	OLIVER DITSON CO.	FROM ORDER BOOK
00-18	6	1926-03-09	DITSON STAMP	OLIVER DITSON CO.	FROM ORDER BOOK
0-21	6	1926-03-09	DITSON STAMP	OLIVER DITSON CO.	FROM ORDER BOOK
00-21	2	1926-03-09	DITSON STAMP	OLIVER DITSON CO.	FROM ORDER BOOK
DD 111	2	1926-08-30	DITSON DREADNOUGHT 111	C. H. DITSON & CO.	FROM ORDER BOOK
DD 111	2	1926-12-21	DITSON DREADNOUGHT 111	C. H. DITSON & CO.	FROM ORDER BOOK
DD 111	2	1927-11-21	DITSON DREADNOUGHT 111	C. H. DITSON & CO.	FROM ORDER BOOK
DD 111	1	1928-02-08	DITSON DREADNOUGHT 111	C. H. DITSON & CO.	FROM ORDER BOOK
DD 111	2	1928-05-28	DITSON DREADNOUGHT 111	C. H. DITSON & CO.	FROM ORDER BOOK
DD 111	2	1928-06-20	DITSON DREADNOUGHT 111	C. H. DITSON & CO.	FROM ORDER BOOK
DD 111	2	1929-01-29	DITSON DREADNOUGHT 111	C. H. DITSON & CO.	FROM ORDER BOOK
DD 111S	1	1930-01-16	DITSON DREADNOUGHT 111S	OLIVER DITSON CO.	FROM ORDER BOOK

Table 27
Ditson Guitars Shipped August 18, 1923 to January 16, 1930

BRIGGS SPECIAL MANDOLINS

Between 1915 and 1919 Martin made seventy-one "Briggs Special Mandolins" for F. K. Briggs of Utica NY. The whole series had regular Martin serial numbers.

The Briggs Special mandolins were not really that "special" as they were broadly based on the regular Martin style A mandolin. The major difference was a scalloped head stock ("like Ditson pattern") instead of the plain Martin rectangular head stock.

A "Briggs Special" steel stamp was prepared and was presumably applied to the back of the head stock and to the interior back strip. In appearance, the Briggs Special stamp was very similar to the Foden Special and Bitting Special stamps.

F. K. Briggs appears to have gone out of business in 1920.

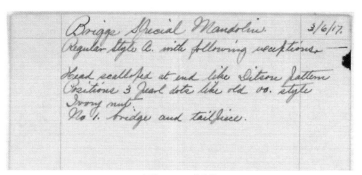

Figure 218
Specification Card for Briggs Special Mandolins

Figure 219
Briggs Special Stamp

BRIGGS SPECIAL MANDOLINS				
STYLE	QUAN	DATE SHIPPED	COMMENTS	SERIAL NUMBERS
BRIGGS SPECIAL	4	1915-11-13	MAND A BRIGGS SPECIAL	4776, 4679, 4680, 4686
BRIGGS SPECIAL	8	1915-11-20	MAND A BRIGGS SPECIAL	4675, 4677-4678, 4681-4685
BRIGGS SPECIAL	12	1916-01-29	MAND A BRIGGS SPECIAL	4749-4760
BRIGGS SPECIAL	6	1916-11-21	MAND A BRIGGS SPECIAL	4878-4883
BRIGGS SPECIAL	5	1917-03-31	MAND A BRIGGS SPECIAL	5119-5123
BS	6	1917-12-12	BRIGGS SPECIAL	5566, 5571, 5579, 5581, 5582, 5592
BS	3	1918-03-14	BRIGGS SPECIAL	5841, 5896, 5897
BS	2	1918-03-18	BRIGGS SPECIAL	5891, 5893
BS	1	1918-03-18	BRIGGS SPECIAL	5890
BS	6	1918-03-26	BRIGGS SPECIAL	5826, 5894, 5895, 5907, 5913, 5917
BS	6	1918-10-04	BRIGGS SPECIAL	6296-6301
BS	12	1919-01-23	BRIGGS SPECIAL	6378-6389

Table 28
Briggs Special Mandolins

SOUTHERN CALIFORNIA MUSIC CO. (1916-1918)

Southern California Music Company (SoCal) was founded in Los Angeles in 1880. By 1916 Southern California Music Co. had become a large retail and wholesale music chain with branches in Los Angeles, Pasadena, Riverside and San Diego.

Southern California Music had been selling Martin guitars since 1901 but sales did not really take off until 1913. There is a possibility that Southern California Music Co. took over Lindsey Music Co., who had been Martin's largest dealer in southern California and ceased buying Martin instruments at about the same time in 1913.

Southern California Music and Sherman, Clay Co. were Martin's two largest dealers on the West Coast. In 1915 Southern California corresponded with Martin and was granted a territory stretching southward from Bakersfield to San Diego. See page 43 for more information on Martin's relationship with the Southern California Music Co.

In Mid-1916 Southern California Music ordered some sample guitars from Martin with spruce tops and koa wood sides and backs. Six of each in styles 0-18, 0-21 and 00-28 comprised the order. These guitars were not serialized and contained neither Martin nor SoCal stamps.

Southern California Music supplied koa to Martin for use on their guitars. Two shipments were received, one some time in 1916 and the second on November 15, 1917. Presumably this wood was pre-seasoned as it was put into use immediately. The records also suggest the wood were supplied as flitches or slabs and re-sawn prior to use. The first shipment must have been substantial since it lasted up to about serial number 192. The second shipment yielded 76 sides and 952 backs (should probably read "tops and backs") and a note was added that indicated "all slabs kept for re-sawing". The second shipment covered the rest of the SoCal production run but there was sufficient wood left over for all Martin koa wood guitars made up to early 1921. Martin did not need to purchase koa for their own account until April 14, 1921.

Martin applied a special series of serial numbers for

the Southern California Music Co. guitars after the first 18 guitars were shipped. Serial numbers from 19 through 262 are recorded in the sales ledger with the exception of serial numbers 124, 137, 141 and 142 (these were probably all model 1350 guitars). Serial number 137 exists but is not in the sales records.

A record of the descriptions of the initial batch is as follows:

"Descriptions of Koa guitars for S. C. Mus. Co. sent 7/10/16

#1350. Style 0-18

- **Plain neck stained dark, 19 frets**
- **Positions style 18. Brass machines.**
- **Plain pins. Ebony nut. Top stained brown**
- **Border & rosette like Foden A**
- **Braces 1-17 style**

#1400. Style 0-21

- **Plain neck stained dark, 19 frets**
- **Positions style 21. Nickel mech. (No promise)**
- **Pearl eye ebony pins. Ivory nut.**
- **Border & rosette like Foden B**
- **Braces 1-17 style**

#1500. Style 00-28

- **Plain neck stained dark, 19 frets**
- **Foden C. Nickel mach. (No promise)**
- **Pearl eye ebony pins. Ivory nut.**
- **Top stained brown**
- **Celluloid (white) binding body and fingerboard**
- **Front border three thin white & 3 thin black**
- **Back border 1 thin white & 1 thin black**
- **Strip in back like C mandolin**
- **Rosette 0.020 white outside with heavy black next to it. Inside 3 - 0.040 white with thin black between. Model Foden C.
  Braces 1-17 style"**

These guitars have spruce tops and the decoration is modeled after Foden style A, B and C guitars. They all have a single ring rosette, while, in comparison, later Southern California Music Co. Style 1400 and 1500 guitars are serialized and have three ring rosettes. Style 1350 guitars retained their single sound

hole ring throughout the production run.

The Martin archive has a hand written order slip, dated July 7, 1916, containing some very interesting information:

"25 Koa wood guitars from wood previously sent, styles not specified. Above number is our own estimate and can be made more or less. Send as many as possible.

Aug 16. Divide as follows:
13 No. 1350 - style like 0-18
7 No. 1400 - style like 0-21
5 No. 1500 - style like 00-28

See letter for ornamentation. Put serial number in each guitar, Stamp S. C. Co. only, Koa wood tops on all. Necks may be mahogany stained dark Sept. 4."

The first batch of guitars (six each of 0-18, 0-21 ad 00-28) was shipped on July 10, 1916, so this letter must be referring to the second order. The second batch, twelve model 1350, seven model 1400 and six model 1500 guitars, was shipped between November 17 and November 24, 1916. As noted on the order slip these guitars have different ornamentation from the first batch and only had a SoCal stamp.

The SoCal labels, decals and the location of the SoCal stamps varied over time. The comments offered below are based on a small sample and may need to be revised as more guitars are uncovered.

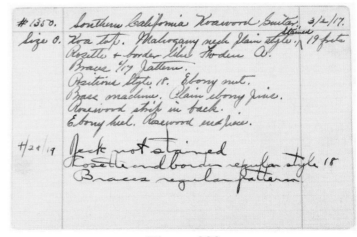

Figure 220
Specification Card for SoCal Model 1350 Guitar

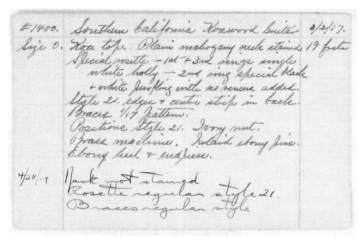

Figure 221
Specification Card for SoCal Model 1400 Guitar

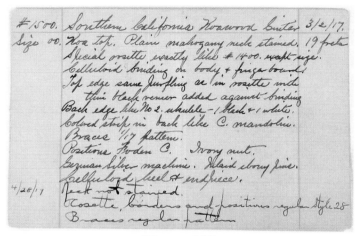

Figure 222
Specification Card for SoCal Model 1500 Guitar

Figure 223
Rolando Label in SoCal Style 1400 Guitar
(Serial Number 237)

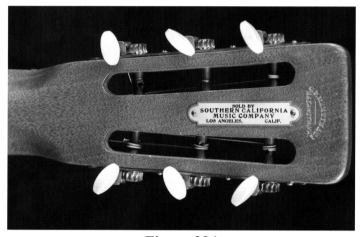

Figure 224
Southern California Music Co. Metal Plaque on Back
of Headstock (Serial Number 162)

Labels

The early serialized SoCal guitars, delivered between November 1916 and May 1917 (serial numbers 19 to 85), have a "M. Nunes & Son/Royal Hawaiian" label. From serial number 86, "Rolando" labels replaced the Nunes type. One style 1400 (serial number 162) is known without a Rolando label but instead has a Southern California Music Co. metal plaque attached to the back of the headstock (see figure 224).

Decals

The earliest SoCal guitars, without serial numbers, have a decal of the coat of arms of Hawaii with additional "M. Nunes " and "1879" decals above and a "Hawaii" decal below. By serial number 19 the "1879" decal had been removed. From serial number 86 to the end of the production run only the Hawaiian

coat of arms decal appeared on SoCal guitars.

The motto of Hawaii is shown on the decal and reads **"Ua Mau ke Ea o ka ʻĀina i ka Pono"**. In English, this can be roughly translated as **"The life of the land is perpetuated in righteousness"**.

Southern California Music Company Stamp

Early SoCal guitars had the Southern California Music Co. stamps on the back strip and on the back of the head stock. From the August and September 1917 deliveries, starting at serial number 86, guitars retained the SoCal stamp on the back strip but had a Martin stamp on the back of the headstock.

Top Bracing Pattern

As indicated on the specification cards SoCal guitars

SOUTHERN CALIFORNIA MUSIC COMPANY LOS ANGELES

Figure 225
Southern California Music Co. Stamp

had a five-strut fan brace as used on Martin 1-17 guitars of the period. However, one style 1500 guitar has been reported with X-bracing so others may exist

Sound Hole Rosette, Purfling and Back Stripe

The SoCal Style 1350 guitars had a rosette and purfling like a Foden Style A, even though none of this Foden model were ever made. The back strip is a single black line of purfling. After SoCal began purchasing regular Martin 0-18K guitars, while still using their own model numbers, the rosette became the usual style 18 rosette of three rings.

SoCal Style 1400 guitars had a three ring rosette with a "special black and white Purfling" making up the center ring. The inside and outside rings were a single line of white holly. Purling was the same as a regular style 21 Martin guitar and the SoCal specification cards called for a style 21 purfling (herringbone) for the back stripe. These are seen in two varieties; black and white or red and green herringbone patterns.

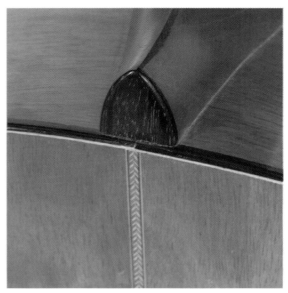

Figure 227
Red and Green Herringbone Back Stripe on SoCal Model 1400 Guitar (Serial Number 237)

Style 1500 SoCal guitars have the same rosette as the Style 1400 models but also used the same special black and white purfling for the edge of the guitar with a thin black line added before the white celluloid binding. The back stripe was the same pattern as that used for Martin Style C mandolins.

Fingerboard Inlays

The fingerboard markers on Style 1350 were the same as regular Martin style 18 guitars while the Style 1400 had Martin style 21 inlays. The fingerboard marker for SoCal Style 1500 guitars were the same as Foden Style C inlays.

Figure 226
SoCal Style 1400 Sound Hole Rosette
(Serial Number 237)

MARTIN STYLE	SoCal STYLE	QUAN	DATE SHIPPED	COMMENTS	SERIAL NUMBERS
(0-18K)		6	1916-06-30	KOA GUITARS SIMILAR TO STYLE 0-18, SPRUCE TOP	(1-6)
(0-21K)		6	1916-06-30	KOA GUITARS SIMILAR TO STYLE 0-21, SPRUCE TOP	(7-12)
(00-28K)		6	1916-06-30	KOA GUITARS SIMILAR TO STYLE 00-28, SPRUCE TOP	(13-18)
0-18K	1350	12	1916-11-17	KOA GUITARS	19-27, 29, 30, 37
0-21K	1400	7	1916-11-24	KOA GUITARS	28, 31-36
00-28K	1500	6	1916-11-24	KOA GUITARS	38-43
0-18K	1350	6	1917-05-10	KOA GUITARS	44, 45, 47, 48, 51, 53, 54, 57
0-21K	1400	2	1917-05-15		65, 73
0-18K	1350	3	1917-05-18		46, 49, 60
0-21K	1400	3	1917-05-18		62, 66, 69
0-18K	1350	1	1917-05-21		55
0-21K	1400	1	1917-05-21		71
00-28K	1500	1	1917-05-21		75
0-18K	1350	1	1917-05-22		61
0-21K	1400	4	1917-05-29		63, 64, 68, 70
00-28K	1500	2	1917-05-29		77, 80
0-18K	1350	1	1917-05-29		58
0-21K	1400	1	1917-05-29		72
00-28K	1500	1	1917-05-29		82
00-28K	1500	3	1917-05-29		79, 81, 84
0-18K	1350	4	1917-05-31		50, 52, 56, 59
0-21K	1400	1	1917-05-31		67
00-28K	1500	5	1917-05-31		74, 76, 78, 83, 85
0-18K	1350	5	1917-08-11		87, 88, 90, 100, 103
0-21K	1400	1	1917-08-11		147
00-28K	1500	2	1917-08-11		149, 150
0-18K	1350	18	1917-09-10		86, 89, 91, 95, 102, 108, 111, 112, 114, 117, 122, 125, 132, 134, 138, 139, 144, 145
0-18K	1350	18	1917-09-24		92, 93, 99, 101, 104, 105, 106, 107, 119, 123, 126, 127, 128, 131, 135, 136, 140, 143
0-21K	1400	15	1917-09-24		146, 154, 156, 159, 160, 161, 162, 164, 170, 174, 175, 177, 178. 179, 180
00-28K	1500	4	1917-09-24		148, 189, 190, 191
0-18K	1350	7	1917-09-29		94, 97, 110, 113, 115, 120, 133
0-21K	1400	15	1917-09-29		151, 152, 153, 155, 157, 158, 163, 165, 166, 167, 168, 169, 171, 172, 173
00-28K	1500	9	1917-09-29		176, 181-184, 186-188, 192
0-18K	1350	6	1917-10-05		96, 109, 118, 121, 129, 130
UKE 1K	21	1	1917-10-13		
UKE 2K	22	1	1917-10-13		
UKE 3K	23	1	1917-10-13		
	31	1	1917-10-13	SPECIAL STYLES	
	32	1	1917-10-13	SPECIAL STYLES	
	33	1	1917-10-13	SPECIAL STYLES	
00-28K	1500	10	1917-11-16		185, 253, 254, 255, 256, 257, 258, 259, 260, 261
0-18K	1350	9	1917-11-16		193, 194, 195, 196, 197, 198, 199, 200, 202
0-18K	1350	32	1917-11-30		116, 201, 203-232
0-21K	1400	20	1917-11-30		233-252
0-18K	(1350)	1	1918-06-29		262

Table 29
Southern California Music Co. Serial Numbers

Bitting Special Guitars, Mandolins and Mandolas
(1916-1918)

Oliver F. Bitting began buying guitars from Martin in 1905. His original store was in Steinway City, New York but by 1907 he had moved to Long Island City. Bitting relocated to Bethlehem PA in 1912 and, finally, to St. Petersburg FL in 1922. Bitting continued to buy Martin instruments as late as 1956 although there was a lengthy hiatus in purchases between 1941 and 1953.

Between 1916 and 1918, O. F. Bitting had Martin make up a number of special model guitars, mandolins and mandolas. The distinguishing feature of these instruments is that they have curly maple sides and backs. The spruce tops were also stained brown while the backs and sides were stained a deep red brown color. A total of 58 Bitting Special instruments were made: 40 mandolins, 3 mandolas and 15 guitars. Of the 15 guitars, five were 0-18 and ten were 0-21 guitars. Most of the Bitting Special instruments have regular Martin serial numbers, with the exception of all five 0-18 guitars and one of the 0-21 guitars.

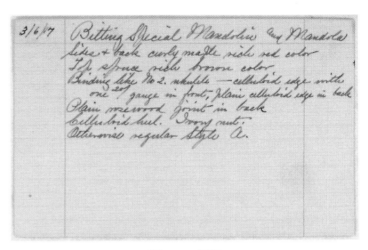

Figure 229
Specification Card for Bitting Special
Mandolins and Mandolas

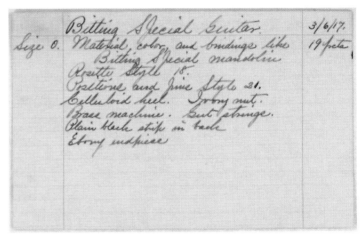

Figure 228
Bitting Special Stamp

Figure 230
Specification Card for Bitting Special Guitars

STYLE	QUAN	DATE SHIPPED	COMMENTS	SERIAL NUMBERS
BITTING SPECIAL	2	SEPT. 27, 1916	MANDOLINS, MAHOGANY STAINED & POLISHED, CELLULOID BOUND FRONT & BACK, IVORY NUT, OTHERWISE LIKE STYLE A	4884-4885
BITTING SPECIAL	8	JAN. 18, 1917	MAPLE MANDOLINS, SPECIAL STYLE	5000-5007
BITTING SPECIAL	5	JAN. 18, 1917	MAPLE 0-18 GUITARS	NONE
BITTING SPECIAL	1	JAN. 18, 1917	MAPLE GUITAR SPECIAL STYLE	NONE
BITTING SPECIAL	2	FEB. 20, 1917	MANDOLINS, STYLE 00	5039-5040
BITTING SPECIAL	1	MAR. 5, 1917	MANDOLA	5041
BITTING SPECIAL	7	APR. 12, 1917	MANDOLINS	5125-5130, 5132
BITTING SPECIAL	5	APR. 12, 1917	BITTING SPECIAL GUITARS	12566-12570
BITTING SPECIAL	2	OCT. 11, 1917	MANDOLINS	5460-5461
BITTING SPECIAL	3	OCT. 11, 1917		5466-5468
BITTING SPECIAL	5	OCT 11, 1917		5472, 5773, 5475, 5476, 5478
BITTING SPECIAL	6	NOV. 2, 1917		5463-5465, 5469, 5474, 5477
BS	1	MAR. 12, 1918	STYLE B SPECIAL	5934
BS	1	JUNE 28, 1918	STYLE B SPECIAL, BORDER LIKE 6a	6169
BS	1	JUNE 28, 1918	STYLE B SPECIAL	6170

Table 30
Bitting Special Guitars, Mandolins and Mandolas

WILLIAM J. SMITH & CO. (1917-1923)

Ukuleles

William J. Smith & Co. was a New York City music publisher and musical instrument retailer. For the decade prior to 1915 Smith had been employed by Charles H. Ditson & Co. and during that time had become expert in playing the ukulele and Hawaiian guitar. In 1915 Smith decided to strike out on his own.

The new company began buying Martin guitars on October 9, 1915, when a large order for 9 guitars and 10 mandolins was placed as a "stock for beginning business".

At this point it is worthwhile looking at an excerpt from a July 14, 1915 letter that Martin wrote to Southern California Music Co.:

"We note your Ukulele enclosure; have you a market for the American made article? We are starting on them for New York trade."

This letter was written in the middle of the Panama-Pacific International Exposition, which ran from February 20 to December 4, 1915. The interest in Hawaiian music had been slowly increasing since the turn of the century but the Exposition ignited that nascent interest into a craze.

The timing of all this ukulele activity is very interesting. Smith was acknowledged as an expert in playing Hawaiian instruments just as Hawaiian music took off as a result of the Panama-Pacific Exposition. Smith must have thought the time was right for him to start his own business in order to capitalize on the new craze. It also begs the question who influenced Martin to begin making ukuleles for "the New York trade". It certainly seems Smith, especially as an employee of Charles H. Ditson & Co., was in the perfect position to encourage Martin to add ukuleles to the line. This theory is amply supported by the fact that the vast majority of Martin's early ukuleles were sold to Charles H. Ditson & Co. and William J. Smith & Co. In effect, these two companies were "the New York trade".

An announcement concerning the opening of William J. Smith & Co. appeared in the Music Trade Review on December 4, 1915. The article states "only genuine native instruments will be handled" by the company although Smith had already been shipped his first Martin ukulele. Considering how many Martin ukuleles Smith purchased from early 1916, it is unlikely native instruments made up any significant part of his business. William J. Smith & Co. also published "The New Kamiki Ukulele Method" in 1916. Smith probably found it much more advantageous to sell Martin ukuleles to go along with the ukulele method, as Martin was known for making quality products and was also much nearer at hand.

NEW SMALL GOODS HOUSE.

Hawaiian ukuleles will be specialized and a general line of small goods carried in the new musical merchandise business opened at 56 East Thirty-fourth street, New York, by William J. Smith & Co. Only genuine native instruments will be handled. Mr. Smith is himself an expert performer on these instruments, being known both as a professional and a teacher. He was formerly connected with C. H. Ditson & Co.

Figure 231
Announcement for William J. Smith & Co.[1]

Smith was shipped his first Martin ukulele (serial number 5) on November 13, 1915 and a second (serial number 13) on January 31, 1916. As production of ukuleles ramped up in early 1916 Smith quickly became Martin's largest customer for the newly introduced ukuleles. (Charles H. Ditson & Co. bought more ukuleles than Smith but their ukuleles had a Ditson stamp and their own serial numbers). Smith purchased 62 of the 143 that Martin ukuleles made with serial numbers. Smith also began to purchase Martin taro-patches in November 1916.

The ledgers records that Smith started ordering ukuleles with a special William J. Smith & Co. stamp in February 1917. The ledger stops mentioning the Smith stamp for ukuleles in February 1918.

It is not entirely clear from the ledgers how many ukuleles were supplied with the Smith stamp. Smith sometimes placed orders for ukuleles that were all to receive a Smith stamp and at other times orders specified a mixture of Martin and Smith stamps. As well, on some orders no mention at all was made concerning the type of stamp to be used. Martin may also have continued to supply ukuleles with the Smith stamp after February 1918. The best that can be said is that at least one hundred and thirty-nine Style 1, thirty-four Style 2 and two Style 3 ukuleles were shipped with the Smith stamp. Curiously, it does not appear that any of the taro-patches ordered by Smith received the special stamp.

UKULELES WITH WILLIAM J. SMITH STAMP			
	UKE 1	UKE 2	UKE 3
1917	125	26	2
1918	14	8	
TOTAL	139	34	2

Table 31
Number of Ukuleles with William J. Smith Stamp

Figure 232
Special William J. Smith & Co. Stamp

Tiples

It is well known that William J. Smith bought the first tiples and examination of the ledger records provides some very interesting information concerning the development of the Martin tiple.

In June 1918 Smith was shipped three ¼-18 (serial numbers 13234 and 13236-237) and three ½-18 guitars (serial numbers 13233, 13235 and 13239). The ¼ guitars, as mentioned elsewhere in this book, had originally been designed in 1917 for Charles H. Ditson & Co. as a "Child's Guitar" but was renamed ¼ size in March 1918. The ½-18 was another small sized guitar designed for Ditson. All of these had "colored tops" and were probably all 6 strings guitars.

On August 9, 1918 an unusual order for William J. Smith & Co. appeared in the Martin bookings ledger:

"Trial order of new South American instrument. Four strings triple, tuned like Ukulele. Six string machine head (i.e., one per side on the head stock). Bridge according to judgment. Build the six then finish one to test bridge. Brace extremely light. Price not set."

A second order, for three ¼-18 guitars, was placed on August 16, 1918. The first order comprised serial numbers 13354-13359 and the second order serial numbers 13387-13389. Up to this point the prototype tiples had the shallow sides of ¼ size guitars.

An order for six ¼-18 guitars was placed on November 29, 1918 and another for six tiples (with 12 strings) on December 19, 1918. Although the number of strings is not mentioned in the November 29 order it can be assumed they were 12-string instruments as well. The shallow sides of the ¼-size guitar didn't produce the tone desired by Smith so the depth of the sides was increased. These two orders were combined and all twelve (serial numbers 13507-13528) were shipped on March 31, 1919 as "Tiple Guitars ¼-size (Deeper Sides)". The overall pattern of the tiple stayed the same as the ¼ size guitar but the depth of the body was increased by roughly 3/4". From this point the instruments were referred to as "Tiples" although ¼-18 and even "guitar-uke" were also used

SIDE DIMENSIONS OF EARLY MARTIN TIPLES		
MODEL	DEPTH OF BODY AT NECK BLOCK	DEPTH OF BODY AT END
¼-18	2 ¼"	2 13/16"
TIPLE	3"	3 5/8"

Table 32
Side Dimensions of ¼-Size Guitars and Early Tiples

at times. One question remaining concerns the source of the design for the Martin tiples. The answer is provided by a note in the ledger that Martin returned "1 Sou(th) Am(erican) Tiple" to Smith in the shipment of December 5, 1918. It appears quite likely that the ¼-size 12-string guitars were modeled after an example of a Tiple Colombiano or a Tiple Colombiano Requinto (sometimes simply called the Tiple Requinto, an instrument about 10-15% smaller than the Tiple Colombiano). Columbian tiples normally have 12 strings in four courses of triple strings. The Columbian tiple itself is an adaptation of the Spanish vihuela. The ¼-size pattern appears to have been smaller than the tiple Colombiano as the former has a scale length of 17" versus about 21" for the latter. The deeper sides adopted for the Martin tiples may have also been to compensate for the smaller pattern size.

It is not known how long the early tiples continued to be made with 12 strings but a specification card in the archive shows that by at least May 19, 1920 the tiple were being made with 10 strings.

The early tiples were sold simply as "Tiples", with no style designation. The specification card indicates

Figure 233
Specification Card for William J. Smith & Co. Tiples

HIGHER GRADE WILLIAM J. SMITH CO. TIPLES			
MODEL	QUAN	DATE SHIPPED	COMMENTS
T-28	1	APRIL 29, 1922	10 STRING
T-28	1	APRIL 29, 1922	8 STRING, DARK TOP
T-42	1	APRIL 29, 1922	8 STRING, DARK TOP, SPECIAL
T-42*	1		SPECIAL (PROBABLY 10 STRING)
T-45K	1	APRIL 29, 1922	10 TRING, DARK TOP, SPECIAL

* A second T-42 was ordered but does not appear in the sales ledger

Table 33
High Grade William J. Smith & Co. Tiples

Figure 234
The Unique T-45K Tiple

Figure 235
U-KA-LU-A Label in T-45K Tiple

only minor differences with what would later be known as T-18 tiples. The T-18 model designation did not come into use until 1923. The backs of the tiples were unbound prior to October 1, 1921. At least 42 "Tiples" were sold to Smith with "dark tops", although many more of the tiples ordered probably had this finish. An order for twelve "Portuguese tiples" was placed on July 23, 1919 but they don't appear in the sales ledger and may not have been made. In addition, Smith ordered a batch of six 8-string tiples with dark tops on February 7, 1922.

The specification card documents that the tiples were to receive only the Smith stamp but examples have been seen with the Martin on the back of the head stock and the Smith stamp on the interior back strip. It is likely that William J. Smith & Co. tiples exist with just the Martin stamp. The use of the William J. Smith & Co. stamp continued until at least 1923.

Smith seems to have had an exclusive arrangement with Martin for the sale of these instruments until July 1921 and bought the majority of early tiples, 171 of a total of 265 made to the end of 1922. Some sample tiples were shipped out in late December 1921 to Oliver Ditson Co., Southern California Music Co. and Sherman, Clay & Co.

In April 1922 Smith experimented with some fancier models.

Smith soon discovered there was little market for higher grade tiples. The T-45K is unique and only these two T-42 tiples were ever made. The "Special" feature noted for the T-45K refers to the double pick guard mounted over the upper bout (see Figure 23). Smith affixed labels, reading "KAMIKI" or "U-KA-LU-A", to the inside of some of their tiples. Smith seems to have had a market for unusual sizes, any size 2½ guitar from the period was likely sold to Smith. Smith continued to buy Martin instruments until 1962, although purchases were scant from 1932. William J. Smith & Co. is no longer in existence, although the timing of the dissolution of the company is unknown.

THE "CUSTOMER'S" OR "C" LINE (1922-1924)

BACON BANJO CO. (1922-1924)

In 1922 Martin corresponded with the Bacon Banjo Co. about participating in the "C" line. In a letter to Martin dated July 7, 1922, Fred Bacon defined the specifications for the guitars he wanted:

"The writer while at the dealers Convention held at the Commodore Hotel, New York City, talked with Mr. Martin Jr. about making some Guitars for us in the white, and we putting on our own special finish and selling them to our trade as Bacon Guitars.

Won't you please send us one style that you would list for about $25, and another (concert size) good spruce top, fine grain and rosewood back and sides, just joined without marquetry thru center of back, something you would list at $35.00 or $40.00. We would prefer both instruments in the white, with bridge glued on and adjusted for proper string heighth (sic), ebony bridges for both instruments and white ivoroid or bone pins for the better grade. Kindly make us proper allowance for finishing the above instruments. We prefer to use our own strings to allow us something for them also.

Just as soon as we receive the instruments and finish them up, we will no doubt be in a position to place an order with you at an early date. Please send both in canvas cases by express…"

On July 24, 1922 Martin replied:

"Your letter of July 7 in regard to Guitars was duly received and we have to apologize for neglecting to reply promptly. After careful consideration of your specification we have decided to make up for you, as samples, one each of two styles according to the following descriptions:

OUR #2-17-C

Amateur size, Mahogany back, sides and top. Rosewood bindings, Single ring rosette of rosewood and ebony. Mahogany neck, rosewood veneered head. Rosewood fingerboard and bridge. Seventeen nickel silver frets. Three white position marks, six small side dots. Black bridge and end pins. Steel Strings. Ebony nut, bone bridge saddle. Net price, in the white.........$10.75

OUR #0-21-C

Concert size. Rosewood back and sides. Selected spruce top. Rosewood bindings. Top edged with narrow rosewood and maple, Single ring rosette of colored marquetry. Mahogany neck, rosewood veneered head. Ebony fingerboard and bridge. Twenty nickel silver frets. Five pearl position dots, six small side dots. Bone nut and bridge saddle. Ivory-celluloid bridge and end pins. Gut and silk-center strings.
Net price, in the white.........$20.00

These prices include an allowance for finishing, but not for strings because we would not care to send the instruments to you without stringing and testing them and there would be little saving in removing the string before shipment.

The samples will be put through as promptly as possible but they can hardly be ready to send to you until the middle of next month."

Martin must have been running a little behind because the two guitars were not shipped until August 31. On September 19 Bacon acknowledged receipt of the guitars:

"The two (2) Guitars furnished on our order of July 7 and invoiced August 31st duly received and are very satisfactory indeed.

We believe, however, it will be better for us to have you finish these for us, and with this in view are enclosing our order #635 for two more of each size which please ship at your earliest convenience, and upon receipt and proper trial, we will be pleased to take the matter of quantity orders up with you. Kindly quote price to us of the finished instruments.

We have not finished the first samples sent to us yet, and would also be pleased to have you quote us your price for the two we have and, if satisfacto-

ry, we will then return same for this work."

Martin responded on September 20 and increased the price of the 2-17-C to $12.50 and the 0-21-C to $25.00 to reflect the fact that these guitars were to be supplied finished.

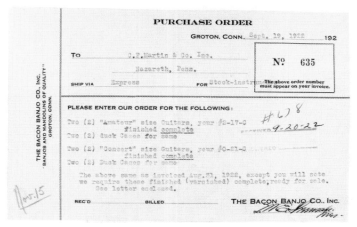

Figure 236
Order 635 for Two 2-17-C and Two 0-21-C Guitars

Bacon ordered two more 2-17-C guitars for Hawaiian playing on September 27, 1922. The guitars would have been set up for gut strings, as Martin did for their own Hawaiian guitars at the time, but since no nut extenders were included with the shipment these must have been supplied by Bacon Banjo.

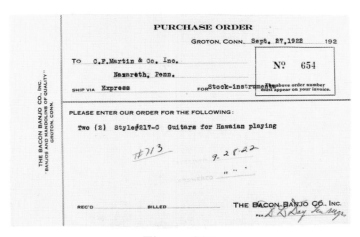

Figure 237
Order for Two 2-17-C Guitars for Hawaiian Playing

The four 2-17-C and two 0-21-C guitars ordered above were shipped on December 7, 1922.

Another four 2-17 guitars were ordered on February 24, 1923 with "no name" and, on May 2, these four 2-17 guitars were shipped to Bacon. The guitars had serial numbers 18251, 18254, 18280 and 18282 and

were regular 2-17 guitars except for the fact that they were supplied with "no stamp". These were supplied from a batch of fifty 2-17's stamped on March 19, 1923 that also included some guitars that received a Ditson stamp.

An 0-21-C was ordered on June 27, 1923 but a regular Martin 0-21 (serial number 18909) with no stamp was shipped on September 7.

Three "no stamp" 0-21 guitars were ordered on November 21. On November 23 three 0-21 guitars with "no brand" were shipped to Bacon (serial numbers 19327, 19333 and 19339).

Three more 0-21s with "no stamp" were ordered on March 4, 1924 and were delivered on March 28 (serial numbers 20090, 20091 and 20094).

"CUSTOMER'S LINE" GUITARS MADE FOR FRED BACON					
STYLE	QUAN	DATE ORDERED	DATE SHIPPED	COMMENTS	SERIAL NUMBERS
2-17-C	1	July 7, 1922	August 31, 1922		N/A
0-21-C	1	July 7, 1922	August 31, 1922		N/A
2-17-C	2	Sept. 20, 1922	December 7, 1922		N/A
0-21-C	2	Sept. 20, 1922	December 7, 1922		N/A
2-17-C	2	Sept. 27, 1922	December 7, 1922	Hawaiian	N/A
2-17	4	February 24, 1923	May 2, 1923	No Brand	18251 18254 18280 18282
0-21-C	1	June 27, 1923	September 7, 1923	No Brand	18909
0-21	3	November 21, 1923	November 23, 1923	No Brand	19327 19333 19339
0-21	3	March 4, 1924	March 26, 1924	No Brand	20090 20091 20094

Table 34
"Customer's Line" Guitars
Made for Bacon Banjo Co. Inc.

A total of nine 2-17 and ten 0-21 guitars were made for the Bacon Banjo Co. as part of the "C" line. Regular Martin models with serial numbers were supplied but without a Martin stamp. The first guitars on the list above were clearly ordered with the single ring rosettes. Until an example of one of the guitars above with a serial number is examined it will not be known if they have a regular Martin rosette.

None of these guitars received any special stamp although the first 0-21-C has "Bacon" inlaid in pearl in the head stock veneer.

PERLBERG & HALPIN (1922)

Perlberg & Halpin was a well-known New York musical merchandise jobbing house formed in 1910 by proprietors Harry Perlberg and Abe Halpin.

The company was originally located at 138 Park Row but moved to 890 Broadway in 1926. The partnership was dissolved in 1927 but the business continued at the same address under the new firm name of Harry Perlberg.

The company sold a wide variety of musical products including the Beltone line of musical instruments. In 1922 they bought Martin-made ukuleles, mandolins and guitars under the Beltone brand name. The arrangement ended in early 1923 when Perlberg & Halpin sought better pricing for jobbing. Martin was not able to agree to their request due to the sole agencies Martin had already established.

Abe Halpin wrote again to Martin in 1924 about jobbing prices but nothing came of it.

"CUSTOMER'S LINE" INSTRUMENTS MADE FOR PERLBERG & HALPIN						
STYLE	QUAN.	DATE ORDERED	DATE SHIPPED	SPECIAL FEATURE	COMMENTS	RETAIL PRICE
UKE 0-C			June 17, 1922		BELTONE STAMP	$10.00
UKE 1-C			June 17, 1922		BELTONE STAMP	$12.00
UKE 2?			June 17, 1922		BELTONE STAMP?	$15.00
UKE 0-C	25	May 2, 1922	June 27, 1922		BELTONE STAMP	$10.00
UKE 0-C	25	May 2, 1922	June 27, 1922	SPECIAL DARK (FINISH)	BELTONE STAMP	$11.00
UKE 1-C	25	May 2, 1922	June 29, 1922		BELTONE STAMP	$12.00
UKE 2-C	12	May 2, 1922	June 29, 1922		BELTONE STAMP	$14.00
UKE 2K-C	12	May 2, 1922	July 17, 1922		BELTONE STAMP	$17.00
UKE 3-C	12	May 2, 1922	June 29, 1922		BELTONE STAMP	$24.00
UKE 3K-C	12	May 2, 1922	Aug. 12, 1922		BELTONE STAMP	$27.00
2-17-C	12	May 2, 1922	June 28, 1922		BELTONE STAMP	$25.00
0-18-C	12	May 2, 1922	Aug. 7, 1922		BELTONE STAMP	$30.00
2-17-C	1	May 2, 1922	July 29, 1922	SPECIAL #1	BELTONE STAMP	$13.50
2-17-C	1	May 2, 1922	July 29, 1922	SPECIAL #2	BELTONE STAMP	$15.50
2-17-C	1	May 2, 1922	July 29, 1922	SPECIAL #3	BELTONE STAMP	$16.50
MAND A-C	12	May 2, 1922	July 29, 1922		BELTONE STAMP	$10.00
MAND A-C	12	May 2, 1922	July 29, 1922	DARK (FINISH)	BELTONE STAMP	$11.00
MAND AK-C	11	May 2, 1922	July 29, 1922		BELTONE STAMP	$12.50
MAND AK-C	1	May 2, 1922	July 31, 1922		BELTONE STAMP	$12.50
MAND A-C	1	May 2, 1922	June 10, 1922	SPECIAL #1	BELTONE STAMP	$20.00
MAND A-C	1	May 2, 1922	June 10, 1922	SPECIAL #2	BELTONE STAMP	$22.00
MAND A-C	1	May 2, 1922	June 10, 1922	SPECIAL #3	BELTONE STAMP	$20.00
MAND A-C	1	May 2, 1922	June 10, 1922	SPECIAL #4	BELTONE STAMP	$22.00
MAND A-C	1	May 2, 1922	June 10, 1922	SPECIAL #5	BELTONE STAMP	$26.00
MAND A-C	1	May 2, 1922	June 10, 1922	SPECIAL #6	BELTONE STAMP	$28.00
MAND BK-C	12	May 2, 1922	1922-06-28		BELTONE STAMP	$35.00
UKE 0-C	25	Aug. 1, 1922	1922-09-14		BELTONE STAMP	$10.00
UKE 0-C	4	1922-08-16	1922-10-06	SPECIAL DESIGN*, 2 STAINED	BELTONE STAMP?	$11.00

* 2 with rosewood headstock veneers and 2 with koa headstock veneers

Table 35
"Beltone" Stamped Musical Instruments Made for Perlberg & Halpin Inc.

When the large order for instruments was placed on May 2, 1922, the bookings ledger recorded instructions for the special Beltone stamp: "Beltone stamp inside, Beltone stamp on plate or head". Presumably, most of the instruments listed in Table 35 will have a Beltone stamp on the interior back strip and on the back of the head stock.

A total of 154 ukuleles, 54 mandolins and 27 guitars were purchased as part of the "Customer's Line" although a few may not have received the "Beltone" stamp. It is not recorded what the differences existed between the various "special" models although, based on price, the more expensive "special" style A-C mandolins probably had increased amounts of inlay work.

Figure 238
Special "Beltone" Stamp in a Style AK Mandolin

BUEGELEISEN & JACOBSON "S. S. Stewart" Brand (1923-1926)

Buegeleisen & Jacobson was a large wholesale music business located in New York City. B & J purchased Martin instruments for over 50 years, from 1901 to 1954.

Buegeleisen & Jacobson sold several brands of guitars to locations around the United States including Kay De Lux guitars, Serenader guitars, S. S. Stewart guitars, and National guitars. The company also sold Serenader ukuleles, Abbott trumpets, clarinets, trombone, accordions, and violins.

Buegeleisen & Jacobson participated in the Customer's Line offered by Martin and purchased guitars and ukuleles with the S. S. Stewart stamp. A total of 100 Martin 2-17 Special guitars and 425 style 0 ukuleles with the S. S. Stewart stamp were ordered between 1923 and 1926. The 2-17 Special guitars were made 1923 in two batches of 50. These received Martin serial numbers (18684-18733 and 19023 -19072) and were shipped in batches of 25 between July and November 1923.

The 2-17 Special guitars were somewhat different than normal 2-17 guitars in that they had spruce instead of mahogany tops. The wholesale price of $13.50 was $1.00 higher than regular wholesale price of $12.50 to reflect the difference. This batch of 100 was the only one ordered with spruce tops. All subsequent orders of 2-17 guitars were regular Martin instruments.

"CUSTOMER'S LINE" INSTRUMENTS MADE FOR BUEGELEISEN & JACOBSON					
STYLE	QUAN.	DATE ORDERED	DATE SHIPPED	SPECIAL FEATURE	COMMENTS
2-17	100	April 17, 1923	July 21-Nov. 13, 1923	Special spruce tops	S. S. Stewart stamp
UKE 0	100	April 24, 1923	July 14-26, 1923		S. S. Stewart stamp
UKE 0	50	Jan. 26, 1924			S. S. Stewart stamp
UKE 0	50	Aug. 2, 1924			S. S. Stewart stamp
UKE 0	50	Nov. 3, 1924			S. S. Stewart stamp
UKE 0	100	Jan. 28, 1925			S. S. Stewart stamp
¼-18*	1	May 23, 1925			S. S. Stewart stamp
UKE 0	50	Sept. 18, 1925			S. S. Stewart stamp
UKE 0	25	Feb. 3, 1926			S. S. Stewart stamp

Table 36
Instruments Made for Buegeleisen & Jacobson with an "S. S. Stewart" Stamp

On May 7, 1923 Martin invoiced Buegeleisen & Jacobson $8.51 for the cost of the S. S. Stewart stamp. The delivery dates for most of the "S. S. Stewart"-stamped ukuleles is unknown as Martin stopped recording order details in the sales ledgers part way through 1924.

*One ¼-18 guitar was ordered in May 1925. It is still in existence and has been examined. The guitar has no Martin or S. S. Stewart stamp nor does it have a serial number, although there is an S. S. Stewart label on the interior under the sound hole.

H. & A. SELMER INC. (1923)

H. & A. Selmer Inc. was a well-known importer and jobber of musical instruments located at 117-119 West 46th St. in New York.

Selmer moved to a new factory Elkhart Indian in early 1927. Selmer woodwinds and saxophones were always made by Henri Selmer (Paris).

The ledgers contain no clear documentation that Selmer participated in the Customer's Line. The original Selmer purchase order is in the Martin archive and makes no mention of special brand markings.

However, Martin historian Mike Longworth did note in his logbook that the instruments above received the Selmer stamp so he must have had a chance to examine at least some of these instruments. As well, some of the 2-17 guitars from the same batch were supplied with Rudolph Wurlitzer stamps so it is not unreasonable to suppose some could have received a Selmer stamp.

"CUSTOMER'S LINE" INSTRUMENTS MADE FOR H. & A. SELMER INC.					
STYLE	QUAN	DATE SHIPPED	DATE SHIPPED	COMMENTS	SERIAL NUMBERS
T-18	1	Sept. 1, 1923	Oct. 20, 1923	H. & A Selmer Stamp	19268
2-17	6	Sept. 12, 1923	Oct. 30, 1923	H. & A Selmer Stamp	19283 19286 19290 19293 19298 19304

Table 37
Instruments with "H. & A. Selmer Inc." Stamp

H & A. SELMER. INC.

Figure 239
Special "H. & A. Selmer Inc." Stamp

W. J. DYER & BROTHER - "Stetson" Brand

W. J. Dyer & Brother were musical merchandise importers, jobbers and manufacturers in St. Paul, Minnesota.

Dyer ordered some sample guitars on May 4, 1922 and, slightly later, specified they were to be supplied with steel strings and stamped with the "Stetson" brand name. Martin mentioned that the design of the guitar would be slightly different from regular guitars but did not detail what this meant. Presumably, the sound hole rosette had only one ring. None of these guitars would have received serial numbers or a Martin stamp.

Dyer supplied the named die stamp to Martin for use on the sample instruments. The die was returned when the samples were shipped.

"CUSTOMER'S LINE" INSTRUMENTS MADE FOR W. J. DYER & BRO.				
STYLE	QUAN.	DATE ORDERED	DATE SHIPPED	COMMENTS
2-17-C	1	1922-05-04	1922-06-27	"STETSON" STAMP
0-18-C	1	1922-05-04	1922-06-27	"STETSON" STAMP
0-21-C	1	1922-05-04	1922-06-27	"STETSON" STAMP
UKE 0-C	1	1922-05-04	1922-06-27	"STETSON" STAMP

Table 38
Instruments Made for W. J. Dyer & Brother with "Stetson" Stamp

GRINNELL BROTHERS "Wolverine" Brand (1922-1924)

The Grinnell Brothers was a large music company with a head office in Detroit and a number of branches in various Michigan towns.

By 1932 Grinnell Brothers had a number of locations

in Detroit and with Michigan branch stores in Adrian, Ann Arbor, Bay City, Birmingham, Flint, Grand Rapids, Hillsdale, Jackson, Kalamazoo, Lansing, Monroe, Muskegon, Pontiac, Port Huron, Saginaw, Wyandotte and Ypsilanti. The company also had stores in Toledo, Ohio and Windsor, Ontario. Grinnell Brothers were a significant account for Martin from 1920 to 1966, the date at which the archival records end. It is not known how long Martin's business relationship with Grinnell Brothers continued after 1966 but the company was no longer in existence by early 1981.

On February 11, 1922 Martin sent Grinnell Brothers a letter to introduce the Customer's Line. H. K. Martin made a sales call on the company and a sample order was nine ukuleles, six guitars and six mandolins, all of the instruments were to be stamped with the "Wolverine" brand name.

On September 19, 1922 Martin invoiced Grinnell Brothers for $11.39 for a steel die which was shipped along with the first six mandolins.

Grinnell Brothers continued to buy regular Martin guitars throughout the 1922 to 1924 period and long afterwards.

The list of instruments in the Tables 39 and 40 details all instruments having the Wolverine stamp, although it needs to be pointed out the ledger entries are not always entirely clear. Some of the guitars and mandolins had serial numbers and some did not. Presumably, like other Customer's Line instruments made for other firms, the guitars should have single ring rosettes but this is yet to be confirmed.

WOLVERINE
Figure 240
Special "Wolverine" Stamp

Along with the "WOLVERINE" stamp, at least some guitars had another three-line stamp impressed on the back strip: "**MADE ESPECIALLY FOR/GRINNELL BROS./AT NAZARETH PA.**"

STYLE	QUAN.	DATE ORDERED	DATE SHIPPED	COMMENTS	SERIAL NUMBERS
				"CUSTOMER'S LINE" INSTRUMENTS MADE FOR GRINNELL BROTHERS	
UKE 0-C	6	Apr. 26, 1922	June 12, 1922	"WOLVERINE" STAMP	
UKE 1-C	3	Apr. 26, 1922	June 12, 1922	"WOLVERINE" STAMP	
2-17-C	4*	Apr. 26, 1922	2 on May 31, 1922	"WOLVERINE" STAMP	17014?, 17051?
0-18C	2	Apr. 26, 1922	Aug. 4, 1922	"WOLVERINE" STAMP	NOT RECORDED
MANDA-C	4	Apr. 26, 1922	Sept. 19, 1922	"WOLVERINE" STAMP	NOT RECORDED
MAND AK-C	2	Apr. 26, 1922	Sept. 19, 1922	"WOLVERINE" STAMP	NOT RECORDED
UKE 0-C	12	July 1, 1922	Aug. 17, 1922	"WOLVERINE" STAMP	
UKE 1-C	6	July 1, 1922	Aug. 17, 1922	"WOLVERINE" STAMP	
0-18-C	2	Oct. 16, 1922	Oct. 17, 1922	"WOLVERINE" STAMP?	NOT RECORDED
0-18-C	4	Oct. 16, 1922	1922-11-18	"WOLVERINE" STAMP	17532-17535
2-17-C	4	Oct. 16, 1922	Nov. 18, 1922	"WOLVERINE" STAMP	17472, 17476, 17486, 17493
2-17-C	2	Oct. 16, 1922	Dec. 7, 1922	"WOLVERINE" STAMP?	NOT RECORDED
UKE 0-C	4	Oct. 16, 1922	Oct. 17, 1922	"WOLVERINE" STAMP	
UKE 0-C	8	Oct. 16, 1922	Nov. 18, 1922	"WOLVERINE" STAMP	
UKE 1-C	12	Oct. 16, 1922	Dec. 7, 1922	"WOLVERINE" STAMP	
UKE 5K	1	Oct. 16, 1922	Nov. 18, 1922	"WOLVERINE" STAMP	
UKE 3	1	Oct. 16, 1922	Dec. 7, 1922	"WOLVERINE" STAMP?	
2-17-C	6	Oct. 16, 1922	Jan. 30, 1923	Dec. or Jan., "WOLVERINE" STAMP	NOT RECORDED
0-18-C	6	Oct. 16, 1922	Jan. 25, 1923	Dec. or Jan., "WOLVERINE" STAMP	NOT RECORDED
UKE 0-C	12	Oct. 16, 1922	Jan. 19, 1923	Dec. or Jan. "WOLVERINE" STAMP	
UKE 1-C	12	Oct. 16, 1922	Jan. 19, 1923	Dec. or Jan. "WOLVERINE" STAMP	
2-17-C	6	Jan. 12, 1923	Apr. 21, 1923	"WOLVERINE" STAMP	18143-18148
0-18-C	6	Jan. 12, 1923	Apr. 24, 1923	"WOLVERINE" STAMP ONLY	18205-18210
UKE 3K	2	Apr. 10, 1923	Apr. 20, 1923	"WOLVERINE" STAMP	
2-17-C	12	Mar. 8, 1923	May 23, 1923	"WOLVERINE" STAMP?	18414-18425
0-18-C	6	Mar. 8, 1923	June 8, 1923	"WOLVERINE" STAMP?	18514-18519
UKE 0-C	24	Mar. 8, 1923	Apr. 24, 1923	"WOLVERINE" STAMP?	
UKE 1-C	12	Mar. 8, 1923	May 17, 1923	"WOLVERINE" STAMP	
2-17	6	May 22, 1923	Aug. 13, 1923	"WOLVERINE" STAMP	18841,18842, 18444, 18845, 18446, 18853
0-18-C	6	May 22, 1923	Sept. 21, 1923	"WOLVERINE" STAMP	19120-19125
00-28	1	June 5, 1923	Sept. 14, 1923	"WOLVERINE" STAMP	18976
UKE 0	12	Aug. 31, 1923	Nov. 13, 1923	"WOLVERINE" STAMP ONLY	
UKE 1	12	Aug. 31, 1923	Oct. 13, 1923	"WOLVERINE" STAMP ONLY	

*Although four 2-17-C guitars were ordered in April 26, 1922 it appears only two were delivered.

Table 39
Instruments Ordered with a "Wolverine" Stamp to August 31, 1923

"CUSTOMER'S LINE" INSTRUMENTS MADE FOR GRINNELL BROTHERS					
STYLE	QUAN.	DATE ORDERED	DATE SHIPPED	COMMENTS	SERIAL NUMBERS
2-17	6	Oct. 1, 1923	Dec. 14, 1923	"WOLVERINE" STAMP	19515,19518, 19519 19524, 19525, 19526
2-17	6	Oct. 1, 1923	Dec. 18, 1923	"WOLVERINE" STAMP	19516,19517, 19521 19522,19523, 19525
0-18-C	5	Oct. 1, 1923	Dec. 14, 1923	"WOLVERINE" STAMP	19503,19504, 19507 19509, 19513
0-18-C	7	Oct. 1, 1923	Dec. 18, 1923	"WOLVERINE" STAMP	19505,19506, 19508 19510, 19511, 19512 19514
UKE 0	10	Oct. 1, 1923	Dec.13, 1923	"WOLVERINE" STAMP?	
UKE 0	2	Oct. 1, 1923	Dec. 14, 1923	"WOLVERINE" STAMP	
UKE 1	13	Oct. 1, 1923	Dec. 8, 1923	"WOLVERINE" STAMP	
UKE 1K	12	Oct. 4, 1923	Dec. 14, 1923	"WOLVERINE" STAMP?	
UKE 2K	6	Oct. 4, 1923	Nov. 30, 1923	"WOLVERINE" STAMP	
UKE 5K	2	Oct. 4, 1923	Nov. 30, 1923	"WOLVERINE" STAMP	
0-21	2	Oct. 4, 1923	Nov. 19, 1923	"WOLVERINE" STAMP	19329, 19344
0-21	1	Oct. 4, 1923	Dec. 4, 1923	"WOLVERINE" STAMP	19336
0-28	3	Oct. 4, 1923	Mar. 29, 1924	"WOLVERINE" BRAND	20114-20116
0-18K	2	Oct. 4, 1923	Nov. 19, 1923	"WOLVERINE" STAMP	19353,19354
MAND A	4	Oct. 4, 1923	Dec. 4, 1923	"WOLVERINE" STAMP	10753-10756
UKE 1	25	Jan. 25, 1924	Mar. 15, 1924	"WOLVERINE" STAMP	
UKE 0	25	Jan. 25, 1924	Mar. 20, 1924	"WOLVERINE" STAMP	
2-17	12	Jan. 25, 1924	Apr. 4, 1924	"WOLVERINE" STAMP	20156-20167
0-18	12	Jan. 25, 1924	Apr. 26, 1924	"WOLVERINE" BRAND	20231-20242
0-28	3		1924-04-26	WOLVERINE" BRAND?	20283,20289 20293
UKE 2	12		1924-04-26	WOLVERINE" BRAND	
2-17	13		1924-04-30	WOLVERINE" BRAND	20307-20319
T-18	2	1924-04-11		"WOLVERINE" STAMP	
UKE 0	25	1924-08-11		"WOLVERINE" STAMP	
UKE 1	25	1924-08-11		"WOLVERINE" STAMP	
2-17	12	1924-01-25	1924-04-04	"WOLVERINE" STAMP	20156-20167
0-18	12	1924-01-25	1924-04-26	"WOLVERINE" BRAND	20231-20242

Note: Shipping dates for the last three orders cannot be determined as Martin ceased recording order details in the sales ledgers towards the end of 1924.

Table 40
Instruments Ordered with a "Wolverine" Stamp from October 1, 1923 to August 11, 1924

RUDOLPH WURLITZER CO.
"Wurlitzer" Brand (1922)

Wurlitzer started to participate in the Customer's Line at the beginning of 1922. Wurlitzer C-Line instruments all received a special "Wurlitzer" stamp on the back of the headstock and possibly on the interior back strip. They did not receive Martin serial numbers and had slightly different appointments, the most obvious difference being a single sound hole ring.

Towards the end of November 1922 Wurlitzer stopped ordering the special "Customer's Line" guitars. Wurlitzer continued to order instruments using their numbering system but beginning with the deliveries in early December 1922 Wurlitzer orders were filled with regular Martin guitars with serial numbers. Wurlitzer continued to intermittently use their numbering system as late as 1926 and it is likely at least some of these received a Wurlitzer stamp. See also pages 45 and 46.

Figure 241
Wurlitzer Model 2093 (00-42) with Single Ring Rosette

"CUSTOMER'S LINE" INSTRUMENTS ORDERED BY RUDOLPH WURLITZER CO.				
WURLITZER STYLE	MARTIN STYLE	QUAN.	DATE ORDERED	COMMENTS
2075	2½-17*	25	Jan. 23, 1922	
2077	0-28K	1	Jan. 27, 1922	SAMPLE LINE
2085	0-18	1	Jan. 27, 1922	SAMPLE LINE
2086	00-18	1	Jan. 27, 1922	SAMPLE LINE
2087	000-18	1	Jan. 27, 1922	SAMPLE LINE
2088	0-21	1	Jan. 27, 1922	SAMPLE LINE
2089	00-21	1	Jan. 27, 1922	SAMPLE LINE
2090	0-28	1	Jan. 27, 1922	SAMPLE LINE
2091	00-28	1	Jan. 27, 1922	SAMPLE LINE
2092	0-42	1	Jan. 27, 1922	SAMPLE LINE
2093	00-42	1	Jan. 27, 1922	SAMPLE LINE
2076	0-18K	1	Jan. 27, 1922	SAMPLE LINE
2075	2-17	50	Feb. 2, 1922	4 MONTHLY SHIPMENTS
835	UKE 0	100	Feb. 2, 1922	4 MONTHLY SHIPMENTS
836	UKE 1	25	Feb. 2, 1922	4 MONTHLY SHIPMENTS
837	UKE 1K	50	Feb. 2, 1922	4 MONTHLY SHIPMENTS
838	UKE 2K	25	Feb. 2, 1922	4 MONTHLY SHIPMENTS
839	UKE 3K	12	Feb. 2, 1922	4 MONTHLY SHIPMENTS
2085	0-18	15	Apr. 5, 1922	
2086	00-18	10	Apr. 5, 1922	
2087	000-18	5	Apr. 5, 1922	
2088	0-21	15	Apr. 5, 1922	
2090	0-28	10	Apr. 5, 1922	
2092	0-42	5	Apr. 5, 1922	
2076	0-18K	15	Apr. 5, 1922	
2077	0-28K	15	Apr. 5, 1922	
835	UKE 0	25	Apr. 18, 1922	
836	UKE 1	25	Apr. 18, 1922	
837	UKE 1K	25	Apr. 18, 1922	
838	UKE 2K	25	Apr. 18, 1922	
839	UKE 3K	25	Apr. 18, 1922	
841	TP 2K	5	Apr. 18, 1922	
835	UKE 0	100	June 8, 1922	MONTHLY SHIPMENTS
839	UKE 3K	12	June 8, 1922	MONTHLY SHIPMENTS
836	UKE 1	12	June 8, 1922	MONTHLY SHIPMENTS, DARK FINISH
835	UKE 0	25	June 9, 1922	

*Wurlitzer style 2075 was changed to Martin style 2-17 very early, no 2½-17 guitars were shipped

Table 41
Instruments Ordered with a Wurlitzer Stamp
Between January 23 to June 9, 1922

"CUSTOMER'S LINE" INSTRUMENTS ORDERED BY RUDOLPH WURLITZER CO.				
WURLITZER STYLE	MARTIN STYLE	QUAN.	DATE ORDERED	COMMENTS
2075	2-17	25	June 15, 1922	
2075	2-17	10	June 26, 1922	
2085	0-18	10	Aug. 23, 1922	
2086	00-18	5	Aug. 23, 1922	
2087	000-18	5	Aug. 23, 1922	
2089	00-21	5	Aug. 23, 1922	
2091	00-28	5	Aug. 23, 1922	
2092	0-42	3	Aug. 23, 1922	
835	UKE 0	25	Aug. 23, 1922	
	TP 2	1	Sept. 11, 1922	
841	TP 2K	3	Sept. 11, 1922	
837	UKE 1K	6	Sept. 11, 1922	
838	UKE 2K	3	Sept. 11, 1922	
841	TP 2K	5	Oct. 6, 1922	
835	UKE 0	80	Oct. 14, 1922	
836	UKE 1	15	Oct. 14, 1922	
837	UKE 1K	20	Oct. 14, 1922	
838	UKE 2K	15	Oct. 14, 1922	
839	UKE 3K	13	Oct. 14, 1922	
841	TP 2K	6	Oct. 16, 1922	
2076	0-18K	15	Oct. 30, 1922	
2086	00-18	5	Oct. 30, 1922	
2087	000-18	3	Oct. 30, 1922	
2088	0-21	5	Oct. 30, 1922	
2085	0-18	10	Nov. 13, 1922	
2075	2-17	12	Nov. 22, 1922	
2092	0-42	2	Nov. 22, 1922	
2090	0-28	3	Nov. 22, 1922	
2088	0-21	3	Nov. 22, 1922	
2087	000-18	3	Nov. 22, 1922	
2086	00-18	12	Nov. 22, 1922	
2085	0-18	3	Nov. 22, 1922	

Table 42
Instruments Ordered with a Wurlitzer Stamp
Between June 15 and November 20, 1922

TOTAL WURLITZER MODELS MADE		
MARTIN STYLE	WURLITZER STYLE	QUAN.
UKE 0	835	355
UKE 1	836	77
UKE 1K	837	101
UKE 2K	838	63
UKE 3K	839	62
TP 2K	841	16
2-17	2075	114
0-18K	2076	31
0-28K	2077	17
0-18	2085	38
00-18	2086	32
000-18	2087	17
0-21	2088	21
00-21	2089	6
0-28	2090	12
00-28	2091	6
0-42	2092	9
00-42	2093	1

Table 43
Numbers of Wurlitzer Instruments
Ordered as Part of the Customer's Line

Figure 242
Special "Wurlitzer" Stamp

H. A. WEYMANN & SON
No Brand (1923-1925)

H. A. Weymann & Son was a musical instrument manufacturer and importer located in Philadelphia.

The company was founded by Henry Arnold Weymann (c. 1829-1892) who was born in Hanover in Saxony. Henry migrated to the U. S. in 1852 and in 1862 started a "small goods" business in Philadelphia selling jewelry, watches, clocks, silver ware, sheet music and imported musical instruments. However, by ca. 1890 the company was manufacturing and importing musical instruments and selling the instruments in its own stores.

H. A. Weymann died in 1892 and his son Harry William Weymann (1866-1939) took over the business, while retaining the name H. A. Weymann and Son.

Weymann began to buy Martin instruments "without stamps" in 1923. Between May 1923 and May 1925 Weymann purchased style 0 and 1 ukuleles, style 1 taro-patches, style A mandolins, T-18 tiples and 2-17 guitars with no stamps. The mandolins, tiples and guitars did not receive serial numbers.

The order and shipping records for Weymann are quite confusing because some orders for the "no stamp" instruments were never shipped and other orders were only partially filled. Weymann also bought other instruments from Martin, including 0-18, 0-18K, 00-18, 0-21 guitars, but these were regular Martin products with a Martin stamp and serial numbers.

The tables below document the order and shipments of Martin instruments to Weymann up to 1927 and the total number of Customer's Line instruments shipped.

After 1927 Weymann continued to buy small quantities of Martin instruments until 1942.

Much more information on H. A. Weymann & Son and their instruments is available at: https://www.leavingthisworld.com/category/weymann-guitars/

MARTIN STYLE	QUAN ORDERED	DATE ORDERED	QUAN SHIPPED	DATE SHIPPED	COMMENTS
UKE 0	1	Apr. 1, 1922	1	Apr. 3,1922	
UKE 1	1	Apr. 1, 1922	1	Apr. 3, 1922	
UKE 0	30	May 28, 1923	30	July 16, 1923	NO NAME OR STAMP
UKE 0	30	Sept. 1, 1923	30	Nov. 10, 1923	NO STAMP
UKE 0	30	Dec. 10, 1923	30	Feb. 29,1924	NO NAME
UKE 0	30	Feb. 7, 1924	30	May 13, 1924	NO NAME
UKE 0	30*	Mar. 4, 1924			NO NAME
2-17	1	Mar. 4, 1924	1	Apr. 17, 1924	NO NAME, SERIAL #20203
MAND A	1	Mar. 4, 1924	1	Apr. 17, 1924	NO NAME, SERIAL #11143
2-17	12	May 24, 1924	12	July 1, 1924	NO NAME
2-17	1	June 21, 1924	1	June 23, 1924	
0-18	1*	June 21, 1924			
00-18	1*	June 21, 1924			
0-18K	1	June 21, 1924		June 23, 1924	
T-18	1*	July 23, 1924			
TP 1	1*	July 23, 1924			
MAND A	1	July 23, 1924		Aug. 18, 1924	
0-18K			1	Oct. 1, 1924	
UKE 1			1	Oct. 1, 1924	
0-18			1	Dec. 5, 1924	
UKE 0	50	Sept. 16, 1924	50	Jan. 17, 1925	NO STAMP
0-18	1	Feb. 11, 1925	1	Feb. 24, 1925	
0-21	1	Feb. 11, 1925	1	Feb. 13, 1925	
0-18			2	Apr. 3, 1925	
0-18			6	May 12, 1925	
UKE 0	900	Feb. 11, 1925	48	May 18, 1925	WITHOUT STAMP, MAY, AUG., OCT.
			52	June 10, 1925	WITHOUT STAMP, MAY, AUG., OCT.
			50	July 7, 1925	WITHOUT STAMP, MAY, AUG., OCT.
			50	July 27, 1925	WITHOUT STAMP, MAY, AUG., OCT.
			50	Aug. 5, 1925	WITHOUT STAMP, MAY, AUG., OCT.
			50	Aug. 18, 1925	WITHOUT STAMP, MAY, AUG., OCT.
			60	Sept. 5, 1925	WITHOUT STAMP, MAY, AUG., OCT.
UKE 1	100	Feb. 11, 1925	50	Apr. 18, 1925	WITHOUT STAMP, JUL.
			50	July 17, 1925	WITHOUT STAMP, JUL.
UKE 1	100	Feb. 11, 1925	40	Oct. 17, 1925	WITHOUT STAMP, SEPT.
			10	Oct. 19, 1925	WITHOUT STAMP, SEPT.
T-18	12*	Feb. 11, 1925			WITHOUT STAMP, MAY-AUG.
TP 1	12	Feb. 11, 1925	6	Apr. 20, 1925	WITHOUT STAMP, APR.-AUG.
			6	July 8, 1925	WITHOUT STAMP, APR.-AUG.
0-18			6	May 12, 1925	
0-21	1	Feb. 26, 1925	1	Mar. 2, 1925	
0-21	1	Mar. 3, 1925		Apr. 28, 1925	
0-21	1	Mar. 16, 1925		Apr. 28, 1925	
TP 1	6	May 19, 1925	6	Aug. 6, 1925	NO STAMP
0-18			5	Aug. 31, 1925	
0-18			1	Sept. 30, 1925	
000-28	1	June 5, 1926	1	Aug. 2, 1926	
UKE 2	1	Oct. 22, 1926	1	Oct. 23, 1926	
UKE 0*	1	Jan. 15, 1927			
T-18	6	Jan. 25, 1927	6	Jan. 27, 1927	
T-17*	1	Feb. 17, 1927			
T-18	6	Mar. 3, 1927	6	Mar. 4, 1927	

*Ordered but not shipped

Table 44
Martin Instruments Ordered by H. A. Weymann & Son Between 1922 and 1927

MARTIN STYLE	QUAN ORDERED	DATE ORDERED	QUAN SHIPPED	DATE SHIPPED	COMMENTS
UKE 0	30	May 28, 1923	30	July 16, 1923	NO NAME OR STAMP
UKE 0	30	Sept. 1, 1923	30	Nov. 10, 1923	NO STAMP
UKE 0	30	Dec. 10, 1923	30	Feb. 29,1924	NO NAME
UKE 0	30	Feb. 7, 1924	30	May 13, 1924	NO NAME
UKE 0	30*	Mar. 4, 1924			NO NAME
2-17	1	Mar. 4, 1924	1	Apr. 17, 1924	NO NAME, SERIAL #20203
MAND A	1	Mar. 4, 1924	1	Apr. 17, 1924	NO NAME, SERIAL #11143
2-17	12	May 24, 1924	12	July 1, 1924	NO NAME
UKE 0	50	Sept. 16, 1924	50	Jan. 17, 1925	NO STAMP
UKE 0	900	Feb. 11, 1925	48	May 18, 1925	WITHOUT STAMP, MAY., AUG., OCT.
			52	Jun 10, 1925	WITHOUT STAMP, MAY., AUG., OCT.
			50	July 7, 1925	WITHOUT STAMP, MAY., AUG., OCT.
			50	July 27, 1925	WITHOUT STAMP, MAY., AUG., OCT.
			50	Aug. 5, 1925	WITHOUT STAMP, MAY., AUG., OCT.
			50	Aug. 18, 1925	WITHOUT STAMP, MAY., AUG., OCT.
			60	Sept. 5, 1925	WITHOUT STAMP, MAY., AUG., OCT.
UKE 1	100	Feb. 11, 1925	50	Apr. 18, 1925	WITHOUT STAMP, JUL.
			50	July 17, 1925	WITHOUT STAMP, JUL.
UKE 1	100	Feb. 11, 1925	40	Oct. 17, 1925	WITHOUT STAMP, SEPT.
			10	Oct. 19, 1925	WITHOUT STAMP, SEPT.
T-18	12*	Feb. 11, 1925			WITHOUT STAMP, MAY-AUG.
TP 1	12	Feb. 11, 1925	6	Apr. 20, 1925	WITHOUT STAMP, APR.-AUG.
			6	July 8, 1925	WITHOUT STAMP, APR.-AUG.
TP 1	6	May 19, 1925	6	Aug. 6, 1925	NO STAMP

Table 45
"Customer's Line" Martin Instruments Ordered by H. A. Weymann & Son Between 1923 and 1925

WEYMAN INSTRUMENTS MADE BY MARTIN WITH NO STAMP		
MODEL	ORDERED	SHIPPED
UKE 0	1100	530
UKE 1	200	150
TAROPATCH 1	18	18
MANDOLIN A	1	1
2-17	13	13
T-18	12	0

Table 46
"Customer's Line" Martin Instruments Shipped to H. A. Weymann & Son with No Stamp

CABLE PIANO CO. - "Made Especially for Cable Piano Co." Stamp (1929)

The Cable Piano Co. was a large manufacturer of various brands of pianos located in Chicago. The Cable Piano Co. store in Atlanta was the southern headquarters for the parent company and offered pianos, stringed musical instruments and sheet music. The company began buying Martin guitars in 1927. In 1935 the store suffered a major fire but was back in business later the same year and continued purchasing Martin instruments through at least 1965, when the archival records end. Purchases of Martin instruments probably continued for a time afterwards but the company went out of business and was dissolved by 1981.

The Martin archive contains a stamp, as illustrated in figure 243, which is a bit of a mystery.

The stamp does not appear in the purchasing records or the yearly inventories so it is hard to put a date on it. On page 228 of Martin Guitars: A Technical Reference by Richard Johnston and Dick Boak it is suggested the stamp was used for the prototype OM-28 (serial number 39081) made for Perry Bechtel in 1929.

That may be the case but it is very odd that this stamp would have been made for a prototype, especially in light of the fact that the Cable Piano Co. never bought another OM (Orchestra Model) guitar! It is also mentioned on page 228 that the stamp has been seen in a Hawaiian guitar. Again, this is curious as Cable Piano never purchased any "special order" guitars after the prototype OM-28 (which was recorded as a 000-28S in the ledgers). The answer to this question can only be answered if and when the prototype OM-28 is ever discovered.

MADE ESPECIALLY FOR CABLE PIANO CO.

Figure 243
Special "Cable Piano Co." Stamp

CARL FISCHER INC.
Carl Fischer Model 0-18T Guitar (1929-1931)

Carl Fischer Inc. was a publisher of music and also operated retail music stores in New York, Chicago and Boston. The company was founded in New York in 1872 by Carl Fischer as a musical instrument repair shop but switched to music publishing in response to a demand for unavailable arrangements of well-known music.

The company also imported musical instruments. In 1929 the C. G. Conn company bought the musical instrument department of Fischer and maintained the Carl Fischer retail stores as a joint venture between Conn and Carl Fischer Inc.

Carl Fischer Inc. began buying Martin instruments in 1922 and purchases continued until at least 1965. The last order from the New York branch was received in 1954 and the Chicago branch ceased buying in 1960.

The development of what became the Carl Fischer Model 0-18T tenor guitar is more than a little interesting, with a lot of twists and turns.

On March 9, 1929 Al Esposito, in charge of the Plectrum Instrument Department of Carl Fisher Inc., wrote to Martin to inquire about a new tenor guitar:

"I have had the pleasure of having Mr. Frank Victor of Paul Spect's Orchestra and Frank Petrucci, of the B. A. Rolfe Orchestra, call at our establishment in regard to a Tenor guitar which they are interested in.

This Tenor Guitar is to be the style of your regular guitar 00-21. The head of the guitar neck to be size of the regular guitar head. The upper or smaller part of the guitar body to be cut short at the 14th fret, in other words the neck to be two frets more and the upper part of the body of the guitar to be two frets shy. In doing this, no doubt, you will have to move the sound hole the difference that you cut down at the upper part of the guitar.

The most important part in constructing this special Tenor Guitar is at your bridge. In the past 6 years that I have been selling your instruments I have found only one fault, and that is the construction at the bridge is not reinforced strong enough, which causes also to warp in time or bulge out from the constant pulling of the strings. This I have remedied at our establishment on a few of Martin Guitars by taking off the top and reinforcing them with some very heavy cross bar wood that has proven very successful.

The idea of this Tenor Guitar is that the professional men want more volume and offer to use heavier strings.

I hope I have made myself plain in the above matter and to hear from you in regard to this special constructive Tenor Guitar and also what it would cost us. I am also sketching below what I mean by cutting down on the body."

Regardless, Martin tried to accommodate the customer by preparing a special 2-18T for their consideration.

Martin replied on March 16:

"The special 2-18T Tenor Guitar which we sent you this morning was selected by the writer yesterday and strung with heavy strings to permit tuning one octave lower than regular. Since the fourth string was rather too heavy to be practical, we substituted a lighter string, tuning it higher, which

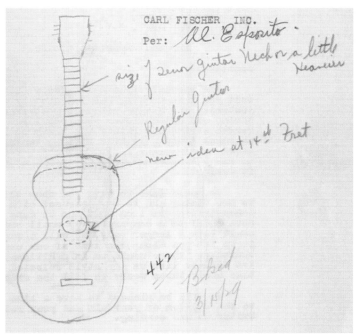

Figure 244
Sketch of Proposed 14-Fret Tenor Guitar

Figure 245
Comparison of 12-Fret (2-18T) and
14-Fret Size 2 Tenor Guitars (2-28T-L)

makes a rather good effect; but it is possible to use the heavy string if a real deep bass tone is desired.

We would like to have you show this instrument to Mr. Victor and to Mr. Petrucci with the idea of demonstrating to them what can be done with a long neck model on a comparatively small body. If they would like a larger body, we will arrange to make it up for you along the line of our conversation on Thursday. There would be an additional charge of ten dollars list on any style selected and it would take about three weeks to fill the order."

By assembling all the clues from the correspondence and considering the explosion of new models launched by Martin from 1927 to 1929, it would appear that something had shaken the Martin company out of its normally conservative approach. Whether it was the growing awareness of the influence of orchestra and big band music, the change in musical tastes or the desire to compete with Gibson is irrelevant. Martin was in the mood to innovate. Martin was listening to their dealers and professional musicians and was prepared to make new instruments as a result.

In order to comply with Fisher's request, it appears that Martin took a regular 12-fret 2-18T guitar and replaced the 12-fret neck with one of 14 frets. Figure 245 illustrates how applying a 14-fret neck to a guitar

body meant for a 12-fret neck results in an awkward location of the bridge. For the 14-fret guitar, the neck and bridge were just moved up by two frets.

Al Esposito reported the reaction to the 2-18T tenor guitar on March 26:

"I am very sorry to have to inform you that this guitar proved very unsatisfactory to them (i.e. Mr. Victor and Mr. Petrucci). It seems that they want the guitar that I was speaking to you about, the 0-21 style, the body being cut down to 14th fret and the scale neck of the 2-18L Guitar which was sent to use attached to it, with the regular guitar head and patent machine head for four strings, the sound hole to be lowered if possible and leave the bridge of the guitar style 0-21 where it is now.

The only arrangement I could make with these gentlemen was that if the guitar proved satisfactory, which they believe it will, they will purchase it. We expect you to take that responsibility. They are very anxious to procure one and I believe they are negotiating with the Gibson concern, as they have something like what they want, but I am holding them back from purchasing one of these, until I hear from you."

This was probably not what Martin wanted to hear. On the other hand, Martin had simply put a 14-fret neck on a 12-fret body rather than cut down the guitar body as suggested and hoped this expedient would satisfy the customer.

However, the reply from Martin on March 28 contains no hint of indignation:

"Thank you for your prompt report on the Tenor Guitar we sent you recently to be shown to Mr. Petrucci and Mr. Victor. We are sorry, of course, that they did not like the instrument, but we appreciate the efforts you are making to sell a Martin Guitar to these gentlemen.

We are proceeding at once to lay out a special instrument embodying the following ideas:

- **Concert size body, Style 0-21**
- **23" Tenor Scale**
- **Location of bridge and brace pattern so that 14 frets will be clear of the body**
- **There will be a special neck with four-string Patent Heads***

We are undertaking this thinking there may be something in the idea because we know many professional players are looking for a Tenor Guitar of this description. We will start work promptly and expect to have the instrument ready in about two weeks."

(*In Martin parlance a "patent head" referred to tuner strips so Martin must have special-ordered two tuner strips with two tuners on each strip or cut down a regular guitar strip of three tuners. Martin did not begin to stock individual side tuners for several more years.)

This reply contains the answer to the sense of urgency felt by Martin in developing the new model. Professional players were driving the demand for tenor guitars with longer necks. Martin clearly understood they had to act quickly, as two weeks is an exceptionally short amount of time to develop and produce a new instrument design. However, this effort served Martin well as it was only a few months until Perry Bechtel visited in June 1929, with the OM guitars being the end result.

The first special 0-21T was shipped on April 20, 1929. Although it was entered in the bookings ledger on March 28 at a retail price of $32.50 there is no shop order detailing this guitar. However, several shop orders from this period are missing from the archive. So, either guitar was treated as a prototype, and received no serial number, or it was recorded on one of the missing shop orders and the serial number remains unknown. There is one serial number, 38266, without an instrument allocated to it, so maybe this is the serial number of the first 0-21T.

Al Esposito responded to Martin on May 1:

"I suppose you are anxiously waiting for my reply in regard to the Tenor Guitar that you sent. This is my first occasion to write to you due to the fact that the gentlemen whom I wanted to try the Guitar delayed appearing at our establishment. I am very pleased to state that the tone of the instrument pleases them very highly.

With the exception of two or three adjustments, I believe we will be able to order from you two or three more of these instruments. First of all, the upper part of the body on this Guitar is entirely out of proportion; these gentlemen critically criticized the appearance of the instrument. The head of the guitar neck, they would prefer more to the actual size of a regular guitar, they would prefer to have you make the neck of the instrument a little wider and thinner as they call it a very slow playing neck due to the thickness of the back part of the neck. They believe by thinning that part of the neck down and making the neck a little wider, it certainly would make it a faster playing neck and the last adjustment which would greatly be appreciated , most of all, by these gentlemen would be, if possible, to lower the sound hole closer to the bridge. You can start to manufacture another one for us and ship it as soon as possible, as I have two or three other people that are very anxiously waiting for this instrument.

I am mailing you, under separate cover, a sketch showing by a dotted line the shape of instrument you have sent us and the regular heavy line showing the shape of instrument that these gentlemen want. I believe personally, as they stated, that it also would be a much finer instrument in playing if

you also could extend the neck an additional fret. We could easily supply strings at our establishment if you could extend this neck one fret longer from the body."

Martin answered on May 6:

"Many thanks for your good report on the special Style 0-21 Guitar we sent you recently. We note the suggestions you make for the improvement of the instrument and appreciate the spirit in which you make them.

You will remember that we insisted, in accepting your order, that the regular Guitar top brace pattern and bridge location be left unchanged for the sake of tone. Since you found the tone of the Guitar satisfactory we presume you will wish to follow the same policy in the second instrument, which means that it will be impossible to change the location of the soundhole or the length of the fingerboard. We can change the shape of the upper part of the body by making it considerably wider, more like the regular Guitar body, and that will improve the appearance of the instrument considerably. The neck can be made a little wider and thinner; although we think it is not safe to make it appreciably thinner than the regular Guitar neck. If it is made a little wider it will seem thinner.

Would there be any objection in making this Guitar with a peg head, using Banjo gear pegs instead of patent heads? The advantage of the gear pegs is that the strings can be changed much easier and in all other respects we think they are at least as good as the patent heads. Please let us know on this point promptly because we are proceeding at once to make up this Guitar and will have it ready for the neck in a few days."

Apparently the prototype 0-21T had an unusual appearance. Possibly Martin shortened the body but did not increase the width of the upper bout. Unfortunately, the sketch mentioned in the letter has not survived. Maybe this instrument will surface one day to answer the question. The prototype should be easy to identify as it has a slotted peg head and side tuners. Carl Fischer Inc. was not able to sell the prototype 0-21T and it was returned to Martin some time in July.

Again, Martin explained the difficulty in finding four string patent heads and offered gear pegs (i. e., banjo tuners) instead.

The second prototype 0-21T (serial number 38541) had a different body shape but retained the patent heads as confirmed in a letter sent by Martin to Carl Fischer Inc. on May 11:

"In accordance with your letter of the 8th, just received this morning, we will proceed to make up a special neck for the Style 0-21 Tenor Guitar we are making for you. We are sorry you cannot use the gear pegs. It will take at least 10 days to get the special two-string patent heads for this Guitar, while with gear pegs we could proceed at once and finish the instrument next week.

The body of this special Guitar is finished and the new design at the upper portion improves the appearance considerably and has the effect of making the soundhole appear lower than it is."

This guitar was shipped on May 28, 1929 and became the first modern 14-fret guitar made by Martin.

Experimentation continued and on June 26, 1929 Carl Fischer Inc. ordered a "**Martin Plectrum guitar – same as the latest new tenor guitar sent to Mr. Esposito**", a 0-21P. The details of this guitar were not documented other than it also had a patent head. Presumably, the longer scale of the plectrum guitar would have yielded the 15-fret neck requested in the letter of May 1. This 0-21P (serial number 38797) was made for Charles Hughes, a star plectrum player of Harry Reezer's office but as it is the only example the longer neck must not have been considered an advantage.

An 0-21T was entered in the bookings ledger on July 13, 1929 but it appears this was changed to an 0-28T (serial number 39128) as the associated shop states "**1 Special Gtr 0-28 Carl Fischer Model**".

In a letter dated July 12, 1929, Carl Fischer Inc. asked if it was possible to make a mahogany guitar with a lower price. Martin answered on July 15 that it was quite possible to make a 0-18T and the price would be $45 compared to $65 for the 0-21T. Martin also offered to lower the price to $40 if an order for five guitars was placed. An order for the first 0-18T, now called the Carl Fischer Model, was booked just a few days later on July 17.

Martin realized that they had a marketable new product and started offering the 0-18T to their dealers through their outside salesman. Change must have been in the wind because on July 29, Peate's Music House Inc. requested a Concert or Grand Concert tenor guitar for a customer. Martin responded with a long letter on the current tenor guitars they made and mentioned the new 14-fret Carl Fischer models just entering production. Peate's must have appreciated the explanation because they placed an order for a Carl Fischer Model 0-18T on August 30. However, it must have been obvious that the new model was something special as orders started to come forth from other Martin dealers. On August 26 McClellan Music House purchased a 0-18T although this guitar was supplied with gear pegs. Although Carl Fischer Inc. had helped develop the new guitar, they purchased very few of them, only a dozen or so to the beginning of 1932.

Figure 246
1931 Martin 0-28T Guitar

Some batches of the Carl Fischer 0-18T guitars received patent heads while others were allocated banjo tuners.

The shape of the Carl Fisher Model 0-18T is quite distinctive as the upper bout appears to be narrower than later 0-18T guitars. It is not known how long the Carl Fischer Model continued in production but this designation stopped appearing in the sales records in March 1930. However, one Carl Fischer Model guitar has been reported from April 1931.

While the Carl Fischer 0-18T guitars were still in production Martin started making 0-28T guitars in late March 1930 with a wider upper bout and a more balanced appearance.

PARAMOUNT STYLE L GUITARS

The correspondence for 1930 is missing but it is known that William L. Lange Music Co., manufacturer of Paramount banjos, contracted with C. F. Martin & Co. to make some special guitars of Lange's own design. Lange marketed them as Paramount Style L guitars and they were available as either 6-string Spanish guitars, with regular or Hawaiian set-up, or as 4-string tenors.

The first batch was stamped in October 1930 and the Style L guitar, in a number of variations, continued in production until mid-1932.

MODEL	SHOP ORDER	DATE STAMPED	QUAN.	COMMENTS
PARAMOUNT 0-21	827	OCT. 17, 1930	4	1 HAWAIIAN, 1 TENOR
PARAMOUNT 0-21	865	DEC. 1, 1930	20	INCLUDING 6 HAWAIIAN AND 2 TENOR
PARAMOUNT 0-21T	907	JAN. 22, 1931	6	TENOR GUITARS, 2 WITH DARK TOPS
PARAMOUNT 0-21	916	FEB. 3, 1931	6	SPANISH
PARAMOUNT 0-21S	917	FEB. 3, 1931	1	SPECIAL
PARAMOUNT 0-21	951	MAR. 10, 1931	6	SPANISH
PARAMOUNT 0-21	980	APR. 10, 1931	6	SPANISH
PARAMOUNT 0-21T	981	APR. 10, 1931	6	TENOR GUITARS, TAILPIECE MODEL
PARAMOUNT 0-21S	982	APR. 10, 1931	1	SPECIAL, SPANISH
PARAMOUNT 0-21	1027	MAY 28, 1931	8	SPANISH, GLUED BRIDGE MODEL
PARAMOUNT 0-21	1064	JULY 25, 1931	6	SPANISH
PARAMOUNT 0-21S	108	SEPT. 29, 1931	1	SPECIAL, TOP BORDER WITH PEARL LIKE STYLE 40, BLACK BINDINGS LIKE REGULAR, NO SOUND HOLE
PARAMOUNT 0-21S	269	JUNE 11, 1932	1	SPECIAL, TOP BORDER WITH PEARL LIKE STYLE 40, BLACK BINDINGS LIKE REGULAR, NO SOUND HOLE

Table 47
Production Orders for Paramount Style L Guitars

Martin always internally referred to these as "**Paramount 0-21**" guitars even though the peg head veneer, supplied by Lange, identified them as Paramount "**Style L**" (one "**Model L**" veneer is known).

The Martin production records indicate that 72 Paramount 0-21 guitars were built although only 71 were ordered. The discrepancy occurred in the first batch where three were ordered but four made, the extra guitar most likely being a prototype or a sample instrument.

MODEL	QUANTITY MADE
PARAMOUNT 0-21	46
PARAMOUNT 0-21H	7
PARAMOUNT 0-21T	15
PARAMOUNT 0-21S	4

Table 48
Number of Paramount Style L Guitars Made

Martin did not record serial numbers for these guitars as the serial numbers were applied by Lange. A "PATENT PENDING" stamp was also added by Lange and appears on the back of the head stock or on the rim of the resonator section at the bottom of the guitar. The serial numbers on examined Style L guitars vary from 101 to 160 which fit well with the number ordered. It will probably be found that the serial numbers range from 100 to 170.

Both the 6-string and the tenor guitars featured a 14-fret neck and a fingerboard long enough for 20 frets. However, Style L guitars come in two completely different shapes and should actually be considered as two separate instruments. The Spanish-style six string guitars have dimensions similar to a 0 guitar shape as the inner body while the resonator width is 2½" wider or about 16" for the lower bout. The tenor guitars have a totally different shape as the body length was reduced in order to accommodate a 14-fret neck with the shorter tenor scale. The bottom of the fingerboard on the tenor guitars is also located closer to the sound hole than the Spanish guitars.

Some of the guitars have solid tops and some have round sound holes. A number of the original shop orders are missing from the archive so it is not possible to determine the how many were made with round sound holes.

The shop order slips for the first two of the four "special" orders (shop orders 917 and 982) are missing. However, in a letter from Lange dated June 15, 1932, it would appear that the special guitar from shop order 269 was intended to be exactly like the one from shop order 108 (i. e., both had solid tops without a sound hole).

The gentleman in the photo at the right owns one of the Paramount Style L guitars with the "glued on

bridge". It is either from the batch of 8 made on shop order 1027 or one of the two special guitars made on shop orders 917 or 982.

Figure 247
Vintage Photograph of Paramount Style L Guitar

Some of the Style L guitars with sound holes have no decoration around the hole at all, while others have a white celluloid ring circling the inside edge of the hole.

DIMENSIONS FOR PARAMOUNT GUITARS

		6 STRING	TENOR
BODY	UPPER BOUT	9 13/16"	9 7/8"
	WAIST	8 1/8"	8 11/16"
	LOWER BOUT	13 5/8"	13 ½"
	LENGTH	19 3/32"	17 1/4"
RESONATOR	UPPER BOUT	12"	12"
	WAIST	10 ¾"	11 3/8"
	LOWER BOUT	16"	16"
	LENGTH	21 3/8"	19 ¼"
	SCALE LENGTH	25.4"	22 15/16"

Table 49
Dimensions of Paramount Style L
Tenor and 6 String Guitars

In a letter dated May 17, 1932 Lange commented on the trouble they were having with the rosewood cracking on the back of the guitar and stated they would try mahogany on the next batch. As can be seen from the table only one more Style L guitar was ordered after this date and no mahogany guitars were ever attempted.

The Paramount Style L guitars made by Martin were more successful than special guitars made for other firms but still could not survive the depths of the Great Depression.

MODEL	SERIAL NUMBER	SIDE	SOUND HOLE	BRIDGE	# HOLES IN RESONATOR	NOTES
PARAMOUNT 0-21	101	SHORT	ROUND	TAILPIECE	20	NATURAL TOP, NO RINGS IN RIM HOLES, "STYLE L" HEADSTOCK, NO SOUNDHOLE DECORATION, SERIAL NUMBER AT BACK OF HEADSTOCK AT TOP, EX-CHINERY COLLECTION
PARAMOUNT 0-21	107	SHORT	SOLID TOP	TAILPIECE	20	NATURAL TOP, CELLULOID RINGS IN RIM HOLES, "PATENT PENDING" STAMP ON RIM, "MODEL L" IN HEADSTOCK INLAY
PARAMOUNT 0-21	110	SHORT	SOLID TOP	TAILPIECE	38	NATURAL TOP, 3 ON A SIDE TUNERS, ALTERNATING BRASS FERRULES ON RESONATOR HOLES, STYLE 27 PURFLING ON TOP EDGE
PARAMOUNT 0-21	112	SHORT	SOLID TOP	TAILPIECE	38	NATURAL TOP, 3 ON A SIDE TUNERS, ALTERNATING BRASS FERRULES ON RESONATOR HOLES
PARAMOUNT 0-21	115	SHORT	SOLID TOP	TAILPIECE	38	NATURAL TOP, 3 ON A SIDE HOLES, CELLULOID RINGS IN RIM HOLES
PARAMOUNT 0-21T	120	SHORT	ROUND	TAILPIECE	18	SHADED TOP, BANJO TUNERS, "PATENTS PENDING" STAMP ON RIM
PARAMOUNT 0-21	126	SHORT	ROUND	TAILPIECE	20	SHADED TOP, 3 ON A SIDE TUNERS, "PATENTS PENDING" STAMP ON RIM, PLAIN SOULD HOLE
PARAMOUNT 0-21	130	SHORT	SOLID TOP	TAILPIECE	20	SHADED TOP, 3 ON A SIDE TUNERS, "PATENT PENDING" STAMP ON RIM, CELLULOID RINGS IN RIM HIOLES
PARAMOUNT 0-21	132	SHORT	SOLID TOP	TAILPIECE	18	NATURAL TOP, "PAGE" BANJO TUNERS, CELLULOID RINGS IN RIM HOLES, SERIAL NUMBER ON BACK OF HEAD STOCK
PARAMOUNT 0-21T	134	SHORT	SOLID TOP	TAILPIECE	18	DARK TOP, "PAGE" BANJO TUNERS, CELLULOID RINGS IN RIM HOLES, SERIAL NUMBER ON BACK OF HEAD STOCK, "L" IN VENEER HAS BEEN ALTERED TO "D", "PATENT PENDING" STAMP ON BOTTOM OF RIM
PARAMOUNT 0-21T	136	SHORT	SOLID TOP	TAILPIECE	18	NATURAL TOP, BANJO TUNERS (OLD GBASE LISTING)
PARAMOUNT 0-21T	146	SHORT	SOLID TOP	TAILPIECE	18	SHADED TOP, BANJO TUNERS, NO "PATENT PENDING" STAMP, CELLULOID RINGS IN RIM HOLES
PARAMOUNT 0-21	150	TALL	SOLID TOP	GLUED STRAIGHT BRIDGE	20	SHADED TOP, HOLES IN SIDE OF BODY, 3 ON A STRIP MACHINE TUNERS, "PATENT PENDING" STAMP ON RIM
PARAMOUNT 0-21T	160	SHORT	SOLID TOP	TAILPIECE	18	SHADED TOP, BANJO TUNERS, "PATENT PENDING" STAMPE ON BACK OF HEADSTOCK

Table 50
Details of Examined Paramount Style L Guitars

CHICAGO MUSICAL INSTRUMENT CO.
Dreadnought Guitars (1931-1932)

Chicago Musical Instrument Co. had an exclusive arrangement with Martin for selling Dreadnought guitars during the period from 1931 until late 1932. This included all the 12-fret D-1, D-2, D-18 and D-28 guitars made in this period. These guitars all received a special stamp on the back strip as shown in Figure 248. There was also one "**Ditson Dreadnought #21 Spec**" guitar (serial number 46590) ordered by CMI just before the first D-1 and D-2 guitars were put into production.

By late December 1932 Martin was beginning to accept orders for Dreadnought guitars from other customers. The first two were a D-18 (serial number 52507) shipped to the Edfred Co. on January 9, 1933 and a D-28 (serial number 52508) shipped to Rudolph Wurlitzer Co. on January 18, 1933.

DREADNAUGHT MODEL
MADE EXCLUSIVELY FOR
CHICAGO MUSICAL INSTRUMENT CO.
BY C. F. MARTIN & CO., INC.
Figure 248
Special "Chicago Musical Instrument Co." Stamp

MONTGOMERY WARD & CO.
Martin 0-17S Guitars (1931-1932)

In mid-1931 Montgomery Ward & Co. ordered some special Martin guitars for inclusion in their catalog. Martin referred to these as 0-17S guitars although they appeared in the Montgomery Ward catalog as "**Catalog No. 856 Martin Guitar Concert**". The new models were same as Martin's regular 12-fret 0-17 guitars except they had spruce tops, lacked binding and came with a distinctively shaped pick guard extending to the outer edge of the guitar.

A total of eighty-six 0-17S guitars were made for Montgomery Ward. Thirty-six Style A mandolins were also ordered by Montgomery Ward in the same period but there appears to be nothing to distinguish them from regular Martin production. Montgomery Ward also purchased some ukuleles.

On July 5, 1933 Martin received a letter from Thomas Music Stores in Albany NY wondering how Montgomery Ward was able to advertise Martin guitars at low prices and provided a clipping of the advertisement (Figure 249). From the advertisement it is clear the guitar being offered was the Martin 0-17S, due to its distinctively shaped pick guard. The retail price was listed as $24.85 but the advertised selling price was only $10.98. Martin offered the following explanation on July 7, 1933:

"**We can only guess at the explanation of the Montgomery Ward advertisement you clipped and our guess is that they are closing out a few Martin Guitars left in their stock. We discontinued selling them in July 1932, having supplied them with several special numbers during the year prior to that and we took back a good many of the Guitars they had in stock. It is possible that some branches neglected to clean out their stock and are now obliged to sell them at less than cost. All the instruments we ever sold them were priced on exactly the same basis as to our regular dealers.**"

Figure 249
Newspaper Clipping of Montgomery Ward Co.
Special Offering of Martin 0-17S Guitars

As the cost to Montgomery Ward of a 0-17S guitar was $16.90, Martin was correct in stating they were being advertised at "close-out" price. Considering it was the depths of the Depression and Montgomery Ward hadn't purchased any Martin guitars for over a year, it is certainly understandable they would want to move out the old stock.

In a letter to Martin dated May 6, 1935, Montgomery Ward approached Martin to purchase higher priced guitars to be included in their catalog under the Martin name.

However, Martin had had enough of dealing with Montgomery Ward and replied to that effect on May 8:

"After giving your letter of May 6 the careful consideration it deserves we are unable to change our opinion that it would not be wise for us to supply you with Martin instruments under our own name or under another name.

Our previous experience brought out very clearly the critical attitude of our established dealers toward the listing of our merchandise in your catalogue at any reduction from our list prices. We also ran into difficulty in cities where we had protected agencies and prospective new dealer accounts seemed to be discouraged by the fact that they would have to compete with you on our line. This would apply also to any special goods we might make for you under your trade name because all products of our factory are easily identified and would be classed as Martin Instruments.

We are somewhat disappointed, too, in the fact that your orders were mostly in small quantities for shipment direct to your distribution points, making it difficult for us to affect certain savings on which we counted."

Table 51 shows that Martin had good reason to discontinue selling the special guitars to Montgomery Ward. It had always been Martin's policy to make special run or customer branded guitars with the understanding the order quantities would be larger. The initial orders were of good size but within 6 months the order size had shrunk to as few as two guitars.

Montgomery Ward's business practices clashed with Martin's normal pricing policy that expected dealers to sell at list. If Montgomery Ward's had followed Martin's usual pricing policy, the retail price for the 0-17S should have been $33.80, not the $24.85 mentioned in the advertisement.

MODEL	SERIAL NUMBERS	QUAN	SHOP ORDER	DATE STAMPED	SHOP ORDER COMMENTS
0-17S	47290-47314	25	1032	JUNE 16, 1931	SPRUCE TOP, ROSEWOOD BINDING ON TOP PLAIN, PICK GUARD, NO BACK BINDING
0-17S	47531-47555	25	1044	AUG. 7, 1931	SPECIAL PICK GUARD
0-17S	49315-49324	10	160	AUG. 12, 1931	SPRUCE TOP, 19 FRET FINGERBOARD
0-17S	49690-49699	10	174	JAN. 7, 1932	
0-17S	50429-50430	2	219	MAR. 9, 1932	SPRUCE TOP
0-17S	50588-50591	4	228	MAR. 30, 1932	SPRUCE TOP, MONTOMERY WARD & CO.
0-17S	50749-50750	2	240	APR. 18, 1932	SPRUCE TOP, MONTOMERY WARD & CO.MONTGOMERY WARD
0-17S	50801-50802	2	241	APR. 20, 1932	SPRUCE TOP, MONTOMERY WARD & CO.MONTGOMERY WARD
0-17S	50889-50891	3	248	MAY 3, 1932	FOR MONTGOMERY WARD
0-17S	51123-51125	3	259	MAY 27, 1932	FOR MONTGOMERY WARD & CO.

Table 51
Martin 0-17S Guitars Made for Montgomery Ward & Co.

RUDICK'S MUSIC STORE
Martin 00-17S (00-55) Guitars (1934-1935)

Rudick's Music Store, located in Akron OH, was one of Martin's more active dealers in the 1930's. Rudick's began buying Martin instruments in 1926 and continued to do so until 1942.

A paragraph in a letter Martin wrote to Rudick's Music Store on April 16, 1934 contains the following information on what was to become the 00-55 guitar:

"When Mr. Markley returns at the end of the week we will talk with him about the special Style 00-17 you are interested in. We understand that you want something distinctive on which you can quote a price that will permit a good trade-in allowance but Mr. Markley's report does not go into enough detail to enable us to quote you now. We will write you further about this next week."

The specifications of the new guitar were further discussed in Martin's letter of April 25:

"After talking to Mr. Markley about the special Guitar you discussed with him we have decided to quote you on a Grand Concert Mahogany instrument rather similar to Style 00-17 but bound on both edges and inlaid like Style 18. To make it different in appearance from the regular 00-17 we propose to finish it dark like Style 18 and to use polished brass vertical machine heads. This will make a distinctive Guitar that we can sell you at $19.50 each in lots of not less than six, for delivery three weeks after receipt of order.

If the idea appeals to you we shall be glad to make you a sample which we could probably rush through in just over two weeks.

It is understood, of course, that this Guitar will have the Orchestra Model neck with oval fingerboard joined to the body at the fourteenth fret. Both the bridge and the fingerboard will be made of rosewood."

Rudick's Music Store replied on April 30 that they wanted to change to nickel plated tuners rather than brass and also specified a wider bridge than a regular 00-17. Martin replied on May 2 that the changes

would raise the price to $20.00 and added the following paragraph to the bottom of the letter:

"Would it be satisfactory to use the style "00-55" thus indicating the size as well as your style number? The serial numbers will be in line with those used in our regular styles."

Therefore, the "00-55" designation was a combination of the Martin size with Rudick's own style number. Although not specifically mentioned in the first shop order, all these guitars were stamped 00-55.

Rudick's ordered the first 6 guitars on May 2 and the initial batch was shipped on June 4.

The finish on the first two batches appears to have been in flat lacquer because the finish for the third order was changed to the "machine polished" finish Martin had just started to use on Style 0-17 guitars.

Martin received a complaint from Rudick's on March 28, 1935 concerning problems being encountered with machines used on a 00-55 guitar. Martin replaced the tuners even though they didn't view them as defective but the same customer returned the guitar again in July with the same complaint (the records clearly indicate the defective machines were style 99T). This complaint may have been the reason that Martin decided to use Grover 100N machines for the last batch of 6.

The 00-55 guitars must not have worked out as well as Rudick's hoped because only four batches of 6 guitars were ever made. Besides, Rudick's was quite successful in selling the larger and more expensive Martin models and probably didn't need a special model to fill the low end of the guitar price range.

MODEL	SERIAL NUMBERS	QUAN	SHOP ORDER	DATE STAMPED	SHOP ORDER COMMENTS
00-17S	56307-56312	6	609	May 15, 1934	BODY BINDING & INLAY LIKE 18, GROVER #99 MACHINES, WIDE MODEL ROSEWOOD BRIDGE, DARK FINISH, FLAT LACQUER
00-17S	57185-57190	6	662	July 31, 1934	STAMPED 00-55, BODY BINDING & INLAY LIKE 18, GROVER #99 MACHINES, WIDE MODEL ROSEWOOD BRIDGE, DARK FINISH, FLAT LACQUER
00-17S	59127-59132	6	812	Feb. 14, 1935	STAMP 00-55, BODY BINDING & INLAY LIKE 18, GROVER #99 MACHINE, WIDE MODEL ROSEWOOD BRIDGE, DARK FINISH, FLAT LACQUER
00-17S	61738-61743	6	988	May 12, 1935	STAMPED 00-55, BODY BOUND & INLAID LIKE STYLE 18, FINGERBOARD INLAY STYLE 18, DARK FINISH, POLISHED, WIDE MODEL ROSEWOOD, GROVER 100N MACHINES

Table 52
Martin 00-17S (00-55) Guitars
Made for Rudick's Music Store

Notes for Chapter 12

1) the Music Trade Review, Vol. LXI, No. 23, pg 51, Dec. 4, 1915

Chapter 13
Martin Instrument Development in the Late 19th and 20th Century

Custom Ordered Guitar Similar to Style 45 (1897)

Although the 00-42S guitars made from 1901 to 1904 are considered the prototypes for what was to become style 45, one custom guitar was ordered in 1897 that could well approximate a style 45.

In a letter dated September 17, 1897 Zoebisch specified:

"We have an inquiry of price of 1-42 Style only more fancy inlaid Pearl around fingerboard left away (author: probably means no pearl around fingerboard extension)

Same inlaying as on top around the back, also around the sides

Inlaying around top about double as broad as an 1-42. Also around sound hole as broad as the pearl & ivory at least

Guitar to have white top & machine head

Fine fancy, not merely dots, on 3, 5, 7, 9 & 12th frets & fancy inlaying up on head upon the middle space

Customer wants it for man who already has 3 of your guitars and is bound to have a very fancy inlaid one."

Zoebisch even included a little sketch for the decoration to be inlaid in the peg head veneer. Although the fingerboard inlay was similar to style 42, the specification clearly called for pearl inlay around the sides and back and a veneered head stock, these both being features of a style 45 instrument.

As the sales records for 1897 are missing it cannot be conclusively proven that this guitar was delivered. However, if it ever appears it should be easy to identify. Like other guitar from the period it will lack a serial number and will be dated in pencil on the underside of the top with "9/97" or "10/97".

Even if this guitar was never made, popular demand

for a fancier grade of Martin guitar existed and Martin was certainly prepared to satisfy that demand.

Harp Guitars (1901-1912)

Martin made a small number of harp guitars from the mid-19th century to the early 20th century. The first four were made for Olaf Erikson in 1859-1860. The last harp guitar was made in 1912 (serial number 11495) and currently resides in the C. F. Martin & Co. collection.

Harp guitars had two necks and were made with 10, 12 or 16 strings. Serial number 9429 may even have 18 strings. Of the twelve harp guitars made after 1901, six were sold to the Grinnell Brothers of Detroit MI and the last three were sold to Henry Spahr of Jersey City NJ.

DATE	SERIAL NO.	MODEL	COMMENTS	SHIPPING DATE
1901	9374	000-28	DUPLICATED SERIAL NUMBER, 10 STRINGS	Dec. 24, 1901
1902	9392	000-21	10 STRINGS, FRICTION PEGS	May 10, 1902
1902	9393	000-21	10 STRINGS	Apr. 18, 1902
1902	9429	000-21	2 NECKS, 12 EXTRA STRINGS	Feb. 3, 1905
1902	9437	000-21	2 NECKS, 12 STRINGS	Sept. 4, 1902
1905	10054	000-21	12 STRING HARP GUITAR	June 20, 1905
1906	10163	000-28	2 NECK 12 STRING HARP GUITAR, VIENNESE (STAUFFER) HEAD ON SECOND NECK	Apr. 28, 1906
1907	10706	000-45	HARP GUITAR, DUPLICATE SERIAL NUMBER	Dec. 31, 1907
1911	11281	000-17	HARP GUITAR, 12 STRINGS, BINDING ON BACK EXTRA $1.00	Sept. 5, 1911
1911	11365	000-21	12 STRING HARP GUITAR	Nov. 24, 1911
1912	11495	STYLE 21	16 STRING HARP GUITAR, STYLE 21, 17" WIDE	Aug 31, 1912

Table 53
Martin Harp Guitars

Martin 00-42S Guitars (1901-1904) and Early Style 45 Guitars

As many guitar collectors and aficionados know Martin style 45 guitars are among the rarest and most sought after pre-WW II instruments.

By the early 1900's Martin had been making style 42 guitars for almost 50 years. What led Martin to add style 45 to a product line that had been well established for such a long time?

Recently, the Martin Guitar Company acquired a very fancy Martin guitar from the auction sale of Richard Gere's guitar collection (Christie's Sale 2519, October 11, 2011, lot 15). This guitar is one of the early 00-42 Specials that evolved into style 45 in the period between 1901 and 1904. The serial number of the guitar is 9373 and the Martin ledger book shows it was shipped in late 1901.

Up to this point in their history the fanciest regular production Martin guitars were designated style 42. Specifications included pearl sound hole decoration, an ivory bridge and pearl purfling around the outside of the guitar and around the edges of the fingerboard extension.

Starting around 1895 Martin began making extra fancy grades of mandolins that included such features as fancy inlay veneers for the head and fingerboard as well as intricate pearl inlaid pick guards. In the early 1900's mandolins made up a substantial part of Martin's total instrument production. The fanciest grades of mandolins (style 6 and style 7) sold reasonably well and Frank Henry Martin may have decided it was time to add a fancier grade of guitar to their long established line in order to profit from the demand for flashier instruments.

A close examination of the Martin ledger for 1898 to 1913 has resulted into some new insights into the development of style 45 guitars.

In 1901 the largest and fanciest guitar regularly made by Martin was the 00-42 which carried a retail price of $80. By reviewing the retail prices of the guitars in the Martin ledger book, it is fairly easy to identify the guitars that were priced higher than $80 and were therefore fancier than style 42. (It should be noted that Martin began experimenting with size 000 guitars around the same time).

The table below documents the 12 instruments, between serial numbers 9242 and 9759, that are presumed to be style 00-42S guitars based on pricing, as they were clearly intended to be fancier that the standard 00-42 guitars. However, specifications and pricing varied somewhat befitting their prototype status. Some may want to consider the last of these, serial number 9759, as a presentation grade guitar since it was so much fancier than the other 00-42S instruments. The table also documents a few of the early style 45 guitars.

The first guitar designated as style 45 in the Martin ledgers was a 00-45 shipped on November 4, 1904 to

MARTIN 00-42S GUITARS (1901-1904)					
SERIAL NUMBER	SHIPPING DATE	DEALER	CITY	STATE	RETAIL[1] PRICE
9242	JUNE 19, 1901	WINTER & HARPER	SEATTLE	WA	$88
9372 (FIRST)[2]	DEC. 24, 1901	RETAIL CUSTOMER	EASTON	PA	$100
9372 (FIRST)[3]	DEC. 31, 1913	RETAIL CUSTOMER	EASTON	PA	$15
9372 (SECOND)[4]	MARCH 6, 1906[5]	RETAIL CUSTOMER	NAZARETH	PA	$30
9373[6]	DEC. 25, 1901	BARTLETT MUSIC CO.	LOS ANGELES	CA	$100
9410	JULY 30, 1902	CALIFORNIA MUSIC CO.	SAN DIEGO	CA	$90
9483[7]					
9486	NOV. 17, 1902	BARTLETT MUSIC CO.	LOS ANGELES	CA	$100
9488	APR. 20, 1903	BARTLETT MUSIC CO.	LOS ANGELES	CA	$100
9590	JUNE 20, 1903	BARTLETT MUSIC CO.	LOS ANGELES	CA	$100
9591	JUNE 20, 1903	BARTLETT MUSIC CO.	LOS ANGELES	CA	$100
9592	AUG. 27, 1903	C. H. DITSON & CO.	NEW YORK	NY	$100
9759[8]	FEB. 27, 1904	RETAIL CUSTOMER	LOS ANGELES	CA	$225
9960[9]	NOV. 30, 1904	BARTLETT MUSIC CO.	LOS ANGELES	CA	$115
9962[10]	DEC. 31, 1904	CLARK WISE & CO.	SAN FRANCISCO	CA	$110
10005[11]	NOV. 24, 1906	WILLIAM LEWIS & SON	CHICAGO	IL	$87
10035[12]	MAR. 27, 1905	SANDERS & STAYMAN CO.	WASHINGTON	DC	$150
10201[13]	OCT. 1, 1906	HENRY SPAHR	JERSEY CITY	NJ	$115
10706[14]	DEC. 31, 1907	BARTLETT MUSIC CO.	LOS ANGELES	CA	$145

1) The retail price for a 00-42 in this period was $80. Prices did not include a case.
2) Returned twice for repairs (including a new top "for tone")
3) Sold as "used" IN 1913 for $15.
4) Returned three times between 1908 and 1934 for repairs (including a new top). This guitar is in the collection of the Museum of Musical Instruments (MoMI).
5) The FIRST 9372 was exchanged to the SECOND 9372 in 1906. The customer pain an additional $30 for the exchange.
6) Recently acquired by the C. F. Martin & Co.
7) No record has yet been found for this serial number in the Martin Archives. It is included in this table because it appears Mike Longworth had a chance to examine it and noted in his logbook "INLAID HEAD, IVORY BRIDGE, PROTO HEAD INLAY".
8) This guitar was even more elaborately decorated that a style 45 instrument. Specifications included "Made to order with pearl inlaid sides and back, solid 14K frets, gold bands around keys, gold and silver position markers, gold plated machines, $225, black leather case for same (seal grained, plush lined, opening on the side, $25.00)
9) First 00-45, friction pegs
10) First 0-45, friction pegs
11) Special order 00-42 with "pearl fingerboard & ebony bridge".
12) Special 00 guitar: "Special style. Made to order with special design in ivory on face, sides, back and head. Pearl inlaying on head & fingbd & at soundhole. Special selection of material."
13) First 000-45, "special to order"
14) Second 000-45 and also a harp guitar. Serial number 10706 is a duplicate serial number, a 1-21 was also made with the same number.

Table 54
Martin 00-42S Guitars (1901-1904) and Early Style 45 Guitars (1904-1907)

Bartlett Music Co. It is interesting to note that many of the 00-42S guitars were sold to Bartlett Music so their input may have had a significant influence on the final development of style 45 guitars. In the period between February and November 1904 Martin finally settled on the specifications for style 45 guitars and increased the retail price to $115.

Details for each of the 00-42S guitars are documented below:

SERIAL NUMBER 9242 (1901)

This is the first 00-42S and was specified with a "special inlaid fingerboard and pick guard, $8.00 extra". The extra charge was added to the normal $80 retail price for a 00-42 guitar. The ledger doesn't mention whether the sides or back were inlaid with pearl. It was shipped to Winter & Harper Co. in Seattle, WA on September 19, 1901.

SERIAL NUMBER 9372 (1901)

There are actually TWO guitars having this serial number. Both have vine inlaid fingerboards, inlaid head stocks and inlaid mandolin-style pick guards. Each had a different headstock inlay and although the fingerboard inlays have identical "vine" or "tree-of-life" inlays they are mirror images of each other. The FIRST guitar was shipped to a customer on December 24, 1901 and was priced at $75 ($100 retail price less a 25% discount), so the customer was probably a music teacher (see Figures 250 to 252.)

This guitar was returned to Martin for gluing of a crack in 1903 and again in 1904 for replacement of the top ("for tone"). The customer continued to have issues with this guitar so he returned it on March 8, 1906 and exchanged it for the SECOND guitar with the same serial number (it cost him an additional $30). Even then, the same customer continued to have issues and returned the SECOND guitar three more times between 1908 and 1934 for repairs (including another top replacement!). It is very curious that the same retail customer owned both of the guitars with serial number 9372, although at different times.

The FIRST guitar was sold again as "used" on December 31, 1913 for the low price of $15.

Is it possible to differentiate between these two guitars? Remarkably, the answer is YES!

An entry in the ledger dated March 8, 1906 provides the clue. The entry details that the same customer exchanged a 00-42 for a 00-45 ("**both with guard plate and inlaid fingerboard**"). This can only mean the SECOND 00-42S guitar was identified as a 00-45 guitar because it had the pearl inlaid sides and back, this being one of the features of style 45 guitars by 1904.

The collection of the Museum of Musical Instruments (MoMI) contains the SECOND guitar with pearl inlaid sides and back.

SERIAL NUMBER 9373 (1901)

The ledger specifies this guitar was "special inlaid" but provides no further details. It was shipped to Bartlett Music Co. on December 25, 1901. Retail on this guitar was also $100. As this guitar in now in the Martin Museum it can now be confirmed it has the level of decoration as the two guitars with serial number 9372.

SERIAL NUMBER 9410 (1902)

The ledger mentions "sides inlaid with pearl" but no further details. It was to The California Music Co., in San Diego, CA on July 30, 1902. Retail for this guitar was $90.

This guitar was discovered by Mike Longworth some time ago but was in very poor shape. The condition of the body was so bad that Mike Longworth built another guitar around the original neck and neck block.

The damaged body, however, is still in existence. The back is off and it does not appear the back was inlaid with pearl. Also, the top does not have a mandolin-style pick guard inlaid into the top. The lack of an inlaid pick guard and the absence of pearl inlay on the back may explain why the guitar was priced $10 less than the other 00-42S guitars.

SERIAL NUMBER 9483 (1902)

The Martin ledger does not contain any information on this guitar. However, it looks like Mike Longworth examined it at some point because he noted in his logbook "inlaid head, ivory bridge, proto head inlay".

SERIAL NUMBER 9486 (1902)

The ledger details this guitar with "guard plate, inlaid head & fingerboard". It was shipped to Bartlett Music Co. of Los Angeles CA on November 17, 1902. Retail was $100 so this must also be a 00-42S.

SERIAL NUMBER 9488 (1902)

The ledger details "sides, back and end inlaid with pearl". It was shipped to Bartlett Music Co. on April 20, 1903.

The fingerboard of this guitar has "snowflake" inlays at the 5th, 7th, 9th, 12th and 15th frets. Although slightly less fancy than the earlier 00-42S guitars with the "vine" fingerboard inlays, it still had a retail price of $100.

SERIAL NUMBERS 9590 & 9591 (1903)

Both were shipped to Bartlett Music Co. of Los Angeles CA on June 20, 1903 and both had "pick guard, inlaid fingerboard & head". Retail price was $100.

SERIAL NUMBER 9592 (1903)

The Martin ledger specifies "special inlaid". It is unclear what this specification meant but it was shipped to C. H. Ditson & Co., New York NY on August 27, 1903 with a retail price of $100.

SERIAL NUMBER 9759 (1904)

This instrument is much fancier than any of the other 00-42S guitars. The ledger has the following specs **"Made to order with pearl inlaid sides & back, solid 14K gold frets, gold wound (?) keys, gold and silver position markers, gold plated machines"**. It was shipped to a retail client on February 27, 1904. Price was $225 plus another $25 for a special plush lined leather case.

SERIAL NUMBER 9960 (1904)

This the first listed style 45, a 00-45 with a solid head stock and ivory friction pegs. It was, not unsurprising-

Figure 250
Headstock Veneer on 1902 00-42S Guitar
(First Serial Number 9372)

Figure 251
Portion of Fingerboard Inlay on 1902 0-42S Guitar
(First Serial Number 9372)

Figure 252
Inlaid Pickguard on 1902 00-42S Guitar
(First Serial Number 9372)

ly, sold to Bartlett Music Co. It was shipped on August 30, 1904 but the retail price had been increased to $115.

Early 12-String Guitars (1913-1941)

Martin made only a few 12-string guitars in the period before 1964. This may be best explained by examining Martin's response to one of their dealer's requests in a letter dated November 9, 1925:

"We are sorry that we cannot supply you with a twelve-string Guitar and hardly know where to recommend you to get a good instrument. Several years ago we thought of taking up this manufacture but found that most of the demand for twelve-string instruments was cheap and, at the price the high grade Guitar would have to command, would not be a good seller."

As can be seen from table 55, Martin did make a small amount of special order 12-string guitars from 1925 to 1941. A few prototype 12-string guitars were made in 1964 and the demand for 12-string guitars,

EARLY 12-STRING GUITARS			
DATE	MODEL	SERIAL NUMBER	COMMENTS
1913	000-18S¹	11605	Modified to 12-string, March 20, 1923
1913	000-18S²	11610	Modified to 12-string, June 26, 1925
1921	000-21³	16098	Special, 12 strings, extra strong bridge
1929	0-17(S)	40112	000 braces, 1½" bridge plate
1932	C-2S	50223	12 strings, 6 pairs, neck as wide as wood will allow, special tailpiece, 12 machine units on regular head
1932	C-1S	50803	12 strings, 6 pairs, neck as wide as wood will allow, special tailpiece, 12 mach. units
1936	000-28S	64231	Special neck, 1 bridge for 12 strings (6 pairs)
1936	000-28S	64916	For 12 strings, 14 fret neck, #5039 Waverly machines
1936	R-18S	64955	For 12 strings (6 pairs)
1937	000-28S	65576	Special neck and bridge for 12 strings (6 pairs), neck width 2" at nut, 2-7/16" at 12ᵗʰ fret
1938	000-18S²	71276	For 12 strings, 6 pairs, neck joined at 12ᵗʰ fret, slotted head, special C-31 patterned heads
1940	000-28(S)	74412	
1940	00-17S	76256	Standard model body for 12 strings, 6 pairs, 12 fret neck, slotted head, special G-31 mach., very unusual bracing pattern
1941	F-1S	78016	
1941	000-18S	78741	For 12 string (6 pairs), neck joined at 12ᵗʰ fret, slotted head, special G-31 pat. Heads, white bridge pins
1964	X-12	193363	D-12-20 prototype
1964	D-12-20A	195323	Prototype
1964	D-12-20B	195324	Prototype

Notes: 1) Sold to retail customer in Easton PA
2) Sold to retail account in South Bethlehem PA
3) Sold to owner of serial number 11610
4) Although this guitar was stamped on September 23, 1938 it didn't clear final inspection until February 21, 1940.

Table 55
List of Early 12-String Guitars

for folk music, was so strong they were quickly added to the product line. Twelve strings guitars made a major contribution to Martin's sales throughout the 1960's and 1970's.

Hawaiian Guitars (1914-1955)

Hawaiian music had been gaining slowly popularity since around the turn of the 20ᵗʰ with the arrival of Hawaiians musicians on the mainland. However, with the exception of the Ditson models Martin produced only a small number of guitars between 1914 and 1920 specifically made for "Hawaiian playing". These amounted to a total of nine instruments: three 1-18, three 0-18, one 1-21, one 0-21 and one 00-21 guitars. From 1914 to 1927 guitars that were ordered for Hawaiian playing had regular frets. The guitars were set up as for guts strings but were supplied with a nut extender and Hawaiian steel strings.

In late 1927 Martin identified the need for a purpose-built Hawaiian guitar that resulted in the 2-17H being added to the Martin line. Martin sent out letters to dealers promoting the 2-17H, the letter below to Loper-Cressett Music Co. dated November 28 is typical:

"Guitars are selling well, particularly in the Tenor and Hawaiian types. We have just added to our line a new Hawaiian guitar fitted with high bridge and nut, and with frets flush in a flat fingerboard. This is our Style 2-17H, retail price thirty dollars. May we send a sample?"

Martin sent a telegram to Chicago Musical Instrument Co. on November 3, 1927 announcing the 2-17H:

"Announcing the new and distinctive Martin Hawaiian guitar. Flat fingerboard. Frets worked flush with wood. Extra strong neck. High bridge and nut. Suitable for Hawaiian playing only. Size, design and materials like regular 2-17 guitar. List price thirty dollars. Will ship sample early next week. Delivery in two weeks."

CMI replied to Martin on December 14, 1927, the letter containing the following comments:

"The style 2-17H guitar is good, but we hardly see any opportunity of any great amount of sales, because in the first place, the present 2-17 with steel nut on it serves the same purpose.

There is no advantage in filing off the frets, because when a guitar is tuned up Hawaiian style to standard pitch and the guitar extension nut used, it is almost impossible to make the bar touch the frets anyway. The $2.50 difference in the price might have some effect if you had a long discount to jobbers so they could offer it to their dealers on

price basis. It is still a Martin, however, and has to be sold on quality basis and you can't well talk quality and price at the same time.

Of course we are going to sell them, in fact we've already sold the one you sent us so you can enter our order for about two more, just so that we'll have them in stock. We have a lot of the No. 2-17, however, and in our retail stock we can really sell them better because the customer can use them either the Spanish or Hawaiian as he pleases which seems to us to be the most logical way of making up the instrument."

The development of the 2-17H is another example of Martin trying to keep costs down on their lower priced instruments by establishing a specification to be applied to whole batches of guitars. However, CMI appears to have been correct about the need for a special Hawaiian model for the Style 2-17 as the 2-17H guitars were only made between 1927 and 1929. A total of 500 of the 2-17H guitars were produced during that period. One more special order for a 2-17 for Hawaiian playing was made in 1930.

The more upscale 00-40H was added in 1928 and was far more successful, at least in terms of longevity. The 00-40H guitars are probably the most commonly encountered of the pre-WW II "pearly" Martins guitars. A total of 282 were made between 1928 and 1939. At least one was made with a solid peg head and banjo tuners and another was made with "curly koa" sides

MARTIN HAWAIIAN GUITARS		
STYLE	PRODUCTION	DATES
2-17H	501	1927-1930
0-15H	12	1940
0-17H	299	1935-1940
0-18H	25	1929
0-28H	2	1928
00-17H	20	1934-1935
00-18H	255	1935-1941
00-21H	2	1952-1955
00-40H	282	1928-1939
000-18HS	3	1937
000-18H	1	1938
000-28H	1	1934
000-45H	2	1937
D-18H	4	1934-1966
D-28H	2	1934-1936
OM-45H	1	1931

Table 56
Hawaiian Guitar Production 1927 to 1955

and back, so is in reality a 00-40HK.

Not all guitars made after 1927 and designated as Hawaiian guitars had flat fingerboards with a raised nut and saddle. Some batches were made as "Spanish" (i.e., regular) guitars.

The last regularly made Hawaiian guitars were 00-18H guitars, with 1941 being the final year of production.

A few more exotic Hawaiian guitars were also produced. One OM-45 was modified to a Hawaiian guitar prior to shipment in 1931 and two 000-45H guitars were sold in 1937.

Ukuleles and Related Instruments (1915)

This subject has already been extensively covered in *The Martin Ukulele by Tom Walsh & John King* (Hal Leonard Books). This book is highly recommended and further information on the ukulele family of instruments in this book will be limited to examination of ukuleles that had serial numbers, covered in other chapters in this book, and a few unusual instruments.

Koa Guitars (1916-1937)

The first Martin koa guitars were made for Southern California Music Co. in the period from 1916 to September 1917. These all received Southern California Co. serial numbers (numbered 1-262). The first 18 or so of these guitars had spruce tops with koa sides and backs while all later guitars were all koa instruments. Southern California Music Co. continued to order their model numbers until 1922 but the koa guitars they were shipped had regular Martin serial numbers.

The first koa guitars made with Martin serial numbers were small batches of 1-18K and 0-28K guitars made in late 1917. The most commonly encountered koa guitars are 0-18K and 0-28K. A number of 00-18K and 00-28K instruments were also made as well as very small quantities of 5-18K, 1-18K, 0-21K, 00-40K, 00-42K, 00-45K and 000-28K models.

The koa guitars were originally intended to be played in the Hawaiian-style. From circa 1927 some koa guitars were made with raised nut and saddles and flat fingerboards while others were made as regular Spanish-style guitars, especially as time went on.

From a letter to Loper-Cressett Music Co. on April 4, 1927 we learn some interesting details about koa guitars:

"The recent call for Hawaiian guitar leads us to believe that this instrument will be quite popular during the coming season. Many people are hearing it on the radio and the phonograph, and orchestra players are finding the fine tone quality of the guitar valuable in their work.

With this in mind we wish to call your attention to our genuine Koawood guitars, specially constructed and adjusted for Hawaiian playing. Style 0-28K is made of selected figured koa, strikingly beautiful, while Style 0-18K is made of plainer wood, all of which we import direct from the Hawaiian Islands. The construction is somewhat heavier than in the standard Martin Guitar, and the adjustment is made with a high level bridge and a high nut, which does not require a re-adjuster."

MARTIN KOA GUITARS		
MODEL	PRODUCTION TOTALS	DATES
5-18K	3	1921-1937
1-18K	48	1917-1919
0-18K	3174	1918-1935
0-21K	66	1919-1929
0-28K	599	1917-1935
00-18K	58	1918-1934
00-28K	41	1919-1933
00-40K	6	1918-1930
00-42K	1	1919
00-45K	1	1919
000-28K	3	1921

Table does not include the koa guitars with Southern California Music Co. serial numbers.

Table 57
Production of Martin Koa Guitars (1917-1937)

The 0-28K guitars were discontinued in 1931 while the 0-18K guitars lasted until 1935. The very last pre-WW II koa guitar was a 5-18K made in 1937.

Tiples (1919)

See section on William J. Smith & Co. (1917-1923) in Chapter 12, pages 179 to180.

T-45K Tiple (1922)

Most of the tiples made by Martin were relatively plain, usually styles 17, 18 or 28. Martin did make a few fancier tiples for William J. Smith in 1922, two T-42 and one T-45K tiples. The vast majority of tiples sold were Styles T-17 and T-28 so there was clearly little demand for fancier and more expensive models. The Style T-15 replaced the T-17 in mid-1949.

The Martin records show that the T-45K was shipped April 29, 1922 to William J. Smith Music Co. in New York City. Although Longworth recorded this instrument as a T-45 the ledger clearly shows it was a

Figure 253
Detail of T-45K Rosette

Figure 254
Detail of End Graft and Back Stripe of T-45K

T-45K. The tiple is listed as having a special feature, probably referring to the double pick guard on the upper bout.

See also figures 234 and 235 on page 180.

The First D-45 Guitar
Could Have Been Made in 1925

It is a well know that the first D-45 guitar was made in 1933 for Gene Autry, the famous cowboy movie and radio star. What is not known is that Martin could have sold fancy grade Dreadnought guitars much earlier, but discouraged the orders!

In a letter dated March 25, 1925, Al Dumas requested a special guitar:

"I want a guitar about two or three inches larger around than an auditorium size as I am trying to get an immense volume of tone, instrument to be made entirely of a selected curly grain of koa wood finished like the Martin 5 ukulele, the inlaying of pearl like your 00-45 guitar priced at $150.00. ..."

In a reply dated March 31 Martin refused to consider making the larger guitar because of the amount of unfilled orders in the factory, although he offered to make a 00-45K in 3 months or a 000-45K at a later date, after an expected new supply of koa was to be received that summer. Martin did not even mention that they were making Dreadnought model guitars for C. H. Ditson & Co.

To be fair, this was before the demand for larger guitars for radio use had taken off. If should also be remembered that 1925 was the peak year for ukulele production and the factory was already back ordered.

In 1929 guitar teacher Irvine Taylor of Birmingham, Alabama custom ordered a 000-45 with a geared peg head, a pick guard and with his name inlaid in pearl in the fingerboard. At is happened Martin was just finishing a batch of 000-45 guitar so was able to deliver the custom guitar in only 3 weeks.

However, in a letter dated July 27, 1929 Mr. Taylor stated:

"I received your guitar and tried it out and while

it is certainly a beautiful solo instrument it is not just exactly what I want. What I want is the guitar with a deeper body and a little larger. If you ever seen the big model Vega guitar that is what I want. I took the guitar too (sic) Nat Williams (the local Martin dealer that helped place the custom order) and he returned it by express ..."

Martin was very accommodating in taking back the special ordered guitar but offered the following comments on large sized instruments:

"Our experience with larger guitars, of which we have made a number, is that the tone becomes deep and hollow, inferior in quality and in carrying power to our regular Auditorium size. For that reason we do not offer a larger Guitar and would not care to make one for you. We have discovered through many years of experimentation that the depth of the Guitar body should be decreased as the width is increased. For that reason our Grand Concert Size is not as deep as Concert Size and Auditorium Size has still less depth. The purpose of this is to prevent the tone from being lost in the body of the instrument. There is a great difference between tone which sounds big and deep to a player and a tone which will carry in a large hall."

By this point in 1929 Martin at least admitted they made guitars larger than 000 size but, based on a conservative notion of the ideal guitar, was still refusing to make a style 45 Dreadnought!

By 1933 the times had obviously changed. The Depression had really begun to affect Martin's business (Martin sales in 1930 were higher than 1929 and in 1931 only slightly lower), popular music had taken over the radio waves, the demand for a large bass guitar for use by radio performers was growing and the first order for a D-45 came from a radio star with whom Martin had already corresponded.

Still, if Martin had been a little less conservative, the first fancy Dreadnought guitar would have been a 1925 D-45K!

Tenor and Plectrum Guitars (1927)

Tenor Guitars

The early history of Martin tenor guitars is much more interesting than previously considered and will be examined here in detail.

Although there is a gap in the records and correspondence, Martin made a decision in late 1926 or early 1927 to consider adding tenor guitars to their products line.

Martin approached H. A. Selmer Inc. in early January 1927 seeking intelligence on the demand for tenor guitars because they received a letter on January 10:

"As far as we can see, there is not an exceptional demand for tenor guitars. However, if you do start making them, we will place a trial order of three. This is not large enough to start heavy production, but no doubt many of the other large dealers in the city will place an order for quite a few. Our string department man suggests that the price be kept within $25, if possible."

Thus heartened Martin responded on February 26:

"Your letter of January 10 in reply to our inquiry regarding Tenor Guitars encouraged us to undertake the production of this instrument. We wish to thank you for your advice.

We have completed the preliminary work are about to proceed with production of two styles, --Style 5-17, an all-Mahogany instrument at $30.00, list, and Style 5-21, Rosewood with Spruce Top, at $55.00.

On the strength of your letter we are booking your order for three of Style 5-17, delivery of which we expect to make early in April. We trust this will be entirely satisfactory to you."

In the meantime, on January 27, 1927, Martin contacted A. D. Grover & Son to advise them that tenor guitars were being considered for addition to the Martin product line and requested a sample of a Grover No. 77 peg (cost: $0.45 ea) to make sure it would work with the peg head design. The No. 77 peg

must have been satisfactory as Martin acknowledged receipt of an order on February 7 and thanked Grover for the prompt delivery.

Pease-Behning Co. Inc. wrote a letter to Martin of Feb. 2, 1927 seeking confirmation that Martin would be starting to manufacture tenor guitars. Martin replied on February 3 that the first six samples would be ready about the middle of the month.

The first six samples were 5-17T guitars (serial numbers 29240 to 29245) and were stamped on January 18, 1927. The sample 5-17T guitars had rosewood bindings and position marks at the 3rd, 5th, 7th and 9th frets. It appears that the scale length of the samples was about 21-3/8".

The samples were ready on February 15 and on that date Martin forwarded one to Chicago Musical Instrument Co. with the request that they put it in the hands of a professional player for garnering feedback on the instrument. Martin also asked for suggestions for improvements. The reply on February 24 produced just a few comments on the quality of strings supplied on the sample and the position dots on the fingerboard. CMI suggested dots at the 1st, 3rd, 5th, 7th, 10th and 12th frets. CMI further commented that the tone was considerably better than the Regal tenor guitars they carried and thought it was because the body was so much larger! Martin replied the next day and admitted they hadn't has time to experiment to find the correct strings. Martin had also decided to make features of the 5-17T guitar exactly like the Style 0 ukulele and the T-17 tiple, with a different rosette than used on the samples.

Southern California Music Co. on March 25, 1927 wrote to Martin:

"We are anxious to learn when we are going to receive our first shipment of tenor guitars. In talking with one of the tenor players the other day, I mentioned to him that you were making up some styles and he said to write you as follows:-'They should be made up with a 23" scale neck instead of 21" scale neck applied to most tenor guitars. This suggestion has been followed out in regard to the tenor banjo and now it is impossible to sell anything else at the present time, as it makes the instrument more efficient and resonant."

Martin replied to southern California Music Co. on March 30:

"A few days ago we sent you by express six Style 5-17 Tenor guitars and in a day or two we expect to send two of the Style 5-21. The balance of four Style 5-21 will be ready in about ten days.

This instrument has a string length of about 21½" which gives a nice firm string and a full tone. In response to the demand for a 23" scale, we are working on several ideas which we hope will prove practical. As soon as we have a sample ready we will send it to you."

Martin has continued to make changes in their design for tenor guitars because in a letter to CMI on April 22, 1927 they stated:

"We are sending you today two Tenor Guitars somewhat different from the style we previously sent you.

One is Style 5-17 with 22½", a little more than one inch longer than the scale we have been using. The other is Style 2-17 with the longer scale. …

We would like to have you get us a report on these instruments from Mr. Rothermel and from any other professional players to whom you care to show them.

We are particularly interested in knowing whether there is an advantage in the longer scale and in the larger body. Other things being equal, it would be our choice to use the small body with the long scale, which you will note has 19 frets."

CMI's interesting reply on April 29 offered the following:

"There's no question at all but that there is more volume to be had from the 2-17 tenor guitar than from the 5-17, however, we doubt that as a commercial proposition there would be any advantage in making the larger instruments because we believe the players all prefer the smaller size.

We are trying to see the various professionals as fast as we can, in fact we have one man that's calling on them pretty nearly every night and he's carrying the tenor guitars with him. We are not yet ready to make a report on the advisability as to which body we'd like to see you use regularly, but so far as the scale length is concerned, we strongly prefer the 22 ½" scale, and think everyone else will say the same, especially so since our new lower priced banjos are all coming through with 22" scales.

We'll write you again in just a few days, but at present our choice would be the same as yours, the smaller body with the long scale."

Curiously, a parallel correspondence with Rudolph Wurlitzer Co. resulted in the same conclusion. In a letter to Martin dated April 26, 1927 they offered:

"We have had the last 2 sample Tenor Guitars carefully tried out by several players and we have decided that the Style 5-17, the smaller bodies instrument, with the 22 ½" scale, is the better of the two."

Martin replied to CMI on May 4 with the following comments:

"Thank you for your recent letter in regard to scales and sizes for our Tenor Guitar. The New York professional players seem to be of the same opinion in regard to the scale so we are going ahead with the No. 5 body and the 22 ½" scale. Later, if we find that there is demand for the larger body, we will be glad to make it up on special order."

On December 5, 1927 CMI queried Martin about the rumor they had heard Martin a tenor guitar with a 26" scale (i. e., a plectrum guitar). Martin replied they had supplied a few large tenor guitars on special order with a scale length of 25". Martin had received some inquiries for plectrum guitars but had not seen sufficient demand to consider production.

H. B. McClellan Music House many some interesting observations on tenor guitars to Martin in a letter dated October 18, 1927:

"As you know, the most of these instruments are sold to professional banjoists to use as a double. All modern professional type tenor banjos have the new long scale. We have had numerous complaints on the Martin Tenor Guitar have too short a neck and the extension of the fingerboard up over the body of the instrument. These banjoists claim that they cannot reach the high position with ease.

It has been brought to our attention that quite a number of banjoists to whom we have sold Martin Tenor Guitars are trading them in on the new Gibson Tenor Guitar which has the neck made the same as on modern long scale tenor banjos and also has a larger body which tends to give the instrument a bigger tone.

We know that you would not want to see the Gibson people get the business on the tenor guitar and we are sure that you can make these instruments with the new long scale fingerboard and with a longer neck without the extension over the top. We have seen the Gibson and upon comparison with the Martin there is no question that the Martin is superior in every way except the neck and fingerboard."

Martin replied on October 26, 1927:

"On his return yesterday from a western trip the writer was shown your interesting and valuable letter of the 18th in regard to the Tenor Guitar.

We understand fully the advantage to the player of the use of several additional frets on the neck of the Guitar. This is accomplished on the Gibson instrument by joining the body to the neck at the fifteenth fret, leaving only a few frets extending over the body. This is possible in the Gibson instrument because of the peculiar shape of the body which is considerably flattened in the upper part, contracted at the sound hole and enlarged at the lower part. It is our opinion that this distortion of the body has a serious effect on the tone of the instrument and for that reason we have we have not considered changing our standard body model.

We understand that the scale length of the Gibson Tenor Guitar is about the same as ours, which is 22½' from nut to bridge saddle. Our first tenor Guitars were made with a 21" scale but this was changed to the longer scale several months ago.

We have found that most dealers report this scale

	5-17T(S)[1]	5-17T[4]	5-17T-L[5]	2-17T(S)[6]	2-17T[7]	2-18T[8]	2-18T-L[9]	2-18T(S)[10]	5-21T(S)[11]	5-21T[12]	2-21T	2-28T[13]	2-28T-L	2-45T
1927	61 (est.)	1000 (est.)		3	24					37	325			
1928		500	12	3		162	6					1	3	3	1
1929	2[2]	298	64			75	56	3				24	28	
1930	1[3]	707				50								

SIZE 5 AND SIZE 2 TENOR GUITARS

1) The first 56 of the 1927 5-17T guitars were identified as "specials" and are shown as 5-17T(S) in the table. Around 250 of the first 5-17T guitars in 1927 appear to have had the 21-3/8" scale length and 22 ½" thereafter.
2) Two 5-17T(S) guitars from 1929 (serial numbers 38539 and 38540) had 14 fret necks. Longworth noted that another batch of fifty 5-17T guitars in 1929 had long necks (included in total although the number of frets clear of the body is not known).
3) One 5-17T(S) in 1930 was made with a 21" scale length.
4) The 5-17T guitars switched to 14 fret necks at some point between late 1929 and early 1930.
5) The 5-17T-L guitars had 15 fret necks. Most of the 1927 5-17T guitars had 12 fret necks except for two (serial numbers 33906 and 33907) which had 15 fret necks.
6) Three 2-17T(S) guitars were made in 1927 with 22 ½" scale length. Three more 2-17T(S) guitars were made in 1928 as Martin experimented with longer scale lengths or longer necks.
7) Of the twenty-four 2-17T guitars made in 1927 half had the 22 ½' scale length and half had "No. 2 Scale" (i.e., 24 ½').
8) The 2-18T guitars had 12 fret necks and 23" scale lengths and, it is assumed the 1930 models had 14 fret necks. The exact split between 12 and 14 fret neck guitars in 1929 is not known.
9) The 2-18T-L guitars had 14 fret necks.
10) There were three 2-18T(S) guitars made in 1929, one with an eight-string neck and two with six-string necks.
11) The earliest 5-21T guitars had the 21 3/8" scale length. The 5-21T guitars come with either 18 fret or 19 frets fingerboards. Twenty-five of the 5-21T(S) guitars noted have 19 fret fingerboards.
12) The scale length of the 5-21T guitars changed to 22 ¾" some time during 1927 although the exact timing of the switch is not known.
13) All 2-28T guitars may have 14 fret necks with 23" scale length except for three made in 1929 with 15 fret necks.
Martin made a batch of 5-17T guitars, stamped February 20, 1928, (35062-35073) with a "long neck" with 15 frets clear of the body. One of this batch is noted with "cross braces moved back ¼"".

Notes: Martin was a little careless in recording scale lengths in correspondence so some lee-way must be given for the information in this table. For example, Martin talked about the 21 3/8" scale length as 21" or even 22". The 22 ½" scale length may be closer to 23".
Martin made a 2-45T (35150) stamped Feb. 29, 1928 and a 2-21T (35151) stamped Feb. 29, 1928.
Of the size 5 or size 2 tenor guitars, only the 5-17T was still being made after 1930. It continued in production until 1949.

Table 58
Size 5 and Size 2 Tenor Guitars

satisfactory in length; but in some places there is a demand for a 27" scale, like the plectrum Banjo. The use of this very long scale would make it possible for us to build a Guitar with standard size body, joined to the neck at the fifteenth fret, but the instrument would no longer be a Tenor Guitar.

We are wondering whether you have in mind the long-scale plectrum instrument or whether you think that our regular Tenor Guitar should have a longer scale than it now has.

After talking with many dealers and a number of players on this subject during his recent trip, the writer concluded that the tone of the instrument is more important than the use of the extra frets so we intend to continue to make our Tenor Guitars as we have been making them, but we are quite likely to make up a Plectrum Guitar as described above. Would this be of interest to you?"

This letter shows that Martin changed the scale length

MODEL	SHOP ORDER	DATE STAMPED	QUAN	SERIAL NUMBER	COMMENTS
2-18T	224	09-03-1928	12	35214-35225	23" SCALE LENGTH
2-18T	238	02-04-1928	25	35426-35450	LONGWORTH NOTED 35432-35437 HAD HEAVY TONE BARS
2-18T	242	19-03-1928	25	35614-35638	23" SCALE LENGTH
2-18T	250	23-08-1928	25	35881-35905	
2-18T	278	20-08-1928	25	36468-36492	
2-18T	315	25-10-1928	25	36997-37021	
2-18T	320	26-11-1928	25	37150-37174	
2-18T-L	332	09-11-1928	3	37200-37202	14 FRETS CLEAR
2-18T-L	352	13-12-1928	3	37465-37467	14 FRETS CLEAR
2-18T-L	361	28-01-1929	25	37779-37803	
2-18T(S)	377	01-02-1929	1	37855	8 STRINGS, SPECIAL NECK WITH MANDOLIN HEAD, SPECIAL EDGE
2-18T(S)	376	02-02-1929	1	37856	6 STRINGS, ROSEWOOD FINGERBOARD, 25" SCALE, METAL TAILPIECE, BANJO TYPE BRIDGE, DARK TOP
2-18T-L	382	12-02-1929	3	37909-37911	
2-18T	385	05-03-1929	25	38024-38048	
2-18T-L	406	21-03-1929	3	38186-38188	14 FRETS CLEAR
2-18T	457	11-06-1929	25	38798-38822	14 FRET NECK
2-18T-L	485	12-08-1929	25	39362-39386	14 FRET NECK
2-18T(S)	524	25-09-1929	1	39721	6 STRINGS, 23" SCALE, 12 FRETS ON NECK
2-18T	535	06-11-1929	25	40168-40192	
2-18T	576	08-01-1930	25	40904-40928	
2-18T	730	17-07-1930	25	43261-43285	

Table 59
Martin 2-18T Tenor Guitars

MODEL	SHOP ORDER	DATE STAMPED	QUAN	SERIAL NUMBER	COMMENTS
0-21T(S)	437	08-05-1929	1	38541	SPECIAL
0-21P(S)	462	08-06-1929	1	38797	SPECIAL BODY
0-21T(S)	481	16-07-1929	1	39128	SPECIAL, 14 FRETS, CARL FISCHER MODEL
0-21T	497	14-08-1929	1	39336	CARL FISCHER MODEL
0-21T	723	25-06-1930	1	43037	MACHINE HEADS
0-21T	857	11-04-1935	1	59635	

Table 60
Martin 0-21T Tenor Guitars

MODEL	SHOP ORDER	DATE STAMPED	QUAN	SERIAL NUMBER	COMMENTS
2-28T	335	16-11-1928	3	37235-37237	
2-28T	362	25-01-1929	6	37745-37750	
2-28T-L	366	25-01-1929	3	37751-37753	LONG NECK, 15 FRETS CLEAR
2-28T	434	29-04-1929	3	38488-38490	LONG NECK, 14 FRETS CLEAR
2-28T	433	29-04-1929	3	38491-38493	
2-28T-L	464	19-06-1929	6	38873-38878	
2-28T-L	484	01-08-1929	15	39271-39285	14 FRET NECK
2-28T	536	25-10-1929	16	40044-40059	14 FRET NECK

Table 61
Martin 2-28T Tenor Guitars

of the tenor guitars to 22½" from the original 21-3/8" scale before August or September 1927.

Martin experimented with a batch of 2-18T guitars (35214-35225) stamped March 9, 1928 with 23" scale. In next batch (35426-35450) it was noted by Mike Longworth that 35432 to 35437 had "heavy tone bars". The next batch (35614-35638) had 23" scales. A small batch (37200-37202) of 2-18T-L guitars stamped Nov. 11, 1928 had 14 fret necks. Three more 2-18T-L guitars (37465-37467) stamped Dec. 13, 1928.

Martin dealer George Stannard wrote on March 16, 1927:

"I have inquiries for tenor guitar 23" scale, standard body size. Do you think you could put together such a guitar with these measurements. If so, kindly give me retail price of styles that you could furnish along this line."

Martin replied the next day:

"Replying to yours of March 16th the Tenor Guitar we have started is one with a scale of something over twenty-one inches.

The next longer one is our regular No. 2, which is about twenty-four and a half inches. We have heard talk about a twenty-three inch scale on Tenor Guitars to make them conform closely to the Tenor Banjo but since we have nothing of that length ready now we made up a sample quite lately for a New York dealer on which we used the No. 2 scale and the No. 2 body, making the neck special for four strings. You probably know our Style 2-17 Guitar but I will mention that it is the size below our No. 1 or Standard. ...

For our personal taste here a No. 5 is more desirable because it is easier to handle and looks more like a special Guitar; if, however, players find a somewhat larger body better, then we have no choice but to make what is wanted."

The correspondence continued with a request from Stannard on March 21:

"My Customer would like a have quotation (retail)

on the following outfit & when can furnish. Style 2-17 Tenor Guitar, 23 in. Scale, position dots 3-5-7-10-12-15 & 17, Keratol case, fleeced lined to fit. ....."

Martin promptly replied on March 23:

"We are going to begin work promptly on a 23"scale Tenor Guitar, but can not tell just how soon we can promise delivery. It will probably not be ready before the end of April. We can supply position dots as specified in you recent letter and the retail price will be $32.50."

On October 24, 1927 Stannard requested a 0-18 tenor guitar with a 23" scale length. Martin replied on October 27:

"We appreciate your order for a Style 0-18 Tenor guitar with twenty-three inch scale. Unfortunately, it is not practical to use a twenty-three inch scale on the Concert Size body. To do so would require changing the layout of the top braces because the bridge would be drawn up much closer to the sound hole.

Would you care to have a Concert Size Guitar with regular Concert Scale, which is about 24¾", fitted with a Tenor neck? Possibly the additional string length would not be a disadvantage. ...
We have in stock Style 2-17 Tenor Guitars with regular No. 2 Size body and No. 2 scale, which is 24½". This body is considerably larger than the No. 5 Size and possibly would fill your order."

Mr. Al Esposito of Carl Fischer Inc. wrote an interesting letter to Martin on March 9, 1929 (see transcription on page 189).

Regardless, Martin tried to accommodate the customer by preparing a special 2-18T for their consider-

SIZE 1, 0, 00, 000 AND OM TENOR GUITARS													
	1-18T	0-17T	0-17T(L)	0-18T	0-18T(S)	0-18T(L)	0-18TE	0-21T	0-28T(S)	00-21T	000-28T(S)	OM-18T	OM-28T	000-18T
1927	3													
1928														
1929				34				3			1			
1930				333	1			1				2	1	
1931				200		1								
1932		4		150	1									
1933		140												
1934		50								2				1
1935		50	1					1						
1936		75		12										2
1937		50	1	31										
1938		50		12										1
1939		25		24										
1940		25		12										
1941		50		12					1					
1942		87		24										
1943		36		12										
1944		60		60										
1945		48		36										
1946		84		72										
1947		134		133										
1948		109		97										
1949		110		72										
1950		123		72										
1951		99		60										
1952		125		72										
1953		150		85										
1954		100		73		1								
1955		75	1	50										
1956		75		24										
1957		37		63										
1958		101		50										
1959		125		125		2	1							
1960		50	1	175										
1961				150	1									
1962				250		1	1							
1963				175		3								
1964				150										
1965				250										
1966				125										
1967				50										

Note: The first six 0-18T guitars probably had slotted peg heads. Thereafter a solid peg head with gear pegs was used.

Table 62
Sizes 1, 0, 00, 000 and OM Tenor Guitars

ation.

Martin replied on March 16 (see transcription on pages 189 and 190).

By assembling all the clues from the correspondence and considering the explosion of new models launched by Martin between 1927 and 1929 it would appear that something had shaken C. F. Martin out of its normally conservative approach. Whether it was the growing awareness of the influence of orchestra and big band music, the change in musical tastes or the desire to compete with Gibson is irrelevant. Martin was in the mood to innovate. Martin was listening to their dealers and professional musicians and was prepared to make new instruments as a result.

In order to comply with Fisher's request, it appears that Martin took a regular 12-fret 2-18T guitar and replaced the 12-fret neck with one of 14 frets. Figure 245 illustrates how applying a 14-fret neck to a guitar body meant for a 12-fret neck results in an awkward location of the bridge. For the 14-fret guitar, the neck and bridge were just moved upward by two frets.

Al Esposito reported the reaction to the 2-18T tenor guitar on March 26 (see transcription on pages 190 and 191).

This is probably not what Martin would have wanted to hear. On the other hand, Martin had simply put a 14-fret neck on a 12-fret body rather than cut down the guitar body as suggested, and hoped this expedient would satisfy the customer.

Martin replied on March 28 (see transcription on page 191).

This reply contains the answer to the sense of urgency felt by Martin in developing the new model. Professional players were driving the demand for tenor guitars with longer necks. Martin clearly understood they had to act quickly as two weeks is an exceptionally short amount of time to develop and produce a new instrument design. However, this effort served Martin well as it was only a few months until Perry Bechtel visited in June 1929, with the OM guitars being the end result.

The first special 0-21T was shipped on April 20,

1929. Although it was entered in the bookings ledger on March 28 at a retail price of $32.50 there is no shop order detailing this guitar. However, several shop orders from this period are missing from the archive. So, either guitar was treated as a prototype, and received no serial number, or it was recorded on one of the missing shop orders and the serial number remains unknown. There is one serial number, 38266, without an instrument allocated to it so maybe this is the serial number of the first 0-21T.

Al Esposito responded to Martin on May 1 (see transcription on pages 191 and 192).

Martin answered on May 6 (see transcription on page 192).

Apparently the prototype 0-21T had an unusual appearance. Possibly Martin shortened the body but did not increase the width of the upper bout. Unfortunately, the sketch mentioned in the letter has not survived. Maybe this instrument will surface one day to answer the question. The prototype should be easy to identify as it has a slotted peg head and side tuners. Carl Fischer Inc. was not able to sell the prototype 0-21T and it was returned to Martin some time in July.

Again, Martin explained the difficulty in finding four string patent heads and offered gear pegs (banjo tuners) instead.

The second prototype 0-21T (serial number 38541) had a different body shape but retained the patent heads as confirmed in a letter sent by Martin to Carl Fischer Inc. on May 11 (see transcription on page 192).

This guitar was shipped on May 28, 1929 and became the first modern 14-fret guitar made by Martin.

Experimentation continued and on June 26, 1929 Carl Fischer Inc. ordered a "**Martin Plectrum guitar – same as the latest new tenor guitar sent to Mr. Esposito**", a 0-21P. The details of this guitar were not documented other than it also had a patent head. Presumably the longer scale of the plectrum guitar would have yielded the 15-fret neck requested in the letter of May 1. This 0-21P, serial number 38797, was made for Charles Hughes, a star plectrum player of Harry Reezer's office but as it is the only example made the longer neck must not have been considered a big advantage.

An 0-21T was entered in the bookings ledger on July 13, 1929 but it appears this was changed to an 0-28T (serial number 39128) as the associated shop states "**1 Special Gtr 0-28 Carl Fischer Model**".

In a letter dated July 12, 1929 Carl Fischer Inc. asked if it was possible to make a mahogany guitar with a lower price. Martin answered on July 15 that it was quite possible to make a 0-18T and the price would be $45 compared to $65 for the 0-21T. Martin also offered to lower the price to $40 if an order for five guitars was placed. An order for the first 0-18T, now called the Carl Fischer Model, was booked just a few days later on July 17.

Martin realized that they had a marketable new product and started offering the 0-18T to their dealers through their outside salesman. Change must have been in the wind because on July 29, Peate's Music House Inc. requested a Concert or Grand Concert tenor guitar for a customer. Martin responded with a long letter on the current tenor guitars they made and mentioned the new 14-fret Carl Fischer models just entering production. Peate's must have appreciated the explanation because they placed an order for a Carl Fischer Model 0-18T on August 30. However, it must have been obvious that the new model was something special as orders started to come forth from other Martin dealers. On August 26 McClellan Music House purchased a 0-18T although this guitar was supplied with gear pegs. Although Carl Fischer Inc. had helped develop the new guitar they purchased very few of them, only a dozen or so to the beginning of 1932.

Some batches of the Carl Fischer 0-18T guitars received patent heads while others were allocated banjo tuners.

The shape of the Carl Fisher Model 0-18T is quite distinctive as the upper bout appears to be narrower than later 0-18T guitars. It is not known how long the Carl Fischer Model continued in production but this designation stopped appearing in the sales records in March 1930. However, one Carl Fischer Model guitar has been reported dated to April 1931.

While the Carl Fischer 0-18T guitars were still in production Martin started making 0-28T guitars in late March 1930 with a wider upper bout and a more balanced appearance.

See Tables 58 to 62 for the production of tenor guitars through 1967.

Plectrum Guitars

Martin wrote to Chicago Musical Instrument Co. on December 9, 1927 concerning a rumor that Martin was about to start producing plectrum guitars:

"The rumor referred to in your letter of the 5th is not correct. We are not making a Plectrum guitar; however, we have supplied to two or three firms on special order a large model Tenor Guitar, exactly the same in size and scale as our Style 2-17 regular guitar, the scale length being about twenty-five inches. This is not properly a Plectrum Guitar but it is preferred by some professional players because it has a bigger tone than the regular Tenor Guitar.

From time to time we have scattered inquiries for the Plectrum Guitar, mostly from the Far West, but it does not yet appear that the demand is sufficient to warrant economical production. Would the demand in your territory warrant your carrying of a stock of this instrument in we were to make it?"

None of these 2-17 plectrum guitars mentioned in the letter appear in the ledgers. Martin must have put a four string neck with a 24.9" scale length on a few regular guitar bodies to test out the concept. Of course these would have had a 12-fret neck.

As with the tenor guitars the correspondence for 1928 is mostly missing so the development of plectrum guitars cannot be fully explained. However, the bookings ledger show that the early plectrum guitar were sold to a fairly large cross section of Martin's regular customers. That would suggest Martin, buoyed by the interest in tenor guitars, had decided by early 1928 there was a large enough market to start producing plectrum guitars and had spread the word to their regular dealers.

The first plectrum guitars made by Martin were 1-17P

PLECTRUM GUITAR PRODUCTION												
	1-17P[1]	1-17PS	1-18P	1-21P	1-28P	1-28P(S)[5]	0-18P	0-21P	O-28P	00-17P	OM-18P	OM-28P
1927												
1928	75 (est.)				5							
1929	81[2]		1		8[4]			1				
1930	50			1	5	1			1		46	3
1931	50										65	3
1932												2
1933												
1934												
1935												
1936												
1937												
1938		1[3]										
1939												
1940							2					
1941										1		

1) 15 fret neck, 27" scale
2) 6 with Bakelite neck reinforcement
3) Special neck & bridge for 5 strings, scale 27", 15 fret body, fifth string 20 ½" long to special peg between 4th & 5th fret, gear pegs except special 5th peg, natural finish
4) 2 with Bakelite neck reinforcement
5) Special, 5 string, guard plate

Table 63
Plectrum Guitar Production

instruments. Mike Longworth noted in his logbook that the first batch of 1-17P guitars had a 23" scale. This seems highly unlikely because, as Martin acknowledged in the letter, even the 24.9" scale couldn't be considered a proper plectrum scale length.

The first batch of 1-17P plectrum guitars (serial number 34946 to 34949) was stamped on Feb. 14, 1928. Another batch (serial numbers 35277 to 35288) followed on March 15, 1928. The third batch (serial numbers 35564 to 35613) was stamped on April 18 and had 15 fret necks and a 27" scale. The scale length of the first two batches was not recorded but is almost certainly 27" (so would also have 15-fret necks). There is a small possibility that the first sixteen plectrum guitars had a shorter scale length but none have come to light to confirm this hypothesis.

The small-bodied plectrum guitars did not sell well and were dropped by the end of 1931. Interestingly, Martin decided to make larger plectrum guitars based on the Orchestra Model body in 1930. Many of the early OM-18 guitars were made as plectrum instruments but even these didn't survive past 1931. After 1932 only a few specially ordered plectrum guitars were made.

Interestingly, the OM plectrum guitars are prime candidates for modification to regular six string guitars because the bridge is in the correct location for a 25.4" scale length.

C. F. Martin & Co. Buys an Old Martin from George Krick (1927)

On April 22, 1927 George C. Krick, a music teacher and Martin dealer in Germantown, Pennsylvania, wrote an interesting letter to Martin offering the company a very old Martin guitar. He carefully described the guitar and, presciently, noted the guitar number was "1278". Remarkably, this guitar is still in the Martin Guitar Co. museum. Krick did make a small mistake in reading the guitar number, which is actually 1275, but the number was hand written and the mistake is understandable. Martin allowed a credit of $30 for it.

Serial number 1275 is on a type 5 label, from its second period of use, and dates the guitar to February 1839, near the end of C. F. Martin's tenure in New York.

It is another example of a notable survivor from the period and indicates Martin, even then, had an interest in its history and risked what seems like a very small amount of money by today's standards to help preserve that history.

Slow Moving 0-42 and 0-45 Guitars (1929-1945)

Martin had always had their own opinion on which size guitar produced the best "tone", the best balance

	CONDITION	1929	1930	1931	1932	1933	1934	1935	1936	1937	1938	1939	1940	1941	1942	1943	1944	1945
	**SLOW MOVING 0-42 and 0-45 GUITARS**																	
	**INVENTORY AT THE BEGINNING OF EACH YEAR**																	
0-42	FINISHED	12	7	21	16	15	13	9	7	7	6	5*	4*	2*	1*	1*	1*	
0-45	FINISHED	16	16	21	16	19	18	15	14	9	9	8*	7*	5*	4*	2*	1*	1*
0-42	IN VARNISH	12	0															
0-45	IN VARNISH	0	0															
0-42	CLEANED	0	15															
0-45	CLEANED	0	10															
0-42	SALES	17	13	6	2	2	4	2	0	1	3	1	2	0	0	0	1	
0-45	SALES	11	10	7	0	1	4	1	4	1	1	0	2	1	1	1	2	1

*Recorded as obsolete models

The sales figures are taken from the bookings ledger. Many of these guitars were shipped on 10 days trial and subsequently retuned at the end of the trial, thus explaining why the reduction in inventory doesn't always match the sales figures.

Table 64
Slow Moving 0-42 and 0-45 Guitars

of treble and bass. In the 19th century Martin always felt and 0-size guitar produced the best tone and continued to believe so even after 00 and 000 size guitars became popular. Once the 000 size was well established and Martin was beginning to produce the early Dreadnought guitars, Martin modified their earlier stance to suggest a 00-size guitar had the best tone. Martin continued to hold on to this idea even after the music industry had begun to change. A good example of this are the 0-42 and 0-45 guitars. Sales of these small but very expensive guitars had been declining since the early 1920's. In 1928 a 0-42 guitar was $110 and a 00-42 $115 while the style 45 guitars were priced at $155 for a 0 size, $160 for a 00 and $170 for a 000. Why would someone buy a 0-42 or 0-45 when then could get the 00-sizes for $5 extra and upgrade from a 0-45 to a 000-45 for $15 extra?

The last ten 0-45 guitars were stamped on August 8, 1929 and the last batch of ten 0-42 guitars was stamped on February 21, 1930.

By 1929, interest in fancy 0-size guitars was dwindling rapidly. The combination of radio, change in musical tastes and competition was putting an end to this segment of the market. The public was demanding larger instruments with more volume while Martin hung on to their slightly antiquated notion of the ideal guitar. That is in no way a criticism of the 0-42 and 0-45 guitars. Anyone who has had a chance to play one usually marvels at the "sweet balanced" tone they produce.

The result, combined with effects of the Depression,

was that demand for these guitars virtually collapsed between 1931 and 1932 while Martin still had quite a few in inventory. Through the 1930's and into 1940's this inventory was reduced only very slowly. By 1939 Martin declared the last five 0-42 and last eight 0-45 guitars as "obsolete" models and offered them at close-out prices, basically the same price as a 0-28 (which itself was obsolete). Even so it wasn't until 1944 that the last 0-42 was sold, followed by the last 0-45 in early 1945.

Orchestra Model (OM) Guitars (1929-1933)

On May 12, 1927 William Lewis & Son, one of Martin's Chicago dealers, wrote to say they had a customer who wanted a 000-28 but wanted the body shape changed so he could reach the higher frets. Martin replied that they knew other manufacturers had tried necks with as many as 15 frets but couldn't recommend a particular maker. Martin went on to suggest this design had been tried by another manufacturer but the design had been found wanting and the maker had returned to the regular 12-fret body.

OM-18 and OM-28 Guitars

On June 6, 1929 C. F. Martin III wrote a letter to Perry Bechtel concerning his travel plans to visit the Martin factory later in the month and arranging to meet with him.

The visit must have been a success because on June 29 Martin wrote to Mr. Shrader, Perry Bechtel's boss at Cable Piano Co., to explain that the plan for a special guitar for Bechtel's personal use was being worked out:

"In the course of Mr. Perry Bechtel's visit with us we worked out a plan for a special Guitar for his personal use. His requirements are rather special because of his great skill, particularly in his left hand technique, and because of the fact that he is used to Banjo construction and finds the regular Guitar neck rather too short for best results. Accordingly we agreed to design a special body for a Style 000-28; this body will be considerably smaller in the upper bout above the sound hole but will not be changed in the lower part. This enables us to assure Mr. Bechtel that the tone will be up to the Martin standard. A special long neck will be provided with fourteen frets clear of the body and Mr. Bechtel will furnish us with a pattern showing the neck width and fingerboard shape he desires.

These special features, together with the pick guard, will be supplied without charge. Extra ornamentation in the form of Ivory-Celluloid binding on fingerboard and head, the same as we use on our style 45 Guitar, is desired by Mr. Bechtel and for this we will make an extra charge of fifteen dollars, list. The list price of the job, therefore, will be one hundred dollars and we explained to Mr. Bechtel that the best arrangement would be to make the bill to you in our usual manner and he will make suitable arrangements with you. We would like to have your usual confirmation on this order so we can start work promptly. We are now working on the design of the special parts and we will be ready to start construction within a few days.

We had a most enjoyable visit with Mr. Bechtel and feel that we profited from the discussions we had on matters of mutual interest. ...."

Although Martin requested a confirmation, the order for a "000-28 Special" was entered in the sales ledger on the same date, June 29.

Mr. Shrader replied on July 1:

"Personally if I were a guitar player I think any Martin guitar would be good enough for me without going to so much trouble of having one built special, but we must have our prima donnas. The sad part of it is that in so many cases these special built instruments do not turn out to be just what the designer anticipated. I hope however that this will not be the case with Perry.

You probably know that I have been after Perry for some time about using that freak shaped Gibson and have been trying for some time to sell him on the idea of using the conventional size and shape guitar, but it looks like that I have failed to do this. However let's hope for the best and maybe this special built instrument will help him to sell more Martins. I will let you know about that part of it a little later on."

It is more than a little ironic that the normally conservative Martin company would put so much faith in Perry Bechtel's instincts on improving guitars while Bechtel's own manager, Mr. Shrader, only sought to humor him and didn't hold out much hope for the success of the new model. Mr. Shrader could scarcely have been more wrong at the birth of a guitar model that was to be so influential!

Martin, on the other hand, made a reply on July 9, 1929 with some very prescient comments:

"We are interested in this special instrument not only for the sake of pleasing Mr. Bechtel, but because there always is a possibility that some new idea may turn out to be a permanent improvement.

We quite agree with you that it is a good policy to get teacher cooperation on the basis of established models and not on the basis of special favors in the way of freak instruments. Sometimes, however, the result of such a special instrument is conclusive evidence to the player that, after all, the standard model is the best. We hope it will work out so in this case."

However, at about the same time Martin turned down an order from another teacher for what could have been the first D-45!

C. F Martin III wrote again to Perry on July 10, 1929. It is clear that Martins was listening to Perry Bechtel's requirements and were still awaiting his specifications for the width and shape of the neck. Remarkably, there is also a mention about tapping the back of a guitar during production to ascertain whether it would have a good tone.

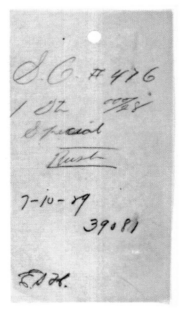

Figure 255
Shop Order Slip for First "Special 000-28" (OM-28)

On July 20 Perry sent a cardboard template for the neck and stated that if the guitar worked out he wanted to "dress up the head a bit". C. F. Martin III replied with some comments on July 22 and mentioned the width of the neck specified was 1/16" less than normal (i.e. 1-13/16").

Perry Bechtel's special guitar was shipped on August 2, 1929 and thus began the story of the Martin Orchestra Models. The serial number of this special guitar was 39081.

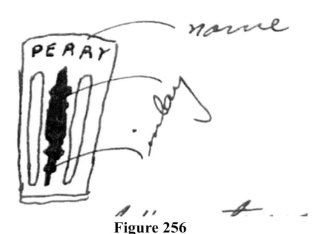

Figure 256
Perry Bechtel's Suggestion for a Head Stock Veneer for the First OM-28 Guitar

On August 9 Perry Bechtel acknowledged receipt of the guitar and discussed some minor changes to the action. Perry was pleased with the bound neck and head stock but wanted Martin to put on a new head stock veneer inlaid with "**Perry**" and a "**grapevine inlay**" in the central part of the head stock. Perry even made a small sketch of what he wanted and it is clear that the first OM guitar had a slotted peg head.

In an August 15 letter Perry changed his mind on the head stock decoration and only wanted the "**grapevine**" and not even that if it took too much time. In the August 17 reply C. F. Martin III stated that a regular style 45 head stock (i. e., a "torch" inlay) would be added to the guitar.

Martin received the guitar on August 27, did a quick turnaround and reshipped it on August 31. Interestingly, Roy Smeck tried out the guitar on August 30 during a visit and commented he liked the guitar and would want one made up for him at a later date. Perry responded later that he was pleased that Roy Smeck had liked the guitar.

Perry returned the guitar in early December to have the action adjusted and there was also a discussion on the thickness of the neck.

In the meantime, Martin must have been promoting the new model because Rudolph Wurlitzer Co. ordered a "**000-28 Special**" on October 10, 1929 for their Detroit store.

Perry Bechtel was not alone in realizing the trend of guitars towards plectrum instruments for orchestra playing. B. A. Rose a Martin dealer in Minneapolis MN had some very insightful comments in his letter of Nov. 1, 1929:

"We are getting inquiries now for regular guitar for orchestra playing. We find that your regular six string instrument is not proving entirely satisfactory. We believe that it will be necessary for you to build, just as you do the tenor-guitar, a special guitar for pick playing. Inclosed (sic) find a notation written by Mr. Gould, our leading teacher. As he is a personal friend of ours and a user of the Martin Hawaiian guitar if you will make the kind of an instrument needed for orchestra playing, he will recommend and indorse (sic) it instead of the

EARLY OM-28 GUITARS					
MODEL	SHOP ORDER	DATE STAMPED	QUAN.	SERIAL NUMBERS	COMMENTS
000-28 SPECIAL	476	JULY 10, 1929	1	39081	SLOTTED PEG HEAD, BOUND FINGERBOARD AND HEAD, STYLE 45 TORCH INLAY
000-28 PERRY BECHTEL	525	OCT. 5, 1929	1	39803	
000-28 PERRY BECHTEL	531	OCT. 15, 1929	1	39904	
000-28S PERRY BECHTEL MODEL	546	NOV. 5, 1929	3	40165-40167	
000-28P PERRY BECHTEL	557	NOV. 21, 1929	5	40441-40445	
000-28P LEFT-HANDED	558	NOV. 21, 1929	1	40440	LEFT-HANDED
000-28 O. M. PERRY BECHTEL MODEL	588	DEC. 23, 1929	5	40814-40818	
000-28 O. M. ORCHESTRA MODEL	594	JAN. 11, 1930	5	40929-40933	
000-28 O. M, O(RCHESTRA) MODEL	606	JAN. 24, 1930	10	41126-41135	
000-28 O. M.	617	FEB. 3, 1930	10	41216-41225	
000-28 O. M.	620	FEB. 11, 1930	10	41326-41335	
000-28 O. M. O(ORCHESTRA) MODEL	624	FEB. 17, 1930	10	417463-41472	
000-28 O. M.	630	FEB. 20,1930	15	41523-41537	
OM-28	643	MAR. 21, 1930	25	41913-41937	

Table 65
Early OM-28 Guitars

Gibson Nick Lucas model or the new Epiphone guitar. Your Spanish model has proved very satisfactory. Regarding making an instrument that fits the need of the banjo player, the following changes will have to be made. The six strings could be just as close together as they are on the banjo. In the old days when they plucked with their fingers, it was necessary to have enough room to put your finger between the strings. Today the celluloid pick is used and by putting the strings close together, it will feel like a banjo and when a chord is struck, the complete chord will respond quicker. On the old guitar they played around the first positions. Now they are playing way up the neck and the top part of the body of the guitar is in the way so they cannot reach the upper positions. The instrument must have geared pages, adjustable bridge as a musician must tune up his instrument to the piano. It should retail for $125 because if it has the qualification and the desired result is achieved, the price is secondary. Now you may know of some more improvements that would be a great help and if you wish to make up a sample for us to see if it proves satisfactory, it would be greatly appreciated."

Martin replied that several 14 fret 000-28 guitars were coming through the factory and offered to send one to the Mr. Gould mentioned in the letter above.

The two guitars shipped to Wurlitzer and Rose can only be serial numbers 39803 and 39904, both of which were identified as "**000-28 Perry Bechtel**". Wurlitzer's Detroit store reported favorably on the new OM model and another three instruments were ordered on November 12. The OM-28 was not yet a stock item and Martin had to make up all three. One of the three was ordered as left handed instrument (serial number 40040) and all three were delivered by December 10.

Martin sent a "**000-28 Prof. Model**" to Rose on November 20. Rose returned it with the comment that it wasn't as loud as the arch top Gibson guitars and the suggestion that Martin consider producing arch tops as well.

In a follow-up letter dated December 11, Rose marveled that Gibson could charge $350 for an arch top guitar and offered the idea that Martin could up-scale the carved top mandolins they were already making. Martin's reply stated the flat top guitar could stand on its own merits and that arch top construction did not produce as responsive a tone as a flat top.

Rose wrote Martin again on December 26 agreeing that nothing on the market exceeded the Martin flat top guitar. He went on to explain that orchestra leaders were driving the demand for Gibson and Epiphone arch top guitars and advised Martin to talk to some band leaders himself before deciding not to consider arch top guitars.

Mike Longworth recorded that shop order 511 from 1929 for twenty-five 000-28 12-fret guitars (serial numbers 39955-39979) had belly bridges. This was either an early experiment in the use of belly bridges or the guitar that Mike Longworth examined had the pyramid bridges replaced because, as will be discussed elsewhere in this book, the belly bridge didn't

Figure 257
Promotional Photograph of
Early OM-28 with Pyramid Bridge

come into use until early April 1930.

The first guitars to actually be designated as "OM" guitars were the first two OM-45 guitars (serial numbers 41697-41698).

EARLY OM-18 GUITARS					
MODEL	SHOP ORDER	DATE STAMPED	QUAN.	SERIAL NUMBER	COMMENTS
000-18 O. M.	601	JAN. 15, 1930	2	41034-41035	
000-18 O. M. PLECTRUM	634	FEB. 25, 1930	2	41578-41579	PLECTRUM SCALE, 15 FRET NECK, NO GUARD PLATE
OM-18 PLECTRUM	651	MAR. 21, 1930	4	41938-41941	O(RCHESTRA) MODEL, PLECTRUM NECK, GUARD PLATE, BRIDGE 6" X 1"-4 HOLE
000-18 O. M. PLECTRUM	656	MAR. 28, 1930	5	42000-42004	
000-18T O. M.	663	APR. 4, 1930	1	42096	MAHOGANY TOP, 23" SCALE, 12 FRETS CLEAR

Table 66
Early OM-18 Guitars

The first OM-28 guitars designated as such were built to shop order 644 (serial numbers 42045-42069). All previous 14-fret style 28 guitars had been called various combination of "**000-28 Perry Bechtel**", "**000-28P Perry Bechtel model**" or "**000-28 O. M. Orchestra Model**".

Figure 258
Promotional Photograph of Sons of the Pioneers without Roy Rogers.
The guitar in this image is one of only two OM-18 guitars made with a pyramid bridge.

Most of the early OM-18 guitars were actually OM-18Ps or, as noted on the shop order, "**000-18 O. M. Plectrum**" (serial numbers 41578-41579).

Banjo tuners were used on OM guitars after the first few prototypes were made. This may have been at the suggestion of Perry Bechtel as he would have been used to this type of tuner on his banjos. However, Martin had always used strips of tuners for their slotted head guitars and from 1929 to 1931 did not have any individual tuners in inventory other than banjo tuners.

As mentioned in the B. A. Rose letter above, dated December 11, 1929, Martin believed that OM guitars could hold their own against arch top guitars. More than two years later Martin was still promoting this idea when he wrote to B. A. Rose again on February 17, 1932:

"**You will be interested to know that we have**

arranged to make our Orchestra Model Guitars, Style OM-18 and Style OM-28, in the dark finish as well as in natural color and the prices have been reduced to fifty dollars and eighty-five dollars, respectively, as you will see by the new price list enclosed. With the shaded brown top these Guitars should make good leaders for you in the professional field. We consider them as fine in tone as anything we make and more suitable for orchestra work than the regular models. The fifty-dollar style particularly should be worth pushing. You can count on prompt delivery of these Guitars in the dark finish beginning about March first."

This letter ties in with Martin's other letters concerning the 14-fret "Model 32" 0-17 and 0-18 that were specified with a dark finish. The OM-18 guitars seem to have been included in this specification as most, if not all, of the OM-18 guitars made in 1932 had the dark finish. However, although Martin may have intended to make dark top OM-28 guitars, they are rarely encountered.

OM-45 and OM-45 Deluxe Guitars

With the possible exception of the early D-45 guitars, the OM-45 and OM-45 Deluxe models are among the most admired and sought-after Martin guitars of the 1930's.

Much has been written about these guitars, some of

it incorrect, and one of the purposes of this book is to correct a few errors in the information hitherto published. Table 67 lists all the OM-45 and OM-45 Deluxe guitars made by C. F. Martin

From the table above it can be seen that total production was 50 guitars: 11 OM-45 DELUXE (one of which was Hawaiian), 38 OM-45 and 1 OM-45H.

These numbers don't match with previously published information. It has long been common knowledge, based on Mike Longworth's original research, that 14 OM-45 Deluxe guitars were made. This was later

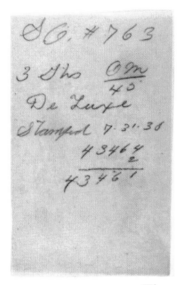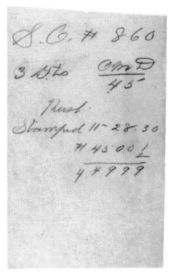

Figure 259
Shop Orders for OM-45 Deluxe Guitars

OM-45 AND OM-45 DELUXE GUITARS					
MODEL	**SHOP ORDER**	**DATE STAMPED**	**SERIAL NUMBERS**	**QUAN**	**COMMENTS**
OM-45	646	MAR. 7, 1930	41697-41698	2	PYRAMID BRIDGE, BANJO TUNERS, SMALL PICK GUARD, TORCH HEADSTOCK INLAY
OM-45 DLX	665	APRIL 9, 1930	42125	1	ONCE OWNED BY ROY ROGERS, DIFFERENT STYLE PICK GUARD INLAY TO OTHER OM-45 DELUXES, BELLY BRIDGE, TORCH HEADSTOCK INLAY
OM-45	665	APRIL 9, 1930	42126	1	
OM-45	710	JUNE 6, 1930	42798-42800	3	BANJO TUNERS
OM-45	724	JUNE 25, 1930	43038	1	SLOTTED PEGHEAD
OM-45 DLX	760	JULY 26, 1930	43386	1	FOR HAWAIIAN PLAYING
OM-45 DLX	763	AUG. 1, 1930	43462-43464	3	MIKE LONGWORTH COUNTED THIS BATCH AS 4 IN HIS LOGBOOK
OM-45	780	AUG. 22, 1930	43709-43711	3	43709 ONCE OWNED BY GENE AUTRY
OM-45 DLX	814	SEPT. 23, 1930	44068-44070	3	
OM-45	815	SEPT. 23, 1930	44071-44073	3	
			44499-44501		MIKE LONGWORTH DUPLICATED SHOP ORDER 860 IN HIS LOGBOOK
OM-45	831	OCT. 23, 1930	44551-44555	5	BANJO TUNER, LARGE PICK GUARD
OM-45 DLX	860	NOV. 11, 1930	44999-45001	3	MIKE LONGWORTH DUPLICATED SHOP ORDER 860 IN HIS LOGBOOK
OM-45	968	APRIL 9, 1931	46555-46559	5	BANJO TUNERS, LARGE PICK GUARD
OM-45	1079	AUG. 26, 1931	48098-48101	4	
OM-45H	1079	AUG. 26, 1931	48102	1	HAWAIIAN, FLUSH FRETS, HIGH NUT & BRIDGE (MAY NOT BE STAMPED OM-45H)
OM-45	300	SEPT. 21, 1932	51831-51835	5	TORCH INLAY
OM-45	453	AUG. 16, 1933	54137-54142	6	"C F MARTIN" HEADSTOCK INLAY

Table 67
OM-45 and OM-45 Deluxe Guitars

amended to 15 with the re-discovery of Roy Rogers' OM-45 Deluxe. However, Mike Longworth made two small mistakes in his calculations. He counted shop order 763 as four guitars (when it was only three) and he counted shop order 860 twice in his logbook, once, incorrectly, as serial numbers 44499 to 44501 and again, correctly, as serial numbers 44999 to 44501.

It is easy to see how this mistake could be made since the serial numbers are exactly 500 numbers apart. Martin does not seem to have used serial numbers 44499 and 44500 but serial number 44501 was assigned to a 1-17P.

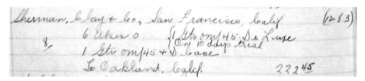

Figure 260
Entry in Bookings Ledger for First OM-45 Deluxe

Figure 262
Roy Rogers with the First OM-45 Deluxe
(Serial Number 42125)

The most recent edition of *Martin Guitars: A Technical Reference (by Richard Johnston & Dick Boak)* records a total of 40 OM-45 guitars but if one is deducted for the Roy Rogers OM-45 Deluxe guitar, originally counted as a OM-45, and one more deducted for the OM-45H recorded above then the numbers above are in agreement.

The booking ledger for May 29, 1930 records an order from Sherman Clay for one OM-45DLX and one OM-45.

OM guitars continued to be made through the end of 1933. At the beginning of 1934 Martin reverted to their old sizing terminology and changed the sizes to the 000 designation. Although the terminology changed, the 000 guitars stamped to August 30, 1934 all retained the 25.4" scale length used on the OM models and had the ebony bar neck reinforcement and bar frets.

Figure 261
Promotional Photograph of Early OM-45 Guitar,
One of Two Made with a Pyramid Bridge

Pick Guards

As specified by Perry Bechtel, the first OM-28 was supplied with a pick guard . However, on July 10, 1930 Martin sold "3 guardplates for OM-28" to Rudick's Music Store in Akron OH. Rudick's music store ordered five OM-28 guitars between December 1929 and June 1930 so the question has to be asked: were pick guards not mounted on some of the early OM-28 guitars? The answer appears to be NO since all known 1929 and early 1930 OM-28 guitars have pick guards but the possibility has to be considered that a few were shipped without pick guards. Most likely Rudick's bought the pick guard to be applied to some of the other Martin guitars they sold. The only Martin guitars that were regularly sold with pick guards in 1929 and 1930 were the OM and tenor instruments.

The early pick guards, often called "small pick guards" or just "OM" pick guards, are relatively small with a tear-drop shape, as seen in figures 257, 261 and 262.

It appears Martin changed to a larger pick guard beginning with the OM guitars stamped on March 18, 1931 (serial number 46287, a OM-18). The archival records don't provide any clues to the reasons for the change but it is obvious that the small pick guards didn't provide as much protection to the top as the larger ones.

Belly Bridges

Assuming the transition to the belly bridge design occurred in early April 1930, only 16 OM-18s, 102 OM-28s (if you include all the prototypes) and 2 OM-45s were made with pyramid bridges.

Of the 16 OM-18 guitars only two were six strings (serial number 41034 and 41035). The remaining fourteen guitars were either OM-18P or OM-18T models and may have received straight bridges instead of pyramid bridges. Figure 258 shows one of the OM-18 six-string guitars with a pyramid bridge.

Tuners

Due to the solid peg head of the Orchestra Model guitars, Martin began to use individual banjo tuning pegs. The OM-18 guitars received Grover #90 "Pro-fessional Tenor Guitar Pegs" and the OM-28 guitars got Grover #89 "Deluxe Guitar Pegs". The OM-45 guitars were mounted with gold plated Grover #89 guitar pegs with either ivoroid or pearl buttons.

Martin had no end of trouble with the Grover banjo pegs failing to hold tension. Grover supplied over 500 replacement tuners to Martin between 1930 and 1932. It did not take very long for Martin to begin replacing the banjo tuners with Grover G-98 "clipped plate" machines, thus explaining why it is not uncommon to see 1930 OM guitars with side tuners, many of which were retro-fitted at the factory. The side tuners worked so much better that Martin decided to drop the banjo pegs entirely in 1931.

It appears that the first OM guitars to be supplied with Grover G-98 tuners were stamped on August 26, 1931, the first being a OM-18 (serial number 48103).

Scale Length

The scale length of all OM guitars was 25.4" although noted luthier T. J. Thompson has demonstrated there is some variation in this scale length. This is important to note when trying to replace a fingerboard on a OM guitar.

Style Stamp

At the suggestion of a dealer Martin began to add a size and style stamp to the neck block of guitars beginning with guitars stamped on October 8, 1930. The first guitar to have received a style stamp was a OM-18P (serial number 44264). One other guitar from the same batch has been examined and it also has a style stamp.

The Switch from Pyramid to Belly Bridges (1930)

By 1929 Martin had been putting their elegantly shaped pyramid bridges on guitars for more than 85 years, although from the late 1920's the less expensive models got a straight bridge instead. The gradual transition from gut to steel strings through the early part of the 20th century had put more tension on the top of the guitar and Martin noted an increased number of bridge gluing surface failures, resulting in the bridges coming lose.

There is a mention in the records from 1930 that Martin tried to address this issue and experimented with a pyramid bridge 1/16" wider than normal that offered an increased gluing surface. However, none of these have been seen to date. Regardless, Martin must have felt that a new bridge design was needed with a greatly increased gluing surface and the belly bridge was born.

It appears the first guitars that received the newly designed belly bridge were OM guitars stamped on April 4 and 9, 1930. The first OM guitar with a belly bridge was serial number 42070 (OM-28). The first OM-18 with a belly bridge was serial number 42122 and the first OM-45 guitar was serial number 42125, which was, in fact, Roy Roger's OM-45 Deluxe.

It is not known if the belly bridge was applied to all other guitar models at the same time or whether there was a transition period.

Octa-chorda (1930)

Mike Longworth pointed out that Martin made one Octa-Chorda 8-string guitar in 1930. It was based on a 000-28 and has serial number 42797.

However, Martin had been aware of the model earlier as a customer had sought information on "an Oc-to-Chorda" in early 1927.

On November 18, 1929 Martin wrote to H. L. Hunt at Oliver Ditson Co. seeking information:

"Please tell us the strings and the tuning used by Mr. Smeck and others who play the eight-string Octa-Chord Hawaiian Guitar."

The first Octa-Chorda made was a Ditson 111S with 8 strings, serial number 41215. It was ordered by Oliver Ditson in New York on January 16, 1930, probably for Roy Smeck. It was stamped on January 30, 1930 and cleared final inspection on February 10, 1930, shipping the same day.

A "000-28 (Octa-Chorda)" was ordered by Oliver Ditson Co., New York on May 26, 1930. It was stamped on June 6, 1930 and cleared final inspection on June 24. It was assigned serial number 42797.

On December 17, 1931 Ed Long of Long's Academy of Music wrote to Martin:

"I heard an instrument over radio called the Octa-Chorda played by Ed of Sambo & Ed and was told you made them. I am very much interested in guitar and this one is the best I have ever heard. Would be grateful to you if you would give me full details of same."

Martin replied on December 22, 1931:

"A number of radio entertainers are using a special Guitar which they call the Octa-Chorda, being a regular Hawaiian Guitar with eight strings. Of course a special neck and bridge are required which makes the instrument somewhat more expensive than the regular six-string model.

We have in stock an Octa-Chorda, Style 000-28, at one hundred dollars list and will be glad to ship it for your approval..."

Mr. Long ordered the Octa-Chorda on approval as Martin wrote to him on January 13, 1932:

"At he request of Sherman, Clay & Company we are today shipping their Seattle store the Octa-Chorda we wrote you about several weeks ago. As far as we know there is no standard tuning for this instrument; we have strung it for the tuning used by Mr. Roy Smeck, of New York City, a popular radio entertainer, in fact the originator of the Octa-Chorda. You may prefer some other tuning; if so, we will be interested to know of it. We certainly hope you will like the Guitar. Thanks for the opportunity to show it to you."

In April 1933 Martin repaired a large Octa-Chorda for Leonard McGinley of Niagara Falls NY. On November 12 of the same year Mr. McGinley contacted Martin:

"I wrote you a letter of appreciation of your splendid workmanship which you so graciously answered.

Now I write you in regard to a new Martin Octo-Chorda. I understand from your representative whom I met in Wurlitzers store that you have one

in stock (Martin noted in pencil in the margin: "000-28 42797 90.00")

Please advise me if such is the case and if so what is the best price you can give me on the same.

I am introducing the Octo-Chorda here & right now things look good for it. I have a customer who is ready to buy one now a Dr. Ruthenberg. Will you please advise me in regard to same & particulars and if you haven't one in stock how long it will take to make one and etc."

Martin replied on November 14 with the following:

"We are glad to hear from you again and we note with interest that you have a prospective customer for an Octo-Chorda. The one mentioned to you by our representative, Mr. J. A. Markley, is still in stock, marked ninety dollars without case. This is an Auditorium Size instrument, not quite as large as your own but the string length is just the same and the arrangement of the strings at the bridge and head are the same.

A Guitar like yours would have to be made up special and would retail at $125.00, delivery in about three weeks.

Our agents in Niagara Falls, The Rudolph Wurlitzer Company, will take care of your order as usual and we refer you to them for your net cost.

If you would like to see the Octo-Chorda we have in stock, which is style 000-28, No. 42797, we are willing to send it to Wurlitzers on 10 days' approval."

In a letter dated November 16, Mr. McGinley made a rather indigent response that nonetheless contains some very interesting information:

"I wish to state that I am very sorry but I will not sell Octo-Chordas through any agency.

I teach all string instruments & I very highly recommend Martin Instruments but I was appointed an agent for the Octo-Chordas by Mr. Sam P. Moore the inventor of same and have been selling them for the past seven years but did not get them

direct from you.

I was in New York in 1926 and Mr. Moore took me to see Mr. Hunt of Oliver Ditsons & made all the arrangements for me & I had been getting them through Ditsons.

Now I have two customers for Octo-Chordas & I write direct to you & you refer me to Wurlitzers. I am very sorry Mr. Martin. I am willing to turn over all customers for Martin Guitars to Wurlitzers as I have been doing but, when it comes to Octo-Chordas, No. They don't even know what they are.

So I say, I am sorry, if I can't make contact with you direct why I must turn someplace else. So you see after all I am the only one around here who can teach it and if I can't make something on them myself, why, I won't bother."

The referral to Wurlitzer's store was well within Martin's policy of protecting local dealers but Martin was not quite ready to give up on a possible sale for an Octa-Chorda so followed up on November 17, 1933:

"We have your letter suggesting that we sell you Octo-Chordas direct instead of through a dealer. This could be done by special arrangement with the dealer and it might be worth your while to take it up with Mr. Simpson at Wurlitzers. You probably know that it is our policy to help our dealers by referring retail and professional business to them in their territory and we do not think it would be wise to make an exception to this rule on any particular part of our line. In addition to Octo-Chordas we make other special instruments from time to time according to customers' specifications and they are always handled on the same basis as our regular line.

There are no exclusive rights to the Octo-Chorda because it is simply a Guitar with eight strings and a special tuning; in fact, we understand that it is made on special order by other manufacturers and there are certainly are no exclusive selling rights.

We do not doubt at all that you say about your acquaintance with Mr. Moore which is the basis of your interest in this instrument and we would like you to continue to use Martin Octo-Chordas so we hope that suitable arrangements can be made with Wurlitzers. We are taking the matter up with Mr. Simpson today."

No further action seems to have been taken.

However, less than a week later Martin received an inquiry for an Octa-Chorda from The Progressive Musical instrument Corporation in New York. Martin responded on November 23:

"We make the eight-string Hawaiian Guitar, sometimes called the Octa-Chorda, in any of our regular styles at ten dollars more than the list price of the six-string model, for delivery in about three weeks.

Right now we have in stock one of these instruments in Style 000-28 on which there is a price of ninety dollars list. We also make this instrument in the extra large Dreadnaught Model, Style D-28, at $125.00 list."

The 000-28 Octa-Chorda (serial number 42797) was sold at least three times and was returned each time! Today, it is on display in the Martin Museum.

Carved-Top Guitars (1931-1943)

B. A. Rose Musical Instruments wrote to Martin on December 26, 1929 concerning the use of OM guitars for big band work and the limited success in penetrating that market:

"As far as your construction of the guitar in concerned, for a guitar, it excels anything on the market and for our idea of a guitar, it is the last word but there is one thing you have overlooked. The ordinary orchestra leader of today is the man responsible for bringing back and it is coming back very rapidly, but they have their ideas regarding what they want. No matter what you and I think the quality should be, in talking the matter over with many of our leaders who are putting in the Gibson and by the way, the Epiphone is making an instrument very much to their liking, they do not want an instrument with very much vibration or in other words, they want a snappy chord and this they are getting on the Gibson instrument.

I would advise you to talk the matter over with some of the up-to-date orchestra leaders who are using the new construction before deciding permanently not to make any changes in your model. You can still make your good old guitars for those who will always play the real guitars but at the same time, get in "Under the wire" on your share of the business which is going to the other fellow."

The correspondence is almost entirely missing for 1930 and 1931 so we don't have the sequence of events that led Martin to getting into the production of carved-top guitars. Based on their past practice, it is unlikely Martin contacted band leaders for their input. Martin always relied on their dealers for market intelligence and probably used that source for ideas on the design of their carved-top guitars.

Clearly, Martin chose not to talk to any band leaders and chose instead to design a new guitar with a carved-top to produce a "snappy chord" while retaining a regular flat top body, probably in an effort to improve the tone of the instrument. Martin also retained the flat top practice of gluing the fingerboard extension to the top of the guitar rather than having an elevated fingerboard like most arch-top guitars. This resulted in an increased neck angle and a somewhat awkward playing position.

Getting into the production of carved-top guitars was not a big impediment to Martin since they already had the seat-carving machine used for producing carved-top mandolins. The first series of carved-top guitars produced by Martin was based on a regular 000-size body and were the named "C" models.

Martin made four "factory test" carved-top guitars in April or May 1931: one C-18, two C-21 and one C-28. Three of the four guitars were ordered by J. W. Greene Co. of Toledo OH (one C-18 and two C-21 guitars) between May 18 and May 25, 1931. These test guitars do not appear in the production records and there are no gaps in the serial numbers of the time. The guitars were shipped but probably don't have serial numbers. The C-18 guitar was priced at $80 retail, same as the C-1, and the C-21 guitars were priced at $100.

See Table 68 for the production totals of C model carved-top guitars.

C Model Carved-Top Guitars

The first C model instruments, six C-1 and two C-2 guitars, were stamped on June 20, 1931 starting at serial number 47365. The first C-3 guitar was stamped on August 4, 1931. All the early C model guitars had round sound holes.

Martin made two prototype C-1 guitars (serial numbers 52259 and 52260) with f-holes instead of round sound holes, these being stamped on November 18, 1932. The changeover to f-holes, however, didn't occur until the batch of C-1 guitars stamped on February 1, 1933, the first serial number being 52830. The C-2 and C-3 guitars changed over to F-holes shortly afterwards.

The C models sold fairly well for a few years but sale had begun to taper off by 1935 and the last carved-top C model, a C-1, was made in January 1943.

C-1 Guitars

1931 Specifications
-mahogany body
-round sound hole
-rosewood fingerboard
-back arched by graduated braces
-round dots at positions 5, 7, 9, 12, 15 and 17
-plain elevated pick guard
-25.4" scale length
-purfling of black and white lines
-black binding
-pearloid or pearl MARTIN vertical head stock veneer on early examples

1933 Specifications
-same as 1931 specifications with following exceptions)
-f-holes from February 1933
-ebony fingerboard
-decal

1934 Specifications
-same as 1933 specification with th following exceptions
-scale length changed to 24.9" from August 1934
-steel T-bar and T-frets from September 1934

1935 Specifications
-same as 1934 specification with one change
-white binding

C-2 Guitars

1931 Specifications
-rosewood body
-round sound hole
-ebony fingerboard
-back arched by graduated braces
-purfling similar to post-1946 style 28 guitars, lines of black and white purfling with white binding
-style 28 zig-zag back stripe
-style 28 diamond and square fingerboard inlays
-plain elevated pick guard
-25.4" scale length
-pearl C. F. MARTIN vertical head stock veneer, although early examples had MARTIN head stock veneer

1933 Specifications
-same as 1931 specifications with following exceptions
-f-holes from February 1933

1934 Specifications
-same as 1933 specification with the following exceptions
-scale length changed to 24.9" from August 1934
-steel T-bar and T-frets from September 1934
-fingerboard and pick guard bound in white

1939 Specifications
-same as 1934 specification with one exception
-diamond and square fingerboard inlays re placed by F-7 fingerboard inlays

C-3 Guitars

1931 Specifications
-rosewood body
-round sound hole
-ebony fingerboard

-back arched by graduated braces
-purfling of black and white purfling with white binding
-back arched with graduated braces
-pearl C. F. Martin head stock veneer
-style 45 "snowflake" fingerboard inlays
-gold plated machines and tailpiece
-elevated pick guard with pearl inlay (later changed to black and white lines of purfling)
-25.4" scale length
-style 45 back stripe

1933 Specifications

-same as 1931 specification with the following exceptions
-f-holes from February 1933
-elevated pick guard with black and white lines of purfling

1934 Specifications

-same as 1933 specification with the following exceptions
-scale length changed to 24.9" from August 1934
-steel T-bar and T-frets from September 1934
-fingerboard and pick guard bound in white

R Model Arched-Top Guitars

Once the C Model Carved-Top had been established Martin, as they had done in the past (e. g., the 2-17 in 1922), began looking to provide instruments with a lower price point. The R-18 had a retail price of $55.00 while the equivalent carved-top model, the C-1, had a retail price of $80.00.

The first prototype R model guitar was a specially made 00-18 guitar stamped on October 14, 1932 (serial number 52010). The shop order slip recorded the specifications of the new model: "**Top arched, neck joined at 14 fret, Rosewood fingerboard, 000 scale, Dark finish, Waverly vertical mach. (i.e., G-98 tuners), elevated guard, Adjustable bridge**". This guitar does not appear in the bookings ledger so was clearly a factory test. It was eventually sold at the factory to a customer from Philadelphia. The "000 scale" is a slight departure from Martin's usual terminology but presumably indicates the guitar had a 25.4" scale length. Martin usually referred to the 25.4" scale length as "00 scale".

The next two R model prototypes, recorded as 00-18S guitars, were serial numbers 54270 and 54271 (stamped December 12, 1932). Serial number 54270 had a "bent top with a 5/16" tone bar" while 54271 had the same top designation but had a "1/4" tone bar". The tops of the R model guitars were not carved but were formed in molds utilizing the same spruce tops as for regular flat top guitars and were then fitted with arched braces.

A third batch of "00-18S new model" guitars were stamped on December 22, 1932 (serial numbers 52560 to 52565).

C MODEL CARVED-TOP GUITAR PRODUCTION															
	C-1 RH	C-1 FH	C-1P	C-1S	C-1T RH	C-1T FH	C-1TS	C-2 RH	C-2 FH	C-2S	C-2P	C-2T	C-3 RH	C-3 FH	C-3S	C-3T
1931	115		3		50			106			1		21			
1932	287	2	5	2	37			152	2	2		12	25		1	
1933		103	1		6 (est.)	12 (est.)		57	2			2		32		1
1934		273		2		42		161	2			2		30	1	
1935		156						89	1							
1936		125		2		12		36				1				
1937		25		1		12		60								
1938		50				6	1	12								
1939		25	1					12	1							
1940								12								
1941		36														
1942		24						12								
1943		12														

Table 68
C Model Carved-Top Guitar Production

The first production batch of R-18 guitars was stamped on January 10, 1933, beginning with serial number 52691. All of the prototype and early production R-18 guitars has round sound holes. It is not known whether the 1/4" or 5/16" tone bar was used on production guitars.

Martin switched to f-holes on R-18 guitars with a batch stamped on October 3, 1933 and beginning with serial number 54439. The original R-18 guitars had the ebony bar neck reinforcement and bar frets but these were replaced with a steel T-bar and T-frets from a batch stamped on August 29, 1934 (serial number 57519). The scale length of the C models changed to 24.9" from 25.4" in August 1934 but it is not known when the change occurred on the R-18 and R-17 guitars.

Martin added the more economical R-17 arched-top guitar to the line at the end of 1933, the retail price of the new model being $40.00. The first two R-17 guitars were stamped on December 17, 1933 (serial numbers 58575 and 58576) and the shop order slip recorded: "**Arched model like R-18, materials & finish like 00-17, edge bound**". A further batch of three prototypes were stamped on December 27, 1934 (serial numbers 59025 to 59027) and the specifications were recorded as: "**Mahogany top, bound with black fiberloid, 2 (with) fingerboards 19 frets long , 1 (with) 20 frets, finish 0-17**". Regular production of the R-17 guitars began with the batch stamped February 15, 1934 and beginning with serial number 59133.

As the first R-17 was stamped on December 17, 1933, after the switch to f-holes, the R-17 guitars were only ever made with that type of sound hole.

At the same time as the prototype R-17 guitars, Martin also made two R-15 guitars with an eye to offering a very basic low-priced model. These two guitars were stamped on December 27, 1933 with serial numbers 58652 and 58653. The shop order slip noted that there were slight differences between the two prototypes. Serial number 58652 had: "**Maple back & sides, spruce top like R-18, one not bound on edges, shaded black finish, flat (finish), rosewood fingerboard & bridge, position dots like 17, ebony nut, (Grover) #99T mach.**" Serial number 58653 had similar specifications but had "**bound top edge only with black fiberloid and polished (finish).**" Only

two R-15 guitars were made and these were eventually sold to J. H. Troup Music House of Harrisburg PA on January 9, 1936. (Also, sold on the same day was a 0-15, four years before this model entered regular production. It appears the 0-15 was sold for $15 retail and the two R-15 guitars were sold for $20.00 ea.)

A R-21 guitar (serial number 70982) was special ordered by Wiegand Brothers of Racine WI on August 13, 1938. It was stamped on August 16, 1938 and cleared final inspection on August 31. The booking ledger only records the guitar as a R-21 but the shop order slip confirms it was actually a special order R-21S with the following specifications: "**Rosewood body, model R, bound & inlaid style 21, scale about 23½"scale, using No. 0 long fingerboard cut off at first fret, neck joined to body at about 12th fret, with steel bar, width at nut 1-15/16", slotted head, D & J No. 31 machines, position marks style 21.**" Although the scale length would seem to indicate a tenor guitar, the nut width points to the guitar being a regular six-string instrument.

R-15 Guitars

1934 Specifications
-only two made (serial number 58652 and 58653), stamped December 27, 1934
-maple back & sides
-arched spruce top with three piece f-holes
-one with no binding and one bound with black fiberloid on top only
-shaded back finish
-one with flat finish and one with polished finish
-rosewood fingerboard & bridge
-fingerboard dots position 5, 7, 9, 12, 15, 17
-finish like 0-17
-raised pick guard
-ebony nut
-Grover 99T tuning machines
-24.9" scale length

R-17 Guitars

1934 Specifications
-first prototypes (serial numbers 58575 and 58576) stamped December 17, 1934
-mahogany back & sides
-arched mahogany top with three piece f-holes

-black fiberloid binding
-rosewood fingerboard & bridge
-fingerboard dots position 5, 7, 9, 12, 15, 17
-finish like 0-17
-raised pick guard
-24.9" scale length
-steel T-bar and T-frets
-similar to R-18 except arched mahogany top, less inlay & plainer trimmings

R-18 Guitars

1933 Specifications
-first R-18s had round holes soon changed to f-holes
-mahogany body, formed spruce top
-arched spruce top with round sound hole
-black binding
-black & white line of purfling
-rosewood fingerboard
-ebony bar neck reinforcement and bar frets
-25.4" scale length
-adjustable bridge
-plain elevated pick guard
-nickel plated hardware
-prototype three piece f-hole R-18 guitars stamped September 12, 1933 (serial numbers 54251 and 54252)
-production three piece f-hole R-18 guitars stamped October 3, 1933 (starting with serial number 54439)

1934 Specification
-probable change to 24.9" scale length around August 1934
-steel T-bar and T-frets from guitar stamped August 29, 1934 beginning with serial number 57519

1936 Specification
-two prototype carved tops stamped May 28, 1936 (serial numbers 63423 and 63424)
-first production carved tops stamped July 14, 1936 beginning with serial number 63844
-one piece f-holes

R-21S Guitar

1938 Specification
-only one special order R-21 guitar was made

	R-15	R-17	R-17S	R-18 RH	R-18 FH	R-18L	R-18P	R-18S	R-18T	R-18TS	R-21S
1931											
1932											
1933				434	46			1	14		
1934	2	2			382		1	4	60		
1935		331			303		2	1			
1936		106			189	1	1	2	24		
1937		175	1		250				24		
1938		100			125						1
1939		100							6	1	
1940		25			25	1			12		
1941		50			12				6		
1942		50			72						
1943											

Table 69
R Model Arched-Top Guitar Production

(serial number 70982)
-rosewood body
-bound and inlaid like style 21
-style 21 fingerboard inlays
-carved top, probably with one piece f-holes
-23½" scale length
-neck joined at 12th fret
-1-15/16" nut width
-slotted peg head
-D & J no. 31 tuning machine
-steel T-bar and T-frets

F Model Carved-Top Guitars

In 1934, the C model carved-top guitars had sold quite well and Martin sought to build on that success by adding a larger sized guitar, probably to compete with the large Gibson and Epiphone jazz guitars. The F model guitars were 16" wide across the lower bout and had a body length of 20".

The first two prototypes were a F-7 (serial number 58755) and a F-9 (serial number 58756) that were both stamped on January 5, 1935. The specification for the F-7 reads as follows: "**Model F extra large size, rosewood bodies, spruce top carved same as C, Style F-7 body bound like C-2, 2 comp. 32½ under binding, top starting at spruce, comp. 0.0325, comp. 0.0325, white 0.040, comp. 0.0325, black 0.025, binding 0.060 3/32" high**". The specification for the F-9 was almost identical to the F-7 with the following exceptions: "**Style F-9 body bound like C-3 with extra black & white lines, back same as C-3 top border.**" (Note: The "comp." designation refers to a black and white lines of purfling cut from a sheet of fiberloid that was black on one side and white on the other.) The shop order slips for the first regular production F-7 and F-9 guitars further fleshed out the specifications for each model. The F-7 specification now included: **"Body bound like C-2, center back strip like C-3, fingerboard & head bound 2 0.040 white lines 1/4" from edge, ivory celluloid position marks 3-15, chromium plate trimmings, guard plain ivory bound"** and the F-9 now included: **"Body bound like C-3 plus extra lines as on order 784 (i. e., serial number 58756), fingerboard & head bound & bordered double white line ¼" from edges of fingerboard, positions 1-17, guard bound & bordered, gold plate trimmings, engraved machines."**

The sales of the F-7 and F-9 models were reasonably good for 1935 but gradually decreased over the next few years. Martin tried to increase interest in the F model guitars by offering less expensive F-1 and F-2 guitars in 1940 and also experimented with a maple body F-5 model at the same time. The F-1 and F-2 guitars sparked an increase in sales from 1940 to 1942 but all F models were dropped from production in November 1942.

F-1 Guitars

1940 Specification
-mahogany body 16" X 20"
-carved spruce top
-bound with ivoroid
-adjustable ebony bridge
-elevated pick guard
-ebony fingerboard with pearl position dots
-wide nickel silver frets
-decal
-lacquer finish, top shaded rich brown color
-24.9" scale length

F-2 Guitars

1940 Specification
-rosewood body 16" X 20"
-carved spruce top bound and inlaid with ivoroid
-ebony fingerboard bound with ivoroid
-wide hard alloy frets
-adjustable ebony bridge
-elevated pick guard bound with ivoroid
-lacquer finish, top shaded, back and sides natural rosewood brown

F-5 Guitars

1940 Specification
-curly maple back and sides
-carved top
-C. F. Martin pearl head stock veneer
-bound and inlaid (i. e., purfling) like C-2 plus extra black lines against light wood
-finish natural color
-Grover G-111 enclosed machines
-#29 nickel tailpiece
-hexagonal fingerboard inlays like F-7
-two prototypes only, never put into production

F-7 Guitars

1935 Specification
-rosewood body
-carved top
-ebony fingerboard bound with ivoroid
-C. F. Martin pearl head stock veneer
-ivoroid hex fingerboard inlays positions 3, 5, 7, 9, 12, 15
-single white line down fingerboard ¼" from edge on both sides
-lacquer finish, top shaded golden brown
-elevated guard, ivoroid bound
-chrome trimmings
-style 45 back strips

1937 Specification
-pearloid fingerboard inlays

F-9 Guitars

1935 Specification
-1935 prototype (serial number 58756)
-rosewood body
-carved spruce top
-ebony fingerboard, ivoroid bound
-all edges bound with ivoroid and bordered with fine black and white lines
-adjustable ebony bridge
-lacquer finish, top shaded golden brown
-pearl hex fingerboard inlays position 1, 3, 5, 7, 9, 12, 15 and 17
-fingerboard w-b-w lines inlaid ¼" from edge each side
-style 45 back strips
-bound head stock with pearl C. F. Martin inlaid head stock veneer
-gold plated trimmings including engraved machines

F MODEL CARVED-TOP GUITAR PRODUCTION								
	F-1	F-1S	F-2	F-2S	F-5	F-7	F-9	F-9S
1931								
1932								
1933								
1934								
1935						91	28	
1936						37	19	
1937						36	6	
1938						12	6	
1939							6	1
1940	54		22		2			
1941	25	1	12	1		6		
1942	12		12			6	6	
1943								

Table 70
F Model Carved-Top Guitar Production

Scale Length

The 1932 sales flyer promoting the carved-top C models noted that the scale length of these guitar was 25.4".

A C-2S guitar (stamped June 26, 1934, serial number 56751) was made with a "**0 scale**" (24.9"). It is not known if this was just a special order or a prototype.

The shop order slips for the next two batches of C models, twelve C-2 guitars stamped August 3, 1934 and twelve C-1 guitars stamped August 10, 1934, noted both had a "**#0 scale**". All of these guitar still retained the ebony bar beck reinforcement and bar frets. All subsequent C model carved-top guitars had the 24.9" scale length.

The early R-18 arched-top guitars had a scale length of 25.4" and it is not known when or if the scale length was reduced to 24.9". The scale length for the R-17 and R-15 guitars was not recorded but are certainly the same as the model R-18 at any given time.

The F model carved-to guitars didn't enter production until January 1935, after the change in scale lengths noted above, and had 24.9" necks.

Transition to T-Bars and Bar Frets

The batch of six C-3 guitars stamped on August 23, 1934 (serial number 57487 to 57492) hold the distinction of being the first regular Martin guitars made with the steel T-bar and T-frets.

Epilogue

It is generally assumed that Martin dropped the carved-top C and F models and the arched-top R models during the war because of a lack of labor and materials. The war years, 1941 to 1945, were considerably better for Martin than the late 1930's. Martin maintained a guitar production averaging over 4,000 guitars per year over that period, compared to under 3,000 guitars per year from 1937 to 1939. Martin may have lost a few skilled employees to the war effort but that didn't affect overall production. It should also be considered that the sales of Martin's carved-top guitars did well when they were introduced but couldn't maintain market share after only a few years. The last straw for the carved-top guitars was probably the war time restriction on metal. The large metal tailpieces had to go and, besides, the carved-top instruments no longer made up a significant portion of Martin's sales.

Although not a great success, the carved-top guitars provided much needed sales to Martin when the company needed them most, during the depths of the Depression. This lack of success was not related in any way to the quality of the product, as any one who had seen a C-2, C-3, F-7 or F-9 can attest, but is mostly due to Martin not being completely in tune with what the market was looking for in a jazz guitar. A letter written to Martin from the Rudolph Wurlitzer Co. in Detroit on December 10, 1935 illustrates the situation perfectly:

"We have a very good customer who now owns a $200 Martin Guitar (i. e., a C-3). He is now determined to purchase one of Gibson's latest model Super-Four Hundred, retailing at $400, and trade-in his Martin. However, I have gained permission to write and ask you what you have to offer at $400. In other words, he would like to know full specification of just what type instrument you could furnish for $400.

You are no doubt familiar with Gibson's new model, its body size and other specifications. It is my personal opinion that you could and would turn out a job far excelling the Super-Four Hundred, at the same price."

Martin replied on December 12:

"We appreciate the opportunity you give us to supply you with an extra fine guitar, similar in a general way, including price to the Gibson Super-400. This we will gladly do for you, using our own ideas rather than just make a copy of a competing instrument.

In size, our Grand Auditorium is the largest we can furnish now because we do not have either the patterns or the extra wide material for a larger size. Players tell us, however, that the tone of our Model F Guitar, Grand Auditorium Size, has a better balance and just as much volume as the tone of the larger guitar. Starting with our Style F-9 we propose to beautify the design by inlaying all borders, top, sides and back, with a narrow line of real pearl. We will also supply real pearl large position marks in the fingerboard. This, with gold metal parts, will make a handsome guitar. Adding a genuine, smooth tan leather case lined with silk plush and trimmed with gold plates fasteners, we would have a guitar that would list at $375 with the case. You know the Gibson 400 includes just such a case; in fact, it is probably the principal item of increased cost in the outfit.

In building this guitar we would use our very best seasoned material and we would like to do the work deliberately, taking about six weeks' time. Since it is being made up special we could include other features that the owner might desire such as inlaying his name in pearl letters in the fingerboard, either in addition or in place of the regular inlay. Such inlay work generally costs about twenty-five dollars so you would have just four hundred dollars for the outfit.

We could also engrave the owner's name in the tailpiece where "Martin" is now engraved. You know we are using a brand new style tailpiece on the Model F Guitars. If there is anything else your customer would like to have, please let us know and we will try to have it done."

It's too bad this guitar was never made, it would have been spectacular!

Dreadnought Guitars (1931 to 1969)

The development of 12-fret and 14-fret Dreadnought guitars is covered on pages 68 to 76. This section will document how many Martin Dreadnought guitars were made and answer some commonly asked questions.

Tables 71 to 73 contain all relevant details that can be gleaned from available archival information.

A list of general notes is attached and some specific notes are added to each table.

General Notes

• To get the number of normal guitars made in a specific year add the regular guitar column and the dark top column (not counting L, S and E guitars).

• The production figures for dark top guitars is an estimate based on production records and the bookings ledger. The highest number from the source information is shown in the table. Since Martin did not always record whether a guitar received a dark top, the number shown in the table should be considered an "at least" figure. In most cases the bookings ledger showed a higher number of dark top guitars than the production records.

• All guitars made from 1931 to August 1934 had the ebony bar neck reinforcement and bar frets. From September 1934 guitars had the steel T-bar neck reinforcement and T-frets except where noted in the war years and for a small number of guitars from 1953. The steel T-bar was replaced by square steel tubing in 1967.

• All guitars made before 1938 had advanced-X bracing. The first rear-X braced guitar was 71358 (although four prototype D-18 guitars with rear-X bracing were made earlier, serial numbers 71165 to 71170).

• Guitars with 12-fret bodies have a neck width of 1-7/8" at the nut. Guitars made between 1934 and mid-1939 have a 1-3/4" wide neck (last 1-3/4" wide neck on a guitar appears to be serial number 72739. Subsequently, all guitars had 1-11/16" wide necks (except for some special ordered guitars).

• All guitars made before 1944 had scalloped braces. Deichman noted the first guitar with non-scalloped bracing was a D-18 with serial number 89926.

• All style 21, 28, 35, 41, 42 and 45 guitars had Brazilian rosewood bodies through 1969 until replaced by East India rosewood on some styles in late 1969 (as noted).

• Some guitars in 1953 had tops made from Vermont spruce, a variety of red spruce. The same source provided Vermont spruce that appeared on some guitars in 1957. The number of 1953 guitars made with this wood is not known but shop order slips from 1957 detail which guitars got Vermont spruce tops (number are noted). Martin began to use German spruce tops in 1957. Where the number of German spruce tops are known they are noted.

• The tables reflect the terminology Martin used

YEAR	D-1	D-18	D-18 DARK TOPS	D-18S	D-18H	D-18L	D-18M	D-18E	D-21	D-21 DARK TOPS	D-21L
D-1, D-18 and D-21 GUITARS											
1931	2(EB)	1(EB)								1[1]	
1932		1(EB)	2(EB)								
1933		3(EB)	6(EB)								
1934		26(EB),20(TB)	7(EB),4(TB)	1[2]	1(EB)						
1935		117	15	1							
1936		252	31	3[3]							
1937		411	20[5]	1[4]							
1938		200(AX),106(RX)	22[5]	1		2					
1939		200(WN),275(NN)	16[5]								
1940		375	5[5]	1		1					
1941		575	17[5]								
1942		100(TB),225(EB)	8[5]			1					
1943		423(EB)	3(EB)[5]								
1944		405(SB),24(NSB)[6]									
1945		325(EB),150(TB)[7]									
1946		423(EB)[8],250(TB)	2(EB)								
1947		748	2								
1948		745	4			2					
1949		446	4								
1950		543	7								
1951		674	1								
1952		823	2			2					
1953		75(EB), 897(TB)	3(TB)			27					
1954		1144	6			1					
1955		1097	3			3			6		
1956		1074	1			3			275		
1957		702(WT),271(ET)[6]	2(WT)			3			180(WT),100(ET),17(GT)	3(WT)	
1958		1075(WT)	9(WT)			1	1(WT)		225(WT)		
1959		440(WT),10(GT)	1[5]				253(WT),48(GT)		25(WT)		
1960		423(WT),277(GT)							81(WT),19(GT)		
1961		564(WT),136(GT)	1[5]			2	1[9]		95(WT),5(GT)		
1962		655(WT),70(GT)				2(WT)			123(WT),27(GT)		
1963		800		1		2			200		
1964		1000				2			125		
1965		1125				1			275		
1966		2175				1			200		
1967		2550		52		2			350		1
1968		1730		150		7			300		
1969		2500		250		6			275(BR),25(IR)		1

Legend: EB = Ebony bar neck reinforcement   AX = Advanced X-bracing   WN = wide neck (1¾")   SB = Scalloped braces
TB = Steel T-bar neck reinforcement   RX = Rear X-bracing   NN = narrow neck (1-11/16")   NSB = Non-scalloped braces
WT = West (Sitka) spruce top   ET = East (Adirondack) spruce top   GT = German spruce top   BR = Brazilian rosewood
IR = Indian rosewood

Notes:
1) The first Martin Dreadnought guitar was a 12-fret D-21. It was made one month before the first D-1 guitar
2) Carved top D-18
3) Two of the 1936 D-18S guitars had 12-fret bodies, the third had left-handed construction
4) 12-fret body
5) Based on number of dark top guitars in the bookings ledger for the specific year. Dark tops ordered late in the year may not have been stamped until the following year.
6) All 1944 D-18 guitars had the ebony bar neck reinforcement
7) At least 150 1945 D-18 guitars had the steel T-bar neck reinforcement
8) At least 425 1946 D-18 guitars had the ebony bar neck reinforcement
9) Mahogany top

Table 71
Detailed Information for D-1, D-18 and D-21 Guitars

for differentiating different types of spruce top. Martin used "East spruce" to indicate red or Adirondack or Vermont spruce and "West spruce" to indicate Sitka spruce. German spruce tops were pre-seasoned and were sourced from Europe. The purchasing records through 1964 never mention Engelmann spruce.

YEAR	D-2	D-28	D-28 DARK TOPs	D-28H	D-28S	D-28G	D-28L	D-28E	D-28SW	D-42S	D-45	D-45L	D-45S
1931	4	1											
1932	2	4											
1933		10	1		1						1[1]		
1934	1[2]	41(EB),24(TB)	7	1[3]						1			1
1935		71	10		2[3]								
1936		59	1	1[3]	2								2
1937		141	6			1							2
1938		96(AX),24(RX)	6[4]		1						6(AX),3(RX)		
1939		48(WN),72(NN)	4[4]		3						3(WN),9(NN)		2(NN)
1940		144	4[4]								18	1	
1941		180	5[4]		2						24		
1942		24(TB),71(EB)	2[4]								6(TB),12(EB)		1(TB)
1943		187(EB)	5(EB)										
1944		219(EB)	1(EB)										
1945		12(EB),172(TB)[5]	1[4]										
1946		275(EB),150(TB)											
1947		447	3										
1948		497	3				6						
1949		422	3		2								
1950		471	4										
1951		450	1[4]				1						
1952		599	1										
1953		50(EB),625(TB)											
1954		800			1		4						
1955		800			2		6						
1956		700			1		2						
1957		516(WT),241(ET), 60(GT)	2(WT)		1		1						
1958		737(WT),12(GT)	1(WT)				2						
1959		404(WT),96(GT)	1[4]				1	175					
1960		249(WT),351(GT)	2 (1S,1EX)		5[6]		4	1(D-28ES)					
1961		340(WT),160(GT)			1	1(D-28GS)	7						
1962		465(WT),210(GT)			4		5	12	2				
1963		649	1				1	25	8				
1964		975			2		1	24	11				
1965		925			20		3		3				
1966		1825			7		2						
1967		2351			67		4						
1968		3078			125		9		6		67		
1969		3029			163		11				162		1

Legend: EB = Ebony bar neck reinforcement   AX = Advanced X-bracing   WN = wide neck (1¾")   SB = Scalloped braces
TB = Steel T-bar neck reinforcement   RX = Rear X-bracing   NN = narrow neck (1-11/16")   NSB = Non-scalloped braces
WT = West (Sitka) spruce top   ET = East (Adirondack) spruce top   GT = German spruce top   BR = Brazilian rosewood
IR = Indian rosewood

Notes:
1) Gene Autry's D-45 guitar
2) The D-2 made in 1934 was special ordered with a carved top like a C-2and is the only D-2 originally made with the steel T-bar neck reinforcement and T-frets
3) 12-fret body
4) From booking ledger
5) The number of 1945 D-28 guitars with the ebony bar neck reinforcement is unclear but is more than twelve.
6) One of the D-28S guitars from 1960 has a 12-fret body.

Table 72
Detailed Information for D-2, D-28, D-42S and D-45 Guitars

YEAR	D-35	D-35L	D-35S	D-35SW	D-41	D12-20	D12-20L	D12-20S	D12-35	D12-35L	D12-35S	D12-45
1964						152						
1965	206					725	1		181			
1966	975	2	1	3	450		1		250			
1967	1325	2	35	3	1100			1	600			
1968	1150		101		1250				825			
1969	1800		137		37(BR),12(IR)	1675			725(BR),50(IR)	3	25	3

Legend: BR = Brazilian rosewood   IR = Indian rosewood

Table 73
Detailed Information for D-35, D-41 and Twelve String Guitars

Model 32 Guitars (1932)

At the beginning of 1932 Martin made six 0-18S guitars with 14-fret necks as prototypes for the Model 32 guitars. The first example, serial number 49750, was stamped on January 13, 1932 with the following specifications: "**Orchestra model neck & scale, gear pegs #90, pick guard**". An OM scale at this time was 25.4". The second 0-18S, serial number 49926, was stamped on January 27 and this was quickly followed by a batch of two, serial numbers 50052 and 50053, on February 9 that further defined the specifications for the new model: "**Celluloid inlay & binding, cream & black 0.025, black 0.015, white 0.020, O. M. neck & scale, mahogany finish, dark top shaded brown, Grover mach. vertical**". A further batch of two, serial numbers 50110 and 50111, was stamped on February 13 with the shop order slip noting: "**New model body, 1 celluloid binding & inlay, 14 frets clear, pick guard, dark finish**", except 50110 had "**O. M. scale & bracing**" and 50111 had "**0 scale & bracing**" (0 scale being 24.9").

From this information it can be deduced that five 0-18S guitars were made with the OM (25.4" scale) and that the first prototype had banjo tuners. The sixth 0-18S was made with the 24.9" scale used on all subsequent production guitars. It is also clear Model 32 guitars were meant to have dark tops.

Figure 263
1932 Martin 0-18S Guitar (Serial Number 50053)
on right and 1938 Martin 00-18 on left

It did not take Martin long to realize they had developed a guitar for which there would be strong demand. In March 1932 Martin send out letters to a number of their dealers promoting the new "**Model 32**" 0-18 guitars. The letter sent to Cable Piano Co. on March 9 is typical:

"**By today's express we are sending you a sample of our new forty dollar guitar. Compared with our old style 0-18 at that price you will notice these features:**

> **1) Long neck, fourteen frets clear**
> **2) Single unit tuning machines, vertical posts**
> **3) Dark finish with shaded top**
> **4) Pick guard as regular equipment**

This new model is really the same as our popular Orchestra Model except for the smaller size (concert) and lower price. In the auditorium size we shall continue to call it Orchestra Model, style OM-18 at fifty dollars; in concert size it is the new style 0-18 at forty dollars. Do you like it?"

Cable Piano Co. replied enthusiastically on March 16 about the new 0-18. Martin was prompted to offer further comments in a follow-up letter:

"**Thank you very much for the encouragement you give us on our new Style 0-18 guitar. Our aim is to make it such good value, with all the latest features, that a prospective customer would feel a real urge to buy it. It seems to take a lot of urge to pry a customer's dollars loose these days so we are hoping that this new Guitar will do the trick, for the common good of dealers and of ourselves.**

The long neck, with fourteen frets clear of the body, is now available on the following Martin Guitars:

> **Style 0-17 at $30.00**
> **Style 0-18 at $40.00**
> **Style OM-18 at $50.00**
> **Style OM-28 at $85.00**
> **Style OM-45 at $170.00**

also on the Carved top Guitars at eighty, one hundred twenty and two hundred dollars. All these guitars have the pick guard as regular equipment; and the OM-18 and OM-28 styles are now avail-

able with the shaded dark top, if desired."

From these letters it can be seen that the new 14-fret 0-18 guitars were meant to compliment the OM-18 guitars that had been in production for several years. It can be inferred that Martin intended to keep the 00 size guitars as 12-fret instruments.

The comment about the shaded top being optional for the OM-18 guitars is interesting because most, if not all, 1932 OM-18 guitars have this feature. The new 14-neck was not available on Style 0-28 guitars.

The Rudolph Wurlitzer Co. tried to place orders in 1932 for 00-28 and 00-42 guitars with 14-fret necks but Martin politely turned them down. Intriguingly, Martin did offer to make a either a 0-42 or a 000-42 with the 14 fret-neck, instead of the 00-42 requested. Martin booked an order for a 000-42 "spec(ial)" from Rudolph Wurlitzer in New York on November 8, 1932. This guitar, serial number 52361, was the very first 14-fret 000-42.

Although Martin demurred from adding the 14-fret 00-21, 00-28 and 00-42 models to the product line, the 14-fret 00-17 guitar was added in January 1933 and the 14-fret 00-18 followed in June 1933.

Martin did make a small number of 14-fret 00-21 and 00-28 guitars in the 1930's on a special order basis. A single 00-42 and one 00-45 14-fret guitars were also made.

Octavario (1932)

Although generally considered a conservative company, the early 1930's, with the introduction of the OM, Martin Dreadnought and carved top guitars, were a period of increased innovation at Martin, undoubtedly as a result of the Great Depression. The unusual Octavario is an example of another novelty instrument Martin tried out.

On October 9, 1932 Joseph Furtner, of Linden NJ, wrote to Martin:

"**What I would like to know is, whether you people are or rather would be interested in a new string instrument, which I have. It will require no other machinery than you already have in making your** famous Guitars. My instrument is named, The Octavario, or reversed Various Octaves. On this instrument one actually can do with ease, things that are daily, poorly imitated. I personally am a Radio Artist on the Country Doctor Programme, on which I play the Theme Song, upon my German Concert Zither. My idea was to have this new instrument before the public thru personal programmes featuring and explaining this instrument on the air, as many times as I can. By the way, it would certainly help Martin Co. with sales. I was wondering if you people would be interested in being the exclusive makers of this instrument, and id you would care to make this demonstration model, as it were for me. I have Patents coming thru on it, and have also a crude model made."

Martin made a fairly encouraging reply on October 11:

"**Your new instrument, the Octavario, may have possibilities. We are always looking for something new and we should be very glad to see your instrument and to try it out. Could you arrange to drive over here some day with it? The writer is usually here every day until five o'clock and on Saturdays until noon.**

Unless you can show us the instrument or furnish more detailed description, we can not say whether we would be interested in making it."

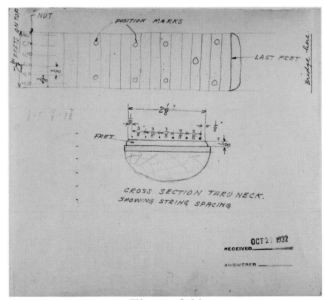

Figure 264
String Spacing and Neck Width for Octavario

Furtner replied on October 22 and enclosed some money for Martin to get started, except that Martin still required more information for spacing of the strings and the neck width. Furtner duly set Martin a sketch of the neck and the how the guitar was to be strung and tuned.

A shop order was created for the Octavario but it does not appear to have had a serial number assigned. It was also not entered in the sales booking ledger, probably being treated as a prototype. This instrument had some very unusual specifications including a 10-fret neck, a flat non-tapered fingerboard and odd tuning!

Unfortunately, this instrument doesn't appear to have worked out for Mr. Furtner and it is not even known for sure if it was completed. The Octavario certainly has to be considered as one of Martin's failed experiments.

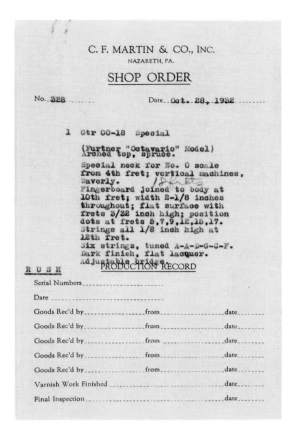

Figure 266
Shop Order for Octavario Based on a 00-18 Guitar

Amplified and Electrically Amplified Acoustic Guitars (1932)

It is generally thought that Martin entered the field of amplification very late in the game. In fact, Martin was quite aware of the developing field of amplification technology and corresponded with several companies. (It should be mentioned that before 1935 "amplified" guitars usually referred to instruments with resonators.)

On April 20, 1932 the Schireson Brothers of Los Angeles CA corresponded with Martin and offered to send them a sample of an "amplified" guitar (i. e., a resonator guitar). Martin declined the offer.

Schireson Brothers tried again later the same year explaining improvements in their amplifying system and this time Martin showed somewhat more interest although they answered they would seek advice from two of their dealer, Southern California Music Co. and Coast Wholesale Music Co.

Martin wrote to Southern California Music Co.

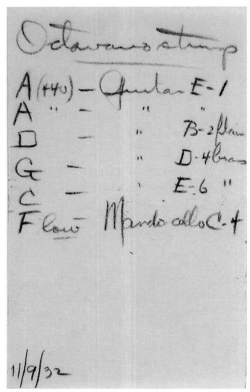

Figure 265
String Tuning for Octavario

on October 3, 1932 asking what they knew of the Schireson amplifying system, and suggesting they might consider it for Martin Hawaiian style guitars.

The reply from the Southern California Music Co. on October 19 stated that Schireson Brothers were using their amplification system on their own line of "Hollywood" guitars and went on to say the system was a competitor to National and Dobro. However, the Southern California Music Co. didn't think the Volutone (i. e., electric pick up and amplifier) system was any better or worse than other systems. Their advice to Martin was to stick to making fine toned guitars and forget about amplification.

This was in line with Martin's thinking on the subject because the Martin reply to Schireson Brothers on October 26, 1932 stated:

"We have decided not to manufacture an instrument of this kind now,….leaving the amplifying guitar field to the manufacturers who specialize in it."

In the meantime, electric amplification had begun to enter the market. On May 3, 1933 a letter from the Rudolph Wurlitzer Co. contained a question to Martin about amplification:

"Do you put out the electric attachment on the Guitar that amplifies the tone similar to the Vivi-tone?"

Martin replied on May 5:

"We are not now putting out a Guitar with an electric amplifying attachment. Do you have calls for this type of instrument and do you think the idea has commercial possibilities? We have been in touch with a manufacturer of such an electrical unit but have not yet made any arrangement to use it. We should be glad to have you opinion."

Schireson Brothers in a letter dated May 17, 1933 now tried to interest Martin in their **"Patented Electrically Amplified Instruments"**. Martin's reply stated that, although they were keeping an eye on developments in the field of electric amplification, they had no plans to add such a system to their instruments.

Arthur Tawn wrote to Martin on October 4, 1933 seeking Martin's view of the "**Vivi-Tone Electrically Energized Guitars**" (note: The Vivi-Tone instruments were developed by Lloyd Loar).

Martin's reply included the following interesting comments:

"…We think the Viva-Tone (sic) device is about the same as the others, consisting of a magnetic pick-up unit attached inside of the Guitar just below the bridge and connected with a radio amplifying set. The sole purpose is to amplify the tone in exactly the same way as a phonograph record may be amplified through a radio set. When the radio set is disconnected the device has absolutely no effect on the tone of the instrument except in so far that it may interfere with the normal tone ordinarily produced. …

It is our opinion and the opinion of some professional players that electrical amplification changes the tone of a Guitar so much as to make it almost a different instrument. True lovers of the Guitar tone are not likely to be interested in this device. We have investigated the matter with a view to adopting it on our instruments and have given it up for the present."

Regardless of Martin's lack of interest concerning electric amplification systems, the company was keeping an eye on developments. A gentleman named Charles Straub wrote to Martin on October 30, 1933 with an idea for an amplification system to be incorporated in the bridge for use on carved-top guitars and included a nicely drafted sketch (Figure 267).

Martin responded on November 4:

"You probably know that there are a number of these devices on the market and we believe that the one patented by Albert E. Allen, 231 Washington Street, Orange, New Jersey, is so similar to yours, at least in principle, that there would be danger of infringement. He uses the principle of a magnetic pick-up attached to the bridge which seems to be your plan. We had this device demonstrated here at the factory and it surely did produce a big tone, but we felt that the distinctive Guitar tone quality was lost.

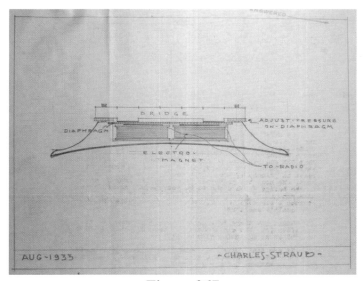

Figure 267
Idea for an Electric Pick Up Built into an Adjustable Bridge for Carved-Top Guitars

Right now there is a good deal of interest in electrical amplification, but commercially it does not seem to be successful so we are going slow on it."

Martin was certainly aware of a number of different electric amplification systems as revealed in this reply to a letter from Frank Reiley on July 26, 1935:

"Your letter has been referred to me since I know you personally and have been on the road noticing different reactions to the new "Rickenbacker." The particular advantage I see is in the sustained tone in glissando on the Hawaiian model. In the Spanish model it seems most practical to have extra microphone for the guitarist. In this way the whole orchestra comes through with the same tonal quality.

Then in Baltimore the current is direct and must be converted to AC before usuable (sic). That will be a drawback until any electrical current is acceptable.

It just occurs to me that these electric instruments will have a short term of popularity and then die down to a low sales volume, confined to theatre and display. This instrument is being put across with much sales energy and I have met some cases of actual sales; but is the instrument really legitimate and will it suit the work?

I have seen more than one electrical amplified guitar come and go. This is the most true toned of them all however. It is possible to insert an electric amplifying attachment in any guitar but we have not given it much consideration, and we would not guarantee true tone color and variations at once. The reaction I have noticed mostly in my travels is that the greatest advantage of the "Rickenbacker" is in sustained tone in Hawaiian playing. In Spanish this is not often desired. The chopped sock tones are still much in evidence and your electric guitar cannot do any better with those tones than a microphone through your public address system."

Martin bought both a Columbia amplifier and a Volu-Tone amplifier in 1935. The Columbia amplifier only appeared in the 1936 inventory while the Volu-Tone was appeared in inventory until at least early 1937.

In late October 1935 Martin was in correspondence with the Columbia Sound Company concerning their amplification system and ordered a **"Columbia Portable Amplifier with 10" Speaker"** on November 7. The Martin purchase order states the pick-ups were **"crystal pick-ups"**. Martin encountered some problems with their system, especially with the amount of electrical hum generated, although the pick-up itself

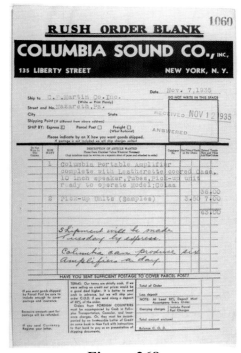

Figure 268
Martin Purchase Order for a Columbia Amplifier with a 10 Inch Speaker and Two Pick-Ups

Figure 269
Columbia Sound Co. Amplifier as
Purchased by C. F. Martin & Co.

A BROADCAST P.A. UNIT FOR MUSICIANS

A new field has opened in the P.A. line—that of supplying musicians with sound-amplifying systems such as this one.

CHAS. R. SHAW AND M. RECHT

WITHIN THE last few years progress in A.F. amplification has gone forward with leaps and bounds. It is only within recent months, however, that the layman has had his interest awakened in this field. The popularity of sound systems has increased to such an extent as to invade the portals of firms which have previously had no particular interest in anything electrical. Music concerns, interested only in manufacturing and selling musical instruments, have gone into the field of audio amplification to satisfy the demand for it created by orchestras and singers. Manufacturers of guitars and other string instruments have had amplifiers and microphonic devices built especially for these instruments so as to increase their tonal volume. People in all walks of life, as well as musicians, have found sound systems valuable adjuncts for their own personal use.

The result of this popularity has been to create new standards for sound systems. Permanent installations are not suitable for personal use. The outfits used by sound engineers are too complicated for the average layman and are too clumsy to carry about. Portable systems are often lacking in power and quality. Musicians, the most critical of any group of *(Continued on page 502)*

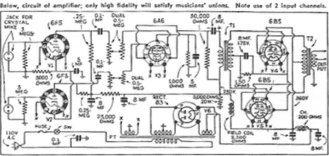

RADIO-CRAFT for FEBRUARY, 1936   481

Figure 270
1936 Article on Columbia Music Co. Amplifiers

A BROADCAST P.A. UNIT FOR MUSICIANS
(Continued from page 481)

people regarding the reproduction of music, find difficulty in getting a system to satisfy them. To meet the demand for an outfit that will fill all requirements, a sound system containing many novel features has been developed. It is simple to operate, versatile, excellent in quality, powerful enough for ordinary purposes, neat in appearance and portable. It attempts the rather difficult feat of satisfying both the layman unfamiliar with electricity (particularly the musician), and the sound engineer.

The heart of this sound system is the amplifying unit, consisting of the amplifier proper, a high-fidelity A.C. or A.C.-D.C. outfit delivering 18 W., and a powerful 10 in. speaker. Provision is made for the use of additional loudspeakers. This amplifier is mounted in a handsome black leatherette-covered case with chromium plated trimmings, and tube and speaker grilles. The case measures 15 x 15 x 8 ins. deep, and yet there is also room for a microphone with cable and a folding microphone stand, thus placing within one neat carrying case a sound system complete in itself, the entire weight being only 29 lbs.

NOVEL APPLICATION

There are really four essential ways of amplifying the sound output of the guitar, for instance. One is the conventional fashion of placing a microphone near the guitar, which is quite unsatisfactory because it picks up other instruments to the same extent. Some guitar manufacturers replace the instrument strings by metal strings and maintain inductive pickup or pickups near the bridge. The sound thus obtained is quite artificial and differs greatly from the natural sound.

A much better method is the use of a "crystal cartridge" such as used in crystal pickups.

The best method, however, is the use of an especially designed crystal cell unit which is simply taped down onto the instrument. Not only can this unit be removed and attached in a jiffy, and at will, but it will give most amazing, realistic, faithful amplification of the weakest tones.

One more interesting way of obtaining the same results is by using a so-called "bridge." Such a bridge can be used both as a normal bridge (which is the part supporting the strings), and as a means of translating the vibrations of an instrument into electrical oscillations so that the tone of the instrument can be reproduced and amplified faithfully.

The 2-channel input mixer in the amplifier provides many useful applications of it for the musician. Two string instruments, such as a Hawaiian guitar and a Spanish guitar, 2 violins, or 2 of any kind can play duets together.

For most purposes a string instrument player can play together with a phonograph or radio set. These things can, of course, be done by any instrument by using ordinary microphones in place of the bridge pickups. With an orchestra 1 microphone can be used for a vocalist and the other for the orchestra, each independently controlled, or 2 microphones can be used to obtain better balance for an orchestra when amplifying it. Many other uses can be found for this mixer.

This article has been prepared from data supplied by courtesy of Columbia Sound Co., Inc.

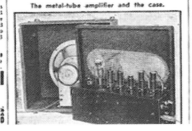

The metal-tube amplifier and the case.

seemed to work better with amplifiers from other manufacturers. In a letter dated December 4, 1935 the Columbia Sound Company identified the manufacturer of the pick-ups as Brush Development Company of Cleveland OH. The main product of the Brush Development Company at the time was piezoelectric phonograph pick-ups.

After experimenting with several amplifying systems Martin seems to have determined the Volu-Tone system gave the best result and, although not yet ready to incorporate an amplification system on their guitars, was prepared to share their conclusion with their dealers and customers. In a letter to Burgers Musical Shoppe on November 15, 1935 Martin wrote:

"In reply to your inquiry about a Martin Guitar with electric amplifier, we can offer you nothing definite at this time. We have had the matter under consideration and we are now trying out several ideas that look promising. We are looking for something different from the electric guitars

now on the market. You will be advised when it is ready.

In the meantime, as you probably know, the Volu-Tone Electric Amplifier, made by Schireson Brothers, 226 North Main Street, Los Angeles, California, is suitable for use on any regular Martin Guitar, either Spanish or Hawaiian style. I you are interested we suggest that you write direct to Schireson Brothers or information and prices."

Martin also experimented with a system offered by Lyon & Healy of Chicago in late 1935. The Lyon & Healy system included a Model 312 amplifier, a separate 10" speaker and what must have been a piezo-electric pick-up. The pick-up was supplied with a clamp and Lyon & Healy recommended clamping the pick-up to the head stock of the guitar for best results!

The Martin archive contains very little correspondence past the end of 1935 so it is not known if Martin continued to experimentation with electric amplification, although Martin was selling De Armond pick-ups by 1940.

Martin entered the electric acoustic guitar field far earlier than anyone has suspected. Martin began selling De Armond RHC guitar "**microphones**" as accessories for their acoustic guitars in September 1940. Martin also sold a number of De Armond FHC pickups for their arched-top and carved-top guitars. Martin even sold a 00-18 on January 17, 1941 with "**RHC mic(rophone) attached**". No other guitar from this period left the factory with a pickup installed. This was the first and only Martin acoustic electric guitar made prior to the introduction of 00-18E, D-18E and D-28E guitars in March 1959. Martin also offered amplifiers and sold a small number of the National #50 amplifiers in 1941.

Martin sold 138 RHC and 102 FHC pickups before the war put an end to production in early 1943. Sales started again late in 1945 but never recovered to the pre-war levels and had almost ceased by 1950. Total sales of De Armond pick-ups between 1945 and 1950 amounted to only 65 RHC and 46 FHC pick-ups. A few of the De Armond RHC-B and FHC-B improved model pick-ups were sold between 1950 and 1959. A very small number of De Armond model 210, 700 and 1000 pick-ups were also sold by Martin.

Amplifiers (1935 to 1964)

In 1935 Martin experimented with two electric amplification systems, one from Schireson Brothers (Volu-Tone) and another from Columbia Sound Co. On November 7, 1935 the Columbia Sound Co. shipped a "Columbia Portable Amplifier with 10" speaker and three pick-ups at a net price of $43.00.

In a letter dated August 9, 1935 Schireson Brothers wrote:

"**Replying to you letter of Aug. 5 we beg to state that the list price of the Volu-Tone, fitted with unit for sound-hole type guitar is $96.00. With unit or "F" hole type guitar, $98.50. Additional units for duet or trio playing through one amplifier is equipped are $25.00 each extra. Every amplifier is equipped to receive three instruments or two instruments and one microphone. ….**

Our discounts are as follows: Single purchases forty and ten percent discount. Quantity buyers get fifty per cent discount. Sample outfit for your use will be $34.56 (60-10%)"

Martin recorded the cost of the Volu-Tone system in their inventory as $44.45 so an extra pick-up, or other accessories, must have been purchased when the system was ordered.

The Volu-Tone system worked in a remarkable and, potentially, very dangerous way. The pick-up did not have magnetic poles. Instead, the strings were "energized" (or magnetized) with a 300 volt power source mounted in the amplifier. A special connector was used for plugging the guitar into the 300 volt power source. The amplifier instructions contained a disconcerting warning on plugging the guitar into the "energizing" socket:

"**DANGER: Do not permit the guitar plug to remain inserted in the energizing socket for longer than a second or two or harm to the instrument will results.**"

Volu-Tone manufactured several different amplifier models in the 1930's. Martin did not record the model number of their system so it is not known which they purchased. A Volu-Tone Model 5 and a Volu-Tone

Figure 271
Front and Back of a Volu-Tone Model 5 Amplifier

Figure 272
Volu-Tone Pick-Up Mounted on a
Lap-Steel Guitar

pick-up (mounted to a lap steel guitar) are illustrated in Figures 271 and 272.

Although Martin began selling De Armond RHC and

FHC pick-ups in 1940, they did not market an amplifier to go with the pick-ups. However, Martin did sell a total of four National #50 amplifiers in 1941, probably on special customer request.

Martin did not enter the amplifier field again until they introduced the 00-18E, D-18E and D-28E acoustic guitars in 1959.

In the period from 1959-1964 offered four different models; 110, 110T, 112 and 112T, manufactured by Rowe Industries Inc. The "T" indicated the amplifier had an additional tremolo circuit. The 110 model amplifiers had a 10" speaker powered by a single 6V6 tube whereas the 112 model amplifiers had two 6V6 tubes powering a 12" speaker. The 110 and 112 models were almost identical to the De Armond R5 and R15 amplifiers respectively.

As well, Martin sold 135 large solid-state SS-140 amplifiers, made by Electromatic Inc., in 1966.

AMPLIFIERS SOLD BY MARTIN		
AMPLIFIER MODEL	QUAN.	PERIOD
NATIONAL #50	4	1941
DANELECTRIC AMP WITH REVERB, TREMOLO & FOOT SWITCH	1	1959
110	75	1960-1963
110T	96	1960-1964
112	197	1959-1963
112T	145	1960-1964
700	34	1962-1963
700 WITH POWER PACK	4	1962-1963
750	5	1962
750 WITH TREMOLO	1	1962
750 WITH POWER PACK	1	1962
SS-140	135	1966
SC2	1	1962
SC3	1	1962
12" PORTABLE SPEAKER	1	1963
LARGE SPEAKER HC-1	1	1962
1045 DC BATTERY UNIT	1	1962
BATTERY PACK BP-1	3	1962
SPEAKER CABINET	3	1962
SPEAKER	1	1962
SPEAKER SC1	7	1962-1963
SPEAKER SC2	7	1962
SPEAKER SC3	3	1962
DE ARMOND 603 PEDAL CONTROL	1	1960
GUITAR REVERB CONVERTER RG-20	1	1962
TREMOLO CONTROL	29	1941-1943
TREMOLO CONTROL 60B	1	1960
TRANSISTOR AMPLIFIER	2	1962
TRANSISTOR AMPLIFIER WITH TREMOLO	1	1962

Table 74
Amplifiers Sold by Martin

C. F. Martin and the Classical Guitar

From the viewpoint of today's acoustic guitar market, with its emphasis on large steel-strung instruments, Martin classical guitars may seem somewhat anachronistic. However, Martin had always considered itself a manufacturer of guitars meant for concert use. In the period when all guitars were strung with gut strings there was no need to define "classical" guitars as a separate type of instrument.

As discussed elsewhere in this book C. F. Martin Sr. was heavily influenced by Spanish guitarists in the late 1830's. In short order Martin dropped the Viennese-shaped guitars in favor of Spanish-shaped instruments.

Martin continued to keep in touch with professional guitarists throughout its long history, adapting to changing tastes and evolving their guitar designs over time.

The most prominent of the early influences were John B. Coupa and Madam De Goni. John B. Coupa was a well-known concert guitarist and teacher, who eventually ran the New York City distribution center for Martin guitars under the name Martin & Coupa. Madam De Goni caused a sensation in the early 1840's with her playing on a Spanish guitar.

It is very likely it was Coupa that introduced De Goni to Martin, probably shortly after she landed in the U. S. in late 1840. Coupa was very active in the concert scene and may have also introduced Martin to Benedid, another Spanish guitarist active in New York at the time. When Marco Aurelio Zani de Ferranti visited the United States in 1847 and 1848 it may be assumed that both Coupa and Martin met him as they later marketed a Ferranti model guitar, as discussed in their 1849 correspondence.

C. F. Martin Jr. continued the tradition of keeping in contact with guitar players. Between 1870 and 1875 there are several letters from an N. Marache. This is almost certainly Napoleon Marache who, although best known for his contribution to the chess world, was also considered one of the best guitar players in the United States at the time. It would appear from the tone of the letters that Marache, more than just a customer, was considered a family friend.

Frank Henry Martin, starting with the death of his father in 1888, was at the helm of Martin guitars for over 50 years and oversaw the development of the Martin Guitar & Co. as it progressed from making small gut-strung guitars in the 19th century to the production a wide variety of steel-strung guitars and mandolins by the 1930's (and also ukes although these were not steel-strung).

During Frank Henry Martin's tenure guitars increased significantly in size to reflect the change in musical tastes. In the 1880's guitars were primarily used in parlors and or small auditoriums. The largest-sized guitars were 00 instruments. By the 1940's large steel-string Dreadnought guitars were well established and gut strings were restricted to specialized classical-style guitars.

Throughout the period from the late 1880's until the 1920's Frank Henry Martin kept in touch with the developments in the classical guitar world through correspondence with well know guitarists and other aficionados.

Frank Martin corresponded with Charles De Janon, Luis T. Romero, Vahdah Olcott-Bickford, William Foden and George Krick, all associated with the classical guitar in the American tradition.

Charles De Janon continued to influence his students to purchase Martin guitar until at least the 1890's. One of his students, E. S. Sanford, kept up a lively correspondence with Frank Martin during 1889 and 1890 and made many interesting observations.

In a letter dated June 18, 1889 Sanford, a proud owner of a 0-28 and a 00-28, stated:

"I have just spent half an hour with Senor Romero, Lyon & Healy's Washburn guitar man. He and de Janon have been playing for each other. It was worth listening to you can depend but what interests you most is that Romero owns and plays only upon a Martin and said that he would give me $75.00 for the "tub" as de Janon and I call my 00. I did not sell it."

A letter dated July 30, 1889 followed:

"Romero that I spoke to you of as a "Washburn"

man is it seems a "Martin" (man) to the back-bone and (don't tell de Janon) the best player I have ever heard.

We entertained him at my mother's home in 53rd St. and amongst the guests was Post of Lyon & Healy (Washburn).

When the show was over Post said to Jim Phipps of W. A. Pond & Co. "by Jimminy Krickets Phipps, that's a Martin crowd I got into". We had Romero's guitar, de Janon's and my 00 and we amused themselves by calling them cheap Washburns."

So players loving their Martin guitars is nothing new, even 130 years ago!

Sanford's letter of September 17, 1889 contains some interesting content on his preference for guitars with friction pegs::

"The 0-28 you sent to Pond at the same time you sent the 1-21 was such a superior instrument in every way that I took it in place of the 1-21 and both de Janon and Romero consider it superior to theirs'. The machine head is a draw back but in the two years when it begins to rattle my bones may be dust."

This is not an unusual comment about tuning machines. There was a general perception at that time that machines would "rattle" after a short period of use as a result of wearing of the gears. In a concert setting it was also much easier to replace broken strings on the fly with a peg head guitar. This provides an interesting contrast to the modern perception that tunings machines are superior. Modern players and collectors, not aware of the limitations of the gut strings available in the 19th century, find friction peg guitars to be finicky and hard to tune. It can be safely assumed Sanford, De Janon and Romero preferred to use Martin guitars with friction pegs.

Another Sanford letter, dated December 4, 1889 provides some interesting comments on Romero:

"Romero writes me from Boston to get him a supply of silver strings. I gave him half of the last consignment you sent me and he says they are the best strings he ever used. He uses an 0-28 (C. F. Martin & Co.) and tunes the E to D so you can give him a very heavy string. The D's you sent me are fine but as I am not as particular as Romero, who when a string wears out puts on an entire new set, so mine are not yet gone.

Jany 25th 1890 a Banjo and Guitar concert will be held at Chickering Hall NY. Romero comes from Boston to play at it and I am sure the guitar will get a great boom that it has been waiting for years. Charlie de Janon will not play in public and to have a man like Romero come in Boston is a great benefit to the guitar. My musical friends who have heard him admit that they are converts whereas before the always turned their noses high at the instrument."

The "silver" strings mentioned above were silver plated steel strings. This may apply only to the higher pitched strings but the mention of a "heavy" E string to be used in a drop D tuning may indicate that all the strings were steel.

A couple more interesting comments are included in a letter dated only a few days later on December 7:

"Romero plays neither in public or private upon anything but a Martin nor does anyone else who has a reputation at stake. I know what you will say about the Lyon & H(ealy) Souvenir but Romero was "more turned against their siminy (sic)" when they got that recommendation from him. He was introduced to me as a Lyon & Healy man but I found out shortly that that was not true."

As implied by Sanford's letter of December 4, the early 1890's seems to have been a difficult time in the guitar business. This was echoed in a letter from Zoebisch on April 3, 1890:

"Mr. Ferrer is in California and a Mexican or of Spanish descent, I helped already twice to present him two fine Concert guitars.

Good players are scarce here two of the best in N. Y. died within 2 years. ...."

It is curious that Zoebisch makes no mention of Romero considering that guitarist's impact on the guitar scene, more on this later.

Luis T. Romero corresponded directly with Martin in February 1890 and ordered several guitars and some strings. (Author's note: Romero's residence in Boston was 24 Dartmouth St.).

Sanford continued his running commentary on Romero throughout 1890. The first letter from January 21 discusses the banjo and Guitar concert first mentioned above:

"The (banjo) & guitar concert will certainly come off on Saturday night (the Lord permitting) at Chickering Hall. ....

The "cracks" are coming from every direction, to hear Romero and I hope that amongst the 1,500 banjoists that will be assembled we may induce 1,000 to take up the guitar. Romero will play "Rigoletto" with as many encores as N. Y. wants for his first number. His selection is the "quartette" from that opera and he plays it "like a dream". His second number will be a selection, if he ever gets to it, for I am afraid the encores of the first may carry him over to Monday A. M."

The period around 1890 was the peak in popularity of the gut-strung "classic" banjo. It may be hard for modern banjo players to imagine a concert of gut-string banjos.

Frank Henry Martin attended the concert. In a follow-up letter dated February 3, Sanford records his reaction to the concert:

"I heard that you enjoyed the concert. I did not. It was the most lamentable failure as far as Romero was concerned as one could imagine.

The "acoustic" effect of the hall is not favorable to the guitar. I want another 0-28 but it (must) be a peghead, must have a rare musical tone and must play very easily."

More commentary was to follow on February 6:

"I am glad that you were able to appreciate that which our friend Romero was doing. I have heard him play "Rigoletto" fifty times and I can assure

you that where I sat I could not tell if he were playing it or something else. ...."

Sanford ordered another 00-28 on March 28, 1890 although he was still very happy with his 0-28.

On April 25 Sanford informed Martin that:

"Romero's health being poor, the Dr's have advised him to "change the air" and he is coming to my house a week from Saturday May 3. Is there any chance of my having my guitar by that time?"

On May 8 Sanford reported:

"I took a day off with Romero to try the new guitar. It's a daisy.

Romero is delighted with it, but as it completely hides his face when he plays on it he says 0-28 is large enough for him. The treble is excellent and I would have note that it is of great power both in treble and bass with the strings low.

Mr. Romero said yesterday that he never saw a Martin with low strings that was not an extraordinary instrument ...."

In this case, "low strings" must refer to a guitar with a low action.

More followed on August 22:

"Romero writes that he goes back to Boston in perfect health today. That I consider good news as his playing awakens the interest in the guitar that is necessary to sell them."

Contrary to Sanford's gushing commentary, Zoebisch had a far different view of Romero. Romero ran afoul of Zoebisch by attempting to deal with Martin directly as discussed in this letter dated February 20, 1890:

"Romero is like all such players & teachers, never can be satisfied & sneak around. He was several times in store, we treated him very nice & kindly, also called last year before he went to Europe & said he wanted one of these days a very fine Guitar for a Lady. Also when he was here last he said he would see that some of his Scholars would get new

Martin Guitars and would send the others or have the orders sent to us.

Now he writes up to you too, just tell him to send us his orders & explain what he wants & you would follow his instructions in making the Guitar. Of course if it is for him I will confidentially do something extra for him in the shape of a present, not concession as we have done with some other noted player, in fact twice gave a Concert night out.

This Teacher business brings us all the time between two fires, they want to have in fact dealer's rate and ignore dealers & be able to say I can but as cheap as you can, and of course this won't do if we go in for that style of business we would soon be left severely alone by the dealers, and they are the parties whom we have to have to work for & keep your Guitar in Front. Inside of a month I would be in trouble in Boston with this Romero business. I am working hard against the "Bay State", "Tilton" "Washburn", "Imperial" & "Orion" Guitars in Boston, all made & sold there, except the Washburn is Lyon & Healy's, whenever I get a chance & Romero says he will recommend them (the Martins) they got him up there & he is not altogether free to act quite openly but he will do justice I think. I have now to send a 1-21 & 0-28 of course to dealers and if Romero can sell guitars he can get them there or order them of us, or through our customers in Boston of us & make his arrangements with them if he prefers. We must do the business fair & square so that can answer for all the transactions otherwise we make enemies out of Dealers and that we cannot afford, as many Guitars are now in the market to be shown & worked & talked up against ours."

"Bay State", "Tilton" and "Washburn" are well known trade names. "Imperial" was a brand name of guitars and mandolins made by the Imperial Company for the John Church Co. of Cincinnati but, so far, no information has been found on "Orion" guitars.

Unfortunately, there is a large and disappointing gap in the correspondence from 1894 until 1922 but Martin did keep in touch with influential classical guitar players and teachers such as William Foden, Vahdah Olcott-Bickford and George Krick. It is also

very likely Martin corresponded with Henry Spahr, the well known Jersey City teacher, although no letters have survived.

It is known from later correspondence that Martin had been in touch with William Foden from at least 1900.

Martin maintained a membership in the American Guitar Society. The American Guitar Society was founded in 1923 by Vahdah Olcott-Bickford and still meets regularly. She was considered one of the foremost concert guitarists in the United States from 1900 to 1950, at which time she retired from the stage to devote the rest of her life to teaching and publishing.

"The purpose of the AGS," as she states in the minutes of the meeting of the board in 1923, "is to promote interest in classical guitar through the educational program, encourage composers to enrich literature and to develop both a scholarship and publication fund."

See the website: http://www.americanguitarsociety. org/history.html.php

Martin was aware that George Krick, a former student of William Foden, had been in touch several times with Andres Segovia, the famed Spanish guitar player. On January 4, 1932 Martin, based on a request from a San Francisco customer, sent a letter to Krick seeking information on the guitar and strings used by Segovia. Martin was also interested in the pricing of Segovia's guitar.

Krick provided some answers on January 8:

"In reply to your letter regarding the Guitar used by Andre Segovia I would say that until two years ago he played on an old Torres instrument. Since that time he has been using a Guitar made for him by Hermann Hauser of Muenchen, Germany. This was made after a Spanish model and is about the same size as your 00 instrument.

A 40% import duty brings the cost of an instrument of this kind up to a little over $200.00 to an American customer.

The gut strings are made by Pirazzi and in length

and thickness properly adjusted to this Guitar. The silk wound bass strings are made by the same Hauser in Muenchen."

Martin was very much interested in this information, especially concerning the strings, and made a reply on January 12:

"**Are the Pirazzi strings available in this country? We have been using Armour strings but do not find them perfectly satisfactory. If we could get a thoroughly reliable, first class string we should be glad to put it up in special envelopes under our name and offer it to our dealers. It is quite difficult for the average music dealer to get gut Guitar strings.**

Do you notice any increased interest in Guitars strung with gut strings? If there were some slight assurance of a steady demand we should be very glad to make up a special model, properly constructed to produce a resonant and responsive tone. We realize that a Guitar made to stand the strain of steel strings is too stiff for gut strings but our experience has been that when we make up Guitars light enough for gut strings they stay on our hands a long time because there is so little call. Right now we have in stock several style 00-42 and 00-45 Guitars especially made for gut strings which are several years old. They have never been out of the factory and we think they are very good in tone. If you would like to try one of them we should be glad to make a selection for you."

This is a most interesting letter because it implies Martin continued to want to promote gut string guitars even when demand was low. The increased interest in Spanish guitars as a result of Segovia's influence and positive encouragement from George Krick may have influenced Martin to introduce the 00-18G and 00-28G classical guitars several years later.

From Table 75 it can be seen that the first guitar with the "G" designation was a 00-21G from late December 1934, while the first batch of 00-18G guitars wasn't made until April 1936.

Earlier books on Martin guitars reported that the "G" model guitars used the usual 14-fret 00 body with the

25.4" scale. However, it appears that the first thirty-three 00-18G had the standard 12-fret body and 24.9" scale. The first 00-18G with the 00 14-fret body shape was serial number 71150.

It also appears only five 00-28G guitars were made with the 12-fret body shape and these likely had the 24.9" scale although this was not recorded. The first 00-28G was made for one of William Foden's students. Beginning with serial number 70366 the 00-28G model had the 14-fret body shape with the 25.4" scale.

It is not known for sure why Martin changed from the old style 12-fret body to the OM 14-fret style body. However, is probably related to the increase in scale length to 25.4" (645 mm) which is closer to the then popular classical guitar scale of 650 mm. The 25.4" scale combined with a 12-fret neck required that the body be shortened.

Figure 273
1938 Martin 00-44G Guitar (Serial Number 70854)
The 45 style fingerboard inlay is original to the guitar.

STYLE	SHOP ORDER	DATE STAMPED	SERIAL NUMBER	COMMENTS ON SHOP ORDER SLIPS
00-21G	811	FEB. 13, 1935	59101	12-FRET BODY, FOR GUT STRINGS ONLY, EBONY NECK BAR, T-FRETS, PIN BRIDGE, NO PICK GUARD
00-18G	182	APR. 21, 1936	63044-63046	FOR GUT TRINGS ONLY, 12 FRET NECK, LIGHT CONSTRUCTION, NO STEEL BAR
00-21G	195	MAY 7, 1936	63180	T FRETS, NO STEEL BAR, FOR GUT STRINGS ONLY
00-18G	273	AUG. 28, 1936	64232-64234	12-FRET NECK, GUT STRINGS ONLY, NO PICK GUARD, OLD STYLE BRIDGE (SOME FROM THIS BATCH X-BRACED, 24.9" SCALE, PIN BRIDGE, "MADE FOR SILK AND GUT STRINGS" STAMPED ON BACK STRIP)
00-42G	356	DEC. 16, 1936	65087	FOR GUT STRINGS ONLY, NO PICK GUARD, OLD STYLE BRIDGE (SOLD TO GEORGE KRICK)
00-28G	357	DEC. 16, 1936	65088	12-FRET NECK, FOR GUT STRINGS ONLY, SELECT MATERIALS, 45 GRADE, NO PICK GUARD, LOOP BRIDGE (ORDERED BY MAJOR FAULCONER THROUGH WILLIAM FODEN)
00-18G	389	FEB. 2, 1937	65428-65433	12-FRET NECK, FOR GUT ONLY, NO PICK GUARD, OLD STYLE BRIDGE (X-BRACED, PYRAMID BRIDGE)
D-28G	406	MAR. 5, 1937	65702	12-FRET NECK, FOR GUT STRINGS ONLY, NO PICK GUARD, NO END PIN
00-18G	418	MAR. 17, 1937	65083	EXTRA WIDE NECK, 2-1/16" AT NUT, 2-7/16" AT 12TH FRET, SPACE BRIDGE PIN HOLES 1/8" WIDER
00-21G	423	MAR. 24, 1937	65879	EXTRA WIDE NECK, 2 1/16" AT NUT, SPACE BRIDGE PIN HOLES 1/8" WIDER, USE NECK MADE FOR ORDER 418
00-28G	429	APR. 1, 1937	65956	GUT STRING, 12-FRET NECK, NO PICK GUARD, CUSTOMER INSTRUCTIONS, SELECT FINE WOOD & SEE THAT INSTRUMENT HAS GOOD QUALITY OF TONE
00-42G	446	APR. 20, 1937	66113	12-FRET NECK, FOR GUT STRINGS, BODY BOUND AND INLAID LIKE STYLE 28, NO PICK GUARD (SOLD AT CHRISTIE'S SALE 2033, HERRINGBONE PURFLING)
00-18G	524	AUG. 2, 1937	67090-67095	
000-28G	589	NOV. 3, 1937	68184	ORCHESTRA MODEL (14 FRET NECK), FOR GUT STRINGS ONLY [a]
00-28G	622	DEC. 17, 1937	68732-68734	12-FRET, FOR GUT STRINGS ONLY, NO PICK GUARD
00-18G	621	DEC. 17, 1937	68735-68740	12-FRET, FOR GUT STRINGS ONLY, NO PICK GUARD
00-21G	687	MAR. 11, 1938	69704	EXTRA LIGHT CONSTRUCTION FOR GUT STRINGS ONLY, NO PICK GUARD
00-18G	688	MAR. 11, 1938	69705-69706	SPECIAL BRACING, TORRES STYLE, NO PICK GUARD, ONE WITH LOOP BRIDGE
00-21G	698	MAR. 18, 1938	69845	FOR GUT STRINGS ONLY, NO PICK GUARD
00-18G	709	APR. 13, 1938	70071-70076	12-FRET, REGULAR X-BRACING, PIN BRIDGE, BRACES EXTREMELY LIGHT, NECK AS WIDE AS WOOD ALLOWS, FINGERBOARD ALMOST FLAT, NO POSITION MARKS, REGULAR SIDE DOTS
00-28G	740	MAY 24, 1938	70366-70368	OM BODY [b], MODIFIED FAN BRACES, 12-FRET BODY, LOOP BRIDGE, NECK AS WIDE AS WOOD ALLOWS, NO POSITION MARKS ONLY SIDE DOTS, ONE (70366) WITH TORRES BACK, 2 WITH 0 [c] SCALE, 70368 WITH SCALE 000 [c]
00-44G	742	JUNE 3, 1938	70469	FOR GUT STRINGS ONLY, OM BODY, REGULAR BRACING AS LIGHT AS POSSIBLE, SLOTTED HEAD, 12 FRET NECK OM WIDTH, 1/16" THINNER THAN USUAL, 19 FRETS, NECK & FINGERBOARD BOUND & INLAID LIKE STYLE 45, OLD STYLE HEAD VENEER, REGULAR PIN BRIDGE, STYLE 28 PINS, D & J MACHINE HEADS
00-28G	754	JUNE 22, 1938	70595-70596	ORCHESTRA MODEL, 000 SCALE, THIN WOOD, REGULAR BACK BRACES, THIN BRIDGE PLATE FOR LOOP BRIDGE, #1 SOUND HOLE, FLAT FINGERBOARD, 19 FRETS, 12TH AT BODY, 2" WIDE AT NUT, 2 3/8" AT BODY, NECK WELL ROUNDED, SIDE DOTS ONLY, D & J MACHINE HEADS, FAN BRACED
00-18G	755	JUNE 22, 1938	70597	STANDARD MODEL [d], 0 SCALE, REGULAR BRACING FOR PIN BRIDGE, FINGERBOARD 2" WIDE AT NUT, 2 3/8" AT 12TH FRET, SLIGHTLY ROUNDED
00-44G	776	JULY 28, 1938	70854	O. M. BODY, LIGHT BRACING FOR GUT STRINGS ONLY, 19 FRET, 0 SCALE, 12 FRET NECK WIDTH 1 3/4", THICKNESS 1/16" THINNER THAN USUAL, NECK & FINGERBOARD BOUND AND INLAID STYLE 45, STYLE 21 BACKSTRIPE
00-18G	797	SEPT. 9, 1938	71150-71152	CLASSIC MODEL, MODIFIED FAN BRACING, TOP 6/64" THICK, #1 HOLE, #000SCALE, 12 FRETS TO BODY, FLAT FINGERBOARD, 19 FRETS LONG, NO POSITION MARKS ONLY, LOOP BRIDGE AS HIGH AS POSSIBLE, D & J #31 MACHINES
00-28G	817	OCT. 26, 1938	71495-71497	CLASSIC MODEL, 19 FRETS, 000 SCALE, TOP 6/64" THICK, OLD MARTIN PATTERN, FAN BRACED, LOOP BRIDGE
00-28G	850	DEC. 29, 1938	71839-71841	
00-18G	851	JAN. 9, 1939	71898-71903	
000-45G	863	JAN. 18, 1939	71954	FOR GUT STRINGS ONLY, ORCHESTRA MODEL BODY AND NECK 14 FRETS CLEAR, EXTRA LIGHT BRACES, REGULAR CROSS PATTERN, NECK 1/16" TO 1/8" THINNER, EBONY STRIP INSTEAD OF STEEL BAR, OVAL FINGERBOARD, NO POSITION MARKS BUT REGULAR SIDE DOTS, NO PICK GUARD, REGULAR PIN BRIDGE, ADJUST A LITTLE HIGHER THAN REGULAR STEEL
00-28G	869	FEB. 8, 1939	72091-72096	
000-28G	875	JAN. 18, 1939	72134	STANDARD MODEL FOR GUT STRINGS ONLY, CROSS BRACE EXTRA LIGHT, TOP 6.5/64", FINGERBOARD 2" WIDE AT NUT, SIDE DOTS ONLY, NO PICK GUARD, PIN BRIDGE, 3/32" + 4/32" AT 12TH FRET, D & J #33 MACHINE HEADS
00-18G	899	APR. 5, 1939	72391-72396	
00-28G	917	MAY 8, 1939	72608-72613	
00-28GS	927	MAY 17, 1939	72665	O.M., FOR GUT STRINGS ONLY, CROSS BRACING, VERY LIGHT, 000 SCALE, 14 FRET NECK, 2" WIDE AT NUT, SLOTTED HEAD, FLAT FINGERBOARD, SIDE DOTS ONLY, LOOP BRIDGE
00-18G	928	JUNE 1, 1939	72703-72714	
5-28G	975	AUG. 30, 1939	73157	TERZ, 19 FRETS, FOR GUT STRINGS ONLY, NECK WITH 1 5/8"-2 1/16", NO PICK GUARD
00-28G	120	DEC. 15, 1939	73953-73958	
00-42G	128	DEC. 20, 1939	74010	STANDARD MODEL FOR GUT STRINGS ONLY, NO PICK GUARD

MARTIN "G" MODEL CLASSICAL GUITARS TO 1939

a) In Martin terminology "Orchestra Model" meant the shortened body length usually associated with guitars with 14-fret necks.
b) In this case the OM body shape was combined with a 12-fret neck
c) "0" scale was always 24.9" and "000" scale was always 25.4"
d) "Standard model" always refers to the old 12-fret body shape, regardless of body size

Table 75
Martin "G" Model Classical Guitars to 1939

The early 00-18G and 00-28G guitars originally had X-bracing while later instruments were fan-braced.

Table 75 documents all the gut string guitars made to the end of 1939. The years from 1935 to 1939 define the period during which Martin tinkered with the specifications of their classical guitars. The table also illustrates some other interesting "G" model guitars, including: four 00-21G, three 000-28G (one 12-fret and two 14-fret bodies), three 00-42G, two 00-44G, one 000-45G, a 5-28G and even one D-28G guitar!

The 00-18G and 00-28G guitars remained in production until April 1962 and were replaced by the "C" Series guitars. A few prototype batches of the 00-16C, 00-18C, 00-28C and 000-28C were made prior to April 1962. The "C" Series classical guitars have 19 frets although a few of the prototype batches have 20 fret fingerboards. Both 00-28C and 000-28C guitars were made as prototypes. The 000-28C instruments were made from 1962 until 1966 but were replaced by 00-28C guitars during 1966 (see Table 76).

MARTIN MODEL "C" CLASSICAL GUITARS				
STYLE	SHOP ORDER	DATE STAMPED	SERIAL NUMBER	COMMENTS
00-16C	956	NOV. 8, 1961	180457-180459	19 FRETS
00-16C	100	DEC. 12, 1961	181101-181102	20 FRETS
00-18C	101	DEC. 12, 1961	181104-181106	20 FRETS
00-28C	102	DEC. 19, 1961	181107-181109	20 FRETS
00-18C	151	JAN. 31, 1962	181792-181793	
00-16C	150	JAN. 31, 1962	181794-181795	
000-28C	152	FEB. 6, 1962	181849-181850	

Table 76
Martin Model "C" Classical Guitars

Electric Guitars (1941 to 1967)

Apart from the single 00-18 guitar shipped in 1941 with a factory installed De Armond RHC pick-up, the first Martin electric guitars were the 00-18E, D-18E and D-28E offered in the late 1950's.

The first prototype electric guitar was a D-18E (serial number 163746) stamped on September 22, 1958. The shop order noted: **"West spruce top, special top prepared for De Armond pick-up and control equipment, finish completely and string as usual, electric parts will be installed at De Armond plant in Toledo, Ohio."**

A 00-18E prototype (serial number 165090) was stamped on November 26, 1958, followed by two more D-18E prototypes (serial numbers 166064 and 166065) and two D-28E prototypes (serial numbers 166066 and 166067), all of which were all stamped on January 26, 1959. The shop orders for the two D-18E and two D-28E guitars stated: **"West spruce top, electric model with built-in De Armond microphones (2) and control (4 knobs and 1 toggle switch)"**. Although not noted in the shop order for the 00-18E, this guitar probably had a single pick-up and two knobs.

The sales of the Martin acoustic electric guitars were moderate for 1959 and quite low for the following few years. As a result, the 00-18E, D-18E and D-28E models were dropped in 1964 (see Table 77).

Martin introduced the "F" model thin hollow-body guitars in late 1961 with three models: F-50, F-55 and F-65. The first three of each model were prototypes and were all stamped on September 27, 1961. The specifications for each prototype model is documented below. In general, construction and specifications were similar across the models except for the number

MARTIN ACOUSTIC-ELECTRIC GUITAR PRODUCTION						
YEAR	00-18E	00-18EL	00-18E(S)	D-18E	D-28E	D-28E(S)
1958	1[1]			1[1]		
1959	249			301[2]	176[2]	
1960	100	1				1[3]
1961	50	1				
1962	25	1	1[4]		12	
1963	50				25	
1964	50				24	

Notes: 1) Prototypes
2) Two guitars from this figure were prototypes
3) Single-unit pick-up (MA-3), special pick guards
4) Single cut-away body like F-50, otherwise like 00-18E

Table 77
Production of 00-18E, D-18E and D-28E
Acoustic Electric Guitars

of cutaways, the number of pick-ups and the number of control knobs:

The specifications for the prototype F-50 guitars (serial number 179828 to 179830), prototypes reads: **"1 cutaway, 1 pickup, 2 controls, maple body, arched top and back, F-scrolls, regular pattern, white body bindings like 2-15, mahogany neck, maple head veneer, rosewood fingerboard #18 inlays, (Kluson) K-324 machines, special tailpiece, plexiglass bridge and guard"**.

The three F-55 prototype guitars (serial number 179831 to 179833) were similar to the F-50 model except for an additional pick-up and two more control knob: **"1 cutaway, 2 pickups, 4 controls, maple body, arched top and back, F-scrolls, regular pattern, white body bindings like 2-15, mahogany neck, maple head veneer, rosewood fingerboard #28 inlays, (Kluson) K-324 machines, special tailpiece, plexiglass bridge and guard"**.

The three F-65 prototype guitars (serial numbers 179834 to 179836) were similar to the F-55 model except for a second cutaway: **"2 cutaways, 2 pickups, 4 controls, maple body, arched top and back, F-scrolls, regular pattern, white body bindings line 2-15, mahogany neck, maple head veneer, rosewood fingerboard #28 inlays, (Kluson) K-324 machines, special tailpiece, plexiglass bridge and guard"**.

The first production batch of each model was stamped in November 1961, although full production didn't commence until January 1962. All three models received a sunburst finish. It is not known whether the plexiglass pick guards were used on production guitars as it appears most guitars received black, probably acetate, guards.

From June to August 1965 Martin took orders for electric guitars they referred to as "New Electric", "Rebel" or "Thunderball". These terminologies are quite obscure because the production records at the time make no mention of these models, only appearing in the bookings ledger. It appears from one entry that the "New Electric" was another name for the "Rebel" model. The only other clue provided in the bookings ledger is that the "Thunderball" model came in red and black colors. The Rebel and Thunderball models were priced about the same as the F-50 and F-55 models respectively and, since they appeared near the end of the F-50 and F-55 production run, may have been an attempt by Martin to freshen up that part of the production line by offering colored finishes instead of the usual sunburst finish. Ultimately, this didn't save the F model guitars and they were dropped from production in 1965.

The sales of the F model guitars were fairly good for 1962 but dropped off rapidly thereafter. To reinvigorate sales of electric guitars Martin launched new GT model hollow-body electric guitars in 1965 just as the F models were being retired.

The first prototypes were three XTE-70 (serial numbers 203803 to 203805) and three XTE-75 guitars (serial numbers 204108 to 204110). The XTE-70 guitars were stamped on August 3, 1965 and the XTE-75 models on August 16. Production got underway with a batch of GT-70 guitars stamped on October 11, 1965.

The bookings ledger records that some guitars were ordered with "B" or "V" suffix. The B suffix indicated guitars that got a Bigsby tailpiece installed while the V indicated a regular tailpiece. The V tailpiece was intended to look like an "M" for "Martin" but cut-out of the tailpiece looked so much like a "V" that Martin even used it in their own terminology. The Bigsby tailpieces were castings with a "V" embossed in the casting and highlighted with black ink. Presumably, the orders that appeared without a suffix were also guitars that received a V tailpiece.

The GT-70 and GT-75 guitars were offered in three colors: black, burgundy and red. The numbers made

of the different colors is unknown from the production records but some clues to the scarcity of the colors can be gleaned from the bookings ledger.

Of the 418 GT-70 guitars recorded in the bookings ledger there were 119 plain GT-70 guitars (i.e., presumably with a V tailpiece) and 94 were GT-70V models with a V tailpiece for a total 213 guitars with a V tailpiece. A further 202 GT-70B guitars were mounted with a Bigsby tailpiece. One GT-70G, one GT-70L and one GT-70S are included in the total. It is not known whether the single GT-70G (it had a Bigsby tailpiece) is an error or whether the "G" suffix had some meaning that went unrecorded.

Of the 213 GT-70 and GT-70V guitars ordered, the ledger records 87 burgundy, 70 black and 13 red guitars (for the remaining 43 guitars the color was not recorded).

Assuming the colors recorded are representative of the total for the GT-70 guitars then black finishes made up 51% of the guitars sold, followed by the burgundy finish with 41% and the red finish with 9%.

Of the 202 GT-70B guitars with Bigsby tailpieces 54 were black, 119 were burgundy and 9 were red; respectively 27%, 59% and 4% of the total. Clearly, the red finish is the scarcest for GT-70 guitars, making up about 5% of the total number made.

It is not known why the ledger book only contains sale for 418 of the various GT-70 models while production totaled 453.

Of the 212 GT-75 plain (as with the GT-70 guitars it will be assumed the plain guitars had V tailpieces) and GT-75V guitars recorded the bookings ledger; 66 had a black finish, while 81 were burgundy and 15 were red. The black finishes made up 41% of the total, followed by 50% for the burgundy finish and 9% for the red color, again assuming the recorded colors are representative of the whole production run of GT-75 guitars.

Of the 269 GT-75B guitars; 69 were recorded as black, 147 as burgundy and 6 in the red finish. The black finish made up 31% of the total, the burgundy color accounted for 66% and the red finish only 3% of the total. For 47 of these guitars the finish color was not recorded.

 As with the GT-70 guitars, the red finish is the rarest of the colors offered for the GT-75 model. Collectors might want to keep an eye out for a GT-75B with a red finish as only about 6 to 8 examples were made.

The sales of GT model guitars were good for 1966 but Martin made a decision to exit the electric market during that year since only 100 GT-75 were produced in 1967. This decision was probably made because the factory enjoyed a large increase in acoustic guitar

sales during 1966 relative to 1965. The electric guitar production must have appeared as a distraction to the factory at a time when acoustic guitars had long back orders times.

Table 78 shows the production of Martin electric guitars. Table 79 shows the comparison between production records and orders recorded in the bookings ledger. Table 79 and also records the finish color options for the GT model guitars and the number made in each color for the various sub-models.

MARTIN ELECTRIC GUITAR PRODUCTION															
YEAR	F-50	F-50S	F-50L	F-55	F-65	F-65L	XTE-70	XTE-75	GT-70	GT-70L	GT-70S	GT-75	GT-75L	GT-75R	GT-12-75
1961	15			15	15										
1962	200	1		325	250										
1963	125			125	100	1									
1964	175		2	150	125										
1965			1	5	75		3	3	125	1		75		1	
1966									325	1	1	575	1		1
1967												100[1]			

Note: 1) Four were 12-string guitars

Table 78
Production of F Model and GT Model Electric Guitars

PRODUCTION RECORDS			FIGURES FROM BOOKINGS LEDGER				
MODEL	PROD. QUAN.	DATES	MODEL	ORDER QUAN.	BLACK FINISH	BURGUNDY FINISH	RED FINISH
00-18 with RHC pick-up	1	1941-01-17					
0-18TE, with MA-3 pick-up like 00-18E	1	1959-08-19					
0-18T, SPECIAL WITH MA-3 PICK UP	1	1962-06-05					
00-18E	525	1958-1964	00-18E	794[1]			
00-18EL	3	1960-1962	00-18EL	2			
D-18E	302	1958-1959	D-18E	404[1]			
D-28E	237	1959-1964	D-28E	326[1]			
D-28ES	1	1960	D-28ES	1			
F-50	515	1961-1965	F-50	621[1]			
		1962-1965	F-50B	15			
		1964-1965	F-50L	3			
F-50S	1	1962	F-50S	1			
(Probably similar to F-50)		1965	NEW ELECTRIC	6			
(Probably similar to F-50)		1965	NEW ELECTRIC-B	8			
(Probably similar to F-50)		1965	REBEL	6			
(Probably similar to F-50)		1965	REBEL-B	4			
F-55	620	1961-1965	F-55	744[1]			
		1962-1965	F-55B	289[1]			
(Probably similar to F-55)		1965	THUNDERBALL	5			
(Probably similar to F-55)		1965	THUNDERBALL-B	1			
F-65	540	1961-1965	F-65	463[1]			
		1962-1965	F-65B	272[1]			
F-65L	1	1963	F-65L	1			
GT-70	450[2]	1965-1966	GT-70	119	70	87	13
		1965-1966	GT-70V	94			
		1965-1966	GT-70B	202	54	119	9
GT-70L	2	1965-1966	GT-70L	1		1	
GT-70S	1	1966	GT-70S	1			
GT-75	750[2]	1965-1967	GT-75	109	66	81	15
		1965-1967	GT-75V	103			
		1965-1967	GT-75B	269	69	147	6
GT-75L	1	1966	GT-75L	1			
GT-75R	1	1965	GT-75R	1			
GT-75-12	1	1966	GT-12-75	1			

Notes: 1) The bookings figure is higher than the production figure because a number of guitars were returned and subsequently resold.
2) It Is not known why the production figure is more than the figures from the bookings ledger.

Table 79
Comparison of Production Records and Bookings Ledger for Electric Guitars

1953 Guitars With Ebony T-Bar Neck Reinforcement

Collectors have noticed that some guitars from late 1953 were made with an ebony T-bar neck reinforcement instead of the usual steel T-bar.

Martin was probably forced to temporarily use an ebony bar for neck reinforcement because of a shortage of steel in the market, probably as a lasting result of the 1952 steel strike.

In 1952, the United Steelworkers of America struck U.S. Steel and nine other steelmakers to win a wage increase. The strike was scheduled to begin on April 9, 1952, but President Harry S. Truman, concerned about the effect on the defense industries and the ability to prosecute the Korean War, nationalized the American steel industry hours before the workers walked out. On June 2, 1952 the United States Supreme Court ruled that the president lacked the authority to seize the steel mills. As a result of the court decision the Steelworkers commenced their strike. Although the strike ended on July 24, 1952, the demand for steel production for the high priority defense industries caused shortages in consumer steel products for some time.

Although the strike had been over for a year by the second half of 1953, it was only in October 1953 the shortage of steel T-bars affected Martin's production.

The shortage may also have been caused by a scheduling problem with the steel mill supplying the T-bar. Even today, mills are sometimes reluctant to roll small shapes because it is more productive to manufacture the larger structural shapes. Small structural shapes, those with a low weight per foot, severely limit the tonnage that can be run through the rolling mills for a given amount of time.

The shortage of steel T-bar affected the guitars made on shop orders 910 through 943 (stamped October 22 to November 18, 1953). Guitars with serial numbers 133302 to 133826 were made with the ebony neck reinforcement. Martin replaced the steel T-bar with an ebony T-bar made of two pieces of ebony. Martin's earlier guitars also had an ebony neck reinforcement but this was in the form of a rectangular bar of ebony.

The information on the guitars that received an ebony T-bar comes from Mike Longworth's "logbook" of serial numbers. There is a slight discrepancy between the "stamped dates" recorded in the logbook and the "production record" sheets, so Longworth must have had access to the original shop order slips at one time, although these are not currently in the Martin archive.

At least some of the D-18 and D-28 guitars with the ebony T-bar also have "mystery" spruce tops (i.e., Vermont spruce, a variety of Adirondack). Considering the small number of these D-18 and D-28 guitars made, there is a good chance a substantial portion of this production have Adirondack tops. It is not known if any of the other style 18 and 21 guitars shown in Table 80 were made with Adirondack spruce tops but it is worthwhile keeping an eye open for them.

The lack of steel T-bar only affected guitars for about a month's worth of production and the T-bar were re-introduced again when available.

1953 GUITARS WITH EBONY BAR NECK REINFORCEMENT			
MODEL	SHOP ORDER	DATE STAMPED	SERIAL NUMBERS
0-18	910	OCT. 22, 1953	133302-133326
D-18	911	OCT. 27, 1953	133352-133376
00-17	912	OCT. 26, 1953	133327-133351
00-18	916	OCT. 29, 1953	133377-133401
D-18	919	OCT. 29, 1953	133427-133451
0-15	920	OCT. 29, 1953	133402-133426
0-18	921	OCT. 30, 1953	133452-133476
D-28	922	NOV. 4, 1953	133502-133526
000-18	924	NOV. 4, 1953	133552-133576
00-17	925	NOV. 3, 1953	133477-133501
000-21	928	NOV. 16, 1953	133752-133776
D-18	929	NOV. 5, 1953	133577-133601
D-28	931	NOV. 11, 1953	133652-133676
0-15	936	NOV. 10, 1953	133627-133651
0-18	937	NOV. 12, 1953	133677-133701
D-18	938	NOV. 16, 1953	133727-133751
00-17	943	NOV. 18, 1953	133802-133826

Table 80
1953 Guitars with Ebony T-Bar Neck Reinforcement

1953 and 1957 Guitars with Vermont Spruce Tops

Even the title of this section is certain to stir discussion among Martin aficionados.

For some time Martin guitar collectors have known that some guitars are encountered from 1953 with so-called "mystery tops". Somewhat later, collectors also identified some guitars from 1957 that had tops with a similar type of spruce top. But it was a question whether the tops were Adirondack or Engelmann spruce.

In the fall of 1984 Eric Schoenberg and Dana Bourgeois conducted an interview with C. F. Martin III. Dana Bourgeois went on to write an article entitled "Which Spruce is That?" that appeared in American Lutherie #14 on page 17 (1988). This is the only known source of information from C. F. Martin III himself on the subject of the type of spruce used for guitar tops. Quoted below is a portion of Bourgeois' article:

"I asked Mr. Martin whether the OMs (all of which were built between 1929 and 1932) were built with Appalachian, or with Adirondack spruce. He laughed and said, 'There's no way to know.' Could he shed any light, then on this identification dilemma?

Mr. Martin said that from the time he was a little boy (probably referring to the first decade of this century) until the mid-40s the Martin Company used Red spruce for topwood. His father liked Red spruce, and he liked Red spruce, and they weren't particular about where they got it from as long as the quality was high and the price was right.

Mr. Martin often accompanied his father on trips to different mills to buy lumber. During his lifetime the company bought Red spruce that was cut as far west as Ohio, as far south as Georgia, and "possibly as far north as New Hampshire", but certainly as far north as New York state. He then went on to rattle off in succession, the list of dealers, from year to year, who supplied the Martin company with Red spruce, and the dates that the purchases were made. The list spanned a sixty or seventy year period!

At that point I was wishing that I had a tape recorder. I cannot, of course, remember all the what Mr. Martin told me, but I do remember that there was no pattern whatsoever to Martin's year to year source of supply of Red spruce. One year it might some from New York state, the next year it might come from North Carolina, and the next year from New York and North Carolina. Furthermore, he didn't use the term Appalachian or Adirondack, and he doubted if there was a difference in appearance between Red spruce grown in one area and

Red spruce grown in another area. That is why, when asked whether Appalachian or Adirondack spruce was used on the OMs, Mr. Martin said there was no way to know.

One footnote that I do remember distinctly is that Mr. Martin said that in '52 or '53 the Martin Company bought a large supply of Engelmann Spruce in the form of government surplus building material. Though he preferred Red Spruce, it was no longer available after the mid-40s because all of the large stands had been harvested. Mr. Martin would have liked to switch from Sitka to Engelmann because he felt that Engelmann was closer to Red Spruce than Sitka was. He could not, however, find anyone who was cutting Engelmann commercially so they went back to Sitka Spruce.

This nugget of information caught my attention because for many years I have owned a '53 D-28. I have always puzzled over the rich color of the top. I have seen a few other '53 Martins with similar looking tops. I have also seen a few Martins from that year on various dealers price lists labeled as having tops made of "Appalachian" or "Adirondack" spruce."

The problem is that the Martin archival material conflicts with a number of points in Bourgeois' article. The following discussion is not criticism of C. F. Martin's remembrances or Bourgeois' notes, written several years after the interview, because much of the other information in the article is verifiable. The archival material, especially the purchasing records and yearly inventories, provide much detail on the spruce purchases and the spruce tops in inventory and will be used to point out where the records don't agree with Mr. Martin's memories.

Table 81 documents all the spruce purchases Martin made between late 1941 and mid-1961; showing the source, description of the purchase and the type of spruce. The descriptions of the spruce orders is exactly as shown in the Martin purchasing records. The type of spruce indicated is based on the source. For instance, Posey Manufacturing Co, located in Hoquiam, Washington always sold Martin Sitka spruce and Martin referred to the spruce bought from Eaton Lumber Co., located in Rochester, Vermont as "Vermont spruce". As this chapter is concerned most with

SPRUCE PURCHASES 1941 TO 1951			
DATE	SOURCE	DESCRIPTION	TYPE
Jan. 10, 1941	Acme Veneer & Lumber Co.	3/16" sawn spruce	Adirondack
Feb. 18, 1941	Acme Veneer & Lumber Co.	3/16" spruce	Adirondack
Apr. 24, 1941	Posey Manufacturing Co.	5/4 rib spruce 2,076 ft.	Sitka
June 3, 1941	Breckwoldt & Son	3/16" spruce	Adirondack
Oct. 14, 1941	Acme Veneer & Lumber Co.	5,489' sawn spruce 3/16"	Adirondack
Dec. 13, 1941	Breckwoldt & Son	3/16" spruce veneer	Adirondack
May 20, 1942	Posey Manufacturing Co.	Rib spruce & guitar tops	Sitka
Dec. 15, 1943	Posey Manufacturing Co.	5/4" rib stock spruce	Sitka
Apr. 12, 1944	Posey Manufacturing Co.	1,000 pairs spruce tops 3/16"	Sitka
Sept. 18, 1944	Posey Manufacturing Co.	1,000 pairs spruce tops 3/16"	Sitka
Nov. 14, 1944	Blair Veneer Co.	10 guitar top blanks spruce	?
Feb. 28, 1945	Posey Manufacturing Co.	504 pcs spruce guitar tops	Sitka
July 25, 1945	Posey Manufacturing Co.	2390' spruce 5/4"	Sitka
Oct. 5, 1945	Posey Manufacturing Co.	1,100 pairs spruce guitar tops	Sitka
Dec. 12, 1945	Posey Manufacturing Co.	3,900 pcs guitar spruce	Sitka
June 7, 1946	North Hudson E. Co.	232' guitar tops spruce 3/16"	Adirondack?
Aug. 20, 1946	North Hudson E. Co.	680' guitar tops spruce 3/16"	Adirondack?
Sept. 24, 1946	Posey Manufacturing Co.	1,500 pairs spruce guitar tops	Sitka
Jan. 7, 1947	Posey Manufacturing Co.	1,000 pairs spruce mandolin tops	Sitka
Apr. 3, 1947	Posey Manufacturing Co.	Spruce tops & rib stock	Sitka
Aug. 5, 1947	North H. W. Corp.	956' 3/16" spruce	Sitka?
Aug. 25, 1947	Posey Manufacturing Co.	2,956 pcs spruce guitar tops	Sitka
Dec. 9, 1947	Posey Manufacturing Co.	Spruce 5/4" & 3/16" pairs	Sitka
July 19, 1948	Posey Manufacturing Co.	3,250 pcs spruce guitar tops	Sitka
Sept. 21, 1948	Posey Manufacturing Co.	3,400 pairs guitar top spruce	Sitka
Apr. 26, 1949	Posey Manufacturing Co.	4,000 pcs spruce guitar tops	Sitka
Nov. 8, 1949	Eaton Lumber Co. (Rochester VT)	2247' 1-3/8" I. S. spruce	Vermont
May 31, 1950	Posey Manufacturing Co.	3,052' Sitka rib spruce	Sitka
Nov. 13, 1950	Eaton Lumber Co. (Rochester VT)	5,135' sawn spruce 1-3/8"	Vermont
Mar. 19, 1951	Eaton Lumber Co. (Rochester VT)	Spruce veneer	Vermont

SPRUCE PURCHASES 1952 TO 1961			
DATE	SOURCE	DESCRIPTION	TYPE
Jan. 14, 1952	Eaton Lumber Co. (Rochester VT)	1-3/8" spruce	Vermont
Dec. 5, 1952	Posey Manufacturing Co.	Spruce tops & rib stock	Sitka
May 8, 1953	Posey Manufacturing Co.	3,000 pairs spruce guitar tops	Sitka
Nov. 4, 1953	Posey Manufacturing Co.	Spruce 3/16" & 5/4"	Sitka
Feb. 19, 1954	Posey Manufacturing Co.	3,000 pairs spruce guitar tops	Sitka
Sept. 24, 1954	Posey Manufacturing Co.	Sundry spruce	Sitka
Mar. 22, 1955	Kockman & Stohr	25 spruce guitar tops	?
May 12, 1955	Posey Manufacturing Co.	Guitar tops	Sitka
Sept. 2, 1955	Posey Manufacturing Co.	Spruce tops & ribstock	Sitka
Nov. 15, 1955	Eaton Lumber Co. (Rochester VT)	2,420' spruce 1-3/8"	Vermont
Mar. 28, 1956	Posey Manufacturing Co.	2,396 pcs spruce guitar tops	Sitka
Aug. 27, 1956	Posey Manufacturing Co.	Posey spruce (rib stock & tops)	Sitka
Feb. 15, 1957	J. H. Monteath Co.	5,786' spruce 5/32"	Sitka?
June 3, 1957	J. H. Monteath Co.	3,440' Sitka spruce 5/32"	Sitka
June 28, 1957	Worldwide Musical Instrument Co.	Wood for instruments	German
Aug. 16, 1957	Posey Manufacturing Co.	Sitka spruce violin rib stock	Sitka
Aug. 30, 1957	J. H. Monteath Co.	Spruce veneer	?
May 19, 1958	Posey Manufacturing Co.	Lumber of designated sizes	Sitka
July 9, 1958	Worldwide Musical Instrument Co.	Spruce guitar tops	German
Sept. 5, 1958	Worldwide Musical Instrument Co.	Guitar tops	German
Dec. 30, 1958	Posey Manufacturing Co.	Sitka spruce	Sitka
June 18, 1959	Posey Manufacturing Co.	Sitka spruce violin rib stock	Sitka
Sept. 15, 1959	Worldwide Musical Instrument Co.	Guitar tops (spruce)	German
Apr. 20, 1960	Posey Manufacturing Co.	Sitka spruce stock	Sitka
July 6, 1960	Worldwide Musical Instrument Co.	Guitar tops (spruce)	German
Oct. 6, 1960	Worldwide Musical Instrument Co.	Guitar tops (spruce)	German
Oct. 21, 1960	Posey Manufacturing Co.	Sitka spruce guitar tops	Sitka
Mar. 17, 1961	Posey Manufacturing Co.	Sitka spruce	Sitka
June 15, 1961	Worldwide Musical Instrument Co.	Guitar tops	German
June 28, 1961	Worldwide Musical Instrument Co.	Guitar tops	German

Notes:

1) The purchase from Acme Veneer & Lumber Co. on October 14, 1941 for 5,489 ft. of 3/16" spruce was the largest order for spruce that Martin had made to that date, almost twice as big as any previous order. It appears that the supply of Adirondack spruce was tightening and Martin decided to stock up whike they could and added another, much smaller, order from Breckwoldt on December 13, 1941. Acme always supplied Adirondack spruce.

2) The last pre-war purchase of Adirondack spruce occurred in December 1941.

3) From mid-1942 to early 1949 only Sitka spruce was purchased by Martin, with the exception of a couple of small orders that could be Adirondack spruce.

4) No information could be found on the North Hudson E. Co. It is not known if they supplied Adirondack spruce or not.

5) The Eaton Lumber Co. was located in Rochester VT and supplied "Vermont" spruce.

6) The late 1955 purchase from the Eaton Lumber Co. is the source of Adirondack spruce used on guitars from late 1956 to mid-1957.

7) The source of German spruce in use from mid-1957 was Worldwide Musical Instrument Co.

8) 1-3/8" spruce was always re-sawn to 3/16" for guitar tops

Table 81
Martin Guitar Co. Spruce Purchases from 1941 to 1961

the Vermont spruce used on 1953 and 1957 guitars these orders are shown in red print.

The other source documents to be considered are the yearly inventories that were held at the beginning of January each year (see Table 82). Martin purchased Adirondack spruce until late 1941 and this spruce was sufficient to last until about 1945. After 1942 Martin purchased Sitka spruce exclusively until 1949.

In late 1949 Martin was able to buy some Vermont spruce (a variety of red spruce) from Eaton Lumber Co. of Rochester, Vermont. Further purchases were made in late 1950, early 1951 and early 1953. Martin must have thought highly of this type of spruce because they started to differentiate the types of spruce in the inventory of January 1950, something they had never done previously. The description of the spruce in inventory is as it appear in the records. Martin referred to Sitka spruce as "West" and Vermont spruce

as "East". The Vermont spruce is shown in red lettering in Table 82.

Much interesting information can be deduced from the purchasing and inventory records.

1. Based on examination of the purchasing records and inventory records, it appears Martin seasoned their spruce for about 12 to 18 months.
2. The first Vermont spruce was bought in November 1949 and must have been processed into tops very quickly as 1,600 East tops appeared in the 1950 inventory. The Vermont spruce can be assumed to be un-seasoned but why then were there 136 joined tops of East spruce in the inventory. Was it Martin's practice to join tops of unseasoned wood?
3. Martin bought some more Vermont spruce in November 1950 which was also processed quickly and accounts for the spike in the number of

YEARLY INVENTORY OF GUITAR TOPS AND BRACE STOCK	Jan. 1948	Jan. 1949	Jan. 1950	Jan. 1951	Jan. 1952	Jan. 1953	Jan. 1954	Jan. 1955	Jan. 1956	Jan. 1957	Jan. 1958	Jan. 1959	Jan. 1960	Jan. 1961	Jan. 1962
5/4" Brace stock	4,900 ft	2,500 ft	1,705 ft												
5/4" Brace stock, Western				1,933 ft	405 ft	1,986 ft	2,400 ft	2,169 ft	1,969 ft	1,767 ft	1,773 ft	1,136 ft	872 ft	707 ft	868 ft
5/4" Brace stock, East				1,100 ft	1,200 ft	510 ft									
Braces, all kinds	9,500 ft	5,150 ft	4,800 ft	8,500 ft	8,100 ft	8,800 ft	7,240 ft	6,970 ft	5,985 ft	5,311 ft	7,550 ft	7,200 ft	11,250 ft	5,556 ft	7,778 ft
Guitar tops, 1/8"	5,758	8,624													
Guitar tops, 1/8" Western			9,811	5,100	2,230	2,050	5,306	4,675	4,304	6,369	4,511	3,376	3,293	4,135	2,750
Guitar tops, 1/8" East			1,600	3,400	1,445	2,622				1,982					
Guitar tops, 1/8" German												1,012	491	996	
Guitar tops, 1"	614	606	607	607	607	603	602	600	600	600	600	599	411	581	391
Guitar tops, #5 Eastern						187									
Guitar tops, 1/8" joined	1,031	550													
Guitar tops, 1/8" joined Western			1,428	1,697	785		802	525	1,535						
Guitar tops, 1/8" joined East			136	130	458				120						
Guitar tops, 1/8" joined East and West										869	390	1,427	95	67	300
Guitar tops, 1/8" joined #5 East							125	183							
Guitar tops, 1/8" joined #5 German															445
Guitar tops inlaid #18	323	786	551	445	990		333	722	533	125	1,058	1,130	1,282	1,538	2,004
Guitar tops braced #18				75	25		50	100	75		150	100	100	75	75
Guitar tops inlaid #18 Western						166									
Guitar tops inlaid #18 Eastern						575									
Guitar tops inlaid #21	12	149	85	51	74		52	167	77	6	20	5		27	170
Guitar tops inlaid #21 Western						46									
Guitar tops inlaid #28	36	308	391	190	95		282	230	339	522	748	316		313	690
Guitar tops inlaid #28 Western						47							288		
Guitar tops inlaid #28 Eastern						196									
Guitar tops braced #28				25			25	25	25	25	25	25	50		50
Guitar tops braced #42	12	11	10	10	10	9	9	9	9	9	9	9	9	9	5

Table 82
Yearly Inventories of Guitar Tops and Brace Stock from 1948 to 1962

Vermont spruce tops in the January 1951 inventory. The quantity of joined tops were lower than the previous year so probably not many of the November 1950 tops were joined from unseasoned wood. The November 1950 order was for about twice the amount of the 1949 order.

4. Martin purchased a small quantity of Vermont spruce, about a quarter of the amount of the 1949 order, in March 1951. This probably didn't have much of an impact on the 1952 inventory. Interestingly, the number of tops dropped significantly between 1951 and 1952. As the 1949 and 1950 Vermont spruce would have been seasoned by late 1951 and it appears that almost 2,000 tops were used by January 1952. (author's note: I am not aware of any 1952 guitars with red spruce tops but they should be out there, something for collectors to watch for). The number of joined tops was higher in the 1952 inventory but in this case the wood was probably seasoned.

5. The early 1952 purchase of Vermont spruce was about the same size as the November 1950 order. This spruce was processed during 1952 and appears in the January 1953 inventory. By this time most of the seasoned wood from the previous three purchases had probably been used up. Where are 1952 guitars with red spruce tops?

6. The 1953 inventory showed 2,622 East spruce tops in stock and Martin also noted a number of joined and inlaid style 18 and 28 tops in stock.

7. All of the Vermont spruce had been used up by January 1954. The only exception were the 187 tops that were only big enough for size 5 guitars.

8. Martin made one last purchase of Vermont spruce in November 1955 (about 2/3 the size of the 1952 order) and, true to past practice, this wood was processed quickly and appeared in the January 1956 inventory. As with point 2 above, 120 joined tops are included in the inventory that can only have been made from unseasoned spruce.

9. In the inventories of 1957 to 1962 Martin created a new inventory category that included a mixture both East and West joined tops. The East spruce tops suitable for Dreadnought guitars had already been used up by mid-1957. However, the processing of the Vermont spruce resulted in a number of tops not wide enough for Dreadnought guitars, these tops being used on progressively smaller guitars from 1958 to 1961 with the final Vermont spruce appearing on mandolins in 1962. The increase in 165 East spruce tops in the January 1960 appears to be a circumstance of "found" stock, as it was recorded with a negative value.

10. By the January 1963 inventory all of the East spruce was gone from stock.

11. The first German spruce tops were purchased in 1957 and first appeared in the January 1958 inventory. The German spruce must have been

purchased in the pre-seasoned condition as it was first used within a month of being received. The German spruce tops were worth about four times as much as a Sitka top.

Conclusions

One of C. F. Martin III's statements was that there was "no way to know" the source of the spruce used for guitar tops. However, Table 81 clearly indicates that Martin was using a very small number of suppliers during the time in question. Even the sources for spruce in the 1930's were remarkably stable with Acme Veneer and Breckwoldt & Son supplying Adirondack spruce and Posey Manufacturing supplying all of the Sitka spruce, mostly in the form of brace stock.

Mr. Martin mentioned in Bourgeois' article that in 1952 or 1953 the Martin Company bought a large supply of Engelmann Spruce in the form of government surplus building material. The November 1950 and January 1952 orders of Vermont spruce were large for the time, although not much larger than some contemporary order for Sitka spruce. The term "surplus" implies that the unit cost of an item is lower than the regular price. This is not the case for the Vermont spruce as Vermont spruce tops were valued 40% to 50% higher than Sitka spruce tops in the 1950 to 1953 inventories. It appears that Martin saw an opportunity to buy a type of spruce they preferred and bought as much as they could, even though the price per top was higher.

Why Mr. Martin thought the company bought surplus Engelmann spruce is a moot point because the records only mention Vermont spruce or Sitka spruce during the 1952 and 1953 time frame. It is possible that Posey Manufacturing supplied some Engelmann spruce with their Sitka spruce but it was never differentiated as such. Besides, none of the contemporary purchases of Sitka spruce can be construed as large orders of surplus material. It might also be suggested that a special purchase of surplus Engelmann spruce might not have appeared in the yearly inventories. Considering that Martin was fastidious in its record keeping, this seems a diminishing small possibility.

This section has been careful to record the types of spruce as they appeared in the records but, in the end,

Vermont spruce is really just a variety of red spruce and indistinguishable from the other sub-varieties of red spruce, including Adirondack spruce.

Re-Issue of 12-Fret Dreadnought Guitars (1960-1966)

One topic of considerable interest to fans of 1950's and 1960's Martin guitars is when Martin began to re-issue Dreadnought guitars with 12-fret bodies. The last pre-WW II Martin Dreadnought guitar with a 12-fret body had been a 1939 D-28S (serial number 72422).

Martin made a number of D-28S guitars in the period from 1949 to 1960 (see Table 83). Previously, it had been thought that some of these might have had the old 12-fret bodies. However, that does not appear to be the case. The "special" feature during this period usually referred to a special neck inlay or special pick guard(s) although details on the "special" feature are missing in a few cases.

The first re-issued 12-fret Dreadnought guitar was made in 1960 and small quantities were made through 1966, as shown in Table 84. The E. U. Wurlitzer D-28SW and D-35SW guitars are included in the table for completeness.

Demand was increasing for the larger body guitars and in 1967 the 12-fret Dreadnought guitars were added to the product line, being offered in D-18S, D-28S and D-35S models.

SPECIAL ORDER DREADNOUGHT GUITARS FROM 1949 TO 1960

STYLE	SHOP ORDER	DATE STAMPED	SERIAL NUMBER	COMMENTS
D-28S	821	June 20, 1949	110160	Special
D-28S	8	Nov. 23, 1949	112435	Special
D-28S	208	July 1, 1954	137966	Special, 14 fret
D-28S	631	June 6, 1955	143977	Special
D-28S	631	June 6, 1955	143978	One inlaid "JIMMIE WALKER "on fingerboard
D-28S?			*	Special pick guard (booked Oct. 10, 1955)
D-28S?			*	Special (booked OCT. 13, 1955)
D-28S?			*	With extra pick guard (booked Nov. 17, 1955)
D-28S?			*	Special fingerboard inlaid "TEX MAGEE" (booked Dec. 8. 1955)
D-28S	843	Feb. 6, 1956	147931	Special, may be the special booked Dec. 5, 1955
D-28S?			*	Special guard (booked July 31, 1956)
D-28S?			*	Special (booked Mar. 11, 1957)
D-28S	395	Aug. 14, 1957	156748	Mahogany top, 00-17 rosette, does not appear in bookings ledger
D-28S?	615	Feb. 21, 1958	160927	Special, double chard (booked Feb. 28, 1958)
D-28S?			*	Special guard (booked Sept. 26, 1958)
D-28S?			*	Special guard (booked Oct. 15, 1958)
D-28S?	865	Oct. 27, 1958	165182	Dark top & extra guard (booked Dec. 17, 1958)
D-28S?	959	Jan. 28, 1959	166513	Special guard, does not appear in the bookings ledger
D-28S?			*	Over size pick guard (booked Apr. 3, 1959)
D-28S?			*	With large pick guard (booked Apr. 7, 1959)
D-28S?	76	May 26, 1959	168550	Gold plated keys, special fingerboard inlaid "JACK GRAY" (booked Aug. 10, 1959)
D-28S?	201	Sept. 29, 1959	170376	2 Special guards, does not appear in bookings ledger
D-28S?			*	With letters "JIM" on pick guard (booked Feb. 2, 1960)
D-28S?	248?		171113?	Special pick guard (booked Feb. 10, 1960)
D-28S?	405	Mar. 29, 1960	173385	Special pearl inlays ("JOAN") in fingerboard (booked June 22, 1960)

*These special guitars were booked but it appears regular guitars were taken off the line to make these, and are probably not stamped D-28S.

Table 83
Special Order Dreadnought Guitars Made Between 1949 and 1960

12-FRET DREADNOUGHT GUITARS FROM 1960 TO 1966

STYLE	SHOP ORDER	DATE STAMPED	SERIAL NUMBER	COMMENTS
D-28S	595	Nov. 9, 1960	175091	Special, 12-fret body, slotted head, neck and fingerboard like 00-28G, wide and flat (booked Nov. 2, 1960 McMurray Music)
D-28GS	912	Sept. 12, 1961	179677	Special, 12-fret body, bindings & inlay like D-21, neck like 00-28G, ebony fingerboard, flat side dots only, loop bridge, no pick guard, Sotted peg head, (booked Aug. 25, 1961)
D-28S	953	Oct. 9, 1961	180204	Special, 12-fret neck, neck like 00-21, no position marks, only side dots, no pick guard, Coast Wholesale (booked Oct. 9, 1961)
D-28S	148	Feb. 6, 1962	181847	Old style, 12-fret neck, no pick guard (booked Jan. 8, 1962) Eddie Bell Guitar-owned by Dick Rosmint
D-28S	148	Feb. 6, 1962	181848	Old style, 12- fret neck, no pick guard (booked Jan. 18, 1962) Folklore Center-owned by Peter Yarrow
D-28S	263	June 5,1962	183267	Special, standard model, 000 scale, bracing like regular D-28, solid head, 12-fret neck, G-102C machines, Cyrus Faryar (booked Apr. 19, 1962)
D-28SW	331	July 19, 1962	184396-184397	Standard model, 12-fret neck, slotted head, FLT lacquer (booked June 5, 1962)
D-28SW	534	Jan. 4, 1963	187435-187438	Four D-28SW guitars (booked July 30, 1962)
D-28SW	894	Nov. 12, 1963	192595-192598	Four D-28SW guitars (booked Apr. 9, 1963), 192598 left-handed
D-28SW	192	Apr. 10, 1964	194917-194919	Three D-28SW guitars (booked Oct. 10, 1963)-mixed solid & slotted heads?, three ordered but six delivered on two shop orders
D-28SW	193	Apr. 10, 1964	194920-194922	Three D-28SW guitars (booked Oct. 10, 1963)-mixed solid & slotted heads?, three ordered but six delivered on two shop orders
D-28SW	273	June 15, 1964	196049-196053	Six D-28SW guitars (booked Feb. 19, 1964), only five delivered
D-28SW	534	Feb. 15, 1965	200473-200475	Three D-28SW guitars (booked Nov. 9, 1964)
D-28S	404	Feb. 1, 1965	200204-200221	Twelve D-28S guitars (booked NOV. 10, 1964), 18 delivered
D-28S	806	Sept. 20, 1965	204696	Two D-28S guitars (booked Nov. 11, 1964)-only one delivered?
D-28S	807	Sept. 20, 1965	204697	One D-28S guitar (booked Nov. 11, 1964)
D-28S			*	Three D-28S (booked Mar. 24, 1965), order cancelled?
D-28S	174	Feb. 17, 1966	208281	(Booked July 26, 1965)
D-28S			*	12-fret neck, no position dots (booked Aug. 23, 1965), order cancelled?
D-28S			*	12-fret neck, 00-21 fingerboard, regular dots & pick guard, folk strings (Feb. 14, 1966), order cancelled
D-28S	535	Nov. 4, 1966	215428-215431	4 guitars, DD body, 00-21 fingerboard, solid head, 102-C machines, regular pick guard (booked Aug. 15. 1966)
D-28S	631	Dec. 27-1966	217013-217014	Two guitars (booked Dec. 15, 1966)

Table 84
12-Fret Dreadnought Guitars Made Between 1960 and 1966

E. U. Wurlitzer D-28SW and D-35SW Guitars (1962-1968)

In 1962 Martin made two special-order 12-fret D-28 guitars for E. U. Wurlitzer Inc. of Boston, Mass. Martin designated these guitars D-28SW; "S" because they were special order guitars and "W" for Wurlitzer. Wurlitzer continued to buy D-28SW guitars until early 1968, sometimes with slotted heads and sometimes with solid head stocks (see Table 85). These guitars should all be stamped "D-28SW" although one is reported as having a stamp of "D-28S" only.

Wurlitzer also bought a small number of D-35SW in 1966 and 1967 (see Table 86).

A total of thirty D-28SW and six D-35SW guitars were made between 1962 and 1968.

E. U. Wurlitzer Inc. was not a branch of Rudolph Wurlitzer Co.

STYLE	SHOP ORDER	DATE STAMPED	SERIAL NUMBER	QUAN	COMMENTS
			E. U. WURLITZER D-28SW GUITARS		
D-28SW	331	July 19, 1962	184396-184397	2	(Booked June 5, 1962 as special, old style, 12-fret neck, flat lacquer) Shop order specified "Standard model, 12-fret neck, slotted head, width like 00-21, steel bar, pickguard, flat lacquer, regular 28 position dots". These guitars had Sitka spruce tops and WG-31 machines.
D-28SW	534	Jan. 4, 1963	187435-187438	4	Slotted head stock
D-28SW	894	Nov. 12, 1963	192595-192598	4	Slotted head stock, 192598 left-handed
D-28SW	192	Apr. 10, 1964	194917-194919	3	Slotted head stock
D-28SW	193	Apr. 10, 1964	194920-194922	3	Solid head stock
D-28SW	273	June 15, 1964	196049-196053	5	Slotted head stock, 196052 stamped "D-28S"
D-28SW	534	Feb. 15, 1965	200473-200475	3	Solid head stock
D-28SW	577	Jan. 22, 1968	232925-232930	6	Slotted head stock

Table 85
E. U. Wurlitzer Co. D-28SW Guitars

STYLE	SHOP ORDER	DATE STAMPED	SERIAL NUMBER	QUAN
		E. U. WURLITZER D-35SW GUITARS		
D-35SW	297	June 6, 1966	211292-211294	3
D-35SW	511	Dec. 1, 1967	230283-230285	3

Table 86
E. U. Wurlitzer Co. D-35SW Guitars

Chapter 14
TECHNICAL INFORMATION

Advertising Material

Through the years Martin used a variety of methods for advertising their business. The archival records are very detailed from 1901 to 1964, although suppliers were rarely mentioned in the 1901 to 1930 records.

Advertising

Martin regularly advertised in a number of publications at certain times. The most prominent publications were Music Trades Review (1927 to 1961) and Piano Trade Magazine (1935 to 1961). Martin also advertised in the American Music Journal (1906), Canadian Music Trades (1908), Crescendo (1922 to 1925), Frets (1925), Music Merchandise (1933 and 1934), Metronome Piano Co. (1934 and 1935), Musical Merchandise Review (1960 and 1961) and Sing Out (1961).

Banners

Between 1929 and 1940 Martin distributed velvet banners to their dealers for window advertising. Most of the banners were 15" X 20" although some smaller sized banners were made in 1930.

A total of about 1,750 of the large format banners and 104 of the smaller banners were made.

Figure 274
1934 Lyon & Healy Window Display of Martin Guitars Showing Banners and Ukulele Signs
Banners are shown on either side of the display. The brass ukulele sign is at the lower left and the brass guitar sign is mostly hidden by the Martin sign near the middle of the photograph.

Figure 275
Detail of Martin Guitar Co. Banner

Figure 277
Detail of Martin String Cabinets Made by Biolite Inc.

Signs

From 1922 to 1930 Martin bought a number of brass guitar and ukulele signs. The signs were 2-1/2" tall by 9-1/2" wide. About 1,250 guitar and 900 ukulele signs were made altogether.

Figure 278
Brass Martin Ukulele Sign

Calendars

Throughout the 20th century one common and inexpensive way to advertise business was through the use of advertising calendars. However, Martin only participated in this form of advertising once, when they bought 300 calendars in late 1904, obviously for 1905. They were good value for money at a cost of only $0.05 each!

Figure 276
C. F. Martin Silk Banner from the 1960's

Biolite Inc. String Cabinets

Martin received a number of Biolite "bubbler" advertising signs on May 5 and June 29, 1937. The number of the Biolite signs bought is unknown but was probably somewhere between 30 and 50 units.

Catalogs

The illustrations for Martin catalogs were printed using wood cuts, half-tone cuts or copper engravings.

1896 Mandolin Catalog

Martin's first catalog was made to promote mandolins that had only recently been added to the product line. The catalogs were printed by Livermore & Knight Co. of Providence, Rhode Island. A total of 2,000 catalogs were shipped on April 18, 1896.

1898 Guitar & Mandolin Catalog

Martin ordered a new 30 page catalog in 1898 illustrating both guitars and mandolins, printed by William J. Schaufele, 102 Hudson St. , New York. It is not known how many were printed but, based on the cost of the order, about 5,000 were made.

1901 Catalog

Catalog of 24 pages made by an unknown printer. A total of 10,000 catalogs were shipped on March 4, 1901

1904 Catalog

A 30 page catalog printed by The Index Press, Pen Argyl PA. Although the catalog is dated in 1904, the 3,800 catalogs weren't delivered until June 15, 1905.

1909 Catalog

The 34 page 1909 catalogs were printed by a company called C. M. Smith. The quantity of catalogs printed were not recorded but, assuming the unit price for the 1904 and 1909 were the same, the quantity was probably about 2,500.

1911 Descriptive Price List

Martin ordered 4,000 non-illustrated 4 page descriptive price lists from the Pen Argyl Index in August 1911.

1911 Mystery Brochure

The Martin archive has a simple three-fold brochure of guitars, with a typewritten date of 1911, that doesn't appear in the purchasing records. The style 45 guitar illustrated has an ivory bridge which dates it to pre-1917 but style 17 guitars are not mentioned nor are 000-size instruments, which would suggest the brochure was made earlier.

1913 "Soloist" Guitar

Although it is well known that style 44 guitars never appeared in a Martin catalog, Martin did order a cut for a "Soloist" guitar on August 1913 and ordered 6 photographs of the same in October 1913. It is not known if these were used for any advertising.

1915 Catalog

In 1915 Martin produced 4,000 catalogs using half-tone cuts for their recently launched flat back mandolins.

During late 1916 Martin ordered a number of new mandolin, ukulele and guitar half-tone cuts and electrotypes for use in their 1917 catalogues.

1917 Ukulele Folder

Martin received 2,000 six-page ukulele folders on March 17, 1917. Another 2,000 were received on August 16, 1917 and a third shipment of 10,000 on August 23. The printer of these folders is unknown.

1917 Catalog

In 1917 Martin produced a new catalog for both guitars and mandolins. The illustrations were copper engravings. A total 3,500 catalogs were delivered in November 1917 and another order followed in February 1918.

1918 Folders

On February 6, 1918, along with second shipment of 3,500 copies of the 1917 catalog mentioned above, Martin received 18,900 "flat mandolin folders with 21 imprints", 16,900 "Italian mandolin (i.e., bowl back mandolins) folders with 19 imprints", 22,700 "guitar folders with 24 imprints" and another 6,000 folders of no description. The Martin does not have a copy of any of these so it is not known what they looked like.

Based on the unit price these folders were probably flyers or circulars.

1919/1920 Catalog

The 1920 catalog was dated October 13, 1919 The Martin updated their catalog in 1920 to include ukuleles with 5,000 being delivered on December 31, 1919 and another 2,000 on May 19, 1921. A number of new half-tone engravings for mandolas and guitars had been made during 1919 in the expectation of the new catalog and the 0-45 guitar half-tone was retouched, probably to show an ebony bridge instead of an ivory bridge. It is not known who printed this 20 page catalog.

This catalog can be viewed on-line at Acoustic Music. org:

https://acousticmusic.org/wp-content/uploads/2016/02/Martin-1919-Catalog.pdf

1923 Catalog

In 1923 Martin prepared 21 new half-tone engravings for an updated catalog. Martin received 10,000 copies of the new 47 page catalog in April 1923. These catalogs were in a 5" X 8" format and were printed by Graphic Sales Co.

This catalog can be viewed on-line at Acoustic Music. org:

https://acousticmusic.org/wp-content/uploads/2016/02/Martin-1924-Catalog.pdf

No catalogs were printed in 1924.

1925 Catalog

Martin received another 10,000 catalogs in September 1925. These were the same as the 1923 catalog except that the last three pages were deleted, resulting in catalog of 44 pages.

1926 Brochure

Martin printed a small two-fold brochure made for advertising their Hawaiian guitars but for this doesn't appear in the purchasing records. The copy of the 1926 brochure has a typewritten date of May 1926 so maybe the 5,000 price lists delivered on June 16, 1926.

1927 Booklet

Martin received 10,000 "booklets" on October 3, 1927 but it is not known what these looked like as there is no copy in the Martin archive.

1928 Folders

On April 17, 1928 Martin received 10,100 Hawaiian guitar six-page folders and 10,500 00-40H guitar "slips". The Martin archive doesn't have copies of either of these. A further 5,000 ukuleles folders were received on April 24, 1928. On May 11, 1928 a further 10,100 Hawaiian guitar folders were received but these were priced at half as much as the April 17 delivery so may have been something different.

1929 Small Catalog

Martin received 9,906 "small catalogues" on January 19, 1929. However, it cost was about one-half of earlier catalogs so may have a simplified format. Another 10,000 catalogs, printed by Hobson, were received on March 15, 1929 but was slightly lower cost so may have differed from the "small catalog".

1930 Booklet

A delivery of 10,164 booklets was delivered by Hobson on January 18, 1930. Price was slightly higher that the 10,000 catalogs delivered by Hobson on March 15, 1929 so may not be exactly the same.

1930 Catalog

Martin received 32,005 catalogs of 31 pages on December 10, 1930. These catalogs were printed by Franklin Press Co. and was the first catalog that featured OM guitars.

This catalog can be viewed on-line at Acoustic Music. org:

https://acousticmusic.org/wp-content/uploads/2016/02/Martin-1930-Catalog-Oct.pdf

1932 Catalog

Franklin Press Co. delivered "catalogs" to Martin on April 8, 1932. These "catalogs" may be the one-fold brochure in the Martin archive that advertised their new C model carved-top guitars. The number of catalogs printed was not recorded.

1934 Catalog

The 1934 catalog was printed by Mack Printing Co. and was delivered on March 17, 1934. The number of pages in the catalog and the quantity printed is not known.

1935 Catalog

Mack Printing Co. delivered another shipment of catalogs, noted as "1935 catalog" in the purchasing records, on July 29, 1935. These catalogs had 32 pages and were probably similar to the 1934 catalog.

This catalog can be viewed on-line at Acoustic Music. org:

https://acousticmusic.org/wp-content/uploads/2016/02/Martin-1935-Catalog.pdf

1936 Catalog

Mack Printing Co. delivered 20,000 catalogs on July 31, 1936. The Martin archive does not contain a copy of this catalog.

1937 Catalog

This catalog can be viewed on-line at Acoustic Music. org:

https://acousticmusic.org/wp-content/uploads/2016/02/Martin-1937-Catalog.pdf

The catalog has 32 pages and is dated July 1937. The expense ledgers do not indicate any catalogs were received in 1937 so the question must be asked whether this could be the 1936 catalog but incorrectly dated.

1938 Catalog

For the 1938 catalog Martin returned to Franklin

Press Co. who delivered catalogues on August 12, 1938. The size of the catalog and the quantity printed is not known but was probably at least 10,000 copies.

1939 Catalog

The 1939 catalog was printed by Kutztown Printing Co. A total of 20,000 catalogs was delivered on August 7, 1939.

1940 Catalog

Kutztown Publishing Co. printed and delivered 18,000 catalogs on July 27, 1940. The value of this order was similar to the 1941 catalog, so probably had 16 pages.

1941 Catalog

This probably the most commonly seen Martin catalog from the 1940's. It has a total of 16 pages illustrating guitars, tiples, mandolins and ukuleles. Kutztown Printing Co. delivered 18,000 of these catalogs on July 26, 1941.

This catalog can be viewed on-line at benjaminle.org:

http://www.benjaminle.org/guitar-archives/1941-martin-catalog.html

No further Martin catalogs were made until 1962. They were hardly needed. From 1943 to 1961 the Martin factory ran at full capacity and was often well behind in deliveries.

1962 Catalog

The folk boom of the early 1960's cause an even larger increase in demand for Martin guitars. Martin hired Walter T. Armstrong Inc. to design a new catalog in 1962. The 18 page catalog was printed by two companies; Schroeder-Lewis and Falcon Press. Another, even larger, quantity of catalogs were printed by Falcon Press in late 1963.

This catalog can be viewed on-line at benjaminle.org:

http://www.benjaminle.org/guitar-archives/1962-martin-price-list-and-catalog.html

Postcards

Martin at times used postcards to advertise their product line. Postcards were an inexpensive advertisement method, especially considering the postage rate for post cards during the period they were used was only one cent.

Martin purchased 25 postcards for advertising in November 1905. These were probably "real photo cards". Another 25 of these cards were purchased in April 1906.

The main period of use of these advertising cards was between 1918 and 1942. Figure 279 is an example of one of these advertising cards.

Figure 279
1928 Advertising Post Card for Martin 5-17T Guitar

Tenor Banjos

Martin records do not contain a lot of information on the development history of their tenor banjo. Information has to be pieced together from a few letters, the bookings, the sales ledgers and notes from the director and shareholders meetings to get a picture of that development.

Banjo development must have stated early in 1922 because Martin booked an order on April 25, 1922 from a dealer in Detroit for three tenor banjos with

a note **"one of each style"**. Obviously, Martin must have been communicating with his dealers before that and was initially planning on three styles with different levels of ornamentation.

Another dealer, O. F. Bitting, wrote to Martin on July 8, 1922:

"How are you getting along with your banjos? Hope you make the best so I can take up your banjo. Would take all the best points in the three of four best banjos such as Vega (Tuba-Phone), Orpheum and Bacon."

Martin listened to their dealers and the January 1, 1923 inventory shows that Martin had a Vega Little Wonder tenor banjo, a Grover "sample" tenor banjo and a Bacon banjo ukulele in stock, maybe the three different styles mentioned in the second paragraph. These sample banjos appeared in the yearly inventories until 1926.

Martin replied on July 14:

"Banjo work is making more rapid progress now since we have secured a license to manufacture under A. D. Grover's patent of a special ring. The construction is different form anything now on the market but does not have the appearance of a novelty. The tone of the Tenor Banjo, which we will start to make first, is very fine indeed, both in quality and volume, and we have great expectations of making a great success with the new instrument.

The first samples will probably be ready about the middle of September."

An excerpt from the director's meeting notes of July 22, 1922 recorded the following:

"The manager made the following report in pursuance of the plan of the Board to make banjos in to time to market in the fall of 1922:

The patent tone-rim feature owned by Mr. A. D. Grover was secured on a non-exclusive license. Production will be started at once beginning with a tenor banjo to sell at a medium price. There will be only samples made at first and these will then be

placed before customers to get the line as near perfect as possible, and at very little expense. It will be pushed as an important branch of the business as soon as it is developed."

The idea of producing three different styles appears to have been set aside but on October 9, 1922 an order was placed by a dealer in Ohio for one "**tenor banjo #3**", so some hope must still have been held out for making a number of different styles.

The development of the tenor banjo proceeded more slowly than originally anticipated as noted in the director's meeting notes from January 15, 1923:

"Our banjo is almost ready to put out, and if the judgement of the officers proves right as to styles and prices it is likely to be a big thing."

One of the reasons for the slow development of the Martin tenor banjo was discussed in a letter A. D. Grover & Son sent to Martin on January 22, 1923:

"Replying to your letter of the 16th, we have ordered six rings to be made of 0.040" brass, which is the heaviest metal they can spin. The other rings are 0.032" thick.

We really think that if the first rings were supported at the point where the strain comes, you would have had no trouble. There is a crushing strain of from one to two tons on the rings when the heads are tight.

We wish you would make a banjo with the rim of full thickness and use one of the rings that are not polished on the inside and advise us of the result. In the meantime, we will lose no time at this end and will send the six heavier rings as soon as possible."

Regardless of the production issues, Martin prepared three sample banjos and shipped them to three different dealers on January 23, 1923, including one to J. A. Handley of Lowell MA, who had been providing steady encouragement to Martin in the development of tenor banjos.

Martin replied on January 25, 1923:

"Yesterday we made up a Banjo with two extra veneer thickness in the rim, making thirteen ply, fully three-fourth-inch thick. After tightening the head as much as possible yesterday and again this morning we find that the tone ring has practically the same appearance as on the other instruments. The pressure seems to be too much for the rim only at the holes, where there is a distinct bulge.

It is true that the average purchaser might not notice this nor think badly of it if he did notice it; but it is subject to just criticism by out competitors. Would it be possible to make the vertical section of the ring a little bit lower, if only an eighth or a sixteenth of an inch? We would also like to have the holes in the flange set in to allow the hooks to stand without bending.

We are preparing six more rims and necks for the rings which you are giving the matter as much careful thought as we are and we want to say again that we are highly pleased with the tone of the instruments and feel sure that they will be very popular with the trade and the profession. The technical difficulties were to be expected and will surely be overcome."

The correspondence from A. D. Grover & Son continued on February 1, 1923:

"I m very glad the tone of the new banjos is so good. That is the principal item. A banjo, no matter how well built it may be, would have no commercial value if tone was lacking.

The rings as made will be strong enough, after ring put through a die operation at a very slight expense - see if you understand this. The ring will be stronger than if made of thicker metal with this operation. This metal is thrown inward at B between the holes, directly behind the straining wires and will absolutely prevent any buckling. Again the ring of 0.032" brass will come much cheaper than 0.040".

I advise that you send back all the rings you have & I will have them put through this process as soon as the dies are finished. In the meantime I will have a little hand punch made & fix up a ring on the banjo you are sending & return same to you in

a day or two.

The matter o the holes in jig I will write you about soon."

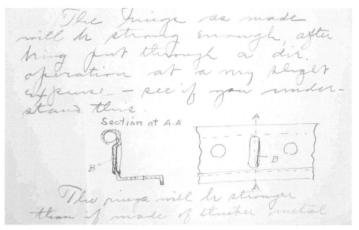

Figure 280
Detail of Sketch in A. D. Grover & Son Letter of February 1, 1923
Explanation of die-stamped dimple used to strengthen the rim of banjo

Martin wrote again to A.D. Grover & Son on March 26, 1923 and included comments from H. A. Handley on the sample banjo sent out on January 23:

"Today's mail brings two letters of congratulations on the Tenor Banjo which we want to pass on to you. One is from J. A. Handley, of Lowell, Mass. who is an old and valued business friend, also a close personal friend who is always candid with us. He writes:

'My first impression of the new Tenor is that it is the finest toned Tenor I have ever heard. The sweetness of the tone seems remarkable and its resonance as well.

I congratulate you on getting out this handsomest and finest toned Tenor on the market and my congratulations to Grover, too.'

The other is from Mr. Howard Wurlitzer, whose words are in a different vein, but very significant considering that he is one of the responsible heads of the Rudolph Wurlitzer Company, Cincinnati. He writes:

Our Mr. J. C. Freeman writes us from New York that you were there recently and showed him your

new Banjo and he thought it was a very fine instrument.

Please keep in mind that we would like to make closer affiliations with you and handle your goods in larger quantities...

Will you please this into consideration and not offer your Banjos to any of your other dealers or any one else until we have had an opportunity to discuss this with you?

Evidently the new instrument would go well just as it is so any further improvement we are able to make will be so much better."

Other issues continued to hamper production of the tenor banjo and these were recorded in the directors' meeting minutes dated July 16, 1923:

"Progress of banjo production is slow on account of the difficulty of securing labor, but some progress; and if present raise in wages brings new workers probably as many as one hundred tenor banjos can be made before 1924."

The director' meeting notes from October 17, 1923 partially blamed the inability to swiftly expand the work force as one of the causes in the delay of tenor banjo production, especially when the factory was already busy with orders for other instruments:

"On account of the large number of orders for guitars, mandolins and ukulele the tenor banjo has not been pushed. As the working force increases this work will be resumed and developed for large production next year."

Although not mentioned in the meeting minutes Martin had managed to ship another dozen tenor banjo between June 6 and September 23, 1923.

The situation had not improved to the directors' satisfaction when the next meeting was held on January 21, 1924, even though a further 19 tenor banjos had been shipped between November 30, 1923 and January 19, 1924:

"The only failure of the year is that we could not get many banjos out. That business is still promising and should be developed; if for any reason other orders fall off we will push it and if they do not fall off the factory should be enlarged."

Only another eleven banjos were shipped between February 18 and April 23, 1924. The need to expand the factory was further discussed in the directors' meeting held on April 24, 1924:

"Provision should also be made to produce more guitars and to begin banjo production on a quantity basis, but this cannot be done with the present facilities."

E. J. Albert offered some comments on a Martin banjo in a letter dated June 19, 1924:

"The Banjo reached us safely and we are extremely well pleased with it. It is true to Martin standards of workmanship and finish, and is creating quite a sensation.

Do you have a Catalogue of your different Models or some kind of price list, that we tell the possible customer who are inquiring?

Most of the Banjoist who come in here are always looking for the high prices stuff and want to get an idea of your higher grades. We are hoping to take orders."

Martin replied promptly on June 20:

"Thank you heartily for your kind words about the Martin Banjo. What we have to reply will probably be rather unsatisfactory to you; that is, that our Banjo production is still very limited. So far this one style, called No. 1, is the only one made up. As soon as we can get to it we intend making finer styles and probably a cheaper style. But that is not likely to happen in 1924. The factory is now being enlarged but the benefit of this enlargement will hardly reach the Banjo field this year.

We have a factory lot of Banjos coming through which will be finished the latter part of July or early in August. We would very much like to book your order for whatever you may need as there will probably not be another lot for several months following.

Under separate cover we are mailing a few circulars which we hope will be useful."

Tenor banjo production continued at a slow pace with only fifteen being sold between April 25 and November 22, 1924. The directors' meeting minutes for January 19, 1925 continued to point out the difficulty of securing sufficient labor:

"As new workers are added ukulele production will be increased and banjo production will be started on a quantity basis."

A further eighteen tenor banjos were sold between March 18 and April 11, 1925 but Martin must had already decided to stop production of tenor banjos because the directors' meeting held on April 12, 1925, as well as subsequent meetings, makes no mention of them at all. This is entirely understandable as 1925 was the peak for ukulele demand. The Martin factory

Figure 281
Advertising Photograph of Martin Tenor Banjo

was already full of orders for other instruments and Martin was already planning on adding a second floor to the factory that had been erected in 1924. Unfortunately, the tenor banjo was just a distraction to Martin management with all the other activity going on and was dropped from the production line.

The last ten banjos were sold off between April 25, 1925 and July 2, 1926, the last two examples to employees.

A total of 94 banjos were sold between January 21, 1923 and July 2, 1926.

Banjo Parts Suppliers

The subject of Martin's sources for banjo parts is easily answered by referring to the yearly inventories. Banjo parts only appeared in the yearly inventories between 1923 and 1926.

A. D. Grover & Son supplied tone rings, resonators, tuning pegs, tailpieces and bridges while Waverly Musical Products Co. Inc. supplied straining hoops, banjo hooks, nuts and wrenches. Banjo heads were supplied by Joseph B. Rogers Manufacturing.

PARTS USED IN MARTIN TENOR BANJOS					
MANUFACTURER	PART	1923	1924	1925	1926
Grover	Tone rings	50	9	54	29
	Resonators		55	110	85
	Pegs	144	123		10
	Neck Sets	10	6	71	46
	Presto tailpieces	100	50	22	5
	Bridges	96	72	28	72
Waverly	Straining hoops U shape	50		92	67
	Straining hoops L shape	50	23		
	Flesh hoops	100	36	81	56
	Hooks	1000	600	9400	8500
	Nuts	1000	600	9500	8400
	Wrenches	160	192	71	46
	Banjo uke hardware	6 sets	6 sets	6 sets	6 sets
	Banjo hardware	2 sets	2 sets	2 sets	2 sets
	Long hooks			115	127
Rogers & Son	Banjo heads	60	3	20	

Table 87
Parts Used in Martin Tenor Banjos

Bellying of Guitar Tops

Collectors of vintage guitars sometimes worry about the bulge or "belly" that develops below the bridge on some guitars. To a large degree most guitars have a slight belly reflecting the flexing of the top to resist the tension of guitar strings acting on the bridge. This is not a new phenomenon and Martin, even 100 years ago, sometimes had to address the concerns of their customers.

Martin on February 19, 1923 replied to a question from George C. Krick, the well-known guitar teacher and long-time Martin dealer, concerning an old Martin guitar he had returned to the factory for some work:

"The swelling at the back of the bridge is not a defect because it indicates fine wood, worked rather thin, this is usually the best for tone, as you know. Many old Guitars have this appearance and are almost always fine in tone.

Similarly, Charles H. Ditson & Co. wrote to Martin on September 22, 1925:

"Will you kindly straighten out the warp in the top, glue bridge and put it in good condition?"

Martin replied on September 28:

"The top is not warped but is slightly bulged below the bridge, due to the tension of the steel strings. This condition can be relieved by proper regulation of the strings. At present they are too high since they were evidently substituted for the original gut strings without lowering the bridge. It would be impossible to restore the top to its original swell nor is it necessary because this bulge does no harm whatever; on the other hand, it indicated a fine piece of Spruce otherwise it would have cracked under strain. Such a top usually has a fine tone."

A retail customer, R. L. Wardwell, wrote to Martin on November 29, 1935 concerned about the bellying of the top of his guitar:

"I notice that after I had used your 00-18 model for a year and a half, that the top of the guitar near the tail piece raised or warped up considerable, thereby raising the strings, making the guitar much harder to finger."

Martin replied on December 3:

"A guitar top that is flexible and thin enough to be sensitive and resonant in tone will sometimes swell enough at the bridge, after use, to make the

strings a little too high. If this happens, our guarantee is effective and we take care of the readjustment without charge, paying the transportation costs ourselves.

The only sure way to overcome this tendency is to make the tops good and stiff and considerably thicker but then the tone would suffer."

Today there are tools and techniques that can help reduce the bellying of vintage guitar tops if the bellying has become excessive.

Bridge Pins and End Pins

19th Century Martin Guitars

The following observations on types of bridge pins and end pins used on 19th century Martin guitars are based on examination of existing guitars as well as clues from the 1889 to 1899 inventories. The information available for 19th century bridge and end pins is not exhaustive and much research still remains to be done.

In general, the 19th century bridge pins used by Martin were either , a) ebony with a pearl inlaid dot, b) ebony with a "double eye" inlay (a pearl dot inlaid with a smaller abalone dot), c) ivory with a pearl or abalone dot or d) bone .

End pins were usually e) ebony with a pearl dot, f) ivory with a pearl or abalone dot or g) bone. However, plain ebony and ivory end pins are also encountered.

Martin guitars from 1833 to 1840 were almost always supplied with bridge pins and end pins. Bridges pins for ebony bridges were usually made of ebony with an inlaid pearl dot. For ivory bridges the bridge pins were ivory with a pearl or abalone inlaid dot. At the end of the 1830's some guitars are known with no end pin but with a bridge pin on the back of the guitar at the end block, a hole being drilled into the end block for mounting the pin. This was used for attaching a "ribbon", as early straps were called.

Most Martin guitars between 1840 and 1843 did not have end pins but did have a back pin mounted in the end block as described above. This short period

of time coincided with Martin's use of a tie bridges rather pin bridges. Once Martin returned to the pin bridge around 1843, end pins became the norm again, although the back pin continued to be used intermittently on "student" model 2½-17 and 3-17 guitars for much of the remainder of the 19th century.

Martin did not purchase bridge and end pins directly throughout this period but, instead, used one of their New York distributors, usually C. A. Zoebisch & Sons, to order pins from New York ebony and "ivory turners". Zoebisch did supply bone bridge pins and end pins in 1891 so it can be presumed bone bridge and end pins were generally available.

20th Century Martin Guitars

The 1892 to 1909 inventories record black, white and double-eye bridge pins as well as black and white end pins. Presumably "white" refers to ivory bridge pins and end pins. The unit price of "white" end pins was about double that of ebony pins and double-eye pins were valued a little higher than "white" pins. White end pins were valued at three times that of ebony end pins. Bone end pins were occasionally recorded in the inventories but don't appear to have been a regular stock item. The inventories from 1910 to 1917 did not identify the type of pins in stock but 1918 found Martin transitioning from ebony and ivory pins to ones made of black and ivory (white) celluloid, with only a small quantity of ebony bridge pins and end pins still remaining in stock.

The purchasing records and yearly inventories provide more information for the period from 1901 to 1964. The purchasing records from 1901 to 1930 provide details on the types of pins bought, while the records from 1930 to 1965 have a little less detail but provide the names of the suppliers. The yearly inventories also provide a fairly good picture of the types of pins used by Martin during this period.

The 1901 to 1930 purchasing records show that Martin continued to buy bridge pins and end pins made of ebony, bone and ivory until mid-1917. From that point until 1930 Martin purchased mostly celluloid bridge and end pins in black or white celluloid (ivoroid). The names of the suppliers were not recorded but a few part numbers were repeatedly ordered, polished ivoroid #25 end pins and #28 bridge pins in black celluloid or ivoroid being the most commonly encountered.

The purchasing records from mid-1930 to 1964 are the opposite of the earlier records, the supplier was always recorded but the part number was not. Martin main supplier for bridge and end pins from 1930 to 1939 was the Auburn Button Works although Waverly received some orders from 1937 to 1939. It is safe to assume Auburn Button Works was supplying celluloid pins to Martin for an unknown length of time before 1930.

During 1940 and 1941 pin orders all went to Keolyn Plastic Co. Kluson became Martin's supplier of bridge and end pins in 1942 and was the sole supplier of these items until at least 1964 (where the records end).

Change from Diamond and Square Inlays to Round Dots (1944)

Since the last few years of the 19th century Martin had been inlaying the fingerboard of their instruments with positions marks. For style 21 and 28 guitars the inlays were in the shape of small slotted diamonds and squares. Lower grade instruments received small dot inlays while styles 30 and above were decorated with beautiful "snowflake" inlays.

By 1944, the style 42 and 45 guitars were no longer in production and in November of that year Martin replaced the "diamonds and squares" with plain abalone dots on style 21 and 28 instruments.

Mike Longworth noted in his logbook that serial number 89553 had "diamond and square" while 89803 had "dot" inlays. It has been reported that serial number 89681 (from shop order 348) also has dot inlays so it appears the transition occurred with guitars stamped around the middle of November 1944.

STYLE	SHOP ORDER	SERIAL NUMBERS	DATE STAMPED	COMMENTS
D-28	340	89542-89553	NOV. 2, 1944	89553 NOTED BY LONGWORTH AS HAVING "DIAMOND & SQUARE" INLAYS
D-28	348	89679-89690	NOV. 14, 1944	89681 REPORTED ON UMGF AS HAVING DOT INLAYS AND SCALLOPED BRACES
000-28	349	89691-89702	NOV. 15, 1944	
D-28	356	89803-89814	NOV. 28, 1944	89803 NOTED BY LONGWORTH AS HAVING "DOT" INLAYS
000-21	357	89815-89826	NOV. 28, 1944	

Table 88
Change from "Diamond and Square" Inlays to Round Dots

Table 88 shows all the shop orders for style 21 and 28 guitars in this period although no examples from shop order 349 or 357 has been reported.

Reasoning Behind Compensated Bridges

In a reply to a customer inquiry dated September 7, 1932, C. F. Martin III made this very succinct explanation for the change to a compensated bridge:

"For about two years now we have been setting the Ivory saddle in our Guitar bridge on an angle in order to give the heavy bass strings extra length to compensate for the inevitable sharping in the upper position on these strings. In recent years the players have been using heavier strings and this made it necessary to make this change in the saddle. You will note that we use genuine Ivory and not celluloid for our bridge saddles."

In the same letter Martin went on to explain the reasoning behind curved fingerboards.

"The top of the bridge us curved because the fingerboard is curved and that is done to make the left hand fingering easier. On a flat fingerboard it is very difficult to make a barre chord of several strings as one has to do so often in the key of F. For that reason we have always made our fingerboards slightly oval but in the last year or so this curve has been made a little greater to meet the needs of the modern player.

There matter are details or refinements of construction which are determined very largely by the wishes of the players. There is no telling when some change in the style of playing will lead to certain changes in the instruments. No principles of tone or durability are involved."

Decals

Martin had been aware of decalomania for a long time before the first Martin head stock decal appeared in 1932.

On October 13, 1897 a company named Palm, Fechteler & Co. sent some sample sound hole transfers (decals) to Martin with the following comments:

"Sound holes can be made much more attractive by 'Transfers' and at a very much lower cost than by any other method.

Some of the best makers are using our goods to good advantage."

Whether it was advantageous or not, Martin did not entertain the use of decals until well into the 20th century.

On June 22, 1932 Martin received a shipment of decals from the same Palm , Fechteler & Co mentioned above. Based on comparing unit cost with later orders, it appears the first batch was for about 3,000 decals.

Martin put the decals into immediate use. The earliest reported guitar with a decal is a 1932 OM-18, serial number 50674, that was stamped on April 11, 1932. This guitar did not leave the finish department until June 29, so there was time for the decal to be applied before the finishing process was complete. Earlier guitars are known with decals but these are mostly guitars returned to Martin for repairs at some later date. Martin did send out decals upon to dealers and these dealers may also have applied decals themselves on some earlier instruments.

Palm, Fechteler & Co. was renamed Palm Brothers Decal Co. in 1934 and was the sole supplier of decals to Martin until 1955. The Chicago Decal Co. received some decal orders in 1958 and 1959 and the Decal Manufacturing Co. supplied some "heavy duty" decals in 1961 although it is not clear what "heavy duty" meant. Palm Brothers shipped more decals in 1960 and 1962 but the last decal order in the purchasing records went to Meyincard Co. in 1963.

The iconic "C. F. Martin" decal was probably designed by Palm, Fechteler & Co. The author had the opportunity to examine the papers and samples of the Cincinnati branch of Palm Brothers Decal Co., that are housed in the Cincinnati History Museum, hoping, unsuccessfully as it turns out, to find correspondence and samples of the C. F. Martin decals. Palm Brothers had several branches and the orders for Martin decals went through the New York branch. About a dozen large boxes of samples were examined and the number of beautiful designs produced by Palm Broth-

ers was quite staggering. Martin probably indicated to Palm Brothers what information was required on the decal and left the artistic work to them, with Martin having final approval on the proposed design.

The purchasing records after 1930 do not supply much detail but #14118 decals were received in November 1941 and #14118-A decals in September 1945. Another decal design, #14416, was mentioned in orders from August 1946, May 1952 and August 1962.

Ukulele decals first appear in the January 1, 1935 inventory so must have been first purchased during 1934.

The earliest Martin decals (Figure 282) were made in just one color, what Palm Brothers referred to as

Figure 282
Decal on Serial Number 52324 (1932)

Figure 283
Decal on Serial Number 60639 (1936)

Figure 284
Decal on Serial Number 97974 (1946)

"bronze". The color was not painted or silk screened but appears to be gold leaf. This type of decal lasted until early 1934.

The next type of decal had changes to the shape of the lettering and was made in two colors, with black edging being added to the gold colored lettering. It is not known precisely when the change occurred. This was the standard decal format thereafter. Some minor variation in design can be seen over the years, especially in the shape of the "&", but these changes might just be due to the manufacturing process.

Regardless, much more research will be required to attempt to match up the decal design changes to the few clues provided in the purchasing records.

Dark Top Guitars

Martin guitars with a sunburst finish are some of the most desirable collector instruments, not only because of their attractive appearance but also because of their relative scarcity.

In the 19th and early 20th century Martin allowed customers to order a darker finish if they didn't want the relatively white top of a new guitar. Some guitars were ordered as "orange tops" and a smaller number were ordered as "yellow tops". Martin regularly used bleached shellac for their French polish finishes. For orange tops Martin used unbleached shellac instead. Presumably, yellow tops were created by using a mixture of bleached and unbleached shellac.

It is difficult to know exactly how many dark top guitars were made by Martin as the company did not always record this feature in the records. The sources of information for dark tops are:

1. The shipping ledgers, which are quite complete from 1898 until April 1924
2. The bookings ledgers covering 1918 to 1967
3. The production record sheets for 1927 to 1974
4. The shop order slips from 1926 to 1948
5. The detailed shop order slips covering 1957 to 1962.

In Tables 89 to 93, the numbers of dark top guitars as noted in the sales ledger books do not have a suffix, the records from the "booking" ledgers are indicated

with a suffix B, the production records with a suffix P and the shop order slips with a suffix S. Where the numbers from the different sources of information don't agree the source with the higher number is shown. The numbers shown in these tables are only an estimate, more may exist.

The most reliable records are the shop order slips, followed, in order of reliability by, the booking ledger records, the production records and the sales ledger records.

Prior to 1926, some guitars were "stained" to create a dark finish but were sometimes referred to as "dark tops". It its not known whether the term "dark top" in this period implies Martin was applying a dark finish with a method other than staining.

Martin began using a spraying-on finish from mid-1926 and had fully changed over to this method by October of that year. Martin almost always used the term "dark top" to designate a sunburst finish although the term "shaded top" is occasionally encountered.

One dark top D-45 is in existence (serial number 71663) but does not appear as such in any of the Martin records. The finish looks original so this is probably a good example of a dark top being produced without that feature being recorded. This instrument was part of a batch of three D-45 guitars and it was noted on the shop order slip that one guitar from the batch got a F-9 fingerboard (serial number 71663 as it turns out). So, maybe it was understood that this guitar was to receive a dark top or maybe there was a last minute change to a dark finish that was communicated by telephone or telegram.

ORANGE TOP GUITARS						
	0-18	0-21	1-28	0-28	2-27	5-34
1898	2					
1899	1		2	1	1	1
1900		1		1		

Table 89
Orange Top Guitars 1898 to 1900

STAINED TOP GUITARS (SOMETIMES CALLED DARK TOPS)																													
	5-17	0-17	00-17	¼-18	¾-18	5-18	2½-18	1-18	0-18	00-18	D-111	5-21	1-21	1-21(S)	0-21	00-21	000-21	5-28	2½-28	2½-28S	1-28	0-28	5-42	0-42	00-42	5-45	0-45	T-18	T-28	T-42
1907		2																												
1908			1																											
1916	5												4								1									
1917					1			3					1														1			
1918					2		2	1					2							1	1									
1919																	2										1		1	
1920						6B	19	3	5B				8B		2B	1B		1	2		5B	13B	2	1				2B	24	
1921			3	3		2		3	14	2B		1		1	1	3			1B			6	1				1	3		
1922			2B																			6B						30	1	1
1923						1B											1B				1B	3B						27B		
1924										1B	2											1B						24B		
1925										1																				

Table 90
Stained Top Guitars (Size 000 and Smaller) 1907 to 1925

STYLE 17 AND 18 DARK TOP GUITARS (SPRAYED-ON FINISH)															
	0-17 14F	0-17T 14F	00-17 14F	5-18	0-18 12F	0-18S 14F	0-18 14F	0-18T	00-18 12F	00-18H 14F	00-18 14F	000-18 14F	000-18HS 12F	000-18L 14F	OM-18	OM-18P
1926																
1927																
1928																
1929							1									
1930							1									
1931					1B				2							1
1932	286 [2]				2	4 [1]	427 [2]	79	5						225 [2]	
1933	21 [2]	1	4 [2]				21				25				38	
1934			3				44					14B				
1935		24	1B				16B			2	3	12		1B		
1936							2B				17S	3B				
1937							12B	18S		31 [3] P	44P	9B	3			
1938							11B			7B	31B	16B	1B			
1939							7B				15B	8B				
1940							14B	1B			7B	3B				
1941							15B				11B	6B				
1942							19B				6B	5B				
1943							1				3B	5B				
1944							7B				7B	7B				
1945							4B				4P	2B				
1946							1P					3P				
1947							1B	1P			2	2P				
1948							4P	1P			5P	9P				
1949				1P			15P				10P	7P				
1950				1P			4P				6P	3P				
1951							10P				1P					
1952							11P					1P				
1953							7P	2P			2,4P	3P				
1954							6P				4P	1P				
1955							2P					1S				
1956							2P				1P	1P				
1957				1S			9S				3S	1S				
1958							1S									
1959							1S									
1960																
1961							1S									

1) Six 0-18S guitars were made of which at least 4 had dark tops.
2) In 1932 all the "Model 32" 14-fret guitars (0-17, 0-18 and OM-18 models) were supposed to have dark tops.
3) It is likely that a large proportion of production of 1937 00-18H guitars had dark tops.
4) A few unique guitars models were made with dark tops: one 1960 5-18S, one 1929 2-18T, one 1938 14-fret 00-18S, one 1939 00-18T, one 1954 00-18G, one 1927 12-fret 000-18 and another in 1931, one 1934 14-fret 000-18T.

Table 91
Style 17 and 18 Dark Top Guitars (Size 000 and Smaller) 1926 to 1961

	1-21	0-21	00-21	00-21S	000-21 14F	0-28	0-28T	00-28S 14F	00-28G	000-28S 12F	000-28 14F	OM-28	00-40H	00-40HS	000-42	00-45	000-45	T-18
STYLE 21, 28, 40, 42 AND 45 DARK TOP GUITARS (SPRAYED-ON FINISH)																		
1926																		
1927															1			2
1928																		
1929																		
1930			10			3												
1931			10				1					10	1					
1932			10										1	1				
1933													1					1B
1934			1B								12				1			
1935										1	3		1B			1B	1B	
1936										1	1B							
1937											4B							
1938		1B									5B		1B					
1939									1		1B		1B					
1940	1B										1B		1B					
1941					3													
1942						1B					1B							
1943											2B							
1944						1P					1B							
1945						2B												
1946																		
1947						1P					1B							
1948											1P							
1949											1P							
1950											1B							
1951						1P												
1952						1P												
1953											1B							
1954																		
1955									1S									
1956																		
1957						1S												
1958																		
1959																		
1960																		
1961				1S														

Table 92

Style 21, 28, 40, 42 and 45 Dark Top Guitars (Size 000 and Smaller) 1926 to 1961

		D-111, D-18, D-21 AND D-28 DARK TOP GUITARS					
YEAR	D-111	D-18	D-18S	D-21	D-28	D-28H	D-28S
1926	4[1]						
1927	2[1]						
1928	2[1]						
1929	2[1]						
1930	2[1]						
1931							
1932		2(EB)					
1933		7(EB)			1		
1934		7(EB),4(TB)			7(EB)		1
1935		15			10		
1936		36	1		1	1	
1937		20B			6		
1938		22B (19AX,3RX)			6B (5AX, 1RX)		
1939		16B (5WN,11NN)			4B (NN)		
1940		5B			4B		
1941		17B			5B		
1942		8B (1TB,7EB)			2B (EB)		
1943		3(EB)			4 (EB)		
1944					1 (EB)		
1945					1B		
1946		1EX, 2P (3EB)					
1947		3P			3		
1948		4P			3P		
1949		4P			3P		
1950		7P			4P		
1951		1P			1B		
1952		2P			1P		
1953		3P (TB)					
1954		6P					
1955		3P					
1956		1P					
1957		3S (WT)		3S (WT)	2S (WT)		
1958		9S (WT)			1S (WT)		
1959		1S (WT)			2		
1960					2 (1S,1EX)		
1961		1B					
1962							
1963					1		
1964					2B		

Legend:
EB = Ebony neck reinforcement   AX = Advanced X-bracing   WN = Wide neck (1-3/4")
TB = Steel T-bar   RX = Rear X-bracing   NN = Narrow neck (1-11/16")
WT = West (Sitka) spruce top
Note:
1) Since earlier D-111 dark tops guitars were stained, it is possible the D-111's made after Martin switched to a spray on finish may still have been stained.

Table 93

Style D-111, D-18, D-21 and D-28 Dark Top Guitars 1926 to 1964

Martin Supplied Spruce Tops to Fairbanks for Mandolins

Although Martin did not begin experimenting with bowl-back mandolins until 1894, there is at least two intriguing clues that F. H Martin was contemplating getting into mandolin production at an even earlier date.

On September 19, 1892 C. A. Zoebisch wrote to Martin:

"This morning by chance Fairbanks came in and he will take 200 Mandolin tops for trial at once, so you can send them Guitars (tops?), pick out nice ones so as to bate (sic) him."

It is an open question why Fairbanks, presumably the banjo, guitar and mandolin manufacturer from Boston, would need to source mandolin tops from Martin. Not much is known about Fairbanks' early mandolin production although they did have a full line of mandolins only a few years later. Maybe Fairbanks was having trouble with the quality of the tops he was receiving from his current sources or maybe he just had an immediate requirement for his production line.

The initial order may have been a success as Zoebisch sent Martin a post card on June 30, 1893:

"Please send at once 500 ffine (very fine) Mandolin tops..."

Zoebisch did not specify whether these tops were for Fairbanks or not so there is a possibility the tops were meant for one of the other mandolin makers in New York City.

Fake Martin Guitars

On September 16, 1893 C. A. Zoebisch wrote a letter to Martin concerning a non-Martin guitar being offered as the original article:

"A customer writes us from lower California that a pawnbroker offers C. F. Martin & Co. Guitars at low prices (which are bogus). I wrote out to buy one, so we could get at the party.

He writes us 'I have quietly interviewed the pawn-broker and find a Guitar, which he represents as a Martin, but it is only stamped inside and the "C" looks like a "G". I sent same one to purchase six of them - he representing that he was a Teacher, but he could furnish but one, and asked $35 for it.'

It is a very poor imitation of a 1-26 celluloid bound.

Today I will send that pawnbroker a price list & circular any way. Perhaps I will write him too, that we heard of bogus C. F. Martin & Co. guitars being sold & want to know if he knows anything about it, & if so, where they came from."

In June 1935, Chalmers Music Co. sent in a Martin guitar for repair. Martin replied on June 28, 1935:

"We have received the old Guitar you sent us a few days ago and we shall be glad to put it in good playing condition for you. We are sorry to report, however, that it is not a Martin Guitar, being branded "G. R. Martin" which is not at all the same as "C. F. Martin". This is the first time we have ever seen this brand and we judge that it was put in by a maker who was imitating the genuine Martin Guitar and chose to use a brand as near like ours as possible. There are many points of workmanship and design in which the Guitar is different from Martin instruments so we are quite sure that it was not made by our firm."

Martin had been aware of G. R. Martin guitars as early as 1893 but had forgotten about them by 1935, so the G. R. Martin guitars could not have been much of a concern for Martin.

Several G. R Martin guitars have appeared over the last few years. On at least one of them there is a stamp on the back strip reading "G. R. Martin/New York". The "G. R Martin" name is in the form of an arc with "New York" underneath, looking very much like the pre-1867 C. F. Martin stamp. On another G. R. Martin guitar an unscrupulous seller has attempted to alter the letter "G. R." to look more like "C. F." in the hopes of fleecing an unsuspecting buyer. However, anyone familiar with 19th century Martin guitars is unlikely to be fooled by a G. R. Martin guitar as these instruments differ from original Martin guitars in design and decoration.

The G. R. Martin stamp indicates these guitars were made in New York but a quick review of the New York directories for 1890 to 1894 did not provide any information as to the location of the G. R. Martin shop. However, considering that a number of G. R. Martin guitars are known, G. R. Martin must have been active at least in the 1890's and possibly a little later.

Fingerboard Inlays

It is generally accepted that Martin did not begin to apply position marks to the fingerboards until after 1898, roughly at the same time serial numbers came into use.

However, with addition of mandolins to the product line in 1895, the introduction of fingerboard inlays to guitars was more of a transition than a clear-cut decision.

Martin guitar had always had plain fingerboards with no position markers except for those few guitars that had ivory or abalone veneers applied to the fingerboards. A few guitars from the 1840's had small abalone dots inlaid in the side of the neck to act as markers.

Figure 285
Abalone Fret Marker on 1843 Martin & Schatz Guitar Made for Madame De Goni

However, by at least 1887 Martin was receiving requests for the addition of fingerboard inlays. In that year Martin received an instruction from Zoebisch on January 18, 1887 to supply a 0-40 guitar with:

"1 star between 5th and 6th fret, 2 star(s) between 6th and 7th fret, 1 star between 7th and 8th fret, 3 star(s) between 8th and 9th fret"

The requests became more and more frequent during the 1890's and were fairly common on the fancier grade of guitars from about 1895. However, the style and number of inlays on the fingerboard was somewhat variable, as can be seen in Figures 286 and 287.

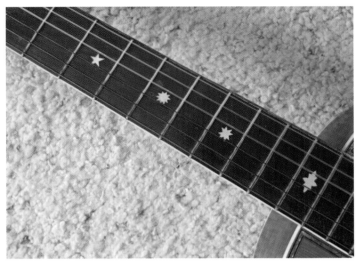

Figure 286
Fingerboard Inlays on 1895 Martin 0-42 Guitar

Figure 287
Fingerboard Inlays on 1897 Martin 1-42 Guitar

Several other pieces of Zoebisch correspondence indicated "position marks" were becoming more common.

Post card dated February 8, 1893:

"...have position dots on the 0-34 Guitars..."

Post card dated February 20, 1894:

"We need quick (one) 0-28 with position dots, they say 5, 7, 10th positions, they mean 5, 7, 9 but was

they say 5, 7, 10 make it so. I believe banjos have it that way."

Correspondence dated January 25, 1897:

"Now we need another 0-42 (with) white top & fine position dots..."

Post card dated January 29 1897:

"Please finish the 1-42 white top, ff (very fine) position dots..."

Post card dated February 8, 1897

"We got an order for a 00-28, we have it on hand, but party writes must have ffine, fancy, neck position dots - 5, 7, 9 frets - so we have to send it up to you to fix either this afternoon yet or tomorrow."

The 1898 catalog images provide the first evidence that fingerboard inlay had become regular Martin features although they are only apparent on the wood-cut illustrations for styles 27, 34 and 42. It does not appear that the other styles of guitars had position markers until the first few years of the 20th century, although the 1904 catalog indicates all the styles had, by that time, some sort of fingerboard inlay.

Styles 17 and 18 guitars had round pearl dots, style 21 had slotted square pearl markers, style 28 had slotted "diamond and square" markers and style 27, 30, 42 and 45 had pearl "snowflake" inlays.

Finishes

From the start Martin used French polish for protecting the wood on his guitars. French polish is a technique whereby shellac, a resin secreted by the female lac bug, is dissolved in denatured alcohol and applied in many thin coats by means of a rubbing pad.

Martin made a number of purchases of shellac while in New York and also bought two different types of alcohol, spiritus (or denatured alcohol) and lamp spirit. The spiritus was used for dissolving shellac and the lamp spirit, as the name suggests, was used for in wicked lamps for heating glue pots. Shellac was mixed with lamp black for the finish applied to wooden "coffin" cases.

Martin usually used bleached shellac for their finish but sometimes unbleached shellac was used when the customer specified a "yellow" or "orange" top. Only a few "yellow tops" were made in the 1850's but, as far as can be determined, none in the 1860's. A couple of "yellow tops" were made in the 1870's and the yellow finish became more common in the 1880's and 1890's, although still few in number. This information may be of limited value since a number of 19th century "yellow" or "orange" top guitars have come to light in recent years which suggests these were more common than the ledger books indicate.

A couple of definitions for different types of finish used by Martin are worth defining prior to proceeding:

Varnish: A wood finish traditionally composed of a resin and a solvent.

Lacquer: In the guitar manufacturing sense of the word, a finish containing nitrocellulose.

In the 1901 catalog Martin made the following observations on finish:

"The mode of finishing is French or hand polish. As this is rather an expensive method it may be well to give the reasons for using it. They are, first, that a thin coating of varnish is less likely to hurt the tone; second, that it will not crack like a thick coat rubbed down; and third, being so thin and transparent it shows all the beauty of the wood when fresh and when old and shrunken can be made like new by simply polishing over."

Guitars from the late 1910's have been noted with finishes that are significantly duller than earlier French polished guitars. A number of events contributed to the change in type of finish Martin applied to their guitars. In response to the demand for ukuleles Martin had begun to expand their work force in June 1916 and by April 1917 the work force stood at 30 compared to just 8 a year earlier. The dilution of skill in the work force, a massive increase in production and the U.S. government's pressure to reduce the labor per instrument (so it could be used for war work) forced Martin to simplify its finishing process. The result was what is sometimes called a "waxed" finish. There is little correspondence from this period so it is not exactly clear what this means, although only shellac and Glidden Skincote varnish appear in the purchasing records. It appears that Martin brushed on several coats of shellac and, after sanding, applied several coats of Skincote that were then brought to the appropriate final finish through the use of a rubbing pad and oil. Guitars examined from the period have a semi-gloss finish on the body of the guitar but a very dull finish on the neck. The finish on the neck does indeed appear to be "waxy" but how this was accomplished is not known. This does not preclude the possibility that the French polish finish may have continued to be used on higher grade guitars and mandolins at this time.

In a January 18, 1923 letter to Southern California Music Co., Martin offered a few comments on finishing:

"**For the last year were have been using the Dull Finish only on the Ukulele line, all Guitars and Mandolins being finished in a rubbed varnish, satin finish, which is considerably brighter than the Dull Finish but it not polished. It is more durable than polish and generally considered just as attractive**".

In a letter to George Stannard dated August 6, 1923 Martin stated a few more details with regards to a customer wanting a 0-45 with a dull finish:

"**In regard to the finish, we are wondering whether your customer desires something absolutely dull or whether our regular oil rubbed, semi-gloss finish will be satisfactory. This regular finish is not a polish and is made by simply rubbing the varnish with a felt pad and oil. The dull finish is made in the same way except that fine sandpaper is used instead of the felt pad, thus producing a dead finish. Personally, we much prefer the felt rubbed surface because it is smoother and brings out the figure of the wood to better advantage; but we will be glad to make the dead finish if you wish.**"

In a letter to Murphy Varnish Co. dated January 31, 1925 Martin wrote:

"**At present we are using Glidden Skincote and have been using it for many years but find that it is running somewhat uneven in quality, with a ten-**

dency to slow drying and tacky finish. Our varnish should dry for rubbing in thirty-six to forty-eight hours. We apply two coats with a brush, rubbing the first with pumicestone and the second with oil for a dull finish.**"

One customer, who owned a Martin, complained about the "waxed" finish of his guitar, a 1921 0-18K serial number 16308, and received the following response from Martin in a letter dated May 21, 1925:

"**We discontinued the use of dull waxed finish about six years ago and have been finishing all our instruments with varnish rubbed down with oil, but not polished. This produces a semigloss or satin finish which we consider better than the waxed finish. If you wish, of course, we can finish your instrument in shellac with a waxed surface; but you will find that it will not wear as well as the rubbed varnish surface.**"

Martin made a number of very interesting comments in a letter dated September 10, 1934 to a customer asking for information on what type of finish to use for a guitar:

"**All Martin instruments are now finished with lacquer that would not be suitable for your use because it must be sprayed on. Formerly we used shellac and varnish, under which there must be a coat of filler on Mahogany but not on Spruce. Two coats of thin white shellac are followed by two coats of a light rubbing varnish, such as Glidden Skincote. The shellac should be thinned in the proportion of two pounds to the gallon, which is just half of the usual mixture sold in the paint supply stores.**

It is possible to make a very satisfactory finish with shellac only, sanding each coat and building up until a satisfactory body is secured, probably five or six coats. The last coat can then be rubbed to a semi-gloss or a high polish finish."

On September 17, 1935 Martin replied to an inquiry from a customer concerning his 1927 guitar:

"**When your guitar was made in 1927 we were using a shellac and varnish finishing process as follows:**

2 Coats Pure White Shellac
Sand Smooth
1 Coat Varnish
Rub down with Pumicestone and Water
1 Coat Varnish
Rub down with Rottenstone and Water
The material used was pure white shellac, cut about one and one-half pounds to a gallon of alcohol, and Glidden Skin-Coat varnish, made by the Glidden Company, of Cleveland, Ohio. While we finish the guitars in a hand rubbed satin finish, they could also be polished in one additional operation."

Martin purchased a spray gun and 4 foot wide spray booth from DeVilbiss Manufacturing Co. on October 9, 1925 and received it on October 22. The equipment was still not uncrated at the end of the year as detailed in a letter written to DeVilbiss on December 30:

"We note your announcement of a new and improved Spray Booth. Since the booth which we recently purchased from you has not yet been uncrated, it occurs to us that it may be possible to arrange an exchange for one of the new type booths. Could this be done?"

This request was honored and Martin purchased the improved, and more expensive, spray booth on February 8, 1926. Martin had purchased a small quantity of Duco nitrocellulose lacquer in early November 1925 but couldn't have used it for more than experimentation as the spray booth was still packed. Some more small amounts of Duco lacquer were ordered from March through early June 1926 but the first large purchase of 50 gallons of lacquer didn't occur until June 21.

Martin last purchased Glidden Skin-Cote and shellac in October 1928 although a very substantial order for this kind of finish had been made in October 1926.

From this information it can be concluded that Martin began to use nitrocellulose lacquer on production instruments from late June 1926 although varnish continued to be used on some instruments for a time. The transition from a varnish finish to a sprayed-on lacquer finish was complete by late 1928.

It may have been tedious to go through all the letters

above but it does allow a number of conclusions to be drawn:

1. Martin used only French polish for finishing guitars until 1917
2. Martin changed to a "waxed" finish, probably by mid-1917
3. By 1922, and probably as early 1919 the "waxed" finished had been dropped and the finish changed to varnish rubbed down with oil (although the correspondence continues to show two layers of shellac were applied before the varnish)
4. Martin began to use sprayed-on nitrocellulose finish around October 1926 although it was not until late 1928 that the transition to nitrocellulose from shellac and varnish finish had been completed

Nitrocellulose lacquer remained the standard finish for Martin instruments until at least 1963. However, documented details of how Martin applied finish to their instruments ends in 1935 so there is no way to know if Martin changed their finishing process in the interim years.

There is one last piece of correspondence concerning the type of finish used by Martin in the 1930's that may be of interest to luthiers. In 1935 Martin carried on some correspondence with William Zinsser & Co. of New York, the manufacturer of Bulls Eye Shellac. In a letter dated August 27, 1935 Zinnser made the following comments:

"We are very appreciative of your inquiry asking for prices of White Shellac in drums and 5-gallon cans.

First we would say that we manufacture only one grade of White Shellac and that is our Pure BULLS EYE White Shellac which is made from our Vac-Dry White Shellac Gum, cut in specially denatured alcohol of 190 proof, to any weight specified.

As to Shellac being used under lacquer, we would say that in our opinion, it is the best material to use under lacquer. One of our reasons for saying this, can best be explained by telling you that the difficulty first experienced with lacquer itself was that it did not have proper adherence after a short aging. After quite a bit of research work, the

lacquer people found that the best material to use to correct this fault, was the addition of shellac to their formula and today, the better lacquers, as far as we know, all contain shellac. It follows therefore, that shellac used as an undercoat or sealer, will still further add to this property. We can also tell you that it is our pleasure to supply a great number of furniture manufacturers with their requirements for shellac which in a great many instances, is used as an undercoat for lacquer."

Martin gave Zinnser an order for one gallon of the Bulls Eye shellac and received some further comments in a letter dated August 30, 1935:

"We have one point about which you probably know, but just in case it has not occurred to you, we want to tell you that ordinarily, shellac when used for wood finishing purposes, is generally reduced with a thinner. This is in line with the general rule that in using shellac, the application of two thins coats is always better than one heavy coat. It is important that the alcohol used in reducing the shellac should be suitable for this purpose. The best alcohol to use for this is the same as we use in our original cutting, that is 190 proof. The use of this however, calls for a permit and putting up a bond because of Government regulations. As a substitute for specially denatured alcohol, we recommend Solvent Alcohol which is obtainable from any alcohol distiller under a trade name such as, for example Solox, Peco Solvent, Shellacol, etc... In any event, just be sure that whatever alcohol you do use, is one that will work properly with the Shellac."

Martin responded with a question on September 11, 1935:

"On August 27th you wrote us that shellac is the best material to used under lacquer and in support of this statement you said:

'..the better lacquers as far as we know all contain shellac.'

Doe this apply to Duco No. 160 Clear Lacquer? We use this material regularly and we have asked the DuPont Company whether it is suitable for use over an all-shellac sealer but they have not yet an-

swered our question. Perhaps you can answer it."

Zinsser replied to Martin's question on September 13, 1935:

"We cannot advise you definitely with reference to the formula of Duco No. 1605 Clear Lacquer, although we imagine you will find this contains considerable shellac in its makeup, as most good lacquers do follow a shellac formula, and can be used over a shellac sealer with perfect safety.

We find that a great many manufacturers of lacquers make the statement in their directions, that the material is to be used only over their specified lacquer sealer, but invariably we find that those lacquer sealers are made up almost entirely of shellac."

Finish Suppliers

Martin bought shellac from a variety of sources in the 19th century, seeing as it was widely available and easily purchased. At least in the 1890's it appears Martin let C. A. Zoebisch buy shellac in New York to be forwarded to the factory. Guitar production was not high so Martin made numerous small purchases of shellac, usually between 1 and 6 lbs per order. Shellac was the primary type of finish Martin used until 1917, although small quantities of Glidden's Skin-Cote polishing varnish were purchased from 1906.

Shellac and Skin-Cote were the only types of finish employed by Martin until 1926. Gradually, these older finishes were gradually replaced by DuPont Duco nitrocellulose lacquer until the transition was complete by 1928 (Duco lacquer was also used for automobiles finishes at this time so was very readily available.) Of course, Martin continued to apply a couple of thin coats of shellac to their instruments prior to a spraying on a coat of Duco lacquer.

DuPont, with their Duco product, was the primary supplier of nitrocellulose lacquer to Martin until 1938. Sherwin-Williams, who provided lacquer under the "Opex" trade name, supplied most of the lacquer to Martin from 1938 to 1949 although small orders were also given to DuPont, Zapon, and Laurence-McFadden. Laurence-McFadden supplied much of the lacquer used by Martin from 1950 to 1963 although

Sherwin-Williams continued to receive frequent orders.

Frets and Fret Material

Martin used frets made of nickel silver which was also known to Martin as German silver or, in the earliest records, Argentan. Nickel silver, contrary to its name, contains no silver. In fact, nickel silver is a type of brass, although the nickel content imparts a silvery luster, hence the name.

Martin mostly commonly used nickel silver containing 18% nickel fret wire but also employed at times alloys containing 10%, 12%, 15% and 30% nickel. Nickel silver with 30% nickel is not a commonly available alloy today and the reference may be for 70-

Alloy	Copper %	Nickel %	Zinc %	Temper	Yield (ksi)	Tensile (ksi)	Hardness Rockwell B
12% Nickel Silver	63.5-	11.0-	20.0-	Annealed	18	52	40
UNS C75700	66.5	13.0	25.0	Full hard	79	93	92
18% Nickel Silver	63.5-	16.5-	13.5-	Annealed	25	58	40
UNS C75200	66.5	19.5	19.5	Full hard	74	85	87
70-30 Cupro-Nickel	66.5-	29.0-	--	Annealed	15	44	15
UNS C71500	70.5	33.0		Full hard	57	60	72

Table 94
Nickel Silver Alloys and Properties

30 Cupro-Nickel which contains no zinc.

Brass is an alloy of copper and zinc whereas nickel silver alloys contain a mixture of copper, zinc and nickel.

Brass alloys, of which nickel silver is one, have higher hardness and better mechanical than pure copper because the zinc forms a solid solution with copper. The mixture of copper, nickel and zinc improves the overall strength of the alloy. The improvement in properties is caused by the interaction of the different sizes of the metal atoms. These alloys cannot be heat treated like steel but mechanical properties can be improved by cold working. Cold work can be any kind of mechanical work imparted to the metal but is most commonly associated with the rolling process.

Brass alloys are available in full hard, half hard or annealed tempers. The half hard or full hard condition is normally used for sheet or spring applications. Martin always bought fret wire in the annealed condition because it was easier to work. Full hard fret wire

would be almost impossible to work with and, because the yield and tensile strengths are so close, the frets would be brittle (i.e. once the full hard material began to yield it would be very close to the maximum tensile strength, the point at which it would break.)

Martin even considered using Beryllium copper for frets in the 1930's. Beryllium copper contains 2% beryllium and has some very unusual properties. It does not work-harden like brass but can be hardened through a process called precipitation hardening or age hardening. The alloy is first heated high enough to fully dissolve the beryllium in the copper matrix. The alloy is then cooled quickly to room temperature and then re-heated to various temperatures at which point the beryllium begins to precipitate out of the matrix as tiny particles. The higher the temperature and the longer it is kept at temperature the more of the beryllium precipitates. Precipitation has a major impact on hardness and mechanical properties. There is, however, a maximum hardness that can be attained and, if too much of the beryllium is allowed to precipitate out of the matrix, the hardness and physical properties will begin to decline, at which point the alloy is considered to be over-aged. Mechanical force (i.e. hammering or rolling) can also allow some beryllium to precipitate although to a lesser degree than thermal treatment. Considering the physical properties and high cost of Beryllium copper it is hard to imagine this material could be used for fret wire.

Martin probably originally used German silver fret wire from Germany but, as with tuning machines, chose to source from local suppliers who imported from Europe rather than import it directly himself. This was likely a matter of economy because, dealing with local suppliers, Martin could order just what was required. It is known that during the 1890's Martin purchased German silver fret wire from C. A. Zoebisch and the Patterson Brothers, a hardware and metal supplier in New York.

Martin seems to have continued to buy from jobbers through to the end of World War I but by the 1920's the factory usage had grown to such an extent that they could buy directly from rolling mills at lower costs. During 1924 Martin started buying 18% nickel silver "solid wire" (bar fret wire) from Chase Metal Works of Waterbury CT. Martin also tried some 12% nickel silver fret wire from the same supplier in later

1924 but found that, although suitable for frets, it was found to be a little softer than 18% nickel silver fret wire. Therefore, Martin opted to continue to use the 18% nickel silver alloy.

However, that did not mean that Martin was unaware of the T-fret wire shapes being used in the market.

On February 1, 1918 Martin sold "**1 fingerboard #00 marked for T frets and fret wire**".

Martin ordered bar fret wire in a variety of gauges, with No. 10, No. 12 and No. 13 being the most common in the 1920's and 1930's. These numbered sizes don't seem to fit with the width of bar frets mounted on period guitars. For instance, 10 gauge American Wire Gauge (AWG), also known as Brown & Sharpe Gauge, has a diameter of 0.120" and 10 gauge Music Wire Gauge corresponds to 0.024" diameter, whereas bar frets mounted on guitars generally measure about 0.048" to 0.050" thick.

On December 31, 1924 General Plate Co. of Attleboro Mass. wrote to offer Martin T-fret material:

"**We wish at this time to bring to your attention a new form of fret wire which we are manufacturing for the musical instrument trade. Sample of this wire you will find enclosed. You will note that the novel feature is the including of a barb on the lower edge suitable for holding the wires in the slot cut for them in the neck of the instrument.**

Our purpose in developing this material was to relieve the manufacturer of the necessity of putting these abrasions on the wire with the usual hand machine employed in most factories. Because of the wedge shape of the barbs on our wire it will be found to press in more easily and will remain more firmly in the slots than will the ordinary form of wire."

Martin took, what was for the period, an inordinate amount of time to consider the offer and did not reply until February 25, 1925:

"**Please send us about five pounds of Fret Wire like the sample enclosed herewith and quote price in full coils.**

Can you make up this wire from 18% Nickel Silver Soft Wire? We are now using wire of this description, supplied by the Chase Co., to form a solid fret which is driven into the fret slot without nicking and holds very well.

It is possible that the T Fret Wire made by you would save us some money on this operation; it should, however, be soft so that it can be easily filed. Many makers of cheap instruments do not smooth these frets with a hand file as we do and probably are not particular about this point."

For whatever reason, Martin does not appear to have been interested in procuring T-fret wire other than the 5 pound sample that was sent to them in February 1925. Collectors should be on the lookout for T-fret wire used on guitars from early 1925, as it is almost certain that Martin would have used up the sample on production guitars.

Martin wrote a letter to Pearson Piano Co. on September 23, 1932 with some interesting comments concerning bar frets:

"**In regard to a new fingerboard with extra wide frets for Mr. McDougal's OM-45 De Luxe Guitar we quote a price of $15.00 net. We have been experimenting with these wide T frets for several months but do not find then as satisfactory in the long run as the solid frets we are using. You know we increased the width of our frets last year and possibly Mr. McDougal's guitar has the old very narrow frets; if so, we can refret the fingerboard for him, putting in our new frets, at a cost of only five or six dollars.**

All the new Martin Guitars, particularly the Carved Top Model, are equipped with these frets."

It is not known what Martin meant by wider frets and this information can't be confirmed by measuring fret widths on existing guitars.

Martin corresponded with Horton-Angell Co. of Attleboro Mass. on August 31, 1934 concerning T-fret wire:

"**After long consideration we have about decided to change from solid nickel silver frets to T frets** and were are interested in your No. 3091 pattern of which you sent us a small quantity last month. We have been using thirty per cent nickel silver wire in the solid frets, rolling it ourselves, and we are very anxious to continue to use this grade of material in the T frets. We understand that it will be harder to work but we would like to have your quotation on one hundred pound lots, No. 3091 pattern. How soon could you make delivery?"

The fact that Martin mentions they rolled their own fret wire may explain why they ordered fret wire wider than the frets they installed. A check of the inventory records shows that Martin did indeed have a "wire rolling machine" on hand by at least 1920. Since they ordered nickel silver wire in the annealed state Martin could re-roll this wire to any desire thickness and end up with work-hardened fret wire, which would last longer. As Martin bought T-fret wire from the end of 1934, they no longer had a use for a wire rolling machine although it did appear on the yearly inventories until 1941.

Horton-Angell Co. replied on September 4, 1934:

"As we have very little call for 30% nickel silver wire, we do not carry this grade in stock. We do carry both 10 and 18% and could make a delivery on either of these items in about a week. The delivery on 30% nickel silver wire would be from three to four weeks."

There may have been a little confusion at this point because in a letter dated July 6, 1934 Horton-Angell Co. had written:

"We are enclosing, herewith, a sample of our fret wire #3091 which is the latest pattern we have made. We would not care to make this in 30% nickel as this grade of material would be very hard on the tools."

Correspondence from 1935 confirms Martin must have prevailed on the alloy used for fret wire, since Horton-Angell did make T-fret wire in 30% nickel silver. However, Martin complained about the hardness of the fret wire in a letter to Horton-Angell Co. dated September 25, 1935:

"Before placing another stock order for Guitar

Fret Wire, No. 3091, made of thirty per cent nickel silver wire, we wish to ask whether you could furnish it a little softer than you did in October 1934. We believe it would work better it were not tempered quite so hard."

Clearly, the 30% nickel silver T-fret wire had work hardened to such an extent during the rolling process that Martin was experiencing some issues using it. Horton-Angell responded on September 26:

"The only thing we can see to do to soften this would be to anneal it after the shape was rolled. This we will do if you think it will be suitable for your requirements."

There is no further correspondence on the subject but purchasing records show that Martin had switched to 18% nickel silver fret wire by early 1936.

The first large order of T-fret wire was received form Horton-Angell Co. on October 3, 1934 and was probably put into use immediately. The introduction of T-frets also coincided with introduction of steel T-bars used for neck reinforcement. It would appear that steel-string Martin guitars completed after mid-October 1934 had both T-frets and the steel T-bar. This would correspond to instruments stamped from August 9, 1934, beginning around serial number 57305.

Horton-Angell Co. was Martin's sole source for fret wire from 1934 until at least 1963. During these years Martin used 10%, 15% and 18% nickel silver fret wire in a variety of patterns, although no detailed information on the differences can be gleaned from the purchasing records.

Number of Frets on the Fingerboard

Martin rarely recorded the number of frets on their guitars, so the observation in this section are based on examination of existing guitars. The sample of guitars, especially for the pre-1840 instruments, is small, so exceptions are bound to be encountered. This information should be considered a basis for further study and discussion.

On the early Stauffer-shaped guitars the number of frets on the fingerboard depended on the period and whether the neck was adjustable or not.

Label Type	Date	Lower Bout (Nominal)	Neck Screw	Number of Frets	Scale (Nominal)
1 to 3	1834-1836	11.69"	Yes	22	24"
4 or 5 (First Period)	1836-1837	11.69"	Yes	21	24"
4 or 5 (First Period)	1836-1837	11.69"	No	20	24"
6	May-Sept. 1838	11.5"-11.75"	Yes/No	20	24"-25.59"
5 (Second Period)	Oct. 1838-May 1839	11.22"-11.65"	Yes/No	18	24"-24.69"
7	May-Aug. 1839	11.25"-11.69"	No	18	24"-24.5"
8	Aug. 1839-May 1850	11.25"-12.13"	No	18 or 19	24"-25"

Table 95
**Number of Frets on the Fingerboards of
Martin Guitars to 1850**

The cittern-shaped Amadill guitar shipped by Martin on August 8, 1836 guitar has only 18 frets.

During the Martin & Coupa period (i. e., 1840-1850) guitars had either 18 or 19 frets, although 18-fret guitars are seen more often. The "Renaissance" shaped guitars usually have 20 frets, although the "Elegant" guitar from 1854 has 19 frets.

From 1851 until around the middle 1880, all guitars featured 18 frets. By at least 1886, the 0-28 guitars gained an extra fret, while the rest of the sizes and style remained at 18 frets until at least 1898.

By 1900 all sizes and styles had 19 frets, although, in that year, William Foden ordered a 0-42 guitar with 20 frets. For the remainder of the 20th century Martin six-string guitars had either 19 or 20 frets, depending on the model and period.

Glue and Glue Suppliers

For most of the period covered by this book Martin used hide glue in the construction of their instruments. Hide glue was not only an excellent adhesive but was widely available.

Hide glue is made using remnants of animal hides from the tanning industry. The process for making glue involved washing the hides, soaking them in lime for 70 days, washing and mixing with acid to neutralize the lime and cooking in water until a liquor was created. The liquor was them dried in special ovens for several hours, resulting in sheets of glue. The dried sheets of glue were then ground to a powder and sold. The glue making process generated a foul odor but the final product had little to no smell.

Martin mostly used ground hide glue although they did occasionally buy sheets of glue.

It has been suggested that the Martin factory converted to "cold glue" shortly after the company moved to the new factory in July 1964. One source claims that on September 29, 1964 Grant Remaley, a foreman in the Martin factory, recorded in his work notes that Martin was beginning to use the cold glue. This assertion may be true but the author could not find this record.

The foremen's note books contain only a few mentions of the type of glue used in the factory in the 1960's:

1) A notebook circa 1965 contains instructions for the use of electric glue pots for hot hide glue

2) A note dated March 26, 1968 states that 6 oz. of water was to be added to 1 gallon of cold glue

INVENTORY DATE	QUAN.	UNIT	PRODUCT
	376	LBS	COOPER GROUND 5A
JANUARY 1, 1964	85	LBS	COOPER GROUND 2A
	20	EA	EASTMAN #910 ADHESIVE BOTTLES
	10	GAL	COOPER GLUE PV1
JANUARY 1, 1965	456	LBS	COOPER GROUND 5A EXTRA
	1	EA	EASTMAN #910 ADHESIVE BOTTLES
	82	LBS	HEWITTS GLUE
	5	GAL	COOPER GLUE PV1
JANUARY 1, 1966	69	GAL	COOPER GLUE PV2
	23	LBS	HEWITTS GLUE
	25	GAL	COOPER PV
	300	LBS	COOPER 5A EXTRA
JANUARY 1, 1967	90	EA	3M #4475 TUBES
	10	GAL	BETASTAY
	5	GAL	POLYMER 14012

Table 96
Types of Glues from 1964 to 1967 Inventories

3) A notebook from around 1970 containing instructions for both PV1 (cold glue) and hot hide glues
As the records concerning glues from the period are not extensive, it is worthwhile examining inventory records from the period in question.

Cooper 5A, Cooper 2A and Hewitts glue are all hot hide glues. Cooper PV1 and PV2 glues were liquid hide glues, similar to today's Titebond. Eastman #910 adhesive was an early variety of cyanoacrylate glue. The 3M #4475 glue is an industrial plastic adhesive, still available, used to join most kinds of plastic. Betastay was the trade name for a synthetic resin emulsion (wood glue) made by the Essex Chemical Co. No information could be found on the Polymer 14012 glue.

It is not known what use Martin made of the Eastman #910 cyanoacrylate adhesive but it was almost all used up during 1964. The 3M #4475 glue may have been used to gluing pick guards to tops.

Keeping in mind that the inventory records are only a single day snapshot, it appears that Martin was beginning to experiment with other types of adhesives by some time in 1963. Martin continued to use only hot hide glue through 1964 but was certainly using liquid hide glue in 1965 and 1966. However, in 1967 hot hide glue still made up the majority of the glue on hand. (The fact that Martin had little hot hide glue on hand on January 1, 1966 may just mean they were short of stock and awaiting another order). Martin was clearly using cold hide glue for gluing some components of their instruments by 1964. There is no information to indicate how long Martin continued to use hot hide glue, other than the note from circa 1970 mentioned above.

Interestingly, Martin did try out small quantities of liquid hide glue during the war years (1942 to 1944).

Hide glue was very commonly available in the 19th century and Martin bought from a variety of sources; F. Hubinger (1875), William A. Baeder Glue Co. (1888), Henry T. Mason (1885, 1890, 1893, 1895, 1896), Herman Behr & Co. (1895), Hammacher, Schlemmer & Co. (1895) and B. Dolan Glue Co. (1896). In the 20th century Martin mostly bought hide glue from the American Glue Co. (1923 to 1925), Coignet Chemical Co. (1923 to 1933), C. B. Hewitt & Bros. (intermittently from 1925 to 1941 and then 1953 to 1959), Peter Cooper Corp. (1932 to 1953 and 1960 to 1964).

Ivory and Ivory Suppliers

In the 19th century ivory was a common commodity used on luxury goods. Martin employed ivory for decoration of their instruments from 1833 until 1918. Ivory decoration was mostly reserved for styles 26 guitars and higher. It was used for binding, purfling, bridges, pins, tuning pegs, tuner buttons (usually supplied by the tuner manufacturer), nuts and saddles. Occasionally, Martin veneered the whole fingerboard of a guitar in ivory and, before 1860 or so, used ivory for making attractive "ornaments" that were placed below the bridge.

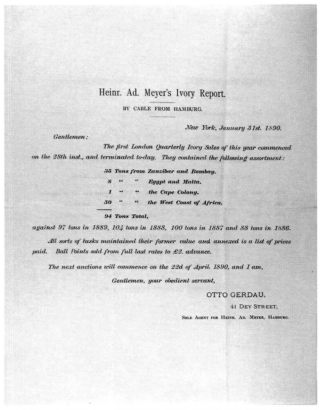

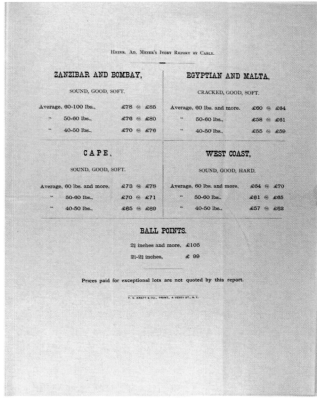

Table 288
Ivory Market Report Dated January 31, 1890

There was a steady demand for ivory throughout the 19th century and Martin received regular market reports on availability and pricing.

These market reports are interesting, if sad, and give some insights into the ivory trade. From the numbers mentioned in Figure 288 it appears the European market for ivory accounted for about 100 tons of tusks per year and that ivory was exported to the United States through the United Kingdom and Germany. Curiously, Egypt and Malta are listed as sources for ivory tusks.

The Martin correspondence includes some interesting information on gluing ivory. In a letter from Henry T. Mason, a dealer in glues, hair and twine, dated March 15, 1895 gives instruction on gluing ivory:

"In reply to your letter of March 13th in reference to glue for Ivory, we would recommend you to use Fine white glue with Russian Isinglass. About one half pound of fine white glue to two ounces of Russian Isinglass, and mix with a little white lead to make it set quick.

This is what is used for glueing piano keys."

Isinglass is made from dried swim bladders of fish and Russian isinglass is specifically made from the swim bladders of the Beluga sturgeon.

Martin usually purchased ivory as tusks, scrivellos (small tusks) or points. From these were made bridges, thin strips for binding or purfling, nuts and saddles. Martin always seems to have purchased bridge pins, end pins and friction pegs (often sourced by C. A. Zoebisch & Co.) from specialized "ivory turners" in New York.

Table 289
Noted Added to a 1917 Catalog Announcing the Discontinuation of Ivory on April 1, 1918

Martin stopped using ivory for bridges, bridge pins, end pins and binding on April 1, 1918. From this point the bridge pins, end pins and binding were made of ivory-colored celluloid (ivoroid).

Martin continued to make ivory saddles and nuts from their own dwindling supply of ivory for a time but began buying ivory nuts and saddles towards the end of 1922, and continued to do so until at least 1967. Martin's main suppliers of ivory nuts and saddles were Rogers Manufacturing Co. (1930 to 1937) and Pratt, Read & Co. (1934 to 1967).

Left-Handed Guitars

In 1925 Martin sent a BK mandolin to the Chicago branch of Carl Fischer Inc. On March 28, 1925 Fischer wrote to Martin with a special request:

"We beg to acknowledge receipt of a special mandolin, which is very satisfactory, except that through a misunderstanding the above should have been ordered for a left handed player.

The party is so well pleased with the instrument that she will accept it as is, only she would like to have the upper saddle (nut?) and the bridge reversed and the instrument strung for left hand playing. Will you kindly advise us if you are willing to do that, and what will be the expense in connection with it, and how long it will take?

Please understand that there is no change to be made in the instrument itself. The only change to be made is the reversing of the upper nut and the bridge."

Martin replied on March 30:

"We can arrange to supply a special bridge and nut for the Style BK Mandolin recently sent you and to string for left-hand playing, at a cost to you of one dollar, net. The work could be done in a day or two.

We must remind you, however, that a Mandolin, like a Violin, is constructed for right-hand stringing and will not produce the same tone when the strings are reversed because the braces are laid

(out) and worked differently on each side of the instrument. When a Mandolin is desired for left-hand playing it is by far the best to make it up specially, then we reverse every step in the construction of the instrument and the result is satisfactory. We are about to start a factory lot of Style BK's and suggest that you take the matter up with your customer and try to have her wait for a special instrument from this lot.

If you wish, we will give you full credit for the return of the instrument you have and will build the special instrument for you at an addition of one dollar, net, to the regular price."

Carl Fischer Inc. took advantage of Martin's kind offer and a left-handed BK mandolin was ordered on April 4, 1925.

As can be seen from the above letter, Martin wanted to reverse the placement of the braces for instruments meant for left-handed playing, so as to not hurt the tone. The majority of left-handed instruments were made as "special orders", although, if a shop order had not proceeded too far in manufacturing process, one instrument from the batch could be selected for left-hand construction. This became a little trickier in late 1930's with the introduction of style stamps for the neck block of instruments. It appears that many guitars from the 1930's to the late 1950's were ordered as either "S" (special) or "L" (left-hand) models. From the late 1950's some guitars were again selected from batches of regular guitars and converted to left-hand construction but it is not known if the style stamp was altered with the addition of a S or L.

Martin made at least 223 left-handed guitars and 8 left-handed mandolins between 1923 and 1966. A few left-handed rarities for collectors to watch out for are a 1929 OM-28P, a 1931 OM-18, a 1931 OM-28, a 1931 000-45L and a 1940 D-45L. The last two guitars mentioned are known to exist.

The Switch to Mahogany for Economy Models (1906)

C. F. Martin Sr. had offered guitars with mahogany bodies as inexpensive student models from his earliest days in New York . From at least 1848 until 1856, Martin produced guitars with mahogany bodies in

styles 14, 15 and 16. Presumably the style 14 guitars had no binding while style 15 was bound on the top only and style 16 was bound on both top and bottom.

The economy 2½-17 and 3-17 "student" guitars with rosewood bodies were common throughout the 19th century but had disappeared from production by 1898. Style 17 was resurrected in 1906 with the introduction of 0-17 guitars, but now the specification for style 17 guitar called for a mahogany body with a spruce top. By the time the new model appeared in the 1909 catalog sizes 1-17 and 00-17 had been added to the 0-17 model in the product line. Style 17 guitars were dropped in 1917. The first serial number for these models was 10121 (a 0-17) and the last was 12798 (a 1-17).

When style 17 reappeared in 1922 with the 2-17 model, the guitar now having a mahogany top as well as body.

Tuning Machines (1850 to 1967)

Tuning machines used on pre-1860 Martin guitars are already covered on pages 96 to 98. This chapter will begin by reviewing "Jerome" tuners which, although in use from the 1840's, overlap with later types of tuning machines.

The tables in this chapter are based on information from the inventories that Martin took at the beginning of each year. The inventory records begin in 1893 and are complete until 1967 except for 1910 to 1917 and 1919. These records are invaluable as they document the history of the tuning machines used by Martin through the years and are currently the only source of information on Kluson model numbers.

Jerome Tuners (1840's to 1850's)

The early Jerome machines are easy to identify because the name "Jerome" is stamped on the top part of the backing plate. Jerome tuners were made in a number of grades: grade 1) plain brass usually with bone buttons, grade 2) brass with ivory buttons an embossed "thistle & leaves" decoration around each screw hole, grade 3) similar to 2) but made of German silver with ivory button and grade 4) similar to 3) but with fancy pearl buttons.

The shape of the tuner buttons are usually "tulip-shaped" on early Jerome tuners while later examples are more oblong in shape. The fancier grade of Jerome tuners have beautifully carved pearl buttons.

The tuning gears can also be used for dating Jerome machines. The early Jerome tuners have "washer-type" gears, named for the smooth outer surface of the gear which looks like a washer has been placed on the outside of the gear (Figures 114, 115 and 116 on page 98). Later Jerome machines have regular exposed spur gears (Figures 117, 118 and 119).

The machines in Figure 120 are regularly encountered on mid-19th century Martin guitars and, although missing a name stamp, were clearly manufactured by Jerome, as the decorative stampings around the screw holes are identical to the earlier Jerome machines. Jerome simply shortened the backing plate by clipping both ends of the old design without changing the decorative features. This change of design occurred in the mid-1850's.

Figure 290, from the Martin Archive, shows an 1850 invoice from J. A. Rohé to C. F. Martin for "guitar mecaniques". Since the description of the tuners is in French the invoice is almost certainly for "Jerome" tuners. An 1852 invoice (Figure 291) from Rohé & Leavitt is identical in quantity and price to the 1850 invoice except the tuners are now referred to as "patent heads", the terminology for tuners used by Martin for most of the 19th century. Rohé and, later, Rohé & Leavitt appear to have been Martin's main suppliers

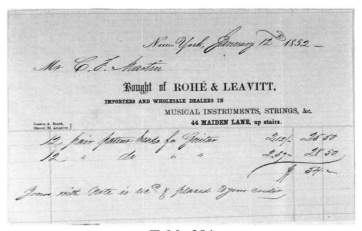

Table 291
1852 Invoice from Rohe & Leavitt for Tuning Machines

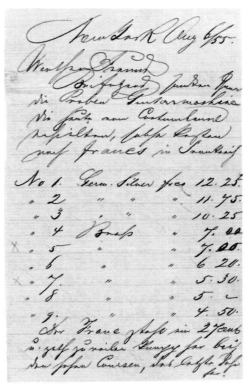

Table 292
1855 Letter from C. A. Zoebisch Discussing the Pricing of French Tuning Machines

of tuning machines from 1850 to 1855, and probably earlier. By 1855 C. A. Zoebisch & Son were taking an interest in supplying tuners to Martin as the 1855 letter in Figure 292 discusses "sample tuning machines" and their cost in Francs, obviously tuners of French manufacture and very likely manufactured by Jerome.

Demet Tuners (circa 1843)

These type of machines have only been seen on one

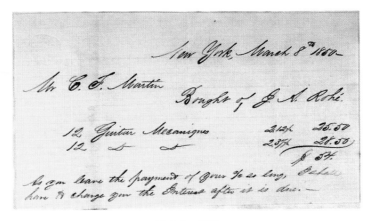

Table 290
1850 Invoice from Rohe & Leavitt for Tuning Machines

GUITAR STRIPS	1893	1894	1895	1896	1897	1898	1899	1900	1901	1902	1903	1904	1905	1908	1909
SEIDEL #2						9	9								
SEIDEL #3 WITH PEARL HANDLES	16	9	2	1											
SEIDEL #3 WITH IVORY HANDLES			2			5			33	9	2				
SEIDEL #3 WITHOUT HANDLES			4	4	9										
SEIDEL #3a									11	11					
BRASS, PEARL BUTTONS							24						34	2	2
SEIDEL #4	4	20	10	3	6	1	43	32	15	5		1			
SEIDEL #5	10	11	4	6		9	15		57	10	19		1		
SEIDEL #6	16	7	14	12	6	8	7		36	38	6	1			
SEIDEL #26	38	21	9		1										
LANG							20								

Table 97
Yearly Inventory of Seidel Tuning Machines from 1893 to 1909

Martin instrument, the Martin & Schatz guitar made for Madam De Goni in 1843 (Figure 122). These tuners were manufactured in France by Victor Auguste Demet (December 15, 1804-November 10, 1884). Demet is recorded in the Mirecourt registry as a sometime watchmaker and sometime luthier (special thanks to Jean-Jacques Poli for providing this information). Mirecourt is a small town in the Vosges mountains of eastern France that for centuries has been involved in the manufacture of stringed instruments, especially those of the violin family.

Seidel Tuners

According to the Martin cash ledger covering 1899 to 1913, the full name of this company was C. Louis Seidel. It is known that these tuners were imported from Germany as Martin paid duty on the orders received and, on at least one invoice, payment was handled through the Leipzig exchange. Possibly Seidel was located in the city of the same name in Saxony.

Based on existing guitars Martin began to use Seidel tuning machines around the mid-1850's and continued to purchase them until early 1905. However, Martin also begun to buy tuners made by Louis Handel in

Figure 293
Seidel Machines on a 1850-1855
Martin Renaissance Guitar

Figure 294
Seidel No. 6 Machines on 1857 Martin 2-17 Guitar

Figure 295
Seidel No. 4 Machines on 1857-1858
Martin 0-27 Guitar

Figure 296
Seidel No. 5 Machines on 1857-1858
Martin 0-27 Guitar

New York tuners from 1899 and purchases of Handel machines replaced those of Seidel during 1905.

It seems Martin purchased tuning machines from a previously unknown supplier, Lang, in 1898 because they appeared in the 1899 inventory records and are included in Table 97 for the sake of completeness. From the number of invoices in the Martin archival records it would appear that C. A. Zoebisch & Sons was importing "patent heads" (i. e., tuning machines) on Martin's behalf from at least 1884 (see Figure 297), but possibly as early as the 1860's, when they became Martin's master distributor. These machines

Figure 297
1884 Invoice from C. A. Zoebisch for Tuning Machines

Figure 298
Seidel No. 3 Machines 1888 Martin 2½-40 Guitar

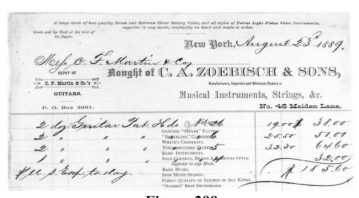

Figure 299
August 23, 1889 Invoice from C. A. Zoebisch & Sons for No. 4, No. 5, No. 6 and No. 26 Patent Heads

Figure 300
Seidel No. 4 Machines on 1890 Martin 2-27 Guitar

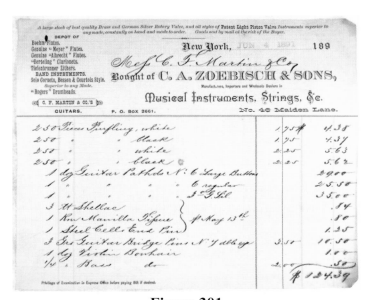

Figure 301
June 4, 1891 Invoice from C. A. Zoebisch & Sons for No. 3 and No. 6 Patent Heads

Figure 302
Seidel No. 26 Machines on 1893 Martin 2½-17 Guitar

were almost certainly made by Seidel since the grades of tuners on the invoices are consistent with the numbering system in Table 97. This situation continued until at least 1897 but, with Zoebisch beginning to fade as a business partner, Martin began importing Seidel tuners directly by 1898 and continued to do so until 1905.

From the invoices above (Figures 297, 299 and 301),

it can be seen that Martin purchased Seidel tuners in grades No. 26, No. 6, No. 5, No. 4 and No. 3. The No. 26 machines were the least expensive and the tuners graded up to the most expensive grade No. 3 or No. 3a machines. Martin also bought a small number of No. 2 tuners that were more expensive than No. 3 machines and, presumably, fancier. It appears grades No. 26 to No. 4 were made of brass while No. 3 and No. 2 were German silver. Seidel tuners are occasionally seen with "Seidel" stamped on the reverse side of the backing plate.

There is no sure way to identify the different grades of Seidel tuners but an attempt will be made here to put them in some semblance of order. The plainer machines were obviously used on the less expensive Martin guitars. Most Seidel tuners, whether brass or German silver, are stamped with a floral decoration as well as two lines of decorative "lozenges", one down each side. However, No. 26 tuners (Figure 302) are stamped with a "butterfly" motif and the two lines of stamped decoration are thinner and closer together. Figure 294 shows a No. 6 tuner and No. 5 is represented in Figure 296. These appear to be identical but since the No. 5 machine is mounted on a 0-27 guitar and the No. 6 machine on a 1-21 guitar the difference is that the No. 5 probably has ivory buttons and the No. 6 bone buttons. A No. 4 tuner is illustrated in Figure 295. It will be noted that the No. 4 tuners have a stamped "bulls-eye" in each corner while the No.5 machine have 5-pointed stars in the corners. The tun-

machines looked like although a grainy photograph of a 1871 Martin 2-42 curiously seems to show a fairly plain German silver backing plate with pearl buttons.

Handel Tuners

Louis Handel was a company on New York engaged in fancy metal sawing and pearl inlay work. Handel had been selling mandolin pick guards and pearl in-

HANDEL TUNERS

GUITARS-STRIPS	1900 QUAN.	1901 QUAN.	1902 QUAN.	1903 QUAN.	1904 QUAN.	1905 QUAN.	1908 QUAN.	1909 QUAN.	1918 QUAN.	1920 QUAN.
HANDEL, BRASS, IVORY BUTTONS	48		10	19						
HANDEL, BRASS, PEARL BUTTONS				2						
HANDEL, GS, PEARL BUTTONS	3		1							
HANDEL, GS, IVORY BUTTONS				24						
HANDEL, BRASS					16					
HANDEL, GS						10	1	5		
HANDEL 4 (0-42)									7	
HANDEL, #6-1/2							1			
HANDEL #6										13
HANDEL #10										39
HANDEL #41										2

Table 98
Yearly Inventory of Handel Tuners from 1900 to 1920

Figure 304
Handel German Silver Tuners with Inlaid Ivory Buttons on 1917 Martin 00-45 Guitar

Figure 303
Seidel No. 3a Machines on 1905 Martin 000-21 Guitar

ers illustrated in Figure 298 is a No. 3 tuner and are very similar to the No. 3a machines shown in Figure 303, the only difference being that the No. 3 machines had pearl buttons while the No. 3a machines had ivory buttons. It is not known at present what No. 2

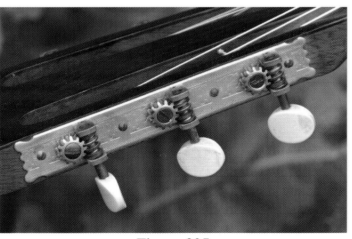

Figure 305
German Silver Handel Tuners on a 1918 Martin 0-18 Guitar

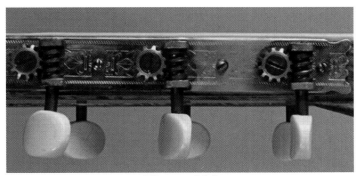

Figure 306
Handel Tuners with German Silver Backing Plate and
Plain Ivory Buttons on 1920 Martin 00-45 Guitar

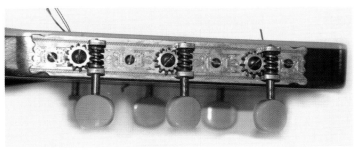

Figure 307
Handel Machines on a 1938 00-44G

lays to Martin since 1895. In 1897 Martin also began buying tuning machines from Handel. Martin didn't buy as many different styles of Handel machines as they had with Seidel tuners. Not all grades of Handel machines shown in Table 98 have been identified and more study is required. However, the fancier grades of Handel machines had a "fleur-de-lis" motif stamped on a German silver backing plate and were sometimes supplied with delicately inlaid ivory buttons.

Dinsmore & Jager Tuners

Dinsmore & Jager was a business located in Northampton MA that manufactured "musical instrument trimmings" with "patent heads a specialty", al-

though in the 1896 business directory for Northampton listed the company as "machinists" located at 29 Walnut St. D & J seem to have concentrated mostly on simple but high quality brass tuners, although they did make some German silver machines.

Dinsmore & Jager sold tuning machines to Martin for almost half a century, 1903 to 1950, but are almost completely unknown. This situation is largely due to the fact that the purchases from D & J overlap with those from Waverly. As collectors and dealers are more familiar with Waverly tuning machines, they naturally assumed that all tuner strips that couldn't be identified as Handel products must be Waverly machines. It also does not help that the backing plates of Handel and D & J tuners are similar. In fact Martin did not begin to buy Waverly machines until 1920, so any non-Handel machines encountered on guitars between 1903 and 1919 must have been produced by D & J.

Martin also bought some brass tuners made by a company called Schmidt in 1925 and 1926 and these inventory figures are included in Table 99.

Author's Note: The theory put forth in this book for the use of D & J and Waverly tuners in the 1920 to 1950 period is based on Martin inventory records.

Figure 308
Dinsmore & Jager #5 Tuners
on 1911 Martin 0-18 Guitar

DINSMORE & JAGER

GUITARS-STRIPS	1904	1905	1908	1909	1918	1920	1921	1922	1923	1924	1925	1926	1927	1928	1929	1930	1931	1932	1933	1934	1935	1936	1937	1938	1939	1940	1941	1942	1943	1944	1945	1946	1947	1948	1949	1950
D & J, GS, PLAIN	93	8																																		
D & J #5, BRASS			65	33	98	51	44		12		302	20											127	68	39	12	25	108	77	59	45	21				
D & J #57, GS				21																																
D & J, GS, FANCY	66	61	28	13																																
D & J #31																								71	48	60	69	152	56	25	5	5	12	87	12	6
D & J #33						129	104		3	10														24	20	2	27	67	56	55	18	3				
D & J #33B							7																													
D & J #9, NOT INLAID					4																															
D & J #9, INLAID					24																															
D & J #9C						2																														
D & J SINGLE UNT																													65				2,088	130		
SCHMIDT, BRASS												247	9																							
D & J 10-STRING, BRASS (TIPLE)												463	138	16		23	23	23																		
D & J #2 (TIPLE)																	159																			

Table 99
Yearly Inventory of Dinsmore & Jager Tuners from 1904 to 1950

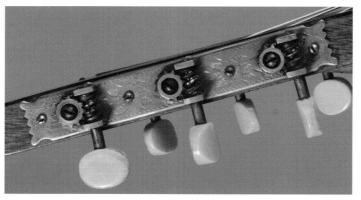

Figure 309
Dinsmore & Jager #33 Tuners on a
1922 Wurlitzer 2093 (00-42) Guitar

Figure 310
Possibly a Set of Schmidt Tuners on a
1924 Martin 0-18 Guitar

Figure 311
Dinsmore & Jager #31 Tuners on
1947 Martin 00-21 Guitar

Figure 312
Waverly #1005 or #1008 Tuners
on 1924 Martin 2-17 Guitar
Ends of backing plate are similar to
later Waverly 5038 machines.

Figure 313
Waverly #1005 Tuners on 1925 Martin 2-17 Guitar

Figure 314
Waverly G-31 Tuners 1926 Martin 00-28 Guitar

Figure 315
Waverly G-32 Tuners on 1927 Martin 000-45 Guitar

These records are only a snap-shot of the tuners in inventory on one day each year. As well, most of the detailed records are missing between 1910 and 1919. The records show that Martin did purchase D & J tuners between 1926 and 1936, even though they do not appear in the inventory records. This is a good example of Martin exhausting their stock of D & J tuners before the end of each year, so that none would be counted in the January 1st inventory count. This illustrates the problem of putting too much faith in the inventory records without comparing them to the

Table 100
Yearly Inventory of Waverly Tuners from 1921 to 1967

	'21	'22	'23	'24	'25	'26	'27	'28	'29	'30	'31	'32	'33	'34	'35	'36	'37	'38	'39	'40	'41	'42	'43	'44	'45	'46	'47	'48	'49	'50	'51	'52	'53	'54	'55	'56	'57	'58	'59	'60	'61	'62	'63	'64	'65	'66	'67
STRIPS																																															
WAVERLY #6	139																																														
WAVERLY #6-10 STRING	6																																														
WAVERLY #10	162																																														
WAVERLY #11	64																																														
WAVERLY #1005		12	136	239																																											
WAVERLY #1008		25	144	190																																											
WAVERLY #1009		6	79	147																																											
WAVERLY 10 STRING, BRASS (TIPLE)		13	45	110	246			136	813	792	626	528	428	408	498	324	266	198	136	85	66	67	42	16	33	8	9	22	42																		
WAVERLY 10 STRING, NICKEL (TIPLE)								55	40	90	88	87	88	88	88	88	88	84	70	64	62	60	60	58	58	58	144		96	48																	
WAVERLY 10 STRING, T-31, NICKEL (TIPLE)																															62	90	168	78	144		23	97	43	114	22	150	8	6			
WAVERLY G-30 (nickel silver)					180	223	440	266	199	510	158	98	77	24		6																															
WAVERLY G-31 (nickel plated)					34	63	322	97	105	67	305		5		16	27										66	52	143	67	65			22	73	54		71	90	4	282	99	215	339				
WAVERLY G-32 (chrome plated)					157	124	64	100	135	79	46	18																																			
WAVERLY G-2 (brass)												192	282	114	7	84	84	84	84	84	84		26																								
WAVERLY G-35																										63	264																				
WAVERLY G-13																																	96	219	108	53	176	66	322	120	302	359	175	200	215	
WAVERLY 5039													426	1062			1113																														
INDIVIDUAL UNITS																																															
WAVERLY 5038																				496	794	1228				2824	4																				
WAVERLY 5038, N.																							1397	19																							
WAVERLY 5038, N. W.																							233																								
WAVERLY 5038D																											3000	2240	1744	1896	900	628	894	1341	2340	1282	382	230									
WAVERLY 5038A																											1212	522	114	10																	

Figure 316
Waverly G-30 Tuners on 1932
Paramount Style L Guitar

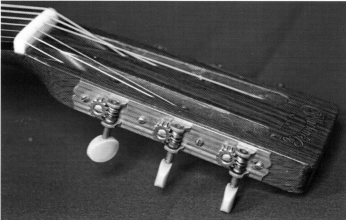

Figure 318
Possibly Waverly 5039 Tuners on 1937 Martin 00-18H

purchasing records.

Waverly Tuners

Martin, according to the purchasing records, began buying Waverly tuners in 1920 and continued to do so through at least 1967. The Waverly tuners from 1920

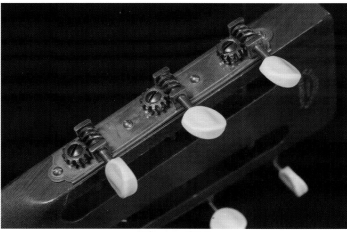

Figure 317
Waverly G-2 Tuners on 1932 Martin 0-18K Guitar

Figure 319
Waverly G-2 Tuners on 1942 Martin 0-15 Guitar

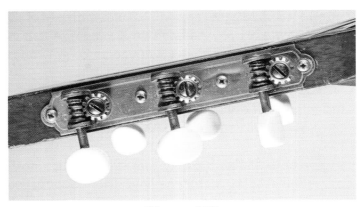

Figure 320
Waverly G-31 Tuners on 1967 Martin D-28S Guitar

to 1939 were all 3-on-a-side machines but from 1940 onwards individual tuners dominated (see Table 100).

It appears the specifications for G-2 tuners changed with time. Originally these tuners were made of brass but by 1942 the tuners appear to be nickel-plated steel (Figure 319). They look similar to the G-30 tuners Martin used in the 1930's but this style of tuner hadn't been recorded in the yearly inventories since 1936.

Grover Tuners

Martin began buying Grover #77 gear pegs in February 1927 for use on their tenor guitars. Interestingly,

Figure 321
Waverly 5038 Tuners on 1940 Martin 00-18 Guitar

Figure 323
Grover #77 Guitar Pegs on 1928 Martin 2-18T Guitar

Figure 322
Waverly 5038D Tuners on 1953 Martin 00-18 Guitar

Figure 324
Grover #91 Leader Tenor Guitar Pegs on
1930 Martin 1-28PS Guitar

INDIVIDUAL UNITS	1929	1930	1931	1932	1933	1934	1935	1936	1937	1938	1939	1940	1941	1942	1943	1944	1945	1946	1947*	1948	1949	1950	1951	1952	1953	1954	1955	1956	1957	1958	1959	1960	1961	1962	1963	1964	1965	1966	1967
GROVER #91 PEGS		494	1401	810	537	437	249	12	6	7	7	2																											
GROVER #90 PEGS	334	188	424	211	210	356	52	43	19	9	3																												
GROVER #89 PEGS	97	83	432																																				
GROVER #89 PEGS (gold, ivoroid buttons)				32																																			
GROVER #89 PEGS (gold, pearl buttons)				16																																			
GROVER 97, HORIZONTAL						85	444	577	834	335	250	192	101	58	52	12	40	40	39	39	37		22																
GROVER 97G, HORIZONTAL				1																																			
GROVER 99T, VERTICAL							2717	521	59																														
GROVER 98, VERTICAL (nickel plated)				117	92	485	972	618	2129	1138	675	826	936	52			9				426	126	48					1500									1797	1357	520
GROVER 98B, VERTICAL (barrel nickel plated)					823	1118	1201	84																															
GROVER 98C, VERTICAL (chrome plated)								260	155	146	127																												
GROVER 98G, VERTICAL (gold plated)		20	6	82	30	10	62	55			20		15	15	15	6																							
GROVER 98N, VERTICAL																													1128	3038	1424	1404	488	1320	1140	1800			
GROVER 98 BUSHINGS																													3000	10000	8500	7500	7500	300	3000	3600	3595	3600	520
GROVER 98G, VERTICAL, (gold plated, engraved)							42	23	48	57	20																												
GROVER 100N, VERTICAL (nickel button)								1470	1285	167	1389	477	35																										
GROVER 105N, VERTICAL (nickel buttons)											1221	266	22	10																									
GROVER G-111													336	924																									
GROVER G-111G (gold plated)													18	72			6	6																					
GROVER 102C (chrome plated)																													1016	1260	501	834	687	1066	240	4176	584		
GROVER 102G (gold plated)																															1432	22	126			144	12	18	4

Table 101
Yearly Inventory of Grover Tuners from 1929 to 1967

the #77 gear pegs never appeared on the yearly inventories. Grover must have been able to ship them quickly from stock when ordered.

The #77 gear pegs were replaced with #91 Leader Tenor Guitar pegs starting about May 1929. The #77 and #91 gear pegs are similar in appearance although the

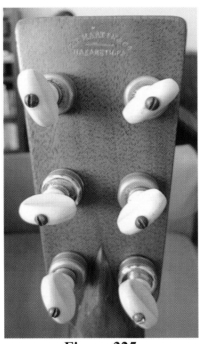

Figure 325
Grover #89 Deluxe Guitar Pegs on
1930 Martin OM-28 Guitar

round cover of the #77 gear peg seems to have a larger radius on its top edge compared to the #91 peg.

Martin received the first #90 Deluxe gear pegs on November 4, 1929, followed by an order for #89 gear pegs on November 26, 1929. The #89 gear pegs were similar in appearance to the #90 but had a deeper

body in comparison to the #90 peg. The #89 Deluxe gear pegs were used on the new OM-28 guitars while #90 gear pegs appeared on the OM-18 model.

The quality of the Grover #89 and #90 gear pegs left much to be desired and there were numerous customer complaints about gear pegs failing to hold string tension. Martin struggled with this problem all through 1930 but began buying Grover individual machines in early February 1931, although orders for gear pegs were being received as late as July 18, 1931. Martin appears to have changed over to side tuners with a batch of OM-18 guitars stamped on June 23, 1931, so it is safe to assume any gears pegs received after this date were used for replacing gear pegs already on guitars. The gear pegs were such an issue that Martin would replace gear pegs on a guitar with side tuners if the customer returned the guitar.

Martin replaced the problematic gear pegs with G-98 individual units from mid-1931. Over the years the G-98 machines were produced with a variety of backing plates and tuner buttons and Martin continued to use them, with the possible exception of a few years in the early 1950's, until at least 1967. The G-98 tuners from 1931 to 1935 have "clipped" backing plates while the version available from 1936 had "pointed" plates.

The G-98 tuners from 1931 to 1934 are seen with seamed butterbean buttons but these were being replaced with un-seamed butterbean buttons by 1935.

Martin also began using G-97 tuners for slot head guitars during 1931 and continued to use them until about 1941. The G-97 tuners during 1931 to 1934 had "clipped" backing plates but this was changed to "pointed" backing plates in late 1934. The types of tuner buttons used for G-97 machines followed a similar time line to the G-98 machines with the 1931 to 1934 G-97 machines having seamed butterbean buttons while un-seamed butterbean buttons came into use in late 1934.

Martin referred to G-98 machines as "vertical" tuners,

Figure 326
Grover G-97 "Clipped Plate" Machines with Seamed Butterbean Buttons on 1932 Martin 00-40H Guitar
Note the beveled edges of the backing plate.

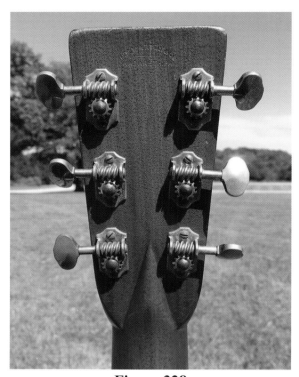

Figure 328
Grover G-98 "Clipped Plate" Tuners with Un-seamed Butterbean Buttons on 1934 Martin D-28 Guitar

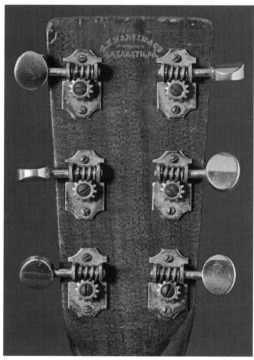

Figure 327
Possibly a Set of Grover G-99T Tuners with Rounded Metal Buttons on 1932 Martin 0-18 14-Fret Guitar
Note the non-beveled edges of the backing plate.

Figure 329
Grover G-98G "Clipped Plate" Tuners with Un-seamed Butterbean Buttons on 1934 Martin 000-45 Guitar

Figure 330
Unknown Style of Grover Tuners with Black Celluloid Buttons on 1934 Martin 00-17 Guitar

Figure 333
Grover G-99T Tuners with Rounded Metal Buttons on 1937 Martin 00-17 Guitar

Figure 331
Grover G-98 "Pointed Plate" Tuners with Seamed Butterbean Buttons on 1936 Martin 000-28 Guitar

Figure 334
Grover G-98G Tuners with Engraved Un-seamed Butterbean Buttons on 1938 Martin 000-45S Guitar

Figure 332
Grover G-98G "Clipped Plate" with Engraved Un-seamed Buttons on 1936 Martin 000-45 Guitar
Buttons are engraved with a stylized "M"

Figure 335
Grover G-111 Tuners with Un-seamed Butterbean Buttons on 1940 Martin D-28 Guitar

Figure 336
Grover G-111G Tuners with Un-seamed Butterbean Buttons on 1940 Martin D-45 Guitar

Figure 337
Grover G-98N "Pointed Plate" Tuners with White Celluloid Buttons on 1963 Martin 00-18 Guitar

Figure 338
Grover 102C Tuners

Figure 339
Grover 102G Tuners

Figure 340
Variety of Grover 102C Tuners with Ivoroid Buttons on 1965 Martin D-35 Guitar

as the string post was perpendicular to the plane of the head stock, and to G-97 machines as "horizontal" tuners to differentiate them.

G-99T machines were similar in appearance to G-98 tuners but had a plain unbeveled edges on the backing plate.

Martin received the first batch of 102-C Rotomatics on March 7, 1958 and would likely have put them into use immediately. The gold-plated 102-G Rotomatic tuners became available in 1959.

Mike Longworth noted that a guitar from the first batch of fifty D-35 guitars had Rotomatic 102C tuners with "pearloid buttons". It appears that at least the first two batches of guitars (i. e., 100 instruments) received this version of Grover 102C tuners. Figure 340 shows these tuners on a D-35 guitar from the second batch.

Kluson Tuners

Martin began receiving Kluson tuners in March 1941 and used them concurrently with Grover and Waverly machines through the remainder of 1941 and into 1942. However, from December 1942 until December 1945 Martin was almost exclusively using Kluson tuners.

The Martin purchasing and inventory records are essentially the only source of information for the style numbers of Kluson machines. War-time Kluson tuners are a study in themselves and numerous variations are encountered as a result of restrictions on the use of metals throughout the war. The early Kluson tuners are well made with a "coined" rim on the backing plate (in the metal stamping industry "coining" refers to a portion of the stamping die that reduces the original thickness of the sheet metal to a specific thickness), thick cog gears, rounded metal buttons and nickel plating. Subsequent tuners retained the coined rim but were made from plain un-plated steel, dispensing with the nickel plating, and the buttons were changed to white celluloid. Late war-time Kluson have plain backing plates, without the coined rim, and were made from lower quality steel. The thickness of the cog gears was also significantly reduced, leading to rapid wear of the gears. The late-war Kluson tuners did have some nickel plating but they were probably "barrel plated" (a less expensive method of plating that used less nickel.)

From 1947 the Kluson 502 tuners were replaced with "octagonal plate" model 190 and 210 machines. These models are similar in appearance but the model 190 tuners had celluloid button while the model 210 machines had metal buttons. Kluson 324 "Deluxe" tuners came into use during 1949 and were still being used on guitars until at least 1967.

The distinctive Kluson 500 tuners, also known as "waffle-backs", were first purchased by Martin in 1950 and remained in used until 1958.

Figure 341
Kluson 511 Tuners with Coined Edge
on 1941 D-28 Guitar

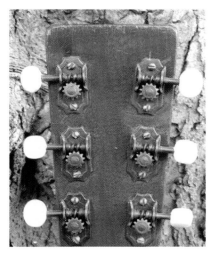

Figure 342
Kluson 501 Tuners with Coined Edge
Un-plated steel backing plate and white celluloid buttons

	1942	1943	1944	1945	1946	1947	1948	1949	1950	1951	1952	1953	1954	1955	1956	1957	1958	1959	1960	1961	1962	1963	1964	1965	1966	1967
STRIPS																										
KLUSON 259	34	43	36	12	66	72	27	24																		
KLUSON 221			120																							
KLUSON 255										59	105	213	131	31	6	6										
KLUSON KG-702 (TIPLE)						4	62	70	40														4	62	70	40
INDIVIDUAL UNITS																										
KLUSON 501			4593																							
KLUSON 502	1494	34																								
KLUSON 502B, BLACK		172	394	2383	6434	3226																				
KLUSON 502N			1117																							
KLUSON 511	2328	420	50																							
KLUSON 511G (GOLD PLATED)	72	12	12	12		6			62																	
KLUSON 190							2372	904	3828	1910	2250	2128	60	50	50	51	25	72			42	30				
KLUSON 210							281	1019	769	2706	4735	210	198	17	11	16	16									
KLUSON 553									1314																	
KLUSON 554					450																					
KLUSON 324									766	332	1005	1428	1050	913	1312	2580	352	1536	1536	350	1721	240	1544	578	1008	1100
KLUSON 324 BUSHING																										2000
KLUSON 500									402	800	1596	700	220	913	1128	504	24	24	10							
KLUSON 601 BUSHINGS					3000																					

Table 102
Yearly Inventory of Kluson Tuners from 1942 to 1967

Figure 343
Kluson 502N Tuners on 1944 D-18 Guitar
"N" suffix probably stands for "nickel-plated"

Figure 344
Kluson 502N Tuners on 1945 000-21 Guitar

Figure 345
Kluson 502N Tuners on 1945 D-28 Guitar

Figure 346
Kluson 210 Tuners on 1947 Martin 000-21 Guitar
Style 190 tuners were similar with white celluloid buttons

Figure 347
Kluson K-324 (also called Kluson Deluxe) Tuners on 1957 Martin D-18 Guitar

Figure 348
Kluson K-500 Tuners on 1956 Martin D-28 Guitar
Also known as "waffle-backs"

Martin Salesmen

Martin's first salesman was Herbert K. Martin (December 5, 1895-January 3, 1927), the second son of Frank Henry Martin. Herbert began his role as salesman on June 20, 1920. He apparently enjoyed his job and continued in this role until his untimely death on January 3, 1927, at the age of only 31.

HERBERT K. MARTIN DIES

One of Most Popular Young Men of Nazareth

Residents of Nazareth on Tuesday morning leaned with much regret of the death of Herbert Keller Martin, son of Mr. and Mrs. H. F. Martin, 201 North Main street, that borough, in St. Luke's hospital, Bethlehem, on Monday night.

Mr. Martin, who was in his thirty-first year, was one of the most popular young men of the borough. He was secretary of the C. F. Martin Company, Inc., makers of musical instruments. He became ill about a week ago and was removed to the hospital when his condition became worse. He was reported to be improving when the complications set in.

Mr. Martin was a graduate of Nazareth High school, class of 1913; Perkiomen school, 1915; and Princeton university, 1919. He was very active in musical circles in high school and at college.

During the war he was in the United States army for a short time. He was also a faithful member of the Moravian church, taking an active interest in the Sunday school. He belonged to the Nazareth Lions club.

Besides his parents, he is survived by a brother, Frederick Martin. The funeral will be held on Thursday afternoon, with services at the home of his parents, followed by services in the Moravian church. Interment will be made in the Moravian cemetery.

Figure 349
Newspaper Announcement of the Unexpected Death of Herbert Keller Martin

For a time C. F. Martin III took over outside sale duties and the archive contains some very interesting sales letters from him during September and October 1927. Martin must have begun looking for a salesman by at least the summer of 1927 because a prospective candidate for the outside salesman wrote a letter to Martin on August 4, 1927 applying for the job. From this letter we learn that Martin was looking for a traveling salesman to locate to Nazareth and whose duties would include helping in the factory when not on the road. The salesman was be paid a salary rather than straight commission.

Martin even put feelers out to see if Lloyd Loar, the ex-Gibson sound engineer, would be interested in a position at Martin and received a very interesting letter from Lloyd dated June 3, 1927. Nothing seems to have come from Martin's approach to Loar but it does make one wonder if musical instrument history might have been different if Loar had joined Martin.

James A. Markley was hired as Martin's second outside salesman. He appears to have been hired in November 1927, as he was first credited with a sale in the bookings ledger on November 21. A notice appeared in the January 21, 1928 edition (Figure 350) of The Music Trades Review announcing his first road trip for Martin and reporting that his territory was to be New York and New England. It is interesting to note that Markley was an amateur musician but had not been involved in music trade previous to his employment with Martin. He was let go at the end of June 1936 to save expense.

James A. Markley With C. F. Martin & Co.

Among the new faces on the road this month will be noted the pleasant smile of James A. Markley, who is now on his maiden trip for C. F. Martin & Co., guitar makers, at Nazareth, Pa. Mr. Markley's previous experience has been outside of the music trade, but a six weeks' course of instruction at the factory has given him first-hand knowledge of the fine points of the Martin line; and as a talented amateur musician he understands string instruments from the player's side. After calling on the trade in New York State, Mr. Markley will visit New England.

Figure 350
Announcement of James A. Markley's First Sale Trip

Frank Henry Martin undertook a sales trip on his own to Portland, Oregon and Seattle, Washington in late July 1929. His notes from the trip are full of astute observation on market conditions in those cities and the local dealers who were selling Martin instruments.

In 1933 Martin came to the conclusion another outside salesman was required to cover the "Middle Western" territory, which extended from Canada to Texas and from Ohio to Colorado. In November 1933 Martin put out feelers to Lyon & Healy in Chicago for a possible candidate for the role of outside salesman. Lyon & Healy recommended John J. Shea, who had previously worked for them.

In 1933 John J. Shea was thirty-eight years old and a resident of Chicago. From 1923 to 1929, he worked for Lyon & Healy in Chicago. In 1929, he left to work for Baldwin Piano Co. but returned to Lyon & Healy in 1930 and was put on the road selling Steinway pianos on commission. With the Depression Shea couldn't make a living on commission so he changed to selling life insurance in 1931. Martin carefully vetted Shea through Lyon & Healy and then arranged to meet with him in Chicago on December 11. This interview must have gone well as Martin offered the job to Shea and he began working for Martin on January 1, 1934. Shea was offered a salary with the possibility of a salary increase depending on sales in his territory. The timing couldn't have been better for Shea, or Martin for that matter, because January 1934 also coincided with the appearance of the first 14-fret Dreadnought guitar. Right from the start Shea was very successful in his sales role and undoubtedly received a higher salary or at least regular bonuses.

It is already well know that Chicago Musical Instrument Co. sold many of the earliest Martin Dreadnought guitars (1931 to 1933). Shea was already located in Chicago, so he could service CMI as well as the many other music stores located between Chicago and Milwaukee. These two cities constituted a major radio hub and the demand for a "bass" guitar for radio work was one of the main reasons for the success of the Dreadnought guitar. There is also the intriguing possibility that Shea had actually influenced Martin to begin producing 14-fret Dreadnought guitars. He began working for Martin on January 1, 1934 and the first 14-fret Dreadnought, a D-28, was stamped on January 22. It is known that this guitar was made as a prototype since it does not appear in the bookings ledger and because it was shipped on approval to Chicago Musical Instrument Co. on February 12, 1934. This theory of Shea's influence is also backed up by the fact that the large majority of D-18 and D-28 guitars sold in 1934 and 1935 were shipped to customers in Shea's territory. As a result, not only did Martin have a winning product but they had just hired a salesman who knew how to sell them.

With war-time conditions, including shortages of labor and materials, Martin could not make enough guitars to meet demand, so they hardly needed a salesman. On March 1, 1943 Shea was put on part-time hours and half pay and was finally "dismissed" on November 1, 1944, partly to save on expense but also because government regulations did not allow price increases during the war that could have helped offset the expense.

Shea only worked for Martin for a period 10 years but a very eventful period it was, Shea selling practically all Dreadnought guitars made during the "Golden Era".

Because of the strong demand for Martin guitars during the 1940's and 1950's, Martin had no need for an outside salesman and it wasn't until the 1960's that a sales force was again established. Unfortunately, there is no information on this sales force in the archival records.

Neck Widths

A letter sent by Martin to Steffens Music House on August 12, 1935 nicely covers the topic of neck widths used on Martin guitars:

"Mr. Markley reports that you have a prospect for a Martin Guitar who wants an extra narrow fingerboard. We would make up one for you, for delivery in three or four weeks, a special guitar in any stock style with the neck and fingerboard 1/8" narrower at the nut and 1/16" thinner, at an extra charge of ten dollars retail. We would like to point out that our model guitars all have narrower necks, 1-3/4" wide at the nut instead of 1-7/8" as in the older models. They are also fairly thin and we find that the professional players, many of whom have been banjoists, do not find this neck too thick or wide. If it is made still narrower at the nut there is a danger that the strings will be so close together that they will be hard to finger."

On the earliest Martin guitars, made between 1834 and 1850, the neck width, measured at the nut, varied from as little as 1-9/16" to as much as 2". From about 1850, and for the remainder of the 19th and early 20th centuries, the neck width was normally 1-7/8".

A 1-3/4" wide neck was introduced with the Orchestra Model guitars in late 1929 and was used on the carved top guitars when they were added to the Martin guitar line in 1931.

Longworth noted that the first regularly produced guitar with a 1-11/16" wide neck was serial number 72740 (a D-45). This guitar was stamped on June 7, 1939.

Guitars with 12-fret necks continued to have a 1-7/8" wide neck, even after 14-fret guitars changed over to the narrower necks.

Table 103 shows neck widths at the nut as well as the neck width at the 12th fret for Martin guitars from 1834. The Martin archive contains a number of dated specification cards and the information contained on them is also shown in the table.

DATES	MODELS	WIDTH AT NUT	WIDTH AT 12TH FRET
1834-1850	ALL	1-9/16" to 2"	2-1/8" to 2-3/8"
1850-1929	ALL	1-7/8"	?
May 16, 1929	TENOR and PLECTRUM	1-1/4"	1-1/2"
Nov. 8, 1919	¼ SIZE GUITAR	1-11/16"	2"
Nov. 8, 1919	½ SIZE GUITAR	1-3/4"	2-3/16"
May 16, 1929	SIZE 2 and SIZE 5	1-13/16"	2-1/4"
May 16, 1929	SIZE 0, 00, 000	1-7/8"	2-5/16"
May 8, 1941	12-FRET 0, 00, 000	1-7/8"	2-5/16"
May 8, 1941	12-FRET ¼, ½, 5	1-5/8"	2-1/16"
May 8, 1941	14-FRET 0, 00, 000, D	1-11/16"	2-1/8"

Table 103
Neck Widths

Pearl & Abalone

Even the name of this chapter is a little misleading. Although Martin referred to both pearl and abalone in company records, all shell used on Martin guitars came from various sub-species of abalone, large sea snails of the family *Haliotidae*.

Martin also purchased pre-cut ornaments for inlaying in fingerboards and often referred to these as being made of "Japan pearl", now commonly called awabi. This refers to shell of the giant abalone (*Haliotis madaka*, formerly *H. gigantea*), which are native to Japanese and Korean waters. This type of abalone does not have the type of heart shell seen on red and green abalone. The nacre of this abalone has a silvery iridescence with reflections of emerald green and red color.

As will be seen later in this chapter Martin used the heart shell from green abalone (*H. fulgens*) for cutting strips for purfling for their higher grade guitars. They were sometimes forced to use red abalone (*H. rufescens*) when green abalone was unavailable but much preferred green abalone for this purpose.

Some interesting information can be gleaned from the letter Martin sent to Union Pearl Works (a company located in Brooklyn that manufactured cloak and suit buttons) on November 24, 1924:

"The California Pink Pearl is very nice but the Green Pearl is not what we want. This stock seems to be selected for green color from the ordinary California Red Back Shell while what we need is Green Abalone in which the blues and greens predominate, with very little pink. To show what we mean we are sending under separate cover a few strips of this shell from the stock which (we) have been grinding here. In order to take full advantage of the heart color we saw the shell into strips and grind these strips to retain the curve. This is an expensive process and we would like to get away from it, if you can supply the same grade of shell; if not, we will have to continue to do our own grinding because our designs call for this kind of pearl."

From this letter we learn that Martin cut and ground "pearl" purfling in-house and insisted on green abalone for the purpose. It is of note that green abalone was difficult to obtain even in 1925. Union Pearl Works replied on November 28 that they couldn't supply the "Green Pearl" because it was very scarce.

As it turns out the inventory and purchasing records show that Martin had been purchasing small quantities of green abalone shell since at least 1898 and also bought 1/16" thick green abalone blanks (known to Martin as "plates") when available. The inventory records indicate that precut blanks were readily available until 1908. However, from 1909 Martin began to inventory raw shell and process it themselves. The quantity of shell in the 1909 inventory amounted to only 3-3/4" lbs. but by 1918 Martin had a total of 54 lbs. of green abalone shell on hand, as well as a small amount of ground shell. It is not known if the larger stock reflected an increased use of shell for making purfling or whether Martin was prompted to stock up when they could as a result of the scarcity of green abalone shell. In 1920 and 1921 Martin had a small quantity of "Japan plates" in stock but for what purpose is unknown.

Fortuitously, one of Martin's ivory supplier, Otto Gerdau Co., contacted Martin on July 14, 1927 that they had just received 2,024 lb. of green abalone shell and offered the company the whole package. There also added a cautionary note to the letter:

"It has taken quite a long time to accumulate this shipment and conditions on the coast are still the same and we do not know when we may receive the next shipment."

Martin replied promptly on July 15:

"Thank you for advising us about the shipment of thirty-two bags of Green Abalone Shells. Our requirements are not large enough to warrant the purchase of your entire shipment but we are willing to lay in quite a stock, if the quality is extra good. We note that the price is very high, doubtless in account of the scarcity; but if the quality is good we will lay in a stock now."

Martin eventually ordered 500 lbs. of this shell and Gerdau recorded the shipping date as September 1, 1927. Curiously, this large quantity of shell did not appear in the yearly inventory until 1929 so, presumably, Martin must have delayed shipment until at least the beginning of 1928.

Regardless, this was the last order for green abalone shell that Martin ever made! Martin slowly processed the shell into strips for purfling but they still had 163 lbs. of raw shell in stock on January 1, 1943. A total of 148 lbs. of shell remained on hand during the count of January 1, 1964. but none appeared on the January 1, 1965 inventory, so the shell was probably written off with the move to the new factory in July 1964.

From 1923 to 1928, Martin always had at least some "pink pearl" (i. e., red abalone) on hand, either as raw shell or processed blanks, for the times when green abalone was unavailable. They continued to carry pink pearl in stock long after the company made a major purchase of green abalone shells in 1927 and some red abalone appeared in the yearly inventories until 1958.

Pearl Suppliers

As mentioned above raw abalone shell and processed strips were supplied by Union Pearl Works from about 1901 to 1936, except for the very large order of green

abalone shell that went to Otto Gerdau company in 1927. From 1937 to 1942 Zaharoff Inc. supplied small quantities of abalone shell and some 1/16" strips to Martin, at least some of which was red abalone.

The pearl ornaments and dots used for inlaying fingerboards were supplied almost exclusively by Louis Handel from 1897 to 1964, although small orders occasionally went to Darlington Pearl Works (1947) and Zaharoff Inc. (1947 to 1952). Martin bought both ornaments and dots during the period to late May 1944 but purchased only dots thereafter.

Martin bought guitar headstock veneers from Louis Handel from 1901 until 1936, although 1936 to 1942 a certain Joseph A. Phetteplace did most of the inlays for headstock veneers. Handel also sold Martin the inlaid fingerboard veneers and pick guards used on fancy Martin mandolins from 1895.

Any special fingerboard lettering was usually supplied by Handel until 1942. However, from 1955 to 1962, J. W. McGonigle did most of the fingerboard lettering used on Martin guitars.

Pick Guards

Mandolin Pick Guards

Until now it has generally been assumed that the early Martin mandolin pick guards were made of genuine tortoise shell. However, period records and correspondence paint a very different picture. In fact, Martin used both celluloid and tortoise shell for pick guards, although celluloid was the more commonly used option.

Martin approached William Unger of New York in November 1894 to quote on pearl ornaments and pick guards for use on the early Martin mandolins. On November 27, 1894 Unger provided a price list detailing a variety of pick guards. Most of the pick guards quoted were made of "celluloid and pearl".

Martin was also in communication with The Celluloid Co. from at least February 1895 about buying celluloid sheets. No purchases from the Celluloid Co. are recorded so Martin was probably just had Handel supply finished guards at this time, since practically all pick guards were inlaid.

Martin corresponded with Frank A. Stratton during 1895 concerning various mandolin parts, including tortoise shell pick guards, but in a letter dated September 27, 1895 Stratton commented: "**We are sorry you can not use the tortoise shell guard plates. The sample returned have been received.**"

Martin was purchasing pick guards and "pearl ornaments" from Louis Handel by March 1895. Handel usually used celluloid for making pick guards, although a few were made of real tortoiseshell in September 1896 when celluloid sheets of the color specified by Martin were unavailable. Martin also avoided using real tortoiseshell pick guards due to the cost, tortoiseshell pick guards being about $0.50 more expensive than celluloid guards.

Josef Scheina, one of Martin's wood suppliers, corresponded with Martin in 1895 about which mandolin parts he could supply. Scheina also recommended J. Bernard Co. to Martin for pick guards and W. A. Lang for mandolin tuning machines. Martin contacted J. Bernard, Manufacturer of Fine Marqueterie according to his letterhead, for a quotation on "guard plates". Martin doesn't appear to have purchased any of the pick guards quoted but did buy some pearl ornaments from Bernard at about the same time. Later, between 1927 and 1938, J. Bernard Co. sold Martin purfling for style 21 and style 28 guitars.

Another shortage of dark colored celluloid occurred in February 1897, so pick guards of real tortoiseshell are likely to be encountered through most of 1897. Handel shipped "butterfly" shaped pick guards for the style G5 mandolins until at least December 1897 so the style G5 must have been in production until the end of 1897. During 1897, Handel discussed the shape of the pick guards several times in the correspondence, so different shapes may be encountered.

Martin regularly bought tortoise shells from Otto Gerdau from 1899 to 1917 and this suggests that Martin was making some of their own pick guards, even when buying large amounts of them from Handel. Why Martin would buy tortoise shell is a bit of a mystery. Martin was already buying sheets of celluloid by 1895 and finished pick guards from Louis Handel. The cost of tortoise shell was also considerably higher than celluloid; tortoise shell being $3.00 to $4.00 per lb. while celluloid was $0.65 to $1.00 per lb. Martin

did buy a "veneer punch for guards" for $10.00 on December 28, 1901 so was obviously making at least some of their own pick guards. The last tortoise shell was purchased on June 16, 1917, just shortly after Martin ceased using ivory on guitars.

Martin purchased very few celluloid sheets between 1901 and 1904, being content with letting Handel supply inlaid mandolin pick guards. The celluloid sheets that were purchased in this period were used for making plain mandolin pick guards in the factory. With the introduction of the lower priced style 0 mandolin in 1905 (also style 00 in 1907 and style 000 in 1909) Martin's use of celluloid increased. Martin's purchases of inlaid mandolin pick guards, on the other hand, sharply decreased in 1913, and, as flat mandolins entered production in 1914, had entirely disappeared by 1917.

Guitar Pick Guards

The first recorded use of pick guards on guitars were the "one fine" and "two medium grade" guitar guards supplied by Handel on November 11, 1896. These were probably similar to the mandolin-style pick guards mounted on the 1901-1903 00-42S guitars.

In 1918 and 1919, Charles H. Ditson & Co. ordered three special guitars for a specific customer: a 000-42 (serial number 13364), a 000-28 (serial number 13365) and a 000-30 (serial number 13610). The 000-42 and the 000-28 were ordered on August 13, 1918 and the bookings ledger contains the following note: "**For Harry K. Gilman, To be built for Hawaiian playing**". The 000-30 was ordered on February 28, 1919 with a simple note: "**For Mr. Gilman**".

The 000-42 was shipped on October 24, 1918 and it was noted in the sales ledger: "**For Mr. Gilman, no charge for guard plate**". The 000-28 was shipped on October 31, 1918 with an ivory bridge (a $5.00 extra charge) and it was noted in the ledger: "**Celluloid guard, steel strings, for Mr. Gilman**". The 000-30 was shipped on July 15, 1919 but this time Martin did not supply the pick guard free of charge: "**Guard-plate to order $3.00**". The 000-42 and the unique 000-30 guitar are still in existence and both have very nice "**cloud**" pick guards inlaid into their tops. If and when the 000-28 ever appears it will likely have a similar type of pick guard.

Harry K. Gilman was born in Hawaii in 1891 and moved to the mainland in 1910 where he began to work for the government in the Census Office and, later, the Treasury Department in Washington DC. He must have been a remarkable young man because he also took up teaching Hawaiian guitar and ukulele with his brother George. He was accounted to be one of the best known musicians in Washington at the time and must also have enjoyed success in his side-line business to have afforded these three expensive Martin guitars. Unfortunately, he did not get to enjoy his Martin guitars for long because he died of the Spanish influenza on October 7, 1919, probably caught while he was playing in the army camps and hospitals around Washington.

Anther unique guitar, a 00-42K (serial number 13640), was ordered in 1919 by R. S. Williams & Sons Co. of Toronto with "**two Guardplates to order**". It is interesting to note that both this guitar and the 000-30 were shipped on the same day.

Cooper Brothers of New Kensington, Pennsylvania were the first Martin dealer to order guitars with pick guards applied to the top rather than being inlaid. In 1920 and 1921 Cooper Bros. ordered sixteen unusual, and mostly expensive, Martin guitars, including 5-18K, 5-28, 5-42, 5-45, 0-45, 00-45, 000-28, 000-28K and 000-42 models. One of the two 000-28K is in the Martin Guitar Museum and has a tear-drop shaped celluloid pick guard quite similar to the design to those seen on early OM guitars, the main difference being that the radiused inside edge of the pick guard follows that outside purfling ring of the rosette while the OM pick guards were a little wider and follow the inside ring.

Celluloid pick guards were seen only intermittently until about 1927 but by that year 90% of Martin guitars were being shipped with steel strings and the problem of scratching the top with a pick was becoming a real problem. Tenor guitars were added to the product line in 1927 and were always mounted with a pick guard, as were plectrum guitars. When the 14-fret Orchestra Models (OM) guitars appeared in 1929 they too had pick guards, as there intended use was for plectrum playing.

Martin was a little slow to adopt pick guards for all its guitars and so came up with a policy, as shown

in Figure 351, whereby guitars would be supplied with a celluloid pick guard upon request but would otherwise be shipped without. Was Martin was really planning to stock the same guitar with and without pick guards? This seems like an unlikely solution to the problem of pick guards in the middle of the Depression. Clearly, the demand for guitars without pick guards was very low in the last half of 1931, because by 1932 pick guards were being applied to virtually all guitars unless specially ordered without a guard. The pick guards on the early OM guitars had a tear-drop shape that were well radiused on the edge closest to the bridge. This type of pick guard didn't provide

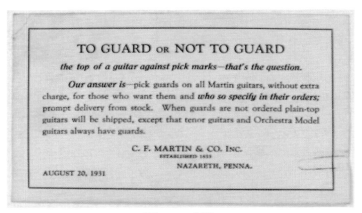

Figure 351
August 20, 1931 Notice from Martin
Concerning Pick Guards on Guitars

enough protection for the top, especially near the sound hole, and was replaced with a larger pick guard in 1931. The exact date for the change to the larger guard is a little unclear but it is known the last guitars with the small pick guard were a batch of OM-18P guitars stamped on February 27, 1931. It is very likely the larger pick guard first appeared on the batch of OM-18 guitars stamped on March 18, 1931. The larger format pick guard was the norm for all Martin guitars from this point.

Since all non-Ditson Dreadnought guitars were made after April 1931, all have the larger format pick guard, with one exception. Figure 352 illustrates what is likely the first Martin Dreadnought, a D-21, which has an unusual pick guard. It maintains the shape of the small OM pick guard at the top of the guard but is considerably wider under the sound hole.

Celluloid Suppliers

From 1895 to 1922, Martin mostly bought celluloid

Figure 352
Possible Photograph of the First Martin
Dreadnought Guitar, D-21 (Serial Number 46590)

from The Celluloid Co. From 1923 to 1930, Martin purchased celluloid from The Fiberloid Co., although a few orders for "viscoloid" were given to DuPont Co. in 1926 and 1927. Fiberloid was again Martin's sole supplier of celluloid from 1930 to early 1938. From 1938 until 1955 Martin's celluloid was supplied by the Monsanto Chemical Co. but Martin changed to Nixon Nitration Works from 1955 to 1960 followed by Nixon-Baldwin Chemical Co. from 1961 and 1964.

For those fans of the television series "Band of Brothers", Captain Lewis Nixon's family owned the Nixon Nitration Works and Major Richard Winters worked for the company for a time after WW II (although he had left the company by the time the company made celluloid for Martin).

In the years before 1927, all celluloid sheets were used for making pick guards for mandolins. The celluloid was commonly supplied in sheets about 20" wide by 36" to 50" long and in a variety of thickness, with 0.025", 0.035" and 0.065" being the commonest. From 1927 pick guards became an increasingly common features on guitars, especially with the introduc-

tion of tenor and plectrum instruments. After 1930, the thickness of celluloid was not often recorded in the purchasing records but the 0.030" and 0.060" thicknesses appear to be the most common.

Purfling and Purfling Suppliers

The making of "adern" or purfling was, and still is, a craft industry in Germany, with many colorful patterns being available. The term purfling also covers plain strips or "lines" of wood that make up much of the purfling used on Martin guitars. Martin made line purflings in-house using dyed maple for the black lines and holly for the white lines.

In the 19th century Martin's main supplier of patterned purfling was C. H. Burdorf of Hamburg, Germany. Martin referred to purfling from this source as either Hamburg or Burdorf purfling. C. F. Martin Sr. purchased purfling directly from this Burdorf and even had one of his employees, Henry Goetz, pick up some purfling from Burdorf when he was visiting Germany in 1854. The C. H. Burdorf Purfling Sample Boards, probably contemporaneous with Goetz's visit in 1854, are in the Martin Guitar Museum and are illustrated in Figures 140 and 141 on pages 108 and 109.

C. A. Zoebisch & Sons, through their own contacts in Germany, were sourcing Hamburg purfling for Martin by the early 1880's and continued to do so until 1893.

"Fischer style" purfling first appeared in the 1893 inventory. It is not known if Fischer was located in Germany or the United States. Fischer purfling appeared in the Martin inventories until at least 1908 and the company at times supplied style 21 and 28 purfling. The last purchase of purfling from Germany seems to have occurred in 1903, so, if Fischer was a German source for purfling, the fact that their purfling appeared in the inventories for several more years might just indicate old stock.

By 1898, Martin appears to have started to switch to local suppliers because Josef Scheina of New York was supplying style 28 purfling by 1898 and continued selling to Martin until 1902. Another supplier, named Dahlman, appeared in the Martin inventory records from 1899 to 1909 and possibly for some years afterwards as there is a nine year gap in the inventory records. No information is available on Dahlman but it is likely Dahlman was a local supplier of purfling to Martin, based on the purchasing records. (No Dahlman involved in this sort of business appears in the 1899/1900 New York City Directory.)

With the 1918 inventory we learn that Martin had on hand 195 dozen pieces of Burdorf purfling in assorted styles and other purfling supplied by Willnus Marqueterie Manufacturing Co. Ltd. of New York and George Jones, also of New York. This inventory indicates that the distinctive purfling used on SoCal Model 1500 guitars was supplied by Jones.

By 1918, the Burdorf purfling in inventory was a remnant stock and continued to decrease over the years until it was down to 50 dozen pieces in 1926, the last time Burdorf purfling appeared in the yearly inventory. Interestingly, to this day, there are a couple of old boxes in the Martin factory that still contain a few strips of the original Burdorf purfling.

Martin continued to used real wood for "line" purfling until 1922 but in that year they began to buy composite sheets of celluloid, black on one side and white on the other, to be made into purfling strips.

From this point, "purfling" always means patterned wood purfling strips, the commonest purflings being style 21 sound hole rings and back stripes plus style 28 "herringbone" for the top edge of the guitar and "zig-zag" back stripes. Although the "herringbone" purfling was dropped from style 28 instruments in 1946, the "zig-zag" back strip continued in use until 1948. In early 1948 Martin changed the back stripe on style 28 instruments to a "zipper" design. The zipper back stripe was referred to as "#305T inlay" and was the only type of purfling bought by Martin from 1948 to 1963.

From 1920 to 1928 much of Martin's purfling purchases went to Willnus although Jones supplied the style 45 back stripes from 1922 to 1926. Jones supplied most of the purfling Martin purchased between 1926 and 1928. However, J. Bernard Co. of New York began to sell purfling to Martin in 1928 and was Martin's sole source until 1938. Dover Inlay Co. began to sell Martin purfling in 1939 and continued to do so until at least 1963.

The Switch to Rear-X Bracing

One subject of particular interest to collector and dealers of Martin guitars is the timing of the switch from forward X-bracing to rear X-bracing. With forward X-braced guitars, the distance from the bottom of the sound hole to the main X-brace is about 1", while for the rear X-braced guitars the measurement is about 1½". The timing of the change has been established as occurring in October 1938 for 000 size and Dreadnought guitars. It has been reported that 00 and 0 size instruments changed to rear X-bracing in 1935, but there is no documentary evidence in the Martin records and the author has not seen enough examples of these guitars to confirm the theory.

A small batch of six D-18 guitars (serial number 71165 to 71170) was made with the shop order slip noting some interesting information: **"Tone Tests, Angles same as R-18 pattern, diagram listed on test pad"**. This batch was stamped on September 13, 1938 and cleared final inspection just a month later, on October 13. A couple of guitars from this batch have been reported and they do have the rear-X top bracing pattern. The reason for the change to rear

X-bracing is not stated in the Martin records.

The "tone tests" must have been successful because the first batch of guitars, twelve D-28's, was stamped on October 13, 1938 and it was noted on the shop order slip: "**New top bracing pattern**". The first Dreadnought guitar with rear-X bracing is serial number 71358. The 000 guitars also seem to have changed to rear-X bracing at the same time. A batch of six 000-42 guitars was stamped on October 7, 1938. An example from the batch (serial number 71356) has been examined and it has advanced X-bracing. The next batch of 000 guitars, twenty-five 000-21 guitars, was stamped on October 21, 1938 and an example seen from this batch confirms the change to rear X-bracing had been made.

Figure 353
Differences Between Advanced-X (left) and
Rear-X Bracing Patterns (right) for a 000 Guitar

Figure 353 illustrates the difference in the bracing patterns for 000 guitars, with the main differences being the included angle of the main X-brace and the angles of the two tone bars. For 000 guitars the included angle of the advanced X-brace is 99°, while the rear-X braced guitars has an angle of 93°. Thus the lower ends of the rear-X braces are positioned further down the sides of the guitar, where they tuck into the kerfing. It is not known if these details are the same for Dreadnought, nor for size 00 and 0 guitars.

Regulation (Set-Up) of Guitars

Martin regulated, or set up, their guitars depending on the type of strings being used. Steel strings were set up to be nearer the frets than for gut strings. Before 1927, when a customer ordered a guitar to be used for Hawaiian playing, the instrument would be set up

as for gut strings but would be supplied with a Kamiki nut extender. As will be seen below, Martin also sometimes supplied a high nut and saddle. After 1927 many Martin Hawaiian guitars had a flat fingerboard with a raised nut and bridge saddle.

Prior to the introduction of T-frets in late 1934, adjusting the regulation of the neck was as simple as replacing a few frets with ones of a different thickness, to change the compression effect of the frets on the fingerboard.

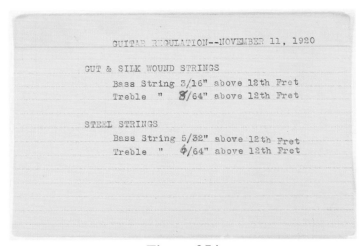

Figure 354
1920 Specification Card for
Regulation of Gut and Steel Strings

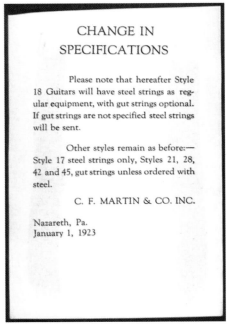

Figure 355
1923 Notice that Style 18 Guitars
Will be Shipped with Steel Strings

C. F. Martin wrote to Thomas Goggan & Brothers of San Antonio TX on February 19, 1924 with the following comment on Hawaiian regulation:

"... all Martin Guitars can be used for Hawaiian playing if that specification is made in placing the order; we make no charge for the regulation."

From this we learn that Martin didn't have heavier construction for Hawaiian guitars, at least at that time. A regular production guitar would be supplied but with a Hawaiian set up.

R. S. Williams & Sons of Toronto ordered a 000-45 on December 8, 1924 and Martin sent a letter requesting some clarification:

"Please advise whether this Guitar is to be used with Gut or Steel Strings, and if the latter whether for Hawaiian Style or the regular Spanish Style. This information will enable us to make the proper adjustments."

C. F. Martin wrote to J. H. Webb January 26, 1925

"In reply to yours of the 23rd, the difference between gut and wire string regulation in our fine guitar is as follows;

The Wire String Guitar has a stiffer neck, one that is fretted stiffer, and with a slight rounding. The neck itself is set back, that is, away from the top of the instrument, and mainly, the bridge is considerably lower than for gut string instruments. Naturally, the slots in the nut are cut lower for wire strings ; for example, if wire strings are put on an instrument that is regulated for gut strings the tuning will not be quite accurate because the gut string guitar will have a higher bridge which will make the steel strings, with their greater tension, sharp on the frets around the middle of the fingerboard."

On June 20, 1925 Charles H. Ditson & Co. complained to Martin about the high action on Martin guitars and received the following reply on June 22:

"We will be very glad to meet your wishes in the matter of the height of Guitar bridges. It is an easy matter, of course, to regulate the strings as high

or as low as the customer wants them when Guitars are made on special order, but when they are taken from stock it will probably be necessary to lower the strings for your orders. This we are quite willing to do and the writer undertakes to see that it is done in the future. In case any Guitars come through with the strings too high, we hope you will not hesitate to send them back at once, at our expense.

It would be a help to us if you could give us an exact measurement for the height of the first and of the sixth strings above the twelfth fret. It is our practice on Gut and Silk String Guitars to lay the first string 1/8" above the top of the twelfth fret and the sixth string 3/32" above the fret. This measurement is the distance clear between the top of the fret and the bottom of the string. Guitars strung with Steel have the first string 1/32" and the sixth string 3/64" lower than the measurements above."**

Ditson's complaint probably arose because they placed steel strings on a guitar set up for gut strings, as many of Martin's better models were stocked with gut strings and gut string regulation.

On March 26, 1927 Martin sent a letter to Artophone Corporation of St. Louis MO to explain the difference between gut and steel string set up:

"These Guitars are regularly carried in stock with Gut Strings. In case Steel Strings are preferred, they can be supplied that way on special order. A guitar strung with gut strings is not properly regulated for use with steel strings so we prefer to change the adjustment here before shipping the instrument. Kindly bear this in mind in ordering our fine Guitars."

On May 28, 1929 Martin wrote to a customer dissatisfied with the set up of her guitar:

"We are sorry to hear that you would rather have preferred to have your 0-45 Martin Guitar strung with steel strings. Ordinarily, we supply all of our Guitars with steel strings unless they are special ordered for gut strings; but in this case the fact that you are a harp player led us to think that you would prefer gut strings and so we sent the instru-

ment that way. We did this entirely on our own judgement and it was not the fault of your dealer.

The only difference between a Guitar strung with gut strings and one strung with steel strings is in the adjustment of the strings at the bridge and nut. Steel strings are adjusted closer to the fingerboard than gut strings. If you do not mind the height of the strings from the fingerboard, you can use steel strings on your Guitar quite easily; however, of you find the action stiff, it will be necessary to re-adjust the bridge and the nut. We would prefer to do this here at the factory and, of course, we will pay the transportation because we are responsible for supplying the gut strings.

As a matter of fact we know of very few Guitarists who play the Guitar in the Spanish style for public solo work who use steel strings. Sometimes a steel treble E is used with two gut strings and silk centre bases; but the best Guitar players use all gut strings. It is true, however, that nine out of ten amateur Guitarists use steel strings and that is why we regularly supply them on out instruments."

One last letter, written on January 15, 1934, describes Martin's string set up for mid-1930's guitars:

"Our rule for adjusting the strings at the nut is to have them just as close to the first fret as possible without striking. This means a gap of about the thickness of the string. At the middle of the scale, or the 12th fret, we set the treble E string 3/32" about (sic) the top of the fret but the bass strings should be a little higher. Guitar strings must be higher from the fingerboard in the upper positions otherwise they could strike the frets in the first and second positions."

No other direct information on string set up is in the Martin records through to 1967 but set up specification probably didn't change too much.

Why did Martin stop scalloping top braces?

Ever since the 1840's Martin had scalloped the braces used in their X-braced guitars. The purpose of scalloping was to lighten the mass of the top braces and make the top more responsive. It is well known among Martin guitar aficionados that Martin stopped

"scalloping" the top braces of their guitars in late 1944. Mike Longworth noted in his book, based on notes kept by John Deichman, that the transition to non-scalloped occurred at serial number 89926. Deichman's notes could not be found to confirm this information. However, serial number 89926 was the last guitar in a batch of twenty-five D-18s. Another guitar from the batch has been reported with non-scalloped bracing so the first guitar braced this way may be serial number 89902.

As with many changes instituted by Martin there is usually some transition period before the changes became the norm. Mike Longworth noted in his logbook that a D-28 (serial number 88112) has non-scalloped braces but this guitar may be an anomaly. It is possible, however, that other guitars before serial number 89902 will be encountered with non-scalloped braces.

Shop order 280 was a small batch of six D-18s stamped on June 20, 1944. The shop order has the following notes: "**Top test for brac(e) shape, shape by J. H. D.**" It seems likely that the guitars from this batch were made to test non-scalloped braces.

STYLE	SHOP ORDER	SERIAL NUMBERS	DATE STAMPED	COMMENTS
D-28	244	88112	JUNE 9, 1944	NON-SCALLOPED BRACES NOTED BY LONGWORTH
D-18	280	88207-88212	JUNE 20, 1944	TOP TEST FOR BRACE SHAPE, SHAPE BY J. H. D.
D-28	348	89679-89690	NOV. 14, 1944	89681 REPORTED ON UMGF AS HAVING DOT INLAYS AND SCALLOPED BRACES
D-28	356	89803-89814	NOV. 28, 1944	89803 NOTED BY LONGWORTH AS HAVING "DOT" INLAYS, 89804 REPORTED BY UMGF AS HAVING SCALLOPED BRACES AND "DOT" INLAYS
D-18	364	89902-89926	DEC. 6, 1944	89926 NON-SCALLOPED BRACES NOTED BY DEICHMAN
D-28	365	90014-90025	DEC. 15, 1944	NON-SCALLOPED BRACES & DOT INLAYS NOTED BY LONGWORTH FOR 90021 AND 90025

Table 104
Timeline for the Transition to Non-Scalloped Braces

It is clear that Martin was experimenting with braces by June 1944 and that the transition to non-scalloped braces was complete by shop orders 364 and 365 in December 1944.

Another question is why Martin chose to stop making scalloped braces. The conventional wisdom is that players were using heavy piano wire on their guitars and the tension these produced caused the tops with scalloped braces to "belly" excessively. This is not mentioned in the Martin records but could be true. The author has purchased and measured antique strings from the 1920's to 1940's that came from the same suppliers Martin used. Although the sample size is small, the largest low E string measured was just 0.056" in diameter, about the same as a medium set today. Martin did not include "heavy" strings on their price lists until the mid-1950's. If the "piano wire" strings were the cause of the demise of scalloped bracing, why are there not more pre-1944 Martin guitar seen with really bad bellying? The author has talked to a number of vintage guitar dealers on this subject and, anecdotally, they couldn't remember seeing many period guitars with damaged tops due to excessive bellying.

There are some other points to consider. Martin couldn't meet demand for their guitars during the war years due to limitations on materials and labor. Martin received very large orders in June and July 1944. The backorder situation at this point became so acute that the factory had to limit orders for the remainder of the year. Martin also changed from "diamond and square" fingerboard inlays on D-28 guitars to "dot" inlays about the middle of November 1944 (see page 269) and then changed to non-scalloped bracing in December as mentioned above. What had changed at Martin to make the design changes in their instruments?

It may have been as simple as a change in management and some new ideas on how to meet customer demands for product. On November 1, 1944 Frank Henry Martin appointed C. F. Martin III "to manage production and sales in additions to his duties as Vice-President and Secretary". It should be remembered that F. H. Martin was 78 years old at the time and saw the necessity of passing on day-to-day control of the company, although he remained President.

So, C. F. Martin III took over the running of the company on November 1, 1944 with an over-full order book and without the ability to hire more workers to speed up production. Martin, at least from the 1920's, performed detailed costing analysis of their instruments and C. F. Martin III may have decided to change to dot fingerboard inlays and stop scalloping braces in order to reduce labor per guitar and increase production, even if only slightly. The slight decrease in unit guitar cost would have partially offset ever increasing costs, which was of some importance, as Martin was not allowed to increase the prices of their instruments due to war-time price control measures.

In conclusion, heavy guitar strings may have contributed to the change to non-scalloped braces but C. F. Martin III's practical approach to solving production issues probably had a larger impact on the final decision.

Special Guitars

Most of Martin's guitar production was made in well established styles and sizes. However, Martin, to suit customer demands, always allowed some variation in specification for the guitars they produced.

In the 19th century the main variation was related to the type of finish applied to the instrument. A "yellow" or "orange" top could be produced by simply using unbleached shellac or a mixture of bleached and unbleached shellac. A few guitars before 1898 were noted as having fingerboard inlays or "guard plates" but these was certainly not the norm.

Special order guitars became more common in the early 20th century but, since most guitars were still not made in batches, specially ordered features were noted but the designation of the guitar was not changed; that is, a special order 0-28 was not recorded as a 0-28S. The 00-42S guitars made between 1901 and 1903 had special inlaid fingerboards and pick guards but were only noted as "00-42" guitars in the sale ledgers.

Martin did not begin to apply a style stamp to their guitars until the first week of October 1930, so the first special order guitar with an "S" suffix applied to the serial number was probably the small batch of three 0-21S guitars that were stamped on December 9, 1930.

From 1900 to the 1950's, a special order guitar could have one or more special features, anything that was different from regular production guitars. Some special order guitars were made in small batches for particular large customers but most special guitars were ordered individually (i.e., there was only one guitar on the shop order slip). A "dark top" finish was not considered by Martin as a special feature since the dark top was offered at no charge. In this case, Martin would just select a random guitar from a batch that had progressed to the finish department and would apply the sunburst finish.

From late 1930's special guitars always had an "S" suffix added to the serial number. The "S" always designated "Special". Some confusion has arisen because some 12-fret guitars, ordered after the transition to the 14-fret body, were noted as "standard body" on the shop order slips. The "S" suffix did not designate a 12-fret body; the 12-fret body was the "special" feature, as that body type was no longer in production. Of course, this only applies to guitars that transitioned to a 14-fret body. The 0 and 00 sized guitars in styles 21, 28, 40H, 42, 44 and 45 continued to be offered in the 12-fret format.

In the 1950's and 1960's most special guitars had more simple specifications; a large or double pick guard or a specially shaped neck were some of the more common features requested. Since Martin production had ramped up significantly from the late 1940's and production batches were taking longer to move through the production process there was less need to generate a new shop order for a "one-off" instrument. Martin had sufficient time to take a guitar out of a regular production batch for adding special features. As a result of this most of the special order guitar from this period have a regular style stamp without an "S" suffix even though they were considered "special" orders by Martin. Of course, this doesn't apply to special order 12-fret guitars and the Wurlitzer D-28SW and D-35SW guitars.

The Transition to Steel Strings

The first mention of steel strings in the Martin archival material is in a letter to Martin from a W. E. Craighead dated April 2, 1889:

"Please put the 'gut' strings on that guitar instead of steel. I think it will be better."

On a post card dated April 27, 1892 William H. Keller, a Martin dealer in Easton PA, made the following request:

"Please make and send as soon as possible another guitar to 2½-17. Do you make them for use with wire strings? If so make this one."

Later in the same year, on December 1, 1892 Keller ordered another guitar with steel strings:

"We forgot to mention on our order for (a) Guitar the other day that we want it for wire strings."

As can be seen from the correspondence above, Martin did occasionally supply steel strings on their in-

struments from the last quarter of the 19th century. By the early part of the 20th century, steel strings, while by no means common, were becoming a fairly regular option on Martin guitars. Mandolins, of course, had always been supplied with steel strings.

Steel strings did cause a few problems and on Martin guitars from the early part of the 20th century. On August 31, 1922 Martin corresponded with Buegeleisen & Jacobson in New York about a 1920 1-28 guitar that had been returned for repair due to a "warped neck". Martin offered the following with regard to handling the issue:

"The only thing wrong with the instrument was the condition of the neck, which had warped slightly under the strain of Steel Strings. This we corrected so that it was better than new and since the rest of the instrument was in first-class condition..."

The "correction" mentioned above would have involved partially re-fretting the fingerboard with slightly thicker bar frets to increase the wedge effect of the frets, thus straightening the neck.

By the early 1920's the market for steel strung guitars had increased significantly and some Martin dealers were beginning to order guitars with steel strings on a regular basis.

On February 18, 1922 Martin wrote to Henry Hunt of C. H. Ditson & Co.:

"We have completed the first sample of our new twenty-five dollar Guitar, known as the Style 2-17, and the writer will be in New York with it Tuesday and will call to show it to you."

At the same Martin sent a similar letter to William J. Smith Music Co. in New York.

On March 6, 1922 Martin replied to the Sherman Clay & Co. request for more information on the new 2-17 guitar:

"We are very glad you give us a chance to send on a sample of the new twenty-five dollar Guitar as soon as it is ready. I believe orders are booked ahead of the first lot in work but very likely we can give you one early. The reason I want this done is

that I think so much of this Guitar. It is our old No. 2 Model, formerly called Ladies' Size. The dimensions are:

Length	18 3/8"
Width behind Bridge	12"
Width above soundhole	8-3/8"

... It is built of Mahogany, top as well as sides and back, and shows up wonderfully – better than the price, as some people express it.

Our economy comes mainly in two things: Using Rosewood for the fingerboard and Bridge, instead of Ebony, and stringing with Steel only. The regulation for Steel Strings must be uniformly low and that is a much easier task for us than to make it medium for either Gut or Steel. This is a feature you will understand at once and you will see how we can give a finely constructed, sweet toned Guitar at a lower price than anything else we have."

In a May 16, 1922 letter to W. J. Dyer and Brother, Martin explained that the construction of guitars was suitable for both gut and steel strings:

"We ... note that you wish to have the sample Guitars which we are making with your trade name 'Stetson' constructed so that they can be strung with Steel strings. This is largely a matter of regulation because all Martin guitars are fully guaranteed when strung with Steel strings as well as gut and silk strings, although we regularly use the latter.

If you find that almost all of the guitars sold by you are used with steel strings we would suggest that you instruct us to regulate and string them that way here. Even if they are especially constructed for Steel strings the regulation would be too high for that purpose if we make it for Gut strings. This you will of course readily understand."

To Martin the difference between gut string and steel strings guitars was only a matter of "regulation", or set up. Most Martin guitars were still set up for gut strings, while the set up for steel strings had to be made somewhat lower. Martin was not concerned about the construction of the guitars, only that an

order for steel string guitars be clearly stated so that the regulation would be correct for the type of strings to be used.

Since the publication of Mike Longworth's first book on Martin guitars it has been widely believed that the first guitars braced for steel string were the style 2-17 guitars introduced in 1922. This idea is incorrect and is the result of misunderstanding of Martin's intent. The misunderstanding that the style 2-17 were the first Martin guitars "constructed for steel strings" may have been caused by the wording on the advertising card Martin printed for promotion of the new model.

Figure 356
1922 Advertising Card for the
Recently Introduced Model 2-17

The card states "steel strings only". However, Martin did not mean that the guitars were "constructed" for steel strings, only that, as the lowest priced guitar in the product line, Martin wanted to keep costs as low as possible by offering only one "regulation". This is confirmed in a letter Martin wrote to Frank Morrow on May 14, 1923:

"The 2-17 is designed only for the Steel String trade and the price does not permit us to go to the expense of the more accurate regulation for Gut strings."

On January 1, 1923 the specification for the style 18 guitars changed so that they were now regularly supplied with steel strings, although gut strings were still an option. The more expensive models continued to be supplied with gut strings unless specifically ordered by the dealer with steel or Hawaiian strings.

In a February 8, 1923 letter to Southern California Music Co., after the return of a 0-44 with a peg head, Frank Henry Martin bemoaned the increase in the demand for steel string guitars:

"It was all right to return the peghead Guitar. You will receive a credit memorandum in due course.

This gives valuable information. I remember well when you got it, and the hope I entertained that there was on(e) place left to appreciate the beauty of pegs on a Guitar. A forlorn hope. Fashion is the master and we must justify our right to live by making what people want. You can trace the effect on us. First, making steel strings optional; second, starting one model with steel strings only; the last, change another style to steel regular with gut optional. It looks as if all styles would end up that way, and why should I worry? A Martin guitar, after all, sounds fine with any kind of strings."

Martin did not even intend different construction for "steel playing" (Hawaiian guitar). In a January 18, 1923 letter to Ira Wasson (a Martin dealer in St. Louis) Martin explained:

"In regard to the Steel Guitar for your pupil, we are sorry to say that we cannot supply a Style 000-42. Style 000-28 and Style 000-45 can be supplied within two weeks, the neck to be especially strengthened for steel playing, without extra charge. We do not advise extra bracing inside because this is almost sure to detract from the tone. A great many Martin Guitars were originally made for gut strings, regular style, are now being used for steel playing by professional players who find the fine tone quality and great volume that they need."

In a January 23, 1925 letter to W. H. Webb, Martin further explained the difference between gut strings and steel strings:

"The Wire Strung Guitar has a stiffer neck, one that is fretted stiffer, and with a slight rounding. The neck itself is set back, that is, away from the top of the instrument, and mainly, the bridge is considerable lower than for gut string instruments. Naturally the slots in the nut are cut lower for wire strings: for example, if wire strings are put on an instrument that is regulated for gut strings the tuning will not be quite accurate because the gut string Guitar will have a higher bridge which will make the steel strings, with their greater tension, sharp on the frets around the middle of the fingerboard."

The movement to steel string guitars must have accelerated because by 1927 Martin admitted in a letter to D. Finlayson on June 1, 1927 that:

"… nine out of ten American players use all steel (strings)."

By 1924 Martin was only carrying style 0-18 in stock with steel strings although gut strings were still available on request. In a letter to the Truman Brothers dated September 16, 1924 Martin wrote:

"We do not carry Style 0-18 with Gut strings in stock but can supply one in a few day's (sic) notice whenever a lot is being finished."

Martin had always maintained a conservative approach, whether with regard to increasing sizes or with the move to steel strings from gut strings. Even in the late 1920's Frank Henry Martin continued to prefer 0 size guitars with gut rather than steel strings.

In a letter to Sophocles Papas dated March 18, 1929, a Martin dealer in Washington DC and passionate promoter of gut string guitars, Martin continued to try to justify their support for gut strings:

"We are glad to see you are advocating in the Crescendo (note: the trade magazine) the use of gut strings. You are absolutely right, of course, and we do hope your advice will be followed by students of the instrument. For many years we took this matter very seriously and endeavored to impress on our dealers and all the players with whom we came in contact that only gut strings are suitable for a fine Guitar. Finally, however, we were forced

to conclude that we might as well try to stem the ocean tides. It is worse than useless to make Guitars which are only suitable for gut strings when it is clear that at least ninety-five per cent of Guitar players will never use anything but steel strings. This is particularly true today because there is an increasing demand for Guitars for use in dance orchestras. You will appreciate the problem this presents to a manufacturer who has musical ideals. The business is there and we must recognize the condition."

Martin eventually bowed to the inevitable as body sizes increased and steel-strung guitars became the norm.

As with other design changes Martin had made over nearly a century of production, the increase in general construction and bracing to more handle the tension of steel strings was made gradually. However, the Martin correspondence does supply some clues that the process had begun by at least 1927 with regard to Hawaiian guitars. On July 25, 1927 Martin wrote to The Denver Music Co. concerning their flat fingerboard Hawaiian guitars that were just being introduced and made a few cogent points on the construction of these guitars:

"**The recent call for Hawaiian Guitars leads us to believe that this instrument will be quite popular during the coming season. Many people are hearing it in the radio and the phonograph, and orchestra players are finding the fine tone quality of the guitar valuable in their work.**

With this in mind we wish to call you attention to our genuine Koawood guitars, specially constructed and adjusted for Hawaiian playing. Style 0-28K is made of selected figured Koa, strikingly beautiful, while the 0-18K is made of plainer wood, all of which we import directly from the Hawaiian Islands. The construction is somewhat heavier than in the standard Martin Guitar, and the adjustment is made with a high level bridge and a high nut, which does not require a re-adjuster."

Martin, in a letter date March 6, 1929 to W. W. Anderson, stated:

"**It is quite true that the early Martin Guitars were hardly strong enough for steel strings. In recent years, however, Guitars have been used almost entirely with steel strings so we have found it necessary to make our Guitars stronger. They are now built in such a way that we guarantee for use with steel strings, either in the Spanish or the Hawaiian style. In fact, all our Guitars are strung at the factory with steel strings unless they are ordered otherwise.**"

The changes Martin made to strengthen their guitars probably refer to several changes instituted in 1928. In March of that year Martin increased the thickness of the spruce tops. The dates shown in Tables 105 and 106 are from specification cards in the Martin archives. These figures are the top thickness specification prior to sanding and finishing. The increase in thickness appears small but has a significant effect on the stiffness of the top.

TOP THICKNESS								
DATE	SMALL		1 AND 0		00 AND 000		TIPLE	
1922-11-27	6/64"	0.09375"	6 ½/64"	0.1016"	7/64"	0.1093"	6 ½/64"	0.1016"
1928-03-22	7/64"	0.1093"	7/64"	0.1093"	7 ½/64"	0.1172"	6 ½/64"	0.1016"

Table 105
1928 Changes to Top Thickness of Guitars

The top thickness specification for the Ditson Dreadnought guitars has not been found in the archive. However, several extant guitars have been examined and the tops measure 0.120" to 0.130" thick, so the specification was likely 8/64" or 0.125"

Martin also made some small changes to the dimensions of their guitars in April 1928.

	SIZE	5	2-1/2	2	1	0	00	000
BODY LENGTH	1921-08-04	16"	17-7/8"	-	18-7/8"	19 1/8"	19-5/8"	20-7/16"
	1928-04-24	16"	17 ¾"	18-3/8"	18 7/8"	19-1/8"	19 ½"	20 ½"
WIDTH, UPPER BOUT	1921-08-04	8 ¼"	8 ¼"	-	9 ¼"	9 ½"	9 ¾"	10 ¾"
	1928-04-24	8 -1/16"	8-3/8"	8 -7/16"	9-3/8"	9 -9/16"	9-7/8"	10 ¾"
WIDTH, LOWER BOUT	1921-08-04	11 ¼"	11-5/8"	-	12 ¾"	13 ½"	14-1/8"	15"
	1928-04-24	11-3/16"	11-11/16"	12 -1/16"	12-7/8"	13 ½"	14-1/8"	15"

Table 106
1928 Changes to Guitar Dimensions

It is not clear if other changes, especially with respect to bracing, were made when the dimensions changed. The only suggestion that bracing was evolving is found in shop order 641 (Figure 357) from 1930 which documents that the batch of twenty-five 0-28 guitar had "**15 backs, 5/16" braces**" and "**10 backs, 1/4" braces**". This might refer to the top two braces on the back of the guitars or could be an error and is

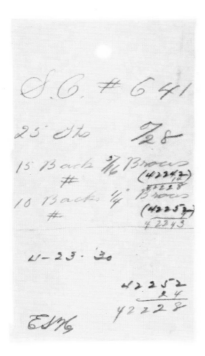

Figure 357
Shop Order 641, Dated April 23, 1930
for Twenty-Five 0-28 Guitars

instead referring to the top braces.

There has been some suggestion that Martin increased the strength of their guitars as a result of heavy gauge steel strings ruining the tops of guitar. The repair records in the archive have been examined and the number of guitars that had tops replaced in the years between 1920 and 1935 is very small (less than 20), almost always as a result of shipping damage or other types of damage caused by the owners.

On the other hand, Martin did not consider a slight belly in the top as a cause for concern. In a letter to George Krick, guitar teacher and Martin dealer in Germantown PA, on February 17, 1923 Martin stated:

"The swelling at the back of the bridge is not a defect because it indicates fine wood, worked rather thin, which is usually the best for tone, as you know. Many old Guitars have this appearance and are almost always fine in tone."

Still, sometimes an owner would be concerned about putting heavy strings on a Martin guitar as discussed in a letter, dated October 30, 1934, from a R. B. Monjoy:

"I would like to get a little information from you.

Now I bought one of your make Guitars last week No. 000-18 (serial number) 55291. Now when I bought the guitar there were over size strings on it and there seemed to be an awful strong pressure on the neck so I became afraid that there were too much strain on the neck with those over side strings. So I exchanged them to the regular size guitar string. Now I like those large over size strings on the guitar but I am afraid to use them. Now will you kindly let me know if the neck of your guitar are reinforced. If so I will put the over side strings on again. Now you make a wonderful instrument. I believe you make the best guitar in the United States. Maybe in the world. I am a man past fifty years and have known your guitar make for 35 years. I hope I can find some of those large frets that you use on your guitar, when the time comes for one to have it refretted again. I like those large frets."

Martin replied on November 5, 1934:

"You need not hesitate to use extra heavy strings on your Martin Guitar. The neck is reinforced with a strip of Ebony inlaid in the centre of the neck under the fingerboard and our guarantee covers neck warping without time limit.

Here at the factory we use the heavy strings regularly in this model."

The guitar being discussed and the timing of the correspondence is very interesting. Serial number 55291 (stamped January 26, 1934) was from the first batch of 000-18 guitars made after the OM-18 model was dropped from the line. As such, it still had the long 25.4" scale length as well as the ebony bar neck reinforcement and bar frets. Martin changed over to the shorter scale length, steel T-bar and T-frets at the beginning of September 1934 and at the beginning of November some of the new models had already been shipped, so it is interesting Martin didn't mention this. Although the first batch of the short scale 000-18 guitar was stamped in October 1934 none were shipped until August 1935. It is curious that the customer knew about Martin's "large" frets at the time.

It is also unfortunate that the definition of "heavy" strings was not discussed further. Anecdotally, the strings that Martin seems to have used in the 1930's would be considered "medium" strings today.

Strings

Strings made a significant contribution to the sales of C. F. Martin's first store in New York City in the 1830's. The earliest ledger books are full of entries for the purchase and sale of strings.

In the 19th century the B, G and high E strings for guitars were made of gut (Martin also sold many gut strings for violins and cellos). Gut strings in the period were usually manufactured in Germany, the U. K. or Italy. It was generally agreed that Italian gut strings were the best quality, but also commanded the highest prices.

Martin bought gut strings from New York sources and also imported some from Germany. Martin was importing gut guitar, violin and cello strings from T. F. Merz in Neukirchen by 1835, with guitar strings being ordered in both regular and terz lengths.

The low E, A and D strings were wound, generally silvered steel wire over a silk core. The November 13, 1835 shipment from T. F. Merz included wound E, A and D strings in regular and terz lengths. The regular strings were noted as being No. 9, No. 11 and No. 16 respectively while the terz strings were recorded as No. 10, No. 12 and No. 17. The "numbers" must refer to the gauge of the strings but it is not known what standard was in use at the time, and none of the modern wire gauge systems seem to fit. Martin continued to import wound guitar strings from Merz until April 1839. Martin rarely ordered wound strings from local sources in New York so either made do with the imported wound strings or supplemented his supply by winding some of his own strings.

The Merz June 10, 1835 shipment to Martin & Schatz contained a quantity of "golddraht" (gold wire), which must have been used for making wound strings, whether by Martin or others. It is not known whether "golddraht" was gold-plated steel wire or designated a higher quality of silvered wire but "golddraht" did command a price about three times that of "silberdraht".

Also included in the November 13, 1835 shipment from Merz was some No. 14 "argantandraht" (an-

other designation for silberdraht), which would also have been used for making wound strings. The wire gauge standards shown in Table 107 came into use from about the middle of the 19th century but it is not known which gauges standards were in use in the 1830's.

In the June 8, 1838 shipment from Merz to Martin was a total of 17 rolls of "silberdraht" and 17 rolls of "golddraht" in a variety of gauges. On November 19, 1838 purchased "silk for guitar strings" and on November 21 "**Paid ($0.75) to a man for turning the String machine**". When Martin sold his New York inventory to Ludecus & Wolter at the end of May 1839 it contained just nine rolls of "spinndraht" or spinning wire. The gauges of wire recorded at that time included 17, 16, 15, 14, 13, 11, 10 and 9 gauges. The fact that Martin had used all the golddraht and almost half of the silberdraht wire between the June 1838 shipment and May 1839, combined with the November expense for a "to a man for turning the String machine", is convincing evidence that Martin was making his own wound strings by the late summer of 1838, and possibly from as early as 1834. The fact that little wire and no silk were purchased before 1838 may just mean that Martin had brought a supply with him when he emigrated in 1833 (like he had with the approximately 400 European spruce tops he brought with him from Saxony and used on all his guitars until 1840.)

It is very interesting that Martin first recorded the manufacture of wound strings just as the Martin & Bruno partnership was just coming to an end. It could be that Martin was reacting to the slow sales conditions, as a result of the Panic of 1837, by making wound strings to boost sales, while at the same time reducing the need to purchase strings. Presumably, Martin already owned the string-winding machine and may have been making wound strings from his arrival in New York. The ledgers do show that, from the beginning of his business in New York, Martin very frequently bought B, G and high E gut strings but very rarely any wound strings.

In a letter from Philip Deringer dated September 22, 1850 it is learned that Martin had installed a steam engine to power a saw and a lathe. A lathe would not seem to have much of a role in a guitar-making shop, since turned products like bridge pins and end pins

Gauge No.	Roebling or Trenton Iron Works		Felter & Guilleaume Wire Gauge		Washburn & Moen Music Wire		New American Steel & Wire Gauge	
	in.	mm	in.	mm	in.	mm	in.	mm
0	0.0085	0.2286	0.009	0.236	0.014	0.366	0.009	0.229
1	0.010	0.254	0.0098	0.2489	0.016	0.396	0.010	0.254
2	0.011	0.2794	0.0106	0.2692	0.017	0.422	0.011	0.279
3	0.012	0.3048	0.0114	0.2896	0.018	0.452	0.012	0.305
4	0.013	0.3302	0.0122	0.3099	0.019	0.477	0.013	0.330
5	0.014	0.3556	0.0138	0.3505	0.020	0.513	0.014	0.356
6	0.016	0.4064	0.0157	0.3988	0.021	0.546	0.016	0.406
7	0.018	0.4572	0.0177	0.4496	0.023	0.584	0.018	0.457
8	0.020	0.508	0.0197	0.5004	0.024	0.617	0.020	0.508
9	0.022	0.5588	0.0216	0.5486	0.026	0.650	0.022	0.559
10	0.024	0.6096	0.0236	0.5994	0.027	0.686	0.024	0.610
11	0.026	0.6604	0.026	0.6604	0.028	0.721	0.026	0.660
12	0.028	0.7112	0.0283	0.7118	0.030	0.752	0.029	0.737
13	0.030	0.762	0.0303	0.7696	0.031	0.797	0.031	0.787
14	0.032	0.8128	0.0323	0.8204	0.033	0.828	0.033	0.838
15	0.034	0.8636	0.0342	0.8687	0.034	0.876	0.035	0.889
16	0.036	0.9144	0.0362	0.9195	0.036	0.914	0.037	0.940

Table 107
String Wire Gauges

were sourced from New York, so it may have been used for winding strings. Regardless, Martin undoubtedly would have had some sort of string-winding machine, possibly the same one he employed in New York.

The ledger books for the 1840's are missing entirely and the ledger books from the 1850's only occasionally mention the sale of strings and always refer to wound E, A and D strings. The purchasing records for the 1850's are very thin so there is no way to know for sure whether Martin continued to buy silk and silvered wire for winding his own strings. However, since he had a lathe and/or a string-winding machine, there is little reason to doubt that Martin continued to make wound E, A and D strings for use on his own guitars just as a matter of economy. It would also have been very practical to make strings as fill-in work at times when guitar sales were slower. When the factory was at capacity Martin could always count on C. A. Zoebisch to buy strings from New York sources, if there was not time to make them in the factory. (It should be remembered that the work week at Martin in the 1850's was 6 days per week and 12 hours per day).

The records show that Martin was purchasing silvered wire regularly by at least 1867 (and likely earlier). The quantities of wire ordered indicate that a fairly large number of wound strings were being made. Since the sale of strings was quite rare between 1867 and 1884, Martin must have been using these strings on his own guitars. Martin purchased the gut strings he needed though C. A. Zoebisch & Son. Martin was mostly using 16, 13 and 10 gauge silvered steel wire during this time frame but the actual diameter of the

wire was not recorded. By this time string wire should have been available in one or another of the standard wire gauge systems, probably Felter & Guilleaume or Roebling, but, again, the gauges above don't seem to fit with Table 107 (for instance, a 16 gauge wire in the F & G chart would be 0.036" in diameter, suggesting that a wound E string would be over 0.070", depending on the thickness of the silk core and the angle of the wire wrapping.)

Martin held their first detailed inventory in 1889. A **"spinning machine"** was recorded in this inventory and in all subsequent inventories for many years, evidence that Martin continued to make their own wound E, A and D strings.

In the early 1890's Martin bought silvered wire through C. A. Zoebisch & Son but by 1894 was also buying wire and strings from Hammacher, Schlemmer & Co. (who were the sole U. S. agent for Felter & Guillaume music wire, which was manufactured in Germany). In December 1894, Martin wrote to Hammacher, Schlemmer & Co. seeking their help in finding a **"machine for string making"** and received a prompt reply providing the names of two companies that could supply this machinery.

Martin continued to buy string wire, in steadily diminishing quantities, until about 1920. Martin may have continued to make some of their own silk and steel strings but steel guitar and mandolin strings were being bought from various string manufacturers by at least 1901. Of course, Martin continued to use large quantities of gut strings throughout the early part of the 20th century.

Martin imported and sold "Superbo" gut guitar strings from at least 1898 through early 1915 as well as "La Favorita" gut guitar strings which were purchased between 1904 and 1912. In 1916, Martin finally found a domestic source for quality gut strings in Armour & Co. This was very timely for Martin as the company's demand for gut strings increased enormously with the addition of ukuleles to the product line in 1917. Armour & Co. was the sole supplier of gut ukulele and guitar strings until 1945, when nylon strings became available. Kaplan Musical Strings Co. received orders for gut uke and guitar strings from 1937 to 1947 and then switched to nylon strings from 1947 to 1950. C. D'Addario & Son supplied uke strings, both straight and packaged, to Martin from 1948 to 1962 and F. W. Jaeger received orders for nylon strings between 1955 and 1957. V. C. Squier Co. supplied nylon uke and guitar strings to Martin from 1957 to 1964.

In the early part of the 20th century, Martin purchased steel mandolin and guitar strings from the National Musical String Co. under the "Black Diamond" trade name (and Martin may have also used some "Bell Brand" strings, another trade name of National Musical Wire). Martin mostly ordered loose strings from National from 1901 to 1914 but later also bought boxes and boxed sets of strings for resale.

National Musical Wire Co. was Martin's primary source of strings until about 1929. The Standard Musical String & Manufacturing Co. began getting some Martin orders in 1926 and became the sole source from 1929 to 1933. The Mapes Piano String Co. replaced Standard Musical String as the supplier from 1933 to 1939. Martin bought steel strings from three sources from 1939 to 1943: Mapes Piano String Co., Music Strings Inc. and, for silk and steel strings, National Music Wire Co. Mapes Piano String Co. enjoyed most of Martin's string business from 1943 to 1946. For the rest of the period until 1964 Martin split string purchases between Mapes Piano String Co, Music String Inc. (to 1961) and National Music Wire Co.

A few other companies, at times, also supplied steel strings to Martin: a) Chicago Musical Instrument Co. (1931-1932), b) Darco Music Strings Co. (uke and guitar strings 1962 -1964) and c) E. O. Mari Inc. (mostly monel strings 1962-1963).

Martin, from at least 1943 had their string boxes, string envelopes and string box labels made locally. Allentown Paper Box Co. made the string boxes from 1943 to 1964. String envelopes and string box labels were printed by Nazareth Item Co. from 1946 to 1953 and Nazareth Publishing Co. from 1953 to 1961.

Strings Guages Used by Martin

One of the enduring controversies of the Golden Age period (1928 to 1944) states that musicians used large diameter piano wire on Martin guitars in an effort to get more volume. Mike Longworth popularized the idea that the extra stress of the large piano strings caused the tops to belly excessively. This lead Martin to the introduce of non-scalloped top braces on guitars from late 1944. See also the section on "**Why did Martin stop scalloping top braces?**" on pages 311 and 312.

Piano strings were certainly commonly available, considering the large number of piano manufacturers in business at the time. However, it would also be obvious to the musician that mounting piano strings on a guitar might cause damage (bellying) to the top of the guitar. A video exists on YouTube where the owner of a guitar tried using piano strings on his instrument, with nearly disastrous results. In this experiment the piano strings did not improve the tone of the guitar.

Style Stamps

Martin began to add serial numbers to mandolins in 1895, at the suggestion of Charles F. Albert, who had a music business in Philadelphia. For some reason Martin delayed adding serial number to guitars until 1898. However, it was still left to the dealers to be able determine the actual size and style of the Martin guitars they were selling.

Martin, probably at the suggestion of one of their dealers, began to add a style stamp to the neck block in early October 1930.

The date of the addition of style stamps was not noted in the Martin records. The latest guitar seen without a style stamp by Mike Longworth was a 00-42 from shop order 808 (stamped October 1, 1930, serial numbers 44174-44188). The first guitar noted with a style stamp was a OM-18P from shop order 816 (stamped October 8, 1930, serial numbers 44274-44298).

So, it seems clear that Martin started to added style stamps to the neck blocks of their guitar at some point between October 1 and October 8, 1930.

The Switch from Brazilian to Indian Rosewood

According to Mike Longworth, Brazil placed an embargo on the export of Brazilian rosewood logs in the 1960's as the government was seeking to attract business to the country by demanding logs be processed in Brazilian mills. This was unsatisfactory to Martin and, as the supply of Brazilian rosewood began to disappear, the company was forced in 1969 to switch from Brazilian rosewood to Indian rosewood for the bodies of their higher end guitars.

A note in a foreman's notebook recorded that the change occurred on November 11, 1969. This is the date that materials were collected for shop orders prior to the start of production. The first batch of guitars effected was shop order 105 which was a batch of twenty-five D-21 guitars beginning with serial number 254498. This shop order didn't appear in the production records until it was recorded that the batch was "glued" on December 1, 1969.

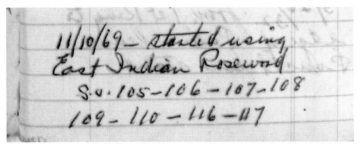

Figure 358
Date of the Switch from Brazilian to Indian Rosewood

However, this date is not a strict line in the sand. A few guitars continued to be made of Brazilian rosewood until early 1970. It appears that at least some of the 000-28 guitars in shop order 208 (serial numbers 256747 to 25671) were made with Brazilian rosewood bodies. Guitars from shop order 208 were noted as being "glued" on January 16, 1970. This is probably a situation where a quantity of Brazilian rosewood was discovered after the switch. As a practical matter, Martin would have simply used up the Brazilian rosewood that was uncovered. There are even reports of Brazilian rosewood guitars made after January 1970. It is possible more Brazilian rosewood was found in various parts of the factory and used for production guitars until the remaining supply was completely depleted.

T-Bar Neck Reinforcement

The introduction of the steel T-bar neck reinforcement is directly related to introduction of T-frets (for information on T-frets see "Frets and Fret Material", pages 280 to 282). Once Martin had decided to switch to T-frets, they were presented with the problem that the compression wedging effect of bar frets was no longer

available. In order to compensate, Martin replaced the ebony bar with a steel T-bar to provide the necessary stiffness and strength to the neck.

That, of course, meant that the previous practice of adjusting a bowed neck by installing different thicknesses of bar fret material was no longer possible and, in the future, the neck would need to be removed to reset the neck angle.

The first order of T-bar material was received on August 31, 1934. On the same day Martin corresponded with Horton-Angell Co. of Attleboro Mass. concerning T-fret wire (see pages 281 and 282).

The first large order of T-fret wire was received form Horton-Angell Co. on October 3, 1934 and was probably put into use immediately.

The first batch of guitars that received the new steel T-bar and T-frets was stamped on August 28, 1934. This batch had only started a few days prior to the arrival of the first T-bars on October 3, so this batch was updated to the new features as it proceeded through the factory.

The 3/8" steel T-bars are not a regular size for structural tees. The story goes that theses T-bars were made for the runners of winter sleighs and were thus available for other uses. Steel T-bars were ordered in 12½" and 14" lengths. However, the records are somewhat unclear and other lengths may have been ordered. The 14" lengths were used for regular guitars and the 12½"lengths for size 5, and possibly tenor, guitars.

From 1934 until at least 1955 the steel T-bars were supplied by Ralph W. Fry only, a business in Easton PA that specialized in industrial and farming equipment and supplies. The steel T-bars were always supplied as cut lengths so Fry was responsible for sourcing the T-bar in full lengths.

The 3/8" T-bar was hot rolled from mild steel at the beginning but by the 1960's the material seems to have changed to cold rolled steel, possibly because the hot rolled section was no longer available.

Virzi Tone Producer

It is well known that The Gibson Co. installed Virzi Tone Producers in some of their more expensive instruments in the early1920's. The Gibson F-5 mandolins are probably the most frequently encountered of the Gibson instruments having a Virzi Tone Producer installed.

In their catalogue for 1924, Gibson offered to install the Virzi device in any of their instruments, although they promoted the installation mostly for mandolins, mandolas, mando-cellos and mando-basses.

One Martin dealer, William D. Hubbs, in a letter dated October 26, 1924, asked what Martin thought of the Virzi Tone Producer and provided some information from a Gibson catalogue. Martin replied on October 28:

"Thank you for your kind letter of the 26th and for the description of the Virzi Tone Producer. It appears that the device could be attached to a Martin Guitar just as it is on the other makes of stringed instruments and might have a good effect. However, a Martin Guitar differs radically in construction from other Guitars in that the bracing of the top is very carefully laid out and delicately constructed, using the principle of the tone bar of the Violin, and it is possible that the imposition of the Tone Producer over these braces would injure rather than develop the tone. The only sure way to determine this is to try it out."

It is interesting that Martin claimed no knowledge of the Virzi Tone Producer in 1924, since J. & J. Virzi Brothers of New York, the inventors of the device, had approached Martin on July 7, 1922 with an offer to demonstrate the effectiveness of the Tone Producer by installing one in a Martin guitar.

Regardless, Martin does not seem to have tried the Virzi Tone Producer in 1922 and was still unenthusiastic in 1924. However, it is interesting to imagine what effect a Virzi Tone Producer might have had on a flat top Martin guitar.

Wood Preferences

TOP WOODS

NOTE: Martin used various terminologies to identify the types of spruce they employed for instrument tops. At various times Martin referred to red spruce as Appalachian, Adirondack, Pennsylvania, White Mountain, West Virginia, New York, Ontario, Vermont, Eastern or East. (All these terms will be used interchangeably, as the spruce used from any of these sources would be indistinguishable from Adirondack red spruce). Sitka spruce was identified as Sitka, Western, West, Washington or Alpine (in this case meaning a type of Sitka cut above a certain altitude and may actually refer to Engelmann spruce although that name never appears in the Martin records.).

EUROPEAN SPRUCE

All Martin instruments made from 1834 until after the turn of the 20th century have spruce sounding boards.

A very small quantity of spruce ($1.50) was purchased on November 28, 1836 but that it the sum total of spruce acquired by Martin while he was in New York. As there are gaps in the early information (there is no ledger covering November 1833-April 1834 and a gap in the ledgers from November 1834 to December 1835), Martin may have purchased locally available spruce during this time frame.

However, close examination of about twenty-five Martin guitars made between 1834 and 1840 shows that all these guitars have the same type kind of spruce top: a very fine-grained spruce very different from spruce used on post-1840 Martin guitars.

James Westbrook in his book "*The Century that Shaped the Guitar*" (pages 156 -162) has a very interesting chapter on the dendrochronology of spruce used on European guitars from the early to mid-19th century. One of the guitars analyzed was a 1834 Stauffer Martin and the results indicate the spruce top on this guitar was European spruce harvested between 1779 and 1794. It is now quite clear that spruce doesn't appear in the early ledger books because C. F. Martin brought a supply with him from the old country. As has been mentioned, all pre-1840 Martin guitars that have been examined have European spruce tops so Martin must have brought at least 400 tops with him from Germany (total production of Martin guitars in New York was about 400 instruments).

RED SPRUCE

From 1840, the spruce Martin used for his guitars was not as fine grained and definitely came from an American sources .Martin likely used local spruce for his guitars or, if the need arose, he could have purchased spruce from piano sound board suppliers located in New York. The purchasing records are spotty from 1840 to the 1880's but it is known Martin was buying spruce from a J. D. Serfas of Effort, Monroe County, Pennsylvania, from 1886 to 1888 (Effort is about 25 kms NNW of Nazareth).

Although most of the spruce Martin used came from local sources, Pennsylvania spruce must have been in short supply by 1889 ad Martin sought other sources as shown by a letter from Zoebisch dated November 2, 1889:

"I will write to my Bro. (i. e., in Germany) & have him look around about spruce which is seasoned and old."

For the short period of time between 1889 and 1893, Martin purchased most spruce tops from piano sounding board suppliers in New York.

From 1893 to 1913, Martin's main supplier of spruce was the Parker & Young Co. of Lisbon, New Hampshire. Parker & Young were a major supplier of piano sounding boards and supplied what Martin called White Mountain spruce.

From 1906 to 1918, Martin switched spruce purchases to Acme Veneer & Lumber Co. of Cincinnati, Ohio. Acme supplied Martin with West Virginia spruce. Martin began buying from Acme in 1906 and it was only in 1913 they became Martin's primary source. Martin also purchased spruce from Acme during the period from 1933 to 1941, although they received only a portion of the total orders. Most of the spruce used by Martin for its "Golden Era" guitars came from Julius Breckwoldt & Son of Dolgeville New York. Breckwoldt harvested and processed Adirondack spruce (Dolgeville being on the southern edge of the Adirondack mountains) and was Martin's main

source between 1919 and 1941.

The availability of West Virginia spruce was becoming unpredictable by the early 1920's as documented in a January 10, 1923 letter that Martin wrote to Fred C. Meyer. Since Martin was already buying Adirondack spruce, this letter may indicate that Martin preferred West Virginia spruce for some reason (possibly freight related).

"Can you refer us to a Philadelphia dealer who handles 3/16" Sawed Spruce, suitable for Guitar tops?

Our source of supply since the Pennsylvania Spruce gave out many years ago has been Cincinnati, which is the market for West Virginia Spruce, but this supply is becoming uncertain and unreliable in quality. We hardly dare hope that there is Spruce available through Philadelphia, but we thought you would know of such a dealer, if there is one."

Occasionally, Martin would receive letters inquiring as to the type of spruce used on guitar tops. In December 1923 F. E. Farrell wrote to Martin wanting to know if the top of his guitar was made of Canadian spruce. Martin responded on December 17:

"In reply to your inquiry we can advise that Guitar Style 00-21, No. 17354, was made in August 1922. It is very likely that the soundboard of this instrument is Appalachian Spruce, probably from West Virginia, which forms the greater part of our supply.

During the war and immediately afterward we used some Pacific Coast Spruce from Washington but found it unsuitable because of its dark color, although there was no particular fault in the tone quality. Appalachian Spruce is distinguished by its comparatively light color and soft texture. We consider it best for all-round use in Guitar construction."

The availability of Adirondack spruce must have continued to be a problem as, on August 23, 1927, Martin even wrote to Frank Adamson of Pictou, Nova Scotia in Canada because they had heard he had some very fine spruce lumber. A sample of the quality of spruce Martin sought was enclosed with the letter but Adamson replied that he had nothing of that quality and advised Martin he did not think any stock could be found east of Quebec.

In 1927 Martin began to buy 5/8" thick Adirondack spruce lumber from Breckwoldt for carved top mandolins and added 1" thick spruce in the 1930's for use on carved top guitars.

A lone Martin 0-21 guitar from 1929 (serial number 40263) is recorded as having a "Romanian spruce" top.

In June 1933, The Pratt & Brake Corp. offered Martin some spruce, a wood they usually did not sell. Martin's reply dated June 27 contains much interesting information:

"The Spruce we use in our Guitar tops reaches us either in four-foot lengths of absolutely clear stock, rough sawn one inch thick and eight inches wide which we use for the tops that are carved like a violin; or in ten or twelve foot lengths of one-eighth inch quarter sawn veneers, eight inches wide for the old style flat tops. The inch wood we get from Hoquiam, Washington, and the price is $150.00 per thousand board feet, f. o. b. Hoquiam. The freight to Nazareth amounts to about thirty-five dollars a thousand. The veneer we get from Breckwoldt & Son, Dolgeville, New York, who take it out of the Adirondack woods or get it from Ontario and manufacture it at their mill in Dolgeville. As a matter of fact it is not veneer sawn but re-sawn out of 1 3/8" lumber which is the way they stock it for the piano trade. In both cases the wood is dried for at least a year."

On December 5, 1935, Palmer & Parker Co. sent Martin some samples of Vermont spruce for use on tops but Martin was unimpressed with the quality of the wood and does not seem to have purchased any at that time.

The last purchase of Adirondack spruce was made in December 1941. This buy and the previous very large order made in October 1941 were sufficient to last into 1945.

Between November 1949 and January 1952 Martin made three purchases of "Vermont" spruce from Eaton Lumber Co. of Rochester, Vermont. The conventional wisdom, based on the remembrances of C. F. Martin III in an 1985 article authored by Dana Bourgeois, was that this wood was surplus Engelmann spruce. However, the Martin records never mention Engelmann spruce through at least 1964 and only Vermont spruce is recorded as the possible source of top wood for the so-called "mystery tops" of 1953.

A check of the inventory records shows that Martin had "East spruce tops" (Martin terminology for Adirondack spruce) in stock from the beginning of 1950 to 1953. The inventory from 1950 must have just been cut and wouldn't have been sufficiently seasoned but from 1951 to 1953 the this wood could have been available for use as guitar tops. Most "mystery" top guitars seem to be from 1953, although a few from 1952 have been reported. That being the case, there very well could be some 1951 Martin guitars with Vermont spruce tops, something to watch out for.

Martin did not begin to list unfinished tops and braces in their yearly inventory until 1918 and did not differentiate between stocks of Western and Eastern spruce until 1951.

A supply of Vermont spruce was purchased from Eaton in late 1955 that yielded 1,382 000-size tops, 600 0-size tops and 562 mandolin tops. According to the surviving shop order slips, Vermont spruce tops are encountered on guitars from the first half of 1957. Since the Vermont spruce should have been ready by the end 1956 there is a possibility that some late 1956 guitars also have this kind of top. Some batches that were made in 1957 with a mixture of Vermont and Sitka spruce tops. Six 00-28G and four 00-18G were made with Vermont tops in 1959 and some Vermont spruce tops appeared on tiples and a few 5-18 guitars in 1958 and 1959 as Martin used up their remaining supply. Mandolin tops continued to be made with the remaining small pieces of Vermont spruce until at least 1961 (in 1962 Martin shop orders ceased indicating the type of spruce used on mandolins).

SITKA SPRUCE

Martin did buy some Sitka spruce from Posey Manufacturing Co. in Washington state between 1918 and 1920 that was used for some guitars tops at that time.

Inventory on Jan. 1 each year	Eastern Spruce Tops	Western Spruce Tops	Mixed Eastern/Western Spruce Tops	German Spruce Tops
1951	3,530	6,797		
1952	1,913	3,015		
1953	2,622	2,050		
1954	312	6,108		
1955	183	5,200		
1956	2,102	5,839		
1957		6,369	860	
1958		4,511	390	
1959		3,376	1,427	1,102
1960	165	3,293	96	491
1961		4,135	67	996
1962		2,750	300	445
1963		6,171		250
1964		4,800		500
1965		2,343		
1966		1,953		
1967		4,830		

Table 108
Types of Spruce Tops Counted
During 1951 to 1967 Inventories

Other suppliers offered Martin Sitka spruce and in one letter the reason for the short period that Sitka spruce was used for flat top guitars is explained. On February 20, 1922, J. C. Iverson of Seattle WA offered Western spruce to Martin for guitar and mandolin tops. Martin replied on March 16:

"We have noted carefully your letters of February 20th and March 7th. The sample of Spruce is indeed fine, but we are not in the market for wood of this kind for several reasons.

In the first place, we have found it entirely satisfactory to use 3/16" sawed stock for our mandolin and Guitar tops. Of this kind of stock we have had several shipments from the Posey Manufacturing Co., Hoquiam, Washington, but we have decided to discontinue the use of Washington Spruce in favor of Appalachian Spruce on account its brownish color as compared with the clear white of the Spruce which is grown in West Virginia."

On June 23, 1924 Ben J. Roy wrote offering spruce to Martin:

"I am sending under separate couver(sic) Samples of Rocky-Mountain Spruce, such as I am supplying the leading Violin-Makers with.

As I am now supplying the Gibson Co., I thought it would be in order to place my self at your service.

If you will submit specifications & prices I will ship you a small order so that you can try it out."

Martin's reply, on July 2, 1924, was much more encouraging than in the 1922 letter to J. C. Everson which raises the question whether "Rocky-Mountain spruce" might really be Engelmann spruce:

"Your samples of Soundboard Spruce are at hand. We can use some of this material if you are able to supply it veneer sawed on the quarter, 5/32" thick, the width to be not less than seven inches.

We are now buying Spruce of this description from a firm in Cincinnati who are supplying very nice wood at fifty-five dollars per thousand. The grade of it is log run which means that the wood varies from coarse to very fine; this suits our purposes very well because it enables us to select for quality according to the grade of our instruments.

Freight from the west would, of course, be considerably higher so we would have to count on finer wood in your wood to make up the difference.

If you are able to supply, as specified, you may send a small flitch of several hundred feet for trial."

No orders for spruce were made between May 1924 and January 1925 so it appears Ben Roy did not receive an order.

On Jun 23, 1924 Posey Manufacturing Co. wrote to Martin seeking another order:

"SPRUCE RIB STOCK LUMBER

It has been sometime since we made the last shipment to you, last December to be exact, and we are wondering of you will not be needing more stock in the near future.

We expect to have a consolidated New York car during the month of August and could protect you on the carload rate to that point if you have your order in soon enough for us to make arrangements accordingly.

In case you should want shipment next month we expect to have a mixed car going to Chicago and could ship in that manner as we did the last time."

This letter is very interesting as it indicates Posey was prepared to pre-pay freight to New York for an immediate order, or, otherwise, would pre-paid freight to Chicago for a later order, Martin's usual arrangement with Posey.

Martin response of July 7 is shown below:

"Thank you for your offer of Spruce Rib stock lumber. We still have on hand a good deal of the last shipment and do not expect to reorder until winter or early spring.

We used some of your stock for Guitar and Mandolin tops about ten years ago but were not well pleased with the results. Since out tops are finished natural color, the dark color of the Washington Spruce compared with the eastern Appalachian Spruce (is) a disadvantage from a sales point of view. In tone we found little if any difference but the western wood seemed to give more trouble from cracks. We work our tops quite thin and prefer the eastern wood because of its apparently greater strength and whiter color."

The reply above clearly explains the reason Martin preferred red spruce to Sitka spruce for guitar tops. However, Martin was perfectly willing to use Sitka spruce for bracing, as long as the freight was subsidized to make its use economical.

This prompted a reply from Posey Manufacturing Co. on July 22:

"GUITAR & MANDOLIN TOPS

Replying to your of July 7th we want to thank you for the explanation set forth because t gives us an opportunity to present our side of the case.

Now, Mr. Martin, you acknowledge you used some of our stock ten years ago. We started in business, as you know, over twenty years ago and we made about fifty sound boards a day and nothing else.

Today our capacity has increased to one thousand boards a day and in addition we make about one hundred and fifty thousand quarter sawed spruce keybeds annually, also harp boards, organ reed boards, violin stock and stock for guitar and mandolin tops.

If you will stop to consider you will readily realize that there must be a very great merit in our products, otherwise we would be going down hill, and finally out of business, rather than showing this splendid growth.

You say our Sitka Spruce is not as strong as what you are using. In answering this we would point to the government tests on our spruce for aircraft work. It is so superior that Sitka Spruce is not only sought by this government for airplane work but is eagerly being purchased by all other countries for this purpose.

Eventually you will use it and we respectfully suggest that you start your experiments now, with the full confidence that it will result in a great benefit to you in as much as it has proved its value to so many of the other manufacturers, as evidenced by the demand outlines above."

This letter seems to indicate Martin was purchasing Sitka spruce from Posey Manufacturing Co. from as early as 1914, although no purchase orders appear in the records at that time. The first recorded order to Posey Manufacturing Co. was dated October 8, 1918 and, at that time, Martin received 880 ft of Washington spruce, yielding 285 guitar tops and 235 mandolin tops.

Posey Manufacturing Co. followed up with another interesting letter on August 12, 1925:

"There is a letter on my desk this morning from Lyon & Healy, Inc. part of which reads as follows:

'We like your material very much for guitars and mandolins and have called it to the attention of some of the other users in the city, in fact, we let one of our Chicago firms have a small quantity recently. We shall be glad to let you know just as soon as we are in further need of any of this material.'

The above call t mind our letter to you of July 22nd and the fact that to date you have not replied. If there is any doubt in your mind as to the superior quality of Sitka Spruce for this kind of work we think you might get some interesting information if you would write to Mr. Kirk of the Lyon & Healy Company, 4100 West Fullerton Ave., Chicago, Ill.

We might further add that we just received a repeat order from one of the largest violin makers for a great quantity of our Sitka Spruce for violin tops."

Martin also had Julius Breckwoldt & Son of Dolgeville NY quote on the 5/4" spruce rib stock but their quote was, of course, for Adirondack spruce. The price quoted was the same as Posey Manufacturing Co. but Posey offered their spruce F. O. B. Chicago or New York. Therefore, Martin purchased Sitka spruce for braces instead of Adirondack spruce, because it was less expensive and the stock was slightly larger in size. On December 11, 1925 Posey Manufacturing acknowledged an order for 1,000 feet of 5/4" rib stock, priced at $150.00 f.o.b. Chicago.

Martin continued to buy Adirondack spruce from Breckwoldt for use on tops, and also occasionally bought bracing stock from them as well.

In general, Martin purchased 1¼" or ½" thick spruce lumber for making braces and 3/16" spruce veneers for making tops. In the 1930's and later, it appears Martin limited the purchasing of bracing material to 5/4" thick spruce.

On March 13, 1925 Martin replied to a request from a Howard Bramhill who wanted to know which combination of woods created the best tone (among other things):

"We wish to reply to your questions as follows: In general the tone value of Guitars according to the material varies as follows:

    Rosewood Body, Spruce Top
    Mahogany Body, Spruce Top
    Koawood Body, Koawood Top
    Mahogany Body, Mahogany Top

Rosewood is the most resonant wood and Spruce the best material for tops; but we often find the Koawood Guitars, adjusted for Hawaiian Playing, have a very brilliant tone. As you know, all Guitars and all materials vary.

In regard to bulging of tops and warping of necks, we guarantee our instruments completely in these matters.

We take particular pains with the regulation, bracing, height of bridge, set of neck and fretting of fingerboard according to the type of stringing that is to be used and therefore find it possible to guarantee our instruments if this stringing is adhered to. As you no doubt found in our catalogue, our less expensive numbers, up to and including Style 000-18, are regularly strung with Steel Strings, as also the Hawaiian Koawood Guitars. Other styles have the Gut Treble and Silk Center Bass. We do not guarantee an instrument on which the type of strings have been changed from the those with which it was equipped at the factory.

In regard to the regulation of the strings of an Hawaiian Guitar, we must explain as follows: Steel String Guitars have a lower bridge and saddle and lower slotting at the nut and stiffer, rounder neck than Gut String Guitars. Gut String Instruments have a fairly high regulation and this regulation is used for Hawaiian Guitars; therefore, if you buy a Martin Guitar equipped for Hawaiian Playing and take the nut adjuster off for the purpose of using it in the regular manner, the regulation will not be right for Steel Strings but it will be right for Gut and Silk Center Strings."

From 1942 onwards, Martin mostly purchased Sitka spruce for guitar tops except when they were able to buy a supplies of Vermont spruce (1949 to 1952 and again in late 1955). Martin also introduced German spruce tops beginning in late 1957, but in relatively small quantities.

GERMAN SPRUCE

Martin began buying German spruce tops from Worldwide Musical Instruments Co. in 1957. These tops must have already been seasoned as they were put into use shortly after being received. According to Martin's yearly inventory records, German spruce tops were about 3 to 4 times more expensive than Sitka tops (See Table 108 for the yearly inventory numbers). After the first order for 100 tops, Martin always ordered in quantities of 250 or 500 tops: 1,000 total in 1958, 500 in 1959, 1,000 in 1960, 500 in each of the years 1961, 1962 and 1963.

Martin received about 100 German spruce tops on June 28, 1957. They were first used on seven 00-28G guitars of a batch of 25 that were stamped on October 30, 1957.

As mentioned above Martin purchased 1,000 German spruce tops in 1958. However, only twelve guitars received German spruce tops in that year: two batches of D-28 guitars which each contained six guitars with German spruce tops and nineteen with Sitka tops.

The number of German spruce tops purchased and the numbers used were more balanced from 1959 to 1962. Most guitars in this period were made in mixed batches of German and Sitka spruce tops. As can be seen from Table 109 Martin did not reserve German spruce tops for any specific models, although D-28E guitars made in 1959 got a larger proportion of these tops. However, by 1968 this policy changed with the re-introduction of D-45 guitars as a foreman's notebook contains the following comment dated August 21, 1968: **"Have all German spruce tops for D-45, measure at 8/64", if possible no less than 7½/64""**. The yearly inventories for 1965, 1966 and 1967 do not contain counts for German spruce tops but, since a large number of guitars from this period appear to have German spruce tops, Martin must have been using up whatever supplies of German spruce were available before the end of each of these years.

The Martin archive, at least through 1967, contains no

mention of Engelmann spruce. If Engelmann spruce can be identified on certain guitars, Martin must have been purchasing it for immediate use or, less likely, grouped Sitka and Engelmann spruce together as "Western" spruce.

In general, Martin preferred Adirondack red spruce for guitar tops, mostly for the clear, white appearance of this wood. By the mid-1940's, Martin was forced to used a mixture Adirondack and Sitka. By the mid-1950's, the Adirondack spruce supply was exhausted and Martin used Sitka spruce along with the more expensive German spruce from 1957.

Sitka spruce was certainly adequate as a top wood but Martin did not prefer it due to its characteristic darker color. On the other hand, Martin had no problem with using Sitka spruce for braces, especially when cost effective. That does not mean that Martin used Sitka spruce exclusively for braces from the 1920's, there being times when Martin found it practical to use Adirondack spruce for that purpose. As a factory, Martin would purchased whatever type of spruce was available when their stock ran low, although Martin always demanded the best quality. Except for the use of Sitka spruce for guitar tops circa 1918 to 1920, Martin used red spruce for guitar tops whenever possible throughout the 1920's, 1930's and 1940's.

Martin did not differentiate between Vermont and Sitka spruce in their yearly inventories until 1951 and this continued until the 1957 inventory (although the Vermont spruce in the 1957 inventory appears to have all been jointed and inlaid into finished tops). Ever practical, Martin used smaller pieces of Vermont spruce on some smaller bodied guitars and tiples until 1959 and on mandolins until 1961.

	GERMAN SPRUCE TOPS PURCHASED	D-28	D-28E	D-28L	D-28S	D-21	D-18	D-18E	000-18	00-18	00-18E	00-18G	00-21NY	00-28G	0-18	0-18T	0-16	0-16NY	5-18S
1957	100	60					17							7					
1958	1,000	12																	
1959	500	96	157	1			30	61		12	76	22		8	17	17			
1960	1,000	360		3	1	19	277		17	112	24	30			23	33			1
1961	500	185				5	166		50	66					54	9	1	74	
1962	500	95	12	1	2				3	43			7		46	3			

Usage for 1962 only covers to June 1962.

Table 109
Number of German Spruce Tops Used on Guitars 1957 to 1962

MAHOGANY TOPS

Martin made a few guitars between 1909 and 1918 with mahogany tops. Also, in 1920, one batch of twenty-four 1-18 guitars with mahogany tops was made for Buegeleisen & Jacobson.

In 1922, Martin introduced the Style 2-17, the first regular production guitars with mahogany tops. Subsequently, all Style 17, and later Style 15, guitars and tiples had mahogany bodies and tops.

For more information see "Mahogany" in the "Wood for Backs and Sides" section.

KOA TOPS

Martin first used koa tops on the Southern California Music Co. Model 1350, 1400 and 1500 guitars in the period from 1916 to 1918. Later, koa tops were used on Martin's own 0-18K and 0-28K guitar up to 1935. The last koa guitar was a 1937 5-18K

For more comments see "Koa" in the section on "Wood for Backs and Sides".

WOOD FOR BACKS AND SIDES

During the 1830's Martin recorded the use of maple, bird's-eye maple, mahogany, pernambuco, rosewood, zebrawood and walnut. By the early 1840's Martin had settled on rosewood, although a few guitars were made of pernambuco or mahogany.

In the period after 1850, most guitars were made of rosewood although lower priced mahogany guitars were made through the end of 1856.

Most of the woods mentioned above are well known. However, pernambuco and zebrawood are worth further examination because of the possibility of confusing these woods with koa and rosewood respectively.

ROSEWOOD

Martin used Brazilian rosewood (Dalbergia nigra) almost exclusively for their higher priced instruments until 1969. At times Brazilian rosewood was called Bahia or Rio rosewood in supplier correspondence.

Martin was offered Indian rosewood occasionally but with the exception of veneers from one supplier always refused to buy this type of rosewood. An exception was made in 1924 when Ichabod T. Williams & Sons sent a sample flitch of 1/20" East Indian rosewood to Martin. Martin responded to the receipt of the sample on July 18, 1924:

"We just received the flitch of 1/20" Sawed E. I. Rosewood which you sent recently and we are immensely pleased with it. It is not only unusually fine wood, but it is also remarkably well sawn, and we wish to compliment you on the shipment. With sawing as nice as this we can use 1/14" stock in place of the 1/12" Rosewood about which we inquired last week and which you promised to lay aside for us when you found something nice. Will you, therefore, please keep an eye open for another flitch like this one, perfectly straight and uniformly dark in color, to be sawn 1/14"? Whenever you get such a flitch you may manufacture it for us without further instruction."

Martin purchased both 1/20" and 1/15" Indian rosewood veneers in 1924. Based on this letter, Martin clearly intended to use the East Indian rosewood for guitar sides and, possibly, backs. Martin also purchased some 1/16" Indian rosewood veneer in early 1926 but must have used it up quickly because it doesn't appear in the 1927 inventory.

From 1925 until 1943, the 1/20" and 1/15" Indian rosewood veneers continued to appear in the yearly inventories. The largest usage of Indian rosewood veneer was between 1925 and 1931, so a number of rosewood guitars from this period may have Indian rosewood bodies. Martin bought some more 1/15" Indian rosewood veneer in 1932.

From 1932 to 1943, the quantity of Indian rosewood in the yearly inventories did not change and Indian rosewood veneers had disappeared by the inventory of January 1, 1946.

Figure 359 provides an interesting view of the appearance of raw Brazilian rosewood logs. On August 13, 1935 one of Martin's suppliers of rosewood, C. H. Pearson & Son Hardwood Co. Inc., wrote to Martin and included this photograph:

"**Enclosed is a photograph of BRAZILIAN ROSE-WOOD logs which we have in our yards. These are very large, of excellent color, best quality and as we are importing direct from the source, can quote a better price than others.**"

Attractive as the logs appear, C. H. Pearson & Son did not receive an order as Martin had received a large order of rosewood in April 1935 from another supplier.

When in the market for Brazilian rosewood C. F.

Figure 359
Brazilian Rosewood Logs from 1935

Martin III, or more rarely Frank Henry Martin, would take a trip to inspect the logs on offer. Martin always purchased Brazilian rosewood as logs and had them processed into veneers at the supplier or at one of the custom sawing companies located in New York.

PERNAMBUCO (FERNAMBUCO)

A few early Martin guitars have been identified by dealers and collectors as having backs and sides of "koa" but these guitars are, in fact, made of pernambuco (fernambuco or fernambuck to C. F. Martin).

Koa, being native to Hawaii, would not have been available to Martin in the 1830's and 1840's. The harvesting and sawing of koa in Hawaii only began around 1837 and the resulting timber was used for local construction.

Fernambuco (*Caesalpinia echinata*, modern pernambuco), on the other hand, is a tree native to coastal

South America. It is also known as brazilwood. The wood has dense orange-red colored heartwood. Pernambuco is still highly valued for violin bows because of its ability to accept a high shine.

Pernambuco was highly prized in Europe in the 16th and 17th centuries for the red dye, brazilin, produced from the wood. It was so heavily harvested that commercial production practically ceased by the 18th century. Brazilwood trees were such an important part of the early economy that the country eventually became known as Brazil.

Brazilwood is a name sometimes incorrectly applied to several other species of wood including: Pink Ipê (*Tabebuia impetiginosa*), Massaranduba (*Manilkara bidentata*), also known as Balatá, Ausubo, cow-tree or bulletwood) and Palo Brasil (*Haematoxylum brasiletto*).

Martin clearly would have had access to fernambuco veneer in New York of the 1830's, where it was probably mostly used on pianos or high grade furniture. But it must have been scarce even then as Martin did not use this type of wood much after about 1840.

MAPLE

A number of early Martin guitars were made of maple. Martin preferred "bird's-eye" and all early Martin guitars examined to date have this variety of maple, although occasionally it is quite plain looking. The "bird's-eye" veneers were very thin and were always lined with spruce when used for guitar backs. Martin seems to have stopped using maple early in the 1840's although a few maple bodied guitars were made in the 1850's.

ZEBRAWOOD

The Martin ledgers record that at least nineteen guitars were made from "zebrawood" between 1836 and 1840.

There has been some discussion as to which type of wood C. F. Martin was referring to but it is almost certainly gonçalo-alves (*Astronium fraxinifolium* or *Astronium graveolens*), also known as zebrawood or tigerwood. This tree is native to South and Central America. The heartwood is a pale brown with dark streaks and can have a straight or wavy grain, sometimes showing some fiddle-back grain. Over time the pale brown matrix deepens in color. Very old zebrawood can easily be mistaken for Brazilian rosewood (see Figure 132).

Another type of wood (*Microberlinia*) that is native to West and Central Africa is also known as zebrawood. Although this zebrawood is sometimes used for modern guitars, the pale yellow wood with narrow lines of dark brown or black is very different from gonçalo-alves.

WALNUT

John Coupa ordered four guitars of "valnut" from Martin on March 26, 1840. It was at this exact point in time that Martin canceled Ludecus and Wolter's agency for New York and gave it to Coupa, so these guitars may be among the first "Martin & Coupa" guitars. The deliveries of these guitars were not recorded and may been entered in the missing ledger from the 1840's.

"Valnut" is the Swedish word for walnut but almost certainly refers to Spanish walnut, a type of wood that had been used in the manufacture of high quality furniture for several centuries, but was quite scarce by the 1840's.

MAHOGANY

Martin made several mahogany guitars in 1834 and about eighty mahogany guitars were made between 1852 and 1856. A few mahogany guitars are also known from the 1840's.

In the 1850's, mahogany was always used on the inexpensive Style 14, 15 and 16 guitars. These styles always had a black neck and an "ice cream cone" heel.

In late 1893, due to the sharp drop in business as a result of the Panic of 1893, Zoebisch suggested Martin should make a mahogany guitar to be priced below Style 17 instruments. It is not known if anything came of this idea.

Martin introduced a style 0-17 guitar in 1906 with a rosewood body but this was changed to a mahogany body by 1908. The 1909 catalogue shows the Style 17 guitars as being mahogany-bodied instruments.

During April 1917, Martin changed the back and sides of the Style 18 guitars from rosewood to mahogany. At the same time, mahogany Style 17 guitars were dropped from the product line.

Style 17 was resurrected in 1922 with the introduction of the all mahogany 2-17 guitar. From this point Style 17 always meant a mahogany-body guitar combined with a mahogany top, with the exception of a few 0-17S guitars made with spruce tops. All mahogany Style 15 instruments were added to the product line in 1940.

Mahogany was purchased in 2½" and 3" wide lumber for necks and in veneer form for tops and sides. Veneers of 1/7" or 1/8" thicknesses were ordered for guitar tops while 1/12" veneers were used for the sides of guitars, and also ukuleles.

On September 19, 1935 Martin's response to a letter from Palmer & Parker Co. contained some interesting information on mahogany:

"We use 3" flat sawn Mahogany lumber twelve inches and up wide for guitar necks, 1/7" and 1/10" quarter sawn Mahogany lumber eight inches up wide for bodies. We require a selected grade, practically free defects, reasonably dark in color and firm in texture, all stock air dried.

Years ago we used some Cuban Mahogany but for some time we have not been able to get it large enough for our purpose so our principal of supply has been Mexican or Honduras wood. Within the last year, however, we have used some Peruvian stock, both lumber and veneer, and we find it to be even better than Mexican in some ways. Do you handle it also?"

As mentioned in the letter above Martin mostly purchased Mexican, Honduras or Peruvian mahogany but also purchased African and Philippine mahogany occasionally for at least a few years in the early 1920s. Most of the Peruvian mahogany seems to have been bought in 3" planks for necks.

African mahogany (Khaya senegalensis) is native to

Madagascar and tropical Africa is the only wood generally accepted as mahogany, alongside true mahogany (genus Swietenia).

Philippine mahogany (genus Shorea) is not a true mahogany. The name "Philippine mahogany" is also applied to a number of different species native to Southeast Asia.

Martin never differentiated between the various types of mahogany in the yearly inventories and used them interchangeably.

KOA

The first koa used by Martin was supplied by the Southern California Music Co. for use on their Model 1350, 1400 and 1500 guitars in the 1916 to 1918 period.

Southern California Music Co. made only two shipments of koa but this was sufficient to cover all SoCal's usage to 1921.

Martin purchased koa veneer from White Brothers in San Francisco in 1921. From 1922, Martin bought koa logs from Bergstrom Music Co., Martin's established dealer in Honolulu, Hawaii. Bergstrom sourced the koa logs from Allen Wall who was located at Kealakekua in the Kona district on the big island of Hawaii. Bergstrom organized the consolidation and shipment of the koa logs. The koa were generally shipped to Los Angeles and then transferred to a ship bound for New York through the Panama Canal. Martin then arranged to have the koa processed by F. A. Mulgrew & Son, Charles Van Brunt, or Herriman-Eifert Manufacturing Co. in New York before shipment to Nazareth.

The demand for koa logs was so high in the 1920's that Bergstrom Music Co. had difficulty finding suitable logs to met Martin's specifications. Curly koa was particularly hard to come by and Martin was sometimes forced to take whatever logs were available. Whatever curly koa veneer the logs yielded was reserved for Style 28 guitars while relatively plain koa was used on Style 18 instruments. Koa was also used for ukuleles and mandolins, as well as a few tiples.

Martin at times corresponded directly with Allen Wall

in Hawaii to ensure that he put aside any particularly good logs of curly koa.

Another consequence of the world-wide demand for koa in the 1920's was its high price. At the same time that Brazilian rosewood logs were selling for about 7 cents per pound, the price of koa logs was 28 cents per pound or more. Martin accordingly priced the 0-18K guitars higher than regular 0-18 instruments but, for some unknown reason, sold the 0-28K guitars at the same price as the rosewood 0-28 guitars.

A small number of other koa guitar models were made: forty-eight 1-18K, sixty-one 0-21K (SoCal), forty 00-28K, one 00-28KS, fifty-seven 00-18K, six 00-40K and one 00-40HK, three 000-28K, one 00-42KS and one 00-45K.

Martin last purchased koa wood in 1931 but still had 775 guitar tops and backs and 1,202 sides in stock at the January 1, 1932 inventory. This was sufficient for the 358 koa guitars made after 1931. There were still a large quantity of koa wood odds and ends, including 2,263 uke tops and backs in the 1938 inventory. By the January 1, 1940 only koa tops and sides remained in stock. However, the remnant koa had been scrapped by the January 1, 1945 inventory.

UNUSUAL WOODS

Martin did buy some non-traditional wood from time to time.

In 1880, Martin bought some snakewood from P. M. Dingee & Sons. The sizes of lumber shipped were not recorded, so no clues are available concerning its intended use. Snakewood (*rosimum guianense*) is native to the Northeast coast of South America.

Some walnut and holly veneer was bought from J. Rayner between 1883 and 1885. The holly, and probably the walnut, was used for making thin strips for purfling or binding.

It appears in 1896 that Martin made up some guitars out of "cazembawood" because Martin requested instructions on how best to bend the wood for making sides. No information could be found on the internet for cazembawood although Cazemba is a town in Mozambique.

Necks and Fingerboards

EBONY FINGERBOARDS

Martin purchased ebony for making fingerboards and bridges. The ebony was always sourced through wood dealers in New York City and was processed at one or another of the sawmills located in that city.

Martin commonly processed the ebony to 7/32" thick and in sizes 2 3/4" X 18", 2 5/16" X 11 7/8" and 2 1/8" X 9 3/4" for guitars, mandolins and ukuleles fingerboards respectively. The remainder pieces were used for making bridges and nuts. Martin did purchase some 1/20" and 1/30" ebony veneers in 1890 but for what purpose is unknown.

Ebony came from a variety of sources. It is known that Martin bought Gaboon ebony (from the west coast of Africa), Madagascar ebony (sometimes associated with a particular locale in Madagascar; such as Tamatave, Minterano or Majunga), and Macassar ebony from what is now Sulawesi, Indonesia (sometimes also call Tomini Bay ebony). Although Martin mostly used Gaboon ebony, at one point they expressed a preference for Madagascar ebony.

On November 19, 1925 Willard Hawes & Co. wrote to Martin about the availability of Gaboon ebony:

"Answering your favor of the 17th, beg to advise that we have no Gaboon ebony, and as far as we know there is none in dealers' hands here in the city.

We have two lots of genuine MADAGASCAR Ebony: one lot of MINTERANO running about 3" to 5" in diameter, 40" to 4 ft. long, jet black for color. This lot, while small, is round, sound and we may repeat the color is all to be desired. The other lot of MAJUNGA wood runs about 6" to 8" in diameter, 40" and up long, round, sound but for color it is not black. This lot runs more or less on a red or brown tint.

We can offer you either of these lots at $120.00 per ton, for the selection."

NOTE: Minterano (modern day Mainterano) and Majunga (or Mahajunga) are towns on the west coast of Madagascar.

Martin must have like the quality of the ebony well enough as C. F. Martin III called at the yard and selected one ton of the Minterano and ½ ton of the Majunga ebony.

ROSEWOOD FINGERBOARDS

Martin began using rosewood for fingerboards on Style 1 and 2 ukuleles by at least 1918.

The first regular Martin guitar with a rosewood fingerboard were the Style 2-17 guitars first offered in 1922.

As Martin strove to reduce costs on some models, ebony fingerboards were replaced with rosewood. As an example, George Gruhn has noted that Style 18 guitars in size 000 and smaller began switching to a rosewood fingerboard around 1935 and the fingerboards were all rosewood by 1940.

CUBAN CEDAR

Martin used Cuban cedar for their early guitars with a Spanish style neck (i.e., without the "ice cream cone" heel). The earliest Martin guitar seen to date with a cedar neck is a Martin & Coupa guitar from the early 1840's. Earlier examples may yet come to light as a "Spanish" neck is mentioned in the 1837 ledger.

Cuban cedar (*cedrela odorata*), also known as Mexican cedar or Cigar-box cedar, is a close relative of mahogany and is native to the Caribbean, Central America and the Pacific coast of Mexico.

Martin used Cuban cedar for necks throughout the 19th century. Longworth notes that the switch to mahogany necks occurred around 1916, but there is no documentary evidence or correspondence to support this. Martin usually purchased Spanish cedar as 3½" planks.

Based on the yearly inventories, it appears Martin continued to use cedar for necks blocks until 1921. Martin may have had a preference for Cuban cedar neck blocks but may also have just been using up the supply on hand.

In the section on mahogany, Martin notes in a 1935

letter that "Cuban mahogany" was used by Martin until it was no longer available in the sizes required. Either there was a variety of mahogany available from Cuba at one time or Martin confused the term with Cuban cedar.

MAHOGANY

See "Mahogany" in the section on "Wood for Backs and Sides".

WHITEWOOD (POPLAR)

The early ledgers contain numerous purchases for "whitewood", which seems to have been used for making necks with "ice cream cone" heels. "Whitewood" is most likely poplar and was ebonized with lampblack and shellac to create the "black" necks used on less expensive guitars, as well as more expensive parlor guitar in Styles 30 and above.

A few early Martins have been examined with ebony veneers on the neck and headstock.

Thinner 3/8" and ½" whitewood lumber was also used for the construction of "coffin" cases.

Wood Suppliers

Table 110 lists the larger wood suppliers used by Martin in the period between 1849 and 1964. The Martin archival records are very spotty at times so there are undoubtedly a number of suppliers missing.

Zithers

The Martin Guitar Museum has on display a very unusual instrument; a zither manufactured by Martin!

The guitar sales books do not record the sale of any zithers but on page 44 of the "Account Book 1849-1885" is an account entry showing that Louis Brachet was shipped five zithers on October 21, 1878 and was invoiced a total of $175. Brachet also bought a few Martin guitars between 1878 and 1884 including a 10-string guitar, two 3-17 guitars (one of which was a terz), a 2½-17, one 2-20 and one 1-21. There is a gap in the Martin records between 1885 and 1898 so it is possible a few more zithers were made by Martin between 1885 and 1888 (see correspondence below).

Philip Louis Brachet was born about 1828 in Prussia and immigrated to the United States in 1860, settling

SUPPLIER	DATES	ROSEWOOD	KOA	MAHOGANY	CEDAR	EBONY	SPRUCE	MAPLE	HOLLY	WHITEWOOD/POPLAR
J. & F. COPCUTT	1849	X								
ODGEN & CO.	1849				X					
P. M. DINGEE & SONS	1880-1887	X			X	X				
J. RAYNER	1883-1896	X			X	X			X	X
J. D. SERFAS	1886-1888						X	X		
C. F. BROWN	1888-1893									X
ISAAC I. COLE & SON	1889-1925	X				X	X	X		
L. F. HEPBURN	1889-1897						X			
J.C. LIVINGSTONE & CO.	1889-1890						X			
WILLARD HAWES & CO.	1890-1935	X			X	X				
AUFFERMAN & CO.	1891	X								
J. H. MONTEATH	1891-1935	X	X	X		X				
PARKER & YOUNG	1894-1895						X			
DANIEL BUCK	1895									X
ALFRED DOLGE & SON	1895									
JOSEPH SCHEINA	1895	X		X	X	X		X	X	
ICHABOD WILLAMS	1923-1935	X		X				X (EBONIZED)		
C. H. PEARSON	1923-1935	X				X				
JULIUS BRECKWOLDT & SON	1923-1935						X			
LEWIS-THOMPSON	1923-1927			X						
ACME VENEER	1924-1934						X	X		
BERGSTROM MUSIC	1923-1929		X							
ASTORIA MAHOGANY	1925-1926			X						
EMPORIUM FORSTRY CO.	1925						X			
GEORGE LOGOTHETI	1925							X		
POSEY MANUFACTURING	1925-1935						X			
PRATT & BRAKE	1925-1935	X				X				
THOMPSON MAHOGANY	1927-1933			X						
DIXIE VENEER	1933	X								
PALMER & PARKER CO.	1935			X			X			

Table 110
Wood Suppliers 1849 to 1964

in Philadelphia, PA. From his home at 602 Callowhill St. he gave music lessons on the zither, guitar and violin. By 1865 Brachet had established a music store at his residence and was selling a wide range of musical instruments. Even though he had a music store, when he did start buying Martin guitars, he was only allowed the 25% teacher's discount instead of the more usual 50% dealer's discount.

Brachet was an active composer of music for both the piano and the zither. One zither piece was titled "Erinnerung an Nazareth" (Memory of Nazareth), suggesting he had been to Nazareth, PA, and possibly visited with Martin while there. As this piece of music was written as a polka it even hints that Brachet's visit with Martin was productive, either ordering or picking up a zither or guitar.

Louis Brachet died in Philadelphia on Wednesday, June 19, 1889, at the age of 61.

The 1878 sale of five zithers is the only ones noted in the Martin records. However, that did not stop Brachet from attempting to get Martin to make more zithers, as documented in his correspondence with Martin in 1888 and 1889.

In a letter dated March 26, 1888 Brachet made the following comments:

"Now Friend Martin, You say - you had no time - to make Zithers? Could not your son Frank and Mr. Schuster make me some by their Evening or Afterwork? (what ever you call it.)

If one or the other only could make me the Zither, ? and other thinks I could have here in Phila. made. I would sent (sic) my Zither, when they make the Fingerboard, so they had no trouble.

Then when I sent up my Zither, I would like to have it polished over – it did warp – bent up, from the Pressure of the Strings – we could fix these easy.

Now Friend Martin – please favor me with and on my ideas to make a Living."

Martin's reason for not making more zithers was that the factory were too busy and that is certainly the

case, as the demand for guitars in 1888 was the largest Martin had ever seen and would only continue to grow every year until 1893.

Brachet continued to correspond with Martin through 1888, but the subject of zithers did not arise again until March 14, 1889, by which time C. F. Martin Jr. had died and Frank Henry Martin had taken over the helm at Martin:

"Frank – do you think, you ever make some Zithers for me yet? Dear Father said, he could not make much on Zithers.

Now Dear Frank – If you think, you do not got the time, or – it would not pay you to make Zithers, then please send me my Pattern, which is in your Possession and I will try to get some made after my Pattern here in Philadelphia."

Frank Henry Martin was clearly not interested in zithers and, since Professor Brachet died only three months after the letter above was written, that put an end to Martin's foray into zither making.

Figure 360
Cabinet Card for Professor Louis Brachet

Chapter 15
SOME MUSICIANS AND THEIR MARTIN GUITARS

Gene Autry (1907-1998)

Orvon Grover Autry (September 29, 1907 – October 2, 1998), better known as Gene Autry, was born September 29, 1907 near Tioga in Grayson County, Texas. He became one of the most famous American performers from the 1930's through the 1960's, starting as a singing cowboy on the radio, before branching into movies and, later, his own television show. Autry was also the owner of a television station and several radio stations in Southern California. From 1961 to 1997 Autry owned the Los Angeles/California/Anaheim Angels Major League Baseball team.

After leaving high school in Oklahoma in 1925, Autry worked for a railroad company as a telegrapher. He sang and played guitar at local dances and was encouraged to sing professionally by the famous humorist, Will Rogers, who had seen him perform. In 1928, Autry was playing on Tulsa's KVOO radio station as "Oklahoma's Yodeling Cowboy". He signed a recording deal with Columbia Records in 1929.

For four years Autry worked in Chicago for the National Barn Dance show on WLS radio as well as his own show. His first hit was in 1932 with "That Silver-Haired Daddy Of Mine," a duet Autry sang with Jimmy Long, who also co-wrote the song. Autry's other hits included "Back In The Saddle Again," and many Christmas holiday songs, including "Santa Claus Is Coming to Town", "Here Comes Santa Claus", "Frosty the Snowman," and "Rudolph the Red-Nosed Reindeer."

Autry made 640 recordings, including more than 300 songs written or co-written by himself. His records sold more than 100 million copies and he has more than a dozen gold and platinum records, including the first record ever certified gold. From 1934 to 1953, Autry appeared in 93 films and 91 episodes of The Gene Autry Show television series. Gene Autry retired from show business in 1964 and subsequently invested widely in real estate and radio and television stations.

The Museum of the American West in was founded in Los Angeles in 1988 as the Gene Autry Western Heritage Museum and features much of Gene Autry's collection of Western art and memorabilia.

Gene Autry must be one of the most photographed celebrities of all time; there are literally hundreds of photographs of Autry taken over his long career.

Gene Autry, from the beginning of this career, appreciated and used Martin guitars. He began a correspondence with Martin during his early days in radio.

On March 9, 1929 Autry wrote to Martin with a request:

"If you have a Guitar Protector for you one hundred ten dollars Guitar please send me one at once C.O.D. My Guitar was stolen last week it has been scratched very bad. Will appreciate your rushing this to me as I use it in Vaudeville and on Radio and can't find one here or Tulsa.

It is the $110.00 Guitar and White Brand would like one White..."

There are many photographs of Autry playing a style 42 Martin guitar but the comment about the "$110 Guitar" identifies it as 0-42, as a 00-42 cost $5 extra at $115.

Martin replied on March 11:

"We are sending you under separate cover a piece of Ivory-Celluloid cut to fit your Martin Guitar. This may be fastened to the Guitar with celluloid cement or any good cement similar to DuPont's Household Cement. The charge for this piece is fifty cents, which we will thank you to remit in stamps.

Have you had good results from your Martin Guitar? We are glad to know that you are using one of our instruments and we hope you have found it satisfactory in every respect".

Autry acknowledged receipt of the pick guard on March 23:

"My shipment received in good condition and am inclosing fifty cents in stamps for same.

I have used several Guitar in Vaudeville, Radio and other entertaining and I prefer a Martin to any of them including the Gibson. And if at any time my instrument is broken or needs new varnishing I would like to return it to the factory for repairs."

March followed up on March 26:

"Many thanks for your remittance of fifty cents in stamps to pay for the guardplate we sent you.

We are much pleased to learn that you prefer Martin Guitars in comparison other makes and we want to assure you that we will be very glad to give you prompt service if your Guitar should be in need or refinishing or repairs."

Autry then contacted Martin on May 27, 1929 to order some custom work for his guitar:

"What would be the cost for having you lower the bridge on my Guitar so as to lower the strings to the fifth, sixth and higher frets.

Also would like to have my name put on it between the frets and pearl keys put on it, would also like to have pearl put around the neck where the strings are.

What would be your price for this work? I am using this Guitar for recording on Paramount records."

Martin's reply on May 27 contains some very interesting information:

"It should not be at all difficult to lower your Guitar bridge and our charge would be nominal. If you decide to send us the instrument we will overhaul the fingerboard while it is here and put it in perfect playing condition.

The expense of special pearl work is considerable and we do not advise it unless there is a probability of a return to the player in increased publicity in his professional work. It would cost about eight dollars to supply a set of patent heads with pearl keys, the metal parts being nickel plated; a gold plated head with pearl keys would cost ten dollars. The fingerboard inlaid with your name in pearl letters between the frets, will cost twenty dollars, complete, attached to the instrument and fretted. It is not practical to supply pearl around the neck but it is possible to border the edge of the head where the patent heads are fastened with a narrow line of pearl inside of an Ivory-Celluloid binding. For this our charge would be ten dollars.

You understand that all of this would be purely ornament and would not improve the tone of your Guitar at all. When it comes to matters affecting the tone of the instrument it is our policy to do everything possible at a minimum cost."

The $20 for the inlaid fingerboard plus $10 for the pearl border on the head stock mentioned above were invoiced on March 20, 1930, indicating that the work on this guitar was delayed for 9 months from the date of the original request. Martin invoiced Gene Autry $10 for "patent heads" on March 4, 1930 so it may have taken a little extra time to get the gold-plated machines with pearl buttons requested by Autry.

Martin invoiced Autry another $45 for "repairing" on June 19, 1930. Since the 1930 correspondence is entirely missing it is not known what repairs were carried on at that time, or even if they were done to the 0-42 guitar.

Gene Autry continued to use his 0-42 Guitar long after he had bought other Martin guitars. This guitar is on display at the Autry Museum of the American West in Los Angeles.

Gene Autry also owned a 1926 00-42 guitar with serial number 25144. It can be distinguished from the 0-42 already discussed as Autry's name on the fingerboard is in pearl block letters. Later, this guitar had a Martin logo in pearl letters added to the head stock.

This guitar was stamped on May 19, 1926. It was ordered by J. W. Jenkins' Sons Music Co. in Kansas City, Missouri on July 19, 1926 and was shipped to Jenkins on August 18, 1926, presumably immediately after the batch it came from was completed. The retail price at the time was $115.

Since Gene Autry's career didn't really get started until late in 1928, it seems unlikely that he was the original owner of this guitar. He may have bought it used after his career was well underway (since we know he owned his 0-42 by 1928 or 1929). It may also have been purchased as new old stock from Jenkins at some later date.

There is no information in the Martin archive related to the custom work on this guitar (the inlaid fingerboard and pearl edging of the head stock). The correspondence files in the Martin archive are entirely missing for 1930, 1931 and most of 1933. The Martin correspondence files are quite complete for 1932 and there is no mention of this guitar.

This 00-42 resides in the collection of The Country Music Hall of Fame.

Gene Autry's OM-45 Guitar

On January 18, 1932 Martin wrote to Gene Autry:

"The work on your Guitar will be finished in two or three days. We shall be glad to have your shipping instructions and your check for the amount of the bill enclosed."

Obviously, Martin had just completed some work on one of Autry's guitars. The return correspondence with Gene Autry is missing but a little detective work in the Martin archive provides some clues.

A letter from Louis Handel Co. to Martin dated January 6, 1932 provides the first clue:

"Per fgbd I would like some more instructions. Enclosed print shows what we made before but how do you make it in script you have to show us. Perhaps you want every letter in a Capital script in place of the (?) letter."

Martin replied the next day:

"Your pencil sketch along the edge of the print of the Gene Autry fingerboard suits us all right except that the frets on this fingerboard are spaced a little further apart so the letters will have to be moved to fit the spaces. Use the regular script letters with capital initials, just as you have

sketched."

Martin's little explanation clearly identifies that the guitar has a long scale and,since this is well before Autry ordered his famous D-45, it must refer to another long-scale guitar. The only other long scale guitars being made by Martin at the time were the Orchestra Model (OM) guitars. As will be confirmed below this guitar was a Martin OM-45!

Having received the OM-45 in the meantime Autry corresponded with Martin again in a letter dated January 31, 1932:

"The Guitar arrived all ok and is a wonderful instrument. I like it fine, now hear is one thing, it has cracked on the face of the guitar just blow the Guard plate and the crack is about one inch long and runs with the grain of the wood. Do you think I should return it now for repairs or do you think it will get larger from time to time. It don't affect the tone any but I just wondering if it will cause trouble later."

Martin responded on February 5:

"We are sorry to hear that your Guitar has a small crack just blow the pick guard. If it does not interfere with the tone we would not advise you to do anything about it right away because it may close up during warmer weather when there is more moisture in the atmosphere and if it returns next winter it will not be too late to repair it. Should it cause trouble of any kind do not hesitate to send the Guitar in for immediate attention. There will be no charge for the work."

Autry opted to return the guitar for repair because Martin received a letter from Rudolph Wurlitzer Co. Chicago dated February 20, 1932. Wurlitzer wanted to return several guitars for repairs and one of these was Gene Autry's OM-45 guitar.

"Gene Autry, who broadcasts over WLS "Prairie Farmer" Station, brought in his new Martin OM-45 Guitar on which the varnishing is checking and the wood cracking near the pick guard. Will you kindly repair and ship back as soon as possible."

As was Martin's habit, a little notation was added to

the margin of the letter, **"2-24-32, OM-45 43709 Varnish checking, Bridge & top cracked Mar 2"**, so not only were the repairs documented but the model and serial number of the guitar were also recorded.

Martin replied to Wurlitzer on February 25:

"Mr. Autry's Guitar, Style OM-45 No. 43709, will be repaired and the top refinished without charge."

This 1930 OM-45 was originally sold to Gene as a stock guitar in late December 1931. It was then upgraded with the addition Gene Autry's name on the fingerboard in January 1932. Subsequently, it was repaired and refinished in February 1932 due to a crack near the pick guard. The guitar originally had a "small OM" pickguard but this was replaced by a larger pickguard when the guitar was refinished in February 1932, the larger pick guard coming into general use in March 1931.

So far only one photograph of Gene Autry with the OM-45 guitar in known. Since it has the large type pickguard and the script pearl fingerboard inlay this photograph must have been taken after February 1932.

The OM-45 would originally have had banjo tuners on the peg head but the photograph of Gene with the OM-45 shows the guitar has been converted to side tuners. The banjo pegs were notoriously difficult to keep tuned and were often replaced by Martin with side tuners. Although the change to side tuners was not documented, Gene Autry must have had the banjo pegs replaced. possibly at the same time it was refinished.

The First D-45

As is well known, the first D-45 was made for Gene Autry. The order was placed by Chicago Musical Instrument Co. on March 23, 1933. CMI sent a sketch (Figure 361) to Martin illustrating the features wanted by Gene Autry.

Although the sketch specifies a "C. F. Martin" pearl headstock veneer, a style 45 "torch" inlay was installed instead, probably because the "C. F. Martin" head stock veneer wouldn't fit on a slotted peg head. The fingerboard inlay for the D-45 was received from Lou-

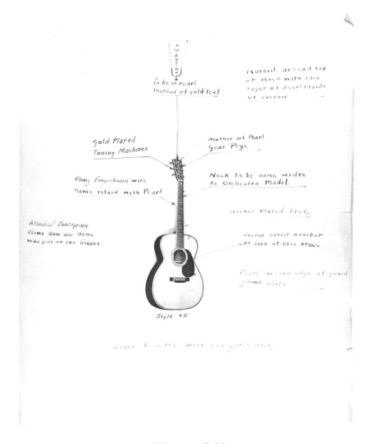

Figure 361
Sketch from CMI with
Specifications for First D-45 Guitar

is Handle Co. on March 31, 1933, at an invoiced price of $10.18.

The first D-45 guitar (serial number 53177) was stamped on March 27, 1933, cleared final inspection on April 15, being finished in less than three weeks! It was probably shipped to CMI on the same day.

Figure 362 illustrates the two sides of the shop order slip for the first D-45 guitar and details its special features.

Other Martin Guitars Played by Gene Autry

Gene Autry continued to show a preference for Martin guitar throughout his long career. It is known he owned and played Gibson and Prairie State guitars, but in photographs he is usually seen with Martin instruments.

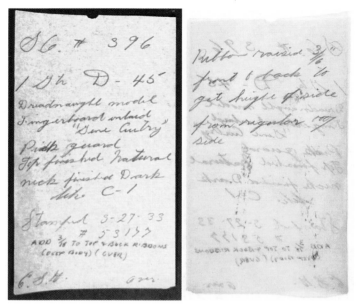

Figure 362
Martin Shop Order Slip for Gene Autry's D-45 Guitar

Bill Boyd, The Cowboy Rambler (1910-1977)

Bill Boyd (born William Lemuel Boyd) was an American Western-style singer and guitarist. He was born on September 29, 1910 and raised on a farm near Ladonia, Texas. With his brother Jim, Bill Boyd appeared on radio station KFPM in Greenville, Texas as early as 1926. During the Depression the family moved to Dallas, where Bill took odd jobs while pursuing his music career. He became active in the local music scene and played on Jimmie Rodgers' recording sessions in Dallas during February 1932. Later in 1932, Boyd formed his own pioneering western swing band named "The Cowboy Ramblers" and was soon found regular work on radio station WRR in Dallas.

In August 1934, Bill Boyd and The Cowboys Ramblers were signed to Victor's budget Bluebird label. Between 1934 and 1951, the band made more than 225 recordings for Bluebird records and also had a popular radio show called "The Bill Boyd Ranch House". Bill Boyd and The Cowboy Ramblers, being major stars on the radio, were offered film work in Hollywood and appeared in six Western movies during the early 1940's.

During World War II, Boyd joined "The Western Minute Men" and promoted the sale of war bonds. In the 1950's, Bill Boyd terminated his radio show and became a DJ for WRR. After suffering a stroke in 1973, Bill Boyd retired from the music business and died in Dallas on December 7, 1977.

Many photos of Bill Boyd show him playing a variety of Martin guitars. In his early photos he is playing what appears to be a Martin 2-17 guitar. Another early photograph shows Boyd playing a Martin 12-fret 00-18 guitar (Figure 363).

In 2014, Heritage Auctions sold a 1929 Martin 00-42 Guitar (serial number 39110) that came from Boyd's estate. This guitar appears on a number of Bill Boyd's old photographs and was later used on the real photo post cards that Boyd sent to appreciative fans (Figure 364).

However, the guitar for which he is best known is the unique 00-42S specially ordered from Martin in 1933.

On December 14, 1933 Martin received an order from the Chicago Musical Instrument Co. for "Special, Orchestra Model" 00-42. Style 00-42 Martin guitars had always been made with 12-fret and the custom order placed by Bill Boyd became the only exception. The guitar was stamped on December 21, 1933, receiving serial number 55038. It was shipped to Chicago Mu-

Figure 363
Bill Boyd Playing a Martin 00-18 Guitar

Figure 364
Photograph of Bill Boyd with His 1929 Martin 00-42
Guitar and His Horse "Texas" on a 1939 Fan Postcard

Figure 365
Signed 8" X 10" Photograph of Bill Boyd
with His 1933 Martin 00-42S Guitar

sical Instrument Co. on January 12, 1934. Not only is Bill Boyd's 00-42S guitar unique because of its 14-fret neck but the fingerboard is also inlaid with his name in script pearl letters (Figure 365).

A small number of 00-21 and 00-28 guitars with the "Orchestra Model" 14 fret-necks were made in the 1930's, but only one 00-42S. This is a little hard to understand as the examples of Martin's rosewood 00-sized guitars with 14-fret necks are well appreciated by modern collectors.

Boyd wrote to Martin on June 23, 1934 concerning to his 00-42 guitar:

"Wish to state that I received the Martin guitar style 00-42 sent you for repairs on the fret board.

Seems to be very nice and plays well. As I have told you before, I am a radio entertainer and teacher here in the city of Dallas, and have used and sold nothing but Martin instruments for four years. I think they can never be beat for tone and quality.

Sure hope the day will come when I make a visit to your wonderful factory. I would enjoy seeing those Martin instruments built from the ground up.

Many many thanks for your kindness and the pick guard you put on the guitar."

Martin replied on June 29:

"Many thanks for your nice letter with the good news that you are pleased with the work we did in repairing your Style 00-42 Guitar. It helps a lot to get a word of appreciation and we are passing it on to the foreman who handled the job.

It certainly was kind of you to take the trouble to write us. We hope, too, that the time will soon come when you can visit our factory and let us show you just how Martin Instruments are made. It is a most interesting business and we know you would enjoy spending a day here with us."

May Belle Carter

Most photos of Mae Belle Carter, of the famous Carter Family, show her playing a Gibson L-5 guitar.

However, on October, 22, 1929 she wrote to Martin with the following:

"At present I am in Need of a good Hiwiian (sic) Steel Guitarrh (sic). I play the Guitarrh in the Carter Family and use both The Gibson and The Martin and personally I like Martin best. We record for Victor.

Do you make or handle the Hiwiian Steel Guitarrh?

If so please advise as I am now on the market and will need it to do a recording for Victor in Atlanta Ga the latter part of November.

We (Carter Family) give music concerts in connection with our recording and have numerous enquiries by letter and in person of what kind of Guitarrh I use so if you can fit me up with a real good "box" I will want my name engraved on the neck also the name of the Guitarrh engraved on it conspicuously.

The Martin (straight) I am using now was purchased for your firm through our recorder (Mr. R. S. Peer) while were recording in Camden NJ last February.

If in position to fit me up advise as to quality of tone, price of the Guitarrh and the additional expense of the engraving."

Martin responded on October 24 and tried to interest Mae Belle in a 00-40H, a number of which Martin had in stock. Martin quoted $20 for inlaying her name in the fingerboard and also quoted a head stock inlay but with an interesting proviso:

"We could inlay your name or initials or anything else you want in the Rosewood head veneer at a cost of ten dollars. We would rather not put our name on the head stock in pearl letters because it is well known that Martin Guitars are branded in the body and on the back of the head so we do not

care to have our name in any other place."

Unfortunately, there is no further mention of this custom 00-40H guitar in the Martin records.

Madam De Goni (1815 -1892)

For C. F. Martin Sr., Madam De Goni was one of the most important celebrities to play Martin guitars in the early years of the company. Her influence on Martin was profound and lasting. Martin even created a De Goni model in the 1840's that survived, as the 1-26 model, until at least 1895. C. A. Zoebisch & Son, Martin's master distributor until the mid-1890's, even used Madam De Goni's name in advertisements until 1893, the year after her death.

Madam De Goni's maiden name was Maria Dolores Esturias y Navarres. She first appeared professionally as Madam De Gone in France in 1837. At different times in her career Madam De Goni's name was spelled De Gone or De Gony.

By 1840, Madam De Goni was giving concerts in the United Kingdom, where she was well received. Late in 1840[1] she and her husband emigrated to the United States seeking opportunities in a country where all things Spanish were currently the rage.

The New York Herald wasted no time in announcing her arrival in the United States in an article published on November 7, 1840[2]:

"Musical - the Spanish guitar

'The light guitar - the light guitar'

A distinguished female, professor of the Spanish guitar, has just arrived from Europe. Her name is Dona Dolores de Goni, a Spanish lady of exquisite beauty, and still more exquisite accomplishments in Spanish music. During the last spring and summer she gave many exhibitions before the royalty and nobility of England, that brought forth great applause. She purposes, we understand, to give a concert here next week."

The article went on to document some of her successes in Europe, copy certainly provided by Madam De Goni herself. The press clippings are all presumably from 1840:

"The following extracts from London papers:

CONCERT ROOMS, HANOVER SQUARE - Madame Nevares De Goni's evening Concert took place on Thursday evening at these rooms, and was brought forward under the patronage of the Marchioness of Hastings and the Baroness Grey de Ruthyn. The selection of music was most judicious and afforded a very high treat to the lovers of harmony and song. A fantasia on the Spanish Guitar by Madame De Goni, exhibited the power of the artist on this instrument, but it was the beautiful air 'Jota Aragonesa', that she displayed her own power of execution, and the capability of the instrument in the hands of a skilful performer. Her execution was exquisite, transfusing into the performance the soul and poetry of harmony, expressing at one moment the zephyr tones of the aeolian harp, and in the next, the deep notes of the most refined expression of musical harmony. Any one who has not heard the performance of Madame De Goni can form no conception of the effect which can be produced upon this instrument, which is likely to become fashionable, through the executions of this highly talented lady. - London Morning Advertiser.

DONA DOLORES DE GONI - On Friday night the celebrated Dona Doloris de Goni, the most exquisite guitarist in Europe, had the honor of performing before the Queen Dowager. - Court Journal

MADAME NEVARES DE GONI'S CONCERT - Under the immediate patronage of the Marchioness of Hastings and Baroness Grey de Ruthyn, the celebrated Spanish guitarist, Madame de Goni, gave a concert yesterday evening at the theatre of the Polytechnic Institution in Regent street. A numerous and most fashionable company attested, by their presence, the favor which the performances of the beneficiaire are regarded in high life. Madame de Goni is a performer of the highest order upon that most difficult instrument, the guitar, which in her hands, becomes the medium of transferring to the senses of her pleased auditors, a correct notion of the romantic and most charming music with which the loves and lovers of Spain are

traditionally connected. We recognized with much pleasure that no attempt was made at a display of outrageous execution, which is altogether opposed to the nature and construction of the instrument. The guitar is only pleasing when it becomes the interpreter of sentiment, or the support of the voice, for which latter its illimitable powers of modulation peculiarly adapt it. Madame de Goni appears to be fully aware of this, for her performances on the instrument were marked throughout by her confining herself to its legitimate application; but this application was characterized by a tone of deep pathos, such as, we believe, a woman can only feel and express. This lady played three airs of her own composition, which were very beautifully written as well as executed; she also accompanied Signor Echarte in a characteristic Spanish song by Gomez, in a way to induce us to listen more to the instrument than the voice. - London Morning Post."

Although the advertisement suggested Madam De Goni would give a concert by mid-November, her first recorded stage performance took place on December 23, 1840 at the annual benefit for the St. George's Society at the National Theatre in New York. On December 29 Madam De Goni performed with her husband at the City Hotel.

Very soon after landing Madam De Goni began to frequent music stores in New York as captured in the following book excerpt[3]:

"The fashionable music stores and lounges for musical people, at the date I am writing, were Atwill's Music Saloon, at the sign of the Golden Lyre, 201 Broadway; Millett's, Broadway (Mr. Millet still remaining in the same store); Firth and Hall, Franklin square; and Davis and Horn, of Broadway.

The first establishment, being next door to my place of business, I quickly became acquainted with its proprietor, Mr. Joseph F. Atwill, (now and for a long time past a resident of California), and many a delightful hour was passed by me there, and I was thus brought into immediate connexion, if not intimacy, with numbers of musical people.

Among the celebrities that in the year 1840 flashed

for a while upon the musical horizon, and who were daily to be seen at Joe Atwill's, were…Madame Dolores de Goni (guitarist)".

From 1841 to 1842, Madam De Goni gave concerts in New York and Philadelphia. By early 1842, De Goni had begun to perform with George Knoop[4], a noted cellist from Germany. From this point in time no more is heard of Senor De Goni.

Madam De Goni and George Knoop toured together from 1842 to 1844 and during their travels gave concerts in New York, Philadelphia, Boston, Baltimore, Cincinnati and even once in Hamilton, Ontario (known as Upper Canada at the time). Madam De Goni also occasionally appeared in concerts with John B. Coupa during the period when Martin & Coupa had the Martin sales agency for New York city. It can be safely assumed that Martin became aware of Madam De Goni through John Coupa and was probably introduced to her in 1841 or 1842 on one of his visits to New York.

De Goni and Knoop settled in Cincinnati in 1844 where they gave concerts and established themselves as teachers. They were married in April 1845. Madam De Goni had several children with Knoop but little can be discovered of them[5]. Knoop continued to give concerts until 1847 and toured this other musicians in 1847 and 1848. Madam De Goni continued to give occasional concerts until 1848. In 1848 and 1849, Knoop appears to have been on the road constantly, performing along the Eastern seaboard, either alone or with other musicians. Knoop's marriage to De Goni appears to have been in trouble during this time as Coupa wrote to C. F. Martin on October 15, 1849 with shocking news:

"Mrs. Degoni has gone to Mexico, she has left her children behind, and a baby 4 months old."

George Knoop died on December 25, 1849 in Philadelphia at the age of 46.

De Goni married the Spanish Consul in New Orleans about 1850 and seems to have spent the rest of her life in that city. She continued to publish guitar music until at least 1866, but always as "Mrs. Knoop".

"Madam De Goni" died in Orleans parish in New Orleans in Louisiana on Nov, 7, 1892. The parish death registry recorded her name as Maria Ysturias Navarres Labord (Volume 102, page 1156).

Two portraits of Madam De Goni are known. One is in a private collection and was painted by Alenson G. Powers. Although supposedly painted in New Orleans in 1840, Powers began painting in northern Ohio around 1842 and was painting portraits in Cincinnati during the summer of 1844, so this painting was probably executed during 1844 or slightly later as Madam De Goni and George Knoop lived in Cincinnati from 1844 to 1848. In this painting Madam De Goni is playing a guitar of European design.

The second portrait of Madam De Goni was painted by James Hamilton Shegogue (1806-1872). It was displayed at the 1844 Exhibit of the National Academy of Design in New York but its current whereabouts are unknown.

Guitars Played by Madam De Goni

Madam De Goni would undoubtedly have brought a European guitar, possibly of Spanish design, with her when she emigrated to the United States. The guitar illustrated in the first of two portraits if De Goni mentioned above confirms this.

Madam De Goni gave a concert in Bethlehem, Pennsylvania in the summer of 1842 and probably followed up with another concert in 1843, as will be shown below. In a book published in 1855 by James Ballard[6] is a comment on the type of guitar played by Madam De Goni:

"In 1843 Madame De Goni brought to New York a large pattern Spanish guitar, from which a number have been made, and distributed over the United States, by Martin, of Pennsylvania, and Schmidt and Maul, of New York."

A "Professor Ballard", possibly the same James Ballard mentioned above, appears in Martin's early ledger books as having purchased "a Spanish guitar" on August 16, 1838 for $35.00. The price suggests this was a guitar made by C. F. Martin.

Several years ago a remarkable silhouette portrait of Madam De Goni with a guitar (Figure 366) was sold at auction in the UK. It has a hand written description at the bottom of the portrait that reads "**Madame Delores De Goñi Philadelphia 7th F(eb)ry 1843**" and is also signed and dated "**Delores De Goñi 7 de Enero de 1843**" at the top.

A 1913 biography of C. F. Martin Sr. by one of his granddaughters[7] charmingly described an event that probably occurred in the summer of 1843. It also provides a clue to the type of guitar Madam De Goni was playing at that time and a description of the guitar that C. F. Martin made and presented to her while she was a guest at his home in Cherry Hill:

"**He took pleasure in having musicians and poor teachers boarded free at his house, which was roomy and comfortable, during their summer vacations. In the day-time, they often strolled into the orchards, read and amused themselves and in the evenings they gave little family concerts to grandfather's infinite delight.**

Madame De Goni, probably the finest professional guitar-soloist of her time, in the South, was also there. It was she, I think, who clung to her Spanish guitar and would have no other. One evening, when all were gathered together, grandfather brought her a guitar that he had made in the exact shape of her Spanish guitar but with his thin sounding-board and other Martin characteristics.

Quite casually, he asked her to try it. Madame De Goni took the instrument but displayed little interest. She struck a few chords, played a piece or two, then got up, took her Spanish guitar and set it in a corner. "I'm through with that", she said, 'I don't care for it anymore. This is the guitar I want.'

That must have been a great triumph for grandfather."

The guitar C. F. Martin made for Madam De Goni in 1843 has survived and is on display in the Martin Guitar Museum (Figure 367). The guitar is remarkable for several reasons.

1) This guitar has a type 7 Martin & Schatz label with the endorsement "**Made for Madam De Gone (sic)**". The late usage of the Martin & Schatz label is a bit of a mystery. The second Martin & Schatz partner-

Image Courtesy of Ellison Fine Art (Used with Permission)

Figure 366
1843 Silhouette Portrait of Madam De Goni

ship had ended in early 1840 so maybe it was the only label Martin had on hand. Based on comparison with the writing in letters in the Martin archive, the endorsement on the label was penned by John Coupa himself. The fact that Coupa signed the label should not be a surprise because of his close association with both De Goñi and C. F. Martin. Madam De Goni used several spellings of her name and "de Gone" appeared in newspaper advertisements during 1842 and 1843.

2) The guitar has the early type of X-bracing and is also the earliest dateable guitar with X-bracing. The guitar proves that Martin was experimenting with this type of bracing by at least 1843.

The Martin archive has a letter from John Coupa, dated November 29, 1849, containing the following excerpt:

"**I have a guitar to be repaired, it is broke in the**

back, can you tell me how I can send it, or if you can do it when you come in the city. It is a fine guitar, one you made for Mrs. Degoni. I had it here more than one month."

This description fits well with the current condition of the De Goni guitar, which has two repaired cracks in the back. The back was removed at some point although the repair appears to be very old. The back purfling and binding match that of the top and also appear to be of the same age. This would appear to be a very rare example of a repair that can be attributed to C. F. Martin Sr. himself.

The Martin & Schatz "De Goni" guitar is a remarkable historic instrument and firmly establishes that C. F. Martin had developed an early form of X-bracing by July 1843.

The Morning Oregonian had an article entitles "The Rise of the Guitar" in its Saturday, November 15, 1902 edition with an interesting comment on Madam De Goni:

"It is often asked 'Why is the Martin Guitar better than others?' This can be answered in one word only, by saying that it partook from the first of the conscientious nature of its founder. Quiet, retiring Mr. Martin lived for his art, and was satisfied with nothing unless it was as nearly perfect as he could make it. In keeping with his character, he moved to a quiet settlement in Pennsylvania in1839 and there worked -until his death In 1873, when he left a well-established business to his descendants. Here Madame de Goni and other famous musicians visited him, with the result that, his guitars became known as artists' models."

Figure 367
1843 Martin & Coupa Guitar
"Made for Madam De Gone"

Figure 368
Daguerreotype of Madam De Goni

Figure 369
Steel Engraving Entitled "The Guitar" from May 1851 Edition of The Ladies' Repository

Salustiano De La Cova (1816 to 1862?)

In the 1850's Martin sold a number of guitars to a certain Salustiano De La Cova of Panama (see Table 111). De La Cova operated his own commission merchant company in Panama, which was involved in transporting mail and freight between New York and California, and for many years was also the Panama agent for the Adams' Express Co. De La Cova also had business interests in Peru, Havana, New York, Boston and Spain and traveled extensively between these locations.

The 1852 guitar ordered by De La Cova was meant for Lieutenant George M. Totten USN. In 1852 Totten was on a medical furlough from the Navy and was captain of the Pacific Mail Steamship Co. steamer "Tennessee" operating between Panama and San Francisco[10,11,12]. (Lieutenant Totten died on August 1, 1857 at Mendham, New Jersey[13].)

During one of his visits to New York De La Cova wrote the following to C. F. Martin Jr. on December 15, 1852:

"Please send me p. 1st opportunity, as I have none, a bundle of 1st tripe strings of the very best Italian medium thickness as this weather is too damp & hot & spoils them very soon. Take care they are not too thick as I cannot use them here.

Remember me particularly to your father & family & Mrs. Coupa if you see her, saying that I may have the pleasure of seeing them all next May.

Please call on Messrs. Adams & Co. for the amount of the strings & if you have something good of that description, send two packs of 30 strings each."

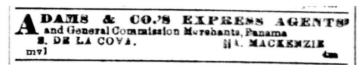

Figure 370
De La Cova Advertisement in the Daily Alta California Dated June 14, 1853[9]

DATE SHIPPED	STYLE	PURFLING	SOUNDHOLE	EDGE	HEAD	EXTRA	CASE	PRICE
Mar. 22, 1852	(1-25)	SPANISH	SPANISH	WHITE HOLLY	EBONY PEGS		FINE	$32.00
May 23, 1853	(1-35)	DE GONI	PEARL	IVORY	IVORY PEGS	NECK SCREW	VERY FINE	$35.00
Feb. 2, 1855	(2-34)	FINE	PEARL	IVORY	IVORY PEGS	IVORY BRIDGE	FINE CEDAR	$70.00
Apr. 6, 1855	2-17	PLAIN	PLAIN	BLACK	EBONY PEGS		LEATHER	$34.00
Aug. 6, 1855	OCTAV	SINGLE LINE	PLAIN	BLACK	IVORY PEGS		MAHOGANY	$15.00

The styles are shown in brackets because they were interpolated from the sizes and prices shown in the sales book.
The (1-25) model was very similar to a 1-26 but had white holly binding instead of ivory.
The (1-35) is probably a 1-26 that was upgraded with an adjustable neck.

Table 111
Martin Guitars Purchased by S. De La Cova from 1852 to 1855

This letter is interesting as it not only comments on quality problems of gut strings of the period but also suggests, as will be confirmed in his later letters, that De La Cova was more than just an acquaintance to C. F. Martin Sr. and John B. Coupa. It is known De La Cova visited New York in 1835[14] and 1841[15] and, with his obvious interest in guitars, would certainly have been known to C. F. Martin, as well as John Coupa. There is even a record that he became a naturalized U. S. citizen in 1843[16] although his main residence appears to have been in Havana, Cuba.

On March 16, 1853 De La Cova wrote to C. F Martin Sr. from Panama:

"I send you today pr Adams & Co. Express one of my two guitars to your address say: "C. F. Martin, music store, Fulton Street, N. York". I shall be there in April next & see if you have invented something better, when I shall exchange with you, You will perceive the varnish in the bottom of the sound board has half gone to the devil I think. You better make it right at once giving it a new varnish front & back. The old one of Pages (the one I constantly use, that one being too hard in the fingering) I shall keep with me, it also wants many repairs which I hope you'll make very soon for I shall not be able to stay with you but 3 to 4 days, the(n) on my return from Europe I may stay longer.

I hope my guitars may arrive safe. Give my best love to your lady & children.

Would you believe "a friend" to whom I sold the little guitar Coupa sent me to Lima, has not yet paid $25 balance of sale; he has only owed me the money since my arrival here in July 1849!!!!! I sold it to him for $70 this currency which is 18% less in American Gold. What a place this for fine guitars & purchasers!!!!!"

The mention of the "music store on Fulton Street" might suggest that De La Cova had not been in touch with Martin for some time but more likely it just let Martin know he could find the two guitars at the Adams Co. Express Office under that address. On May 23, 1853 Martin sold a guitar to De La Cova in New York so he must have thought Martin had "invented something better". The guitar had a size 1 body and appointments like a style 26 instrument. However, it commanded a price of $35 because it was supplied with a neck screw.

On May 28, 1853 De La Cova was in New York and sent C. F. Martin Sr. the following letter:

"I send you my old & lovely pet guitar. I believe it needs a new box - the lock of this one id bad. I send you the key with it. How do you like those old pegs of Pages? I send them in because they do not fit now. I hope I'll see you in August next when I come. I am off at 12 a. m. today.

God bless you, may you be happy & prosperous. Same all your family.

I shall take good care with the guitar you had the kindness to send me as loan with your son & try to get you $35 if not $40 for it."

Evidently, Martin loaned De La Cova the 1-26 guitar with the neck screw for his trip to Europe.

De a Cova was again in New York when he wrote to C. F. Martin Sr. on November 29, 1853:

"I arr^d today & hasten to inform you that I sh'd be most happy to see you down with my two guitars & receive yours which has been so much admired in Europe by every one who has seen it & heard it, even in Spain. I want you to take a dinner with me. I am staying at the same old place where your son met me, Judson's Hotel 61 Broadway. I don't know whether I will stay here 3 or 4 days before I go to Boston on some business visit.

We'll have a long, very long talk about old folks, old things."

After his return from his business trip to Europe, De La Cova desired to meet up with C. F. Martin Sr. to return the borrowed 1-26 guitar and also to pick up the two guitars he had sent to Martin for repairs (an old Martin guitar and an old Pages guitar).

De La Cova must have been quite concerned he might not be able to meet with C. F. Martin because he wrote again on Dec. 1, 1853:

"I'm waitg for you. I hope you recd my letter of the 28th ulto. I am in Judson's Hotel 61 Broadway. I have to go to Boston for 2 days, but shall not start in three days yet. When can I expect to see you? I want you to take a dinner with me without fail. I have your guitar ready for you. Have you my two ready? I want to send the one with the round plate of Martin & Co. well packed to Panama & the old Pages I will take with me to Havana (after 17 years!!!!)

Whenever you come if I am not in my hotel, enquire next door no. 59 Adams & Co. Express & they will tell you my whereabouts; come soon, I want to see you very bad after 10 years!! No wonder I have not had time yet to see the Cryistal (sic)

Palace & that beauty (I suppose) of your own manufactory."

An interesting comment in the letter is the reference to the fancy guitar that Martin made for the 1853 Crystal Palace Exhibition in New York.

De La Cova wrote to C. F. Martin Sr. from Havana on January 29, 1854 requesting some very interesting strings made by Martin:

"Here I am since the 18th Inst. & shall leave in a week.

I have seen Crucet my old friend & he desires to some of your strings which I have promised him & now beg of you vizt:

1 doz 6s good silk & gold wire (6th strings)
1½ doz 5s d0......do......do   (5th strings)
2½ doz 4s do......do......do   (4th strings)

Please send them to H. Dixon of Messrs Adams & Co. New York, he will pay you them when you send the bill.

My guitar has a crack 5 inches in length. I believe in R. Road from Baltimore to Charleston. Is this not too bad!!!"

From the early ledger books it is known Martin bought "golddraht" (gold wire) for making wound strings. The "gold wire" reference likely means gold plated steel wire. The purchasing records are missing for most of the period between 1840 and 1890 but it appears Martin continued to make strings of "gold wire" until at least the middle 1850's.

The last guitar Martin sold to De La Cova was an "octav" guitar that he purchased on August 6, 1855. It is not known what is meant by "octav" as Martin left no description in the ledgers.

De La Cova wrote to C. F. Martin Sr. from Panama on October 2, 1855 with some unusual requests for altering the "octav" guitar he purchased in August 1855:

"I made an awful mistake with that little guitar I asked you for in June & now return thr(u)' my friends Freeman & Co. & wish you to correct

same.

Instead of putting the 12th fret in the edge of the guitar circles as now is, the 9th fret should be there and the 12th fret near the mouth of the guitar & by these means, you could afford to make the frets much wider (than) they now are, there are no human fingers thin enough to be placed thereon. Another improvement is to place the bridge near an inch lower down, than where now is as I don't think it would give a bad look to the guitar & this would afford us more room to make the frets a little wider & easier to the left hand besides making the handle a little wider, putting the strings little more separate or apart from each other. If the whole body of the guitar or the sounding box was a little higher than it is now, it would sound much better. If you would after reflecting in these improvements, find them correct & do them for me I should be under many thanks to you for if I must speak (to) you candidly, as the guitar now stands, it is perfectly useless to me as playing on it is utterly out of the question. You will notice the varnish has been a little scratched with the piece of horn which is sometimes required to play with. Could you revarnish it? Do, if you please."

On September 3, 1857 De La Cova booked passage on the SS Central America[15] bound from Panama to Havana. The SS Central America was a 280-foot side-wheel steamer that operated between Central America and New York. After De La Cova disembarked in Havana, the ship continued on to New York but was caught in a hurricane off the Carolina coast and sank on September 12, 1857. The SS Central America went down carrying 10 short tons of gold from the California gold fields. It is fortunate that De La Cova did not have pressing business in New York at that time because 425 of the 578 passengers and crew on board were lost in the sinking.

On November 5, 1857 De La Cova wrote to C. F. Martin Sr. from Havana:

"I wrote you last month begging you to send me my guitar to Freeman & Co. N. Y. as I suppose you must have finished it ever since the month of Augt & I cannot conceive why has it has been delayed so long it keeps me in the greatest anxiety for you know I w'd not take any money for that Instru-

ment as neither for yours tho' I would replace it, but not so with that of Pagés.

I hope ere this reached you that you have sent it to Freeman & Co. Express with the bill.

I'm doing nothing yet & shall not commence to work before next January most likely. Times are very bad here with the panic here & in the U.S. which has caused a few failures, but I hope all will pass over soon."

In this letter De La Cova is bemoaning the state of the market resulting from the Panic of 1857. It is ironic that the gold lost in the sinking of the SS Central America was one of the contributing factors to the Panic of 1857.

The last letter to C. F. Martin from De La Cova was written in Panama on July 20, 1858:

"I hope this may reach you in time to send me ½ dozen more of the 3ᵈ pure silver wire & silk strings that is to say, instead of one dozen ordered, send on 1½ dozen.

I hope you've tried the experiment & found it super-magnificent. I am anxious to receive these strings with the others ordered in my last to you, to see how does that splendid Spanish silk turn out. I think I shall be off for Peru again in about a month from this & hope to get those strings from you before I go.

Gallegos repaired your guitar of mine very well."

The New York Times correspondent in Panama reported on February 25, 1862 that "... Mr. S. DE LA COVA, of Havana, for many years agent of Adams' Express Company in Panama, lately died at Chorrillos, in Peru..."

It may be that De La Cova did die in Peru in 1862 but the ship's manifest for the steam ship "Eagle" recorded that a "S. De La Cova" landed in New York on June 24, 1864 after a voyage from Havana. His age was noted as 46 and his occupation as "merchant" so this could well be Salustiano De La Cova.

Taken altogether, De La Cova appears to have been a family friend of both C. F. Martin and John B. Coupa. He certainly had a more interesting business relationship with C. F. Martin than is usual for other guitar players and dealers. De La Cova had the resources to indulge his interest in guitars and C. F. Martin and John Coupa may have valued his connections with international business.

Manuel Ygnacio Ferrer (ca. 1832-1904)

From the middle of the 19th century until the early years of the 20th century, Manuel Y. Ferrer was a prolific composer and arranger for the guitar and mandolin, as well as a virtuoso guitarist and respected teacher . Although little known today, except in classical guitar circles, Ferrer must rank as one of the most influential American guitarists.

Manuel Ygnacio Ferrer was born around 1832 in San Antonio in Baja California (Mexico) of Spanish parents. Ferrer displayed musical talent from the young age of four years and began serious study of the guitar only a little later[17]. When he was about eighteen years old he traveled to Santa Barbara in California. In the Santa Barbara mission Ferrer became acquainted a priest who provided him further instruction on the guitar. In 1850 Ferrer moved to San Francisco where he continued to study the guitar and began to gradually build a musical reputation. His public debut at a guitar concert took place on September 18, 1854 at the Metropolitan Theatre in San Francisco.

Ferrer continued to perform and teach in San Francisco for a period of fifty years. His wife, Jesusita de Vivar, and several of his children were also talented musicians. Ferrer and his family toured in the eastern United States in 1891 and even performed in the White House.

In the early 1880's Ferrer was also one of the earliest teachers and composers of mandolin music in the United State. In a 1905 article in the Music Trade Review[18] the following comments were made concerning Ferrer:

"Manuel Y. Ferrer, the late eminent guitarist and composer, and Luis Romero, the late gifted guitar soloist, and the writer (Samuel Adelstein), were the three original mandolinists on the Pacific Coast. At that time (20 years ago) there was absolutely no music published for mandolin in this country, no manufacturers of instruments, and in comparison to the population, few or hardly any teachers east of the Rocky Mountains, excepting a few Italians in New York, amateurs in the Latin quarter, who played the mandolin for pastime among themselves."

Figure 371
Photograph of Manuel Ygnacio Ferrer

For several years Ferrer conducted a mandolin band, El Mandolinita, which performed only Ferrer's compositions and arrangements.

Ferrer published many compositions and arrangements for the guitar[19]. He continued to teach right up to his death in San Francisco on June 1, 1904.

Among Ferrer's students in the latter part of his life was Ethel Lucretia Olcott (later Vahdah Olcott-Bickford), who organized the American Guitar Society in 1923, wrote a description of Ferrer[17]:

"In appearance Ferrer was short of stature and dark, with small piercing black eyes, and when I knew him, his jet black hair was tinged with grey. He was kind and gentle to a degree and a man of very few words. In his teaching, however, he was very methodical and strict, although not necessarily harsh, invariably playing with the pupil, and though three or four years previous to his death

he broke his arm, so that his hand was apparently stiff, he still possessed a wonderful execution. He did not retain the astonishing brilliance and dazzling technique of his youth, as he was a man past his seventieth year then; but to me there is a quality more beautiful and effective than dazzling brilliance - the soulful quality - and Ferrer possessed this in a high degree with a sufficient amount of the former. When Ferrer touched the strings of the guitar the sounds entered the heart, and his chords made music which lifter the soul to a higher plane. One of his favorite solos was his arrangement of a selection from Puccini's La Boheme, which remains in manuscript. His last original composition entitled: Arbor villa, mazurka, was written two years before his death, and is also published, and I am proud to possess a copy written by his own hand. He taught the guitar up to the time of his death, which occurred very suddenly on June 1, 1904. He had gone from his home in Oakland to San Francisco to teach, and gave several lessons, when he suddenly taken ill, and went to the home of his daughter. Later he was removed to the hospital, where he died the same day, his third wife surviving him for several years. Though he lived to a ripe old age, his death was a great loss: but I love to think of him now playing with angelic choirs in the Holy City."

Ferrer is mentioned several times in the Martin archive. One April 3, 1889 C. A. Zoebisch noted the following:

"Mr. Ferrer is in California and a Mexican is of Spanish descent, I helped already twice to present him two fine Concert Guitars."

Zoebisch wrote again to Martin concerning Ferrer on August 17, 1892:

"Mr. Ferrer complains over the thin D String we sent his daughter (note: probably Adele Ferrer) some time ago, says every D string broke as soon as stretched on the guitar. Please broken 6 successive A Strings which makes me think the silk is of poor quality.

Please see that those I ordered are made of good strong silk."

Ferrer and at least one of his daughters owned and

used Martin guitars. Ferrer was prominent in the advertisements for Martin guitar placed by C. A. Zoebisch in the Music Trade Review between 1892 and 1898. In a post card to Martin on January 24, 1893 C. A. Zoebisch wrote "**Please send quick 2 doz. D, 1 doz. A & 1 doz. E, thin, same as made before for Miss Ferrer. She doesn't use the 0 (size) A stgs, although she plays a No. 1**". Miss Ferrer was most likely Adele, one of Ferrer's musically talented children. No direct correspondence between Ferrer and Martin is in the archive so string orders were probably handled directly by Zoebisch.

Tex Fletcher (1910-1987)

Tex Fletcher was a singing cowboy, and, as his career progressed, he was also a recording artist, a Broadway and movie actor, a night club performer, a radio and television entertainer and a restaurant owner.

In Martin guitar lore he is known as the owner of a left-handed 1935 D-42S guitar, the only style 42 Dreadnought guitar built in the Golden Era.

Tex Fletcher was born Geremino (Jerry) Bisceglia on January 17, 1910 in Harrison, New York.

He left school in the 3rd grade to work with his father and older brothers as a stonemason. As a child he learned guitar from Salvatore Figliola, a local musician and family friend.

Around the age of 15 years he ran away from home but was rounded up and sent to a reform school. Jerry escaped and found his way to Danbury, CT where he joined the Sells-Floto Circus. He had a menial job with the circus but his meager pay included three meals a day and passage on the circus train, which took him far away from home. The circus traveled west through the northern US states and Canada. Jerry left the circus upon reaching Oregon but within a year or so he ended up in Buffalo, South Dakota.

Due to the kindness of a local business owner Jerry decided to stay in Buffalo. He began by taking odd jobs but eventually became a ranch hand, where he learned to handle cattle and horses while also learning cowboy lore and campfire songs.

Early press information on Tex indicates he may have begun his music career over radio station WNAX in Yankton, South Dakota in the late 1920's, although corroborating information is difficult to find.

Tex returned to New York in the early 1930's and took a radio job as a singing cowboy on WFAS in White Plains, New York. Cowboy songs were popular and his performances were often used as "filler" for time slots that couldn't be sold to local advertisers, so Fletcher's time slots varied widely in the months he worked for WFAS.

For a time in the early 1930's Tex was also a member of Rex Cole's Mountaineers.

By 1933, Fletcher started his solo career when he moved to New Jersey to become "Cowboy Answer Man" at WOR, a major New York radio station. In 1934 WOR became part of the Mutual Broadcasting Company. Tex's lucrative career with WOR spanned three decades and included voice-over work and some dramatic acting. Fletcher also played Madison Square Garden and landed a record deal with Decca that lasted into the 1950's .

Fletcher, as well as being on big-time radio, starred in the Broadway production of "Howdy Stranger" in 1937. He then toured the country as a soloist with the popular radio hillbilly group, "Tom Emerson's Mountaineers", who were broadcast nationwide over WMCA and its affiliates. With this group he appeared in the Hollywood musical film "Down on The Barn" in 1938. As a result Fletcher was signed to star in six B-Western musicals planned by Acadia Productions that were to be made by Grand National Pictures. The first film in the series, "Six Gun Rhythm", was released in 1939 just before Grand National went bankrupt. This film might not even be remembered today except for the fact that Tex set out on an a one-man tour through the North-East United States and Canada to promote the film. Afterwards, Fletcher avoided Hollywood despite numerous offers.

Tex entered the United States army during World War II and rose to the rank of sergeant in the military police. Upon leaving the army in 1945 he returned to his radio career on WOR. He also performed in night clubs, including the Village Barn in New York, and was regularly seen on television stations WWOR, WNBC and WPIX from 1949 to 1956. In 1956 Tex moved to South Dakota and broadcast on radio station KDSJ in Deadwood and on TV over KOTA in Rapid City for several years before retiring from broadcasting. He moved back to New York city in 1960 or 1961 and returned to work as a cowboy performer at the Village Barn. With his musical career beginning to wane, Tex began a second career working as head of security for Westchester Country Club in Rye, New York, although he continued to perform and record. Tex was still performing at the Village Barn in 1965, but with the times changing even tried to re-invent himself as a folk singer.

Fletcher was a prolific songwriter and recorded for many record labels, including ARC, Decca, Vocalion, Majestic, Montgomery Ward, Flint, SESAC, Waldorf Music, Grand Award and his own Dakota label.

A "Ripley's Believe It or Not" entry credited Tex with the ability to recall more than 4,000 songs from memory, so his lack of formal training as a musician was certainly no hindrance to his musical career.

Tex died in Newburgh, New York on March 14, 1987.

The earliest photos of Fletcher show him playing a Gibson guitar but for the remainder of his long career he only played Martin guitars. While a member of Rex Cole's Mountaineers he appears to have played a right-handed 00-size Martin.

Figure 372 shows Tex playing a left-handed 000-28 guitar. This guitar must be a 1934 or 1935 000-28 as only two left-handed versions of this model were made before 1950.

In the movie "Six Gun Rhythm" Fletcher played what appears to be a 0-42 with a pyramid bridge (Figure 373).

But the Martin guitar most associated with Tex Fletcher is his unique 1935 D-42S guitar, which comes with an equally unique and interesting story. It was ordered as the second D-45 in 1934 but the order was canceled and the unused already-made body was recycled into the D-42S in 1935. This explains why the guitar has a 1934 serial number but is really a 1935 guitar, as it wasn't ordered until late in 1935.

Rudolph Wurlitzer Co. in New York started the ball

Figure 372
Tex Playing His Left-Handed 000-28 (ca. 1946)

Figure 373
Tex wih 0-42 in "Six Gun Rhythm"

rolling with a letter to Martin on November 20, 1935:

"I just had a visit from Tex Fletcher who seems to have arrived at a decision regarding his new guitar.

As far as I can understand he would like to have the D-28 Dreadnaught, finished similar to the 00-42; that is, with the pearl-inlay, etc.

His name to be inlaid on the fingerboard in block letters and as Tex is a left-handed player the name will have to read from that position.

I would like to know what the approximate cost of a guitar of this type would cost; also, how soon can you make delivery."

Martin replied on November 21:

"The special guitar Tex Fletcher is interested in would be called the D-42 and the list price would be $150.00, including the name in pearl block letters on the fingerboard. Delivery could be made about four weeks after receipt of the order. Special details such as placing the pearl letters properly and anything else desired by Mr. Fletcher will have our close personal attention."

After confirming the specifications with Tex, Wurlitzer placed an order for a special left handed D-42 guitar with Martin on December 6, 1935:

"We are sending you purchase order #2401-19 for the model D-42 Guitar for Tex Fletcher which Mr. Magrane wrote you about recently.

As you know he wants his name in pearl block letters on the finger board. We wish to explain that Mr. Fletcher plays the Guitar left handed, but he does not reverse the strings. Attached is a sketch to show just what position the name should have on the finger board.

Is there any chance of getting this Guitar before the end of the month, it would be very much appreciated because Mr. Fletcher has an important engagement New Year's Eve and would like to have the new instrument for the occasion."

The guitar was entered as a D-42S in the bookings ledger. Although the 14-fret body was originally made as a D-45 for shop order 605 in 1934, it was set aside as Jackie "Kid" Moore decided he wanted a 12-fret D-45 instead, so shop order 611 was created to correct the problem. For Tex Fletcher's D-42S guitar, shop order 989 was opened in 1935 and utilized the earlier 14-fret body that had been made in error.

The shop order contains the following comments: **"Dreadnaught model without Pick guard, fingerboard inlaid "Tex Fletcher" in pearl block letters, side dote on treble side of fingerboard, pearl bridge pins, two black & white strips under binding like F-9 on sides, back inlaid like C-2 top"**

Martin ordered the inlaid fingerboard from Louis Handel Co. in New York about December 10 and followed up with a letter on December 13:

"The special guitar fingerboard we ordered a few days ago to be inlaid with the name "Tex Fletcher" in pearl bock letters is needed at once. If you can

Figure 374
Tex with His Brand-New D-42S Guitar (ca. 1936)

possibly send it by return mail, we will appreciate it very much".

Martin received the inlaid fingerboard on December 17 and the completed guitar was duly shipped December 24, 1935.

The error made in 1934 seems fortuitous in retrospect, since having a high-grade 14-fret Dreadnought body on hand certainly helped speed up production of Tex Fletcher's D-42S guitar.

Although the guitar was originally made without a pick guard, it must have been added at an early stage as all later photos of the D-42S guitars shows it having a pick guard.

Mike Longworth contacted Tex Fletcher in the early 1970's and Tex subsequently donated his D-42S to Martin where it remains on display to this day.

All photographs in this section are courtesy of the Fletcher Family Archive. Much more information on Tex is available at texfletcher.com.

TEX FLETCHER
YOUR FAVORITE WESTERN SINGING STAR
SINGING HOST APPEARS NIGHTLY
THE VILLAGE BARN
GREENWICH VILLAGE
NEW YORK, U.S.A.

Figure 376
Tex wih His D-42S (ca. 1960)

Joe Harvey

Joe Harvey, who styled himself as "America's Blue Yodeling Cowboy", was a musician, singer and yodeler who performed on KNX Hollywood and XEBC Agua Caliente (Tijuana, Mexico) during the middle 1930's.

Like many other performers, Joe Harvey wrote to Martin in the hope of getting a special deal on a guitar he wanted to buy. He summed up his pitch in a letter dated January 31, 1935:

"I am enclosing two pictures of myself, one from KNX Hollywood and one from XEBC, the station with which I am now connected. You will notice the picture I am sending is a Martin Guitar which

Figure 375
Another Shot of the D-42S Guitar (ca. 1936)

I have used for eleven years. This guitar was presented to me in Atlanta, Georgia, and has rang out over 336 American Radio Station, 11 foreign stations. This guitar has never been repaired in any way or refrated and frats true from end to end. However I would like to have a later model and I wonder just what kind of deal I can make with you people on a new guitar. I have been offered several good propositions with different guitar manufactures but I would still like to cling to the "old Martin", as I believe it to be the best there is on the market.

I can do you a lot of good in advertising as I have already did in the past and I will add a word for Martin on my program each evening from 7:30 to 8:00 except Sundays. If we can make a deal I will also change my motion picture sound trailer that I use on my personal appearance tour for coming attractions. I send out at least 30,000 of the enclosed pictures each year besides 3,000 of the 8 X 10 size. Your new Martin would stand out much better in these pictures as it shows the name on the front of the guitar.

If you are interested I will take this up with your local music store, Thearles or Southern Music Co. or any one you suggest. Will you please advise me why they have discontinued using Martin strings on the Pacific coast? I would like very much to have a set or two of these strings.

I will be awaiting your reply as to what kind of deal you can make me. You will notice on the back of my picture a list of a good many of my songs that will soon be published in a folio. I would like to advise you that I am a personal friend of the late Jimmie Rodgers and his family and I am authorized to give out information on Jimmie's life. This authorization comes from his brother Tal. Awaiting your offer before I make my decision."

As they had done so often done in the past, Martin patiently replied on February 6, 1935:

"Your kind letter of January 31st has been forwarded to us by our good friends the Martin Band Instrument Co., of Elkhart, Indiana.

Many thanks for sending us your pictures and for your interesting account of your radio activities. We certainly are proud to know that a Martin Guitar has been a help to you, as it has been to many other prominent radio artists, including Jimmy Rodgers whose untimely death we all lament. Our pride is the greater because we know that none of these artists have ever received any inducement of any kind from us to use Martin Guitars; they have chosen them voluntarily because they like the Martin tone. We think it best to continue this policy and to refrain from any kind of subsidy or financial inducement to professional players so we are unable to make you an offer along the line you suggest. While we realize that the advertising you can give us would be valuable, we would prefer to pay for it on a cash basis but we cannot now include any expense of this kind in our advertising budget.

We think, too, that it would be to your advantage to have a late model Martin Guitar and we hope you will see our dealers soon about the matter. If we can help you with any information about the new models, or if you have any other questions you would like to ask about Martin Guitar, we shall be very glad to hear from you."**

It doesn't appear that Joe Harvey bought a Martin guitar at that time but on February 16, 1938 W. G. Thompson, a dealer in Montrose, Georgia, ordered a 00-18S guitar with "Joe Harvey" inlaid in the fingerboard in pearl letters. The shop order slip was allocated to serial number 69464 and called out the following specifications: **"special fingerboard, (1)-7/8" wide at nut, inlaid 'Joe Harvey', shaped less oval than usual"**. This guitar was stamped on February 18, 1938, cleared final inspection March 4, just 2 weeks after the start of production.

Harvey was not able to negotiate a deal with Martin for a custom guitar but may have done so with the dealer since this was the only Martin guitar ever purchased by W. G. Thompson.

The guitar shown in the Figures 377 and 378 appears to be a Martin 00-21. The different pick guards is curious as it appears the photos were taken at about the same time.

Figure 377
Joe Harvey with a Martin 00-21 in a ca. 1935
Real Photo Post Card (KNX Hollywood)

Figure 378
Joe Harvey with a Martin 00-21 in a ca. 1935
Real Photo Post Card (XEBC Agua Caliente, Mexico)

Ernest Kaai (1881-1962)

Along with Mekia (Major) Kealakai and Joseph Kekuku, Ernest Kaai was one of the pioneers who popularized Hawaiian music. Kaai was a talented musician, teacher, entrepreneur, manufacturer, impresario, booking agent and publisher, of music and numerous method books[20].

He was probably the foremost proponent of the ukulele at the beginning of the 20th century and published the first ukulele method in 1906, although early in his career he was better known as a virtuoso mandolin player.

Ernest Kaleihoku Kaai was born in Honolulu on January 7, 1881. His musical talent was recognized early and, when only 13 years old, he traveled to San Francisco to perform in mandolin recitals. By 1899 he was advertising himself as a "teacher of Guitar, Mandolin, Zither, Ukulele and Taro Patch"[21].

In the period to 1919, Kaai was an important luminary in the Hawaiian music scene. As well as a busy teaching business, Kaai performed at numerous religious concerts, private parties, social events, benefits and concerts. Kaai also provided stringed bands, glee clubs and dance orchestras for many Hawaiian hotels and dance clubs, as well as entertainment for docked cruise ships. Quintettes and quartettes were often supplied to these venues and the performances included instrumental music, singing and hula dancing.

Kaai's music school also regularly held their own concerts where the talents of both Kaai and his students was displayed. The repertoire of concerts included Hawaiian music and also ragtime, jazz, waltzes, popular songs and other European works. Many of Kaai's students worked as members of the glee clubs and dance orchestras and Kaai's entrepreneurship gave many an entry into the music business.

Kaai formed many small musical groups depending on the type of music to be performed and the demands of the venue being played. Some of the names of these groups were Kaai's Quartet (1905), Ernest Kaai Glee Club (played in Los Angeles, 1906-1907), Kaai Mandolin Orchestra (1907) Ernest Kaai's Quintet Club (1910), Ernest Kaai Hawaiian Serenaders (1911), Ernest Kaai and Troubadors (toured Australia

Figure 379
Ernest Kaai Playing a Martin Guitar,
from a 1907 Newspaper Advertisement for
"The Ernest Kaai Music School[22]"

and New Zealand in 1911) and Ernest Kaai and Royal Hawaiian Singers (1912).

Hawaiian music had been slowly growing in popularity due to the Hawaiian presence at various international expositions held in the United States at the turn of the 19th century: Chicago World' Fair (1893), San Francisco Midwinter Fair (1894), Trans-Mississippi Exposition held in Omaha (1898), Pan-American Exposition, Buffalo (1901). The next exposition, the Alaska-Yukon-Pacific Exposition was held in Seattle in 1909 and saw Kaai acting as the music director of the Hawaiian Pavilion, where he was judged a great success.

In 1911 Kaai commenced a more than 25 year period of touring the Asia Pacific region by performing in Australia and New Zealand with Ernest Kaai and Troubadours, a double quintette group of musicians and dancers.

As if his musical career was not busy enough Kaai formed the Kaai Ukulele Manufacturing Co. in 1912.

This business may have been too much of a distraction from his other music endeavors, or competition from other makers was perhap too fierce, so sold Kaai sold his company to Paradise Ukulele Manufacturing Co. (later the Aloha Ukulele Manufacturing Co.) in 1917. Later, Kaai would put his label in the ukuleles of other makers, including those made by Larson Brothers and Kumulae.

The next big exposition was the Panama-Pacific International Exposition held in San Francisco during 1915. Kaai didn't participate in this exposition because for several years he had been involved with organizing a separate exposition, the Panama-California Exposition, to be held in San Diego, also in 1915. Kaai managed the Hawaiian Village on this site and performed with Kaai's Serenaders. The Royal Hawaiian Quintette, Glee groups and hula dancers also performed at the Hawaiian exhibit during the exposition. When the Pan-Pacific Exposition closed in December 1915 many exhibits, who could not return home due the First World War, took up residence at the Panama-California Exposition until it closed on January 1, 1917. In 1916 Kaai also began supplying Hawaiian musicians for the "Chautauqua" circuit in the United States due to the increased interest in Hawaiian music.

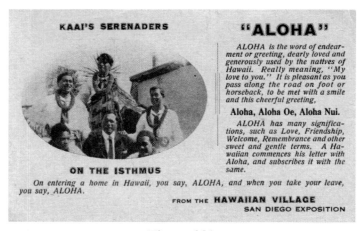

Figure 380
Kaai's Serenaders Advertising Postcard
from the 1915 Panama-California Exposition

Kaai would sometimes perform with visiting musicians, as happened in 1917, after his return from the Panama-California Exposition, when he collaborated with Ellen Beach Yaw, a famous coloratura soprano[23].

From 1919 to 1924 Kaai toured Ceylon (Sri Lanka), Borneo, Java, Burma, India and Singapore with Kaai's

Figure 381
Cover Photograph from "Kaai's Enchanted
Melodies for Hawaiian Guitar" (1917)

Figure 382
Cover Artwork for Kaai's Hawaiian
Guitar Method 1919 (rev. 1926)

Royal Hawaiian Troubadours.

On January 14, 1924, while still on tour, Kaai wrote Martin from Kuala Lumpur to begin the purchase of some Martin instruments:

"Seeing your ad in the columns of the CRESCEN-DO will you kindly send me your catalog of UKU-LELES also your prices to the profession and oblige. c/o Thomas Cook & Son HONG KONG"

Martin replied on February 25, 1924 and sent the missive to Hong Kong:

"In accordance with your request illustrated catalogue with price list is being mailed under separate cover. These prices are subject to the regular professional discount of 20%. Price list of cases to fit Martin Instruments in enclosed.

We are at your service for further information."

After a long delay, Kaai wrote to Martin on October 14, 1924 to order some instruments:

"I am ordering three instruments from the catalog you so kindly forwarded to me the early part of this year. Have noted your price list as well as the professional discount you allow. And with this same mail I am instructing my bankers in Honolulu to forward you a certified check for $135.00. This amount being in excess of the order, but it is really to cover any additional expenses such as prepaid freight, insurance and etc. I believe there will (be) some duty to pay at this end, and not being familiar with conditions and procedures by shippers, I am leaving the matter entirely in your hands, knowing full well that you will dispatch this order by the most expeditious method and route.

The order

1 Grand Concert Martin Guitar Style 28 No. 00
1 Keratol, Plush Lined case (to fit)
1 Martin Taropatch No. 2
1 Keratol Plush Lined Case (to fit)
1 Martin Tiple
1 Keratol Plush lined Case to fit
Strings - 2 extra sets Tiple
(Strings) - 2 (extra sets) Taropatch

Remarks and suggestions
Re the Guitar - I use steel strings - intended as a solo instrument - fingerboard must be true and without WARP - may use it for steel playing as well - the BRIDGE such as in the catalog is the only thing that has given me any trouble, I use three Martin guitars in my organization and I have had to rivet (Brass screws) on the ends of all of them."

Kaai also included a sketch of a bridge one of his mu-

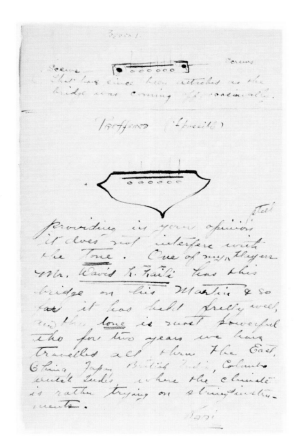

Figure 383
Letter from Ernest Kaai Suggesting a Bridge Shape like the Bridge of the Kealakai Guitar

ERNEST KAAI, GUITARIST
MIAMI 35. FLA.

Figure 384
Ca. 1959 Real Photo Advertising Card for Ernest Kaai

sicians was using on his guitar that looks very much like the bridge that Major Kealakai ordered with his "extra large" guitar in 1916.

Kaai wrote to Martin again on October 17, 1924 but this time from Brisbane, Australia:

"With this same mail I am instructing the Hawaiian Trust Co. Ltd. to cancel sending you the certified check mentioned in my letter of the 14th inst. Our movements are uncertain at present and it may be that we should be starting for Hawaii before very long. However should the check arrive and you have not yet forwarded the instruments, kindly place the amount to the credit of my account, till further advised when and where to ship the instruments."

Kaai began a two year tour of Australia and New Zealand in 1925 with his long-running show "A Night in Honolulu". Kaai's Hawaiian Troubadours disbanded in 1930 but Kaai continued to tour the "Eastern circuit" until 1937, at which time Japan's invasion of China was making touring more difficult.

At the end of 1937 Kaai landed in San Francisco and, sometime between 1937 and 1940, settled in Miami, Florida where he opened Kaai Music Studio Inc. Kaai Music was a regular buyer of Martin guitars from 1955 to 1962. Kaai Music may have wanted to purchase Martin instruments before 1955 but Martin already had a long-time dealer in Miami, S. Ernest Philpitt & Son. However, there is a good chance Philpitt was selling wholesale to Kaai Music before 1955, considering Kaai's preference for Martin instruments.

Ernest Kaai died in Miami in September 1962.

Mekia (Major) Kealakai (1867-1944)

Mekia (Major) Kealakai was one of the foremost contributors to the popularity of Hawaiian music, especially in the period after the Panama-Pacific International Exposition in 1915. Kealakai was a talented musician, composer and, later, conductor of the Royal Hawaiian Band.

Mekia Kealakai was born on October 15, 1867 on

Oahu. He was sent to the Reform School of Honolulu for truancy at twelve years of age. There he learned music, including theory and harmony, under the tutelage of Heinrich Berger, who was the conductor and composer of the Royal Hawaiian Band from 1872 to 1915. Kealakai played the trombone in the band but was also a virtuoso on the flute and guitar. By 1892 Kealakai was a featured member of the Royal Hawaiian Band, often playing the final musical selection in concerts[24]. Kealakai was also in the band when they toured the mainland United States with in 1895 and intermittently played with the band until at least 1900.

Kealakai was part of the troupe of 28 Hawaiian musicians and dancers that performed in the Hawaiian pavilion at the 1898 Trans-Mississippi Exposition in Omaha, Nebraska[25]. The troupe continued to tour the United States for a time after the exposition and Kealakai did not return to Hawaii until late in 1899[26].

In 1901 Kealakai joined another troupe that performed at the 1901 Pan-American Exposition in Buffalo, New York[27]. At least some of the troupe, under the management of John Wilson, continued to tour the United States after the exposition closed on November 1, 1901 and did not return to Hawaii until late March 1902[28]. Mekia played mostly with the Kawaihau Orchestra and Glee Club after his return to Hawaii and was noted as being the leader of the orchestra for part of 1905[29]. Later in 1905 the Kawaihau Orchestra began a world tour with Kealakai as a member of the group. In May 1906 Mekia was a member of a glee club led by Thomas Silva that was touring the United States[30]. Information is scanty but it appears Kealakai continued to tour the Mainland for a number years after 1906, teaming up with other Hawaiian musicians to form small bands for a variety of venues[31].

Kealakai based himself in San Francisco during 1912 and 1913[32] where he "furnished Hawaiian music for all occasions" and also taught ukulele, taro-patch and

REORGANIZATION OF THE POPULAR KAWAIHAU GLEE CLUB

REORGANIZED KAWAIHAU GLEE CLUB. (Williams Photo.)

Figure 385
1904 Photograph of the Kawaihau Glee Club (Mekia Kealakai seated in the second row, second from the left)[32]

guitar[33]. He also continued to do some local touring[34]. Around 1914 Mekia formed his own group, Kealakai's Hawaiians. This troupe was a fixture on the Chicago Vaudeville and Chautauqua circuits until 1919[35]. The group seems to have been particularly popular at state and county fairs in Iowa[36].

Somehow, Kealakai also found time to publish a ukulele method in 1912[37].

At the end of 1915, Kealakai had Martin make him "an extra large guitar", that subsequently evolved into the Ditson Dreadnought. See the section on "The Kealakai Guitar" (pages 68 to 73) for more information.

Kealakai's Hawaiians performed for several years in London and Europe. However, Kealakai was convinced by John Wilson, by then mayor of Honolulu, to return to Hawaii in 1920 to be the Bandmaster of the Royal Hawaiian Band. Kealakai lead the band from 1920 to 1926. Afterwards, Kealakai undertook another musical tour of Europe but returned again to lead the Royal Hawaiian Band from 1930 to 1932 before retiring.

Mekia Kealakai died in Honolulu on March 31, 1944.

Joseph Kekuku (1874-1932)

Kekuku was born in 1874 on the Hawaiian island of Oahu. While attending the Kamehameha School for Boys in Hawaii, Kekuku, quite by accident, discovered the sound of the steel guitar about 1885. About 1930 Kekuku wrote the following comments for an advertisement for a guitar teaching method he was promoting while in Chicago:

"I originated the Hawaiian Steel Guitar method of playing in the year 1885 at the age of 11 years. At the time, I was living in the village where I was born, a place called Laie only a short distance from Honolulu. It took me seven years to master the guitar as I had no teachers to show me and no books to refer to for information. In 1904 I came to your beautiful country and played in every theater of renown from coast to coast."

The first mention in the local Hawaiian newspapers of Joseph Kekuku playing the guitar occurred in 1900[38] but it is very likely he had already been active on the

local musical scene due to his unique style of guitar playing. However, performing was only a part-time profession for Kekuku at the time; his full-time job was as a copyist in the Registry of Conveyances (land records). Kekuku ran into some financial difficulties in 1904[39] and left Hawaii precipitously in June of that year by stowing away on the steamship "Korea" bound for San Francisco. Kekuku never returned to Hawaii.

Once in San Francisco, Kekuku set up shop as a guitar teacher, while at the same time attempting to maintain a link to his old profession by presenting himself as an "Expert Searcher of Records"[40]. Kekuku was playing the Vaudeville circuit on the West Coast by 1906[41,42] and was a performer at the 1909 Alaska-Yukon-Pacific Exposition, remaining in Seattle for a time after the fair closed to give lessons on the steel guitar.

GONE TO FRISCO

JOSEPH KEKUKU, WHO DISAPPEARED FROM THE REGISTRAR'S OFFICE AFTER ASSIGNING HIS SALARY TO SEVERAL DIFFERENT PERSONS SEEN IN SAN FRANCISCO—EARNING LIVING AS A MUSICIAN NOW.

Joseph K. Kekuku, the copyist in the Registrar's office, who stood not upon the order of his going but went without bidding anyone farewell, is not, as some thought, living anywhere in the islands, but is located in San Francisco. A letter from a Honolulu man now in the Coast city states that he saw and conversed with Kekuku there a short time ago and that the young man is ekeing out some sort of a living by his musical talents.

Kekuku's disappearance was coincident with the presentation of duplicate pay checks for his month salary which had been cashed by different parties. The treasurer's office was so unfeeling as to refuse to accept more than one and the young man meanwhile found the climtae unhealthy.

Figure 386
July 16, 1904 Article Concerning
Kekuku's Departure for San Francisco[2]

The explosion in interest for Hawaiian music after 1915 Panama-Pacific International Exposition was the catalyst that raised Kekuku's career to the next level. By 1916 Kekuku had formed Kekuku's Hawaiian Quintet. The Quintet became a staple head-line act on the Vaudeville and Chautauqua circuits, especially in the western half of the United States.

In 1919 Kekuku left the U.S. and spent eight years touring Europe with "The Bird of Paradise" show. "The Bird of Paradise" show was very popular in Europe due to its brilliant stage scenery, authentic

THE members of Kekuku's Hawaiian Quintet, coming to Chautauqua, are principally drawn from the Alisky and Toots Paka Troupes, who roused such a wild fervor of enthusiasm throughout the United States several years ago. Kekuku was the instrumentalist featured in both companies. He, together with his players, toured with the "Bird of Paradise" Company. Joseph Kekuku is the originator of the steel pick, sliding, two hand fingering method of the guitar that has made Hawaiian music famous the world over. To this artist belongs that half ready, dreamlike, whispering hum of the guitar and ukelele, that plaintive, witching charm, which in its lulling sweetness even rivals the possibilities of the human voice.

Figure 387
1916 Photograph of Kekuku's Hawaiian Quintet,
Kekuku with a Style 42 or 45 Martin Guitar[43]

Hawaiian costumes and novel music.

It appears that Kekuku only played Martin guitars. The photographs of Kekuku's Hawaiian Quintet from 1916 to 1919 show Kekuku playing a style 42 or 45 Martin guitar with an ivory bridge. Usually the photographs show Kekuku playing the instrument as a steel guitar so it is not easy to identify the model he used.

On February 12, 1920 Kekuku ordered a Martin 00-45 guitar while he was in Cannes, France. A 1919 Martin 00-45 guitar with serial number 14434 (stamped on December 5, 1919) was shipped a few days later on February 24. As a performer Kekuku received a 20% discount from Martin. Photographs from Kekuku's time in Europe are rare but it is likely this guitar was made with an ivory bridge. Martin had begun using celluloid binding in place of ivory in May 1917 but it appears the company continued to use ivory bridges for a time. When a new catalogue was printed in September 1920, the style 42 guitars no longer had an ivory bridge (style 45 guitars did not appear in this catalogue) so it seems ivory bridges were still featured on style 42 and 45 guitars well into 1920.

Kekuku returned to the United States in 1927. He settled in Chicago for a time and ran a popular and successful music school. Around 1930, he left Chica-

go and moved to Dover, New Jersey where he gave Hawaiian guitar lessons and, probably, continued to perform on the Vaudeville circuit.

On January 26, 1927 Martin wrote to Bergstrom Music Co.:

"In the New York Times of last Sunday, January 23, we note an article entitled, "Steel Guitar Playing Invented by Hawaiian". From this article we copy the first paragraph, as follows

'The origin of steel guitar playing, Hawaii's foremost contribution to instrumental music, in described in manuscripts just published in Honolulu by the Bishop Museum, dealing with a survey of native music made by the Hawaiian Folklore Commission. These manuscripts show that the steel guitar was played first in 1893 by a native boy, who found that by placing an article on the fingerboard of the guitar he could produce a novel sound.'

The boy referred to in this paragraph is mentioned as Joseph Kekuku. Can you help us to secure several copies of the manuscript referred to, just published by the Bishop Museum? We have a number of customers who are interested in this subject and would be glad to have you send us half a dozen copies, if they can be secured."

On February 18, 1927 Bergstrom Music Co. wrote to Martin:

"We have your letter of January 26, with reference to securing an article gotten out by the Bishop Museum dealing with the origin of steel guitar playing in Hawaii. This, they claim they are selling for four dollars a copy, so before ordering we thought we would give you this information.

We have with us a Hawaiian by the name of Major Kealakai who was a boy and grew up with Joseph Kekuku mentioned in your letter. The straight guitar was then in use having been brought over by the Portugese and these boys first got the idea of playing a guitar in steel fashion by trying to imitate the actions of some German sailors off a German ship here at that time, about 1882. These men made up a bass violin out of a cracker box and a bass drum from an empty salmon barrel,

and a narrow long box strung with two steel wires and a metal belaying pin run up and down and the strings strummed with the thumb. This latter instrument is what the boys tried to imitate on the guitar, first with a pen knife and another tired (sic) a file and Mr. Keakuku (sic) was the first to try a file. Mr. Keakuku (sic) is now in New York and has been for many years and possibly could give you a verification of this or his version of it if you could give you a verification of this or his version of it if you could get in touch with him. You might be able to locate him through the National Vaudeville Artists' Association of New York."

Martin replied on March 8, 1927:

"We thank you very kindly for your interesting letter of February 18th in regard to the origin of the Hawaiian Steel Guitar. We hardly think that the report prepared by the Bishop Museum would give us sufficient additional information to warrant the charge of four dollars.

We are making an effort to get in touch with Mr. Joseph Kekuku to verify the very interesting version you give of the beginning of Steel Guitar Playing.

We are interested to learn that Major Kealakai is with you. The writer has a very pleasant recollection of meeting the Major ten or eleven years ago in the M. Doyle Marks Company's store in Elmira, N. Y. He was at that time on the vaudeville stage and the writer was on a business trip. We had a very pleasant conversation together. We trust he is enjoying his work with you and would appreciate your conveying to him our kind regards."

Joseph Kekuku died in Morristown, New Jersey on January 16, 1932 of a cerebral hemorrhage and was buried in the Orchard Street Cemetery.

On February 5, 1932, Kekuku's wife, Adeline, wrote to Martin:

"My husband, Joseph Kekuku, passed into Eternity and I have his Guitar which some years ago was sent to us in Europe while he was En Tour there.

I wonder if for a consideration you could use the

Guitar for adv. purpose. The Guitar had a wonderful tone even tho it has been patched up after Joseph Kekuku fell down two long flights of concrete steps with it. When we returned from Europe he made a tour here and I can show you a full page in an Orpheum Programe stating Joseph Kekuku "always plays on The Celebrated Martin Guitar. If you wish to see the Guitar and talk the matter over, my friends can drive me there any day, Saturday excepted and any hour by appointment."

Martin replied on February 11:

"Although we never had the pleasure of meeting your distinguished husband, Joseph Kekuku, we had great respect for his ability as a Guitarist and as a pioneer in the Hawaiian style of playing. We are very sorry to hear of his untimely death and we wish to extend our sincere sympathy in your bereavement.

For advertising purposes his Guitar would be of little value to us because Guitars are now built somewhat differently and it would hardly do to advertise the new style with an old instrument, as you will understand.

If you are anxious to dispose of the Guitar we would suggest that you offer it for sale through one of our metropolitan dealers, a list of which is given below. Of course we cannot assure you that they will be interested but we think there is a possibility. We regret that we cannot make you an offer for it."

George C. Krick (1871-1962)

Another important, but little known, influence on Martin guitars was provided by George C. Krick, a student of William Foden, who corresponded with Martin over a very long period of time.

George C. Krick, a concert guitarist and teacher of classical guitar, was born in Germany in 1871. In 1887 he moved to St. Louis, Mo., at the age of 16. He began studying the mandolin with William Foden but quickly became more interested in the guitar. Krick was a member of the "Beethoven Mandolin-Guitar Quartet" organized by Foden in 1887. The quartet was very popular and performed extensively in St. Louis and the surrounding area. The group later expanded during the 1890's and its name was changed to "The Foden Mandolin and Guitar Orchestra."

Later, he joined Foden on the New York concert stage and also performed in independent concerts.

Krick left St. Louis around 1904 and moved to the Philadelphia PA area where he headed the Germantown Conservatory in Germantown PA and later ran the George C. Krick Music Studios, also in Germantown. For several years he was president of the American Guild of Philadelphia PA and Washington DC.

Well known for his article about guitars, Krick published in various American guitar journals and the German guitar journal Mitteilungern (Communications). From 1937 to 1942 he contributed a monthly column in Etude magazine devoted to fretted instruments.

Although these articles dealt with all fretted instruments, Krick's emphasis was on the classical guitar and its composers and players. He made many trips to Europe where he collected music and met with many of the European concert artists of his time. Krick's articles on the guitar were central to providing one of the rare links between the old 19th century school of American guitars and the pre- and post-World War II generation of guitarists learning the Andres Segovia method of playing.

George Krick kept up a regular correspondence with "Bill" Foden until 1946, buying music and commiserating on the state of the teaching business during the war years.

Krick returned to St. Louis in 1950. He continued to teach until his death at the age of 90 on April 2, 1962.

Sources:

University of Colorado at Boulder, University Libraries, AMRC, George C. Krick Collection

Washington University, Gaylord Music Library, St. Louis, Missouri, George C. Krick Collection

Lei Lehua (1893-1963)

Princess Lei Lehua (born Lizzie Kaiama) was a Hawaiian dancer, performer and teacher.

Not much information can be found on Lei Lehua's early life but the 1910 census recorded that Lizzie Kaiama, and her brother Willie Kaiama, were the adopted children of a Sam Luahine of Honolulu.

Lei Lehua extensively toured the United States on the Chautauqua and Vaudeville circuits from at least 1913[44]. Lei Lehua was a very popular hula dancer who was featured in a number of different troupes: Lei Lehua and the Hawaiian Four (1913), Bell's Famous Hawaiians (ca. 1917-1920), the Peerless Quartet (ca. 1922-1924) and Kaiama's Native Hawaiians (ca. 1927-1929).

Figure 388
1918 Advertisement for Bell's Famous Hawaiians, Featuring Lei Leihena (sic)[45]

Lei Lehua married another Hawaiian musician, Lani Kamiki. Both were part of the Peerless Quartet along with her brother Willie. Later, the three of them managed the Hawaiian Studios in Jacksonville Florida.

It appears that the Hawaiian Studios my have only lasted from about 1925 to 1927 since Kaiama's Native Hawaiians appear to have toured extensively in 1928 and 1929. On the other hand, the Hawaiian Studios may have remained in business while the troupe was out touring during the summer months.

Figure 389
1928 Newspaper Photograph of Lei Lehua
with Kaiama's Hawaiians[46]

"TIN CAN" THEIR WAY FOR 150,000 MILES

Figure 390
1929 Photograph of Lei Lehua, Willie Kaiama and
Ernest Kamiki[47]

Early in 1925 Willie Kaiama, Lei Lehua's brother
and manager of the Hawaiian Studios, bought a 1924
0-28K Martin guitar, serial number 21271, and wrote
to Martin to express his satisfaction with the new

guitar.

On May 23, 1925 Lei Lehua wrote to Martin concerning her Martin instruments and included an interesting newspaper clipping:

"**I am returning my Ukulele to you today for repairs. It has a wonderful tone. And I like the Martin Instruments best of all. I have a beautiful Martin Guitar and I sure advertise Martin Instruments. I think they are the best made. I have a Studio here of over 700 pupils my brother and I are teaching here. We were formerly on Swarthmore Chautauqua and Keith Vaudeville. Our business here picks up every day. We had an enormous business for the past month and have just finished with our new set of Books and auditing. I am in-**

Figure 391
Newspaper Clipping of Lei Lehua with Her Brother,
Husband and Students (ca. 1925)

Figure 392
Photographs of Lei Lehua
from Hawaiian Studio Letterhead (ca. 1925)

closing (sic) you a few newspaper clips so you can see what I have done and are doing now.

You can repair this Ukulele as you think best. It may not need a new back. I guess you can glue it so it will not show. Please put in a set of wood keys. I don't like patent keys, and string it up."

Martin replied on June 9:

"Your Ukulele arrived last week and was immediately placed in work. We will probably be able to return it to you with in two or three days We will glue the broken places, refret the fingerboard and fit wooden pegs, as directed.

Enclosed here you will find one wooden peg for your Taro Patch.

We are much interested in the description of your business and trust that you will have continued success as the business grows. It will be a pleasure to us to supply you, whenever you have need, with Ukuleles, Guitars or Mandolins. In Jacksonville we are represented by S. Ernest Philpitt & Son, who carry a fair stock and will always be willing to order special numbers for you."

Neither Willie Kaiama nor Lei Lehua seems to have bought any more Martin instruments. However, they did regularly return ukuleles, taro-patches and guitars to Martin for repairs until 1929.

Lei Lehua again wrote to Martin on October 26, 1929:

"I am returning herewith by express today my Martin Guitar, and am asking that you repair it for me and put it in A-1 condition. It is split in several places. What I want is to have it repaired so that the tone will not be damaged, as it has a wonderful tone. I also need a new bridge, as the other one split thro (sic) the centre. And please do your best to glue the bridge on so that it will not be continually pulling off. Also please notice that some of the frets are bad.

Your will notice that I have a piece of celluloid put on by you to save the top of my guitar from being scratched by the pick. Before you refinish the guitar will you please place another similar piece

down near the bridge for the same purpose, as you will notice that it is tearing up the top.

I have been intending to send this guitar in for some time, but have been unable to do without it, and I am closing my summer season this week, and will have a two weeks vacation, and hope that you can give me quick service on my instrument, as I have no other Standard Guitar. I have another Martin Steel, but have no Standard. I just secured a box to ship the guitar in from the one of the music stores here, and am sending my express today. Please notify me at once when you will receive same, and when you think you can finish the repairs etc, and return to me."

C. F. Martin III made a note in the margin of this letter: "0-21 #24853, Put in Work, 10-30-29."

Martin replied on October 30:

"Your Guitar is here and is having our immediate attention. We will remove the back in order to repair and reinforce the broken side from within, also to examine and repair both the top and back braces. The frets will be overhauled and we will supply a new bridge with bridge pins and a set of strings. On the top we will inlay an additional piece of celluloid for a guard between the old piece and the bridge.

We note that the Guitar has a good many marks from use; since it will be necessary to do quite a bit if touching up on account of the repairs to the side, there will be only a little additional cost to refinish the Guitar completely, using our new lacquer finish. We estimate that the total cost, including string and other new parts, will not exceed fifteen dollars.

Probably, we can have the work finished by the end of the week. We will do out best for you."

The Hawaiian Studio may not have survived the start of the Depression and it would appear Kaiama's Native Hawaiians returned to touring. The group was also playing on the radio from at least 1934 to 1936.

Lei Lehua moved to St. Petersburg, Florida about 1951 where she opened the Lei Lehua Hawaiian

Studio (Oriental and Hawaiian Dancing). Later in her career she toured as a secretary with Ringling Brothers Circus in 1956 and, for a time, was a teacher at the Fred Astaire Dance Studios in St. Petersburg Beach. She also continued to perform for local St. Petersburg organizations until her death in St. Petersburg[48] on June 11, 1963.

The Tale of E. C. Lilly

Just how much abuse can a Martin guitar take?

In November 1922 Martin received the following letter:

"Leavenworth, Kansas, November 5, 1922

I am writing you in regards to my guitar. I have one of the old Martin guitar (sic). The number inside it is 8198 (i.e., 0-28) its (sic) a concert size. I am a guitar soloist and I have used the Gibson and Washburn but I can safely say the Martin is my favorite. I bought this guitar I have from a teacher in Eugene Oregon about 8 years ago. I turned over in a car a few years ago and busted the top but I had a piece put in the top and it never hurt the tone. I was touring Alaska in a small launch. One day the guitar and I went over board. It was some time before I got the guitar out of the water. I poured the water out of it, then let it dry slowly. The water done no harm to it. To day the guitar has a wonderful tone. I wanted to find out if you repair guitars. I need a new finger board. I have had four sets of frets put on and the finger board has been planed down. Do you sell finger boards or would you put one on my guitar if I ship it to you? I am in the penitentiary. How much would it cost? I am doing life and I have no financial income. My cell mate is learning and he is going to get a good guitar in the spring. He ask (sic) me what kind of a guitar was best. I told him to get a Martin. He received one of your new catalogues the other day. He says he will get the best you got, style 45, Price $138. There is about 25 hundred men hear (sic).

I have the only Martin guitar hear (sic).
It is possible that I can sell some guitars for you, the boys say my guitar sounds like a piano.

On a Sunday, when we get the yard they gather around me to hear me play.

I will close, hoping to hear from you soon and let me know what you can do.

C. F. Martin III replied on November 19, 1922:

"We are interested and pleased to learn of the pleasure you derive from your Martin guitar. It is also gratifying to learn that the instrument has stood up well under such trying conditions. Evidently it has had good care for the greater part of its life. Our records show those instrument is twenty-five years old.

The replacing of a fingerboard is an operation requiring great care and some time and we would very much prefer to have you send us the instrument, if you can possibly arrange to do so.

In view of the fact that you are using this Guitar for the entertainment and amusement of your comrades, as well as for your own pleasure, we will arrange to do the work for you without charge.

The time necessary to complete the work will be about two weeks provided nothing further is found to be done; however, we will give the instrument a thorough examination and repair it wherever necessary. Please send it to us by express, well crated or boxed."

C. F. Martin III was certainly not obligated to cover the cost of the repairs but was clearly very touched by the circumstances of the writer and displayed an admirable degree of empathy.

The ledgers don't contain any mention of the repair to this guitar although, since C. F. Martin III had offered to do the repair for free, a ledger entry shouldn't necessarily be expected.

The writer of the touching letter was E. C. Lilly. He was born in Wheeling, West Virginia on December 12, 1888 and had a rough early life. His parents separated when he was 4 or 5 and he ended up living mostly with his father. He only received a 2nd grade education and ran away from home when he was about 11 or 12.

Lilly got into trouble with the law early. He was convicted of manslaughter in 1906 and sentenced to a 10 year prison term. He was incarcerated in Folsom State Prison in California on December 20, 1906 but was paroled on June 20, 1912.

Lilly received a second prison term in 1914 when he was convicted of petty larceny. He served a one year sentence at Folsom State Prison and was released on October 16, 1915.

Lilly's final sentence was also his last; he received a life sentence for first degree murder in 1920. Originally jailed at McNeil State Prison in Alaska, he was transferred to Leavenworth Penitentiary on March 5, 1921 and there became prisoner number 16048.

A parole report was prepared 1935 when he had his first parole hearing. It contained a number of important details about the crime. Interestingly, his musical ability and his Martin guitar played a prominent, if sad, role in the story!

"Parole report March 20, 1935

This prisoner and one W. B. Woodworth (the murdered man) and a man by the name of Jack, true name unknown, came up to S. E. Alaska on a gasboat visiting different canneries and small settlements giving musical entertainments and picture shows; on the 25th of August, 1920 these three men left Washington Bay on said gasboat, at about 2. P. M., on or about 5 P. M., of the same day one Capt. Herrington discovered what he thought to be a boat on fire and started out immediately reaching it in about 25 minutes, and discovered it was the same gasboat that had left Washington Bay shortly previous. He could see no one on the boat and after searching around discovered an object which he took to be a man in a canoe; he gave chase and discovered that Lilly was in it; he was alone in the canoe and had in his possession his suit case and presumably all his clothes, a guitar, some bread, canned goods and provision, also a pistol which Lilly stated belonged to Mr. Woodworth. Woodworth owned the boat and he and Lilly had some trouble about a week's wages claimed to be due, and while it was proved Lilly had no money just prior to the homicide, upon being searched when taken out of the canoe $516.00 was found secreted

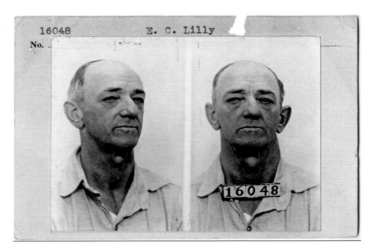

Figure 393
Prison photo of E. C. Lilly circa 1935

on his person. The gasboat burned to the waters edge and sank within a few minutes after the arrival of Captain Herrington so neither the body of Mr. Woodworth or the other party named Jack was found."

Lilly was turned down for parole in 1935. He was denied parole several more times and eventually committed suicide on February 28, 1944 by jumping from the 4th tier of the cell house, when it appeared he would never be let out of prison.

Here's hoping that E. C. Lilly found some solace in his Martin guitar during his long prison sentence.

Lloyd Loar (1886-1943)

Lloyd Alayre Loar (January 9, 1886 – September 14, 1943) was a musician, inventor, lecturer, professor of acoustics and "musical authority and composer"[49].

He is best known to instrument collectors for his association with the Gibson Guitar Co.

Loar was a well-regarded performer on the mandolin, viola and musical saw. He toured the United States and Europe with several different musical groups and performed on the Chautauqua and Lyceum circuits. Loar also performed as a feature artist at many American Guild of Banjoists, Mandolinists and Harpists Conventions during the 1920's and 1930's[50].

From 1919 to 1924 Loar worked for the Gibson Guitar Co. as an instrument designer and sound engineer.

He introduced many innovations at Gibson including: F-shaped holes on the tops of guitars and mandolin family instruments, longer necks and elevated fingerboards. He also promoted the use of the Virzi Tone Producer in Gibson instruments. (A Virzi Sound Producer was a oval disk of spruce attached to the underside of instruments by two or three feet. It was sensitive to vibration and was theoretically supposed to amplify the tone produced.)

Loar is most famous for the "Master" grade instrument he created for Gibson, including the F5 mandolin, L5 guitar, H5 mandola, K5 mando-cello and A5 mandolin. Between 1922 and 1924 the "Master" instruments received a special oval label signed by Loar himself. A F5 "Lloyd Loar" mandolin, or any of the other Master instruments from this period, are often spoken of in reverential terms and are highly sought after by collectors and musicians.

After leaving Gibson, Loar was involved in a wide variety of musical enterprises all while continuing an active concert schedule.

From 1925 until at least 1927 Loar was a contributor to Walter Jacobs' Music Magazines[51].

Between 1925 and 1930 Loar created a number of teaching methods for the Nicomede Music Co. publications. In 1925 he wrote "Loar's New Method Ukulele, Ukulele-Banjo and Tenor Banjo" in four volumes[52]. This was followed in 1927 with the four volume "Loar's Orchestral Tenor Banjo Method"[53] and, in 1930, a six volume method named "The American Violin System"[54].

After the death of Herbert K. Martin in early 1927 Martin began a search for an outside salesman to replace Herbert. One result of this search was an interesting letter written by Lloyd Loar to Martin on June 3, 1927:

"Mr. Buttelman, with whom I am associated in Walter Jacobs' Music Magazines, tells me that you were recently inquiring as to the probability of my being interested in a proposition from you.

As you doubtless know, I have had considerable experience in all angles of small stringed instrument manufacture, and while I have not been **actively engaged in it for the past two years, I have still kept in touch with affairs connected with it and have by any means not lost my interest. Of course, I am unable to say without further information as to whether I could be definitely interested in a proposition from you; if the position you had in mind, however, was such that I would feel I was competent to fill it satisfactorily both from yours and my own standpoint, I would be glad to hear further about it and to give you such other information concerning myself as you might be interested in having."**

Nothing further seems to have happened with regard to Loar working for Martin. Loar was very busy at the time and probably has his own ideas on what he could contribute to Martin while Martin was focused on finding an outside salesman. However, it is interesting to speculate what contributions to instrument design Loar might have made for Martin if he had joined the company. In early 1927, Martin was still a very conservative company and were only just entering into the production of tenor guitars and carved-top mandolins. Within a few years, however, Martin was innovating many new designs (Orchestra Model, C model, Dreadnought and F model guitars) in order to survive the Great Depression.

Loar wrote for other publications as well; including five articles entitled "Fretted Instruments: Their Origins, Development and Marketing" [55,56,57,58,59] for the Music Trade Review magazine between 1929 and 1930, .

From 1929 until 1943 Loar was also Professor of Acoustics in the Music School at Northwestern University in Evanston, Illinois .

B. A. Rose Music Co., a long time dealer of Martin guitars, wrote a letter to the company on February 27, 1933 with some interesting information on Lloyd Loar:

"Mr. Lohr (sic) who was the engineer and designed all the Gibson instruments, especially the $300 model, was in town last fall and gave a talk at the State Music Teacher's Convention. He is now with the Vibrola Company in Kalamazoo, Michigan. He said he had an idea for using soundposts in guitars and fretted instruments but at that time he was

very busy with experimental work for the Vibrola Company but at a future date, he would again go back to the manufacturing of guitars and come out with instruments with soundposts."

Nothing more was heard of Loar's idea for making guitars with sound posts but this letter does establish that he was working for the Vibrola Co. in Kalamazoo in early 1933. Loar didn't work for that company very much longer since he co-founded the Vivitone Company with Lewis Williams, a former Gibson executive, on November 1, 1933.

See Roger Siminoff's Biography of Lloyd Loar (https://www.siminoff.net/lloyd-loar) for much more information on Lloyd Loar, especially his interesting later career.

Loar died in Chicago on September 14, 1943.

Napoleon Marache (1818-1875)

Napoleon Marache was born in Meaux, France on June 15, 1818 and immigrated to the United States with his parents in 1831[60]. He had already exhibited musical aptitude on the violin but switched to playing the guitar in his new country. He became very skilled on the guitar and was considered to be one of the best guitarists in the U. S.[60]

Marache is most well known for his contributions to the game of chess. He learned the game of chess around 1844, learned quickly and started composing chess problems for publication in newspapers by late 1845. In October 1846, he started the publishing the first chess magazine in the U.S. In the mid-19th century, Marache was a leading chess player as well as one of America's first chess journalists. In 1866 he published *Marache's Manual of Chess*, one of the country's first books on chess. Included in this manual were rules and strategies for the game of backgammon.

Marache corresponded with C. F. Martin from at least 1863 and continued to do so until just a few several months before his death on May 11, 1875.

Marache purchased at least five Martin guitars over the years. In 1864 he bought two 0-24 guitars. One had ivory pegs and was kept by Marache for his own

Figure 394
Photograph of Napoleon Marache

use while the second had ebony pegs and was supplied to his friend, a certain Mr. Elverson. It is most unusual that no price was recorded in the day book for these two guitars so it is possible they were presentation guitars. He purchased a third guitar in 1864 but the model was not recorded, although he paid $35 for it. Marache purchased a 2-34 with ivory pegs in 1874, which should be easy to identify because it was the only 2-34 made with ivory pegs after the formation of C. F. Martin & Co. in 1867. His last purchase was a 2½-20 with ivory pegs that he bought in 1875 for his niece that was the subject of several letters to Martin. Not only were the ivory pegs an unusual option for a plain guitar but it was the very last 2½-20 ever made!

The fact that Martin sold directly to Marache is notable in itself, as Martin rarely made retail sales to customers.

Jackie "Kid" Moore

Jackie "Kid" Moore was a twelve year old cowboy singer in 1934 when he ordered a very famous guitar, the second D-45 guitar, a D-45S to be exact, ever made!

Moore began by performing in Milwaukee bars but had a meteoric rise in fame and even reportedly gave guitar lessons to Gene Autry, the owner of the first

D-45. Unfortunately, Moore had a lamentably short career that ended when his voice changed.

The story of Moore's D-45 guitar is very interesting and a miscommunication resulted in the guitar being changed from a 14-fret to a 12-fret body part way through construction! The 14-fret body was already partially completed and would be saved and used for the unique 1935 D-42S guitar! (See section on Tex Fletcher, the owner of the D-42S.)

On January 30, 1934 the Rudolph Wurlitzer Co. in Milwaukee began a correspondence with Martin for a special D-45:

"Jackie 'Kid' Moore, is quite a theatrical celebrity in Milwaukee, using a $210.00 Gibson Guitar. I am pretty sure that we can take this Gibson in on the Dreadnaught which we have in stock. However, he wants the fingerboard to be covered with pearl with his name on it in large letters just like his present instrument.

If we can make the deal, will you put the pearl on the fingerboard with his name on it?"

Martin replied on February 1:

"We are sorry to say that we are not in a position to furnish an all-pearl Guitar fingerboard, but we could arrange to furnish a special Ebony finger-board with large letters inlaid in genuine pearl. The cost of this inlaying is about one dollar net for each letter and if it must be done on a finished Guitar there is a charge of five dollars net for taking off the old fingerboard and putting on the new one.

This makes it rather impractical for your deal with Mr. Moore but you might keep it in mind for the future when you have such a request. In our own opinion the cost of the work is higher than the results justify and we usually advise against it when our opinion is asked".

So it can be seen that at first the addition of pearl letters was contemplated to be put on a Dreadnought guitar that Wurlitzer had in stock, probably a D-28. Wurlitzer continued the correspondence on February 5:

"Thank you for your letter of Feb. 1st, regarding the Dreadnaught Guitar that we are trying to sell to Jackie 'Kid' Moore. It is satisfactory to have the ebony fingerboard with the letters inlaid in pearl. However, this boy wants the instrument to have a lot of 'flash' and eve though we advised against it, he insists that we have an instruments made up for him with pearl around the body to give it a lost of 'flash'.

He has reference to something that gives a tinsel appearance. Will you do this?

We are very anxious to make a deal with this boy, because we are satisfied that we will get a lot of Martin business if we are successful in selling him one."

Martin replied again on February 7:

"It is not at all unusual for a prominent Guitarist such as your prospective customer, Jackie 'Kid' Moore, to urge the use of flash ornament on a Guitar but we have consistently stood out against this practice because it has a tendency to interfere with the tone of the instrument and to detract from the fine dignity that is characteristic of Martin designs.

Our Style 45 Guitar is bordered with pearl along all edges and there is a good deal of inlaid pearl in the fingerboard and head, making a very beautiful instrument, and we would suggest this for Mr. Moore's personal use.

We would not care to add any tinsel ornament or imitation inlay to this Guitar but we could have Mr. Moore's name inlaid in the fingerboard as suggested in your previous letter. Such a Guitar, including the inlaid fingerboard, in the Dreadnaught model would be a D-45. The list price would be $215.00, delivery in about three weeks after receipt of the order."

The next letter from Wurlitzer was written on March 27, 1934:

"Sometime ago I wrote you about making up a special Dreadnaught for Jackie 'Kid' Moore. You gave me a price of $215.00 for a special made instrument with pearl on the top. I think that I will close

this deal Saturday.

I have been keeping my price higher than what you gave me because of a Gibson trade-in. I don't know why they are putting this deal off until Saturday, but there is a thought in my mind that they might be dealing with a competitor for a better price. If they should be, you would naturally hear about it because of it being a special made Guitar, and I would like you to protect me on this deal. The entire deal is going to amount to $310.00 including the case and name on the fingerboard, with a $105.00 allowance for his Gibson.

Jackie's father has promised me the deal for sure, Saturday, but if anyone else had written you about the matter, I would appreciated anything you can do to help me."

Martin replied on March 31:

"We are glad to hear that you are making good progress on the sale of a special Dreadnaught Model Guitar to Jackie 'Kid' Moore. No one else has inquired about this particular deal and if we should get an inquiry we would keep in mind the work you have done on it as outlined in your letter."

Wurlitzer followed up with a letter on April 11:

"We have hit a 'snag' in the Jackie 'Kid' Moore deal. Our competitor, Flanner-Hafsoos, told him that he can get him the same instrument and is allowing him $50.00 more for the trade-in than we are. We do not want to lose this deal, but at the same time, will not sacrifice $50.00 to get it. You know yourself that Flanner-Hafsoos push Gibson and Epiphone almost exclusively, Gibson preferred. They carry one or two Martins and Vegas in stock as a sale argument to let customers know they handle all makes of Guitars.

I understand that Mr. Nemick of Flanner-Hafsoos has written you regarding a Guitar for Jackie 'Kid' Moore, but as yet had not received an answer.
Considering the fact that we are doing a fairly good job on Martins and that we are going to push them stronger than ever, handling them exclusive-ly, with the exception of a few cheaper Guitars for lead business, don't you think there is a possibility of our having the Martin agency exclusively, in Milwaukee?"

Martin had indeed received an inquiry from Flanner-Hafsoos but wrote them to explain the situation. Flanner-Hafsoos penned a reply to Martin on April 13, 1934:

"In reply to your letter of April 11th we were un-aware that Jackie 'Kid' Moore had been figuring with the Wurlitzer firm on the same type of guitar.

We sold this young man his first guitar, and now he wants something more elaborate and high grade and what were we to do but try to get the deal.

Inasmuch as Wurlitzer has been working on this deal and it is a special order, we feel perfectly willing yo let the matter drop as far as we are concerned."

Martin passed on this information to Wurlitzer on April 16 and received the following letter from Wurlitzer on April 23:

"We have obtained the Jackie 'Kid' Moore guitar deal. The specifications are as follows: Special D-28 Dreadnaught Guitar with top to have the same specifications as the orchestra model Style 45.

The tuning machines are to be gold plated. The gear pegs are to be covered with Mother of Pearl. The word "Martin" which ordinarily is in golf leaf on the top of the neck is to be in Mother of Pearl. The neck is to be the same width as the orchestra model OM28 Guitar.

The finger board is to be of black ebony with the name JACKIE "KID" MOORE inlaid on the ebony finger board with pearl. The attached photograph which shows this boy with his Gibson guitar will give you an idea as to how the name was put on the Gibson. However, the Gibson had a pearl fingerboard with dark lettering whereas the Martin is to be just the opposite. The frets are to be nickel plated.

The top of the guitar is to be light just like the

Style 45 with the exception that Mr. Moore would like to have a thin layer of pearl around the guard plate.

On one of Gene Autry's Martin Guitars, he has a layer of pearl next to the Ivaroid (sic) on top of the neck. Mr. Moore would like this feature also. He would also like a secret serial number in the guitar in addition to the regular serial number. Both numbers are to be the same, of course, but one number is to be put on the side of piece going across the bottom of the guitar directly underneath the sound hole. You will only be able to read this serial number with a looking glass.

Mr. Moore wants red silk plush lining in a Style D case.

A lot of time and expense was spent to get this deal and inasmuch as several Gibson guitars have been sold because the boy use one, I am positive that you, as well as we, will benefit greatly from this sale. We realize that were are asking for many special things in this order but at the same time we were not able to get a very profitable deal because of this trade-in."

Martin responded on April 30:

"We have studied carefully the specifications for the special Dreadnaught Guitar you have sold to Jackie 'Kid' Moore. All the special features you mention are quite practical except the pearl border around the pick guard. Both the Spruce top and the celluloid guardplate are too thin to permit inlaying pearl. In all other respects we can make the Guitar exactly as specified for delivery about three weeks after we receive the necessary confirmation from Cincinnati; the price for this Guitar will be seventy-five dollars net and for a special red silk plush lined case, fifteen dollars net, or ninety dollars for the outfit.

Actually this will be a Special D-45 rather than a D-28 because it will be just like Style 45 except or the pearl inlay on the back and sides. The special features mention are all standard on Style 45 except the name inlaid in the fingerboard and th pearl inlay around the neck head. These two items alone just about equal the saving we will have in

omitting the pearl on the back and sides.

We are prepared to go ahead with this Guitar as (soon as) we receive the confirmation".

The correspondence from Wurlitzer continued on May 2:

"In answer to you letter of April 30th regarding the Special Dreadnaught Guitar for Jackie 'Kid' Moore, it is satisfactory for you to go ahead with the instructions even though we cannot have the pearl inlaying around the celluloid pick guard.

You state in your letter that this guitar will be called a D-45 rather than a D-28 because it will be just like the Style 45 except for the pearl inlay on the back and side. This customer wants that feature. I forgot to mention that in the original specifications but as he has seen the Style 45 and told me he wanted all those features.

When you mention that it will be called a D-45 instead of a D-28, you make me think that I may not have made myself clear regarding the shape of the body of this guitar. In the event that I did not make myself clear; the body of the guitar is to be shaped exactly like the Dreadnaught except that it is to have the features of the D-45.

P. S. The customer has partially changed his mind about the color of the top. He doesn't know for sure whether he wants a light or a dark top and wants you to use the one which you think will show up the best with the pearl etc."

Martin acknowledged receipt of the order on May 5:

"In accordance with your letter of May first we are booking your order for a Dreadnaught Guitar Style D-45 and work on it will be started right away. Your specifications are entirely clear both as to the shape and size of the Guitar and as to the details of special ornamentation.

Since your customer wants all of the Style 45 inlay the price of the Guitar will be as quoted originally, $215.00 list, and we will make the case $35.00 list, or $250.00 for the outfit.

You can rest assured that this special job will have the writer's personal attention."

Martin did book the order for a D-45 on May 5. Shop order 605 was created for the guitar and the guitar was stamped on May 8. Serial number 56287 was assigned to the guitar.

Wurlitzer encountered a problem and communicated with Martin on May 7:

"Jackie 'Kid' Moore was in the store Saturday and looked at the new Dreadnaught which we received from you several days ago. He notices that this new Dreadnaught had 14 frets instead of 12 and also that it was smaller than the 12 fret model which he traded some time ago.

We would prefer the 12 fret made up the same, as to size, like the old one."

Martin replied to this unwelcome news on May 9:

"The special Guitar for Jackie 'Kid' Moore has already been glued up so it is really too late to change it to the twelve-fret model as suggested in your letter of May 7th.

Nothing was said about the length of the neck of this Guitar but we assumed that you would want the latest model with fourteen frets clear of the body. We now make all our Dreadnaught Guitars that way, in fact we have done so for several months and we surely thought this was the model you were inquiring about, although we still make the twelve-fret model in special order and it would have been just as easy to make this one that way. It is now too late to change. It may be, however, that your customer has his mind set this so we will hold up the work until we hear further from you. If you want us to go ahead as we have started, let us know promptly."

Wurlitzer clarified everything in a letter dated May 14, 1934:

"When we placed Jackie 'Kid' Moore's order and gave you specifications, we did not know that you made the Dreadnaught with 14 frets. In fact, about a year ago when we sold a Dreadnaught to

Dr. Minor, we wrote asking if you would make it with 14 frets and your reply was 'No'.

It was not until after the specifications for Moore's guitar was sent in that we received two new Dreadnaught instruments from you both having 14 frets. We did not notice then that there were 14 frets until our customer tried one and (we are loaning him a Dreadnaught until his comes in) he noticed it was smaller because he was able to put it in his Gibson case and the first Dreadnaught he tried, which was four or five months ago, did not even begin to go in this case.

When I wrote the letter asking if you had started work on the guitar I felt that there was a slight possibility of changing his mind, if you had. I left town on the 9th, the day your letter was written, returning this morning finding your letter. I went out to see the customer but had to wait until school was out. I could not possibly change his mind to accept a 14 fret instrument. Upon returning to the store I found a telegram had been sent to you to the effect that you were to go ahead with the 14 fret instrument.

I regret this mix-up very much but as explained above, I naturally, took it for granted that the instruments would come with 12 frets and inasmuch as 14 frets is standard now, you, naturally, thought he would want 14 frets. I sincerely hope, Mr Martin, that this change will not cause you a great deal of inconvenience and you can rest assured that we will be very careful in any special orders in the future."

Martin replied on May 16 to assure Wurlitzer that Moore's desires would be followed:

"In response to your telegram and letter we have arranged to make up another special D-45 Dreadnaught Guitar in the old model with 12 frets clear of the body. The work will be started promptly and we expect to finish it in about three weeks."

Martin created a new shop order, 611, for a D-45S 12-fret guitar and assigned it serial number 56394. The guitar was on May 18, 1934 and was shipped on June 8.

Figure 395
Jackie "Kid " Moore and His D-45S Guitar

Vahdah Olcott-Bickford (1885-1980)

Vahdah Olcott-Bickford will forever be associated in Martin lore with Style 44 guitars. However, she was also a well known concert artist and teacher and founded the American Guitar Society in 1923.

Ethel Lucretia Olcott was born on October 17, 1885 in Norwalk, Ohio. She moved with her parents to Los Angeles when she was three years old. She started taking lessons at the age of eight with the well-known classic guitarist George Lindsay. She lived with Manuel Y. Ferrer in Berkeley from 1903 to 1904 and expanded her repertoire to include European classical guitar music. She moved to New York in 1914, where she engaged in giving concerts and teaching.

In 1915, she married Myron Bickford, a well-known mandolin artist. When Ethel changed her name to Vahdah her husband Myron changed his name to Zarh.

Olcott-Bickford returned to Los Angeles in 1923 and,

with other local guitarists, started the Los Angeles Guitar Society, later becoming the American Guitar Society (AGS). She was a major contributor to the AGS and was the secretary and Musical Director of the AGS for many years.

Zarh Bickford passed away in the 1961. She later married Robert Revere, changing her name to Vahdah Olcott-Bickford Revere. Olcott-Bickford continued to play guitar and was associated with the AGS until her death in 1980.

A number of early photos show Olcott-Bickford and her students playing Style 42 Martin guitars with ivory bridges (indicating these guitars were made before 1920).

There is almost no correspondence from Olcott-Bickford in the Martin archive between 1898 and 1922. One of the few exceptions is a 1916 letter written by Olcott-Bickford to a guitar player who requested information on the kind of guitar she played. Olcott-Bickford not only mentioned she played Martin guitars but also highly recommended Martin guitars in general.

On February 6, 1922 Martin wrote a letter to Charles Ditson & Co. concerning some style 44 guitars about to be completed:

"In about 10 days we will have ready to send you a Soloist Guitar to fill your order for an instrument of this style to be supplied to you "in the white", finishing to be done by your expert.

With this instrument we built a companion because of the advantage in building two at a time and will hold the extra for your order. Perhaps you would like to have them both now.

A few days ago we tested both instruments and found them very satisfactory in tone, both as to quality and volume. We feel sure Mrs. Bickford will be well pleased with them."

Ditson replied the next day and took both instruments.

Martin also wrote an interesting letter to Vahdah Olcott-Bickford on February 7:

"I have considered your letter but will have to write twice to answer it in full. The time will be needed to get our ad ready for your program and to see whether we can device some sort of plan for the head of your Guitars. The name is rather long and the original style had only the word "Soloist" but perhaps we can think out something. If not, it will fall to Mr. Hunt to get it painted in or to have a metal plate made.

It is gratifying to hear that you are getting orders already, in advance of the first example.

We, here, are really interested in one thing above all others – to make good Guitars. Regular style or special style, a small number or a large number, nothing counts except to see that it is a good Guitar. These that are being built for you will have the benefit of all our knowledge, always admitting that wood is not certain and we are never able to promise that one Guitar will sound just like another.

Figure 396
Photograph from 1923 meeting of the American Guitar Society, Vahdah Olcott-Bickford standing at far right

Your style will have Ebony Pegs. We found it not practicable to make Ivory at this time and celluloid is not very nice and I believe is apt to stick, Ebony is standard material on Violins and we have used it on Guitars and know it will answer nicely."

Martin reported to Ditson on the same day:

"Mrs. Bickford has written us asking to have her name inlaid on the back of the special Guitars now being made for her. In reply we have just told her that the plan will be considered, but the name is rather long and we are not sure we can do anything. In that case, Guitars will be sent without it and it will fall to you to have the name painted on or a plate made, or whatever you may decide on with Mrs. Bickford."

Ditson made an interesting reply on February 9:

"Replying to your letter of the 7th inst., in reference to Mrs. Bickford's name on the Guitars, would say that she has already approached us and we have had an artist draw us up a design which will be made in decalomania, the same as the gilt is put on in piano keyboards.

This will be put on under the varnish so that it will receive good protection and, also, look very neat. Therefore, you may cease to worry on this point."

See pages 161 to 163 for more information on Olcott-Bickford Style 44 Guitars (1914-1938).

Jimmie Rodgers (1897-1933)

Another musical celebrity that Martin corresponded with was Jimmie Rodgers, the famous country singer, who was also popularly known as "The Singing Brakeman" or "The Blue Yodeler".

James Charles "Jimmie" Rodgers was born on September 8, 1897 at either Pine Springs, Mississippi or Geiger, Alabama, there still being some question as to which is correct. Jimmie began to work for a railroad at a young age, beginning as a water boy and working his way up to brakeman. At the same time he displayed a talent for entertaining and had ample time to learn the guitar from railroad workers and hobos.

Rodgers contracted tuberculosis in 1924, which temporarily ended his railroad career. However, this offered Jimmie the opportunity to try the entertainment industry again. He organized a traveling show and for a time performed across the Southern states. He returned to railroad work but did not keep this job long due to his tuberculosis and settled at Meridian, Mississippi in early 1927.

The year 1927 was the pivotal one for Jimmie Rodgers' performing career. In April of that year he traveled to Asheville, North Carolina to perform on radio station WWNC. In early August 1927 he made his first recordings for Ralph Peer of the Victor Talking Machine Co. in Bristol, Tennessee (later Peer became Jimmie's manager). The first records were released in October that year and enjoyed some modest success so in November recorded four more songs in the Victor studios in Camden, New Jersey, including his first major hit, "Blue Yodel", also known as "T for Texas".

Over the next few years Jimmie Rodgers was very busy performing and recording but his health was failing. Rodgers last recording sessions began on May 17, 1933 and was in a very weakened condition when they ended on May 24. Jimmie Rodgers died on May 26, 1933 of a pulmonary hemorrhage.

Just before his first records were released Jimmie Rodgers wrote to Martin on September 12, 1927 from Washington DC:

"I sent you by Parcel Post Sept. 10 one Martin Guitar. Please repair the busted side and send me C.O.D., also prices on ukes & Guitars. I want to buy some ukes for fair concessions about 3 or 4 hundred. Please let me hear from you at once."

The model number and the serial number of the repaired guitar was not mentioned. A Martin 00-18 guitar once owned by Jimmie Rodgers is in the Country Music Hall of Fame.

Martin replied on September 14, 1927:

"The Guitar referred to in your letter of the 12th arrived yesterday and has been placed in the shop for necessary repairs. We expect to have it finished about October 1st and will return it to you by express, C.O.D., in a new Keratol Plush lined Case, as requested. The price of this case, to members of the profession, is $17.50 net; the same case with fleece lining costs $11.06.

In answer to your request for prices on Ukes, we send our complete catalogue and ask that you kindly call on S. Ernest Philpitt & Son, 1300 G Street, who hold our agency for the city of Washington.

Thank you for your kind words about our instruments."

There must have been another letter, no longer in the Martin archive that is being referred to by Martin. Philpitt didn't order a large quantities at this time so Jimmie Rodgers must have found the price quoted not very attractive. The repaired guitar was shipped on October 3 and was billed at $25.00. Part of this cost was the $17.50 case and the remainder was the repair cost. A repair bill for $7.50 was very high for the peri-

Figure 397
Jimmie Rodgers with His Martin 00-18 Guitar

od and indicates the guitar underwent major repairs.

On June 12, 1928 Jimmie Rodgers placed an order with Martin for a 000-45S (serial number 36112) with "special ornament". The "Special Head and Fingerboard" were delivered to Martin on July 14, 1928 with an invoiced price of $20.00. These items were probably made by the Louis Handel Co. of New York City. The guitar was invoiced and shipped on July 27, 1928. The fingerboard had Jimmie Rodgers' name inlaid in the fingerboard in pearl capital letters. The head stock had "BLUE YODEL", the title of Rodgers' first big hit, inlaid in it in pearl letters.

The fact that Martin allowed Jimmie Rodgers to place an order without going through a dealer is very unusual. The guitar was invoiced at $168.75. The retail price for a regular 000-45 was $170 in 1928. If a $30.00 plush case and the $20 special inlaying were added in the total price should have been at least $207.50, so it appears that Rodgers was allowed a discount of 25%, also very unusual. Maybe this was just a reflection of the meteoric path of Jimmie Rodgers' career and Martin's desire to have their guitars associated with him (as will be seen later Rodgers really loved his Martin guitars). On the other hand, it appears that Martin had developed a friendly relationship with Rodgers in their earlier correspondence, so the discount may have just been a friendly gesture. Regardless, this sort of special treatment had only been accorded to the likes of Madam De Goni, Henry Worrall and William Foden up to this point.

Rodger again wrote to Martin on June 12, 1929:

"Am still using my Martin Guitar. I have heard so much about your new mandolins wish you would send me one of them to San Antonio Texas c/o New Magistic (?) Theatre. I am headlining the Bill there week of 15th if I don't like the one you send me I will send it back and wait till I get to the Factory pick out or have you make me one like I wont (sic). Am building my new home in Kerrville Texas 70 miles South west of San Antonio. Am sending you invitation to the house warming soon as it is completed. If your representative is any where close to me next week I would love to see & talk with him. Am getting along fine but need lots of Rest."

Martin replied on June 17:

Figure 398
Jimmie Rodgers and His Martin 000-45S Guitar

"It is a real pleasure to hear from you again. Evidently you are prospering in your work and enjoying Texas; otherwise, you would not be building a home way down there. It is a big state and the amount of business we do there in several cities is evidence that Texans appreciate and enjoy string instrument music. We certainly wish it were possible for us to sit in on one of your shows in Dallas. Today we are selecting s Style 20 Mandolin which we will ship to you by express in a silk plush lined case. We will be very glad to have you try it our thoroughly and we want you to feel perfectly free to send it back to us if it is not all that you expect. You suggestion that you may be able to pick a better instrument for your self here at the factory is a good one and we want to assure you that we will always be pleased to give you that privilege. We will bill this and case to Mr. Ralph Peer and will notify him in case you return it.

Your kind message to our salesman, Mr. Markley, will be delivered to him when he returns to the factory late next week. He always enjoys meeting you in his travels and we are sure he would be more than pleased to see you in Texas. It is not likely that he will be down there until October or November. When he goes he will try to lay out his trip so that he can have a day to visit you in your new home, if you happen to be there then."

An order for a style 20 mandolin was booked and shipped to Rodgers on the same day.

Jimmie Rodgers acknowledged the receipt of the mandolin on June 22:

"I rec'd the Mandolin in San Antonio and think it is the sweetest thing I ever saw in the way of a mandolin, but it is too small for the purpose I wanted. I understand you are making a big Concert Mandolin that is what I had in mind to use in my Vaudeville work. I had one of my friends to pack and ship back to you. If you have a larger Mandolin in stock, wish you would send me one c/o Orpheum Theatre at New Orleans La. If you haven't I've decided to wait until I can come to the factory, which I expect to be in October some time. I am breaking house records on box office receipts and going along nicely."

This letter prompted a reply from Martin on June 26:

"Your word of praise for the Mandolin we sent you is appreciated and we are sorry it was not large enough for your purpose. The size of the Mandolin is limited by the fact that the scale must not be over thirteen or thirteen and one-half inches so it is not advisable to build a very large body. The Tenor Mandola, which has a longer scale and a lower tuning, is a considerably larger instrument and perhaps it would do for your purpose. We believe, however, that it would be better to allow this matter to rest until you visit us in Fall when we can show you all the different Mandolins we have. At present we have no larger Mandolin than the one we sent you."

On July 4, 1929 Rodgers sent his 000-45S to Martin for repairs:

"I am shipping to you today my Guitar. The Bridge is loose and very hard to keep in tune, please examine for any further defect and repair and return to me early as possible.

I open in Little Rock Ark. July 6 Majestic Theatre, Birmingham Ala. July 13th Ritz Theatre, July 20 Atlanta Ga. Keith Ga. Theatre. After then address me at Kerrville Texas."

Martin wrote back on July 12:

"Today we are shipping your Guitar by pre-paid express to the above address (Ritz Theatre, Birmingham, Alabama). We have re-glued the bridge and the writer has tested the Guitar thoroughly. It seems to be in perfect condition. The neck and fingerboard are absolutely straight and true and the strings seem to us to be properly adjusted both at the nut and at the bridge.

We are sorry the bridge gave you some trouble but we think we have fastened it now so that it will not come loose again and we hope you will find the Guitar as good as new. We will be glad to have a report from you as soon as you have tested it thoroughly."

Martin did not charge Rodgers for this repair work.

Rodgers accommodated Martin's request on July 18, 1929:

"I received my guitar a few days ago in perfect condition.

Many thanks for fixing it up so nice for me. I'm telling the world that I have the best guitar."

Another repair request from Jimmie Rodgers was mailed to Martin on October 17, 1929:

"I am sending you by today's pre-paid express, my Guitar, for repair.

You will please take off the patented keys, and put on keys same as on my Special Guitar, returning same to me when completed, and oblige."

This repair was not needed for a Martin guitar as explained when Martin replied on October 22:

"Your Weymann Guitar came in yesterday afternoon and we will give it our best attention. The gold plated Patent Heads we used on your special Guitar were ordered specially for that instrument and we are placing a duplicate order with the head makers for this Guitar. As soon as they arrive, which should be in a week or ten days, we will fit them on the Guitar. That means that we should have the work finished in not more than three weeks.

We are interested to note that you are spending some time at your home in Kerrville. It happens that our salesman, Mr. Markley, is planning a trip to Texas, leaving here next Monday, October 28th. He is schedules to reach San Antonio on Sunday morning, November ninth, and will remain there until the next afternoon. No doubt he would enjoy visiting you at your home, if you find it convenient to have him. He is planning to stop at the Rice Hotel in Houston November 8th so you can reach him there."

Martin billed Jimmie Rodgers $20.00 for the repair through Ralph Peer on December 13, 1929. This is mostly likely the cost of the repair for Rodgers' fancy Weymann guitar but the delay in billing is not explained.

It is interesting that mention is made of the 000-45S having originally been made with gold-plated tuners and that another set was ordered for use on the fancy Weymann guitar. Neither of these special tuners are recorded separately in the purchasing records so they must have just been included in a shipment with some other regular tuning machines.

No further correspondence with Jimmie Rodgers is in the Martin archive and, as mentioned previously, Rodger passed away on May 26, 1933.

On January 9, 1935 the Southern Literary Institute wrote to Martin announcing the upcoming biographical book on Jimmie Rodgers' life:

"Within a few weeks we shall bring out the book "My Husband, Jimmie Rodgers", by Mrs. Jimmie Rodgers. This book is one of the most unusual and strikingly interesting biographies I have seen in an experience covering more than twenty-five years, most of it spent with the big publishing companies in the East. ...

It will be utterly impossible for interest of this kind to be stimulated without reacting in a most definite manner in favor of every industry represented, and particularly in favor of the guitar manufacturers.

In short, the pushing of this book, in line with the various other companies and groups who are getting behind it, will constitute one of the strong and most effective forms of advertising and publicity you can gain in 1935.

We are not advocating any definitive form of co-operation, leaving that largely to the various companies who, of course, know their own plans and programs far better than we can. Several plans are possible.

One, which seems to be meeting with favor, is that under which the manufacturers, in sending out their regular advertising and literature, include an announcement of this book and urge their distributors and dealers to stock at least a few copies with their regular line. We, of course, will allow them the regular 40 per cent discount. ...

The book will be in two editions; the Regular Edition, which will retail for $2, and the Popular Edition, which will be virtually the same except in the matter of binding and a few minor details, which will retail for $1.25. It is expected that the latter edition will prove the larger seller.

The Special Edition, of which announcement is enclosed, is not expected to run to any great sale and is intended chiefly for the benefit of personal friends and associates of Jimmie Rodger, who will want a book that can be regarded as being somewhat in the nature of a personal tribute to him.

We believe that you will be interested in co-operating in the promotion of this book which, in line with the strong campaign being arranged in its behalf will be bound to benefit your interest directly. ..."

The Southern Literary Institute sent another letter to

Martin on January 19, 1935:

"Portions of the manuscript received since my former letter, however, show that the Martin Guitar is coming in for some mention. Under ordinary circumstances I would edit that out immediately, as I am opposed to such definite mention in a book.

However, we have a peculiar situation, where Jimmie Rodgers and guitars are tangled up all the way through in such a manner that definite mention can be made without giving the book the appearance of being commercialized.

On the other hand, it is highly obvious that such definite mention will make one of the strongest and most effective pieces of publicity you can obtain in 1935, as this book is certain of a wide distribution among exactly the prospective customers it will be most to your advantage to reach, specifically with the virtual O.K. of Jimmie Rodgers attached. Certainly it will be worth considerably more to you than several pages in trade journals, as here you will be reaching the very cream of a list of live prospects.

As I explained before, we are planning a very elaborate publicity campaign in behalf of this book, in which the Victor dealers and many others will participate. Such a campaign calls for money, and the more money we can obtain for use in it, the greater will be the campaign, and the more profitable the results for all concerned.

We are willing to let the Martin Guitar ride into this publicity with the book, but we believe it only fair to ask you to contribute to the publicity campaign an amount equal to the cost of two or three trade journal pages, which could not bring you anywhere nearly as great results. We are asking you to contribute $200, which money will be used for publicity and no other purpose."

Another letter was sent to Martin the same day:

"In my earlier letter to you today I unintentionally failed to quote the passages from "My Husband, Jimmie Rodger" relative to the Martin guitar.

Here they are:

'...somehow the Martin seemed to "fit" better; it was to his Martin that he loved to turn to soothe him through a trying hour. ...to tell the truth it was the Martin he loved; that was his "old guitar" - no matter how many new ones of the same make he owned; the Martin "went into the mike" with Jimmie, whether on the road or in the old church at Camden.'

This was not to say instruments of other makes were not good; it just so happened that he was a bit more fond of his Martin.'

If that, in this particular book, is not worth the full amount of the co-operation I have suggested, and as much more as you can give us, I know nothing at all about the value of publicity."

Martin replied on January 29, 1935:

"Thank you for telling us about the book, "My Husband, Jimmie Rodgers" you are about to publish. We recall clearly the visit Rodgers and Mr. Ralph Peer made here five or six years ago to order a special Guitar, and a little later the writer delivered another Guitar to Rodgers at the Hotel Walt Whitman in Camden. He certainly had an engaging personality which he was able to put across through his records.

Of course we are proud that he used Martin Guitars, although we never offered him any special inducement to do so.

Because of this personal contact with him we would like to have a copy of the Author's Edition for our office library and we are ordering also two copies of the Popular Edition which we intend to hand to our travelling salesmen in the hope that they give the book some publicity in the trade.

As for the use of our name in the book, we appreciate Mrs. Rodgers' sincerity but we fear her words might be misconstrued and we would not want her to be suspected of including paid publicity in her book. Of course, it is for her to say whether she wishes to mention our name or not but we do not care to pay anything for this purpose."

Curiously, this was not the end of the correspondence.

Southern Literary Institute was most persistent in getting Martin to pay money to help the "publicity campaign" of the book and wrote several more letters to the company. The issue was finally laid to rest when Martin wrote them on June 24, 1935:

"We have considered your offer to publicize the Martin Guitar in the second edition of My Husband, Jimmie Rodgers at a net price of one hundred dollar. While this would seem to be a reasonable price, we really are not interested at all in publicity of this kind; in fact, we would be just as well pleased if our name is not mentioned in subsequent editions of the book. This is not meant unkindly, only expressing our personal views in the matter of advertising publicity.

We are glad to hear that the book has had a good sale and we wish to congratulate you and Mrs. Rodgers on its success."

Luis T. Romero (1854-1893)

Today little is known of Luis Romero but during his lifetime he was considered to be in the first rank of 19th century American guitar virtuosos. The Martin Guitar Co. Archive contains a remarkably large number of letters related to the last few years of Romero's life, when he was at the pinnacle of his lamentably short career. Romero featured prominently in Martin's correspondence with E. S. Sanford and C. A. Zoebisch between 1889 and 1893. Edward S. Sanford was an agent for the Adams Express Co. in New York with the income and taste to indulge an interest in the guitar and the contemporary players of the time. Sanford was also an amateur guitarist and friend of both Romero and Charles de Janon. Sanford provided most of the commentary on Romero's career but Romero also wrote Martin directly and C. A. Zoebisch even offered some comments on Romero's business practices. These letters that will be quoted extensively in the text below and contain many interesting observations on musical culture and the music business at the time.

Romero was born in San Luis Obispo, California, of immigrant Spanish parents, in 1854. As a boy he played the guitar and when he moved to Los Angeles, studied with Miguel S. Arrevalo, the noted Mexican guitarist, teacher, composer and singer who taught in Los Angeles from 1871. Later, he moved to San Jose,

California to perform and teach and here also began to publish musical works. Romero was teaching mandolin, as well as guitar, in California by 1885 and formed a mandolin club with Samuel Adelstein in 1887[61]. He subsequently moved to Boston about 1889 and established a teaching practice while at the same time continuing his concert career. He was a guest soloist in at least three concerts in New York.

Figure 399
Signed Photograph of Luis T. Romero

He appeared in a "Banjo and Guitar Concert" on January 25, 1890 that also included the banjo clubs of Stevens Institute and Columbia College, another concert held on January 8, 1890 and again on April 13, 1891 in a "Banjo, Mandolin and Guitar Concert" sponsored by the instrument clubs of Princeton, Columbia, Haverford and Brown University. Romero's original and arranged works were published by Clark Wise of Oakland, Oliver Ditson Co. of Boston and Jean White Publishing Co. of Boston.

He died prematurely of pulmonary tuberculosis in Boston on November 19, 1893.

The letters quoted below expand further on the commentary on Romero seen in the "C. F. Martin and the Classical Guitar" section on page 242.

On June 18,1889 Sanford first wrote to Martin about Romero:

"I have just spent half an hour with Signor Romero, Lyon & Healy's Washburn guitar man. He and de Janon have been playing for each other. It was worth listening to you can be sure but what interests you most is that Romero owns and plays only upon a Martin and said he would give $75.00 for the 'tub' as De Janon and I call my 00. I did not take it."

Figure 400
Luis T. Romero Arrangements for Guitar
Published by Clark Wise in 1889

Sanford followed up with another interesting letter on July 30, 1889:

"Romero that I spoke to you of as a "Washburn" man is it seems a "Martin" (man) to the back-bone and (don't tell de Janon) the best player I have ever heard.

We entertained him at my mother's home in 53rd St. and amongst the guests was Post of Lyon & Healy (Washburn).

When the show was over Post said to Jim Phipps of W. A. Pond & Co. "by Jimminy Krickets Phipps that's a Martin crowd I got into". We had Romero's guitar, de Janon's and my 00 and we amused themselves by calling them cheap Washburns."

So, players loving their Martin guitars is nothing new, even 130 years ago.

Sanford next letter to Martin on mailed on September 17, 1889:

"The 0-28 you sent to Pond at the same times you sent the 1-21 was such a superior instrument in every way that I took it in place of the 1-21 and both de Janon and Romero consider it superior to theirs'. The machine head us a draw back but in ten years when it begins to rattle my bones may be dust."

This letter illustrates the bias that many players had at the time against mechanical tuners. It can be assumed Sanford, De Janon and Romero mostly used Martin guitars with friction pegs.

In a letter dated December 4, 1889, Sanford wrote to Martin about Romero's preference for Martin strings and the date of an up-coming concert:

"Romero writes from Boston to get him a supply of silver strings. I gave him half of the last consignment you sent me and he says they are the best strings he ever used. He has an 0-28 (C. F. Martin & Co.) and tunes the E to D so you can give him very heavy strings(s). The D's you sent me are fine but as I am not as particular as Romero, who when one string wears out puts on an entire new set, so mine are not yet gone. Send $2.00 worth by mail and I will forward them to him....

Jany 25th 1890 a Banjo and Guitar concert will be held at Chickering Hall N. Y. Romero comes from Boston to play at it and I am sure the guitar will get a boom that it has been waiting for years. Charlie de Janon will not play in public and to have a man like Romero is a great benefit to the guitar."

Sanford wrote to Martin December 7, 1889 further emphasizing that Romero was using Martin guitars:

"Romero plays neither in public or private upon anything but a Martin, not does anyone else who has any reputation at stake. I know what you will say about the Lyon & H. Souvenir...

He was introduced to me as a Lyon & Healy man but I found out shortly that was not true."

On January 21, 1890 Sanford wrote to Martin with further comments on the concert to take place on January 25:

"The 'cranks' are coming from every direction to hear Romero and I hope that amongst the 1,500 banjoists that will be assembled we may induce 1,000 to take up the guitar. Romero will play 'Rigoletto' with as many encores as N. Y. wants for his first number. His selection is the 'quartette' from that opera and he plays it 'like a dream'.

His second number will be a selection if he ever gets to it, for I am afraid the encores of the first may carry him over to Monday A. M.

Charley de Janon is the only man I knew to play the guitar until I met Romero (de J. is nowhere)."

F. H. Martin attended the concert but Sanford still communicated his disappointment in the concert on February 3, 1890:

"I have heard that you enjoyed the concert. I did not. It was the most lamentable failure as far as Romero was concerned as we can imagine. The acoustic effect of the Hall is not favorable to the guitar."

Sanford offered more comments in a letter on February 6, 1890:

"I am glad that you were able to appreciate that which our friend Romero was doing. I had heard him play "Rigoletto" fifty times and I can assure you that where I sat I could not tell if he were playing it or something else....

I went to Zoebisch & Co. yesterday, the 00-28 is a daisy. If you run against (sic) a particularly fine one, that plays very easily I will take it provided I have not an 0-28 in the mean time. I have written

Romero that you have at last turned out a 00 with a good treble and I hope you will continue to improve upon it. My eye tells me that you have made the instrument more shallow and there is a small divergence of model on the deck.

I want a peg-head but will sacrifice that desire to get one just right."

Romero also corresponded directly with Martin. The following is from a letter he sent Martin on February 15, 1890:

"I suppose you remember the guitar Mr. Sanford was trying at Wm Pond's on the 25th of last month. I bought the same for a pupil. Could you send me another only larger and what would be the cost for me.

I want ivory bound all around even the head and pegs of course.

If you have non(e) ready, please have two or three made that I am sure to dispose of them.

Remember they must be one size smaller than concert size and larger than ladies size."

Martin must have promptly replied to Romero as Romero sent this reply on February 20, 1890:

"Your favor of 18th on hand and thank you for your promptness.

In regard to guitar you can make it 1-26 that being size smaller than concert, is it not?

If you will let me know how long it will take you to make it. It might be I want two or three - you can have ivory head and charge the extra.

Hoping you will send strings soon and price of the guitar with discount."

Clearly C. A. Zoebisch must have been aware of the letter Romero sent Martin on February 15 (but not the one from the 20th) when he spelled out his much different opinion of Romero in a letter dated February 20, 1890:

"Your favor of 18th duly rec'd & contents noted - Romero is like all such players & teachers, never can be satisfied & sneak around. He was several times in store, we treated him very nice & kindly, also called last year before he went to Europe & said he wanted one of these days a very fine Guitar for a Lady - also when he came here last he said he would see that same of his Salidars, would get new Martin Guitar & would send the orders or have the order sent to me.

Now he writes up to you too, just tell him to send us his order & explain what he wants & you would follow his instructions in making the Guitar - of course if it is for him I will confidentially do something extra for him in the shape of a present, not (illegible) as we done with some other noted player, in fact twice gone a concert night out.

This teacher business brings us all the time between two fires, they want to have in fact dealers' rate and ignore dealers & be able to say I can buy as cheap as you can, and of course this won't do if we go in for that style of business we would soon be left severely alone by the dealers, and they are the parties whom we have to have to work for & keep your Guitar in Front. Inside a month I would trouble in Boston with this Romero business. I am working hard against" Bay State", "Tilton", "Washburn", "Imperial" & "Orion" in Boston, all made & sold there, except the Washburn is Lyon & Healy, whenever I get a chance & Romero said he will recommend them (the Martins) they get him up there & he is not altogether free to act quite openly, but he will do justice I think. I have now to send a 1/21 and a 0/28 of course to dealers and if Romero can sell guitars he knows he can get them there or order them of us, or through our customers in Boston of (illegible) & make his arrangements with them if he prefers. We must do the business open and square so that we can (illegible) for all transactions otherwise we make enemies out of Dealers and that we can not afford, as many Guitars are now in market to be shown & worked & talked up against ours."

The two things guaranteed to raise Zoebisch's ire was a performer or teacher trying to get the dealers' discount or trying to deal directly with the factory, these were on-going themes in the C. A. Zoebisch correspondence and very often repeated. Martin was in the midst of a significant growth of sales and Zoebisch was at the peak of his influence with Martin. On the other hand, Zoebisch's comments above on business are appropriate for the time. From today's perspective, Martin guitars are more commonly seen than examples from other competitors. It is not always appreciated just how competitive the instrument market was during the 1890's, being dominated by industrialization and mass marketing. Of the competitors mentioned by Zoebisch, only Washburn, Bay State and Tilton might be recognizable to modern collectors, the other names having faded with time.

Romero wrote again to Martin on February 27, 1890:

"Enclosed Postal Note for strings you sent me and hope you will pardon my not doing so before as I have been sick.

I shall wait for guitar in five weeks and hope Mr. Zoebisch will be liveraly (sic, should be 'liberal') in his discount."

Clearly, Zoebisch had won the battle and Romero had to place his guitar order through Zoebisch.

On April 25, 1890 Sanford wrote to Martin again:

"Romero's health being poor, the Dr's have advised him to "change the air" and he is coming to my house a week from Saturday May 3rd. Is there any chance of my having my guitar by that time. Mr. Zoebisch told me the other day that it would be done about that time."

Happily, Sanford received his new 00-28 guitar on time as he reported in a letter dated May 8, 1890:

"I took a day off with Romero to try the new guitar. It's a daisy.

Romero is delighted with it, but as it completely hides his face when plays on it he says 0-28 is large enough for him.

The treble is excellent and I would have note that it is of great power both in treble and bass with the strings low.

Mr. Romero said yesterday that he never seen a Martin with low strings that was not an extraordinary instrument and calls my attention to the effect of the slide on a high and a low instrument."

Zoebisch continued to have issues with Romero wrote Martin on June 14, 1892 about Romero not paying for a guitar:

"Just came to my mind. Romero has not yet paid for that guitar. Practically think he will not pay for it, I always had an idea he wanted it for nothing when he all at once wrote to you direct, I will wait yet a while then write him again."

Zoebisch wrote to Martin on September 27, 1892:

"That sneak Romero hasn't paid up yet & presume he never will."

Zoebisch wrote Martin on October 29, 1892:

"Of course it won't do to offend Romero, but the fellow is (illegible) greedy & seems is not satisfied that he makes money with teaching & the good Commission he gets from Boston Stores when he sells Guitars."

Whatever Zoebisch felt about Romero, he used his name in the Martin advertisements in the Music Trade Review magazine from 1893 until 1898[62].

Roy Smeck (1900-1994)

Leroy (Roy) George Smeck was an American instrumental musician who became a major Vaudeville, radio and recording star as well as a pioneer sound movie performer. Smeck was promoted as the "Wizard of the Strings" for his skill playing the ukulele, banjo, guitar and steel guitar.

Smeck was born on February 6, 1900 in Reading, Pennsylvania. His military records from 1918 show he was living with his mother in Binghamton, New York and was employed as a shoe maker. Not much else is known about Smeck's early life but some details were provided in a 1934 newspaper article[63]:

"Roy Smeck worked in a shoe factory long before he dreamed of holding the spotlight at Loew's

Fox or any other theater. The insistent beat of hammers sounded in his ears; rhythmic, varied in tempo, by no means musical. But young Mr. Smeck liked music. His father gave him a guitar and taught him three chords, all that he knew. Roy, aged 15, practiced at home, slipped the guitar to work and practiced some more when he could sneak a few moments on the side. One day his boss caught Roy strumming the guitar in a very peculiar place. He was fired.

Like an arrow from a bow and unable by any will of its own to change the course, he gravitated into a music store, got a job as a clerk. When he had learned the tricks of his clerkship routine, he began to lift every available phonograph record with banjo, guitar or ukulele instrumentation, disappear into booths and practice - with the ukulele. He found it possible to learn the pieces by ear. His boss also found the wear and tear on records terrific, and began deducting so much from Roy's salary every week that on Saturdays the uke student had more new numbers than dollars.

Equipped with more virtuosity than knowledge, Smeck found a place in a stage orchestra. The boys all around him read their notes, worked arduously on elaborate arrangements of popular tunes, while he 'faked' along blithely and convincingly. Next he drifted into the Paul Sprecht Band when that maestro was in his hey day, and thereafter into vaudeville.

One of the Warner brothers heard him one night in a New York house and sent word he could be used in a new-fangled stunt called talking pictures. The Warners were making a talkie with Martinelli, Marion Talley, Mischa Elman, and thought they might include Smeck to prove the range of their sound recordings. Smeck's part of the film was a hit.

He accumulated a great variety of instruments - the banjo, Hawaiian guitar (which is quite a different proposition from the from the usual type, requiring one to manipulate a single piece of steel in place of five fingers) and even the harmonica. Smeck already knew something about the harmonica. Once when he was working with it he absently picked up his ukulele, played both at the same

time. He has been doing it ever since, but the harmonica portion of his act is something of a trial. Hard on the lungs and diaphragm.

In a later talking picture, there was a 'Smeck Quartette'. He played harmonized parts on four instruments, and the technicians combined them so that he appeared quadrupled on the screen, and all the instruments were heard at once[64].

The 'Bill Robinson tap dance', best applause winner in the present act, and a really remarkable achievement in imitation, sprang into existence one evening when Smeck was listening to Robinson's hoofing via radio. He heard, remembered, and did it himself with his finger and ukulele sounding board. Memory is his strong point. He could sit down tomorrow and play you a hundred tunes without a sheet of music in sight. But he carries with him a skilled composer, who writes down what Smeck knows. Together they have produced the instruction books, Smeck banjoes, Smeck picts and all that."

Smeck could not sing well, so he developed trick playing (e.g., exaggerated playing style, string tapping, etc.), to offset for this weakness in his act[65].

The newspaper article above mentions he played with the Paul Sprecht Band. This must have been before 1922 as the band went on tour to the UK that year. Also, he does not appear in any of the photographs of the band from the early 1920's. It appears Smeck had launched his own Vaudeville career by at least 1922.

Martin became aware of Smeck very early in his career because he ordered a Ditson D-111 Dreadnought guitar through Charles H. Ditson & Co. in 1923. Martin booked the order on July 7, 1923 but sent a letter to Ditson requesting some more details before starting production of the instrument. Henry Hunt himself replied on a letter dated July 12:

"Replying to your letter of the 9th inst., would say that we desire the dark finish on face and all. (Dark mahogany finish.)"

The guitar was not shipped until December 22, 1923. Based on its position in the serial number sequence (serial number 19734), it does not appear that the guitar was even put into production until late November that year.

The order of this Ditson Dreadnought for Roy Smeck caused a minor rift between Martin and Ditson that almost resulted in the end of the Dreadnought model!

On January 23, 1924 Ditson attempted to order another Dreadnought to be made just like the one for Smeck. Martin wrote to Ditson on January 25:

"Thank you for your order of January 23rd; however, before booking we wish to call this matter to your attention, that on the last order of this kind, that is the instrument made up for Roy Smeck in December, we found no profit for ourselves. Would you consider it advisable to order at least half a dozen at one time? If not, we will have to quote an somewhat higher price on this single order."

Henry Hunt responded on January 29:

"Replying to your letter of the 25th inst., in reference to the guitar made up for Mr. Smeck, beg to say that we would like to order these in half-dozen lots if we had sale for them.

We need one more for a special order. Unless there is a demand for these instruments, we will retire them, therefore, would kindly ask you to make the instrument and charge us the price that you think will cover your trouble and show profit for yourself.

There are one or two Vaudeville players who insist on this sort of an instrument and if we find that there is enough of them, we do not mind ordering them in half-dozen lots but, at present, we are undecided."

Again, there as a delay and Martin did not put this guitar (serial number 20306) into production until March 14, 1924, although it was shipped on April 24. Martin had charged Ditson $21 for the Roy Smeck Dreadnought but increased the wholesale price to $25 for the follow up order. Ditson continued to make individual orders for Dreadnought guitars until 1926 and only, at that point, increased the order quantity to two Dreadnought guitars per order.

When Warner Brothers released the talkie film "Don Juan" in 1926 using the Vitaphone sound system the program also included a short Vitaphone film, "His Pastimes", starring Roy Smeck. Smeck was already enjoying a very successful Vaudeville career but his appearance in this film made him a major radio and Vaudeville star. He also appeared in several films in the early 1930's.

On August 30, 1929 Roy Smeck visited the Martin factory and selected a 2-28T guitar and a ukulele 1 for his use. Martin shipped both instruments to Smeck but booked the order through Ditson on September 6, 1929.

This impromptu visit also had a passing connection with the first OM-28 guitar. In a letter to Perry Bechtel dated September 3, 1929 Martin wrote:

"By good fortune we were able to have your Guitar tried out by Mr. Roy Smeck who paid us an unexpected visit, accompanied by Mrs. Smeck, on Friday. He liked the Guitar very much and seemed to think you were farsighted in having it made up. He expressed his desire to a have a similar Guitar for his own use at a later date."

Martin wrote a very interesting letter to Smeck on September 4 as a result of his recent visit to the factory:

"Your tenor guitar is ready to ship; but the ukulele had to have the head refinished on account of marks made by the patent peg washers, so it will not be ready until tomorrow. We will ship them, with a case for the guitar, by express to your home address, and the bill will go to Chas. H. Ditson & Co. The retail price of the guitar (style No. 2-28) is seventy-five dollars, of the ukulele (style No. 1) thirteen dollars and fifty cents, and of the guitar case (style 2C) twenty dollars. There is no charge for the special uke pegs, nor for extra position marks on the guitar.

We wish you could have had more time to give to the selection of these instruments, altho we feel sure they are both above average in tone. If you do not find them perfectly satisfactory for your work do not hesitate to tell us; we will gladly exchange them at any time for others selected by you. Also,

we would like to have you send us your old Martin guitar for re-adjustment; if you wish we will rework the neck to the narrower width used on Perry Bechtel's guitar.

We surely did enjoy your visit and hope you will repeat it soon, with Mrs. Smeck. Meanwhile we will enjoy your radio broadcasts and your records more than ever. Many thanks, again, for the records you left with us and for the wonderful entertainment you gave us on Friday evening; you may be sure we all appreciated your generosity."

On September 25, 1929 Ditson wrote to Martin to order a 00-40H for a particularly important customer:

"Please send us one (1) Martin Guitar, Style H 00-40H listed $100. Please note this guitar is for Mr. Ralph Colucchio (sic, should be Colicchio) who is a partner of Roy Smeck.

We would esteem it a great favor if you would make a most careful selection for Mr. Colucchio (sic), as we are very anxious to please him and we know you are."

A 00-40H guitar (serial number 38495) was shipped to Ditson on September 26. This guitar may be the same 00-40H that appears in photographs with Smeck dating to the late 1920's.

Ralph Colicchio was a banjoist and mandolinist who was also a prolific publisher of sheet music, arrangements, song books and method books for the tenor banjo in the 1920's. Colicchio was also a member of many different bands between the 1920's and 1950's, including the Ernie Golden's Band (1920's) and the Luck Strike Dance Orchestra (ca. 1931). As mentioned in the newspaper article at the beginning of this chapter, Roy Smeck was not a classically trained musician and it appears very likely that Ralph Colicchio was the "skilled composer" that helped Roy arrange his own music and method books.

On December 11, 1929 Smeck wrote to Martin again, but this time about Octa-chordas:

"Mr. Smith (author's note, at Charles H. Ditson & Co.) was telling me you are putting out an octa-chorda. I was surprised for outside of Sam

Moore I do not know any one else that plays the instrument."

Martin replied on December 12:

"Mr. Smith was not quite correct in telling you that we are putting out an Octo-Chorda Guitar. When the writer visited him some time ago and met you in his office we spoke about the instrument and asked us to make one of our Grand Concert Size Guitar with eight strings so that he could tune and play it like an Octo-Chorda, This we did; but there was nothing special in the instruments except the bridge and neck for eight strings. As far as we know no one else is using this Guitar and we do not intend to make it regularly. We are satisfied to have you develop it through Mr. Hunt and Mr. Smith."

The Octa-Chorda was not ordered until May 26, 1930. However, the order was placed by Oliver Ditson Co. (since the December 1929 letter Oliver Ditson Co, had taken over the Charles H. Ditson & Co. business in New York.) The Octa-Chorda (serial number 42797) was shipped to Ditson on June 24. Smeck must not have liked the guitars because it was returned by Ditson on October 27. This is confirmed in a letter written by Martin to Roy Smeck on January 2, 1932:

"Hearing you all (that means Olga too) on the radio yesterday inspired in us a New Year's resolution to do something about your Octa-Chorda -- if you are still interested. We have no hope of improving the first one very much so our plan is to build one with out new carved top construction and let you try it out. The new model seems to be a success for plectrum playing, but it hasn't had a good test in the Hawaiian style and, of course, no one can even guess what sort of an Octa-chorda it will turn out to be. There's only one way to find out, so we are willing to make one up either in the mahogany C-1 style or in the rosewood C-2. For plectrum playing C-2 has a brighter tone, and we think that would be the best bet. The list price of C-1 will be one hundred dollars and of C-2 one hundred fifty dollars, without case."

Nothing seems to have come from this suggestion by Martin for a new guitar. However, the mention of "doing something about your Octa-Chorda" can't refer to serial number 42797 so it is not clear what other Octa-Chorda guitar Roy may have had.

Subsequently, the Octa-chorda was ordered by Sherman, Clay & Co. of San Francisco on January 12, 1932. It must have been returned at some point because it was sold to Pearson Piano Co. of Indianapolis on September 14, 1933 (returned October 24). This interesting instrument was not sold again and now resides in the Martin Guitar Museum.
Having achieved the peak of popularity and success, Smeck sought to brand his name for use in other ventures. As mentioned previously Smeck, with the help of Ralph Colicchio, published a number of method books under his name for the ukulele, tenor banjo, guitar and Hawaiian guitar.

For a time in the mid-1930's there was even a Roy Smeck School of Music in Jersey City, New Jersey. It is also very well known that Smeck had a number of manufacturers produce instruments under his name. Gibson made Roy Smeck Stage Deluxe and Recording King guitars. Roy also designed and en-

Figure 401
Cover of Roy Smeck Ukulele and
Ukulele-Banjo Method (1928)

dorsed Vita-Guitar and Vita-Uke instruments marketed by the Harmony Co., starting in 1928. Harmony continued to make Roy Smeck ukes, guitars and banjos until well into the 1960's.

In 1932 Roy Smeck, through an intermediary, even approached Martin to see if the company would be interested in making Roy Smeck guitars. On September 22, 1932 Alex Kolbe of Musical Merchandise in New York wrote a most interesting letter to Martin:

"--no doubt you have heard of my personal interest in Roy Smeck. I personally am responsible for the house of Carl Fischer putting out a Roy Smeck Hawaiian Guitar book and for the firm of L. A. Elkington putting out a line of Roy Smeck picks and bars for the Hawaiian Guitar.

--I have interested a very large manufacturer in the East to manufacture a commercial line of banjo outfits with the name of Roy Smeck for the school trade.

--now here is the reason for my writing you the forementioned. Gibson in Kalamazoo and Schireson Bros. in Los Angeles and two Eastern houses have been after Mr. Smeck for the purpose of putting out a line of guitars bearing his name. Two other companies in question were agreeable in organizing a Roy Smeck firm and for some unknown reason, Roy Smeck prefers his Martin guitar.

--last night Roy asked me to communicate with you for the sole purpose of interesting your Company in putting out a commercial line of guitars both standard and Hawaiian, bearing his name. What do you think of this plan? Now is the time -- with the growing interest in guitar playing there is a golden opportunity for some one manufacturer at this time to cash in on the name Roy Smeck.

--you know he is doing very well on the radio and records -- you know he is very popular in vaudeville and plans a long tour on the R. K. O. circuit -- in fact you know him better than I and there is no reason for me to go into more detail concerning Roy Smeck.

--another point of interest is the introduction of

Roy Smeck strings for guitars. This string to bear a little tag at the end saying that it has been approved and tested by Roy Smeck."

Martin replied on September 23:

"Thank you for your interesting letter with the suggestion that we put out a Roy Smeck line of Guitars. Considering the matter impersonally because the fact that we like Roy and wish him all possible success would not be a sufficient motive, we must be guided by our policy in such matters and that is to put the greatest possible intrinsic value in Martin Instruments but not to use the name of any individual in addition to or in place of our own. While there is undoubted advertising value in names like Nick Lucas and Roy Smeck, we still think that our policy of sticking to our own name is right.

In years past we have made for certain customers special lines bearing their name; for example a Ditson line, and we are willing to do that now if Mr. Smeck himself of any suitable dealer or jobber wishes to market a Roy Smeck line. In such cases we advise the use of our name as well as the special name because our experience has been that the name Martin helps to put the goods across. That gives you something more to think about."

Smeck's career continued into the 1960's where he appeared on the Ed Sullivan, Steve Allen and Jack Paar television variety shows. He even had a comeback concert at the age of 82[65].

Roy Smeck died on 5 April 1994 in Washington, DC.

Henry Worrall (1825-1902)

Henry Worrall was an American visual artist and musician in Ohio and Kansas during the 19th century.

Worrall was born in Liverpool, he emigrated to the United States with his parents in the 1830's.

He taught guitar at the Ohio Female College and co-founded the Cincinnati Sketch Club.

He settled in Topeka in 1868. Worrall established a new career as a designer, artist and illustrator. He de-

signed the Kansas exhibits for both the Philadelphia Centennial in 1876 and the World's Columbian Exposition in 1893.

Some of his musical compositions were published by Oliver Ditson in Boston and J. L. Peters & Bros. in St. Louis. He died in Kansas in 1902.

See pages 121 to 123 for details on the guitar presented to him in 1856.

Notes for Chapter 14

1) "Senor and Madam Gonie" landed in New York on November 2, 1840 aboard the ship "Sheffield" out of Liverpool. Their ages were listed as 30 and 25 respectively and both are recorded as having Spanish nationality.

2) The New York Herald, November 7, 1840

3) Massett, Stephen C. Drifting About. New York, Carleton, 1863, Pg. 27

4) George Knoop arrived in New York, September 10, 1841, from Hamburg aboard the bark "Washington". His first name was not recorded but he was listed on the ship's manifest as being 38 years old. His occupation was noted as "Musician".

5) First District Court for the Parish of New Orleans, Marriage license for Georgina Knoop, February 16, 1874

6) Ballard, James. A History of the Guitar : From the Earliest Antiquity to the Present Time. New York : W. B. Tilton, 1855

7) Whittaker, Clara Ruetenik, hand written "Biography of my Grandfather, Christian Frederick Martin" pages 15-16, December, 1913

8) The Ladies' repository: a monthly periodical, devoted to literature, arts, and religion, Volume 11, Issue 5, May 1851

9) Daily Alta California, Volume 4, Number 164, June 14, 1853, page 2

10) October 18, 1851, Daily Alta California, San Francisco, California - ARRIVAL OF THE TENNESSEE!

11) March 16, 1852, Daily Alta California, San Francisco, California - P.M.S.S. Tennessee, San Francisco Bar, Monday, March 14, 1852

12) November 7, 1852, Daily Alta California San Francisco, California - ARRIVAL OF THE TENNESSEE!

13) Obituary for Lieutenant George M. Totten, Sacramento Daily Union, Sacramento, California, September 1, 1857

14) From New York ship's manifest, December 15, 1835

15) From New York ship's manifest for the Barque Louisa, May 4, 1841

16) New York Naturalization Record, May 6, 1843 http://www.immigrantships.net/v10/1800v10/centralameri-ca18570912_03.html

17) Philip J. Bone: The Guitar & Mandolin: Biographies of Celebrated Players and Composers, London: Schott & Co. Ltd. First edition 1914 pages 106-108, second enlarged edition 1954, reprint of second edition with new preface, 1972.

18) Music Trade Review magazine, Sept. 30, 1905, page 101 (https://mtr.arcade-museum.com/MTR-1905-41-13/101/)

19) Compositions and Arrangements for the Guitar published in San Francisco in 1882 and reprinted in Boston by Oliver Ditson in 1915, 227 pages

20) A partial list of Kaai's publications include: a) *The Ukulele: A Hawaiian Guitar and How to Play It*, publisher: Wall, Nichols Co., Honolulu 1906, revised 1910, b) *The Ukulele and How Its Played,* publisher: Hawaii News Co. Ltd, Honolulu, 1916, c) *Kaai's Hawaiian Guitar Method*, publisher: Chicago: Chart Music Publishing House, Chicago, 1919, 1926, d) *Kaai's Method and Solos for Ukulele or Tiple*, publisher: Chart Music Publishing House, Chicago, 1926, e) *Kaai's Method and Solos for Hawaiian Guitar*, publisher: Chart Music Publishing House, Chicago, 1926.

21) The Evening Bulletin, Honolulu, Hawaii, July 10, 1899, pg 2

22) The Pacific Commercial Advertiser, Honolulu, Hawaii, 20 April 1907, pg 7

23) Honolulu Star-Bulletin, Honolulu, Hawaii, November 24, 1917, pg 5

24) The Pacific Commercial Advertiser, Honolulu, Hawaii, October 3, 1892, pg 2

25) The Evening Bulletin, Honolulu, Hawaii, August 4, 1899, pg 3

26) The Hawaiian Star, Honolulu, Hawaii, December 20, 1899, pg 2

27) The Pacific Commercial Advertiser, Honolulu, April 16, 1901, pg 4

28) The Pacific Commercial Advertiser, Honolulu, Hawaii, March 6, 1902, pg 5

29) Sunday Advertiser, Honolulu, Hawaii, May 28, 1905, pg 11

30) The Pacific Commercial Advertiser, Honolulu, Hawaii, May 19, 1905, pg 9

31) Honolulu Star-Bulletin, Honolulu, Hawaii, January 4, 1913, pg 5

32) Pacific Commercial Advertiser, Honolulu, Hawaii, June 8, 1904, pg 5

33) 1913 Crocker-Langley San Francisco Directory, publisher: H. S. Crocker Co., pg 1002 and pg 2240

34) San Francisco Chronicle, San Francisco, California, March 23, 1913, pg 67

35) Honolulu Star-Bulletin, Honolulu, Hawaii, January 4, 1913, pg 5

36) Audubon County Journal, Exira, Iowa, August 28, 1919

37) *The Ukulele and How to Play It: Self Instructor for the Ukulele and Taro-Patch Fiddle*, publisher: Southern California Music Co., 1912, revised 1914

38) The Hawaiian Star, Honolulu, Hawaii, June 5, 1900, pg 1

39) The Hawaiian Star, Honolulu, Hawaii, July 16, 1904, pg 5

40) Evening Bulletin, Honolulu, Hawaii, July 22, 1904, pg 1

41) Aberdeen Herald, Aberdeen, Washington, April 5, 1906, pg 1

42) Los Angeles Herald, Los Angeles, California, June 11, 1907, pg 5

43) Nezperce Herald, Nezperce, Idaho, May 25, 1916, pg 6

44) The Arizona Republican, Phoenix, Arizona, June 23, 1913, pg 2

45) Wheeling Intelligencer, Wheeling, West Virginia, March 29, 1918, pg 7

46) The Independent, Elizabeth City, North Carolina, May 25, 1928, pg 2

47) The Evening Star, Washington DC, July 19, 1929, pg 15

48) St. Petersburg Times, St. Petersburg, Florida, June 12, 1963, obituary, pg 13-B

49) The International Arcade Museum (https://mtr.arcade-museum.com/MTR-1930-89-8/26/)

50) The International Arcade Museum (https://mtr.arcade-museum.com/MTR-1920-70-24/45/)

51) The International Arcade Museum (https://mtr.arcade-museum.com/MTR-1925-81-18/25/)

52) The International Arcade Museum (https://mtr.arcade-museum.com/MTR-1925-80-26/42/)

53) The International Arcade Museum (https://mtr.arcade-muse-um.com/MTR-1927-84-18/36/)

54) The International Arcade Museum (https://mtr.arcade-muse-um.com/MTR-1930-89-8/26/)

55) The International Arcade Museum (https://mtr.arcade-muse-um.com/MTR-1929-88-28/67/), pages 65 and 77

56) The International Arcade Museum (https://mtr.arcade-muse-um.com/MTR-1929-88-29/91/), pages 91 and 95

57) The International Arcade Museum (https://mtr.arcade-muse-um.com/MTR-1930-89-2/37/), pages 37 and 39

58) The International Arcade Museum (https://mtr.arcade-muse-um.com/MTR-1930-89-4/39/),pages 37 and 39

59) The International Arcade Museum (https://mtr.arcade-muse-um.com/MTR-1930-89-6/57/), pages 55 and 61

60) Dubuque Chess Journal, June 1875, pgs 303-304

61) Music Trade Review magazine, Sept. 30, 1905, page 101 (https://mtr.arcade-museum.com/MTR-1905-41-13/101/)

62) Music Trade Review magazine, most editions between July 29, 1893 and April 9, 1898 (https://mtr.arcade-museum.com/)

63) The Washington Star, Washington, DC, August 25, 1934, pg B-12

64) Excerpt from the film That Goes Double (1933)

65) See The Wizard of the Strings (1983), Academy Award-nom-inated documentary film by Alan Edelstein and Peter Friedman about Smeck and his career, made when Roy was 82

Chapter 16
MARTIN EMPLOYEES

The Martin archives contains detailed time books covering January 1890 to December 1891 and July 1905 to December 1922. The remainder of the information presented in this section was put together by closely examining the ledgers and account books..

EMPLOYEES IN NEW YORK 1834-1839

C. F. Martin landed in New York along with his apprentice Louis Schmidt in November 1833. Martin and Schmidt concentrated on guitar production while Jacob Hartman was hired to look after the shop.

In 1836 Charles Bruno replaced Jacob Hartman as shop manager and in mid-1838 Louis Schmidt left to start his own business. This affected guitar production but C. F. Martin Jr. may have begun to help out since he was 13 years old.

Regardless, C. F. Martin Sr. was prepared to accept the decrease in revenue because he had likely already decided to leave New York for the Nazareth area. Unfortunately, the collapse of the Martin & Bruno co-partnership in late 1838 meant that Martin needed to stay on longer to sell the store inventory, which he did in May 1839, to Ludecus & Wolter.

Louis Schmidt (1815-?)

Louis Schmidt arrived on the same ship as the Martin family in November 1833[78]. It is more than likely he had already been Martin's apprentice in Neukirchen. An entry in the 1834 Martin ledger records that Schmidt was paid $4 per week plus room and board[79].

Louis Schmidt worked for Martin from 1834 to 1838 before setting up his own business. It is not clear exactly when Schmidt ceased working for C. F. Martin

as there are no employee records the ledgers after 1834.

During the Martin & Bruno partnership Bruno recorded several payments to Louis Schmidt that were charged to C. F. Martin's account.

Payments to Schmidt of $5 on May 19, 1838 and $5.00 on June 7, 1838 appear to be for wages. A payment of $100.00 to Schmidt on August 23, 1838 may indicate C. F. Martin was extending a loan to Schmidt for his new store, especially since the payment was charged to C. F. Martin's account rather than being part of the Martin & Bruno business expenses.

During the time period from May 12 to November 14, 1838 Schmidt made several musical merchandise purchases from Martin & Bruno. A purchase made on June 12, 1838 records Schmidt's address as 92 Chatham St., the location of Schmidt's first music store.

Based on the information above, Louis Schmidt probably left C. F. Martin in June 1838 to start is his own musical instrument business at 92 Chatham Street.

The New York directories shows the Schmidt & Maul partnership was established by 1839, so Schmidt wasn't in business on his own for very long.

Schmidt also imported musical instruments and supplies from T. F. Merz in Markneukirchen.

George Maul

There is no evidence in the 1834-1836 ledger to suggest that Maul ever worked on a full time basis for C. F. Martin. The New York directories covering 1833 to 1838 list him as a cabinet maker at 184 Canal St.

MARTIN EMPLOYEES 1834 TO 1839						
	1834	1835	1836	1837	1838	1839
C. F. MARTIN SR. (1794-1873)	X	X	X	X	X	X
C. F. MARTIN JR. (1825-1888)					X	X
LOUIS SCHMIDT	X	X	X	X	X	
C. F. HARTMAN (1820-1893)						X

Table 112
C. F. Martin Employees from 1834 to 1839

Martin did make a payment of $20 to Maul on June 7, 1838. The address specified was 190 Canal St. His business address was 184 Canal St. so 190 Canal St. may have been his residence. Another payment of $17.61 was made to Maul on July 12, 1838.

It was not noted what sort of work Maul performed for C. F. Martin.

Schmidt & Maul

From 1839 to 1849 Schmidt & Maul had their shop at 412½ Broadway. In 1849 they moved to 385 Broadway, the same address as the Martin depot run by John Coupa.

Samuel C. Jollie had a music store at 385 Broadway from 1839-1845. Thomas H. Chambers (a piano-maker and music seller) also occupied 385 Broadway from 1842-1856. Additionally, John Face Brown, a harp manufacturer, was at the same address in 1843. From this it is clear the building was sub-divided into separate floors. Samuel C. Jollie occupied the shop fronting the street until 1845. Thomas Chambers, John Brown and John Coupa occupied the floors upstairs.

Schmidt and Maul were not just colleagues of C. F. Martin and John Coupa but were also close friends. In a letter dated August 28, 1849 Coupa informed Martin he would be going to the country but would "leave the keys with Maul" who, by that date, was at the same address.

Jacob Hartman

Jacob Hartman was another of C. F. Martin's early employees. A translated entry dated June 1, 1834 states that Hartman was to be paid $1 per week plus room and board for "handling all (Martin's) business

affairs in the city". These duties probably included helping in the shop and collecting monies owed.

As the ledger starting January 1, 1836 is in different handwriting Hartman had ceased working for Martin by that date.

After April 1836 Hartman appears frequently in the ledgers for repairs made to horns and trombones. He also supplied some guitar parts to Martin. For instance, it is recorded on July 3, 1837 he "made 11 neck screws" and received $1.25 in payment.

Frederick William Rasche

Rasche was an employee from May 21 to September 17, 1838 at 212 Fulton St where he "attended the store". His salary was $2 per week. He performed some special work for Martin and also did some pearl cutting.

It is not entirely clear what Rasche's position comprised but the work he did perform was charged to Martin's account.

MARTIN EMPLOYEES 1839-1887

In Cherry Hill the 1839 work force included C. F. Martin Sr., C. F. Martin Jr. and C. F. Martin Sr.'s nephew, C. F. Hartmann, who had emigrated to the United States that year. The 1840 census shows a young man of Hartmann's age as part of the Martin household so, not surprisingly, Hartmann was living with the Martin family. It appears Martin and Henry Schatz formed a brief partnership between mid-1839 and early 1840 but there may not have been enough sales at the time for the partnership to be a success.

At times during the 1850's and 1860's Martin also employed August Clewell and Cristian Blum to make

MARTIN EMPLOYEES 1840 TO 1867																												
	1840	1841	1842	1843	1844	1845	1846	1847	1848	1849	1850	1851	1852	1853	1854	1855	1856	1857	1858	1859	1860	1861	1862	1863	1864	1865	1866	1867
C. F. MARTIN SR. (1794-1873)	X	X	X	X	X	X	X	X	X	X	X	X	X	X	X	X	X	X	X	X	X	X	X	X	X	X	X	X
C. F. MARTIN JR. (1825-1888)	X	X	X	X	X	X	X	X	X	X	X	X	X	X	X	X	X	X	X	X	X	X	X	X	X	X	X	X
C. F. HARTMAN (1820-1893)	X	X	X	X	X	X	X	X	X	X	X	X	X	X	X	X	X	X	X	X	X	X	X	X	X	X	X	X
HENRY GOETZ (1815-1894)													X	X	X	X	X	X	X	X	X	X	X	X	X	X	X	X
A. CLEWELL (CASE MAKER)																				X								X
REINHOLD A. SCHUSTER																												X

Table 113
C. F. Martin Employees from 1840 to 1867

cases. As their pay tapered off in the summer, Clewell and Blum were clearly local farmers who supplemented their income making cases between the harvesting and planting seasons. When guitar production was low as occurred from 1876 to 1879, the company employees made the guitar cases instead.

It is remarkable to think that all the lovely Martin guitars made between 1867 and 1887 were made by only four employees, namely; C. F. Martin Jr., C. F. Hartmann, Henry Goetz, Reinhold Schuster. Frank Henry Martin probably supplemented the work force when he turned 15 years old in 1881 but the work force of comprised only 5 people through 1887. Sales were on the increase by 1888 and the work force was expanded the to 8. The work force varied between 11 and 13 persons from 1889 to 1898.

C. F. Hartmann (Oct. 5, 1820-Dec. 30, 1893)

Christian Frederick Hartmann was born October 5, 1820 in Neukirchen. He was C. F. Martin Sr.'s nephew, being the son of Christiane Friedericke Hartmann (nee Martin), the older sister of C. F. Martin.

Somehow, Hartmann also found time to make a number of violins and cellos while in Nazareth.

Hartmann became a partner in C. F. Martin & Co., along with C. F. Martin Sr. and C. F. Martin Jr., when it was formed in July 1867.

Hartmann seems to have given up his share of the company in 1885 but continued his employment.

Hartmann retired in 1892 and died on December 30, 1893 in Nazareth. Hartmann's employment with Martin stretched from 1839 to 1892, a total of 53 years!

Heinrich B. Goetz (April 23, 1820-Feb. 16, 1894)

The census of 1850 indicated that "Henry Getz" was part of the Martin household so it is clear that Goetz began working for Martin by that time or even a little earlier.

In 1854, Henry Goetz was in Germany on family business and purchased marquetry and other supplies for Martin. The archive contains several invoices from suppliers in Germany, including one long in-voice from Burdorf detailing the type and quantities of purfling billed to Martin.

The sales and accounting ledgers are almost entirely missing for the 1840's but the archive does contain a number of cancelled checks. Henry Goetz first appears in the cancelled checks on April 27, 1852 but the $150 check indicates he was being paid for work already performed.

The Martin records from the 1840's to 1851 are spotty at best. However, from 1852 Martin kept account books that recorded various transactions with employees. One of the most common transactions was for sales of flour to C. F. Hartman and Henry Goetz. Since the usual work week for Martin employees was 12 hours per day and 6 days a week, Martin made life a little easier for Hartman and Goetz by buying flour in bulk and selling them this staple.

Goetz continued working at the factory until November 1890 so had a forty year career with the Martin company.

Reinhold Schuster

C. F. Martin Sr. suffered a stroke in the late 1850's. An account book of the time shows he missed many days off work from 1859 to 1861. He returned to part time work in 1862, was working a 5 to 6 day week during 1863 and was working pretty much full time from 1864 to 1867.

It is likely the formation of C. F. Martin & Co. in 1867 marked the retirement of C. F. Martin Sr. He had been suffering with declining health for some time and, as he was now over 70 years old, had earned a rest from his labors. At the same time Reinhold Schuster began to work for the company in order to maintain an appropriate work force.

Reinhold must have been held in high esteem because, on May 1, 1873, he was allowed to purchase two lots on North Main St. from the estate C. F. Martin Sr., one of which contained the house, up to that point, of C. F. Martin Jr.

Schuster continued to be employed by the company until retiring in July 1901.

MARTIN EMPLOYEES 1867 TO 1898	1867	1868	1869	1870	1871	1872	1873	1874	1875	1876	1877	1878	1879	1880	1881	1882	1883	1884	1885	1886	1887	1888	1889	1890	1891	1892	1893	1894	1895	1896	1897	1898
C. F. MARTIN JR. (1825-1888)	X	X	X	X	X	X	X	X	X	X	X	X	X	X	X	X	X	X	X	X	X	X										
F. H. MARTIN (1866-1948)																							X	X	X	X	X	X	X	X	X	X
C. F. HARTMAN (1820-1893)	X	X	X	X	X	X	X	X	X	X	X	X	X	X	X	X	X	X	X	X	X	X	X	X	X	X	X					
HENRY GOETZ (1815-1891?)	X	X	X	X	X	X	X	X	X	X	X	X	X	X	X	X	X	X	X	X	X	X	X	X	X							
A. CLEWELL (CASE MAKER)	X	X	X	X	X	X																										
REINHOLD A. SCHUSTER	X	X	X	X	X	X	X	X	X	X	X	X	X	X	X	X	X	X	X	X	X	X	X	X	X	X	X	X	X	X	X	X
HARRY L. KELLER																							X	X	X	X	X	X	X	X	X	X
EDWARD L. MIKSCH																							X	X	X	X	X	X	X	X	X	X
ROBERT J. KNECHT																							X	X	X	X	X	X				
A. C. GIERSCH																							X	X	X	X	X	X	X	X	X	X
CLEMENCE T. BEITEL																							X	X	X	X	X	X				
WILLIAM KNECHT																								X	X	X	X					
H. J. WOODUS																								X	X							
W. ENVRIC NICHOLAS																									X	X						
SYDNEY B. BEITEL																									X	X						
H. ALBIN VOIGT																											X	X	X	X	X	X
WILHELM VOIGT																											X	X	X			
G. L. BEITEL																												X	X	X	X	X
HERBERT C. SNYDER																											X	X	X	X	X	X
J. J. KNECHT																											X	X	X	X	X	X
MICHAEL R. HAGETER																												X	X	X	X	
CHARLES D. RUTH																												X	X	X	X	
JULIUS HAGETER																												X				
CHARLES BERGER																														X	X	
W. H. CLEWELL																														X	X	X
R. G. WUNDERLEY																																X
CHARLES SAVITZ																																X
TOTAL	5	5	5	5	5	5	4	4	4	4	4	4	4	4	4	4	4	4	4	4	4	4	9	11	13	11	13	15	12	13	13	12

Table 114
C. F. Martin & Co. Employees from 1867 to 1898

MARTIN EMPLOYEES 1898 TO 1922 (WORKERS HIRED TO 1915)	1898	1899	1900	1901	1902	1903	1904	1905	1906	1907	1908	1909	1910	1911	1912	1913	1914	1915	1916	1917	1918	1919	1920	1921	1922
F. H. MARTIN (1866-1948)	X	X	X	X	X	X	X	X	X	X	X	X	X	X	X	X	X	X	X	X	X	X	X	X	X
C. F. MARTIN III															X	X	X	X	X	X		X	X	X	X
H. K. MARTIN																X	X	X	X	X	X	X	X	X	X
MENHENNIT, MAUD (SECRETARY)																					X	X	X	X	X
REINHOLD A. SCHUSTER	X	X	X	X																					
HARRY L. KELLER	X	X	X	X																					
EDWARD L. MIKSCH	X	X	X	X	X	X	X	X	X	X	X	X	X	X	X	X	X	X							
A. C. GIERSCH	X																								
H. ALBIN VOIGT	X	X	X	X																					
G. L. BEITEL	X	X	X	X																					
SNYDER, HERBERT C.	X	X	X	X	X	X	X	X	X	X															
J. J. KNECHT	X	X	X	X																					
J. P. NEUMEYER		X	X	X																					
J. G. HAGETER						X																			
W. H. CLEWELL	X																								
R. G. WUNDERLEY	X	X																							
CHARLES SAVITZ	X	X	X	X	X	X	X	X	X	X	X	X	X	X	X	X	X	X	X	X	X	X	X	X	X
H. W. ACHE		X																							
E. WERKHEISER		X																							
C. D. FRANTZ		X	X	X	X	X	X	X	X																
JOHN ABEL			X	X	X				X																
S. E. ALBERT			X	X	X	X	X	X																	
R. J. GINTHER			X	X	X																				
E. HOUCK			X																						
O. H. RADER				X	X																				
A. C. KESSLER				X	X	X																			
W. DEREAMER				X	X																				
WILLIAM MAXWELL					X																				
A. P. SUNDBERG						X																			
EMIL PETERSON						X	X	X	X	X	X	X	X							X	X				
A. ASPEREN						X																			
F. CATALANELLO						X	X																		
M. JOHANSSON						X																			
L. C. SCHMICKLY							X																		
R. W. KUNKLE							X	X																	
H. E. YOUNG							X	X	X																
BURT HESS							X	X																	
SAMUEL SMORTO									X	X															
GEORGE HEINLINE (HINELINE)									X	X	X	X	X	X	X	X	X	X	X	X	X	X	X	X	X
C. N. ANGELMIRE									X	X	X	X	X	X	X	X	X	X							
J. P. TROXELL				X	X	X	X	X	X	X	X	X	X												
DOMENICO SAMA									X	X															
PASQUALE POLIMENI									X	X															
ROBERT G. MISSINGER									X	X	X														
JACOB EILENBERGER								X	X																
CHARLES FARBER								X																	
REPH, SPENCER M.								X																	
SILFIES, CHARLES									X																
TROXELL, FRED S.									X																
FRANCIS YOUNG									X																
TROXELL, ALLEN D.									X																
GINTHER, R. J.													X												
COOS, CHARLES													X												
METZ, CLARENCE L.													X	X	X	X						X	X	X	X
RADER, OWEN H.													X	X											
ETSCHMAN, CARL													X												
COLVER, ROBERT														X	X	X									
DEICHMAN, JOHN																X	X	X	X	X	X	X	X	X	X
JONES, ROBERT O.															X										
DURS, CASINO																	X	X							

Table 115
C. F. Martin & Co. Employees from 1898 to 1922 (workers hired to 1915)

MARTIN EMPLOYEES 1898 TO 1922 (WORKERS HIRED 1916 TO 1918)																									
	1898	1899	1900	1901	1902	1903	1904	1905	1906	1907	1908	1909	1910	1911	1912	1913	1914	1915	1916	1917	1918	1919	1920	1921	1922
SWEITZER, JOHN																			X						
PLATTENBERGER, J. A.																			X	X	X	X	X	X	X
EVERITT, BURTON																			X						
KALE, VICTOR																			X	X	X	X	X	X	X
KALE, ALLEN D.																			X						
HOFFMAN, AUGUSTUS																			X						
CLEWELL, LUTHER																			X						
KALE, OSCAR R.																			X	X					
WALTER, FRED																			X	X	X	X			
WALTER, VICTOR																			X						
LAMBERT, OSCAR																			X	X	X	X	X	X	X
WERNER, CLINTON																			X						
JOHNSON, RAYMOND																			X	X	X		X		X
BARTHOLOMEW, E. B.																			X						
WILLIAMSON, RAY																			X	X	X				
COLVER, R. L.																			X	X	X	X			
RADER, RALPH																			X						
KOCH, DAVID																			X						
REDLINE, JOHN																			X	X		X	X	X	
RICE, JAMES																			X	X	X	X	X	X	X
WERKHEISER, WILLIS I.																			X	X	X	X	X	X	X
BERGER, JOHN H.																			X	X	X	X	X	X	X
WERKHEISER, CLARENCE																			X	X	X	X	X	X	X
WERKHEISER, ELMER																			X	X	X	X	X	X	X
SCHUMAN, CLARENCE																			X	X	X	X	X	X	X
RICE, FLOYD																			X	X		X			
SANDT, WILLIAM R.																				X		X	X	X	
RUPELL, WILLIAM L.																				X					
MABUS, ALBERT																				X					
RASH, CLARK																				X	X	X	X	X	
HUGO, JAMES																				X					
SYNDER, HOWARD																				X	X	X	X	X	X
MISSINGER, WILLIAM J.																				X					
KNECHT, FLOYD																				X					
FLORY, PRESTON																				X					
BOWLBY, CHARLES P.																				X					
CLEWELL. ESCHOR																				X					
ZIEGLER, ROBERT																				X					
WEIDLICH, LUTHER																				X					
STOUDT, GEORGE																				X	X				
RICE, MORRIS																				X					
TEEL, PAUL																				X	X				
WERNER, LEWIS																				X	X				
FRACK, EDGAR																				X	X				
KELLER, JOHN A.																				X	X	X	X	X	
SEYFREID, FRANK R.																				X					
SHAFER, HENRY																					X				
MENHENNIT, DOROTHY																					X				
METZ, MABEL																					X	X			
METZ, MYRTLE																					X	X			
SHEA, MRS. THOMAS																					X				
KNECHT, ESTHER																					X				
GOLD, HELEN																					X	X			
HARUR, LULU																					X	X			
HARMAN, E.																					X				

Table 116
C. F. Martin & Co. Employees from 1898 to 1922 (workers hired from 1916 to 1918)

MARTIN EMPLOYEES 1898 TO 1922 (WORKERS HIRED 1919 TO 1922)																									
	1898	1899	1900	1901	1902	1903	1904	1905	1906	1907	1908	1909	1910	1911	1912	1913	1914	1915	1916	1917	1918	1919	1920	1921	1922
FRANTZ, EZRA																						X			
BENNER, A.																						X			
SEIBOLD, JOSEPH																						X	X	X	X
STETTLER, GEORGE																						X	X		
KNECHT, MARK																						X			
LAUDENBACH, GEORGE																						X	X	X	
WATSON, FLOYD																						X			
BREIDINGER, FRANCIS																						X			
YOUNG, WALTER																						X			
HERTZOG, WILLIAM																						X	X	X	
HALDIMAN, W.																						X	X		
FRANTZ, HARVEY																						X			
KENT, ARTHUR																						X			
TOTH, JOSEPH																						X			
WOLF, ROBERT																						X	X	X	
FRACK, CHARLES																						X			
WERKHEISER, PAUL																						X	X	X	X
BONSTEIN, FREDERICK																						X	X	X	X
DOTTER, WALTER																						X			
HARTZELL, EARL																						X	X	X	X
LEMINGER, WALTER																						X	X	X	
STARK, VICTOR																						X			
WOLF, FREDERICK																						X			
WERKHEISER, NEVIN																						X			
BARWICK, HAROLD																						X			
HEFFELFINGER, L.																						X	X	X	X
HEYER, LEON																						X	X	X	
LEVERING, ROY																						X			
ANDREWS, B.																						X			
LAMBERT, RAY																						X	X	X	
KOCH, EARL																						X	X	X	X
STECKEL, FRANK																						X			
ZEINER, HOWARD																						X			
MILLHEIM, WILLIAM																						X	X	X	X
GUM, RAY																						X	X	X	
REMALEY, R.																						X			
JONES, CHARLES																						X	X	X	
RADER, ASHER																						X	X	X	
WERKHEISER, H.																						X	X	X	X
METZ, STEWART																						X	X	X	
RADER, RALPH																						X			
YOUNG, JOHN																						X			
REMALEY, J. F.																							X	X	
HALDEMAN, W.																							X	X	
KALHER, SAMUEL																							X	X	
REMALEY, FRANK																							X	X	
PARSEGIAN, M.																							X	X	X
GOODHARD, WILLIAM																							X	X	
CLEWELL, A.																							X		
WALTERS, GEORGE																							X		
WERKHEISER, G.																							X		
WERKHEISER, R.																							X		
KLUMP, ELMER																							X		
SASSAMAN, E.																							X		
WERKHEISER, L.																									X
CLEWELL, WALTER																									X
BERGER, STEWART																									X
KUTI, WILLIAM																									X
FISHER, RAYMOND																									X
HOWELL, HAROLD																									X
MOHN, EARL																									X
NICHOLAS, ARLING																									X
SNYDER, JOHN																									X
WILLIAMS, JERRY (PACKER)																									X
ANDREWS, WILLIAM (JANITOR)																							X	X	
BILL, JOHN (JANITOR)																							X	X	X

Table 117
C. F. Martin & Co. Employees from 1898 to 1922 (workers hired from 1919 to 1922)

There are no time sheets ledger books after 1922 but, from other reports, it is possible to show the number of Martin workers from 1923 to 1941. The foremen were not considered workers so the number of foremen was only occasionally recorded.

MARTIN EMPLOYEES 1923 TO 1941		
DATE	NUMBER OF WORKERS	# FOREMEN
October 17, 1923	32	-
April 21, 1924	33	3
End of 1925	62	-
April 19, 1926	68	-
July 17, 1926	66	-
October 19, 1926	72	-
January 17, 1927	70	-
July 18, 1927	53	-
January 21, 1929	37	-
January 23, 1930	36	-
January 19, 1931	38	-
January 25, 1932	34	-
January 23, 1933	34	-
January 22, 1934	34	-
January 23, 1935	34	6
January 20, 1936	35	-
January 18, 1937	33	-
January 17, 1938	36	-
January 16, 1939	27	-
January 22, 1940	26	-
January 17, 1941	26	-

Table 118
Number of workers employed by C. F. Martin & Co. from 1923 to 1941

There is, however, one report for the week of December 16 to 22, 1934, that had to be submitted to the government, that shows the names of 32 employees. Unsurprisingly, many of the Martin employees from 1922 were still with Martin in 1934.

Table 119
Names of Martin employees for the week of December 16 to 22, 1934

Figures

Figures (cont.)

Figures (cont.)

Figure	Description	Source	Page
150	1835-1836 Martin & Schatz Guitar Type 3 Label (private collection)	Martin Guitar Archive	117
151	1836 Martin & Schatz "Amadill" Guitar Type 3 Label	Museum of Pop Culture collection	117
152	1836 Martin Guitar Type 4 Label	Museum of Pop Culture collection	117
153	1836 Martin Guitar Type 4 Label, Serial Number 1114 (Martin Guitar Museum)	Martin Guitar Archive	118
154	1837 Martin Guitar Type 5 Label (first period of use), Serial Number 1160 (private collection)	Lynn Wheelwright	118
155	1838 Martin & Bruno Terz Guitar, Type 6 Label, Serial Number 1231 (private collection)	Author	118
156	1839 Martin Guitar, Type 5 Label (2nd period of use), SN 1275 (Martin Guitar Museum)	Martin Guitar Archive	118
157	1839 Martin & Schatz Guitar, Type 7 Label, Serial Number 1296 (private collection)	Chris Andrada	119
158	1938 Martin & Schatz Guitar, Type 7 and Type 8 Labels, Serial Number 1304 (private collection)	Author	119
159	1840 Martin & Schatz Guitar, Type 7 Label, Serial Number 1341 (private collection)	Leonard Joel Auctions, Melbourne, Australia	119
160	1843 Martin & Schatz "De Goni" Guitar, Type 7 Label, (Martin Guitar Museum)	Folkways Music	119
161	Colonel Wilkins ca. 1846 Martin & Coupa Period Guitar- (private collection)	Vintz Huang	121
162	Engraving of Henry Worral and His Guitar	Kansas State Historical Soc., Collection no. 23.	123
163	1870's Photograph of Henry Worrall	Kansas State Historical Soc., Collection no. 23	123
164	Henry Worral and His Wife Playing Martin Guitars	Kansas State Historical Soc., Collection no. 23	123
165	Type A Case Label	Author	126
166	Type B Case Label	Gruhn Guitars	126
167	Type C Case Label	Gruhn Guitars	127
168	Advertisement for C. F. Martin Guitars in February 1850 Edition of "The Baltimore Olio"	Martin Guitar Archive	127
169	TYPE 1 Case Label - 1867 to 1873?	Frank Ford	127
170	TYPE 2 Case Label - 1875? to 1886	Author	127
171	TYPE 3 Case Label - 1887 to 1888	Laurence Wexer	128
172	TYPE 4 Case Label - 1889 to 1893	E-Bay	128
173	TYPE 5 Case Label - 1895 to 1898	Gryphon Stringed Instruments	128
174	Style G1 Mandolin from 1896 Catalogue	Author	139
175	Style G2 Mandolin from 1896 Catalogue	Author	140
176	Style G3 Mandolin from 1896 Catalogue	Author	140
177	Style G5 Mandolin from 1896 Catalogue	Author	140
178	Mandolin Style 1 from the 1898 Catalogue	Author	140
179	Mandolin Style 2 from the 1898 Catalogue	Author	141
180	Mandolin Style 3 from the 1898 Catalogue	Author	141
181	Mandolin Style 4 from the 1898 Catalogue	Author	141
182	Mandolin Style 5 from the 1898 Catalogue	Author	141
183	Mandolin Style 6 from the 1898 Catalogue	Author	141
184	1904 Style 7 Mandolin	Gruhn Guitars	142
185	1898 and 1905 Style 6 Mandolins	E-Bay (both)	143
186	1903 Martin 6A Mandolin (Serial Number 3127)	Carter Vintage Guitars	143
187	Styles A, B, C, D and E from 1915 Mandolin Price List	Martin Guitar Archive	145
188	Patent Announcement for Harp Mandolin	Music Trade Review June 1896	149
189	Back of Style 21 Harp Mandolin	Author	150
190	One of the Style 21 Harp Mandolins Shipped on November 7, 1899	Author	150
191	Label in 1907 Model America	Schoenberg Guitars	153
192	Label in 1909 Model America	Chris Andrada	153
193	1907 Model America Guitar	Schoenberg Guitars	153
194	Detail of Extended Neck Heel of 1907 Model	Schoenberg Guitars	153
195	Head Stock on 1907 Model America Guitar	Schoenberg Guitars	154
196	Detail of Bridge on 1907 Model America Guitar	Schoenberg Guitars	154
197	Wanamaker's in Philadelphia (ca. 1920)	Vintage Post Card	154
198	Type 1 and Type 2 Stamps Used in Wanamaker Guitars	Martin Guitar Archive	155
199	Wanamaker Stamp on Neck Block of Style F Guitar	Bruce Roth	155
200	Wanamaker Style F Guitar (Shipped December 18, 1909)	Bruce Roth	155
201	William Foden Playin a Washburn Guitar, Photograph by Fitz W. Guerin	Missouri History Museum	156
202	Poster for April 25, 1911 Performance of "The Big Three"	Washington Univ., George C. Krick collection	156
203	"The Big Three" Touring Car with Fred Bacon, Giuseppe Pettine and William Foden in Back Seat	Foden-Hoskins Archive, Missouri Hist.Mus.	157
204	William Foden Playing His 0-42 (Serial Number 8721)	Martin Guitar Archive	158
205	Type 1 and Type 2 "Foden Special" Stamps	Martin Guitar Archive	159
206	Foden Special Price List	Foden-Hoskins Archive, Missouri Hist.Mus.	160
207	Olcott Quartette (ca. 1910)	Martin Guitar Archive	161
208	Purfling, Sound Hole Decoration and Back Stripe of Style 44 Guitar	Elderly Instruments	161
209	Specifications for Ditson Small Guitars from December 1, 1917	Martin Guitar Archive	167
210	Specification for Ditson Small Guitars from March 9, 1918	Martin Guitar Archive	167
211	Ditson Small Guitars Renamed on March 30, 1918	Martin Guitar Archive	167
212	Specifications for Style 1 and Style 2 Ditson Guitars	Martin Guitar Archive	167
213	Specifications for Style 3 Ditson Guitars	Martin Guitar Archive	168
214	Oliver Ditson Special (ODS) 1-18 Guitar (Serial Number 367)	Tony Romano	168
215	Fingerboard of Ditson 33 Guitar (Serial Number 20)	Chris Andrada	168
216	Chicago-style Pyramid Bridge on Ditson 33 Guitar (Serial Number 20)	Chris Andrada	169
217	From Oliver Ditson Co. and Charles H. Ditson & Co. catalogue circa 1918-1920	Tony Romano	169
218	Specification Card for Briggs Special Mandolins	Martin Guitar Archive	172
219	Briggs Special Stamp	Martin Guitar Archive	172
220	Specification Card for SoCal Model 1350 Guitar	Martin Guitar Archive	173
221	Specification Card for SoCal Model 1400 Guitar	Martin Guitar Archive	174
222	Specification Card for SoCal Model 1500 Guitar	Martin Guitar Archive	174
223	Rolando Label in SoCal Style 1400 Guitar (Serial Number 237)	Elderly Instruments	174
224	Southern California Music Co. Metal Plaque on Back of Headstock (Serial Number 162)	E-Bay	174

Figures (cont.)

Figure	Description	Source	Page
225	Southern California Music Co. Stamp	Martin Guitar Archive	175
226	SoCal Style 1400 Sound Hole Rosette (Serial Number 237)	Elderly Instruments	175
227	Red and Green Herringbone Back Stripe on SoCal Model 1400 Guitar (Serial Number 237)	Elderly Instruments	175
228	Bitting Special Stamp	Mandolin Brothers	177
229	Specification Card for Bitting Special Mandolins and Mandolas	Martin Guitar Archive	177
230	Specification Card for Bitting Special Guitars	Martin Guitar Archive	177
231	Announcement for William J. Smith & Co. in the Music Trade Review	MTR (Vol. LXI No. 23, pg 51, Dec. 4, 1915)	178
232	Special William J. Smith & Co. Stamp	Martin Guitar Archive	179
233	Specification Card for William J. Smith & Co. Tiples	Martin Guitar Archive	180
234	The Unique T-45K Tiple	John Bernunzio	180
235	U-KA-LU-A Label in T-45K Tiple	John Bernunzio	180
236	Order Number 635 for Two 2-17-C and Two 0-21-C Guitars	Martin Guitar Archive	182
237	Order for Two 2-17-C Guitars for Hawaiian Playing	Martin Guitar Archive	182
238	Special "Beltone" Stamp in Style AK Mandolin	Martin Guitar Archive	183
239	Special "H. & A. Selmer Inc." Stamp	Martin Guitar Archive	184
240	Special "Wolverine" Stamp	Martin Guitar Archive	185
241	Unique Wurlitzer Model 2093 (00-42) with Single Ring Rosette	Gruhn Guitars	186
242	Special "Wurlitzer" Stamp	Martin Guitar Archive	187
243	Special "Cable Piano Co." Stamp	Martin Guitar Archive	189
244	Sketch of Proposed 14-Fret Tenor Guitar	Martin Guitar Archive	190
245	Comparison of 12-Fret (2-18T) and 14-Fret Size 2 Tenor Guitars (2-28T-L)	Steve Swan Guitar/Intermountain Guitar	190
246	1931 Martin O-28T Guitar	Dan Reimborn	193
247	Vintage Photograph of Paramount Style L Guitar	Steve Kovacik	194
248	Special "Chicago Musical Instrument Co." Stamp	Martin Guitar Archive	195
249	Newspaper Clipping of Montgomery Ward Co. Special Offering of Martin 0-17S Guitars	Martin Guitar Archive	196
250	Headstock Veneer on 1902 00-42S Guitar (First Serial Number 9372)	Author	201
251	Portion of Fingerboard Inlay on 1902 0-42S Guitar (First Serial Number 9372)	Author	201
252	Inlaid Pickguard on 1902 00-42S Guitar (First Serial Number 9372)	Author	201
253	Detail of T-45K Rosette	Bernunzio Music	204
254	Detail of End Graft and Back Stripe of T-45K	Bernunzio Music	204
255	Shop Order Slip for First "Special 000-28" (OM-28) Guitar	Martin Guitar Archive	216
256	Perry Bechtel's Suggestion for a Headstock Veneer for the First OM-28	Martin Guitar Archive	216
257	Promotional Photograph of Early OM-28 with Pyramid Bridge	Martin Guitar Archive	218
258	Promotional Photograph of Sons of the Pioneers without Roy Rogers	Martin Guitar Archive	218
259	Shop Orders for OM-45 Deluxe Guitars	Martin Guitar Archive	219
260	Entry in Bookings Ledger for First OM-45 Deluxe	Martin Guitar Archive	220
261	Promotional Photograph of Early OM-45 Guitar, One of Two Made with a Pyramid Bridge	Martin Guitar Archive	220
262	Roy Rogers with the First OM-45 Deluxe (Serial Number 42125)	Martin Guitar Archive	220
263	1932 Martin 0-18S Guitar (Serial Number 50053) and 1938 Martin 00-18	Private Collector	234
264	String Spacing and Neck Width for Octavario	Martin Guitar Archive	235
265	String Tuning for Octavario	Martin Guitar Archive	236
266	Shop Order for Octavario Based on a 00-18 Guitar	Martin Guitar Archive	236
267	Idea for an Electric Pick Up Built into an Adjustable Bridge for Carved-Top Guitars	Martin Guitar Archive	238
268	Martin Purchase Order for a Columbia Amplifier with a 10 Inch Speaker and Two Pick-Ups	Martin Guitar Archive	238
269	Columbia Sound Co. Amplifier as Purchased by C. F. Martin & Co.	Lynn Wheelwright	239
270	1936 Article on Columbia Music Co. Amplifiers	Lynn Wheelwright	239
271	Front and Back of a Volu-Tone Model 5 Amplifier	Doug Beaumier - Steel Guitar Forum	241
272	Volu-Tone Pick-Up Mounted on a Lap-Steel Guitar	Doug Beaumier - Steel Guitar Forum	241
273	1938 Martin 00-44G Guitar (Serial Number 70854)	Brian Chazba	246
274	1934 Lyon & Healy Window Display of Martin Guitars Showing Banners and Ukulele Signs	Martin Guitar Archive	258
275	Detail of Martin Guitar Co. Banner	Martin Guitar Archive	259
276	C. F. Martin Silk Banner from the 1960's	Martin Guitar Archive	259
277	Detail of Martin String Cabinets Made by Biolite Inc.	Martin Guitar Archive	259
278	Brass Martin Ukulele Sign	Martin Guitar Archive	259
279	1928 Advertising Post Card for Martin 5-17T Guitar	Martin Guitar Archive	263
280	Detail of Sketch in A. D. Grover & Son Letter of February 1, 1923	Martin Guitar Archive	265
281	Advertising Photograph of Martin Tenor Banjo	Martin Guitar Archive	266
282	Serial Number 54482 (1933), Stamped October 24 1933, Cleared Finish Depart. January 17, 1934	Unofficial Martin Guitar Forum	270
283	Serial Number 60639 (1936)	Unofficial Martin Guitar Forum	270
284	Serial number 97974 (1946)	Unofficial Martin Guitar Forum	270
285	Abalone Dot Fret Marker on 1843 Martin & Schatz Guitar Made for Madame De Goni	Folkways Music	275
286	Fingerboard Inlays on 1895 Martin 0-42 Guitar	E-Bay	275
287	Fingerboard Inlays on 1897 Martin 1-42 Guitar	Unofficial Martin Guitar Forum	275
288	Ivory Market Report Dated January 31, 1890	Martin Guitar Archive	284
289	Noted Added to a 1917 Catalog Announcing the Discontinuation of Ivory on April 1, 1918	Martin Guitar Archive	285
290	1850 Invoice from Rohe & Leavitt for Tuning Machines	Martin Guitar Archive	287
291	1852 Invoice from Rohe & Leavitt for Tuning Machines	Martin Guitar Archive	287
292	1855 Letter from C. A. Zoebisch Discussing the Pricing of French Tuning Machines	Martin Guitar Archive	287
293	Seidel Machines on a 1850-1855 Renaissance Guitar	Martin Guitar Archive	288
294	Seidel No. 6 Machines on 1857 Martin 2-17 Guitar	Lowell Levinger	288
295	Seidel No. 4 Machines on 1857-1858 Martin 0-27 Guitar	Author	288
296	Seidel No. 5 Machines on 1857-1858 Martin 0-27 Guitar (different guitar than above)	Martin Guitar Archive	288
297	1884 Invoice from C. A. Zoebisch for Tuning Machines	Martin Guitar Archive	289
298	Seidel Machines 1888 Martin 2½-40 Guitar	The Music Emporium	289
299	August 23, 1889 Invoice from C. A. Zoebisch & Sons for No. 4, No. 5 and No. 6 Patent Heads	Martin Guitar Archive	289

Figures (cont.)

Figure	Description	Source	Page
300	Seidel Machines on 1890 Martin 2-27 Guitar	Unofficial Martin Guitar Forum	289
301	June 4, 1891 Invoice from C. A. Zoebisch & Sons for No. 3 and No. 6 Patent Heads	Martin Guitar Archive	289
302	Seidel Machines on 1893 Martin 2½-17 Guitar	Unofficial Martin Guitar Forum	289
303	Seidel Machines on 1905 Martin 000-21 Guitar	Lark Street Music	290
304	Handel German Silver Tuners with Inlaid Ivory Buttons on 1917 Martin 00-45	Unofficial Martin Guitar Forum	290
305	German Silver Handel Tuners on a 1918 Martin 0-18 Guitar	Antebellum Guitars	290
306	Handel Tuners with German Silver Backing Plate and Plain Ivory Buttons on 1920 Martin 00-45	Unofficial Martin Guitar Forum	291
307	Handel Machines on a 1938 00-44G	Brian Chazba	291
308	Dinsmore & Jager #5 Tuners on 1911 Martin 0-18 Guitar	Unofficial Martin Guitar Forum	291
309	Dinsmore & Jager #33 Tuners on a 1917 Foden Style E Guitar	Gruhn Guitars	292
310	Possibly a Set of Schmidt Tuners on a 1924 Martin 0-18 Guitar	Mark Rohrer	292
311	Dinsmore & Jager #31 Tuners on 1947 Martin 00-21 Guitar	Unofficial Martin Guitar Forum	292
312	(Possibly) Waverly #1005 or #1008 Tuners on 1924 Martin 2-17 Guitar	Unofficial Martin Guitar Forum	292
313	Waverly #1005 Tuners on 1925 Martin 2-17 Guitar	Unofficial Martin Guitar Forum	292
314	Waverly G-31 Tuners 1926 Martin 00-28 Guitar	Dick Boak	292
315	Waverly G-32 Tuners on 1927 Martin 000-45 Guitar	David Ziegele	292
316	Waverly G-30 Tuners on 1932 Paramount Style L Guitar	Elderly Instruments	293
317	Waverly G-2 Tuners on 1932 Martin 0-18K Guitar	Folkway Music	293
318	Possibly Waverly 5039 Tuners on 1937 00-18H David Ziegele	David Ziegele	293
319	Waverly G-2 Tuners on 1942 Martin 0-15 Guitars Folkways	Folkway Music	293
320	Waverly G-31 Tuners on 1967 Martin D-28S Guitar	Unofficial Martin Guitar Forum	294
321	Waverly 5038 Tuners on 1940 Martin 00-18 Guitar	Ted Hutson	294
322	Waverly 5038D Tuners on 1953 Martin 00-18 Guitar	Steve Swan	294
323	Grover #77 Guitar Pegs on 1928 Martin 2-18T Guitar	Steve Swan	294
324	Grover #91 Leader Tenor Guitar Pegs on 1930 Martin 1-28PS Guitar	Jake Wildwood	294
325	Grover #89 Deluxe Guitar Pegs on 1930 Martin OM-28 Guitar	Lawrence Wexer	295
326	Grover G-97 "Clipped Plate" Tuners on 1932 Martin 00-40H Guitar	David Ziegele	296
327	Possibly a Set of Grover G-99T Tuners with Rounded Metal Buttons on 1932 Martin 0-18 Guitar	Folkway Music	296
328	Grover G-98 "Clipped Plate" Tuners with Un-seamed Butterbean Buttons on 1934 Martin D-28	Josh Storm	296
329	Grover G-98G "Clipped Plate" Tuners with Un-seamed Butterbean Buttons 1934 Martin 00-45	Lowell Levinger	296
330	Unknown Model of Grover "Clipped Plate" Tuners with Celluloid Buttons on 1934 Martin 00-17	Folkway Music	297
331	Grover G-98 "Pointed Plate" Tuners with Seamed Butterbean Buttons on 1936 Martin 000-28	Unofficial Martin Guitar Forum	297
332	Grover G-98G "Clipped Plate" with Engraved Un-seamed Butterbean Buttons on 1936 000-45	Elderly Instruments	297
333	Grover G-99T Tuners with Rounded Metal Buttons on 1937 Martin 00-17 Guitar	Folkway Music	297
334	Grover G-98G Tuners with Engraved Un-seamed Butterbean Buttons on 1938 Martin 000-45	Lawrence Wexer	297
335	Grover G-111 Tuners with Un-seamed Butterbean Buttons on 1940 Martin D-28 Guitar	Unofficial Martin Guitar Forum	297
336	Grover G-111G Tuners with Un-seamed Butterbean Buttons on 1940 Martin D-45 Guitar	Gruhn Guitars	298
337	Grover G-98N "Pointed Plate" Tuners with White Celluloid Buttons on 1963 Martin 00-18 Guitar	Matti Harkonen	298
338	Grover 102C Tuners	Unofficial Martin Guitar Forum	298
339	Grover 102G Tuners	Unofficial Martin Guitar Forum	298
340	Variety of Grover 102C Tuners with Ivoroid Buttons on 1965 Martin D-35 Guitar	Unofficial Martin Guitar Forum	298
341	Kluson 511 Tuners with Coined Edge on 1941 D-28 Guitar Folkways	Folkway Music	299
342	Kluson 501 Tuners with Coined Edge on 1943 0-17 Guitar	Schoenberg Guitars	299
343	Kluson 502N Tuners on 1944 D-18 Guitar	Steve Swan	300
344	Kluson 502N Tuners on 1945 000-21 Guitar	Schoenberg Guitars	300
345	Kluson 502N Tuners on 1945 D-28 Guitar	Schoenberg Guitars	300
346	Kluson 210 Tuners on 1947 Martin 000-21 Guitar	Schoenberg Guitars	300
347	Kluson K-324 (also called Kluson Deluxe) Tuners on 1957 Martin D-18 Guitar	Folkway Music	300
348	Kluson K-500 Tuners on 1956 Martin D-28 Guitar	Steve Swan	300
349	Newspaper Announcement of the Unexpected Death of Herbert Keller Martin	Martin Guitar Archive	301
350	James A. Markley's First Sale Trip, from the January 21, 1928 The Music Trades Review Magazine	https://www.arcade-museum.com/	301
351	August 20, 1931 Notice from Martin Concerning Pick Guards on Guitars	Martin Guitar Archive	306
352	Possible Photograph of the First Martin Dreadnought Guitar, D-21 (Serial Number 46590)	Unofficial Martin Guitar Forum	307
353	Differences Between Advanced-X and Rear-X Bracing Patterns for a 000 Guitar	Author	309
354	1920 Specification Card for Regulation of Gut and Steel Strings	Martin Guitar Archive	309
355	1923 Notice the Style 18 Guitars Will Henceforth be Shipped with Steel Strings	Martin Guitar Archive	309
356	1922 Advertising Card for the Recently Introduced Model 2-17	Martin Guitar Archive	314
357	Shop Order 641, Dated April 23, 1930 for Twenty-Five 0-28 Guitars.	Martin Guitar Archive	317
358	Date of the Switch from Brazilian to Indian Rosewood	Martin Guitar Archive	321
359	Brazilian Rosewood Logs from 1935	Martin Guitar Archive	330
360	Cabinet Card of Professor Louis Brachet, Teacher of Music	Washington Historical Society	335
361	Sketch from CMI with Specifications for First D-45 Guitar	Martin Guitar Archive	339
362	Martin Shop Order Slip for Gene Autry's D-45 Guitar	Martin Guitar Archive	340
363	Bill Boyd Playing a Martin 00-18 Guitar	Dick Boak	340
364	Photograph of Bill Boyd with His 1929 Martin 00-42 Guitar and His Horse "Texas"	Martin Guitar Archive	340
365	Signed 8" X 10" Photograph of Bill Boyd with His 1933 Martin 00-42S Guitar	Martin Guitar Archive	341
366	1843 Silhouette Portrait of Madam De Goni	Ellison Fine Art (with permission)	345
367	1843 Martin & Schatz Guitar Made for Madam De Gone	Folkway Music Co.	346
368	Daguerreotype of Madan De Goni	Martin Guitar Archive	346
369	Steel Engraving Entitled "The Guitar" from May 1851 Edition of The Ladies' Repository	Author's collection	347
370	De La Cova Advertisement in the Daily Alta California Dated June 14, 1853	Daily Alta California June 14, 1853	347
371	Photograph of Manuel Ygnacio Ferrer	Internet	351
372	Tex Playing His Left-Handed 000-28 (ca. 1946)	Fletcher Family Archive	353
373	Tex wih 0-42 in "Six Gun Rhythm"	Fletcher Family Archive	353
374	Tex with His Brand-New D-42S Guitar (ca. 1936)	Fletcher Family Archive	354

Figures (cont.)

Tables

Tables (cont.)

APPENDIX A

SOURCE DOCUMENTS

The titles written on the ledgers in the Martin archive are used below. Each ledger has also been numbered according to sequence.

01) STORE LEDGER 1834-37
    1) Shop Expenses, APRIL 29-JULY 27, 1834
    2) Customer Accounts, MARCH-DEC. 1835
    3) Store Sales, MAY 26-OCTOBER 18, 1834
    4) Guitar Sales & Repairs, JUNE 2-OCT. 16, 1834
    5) Commission Guitar Sales, MAY 9-SEPT. 25, 1834
    6) Employee & Contractor Expenses, JUNE 1834-MAY
       1837 (mostly 1834-35)
    7) Employees (SCHATZ, SCHMIDT, HARTMAN,
       TOLERR, etc.)
The writing in the ledgers is in two different hands. C. F. Martin is one of the writers but another person, probably Jacob Hartman, made some of the entries.

02) JOURNAL 1836-39
Includes 1) Detailed Sales Records for 196 HUDSON ST.,
      Jan. 1, 1836 to June 9, 1837
    2) Guitar Orders & Deliveries, May 10, 1838-April 11,
      1839
Entries were made by Charles Bruno.

03) ACCT 1837-39 NEW YORK
Sales organized by customer for 212 Fulton St. location only.

04) JOURNAL 04-1837 TO 11-1838 BRUNO
-Sales activity for 212 FULTON ST from APRIL 1, 1837 to NOVEMBER 29, 1838
-It appears the store at 196 Hudson St. was closed Friday June 9, 1837, the last day of recorded sales although rent for 196 Hudson St. was paid through July 31, 1837. Martin may have continued to use this address for making guitars after this date. However, Rent on 212 Fulton St. started February 1, 1837 and the journal records sales from April 1, 1837 at that location. From April 1 to June 9, 1837 Martin operated at both 196 Hudson St. and 212 Fulton St.
-the MARTIN & BRUNO partnership lasted from May 1 to late September, 1838 although Bruno continued to work for Martin until the end of November.

05) INVENTORY PURCHASES 1837-38
-Located in 09 SALES 1852-59 ledger
Includes 1) Records musical instruments imported from
      Germany
    2) List of guitars brought into stock in 1837

06) LUDECUS & WOLTER INVENTORY LISTING 1839
-Located in 09 SALES 1852-59 ledger
-A list of musical stock-in-trade sold to Ludecus & Wolter in May 1839

07) ACCOUNT BOOK 1849-1885

08) DAYBOOK 1850-51
-Located in SALES 1859-1864 ledger
-Guitars received by C. F. Martin Jr. starting June 1850, the actual sales of guitars are recorded on some loose pages in the archives

09) SALES 1852-59
-Day book showing guitar shipments from 1852-1859
Includes 1) Inventory Purchases 1837-1838
      2) Daybook 1850-1851

10) LEDGER 1852-57
-Ledger book of customer accounts

11) SALE BOOK 1859-64
-Includes Daybook 1850-1851

12) JOURNAL 1859-67

13) DAYBOOK 1867-74

14) C. F. MARTIN & CO. INVENTORY JULY 20, 1867
-Located in JOURNAL OF SHOP EXPENSES 1867-69

15) JOURNAL OF SHOP EXPENSES 1867-69
Includes 14-C. F. Martin & Co. Inventory July 20, 1867
      17-Day Book of Guitar Sales 1874-1884

16) LEDGER OF EXPENSES 1869 TO 1874

17) DAY BOOK OF GUITAR SALES 1874-1884
-Located in 15-Journal of Shop Expenses 1867-69

18) DAYBOOK OF EXPENSES 1874-01-01 TO 1878-01-05

19) LEDGER 1873-1884

20) ACCOUNTS 1885-04-16 TO 1898-04-28

21) LEDGER 1885-04-27 TO 1896-12-31

22) LEDGER 1897-01-15 TO 1899-06-01

23) LEDGER 1897-1899

24) SALES 1898-1913

25) CASH 1899-1913

26) CASH 1913-1918

27) SALES 1914-1922

28) LEDGER 1915-12-01 TO 1918-11-30

29) SALES 1922-1930

30) SALES BOOK 1923-05-01 TO 1925-06-29

31) BOOKED ORDERS 1918-1967

32) EXPENSES 1901-1930

33) PURCHASES 1930-1964

34) AR-AP 1930-120-01 TO 1932-11-25

35) AP 1930-10-01 TO 1934-05-31

36) AP 1934-06-01 TO 1938-02-28

37) AP 1937-11-01 TO 1940-07-31

38) CASH DISBURSMENTS 1932-1965

39) CORRESPONDENCE 1833 TO 1935

40) MANUFACTURING EXPENSES 1918-1947

41) RECHNUNGSBUCH MERZ 1833-1843
-Located in Musikinstrumenten Museum, Markneukirchen, Germany.

This ledger details shipments of musical products from T. F. Merz in Neukirchen to a number of customers including:
i) Henry Schatz, Philadelphia, July-November 1834
ii) Martin & Schatz, New York, April 1835-September 1836
iii) C. F. Martin, New York, October 1836 to July 1837
iv) Martin & Bruno, New York, June 1838
v) C. F. Martin, New York, April 1839
vi) Charles Bruno, Macon GA, June-August 1839
vii) Ludecus & Wolter, New York, October 1839-March 1840

MISSING INFORMATION

The Martin archival material is a wonderful resource but contains a number of gaps:

1) Guitar sales are missing from late October 1834 to January 1836, except for some sales records that can be gleaned the customer account ledger.

2) Except for a few pages of notes in the first ledger, information on employees is almost entirely missing.

3) The sales day books and ledgers for the 1840's are missing entirely. There are a few notes for guitar ordered and sold in early 1840. The earliest business letter dates to 1848.

4) The sales sheets kept by C. F. Martin Jr. from mid-1850 to 1851 contain spotty information and only record sales from 385 Broadway.

5) The sales records from June 28, 1864 to August 4, 1867 are missing.

6) The custom
er account ledger books are missing from 1857 to 1885.

7) Sales records are missing from 1884 to 1898 except for some

information that can be pieced together for the years 1891-1893

8) Shipping documents and correspondence after 1935

APPENDIX B

\multicolumn{5}{c}{T. F. MERZ SHIPMENTS TO THE UNITED STATES}				
DATE	**CUSTOMER**	**CITY**	**BOX**	**GUITARS**
1834-07-16	SCHATZ	PHILADELPHIA	3	
1834-09-29	SCHATZ	PHILADELPHIA	4,5,6	
1834-11-17	SCHATZ	PHILADELPHIA	7	
1835-04-25	MARTIN & SCHATZ	NEW YORK	9	
PAGES 10 AND 11 MISSING				
1835-06-30	MARTIN & SCHATZ	NEW YORK	8,12,13	
1835-09-14	MARTIN & SCHATZ	NEW YORK	14	
1835-10-25	MARTIN & SCHATZ	NEW YORK	15	
1835-11-13	MARTIN & SCHATZ	NEW YORK	16	6 ff GUITARS?
1836-05-06	MARTIN & SCHATZ	NEW YORK	17,18	21 GUITARS BY MAKER (GUTTER, VOIGT, FICKER, LEDERER)
1836-06-23	MARTIN & SCHATZ	NEW YORK	19	11 GUITARS BY MAKER (GUTTER, VOIGT, FICKER, LEDERER)
1836-09-03	MARTIN & SCHATZ	NEW YORK	20,21	3 GUITARS
1836-10-11	C. F. MARTIN	NEW YORK	22,23	1 GUITAR
1836-10-22	C. F. MARTIN	NEW YORK	24	
PAGES 29 AND 30 ARE MISSING FROM BOOK				MARTIN RECORDS SHOW RECEIPT OF BOXES 25 & 26
1837-04-06	C. F. MARTIN	NEW YORK	27	3 DIFFERENT KINDS OF MACHINES
1837-07-26	C. F. MARTIN	NEW YORK	28	6? GUITAR MACHINES
1838-06-08	MARTIN & BRUNO	NEW YORK	29	
1838-07-16	MARTIN & BRUNO	NEW YORK	AR130	
1839-04-09	C. F. MARTIN	NEW YORK	30,31,32	
1839-06-04	C. BRUNO	MACON	1,2,3	12 GUITARS
1839-07-05	C. BRUNO	MACON	4	8 GUITARS
1839-08-16	C. BRUNO	MACON	5	
1839-10-23	LUDECUS & WOLTER	NEW YORK	33,34	
1839-11-21	LUDECUS & WOLTER	NEW YORK	35,36	
1840-03-05	LUDECUS & WOLTER	NEW YORK	37	

APPENDIX C

\multicolumn{9}{c}{SHOP LOCATIONS IN NEW YORK CITY (FROM LONGWORTH'S AMERICAN ALMANAC)}								
YEAR	**C. F. MARTIN**	**MARTIN & SCHATZ**	**LOUIS SCHMIDT**	**SCHMIDT & MAUL**	**CHARLES BRUNO**	**MARTIN & BRUNO**	**JOHN COUPA**	**MARTIN & COUPA**
1834-1835	Violin & guitar maker 196 Hudson							
1835-1836		Violin makers 196 Hudson						
1836-1837	Mus. Instr. 196 Hudson							
1837-1838	Mus. Instr. 196 Hudson & 212 Fulton				Books 212 Fulton			
1838-1839	Mus. Instr. 212 Fulton		Mus. Instr. 92 Chatham		Mus. Instr. 212 Fulton	Mus. Instr. 212 Fulton	385 Broadway	
1839-1840	Mus. Instr. 320 Broadway & 212 Fulton			Mus. Instr. 412 ½ Broadway			385 Broadway	
1840-1841	Mus. Instr. 385 Broadway			Mus. Instr. 412 ½ Broadway			385 Broadway	Mus. Instr. 385 Broadway
1841-1842	Mus. Instr. 385 Broadway			Mus. Instr. 412 ½ Broadway			385 Broadway	
1842-1843	Mus. Instr. 385 Broadway			Mus. Instr. 412 ½ Broadway			Prof. Guitar 385 Broadway	
1843-1844				?			Prof. Guitar 385 Broadway	
1844-1845				Mus. Instr. 412 ½ Broadway			Prof. Guitar 385 Broadway	
1845-1846				?			Prof. Guitar 385 Broadway	
1846-1847				?			Prof. Guitar 385 Broadway	
1847-1848				?			Prof. Guitar 385 Broadway	
1848-1849				Mus. Instr. 412 ½ Broadway			Prof. Guitar 385 Broadway	
1849-1850				?			Teacher 385 Broadway	

APPENDIX D
EARLY MARTIN DEALERS & SUPPLIERS

The following are names of early Martin dealers and suppliers that appear in the Martin ledgers to 1839.

JOSEPH F. ATWILL
Atwill was one of Martin's earliest customers. The city directory lists his music store at 201 Broadway as a "music saloon".

Atwill sold 11 Martin guitars from 1834 to 1838. Many of the guitars sold were high grade instruments and Martin often let Atwill take these "in commission".

MR. AUSTRUP
Martin sold a variety of musical instruments to Mr. Austrup, first at West Point and later at New Haven. A total of 4 Martin guitars were purchased by Austrup between 1836 and 1838.

EDWARD BAACK
Edward Baack had a music store at 28 Cherry Street. From 1836 to 1838 Martin bought a number of flutes and fifes from Baack and also had him repair flutes and other woodwind instruments.

BRAUNS & FOCKE
Brauns & Focke of Baltimore purchased 16 guitars from Martin from 1836 to 1838. Based on the price paid, at least 14 of these guitars appear to have been made by Martin.

S. BROMBERG & CO.
S. Bromberg & Co. was a store at 112 Fulton Street selling pianos and musical goods.

From 1836 to 1838 C. F. Martin purchased varnish, instruction books and woodwind reeds from Bromberg and sold him, in turn, violins, violin bows, brass instruments, strings and two $20 guitars.

CHARLES G. CHRISTMAN
Charles Christman was a well known instrument maker specializing in wind instruments. During Martin's time in New York he was located at 398 Pearl (1829-1836) and 404 Pearl St. (1837-1842).

Martin purchased flutes and music instruction books from Christman and used him for repairs to wind instruments. Christman in turn purchased strings from Martin.

GEORGE COE
George Coe was located at New Haven CT and in 1836 and 1837 bought a variety of musical instruments and parts from C. F. Martin but only 1 (Zebrawood) guitar.

WILLIAM J. DAVIS
Although primarily a flutist, Davis was also periodically involved with the making and selling musical instruments. This included Davis & Horn, a music store located at 367 Broadway that only lasted for one year (1839).
It is very probable that the Mr. Davis in the Martin ledgers is this same William J. Davis. Martin sold Davis flutes and violins during 1836 and 1837.

EDWARD FEHRMAN
Fehrman was Martin's earliest customer in New York, purchasing at least one guitar before the 196 Hudson Street store even officially opened.

The city directory for 1834 lists him as a "Teacher of Music and the German language" at 177 Grand Street although the Martin ledger has 76 Walker Street as his address.

Fehrman sold many guitars to young ladies residing at Mrs. O'Kills Boarding School and Mary McClenachan's Boarding School so may have been a music teacher at both schools. Between 1834 and 1839 Fehrman sold 28 guitars, mostly on a commission basis.

WILLIAM FEURING
William Feuring is listed in the 1839 and 1840 Philadelphia Directories as a pianoforte maker at the southeast corner of 8th and High Streets. Feuring was probably a friend of C. F. Martin as Martin sourced ivory piano key sets and piano wire from New York suppliers and shipped them with no mark up during 1836 and 1837.

GEIB & WALKER
Geib & Walker had a piano and music store at 23 Maiden Lane from 1829-1843. Martin purchased strings from this store in the period from 1836 to 1838.

GASPAR (JASPER) GODONNE
Gaspar Godone was a piano maker and later a music dealer specializing in violins, cellos and music stands. He was located variously at 412 Broadway (1832-1834), 412½ Broadway (1835-1837), 403 Broadway (1838) and 403½ Broadway (1839-1849).

Martin sold Godonne strings and violin bows and also purchased some items from him.

HENRY G. GUETTER
From 1836 to 1838, Martin purchased musical instruments, guitars strings and guitar cases from Guetter in Bethlehem PA.

Further research is needed to determine if Henry Guetter is the same "Gutter" mentioned as a maker of some of the guitars Martin imported from T. F. Merz in Neukirchen.

AUGUST HARTMAN
Martin imported musical merchandise from Hartman in Neukirchen between 1836 and 1838 although it is not known exactly what sorts of goods were purchased. It is unlikely that C. F. Martin imported any guitars from Hartman as the number of guitars imported from T. F. Merz very closely matches actual sales.

HELFRICH & CO.
Helfrich & Co. was located at West Point and purchased strings

and flutes from Martin during 1836 and 1837.

CHARLES F. HOYER

In the period from 1836 to 1838 Martin often purchased music, music paper, various musical instrument instruction books and strings from Hoyer. The Martin ledgers initially record Hoyer at 393 Broadway and, from late 1837, at 301 Broadway.

Charles F. Hoyer is listed as a "music-st(ore) & consul for Baden" at 301 Broadway in Longworth`s Almanac for 1839.

"FIFTH" GUITAR
        C. F. Martin sold five guitars during 1836 and 1837 that he termed "fifth" guitars. It is not known what this refers to unless, like "terz" guitars that were tuned three half-tones higher, this type of guitar was tuned five half-tones higher.

HENRY INMAN (1801 - 1846)

Henry Inman was the leading American portrait and lanscape artist of his time.

Although not a Martin dealer Inman did buy a Martin "fifth" guitars on November 9, 1836 from another artist Cornelius Ver Bryck, who received a commission on the sale.

Inman painted a potrait of Ver Bryck in 1837.

SAMUEL C. JOLLIE & CO.

Samuel C. Jollie & Co. had a music store at 385 Broadway from 1839 to 1845. Their store occupied the ground level at this address and the Martin & Coupa warerooms were located above the store (as confirmed by the Martin & Coupa case labels).

CHARLES H. KEITH

Charles H. Keith had a music store at 61 Court Street in Boston.

Keith was one of C. F. Martin's better accounts from 1835 to 1838 and bought a wide variety of musical goods, but only 2 guitars, during this period.

NANNING KOSTER & CO.

Nanning Koster & Co. was Martin's largest source for German silver wire from 1836 to 1838. The business was located at 16 Cedar Street.

MARY McCLENACHAN

Mrs. McClenachan ran a boarding school at 13 Carroll Place. At least two guitars were sold to young women at this location. Edward Fehrman received a commission on these two guitars so may have been a music teacher at the school.

JOHN McVICKAR

Martin's landlord at 196 Hudson was probably Rev. Dr. John McVickar D. D. of 8 Columbia College. The 1834 edition of Longworth's American Almanac describes him as a "professor of moral philosophy". Reverend McVickar was a "Professor of Moral and Intellectual Philosophy, Rhetoric, Belles Lettres and Political Economy" at Columbia College and held a number of important positions with the Protestant Episcopal Church including vice president of the "New York Protestant Episcopal

City Mission Society", fifth vice president of the "Education and Missionary Society of the Protestant Episcopal in the State of New York" and membership in the "Committee for Domestic Mission" (1837) and was also vice president of the "New York Literary & Philosophical Society" (1837).

JOHN G. MILLER & SON

John G. Miller & Son were located at 35 North 4th Street in Philadelphia from at least 1837. They don't appear in the Philadelphia directory for 1835-1836 although they were one of Martin's better accounts in the period from 1835 to early 1837.

J. G. Miller & Son purchased 11 Martin guitars in early 1835. These guitars would have had the Martin & Schatz label in them as confirmed by the advertisement below.

JOHN F. NUNNS

John F. Nunns had a music store located at 70 3rd Street in Philadelphia.

From 1836 to 1838 Nunns bought mostly flutes and brass instruments from Martin but also 9 guitars made by Martin.

NUNNS, CLARK & CO.

Brothers Robert & William Nunns and John Clark formed Nunns, Clark & Co. in 1833. The city directory lists Nunns, Clark & Co. as piano makers at 137 Broadway.

In 1836 Martin sold Nunns, Clark & Co. some violin bridges and tailpieces plus 3, or possibly 4, Martin guitars.

JOHN PHYFE

The city directories between 1834 and 1839 show John Phyfe, ivory turner, at 19 Murray Street.

John Phyfe was the source of the piano keys C. F. Martin sent to William Feuring in Philadelphia but was also one of the Martin's suppliers of ivory for use on guitars

Interestingly, Duncan Phyfe & Son, the famous cabinetmakers, were located at 194 Fulton in the same period, very close to Martin's store at 212 Fulton.

WILLIAM RADDE

In 1849 he had a store at 322 Broadway that sold books in German and homeopathic medical supplies.

ANTHONY REIFF

Anthony Reiff was a music teacher located at 9 Thompson Street (1834) and later at 65 Vestry (1839). He sold at least two Martin guitar to students but also purchased other types of instruments from Martin.

RICHARD SCHROEDER

A Richard Schroder, instrument maker, is listed in the 1834 edition of Longworth`s American Almanac at 191 Mulberry Street. Between 1836 ans 1838 Martin purchased a large number of flutes from him and used him for repairs to a variety of woodwind instruments. Martin also purchased some bone and ivory buttons for guitar machines from Schroeder.

VINCENT SCHMIDT

Vincent Schmidt is listed in the 1842 Baltimore directory as a "professor of music" on Saratoga Street. Schmidt was also a concert musician[90].

In 1836 Schmidt bought two unusual guitars from Martin. One was a "fifth" guitar with a mahogany case and the other was an "Amadill" guitar.

The "fifth" guitar was priced at $7.00 and may be a foreign-made guitar although the addition of a $6 mahogany case suggests the guitar was probably made by Martin. It is not know what "fifth" refers to but it may be that it is an instrument tuned 5 half-tones higher than a regular guitar in the same way that a "terz" guitar is tuned 3 half-tones higher than normal.
The meaning of "Amadill" has yet to be determined.

MR. SCHNEPF

Schnepf does not appear in the city directories from 1834-1840 but is noted in the Martin ledger as being a "Professor of Guitar" at 41 Greenwich Lane. In the period from 1836 to 1838 he sold 19 guitars, mostly to his students, and received commissions from Martin.

P. H. TAYLOR

From 1836 to 1838 Martin sold a variety of musical instruments and parts to P. H. Taylor in Richmond VA. Taylor purchased 14 guitars made by Martin including one that could be considered a presentation grade instrument.

CORNELIUS VER BRYCK (1813-1844)

Ver Bryck was an artist best known for his landscape, historical and portrait paintings.

As well as making a living as a painter, he also seems to have had some sort of connection with Martin as he sold several Martin guitars while he was in New York during 1836 and 1837.

One November 9, 1836 Martin sold a "fifth" guitar to Henry Inman, another well known artist, to which Ver Bryck received a commission on the sale. He bought another guitar on January 20, 1837 and another guitar was sold a Mr. Robinson through Ver Bryck on February 14, 1837.

Ver Bryck died of tuberculosis at the age of only 31.

APPENDIX E
EARLY MARTIN DEALERS

DEALER	CITY	DATES	GUITARS SOLD
D. Alexander & Son	Franklin IN	1856-57	3
Alexander & White	Franklin IN	1856	17
John B. Anderson	North Albany NY	1850	3
Balmer & Weber	St. Louis MO	1850-64	123
Beck & Lawton	Philadelphia PA	1856-60	15
C. D. Benson & Co.	Nashville TN	1859-61	30
E. A. Benson	Memphis TN	1854	6
F. D. Benteen & Co.	Baltimore MD	1850-52	12
Joseph Borra	Chapel Hill NC	1858	4
S. Brainard & Co.	New York NY	1852-62	54
Charles Bruno	New York NY	1858-60	176
Charles Bruno	New York NY	1863-67	88
Bruno & Morris	New York NY	1860-62	62
B. F. Colburn	Cincinnati OH	1855	6
Colburn & Field	Cincinnati OH	1852-55	62
A. G. Crane & Co.	Indianapolis IN	1855	4
Richard Davis	Washington DC	1859	6
Chares De Janon	New York NY	1851-60	13
Salustiano De La Cova	Panama	1852-55	5
Ossia E. Dodge	Cleveland OH	1853-57	3
Charles Dummig	Philadelphia PA	1852	3
George Dutch	Marietta OH	1850-51	?
D. P. Faulds	Louisville KY	1855	12
Faulds, Stone & Co.	Louisville KY	1854	10
A. Fiot	Philadelphia PA	1850-53	11
C. G. Fonda	Cincinnati OH	1862-63	18
Francis Funck	Vicksburg MS	1853	4
Gould & Co.	Philadelphia PA	1853-56	6
J. E. Gould	Philadelphia PA	1853-56	70
R. G. Greene	Chicago IL	1855	6
C. Hall & Co.	Norfolk VA	1855-61	16
John Harvie	Port Gibson MS	1853-53	8
H. N. Hempsted	Milwaukee WI	1857	3
J. H. Hidley	Albany NY	1850-54	4
Hilbus & Hitz	Washington DC	1851-54	12
John Hitz Jr.	Leesburg VA	1856-60	4
F. J. Ilsley	Albany NY	1850-54	25
J. M. Jaques	New York NY	1852-53	17
Jaques & Brother	New York NY	1852	4
Klemm & Brothers		1864	8
Lee & Walker	Philadelphia PA	1851-63	65
Loud's	Holly Springs MS	1851-52	
I. H. Macmichael	Natchez MS	1854	6
Marvin & North	(New York NY)	1850	2
Mayer & Collier	Albany NY		6

DEALER	CITY	DATES	GUITARS SOLD
J. H. Mellor	Pittsburgh PA	1848-54	38
Jason Mellor	Wheeling WV	1854-55	8
Charles F. Meyer	Lexington KY	1852-59	19
Joseph Mickly	Philadelphia PA	1853	2
J. G. Miller	Philadelphia PA	1835	10
C. E. W. Miller	Germantown PA	1858-59	7
Miller & Beacham	Baltimore MD	1853-63	81
Mould & Greene	Chicago IL	1854-56	12
E. P. Nash & Co.	Petersburg VA	1836-59	63
Henry Parsons	New Orleans LA	1853-56	30
A. W. Penniman	Columbus OH	1853-54	10
A. C. Peters & Brother	Cincinnati OH	1860-64	87
W. C. Peters	Baltimore MD	1850	
W. C. Peters & Sons	Cincinnati OH	1851-60	209
W. M. Peter	Louisville KY	1836	
W. M. Peters	New York NY	1856-63	27
Peters & Field	Cincinnati OH	1850	
Peters, Webb & Co.	Louisville KY	1851-54	54
Edouard Pique	Philadelphia PA	1851-58	8
G. P Reed & Co.	Boston MA	1851-55	37
A. B. Reichenbach	Phildelphia PA	1858-64	12
C. Reichenbach		1860	5
Rohe & Leavitt	New York NY	1850-61	17
Henry Sanford	Reading PA	1851-52	
M. Schmitz	Philadelphia PA	1852	4
William Schubert	Philadelphia PA	1852-64	44
P. H. Taylor	Richmond VA	1836-59	50
David A. Truax	Cincinnati OH	1853-56	18
Truax & Baldwin	Cincinnati OH	1856-58	50
Horace Waters	New York NY	1851-58	110
H. Weber		1856-60	10
John B. West	Nashville TN	1850-57	32
Rev. S. Wolle	Bethlehem PA	1852-60	8
James Woodhouse	Richmond VA	1857-60	42
C. A. Zoebisch	New York NY	1849-67	921

APPENDIX F

DATE	DESCRIPTION	ADDRESS
1845	Guitar and violin maker	h. 1 Beach
1846	Guitar maker	h. 327 Wash. h. Canton ct.
1847	Guitar and violin maker	323 Washington & 3 Amory Hall
1848	Guitar and violin maker	Amory Hall, 323 Washington
1849	Guitar and violin maker	17 Boylston Square
1850	Guitar and violin maker	17 Boylston Square
1851	Guitar and violin maker	17 Boylston Square

HENRY SCHATZ' SHOP LOCATIONS

(From Boston Almanac City Directory)

APPENDIX G
ESTIMATED GUITAR PRODUCTION
(1833-1898)

The chart below documents all the guitar sales recorded in the Martin ledgers. It should be noted that the records are somewhat spotty and are not complete as indicated below:

1) 1834-Records appear to be quite complete until October.

2) 1835-Appears to cover only sales made in March and April.

3) 1836 and 1837-Quite complete

4) 1838-Complete to about November but for some reason not all guitar sales recorded in the accounts book are in the sales day book.

5) 1839 and 1840-Only a few records

6) 1841-1847-No records

7) 1848-1849-No records except for orders recorded in co rrespondence

8) 1850-Partial records only (C. F. Martin Jr. recorded sales in New York from June to October)

9) 1851-Missing except for orders recorded in correspondence

10) 1852-June 28, 1864-Records are complete

The guitar sales listed the above total 3,267 instruments. However, by making some estimates on production for the periods where records are incomplete or missing, it is likely that Martin's actual production was closer to 6,000 guitars.

GUITAR SALES 1833-1839 and ESTIMATED PRODUCTION of MARTIN GUITARS				
YEAR	MARTIN GUITARS SOLD	GERMAN GUITARS SOLD	COMMENTS	EST. MARTIN GUITAR PRODUCTION
1834	26	3	Fairly complete records May-Oct.	30
1835	12	0	Partial records	72
1836	110	12	Records complete	98
1837	68	21	Records complete	68
1838	52	7	Records complete to Nov.	90
1839	6	1	Partial records	35
Total	274	44		393

ESTIMATED GUITAR PRODUCTION 1840 TO 1867		
YEAR	GUITARS	COMMENTS
1840	90	Partial records, 12 Guitars to Mar. 1840
1841	100	Estimated production
1842	100	Estimated production
1843	150	Estimated production
1844	150	Estimated production
1845	150	Estimated production
1846	150	Estimated production
1847	150	Estimated production
1848	150	Estimated production
1849	150	Records missing
1850	200	Partial records, 28 guitars
1851	200	Estimated production
1852	220	Actual production
1853	304	Actual production
1854	273	Actual production
1855	204	Actual production
1856	270	Actual production
1857	235	Actual production
1858	241	Actual production
1859	319	Actual production
1860	315	Actual production
1861	85	Actual production
1862	95	Actual production
1863	221	Actual production
1864	300	Complete to June 26 (150 guitars)
1865	250	Estimated production
1866	250	Estimated production
1867	250	Records missing until August
TOTAL	5572	

ESTIMATED GUITAR PRODUCTION 1868 TO 1898		
YEAR	GUITARS	COMMENTS
1868	197	Actual production
1869	304	Actual production
1870	190	Actual production
1871	227	Actual production
1872	231	Actual production
1873	244	Actual production
1874	226	Actual production
1875	223	Actual production
1876	112	Actual production
1877	129	Actual production
1878	108	Actual production
1879	115	Actual production
1880	149	Actual production
1881	159	Actual production
1882	193	Actual production
1883	253	Actual production
1884	276	Actual production 239 to Oct. 10
1885	200	Est. production (based on 1885-98 ledger)
1886	280	Est. production (based on 1885-98 ledger)
1887	290	Est. production (based on 1885-98 ledger)
1888	220	Est. production (based on 1885-98 ledger)
1889	405	Est. production (based on 1885-98 ledger)
1890	540	Est. production (based on 1885-98 ledger)
1891	545	Est. production (based on 1885-98 ledger)
1892	543	Estimate from C. A. Zoebisch post cards
1893	450	Estimate from C. A. Zoebisch post cards
1894	275	Martin closed for 2 months
1895	388	Est. production (based on 1885-98 ledger)
1896	275	Estimated production
1897	300	Estimated production
1898	350	Estimated production
TOTAL	8397	

APPENDIX H

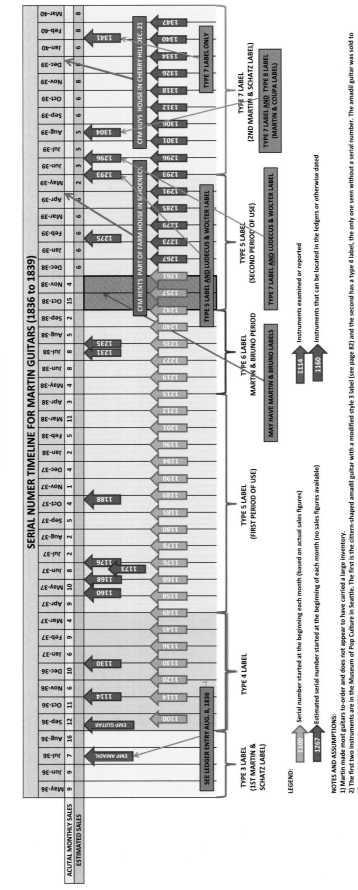

SERIAL NUMER TIMELINE FOR MARTIN GUITARS (1836 to 1839)

BIBLIOGRAPHY

1) *Acoustic Guitars and Other Fretted Instruments* by George Gruhn and Walter Carter

2) *Best Companions: Letters of Eliza Middleton Fisher and Her Mother, Mary Hering Middleton, from Charleston, Philadelphia and Newport, 1839-1846*, Edited by Eliza Middleton Fisher

3) *C. F. Martin and His Guitars 1796-1873*, Centerstream Publishing, Philip F. Gura, 2003

4) *C. F. Martin & Co. A History*, Mike Longworth,4 Maples Press Inc., 1988

5) *Cleave's Biographical Cyclopaedia Homeopathic Physicians and Surgeons*, Galaxy Publishing Company, Philadelphia Pa., 1873

6) *A Collection of Fine Spanish Guitars from Torres to the Present*, Sheldon Urlik, Sunny Knoll Publishing, 1997

7) *The Complete Encyclopaedia of Music*, John Weeks Moore (1854), Oliver Ditson, Boston

8) *Desilver's Philadelphia directory, and strangers' guide 1833 & 1834*

9) *Drifting About*, Stephen C. Massett (autobiography), Carleton Publishers, New York, 1881 (page 27 mentions De Goni being at Atwill's in 1840)

10) *European Music & Musicians in New York 1840-1900*, edited by John Graziano, University of Rochester Press 2006

11) *The Guitar & Mandolin* by Philip J. Bone

12) *The Guitar in America: Victorian Era to Jazz Age*, Jeffrey Noonan, University Press of Mississippi (notes on De Janon)

13) *Graham's American Monthly Magazine of Literature & Arts 1845* (some notes on Madam De Goni)

14) *Historical Review for the Joint Celebration of the Musical Instrument Makers' Guild (formerly Violin Makers' Guild) and the String Makers' Guild, of Mark Neukirchen, commemorating the years of their foundation, 1677 and 1777*, published in German by the Guilds in 1927

15) *The Letters of Henry Wadsworth Longfellow 1814-43, Vol. 2 1837-43* (see page 378)

16) *Marci Aurelio Zani de Ferranti* by Simon Wynberg and Gary Southwell

17) *Martin Guitars A History*, Richard Johnston & Dick Boak, Hal Leonard, 2008

18) *Martin Guitars: A Technical Reference*, Richard Johnstone & Dick Boak, Hal Leonard, 2009

19) *Music in German Immigrant Theater New York City 1840-1940*, John Koegel

20) *The Musical Instrument Makers of New York: A Directory of the 18th and 19th Centuries*, Nancy Groce (there is a broadside engraving of Jollie & Co. Music store at 385 Broadway on page 85)

21) *The New Langwill Index*, William Waterhouse.

22) *The New York City Directory for 1842 and 1843*, published by John Doggett

23) *New York, Past, Present & Future: Comprising a History of the City of New York*, Ezekiel Porter Belden, 1849 (see note on page 174 "Schmidt & Maul musical instruments has removed from 412 ½ to 385 Broadway", page 100 has ad for William Radde book seller, 322 Broadway, page 103 has ad for Joseph Rohe, importer of French musical instruments, 44 Maiden Lane)

24) *Performing Arts Annual* by Library of Congress page 57

25) *Rechnungsbuch Merz 1833-1843*, Musikinstrumenten Museum, Markneukirchen, Germany

26) *A Sketch of the Musical Fund Society* (page 22, 1841 concert mentions Delores Nevares de Goni and Knoop)

27) *Sound Travels, Ernest Kaleihoku Kaai and the transmission of Hawaiian music in the early twentieth century*, PhD thesis, Andrea Eden Low, University of Auckland, 2016

28) *Strong on Music: Resonances, 1836-1850*, by Vera Brodsky Lawrence, George Templeton Strong (see pages 96, 107, 142, 223, 353 and 660 for comments on De Goni)

29) *Stauffer & Co.* (2011) Erik Pierre Hofmann, Pascal Mougin, Stefan Hackl

30) *Vogtlandischer Geigenbau*, Bernhard Zoebisch

OTHER SOURCES OF INFORMATION

Tex Fletcher: texfletcher.com and Fletcher Family Archive

William Foden: Foden-Hoskins Archive, Missouri History Museum

George C. Krick Collection, University of Colorado at Boulder, University Libraries, AMRC

George C. Krick Collection, Washington University, Gaylord Music Library, St. Louis, Missouri

E. C. Lilly: National Archives at Kansas City, https://www.archives.gov/kansas-city/finding-aids/leavenworth-penitentiary/inmates-l.html

Lloyd Loar: Roger Siminoff's Biography of Lloyd Loar (https://www.siminoff.net/lloyd-loar)

Michael Lorenz, http://michaelorenz.blogspot.co.at/2014/03/stauffer-miscellanea.html

Weymann Guitars, https://www.leavingthisworld.com/category/weymann-guitars/

Henry Worrall: The Kansas Historical Society

Index

Virzi tone producer 322
Vogtlandischer Geigenbau 27, 47
volute 101, 103, 153
von Lacasse
  Franz 2

W

Wanamaker 135, 154, 155
War Production Board 21
Washburn 63, 64, 134, 135, 136, 137, 151,
    156, 242, 243, 245, 368, 384, 386,
    387
Weiner Zeitung 1
Werlein
  Philip 136
West & Scholey 4
Weymann
  H. A. & Son 135, 187, 188
whitewood 49, 52, 54, 103, 124, 334
Wilkins
  Colonel 84, 95, 120, 121
wood
  bird's-eye maple 48, 52, 329
  Brazilian rosewood 23, 24, 48, 52, 53,
    54, 55, 56, 232, 320, 321, 329, 330,
    331, 332
  Cuban cedar 103, 333, 334
  ebony 21, 49, 52, 54, 55, 101, 157, 159,
    173, 181, 251, 253, 314, 317, 333,
    372, 378
  Indian rosewood 23, 24, 55, 321, 329
  koa 44, 57, 145, 172, 203, 204, 205, 329,
    330, 332
  mahogany 13, 48, 49, 52, 53, 54, 55, 56,
    77, 78, 79, 87, 101, 124, 144, 155,
    158, 168, 169, 173, 183, 192, 195,
    212, 225, 227, 228, 229, 234, 248,
    286, 329, 331, 332, 333, 334, 388,
    390
  pernambuco 48, 52, 329, 330
  poplar 49, 52, 54, 103, 124, 334
  Spanish cedar 52, 54, 333
  spruce 52
    Adirondack 54, 56, 233, 251, 252, 253,
      255, 323, 324, 327, 328
    Appalachian 252, 322, 323, 325, 326
    Engelmann 233, 251, 255, 322, 324,
      325, 328
    European 49, 52, 318, 322
    German 56, 232, 233, 254, 255, 327,
      328
    red 52, 54, 56, 232, 253, 254, 255, 322,
      323, 326, 328
    Rocky-Mountain 325
    Sitka 56, 233, 252, 253, 255, 322, 324,
      325, 326, 327, 328
    Vermont 56, 232, 251, 252, 253, 254,
      255, 324, 327, 328
    West Virginian 56

White Mountain 54, 56, 323
valnut 48, 52
whitewood 49, 52, 54, 103, 124, 334
zebrawood (gonçalo alves) 48
wood suppliers 334
Worrall
  Henry 121, 122, 123, 156, 379, 392
Wurlitzer
  E. U. 255, 257
  Rudolph Co. 16, 45, 46, 132, 186, 195,
    207, 216, 230, 235, 237, 257, 354,
    372

X

X-bracing
  early 86
  forward 4, 122, 308, 343, 359, 385
  plain 87
  rear 5, 93, 94, 231, 308, 309

Z

zithers 25, 334, 335
Zoebisch
  C. A. 11, 12, 13, 14, 27, 30, 32, 34, 35,
    43, 47, 63, 64, 77, 99, 106, 111, 115,
    133, 151, 152, 198, 243, 244, 268,
    274, 275, 279, 280, 285, 287, 289,
    308, 319, 323, 331, 342, 351, 352,
    383, 385, 386, 387
  C. A. & Sons 11, 12, 14, 32, 34, 35, 99,
    111, 115, 268, 289, 308

Figure 402
David Manaku with Second Kealakai Dreadnought Guitar